PHILIP'S

STREET
Cornwall

G000255172

Falmouth, Newquay, Penzance, Plymouth, St Austell, Truro

www.philips-maps.co.uk
First published in 2003 by Philip's,
a division of Octopus Publishing Group Ltd
www.octopusbooks.co.uk
Endeavour House, 189 Shaftesbury Avenue
London WC2H 8JY
An Hachette UK Company
www.hachette.co.uk

Third edition 2010
First impression 2010
CORCA

978-1-84907-086-7 (pocket)

© Philip's 2010

Ordnance Survey®

This product includes mapping data licensed from
Ordnance Survey® with
the permission of the Controller of
Her Majesty's Stationery Office.
© Crown copyright 2010. All rights reserved.
Licence number 100011710.

No part of this publication may be reproduced,
stored in a retrieval system or transmitted in any
form or by any means, electronic, mechanical,
photocopying, recording or otherwise, without
the permission of the Publishers and the copyright
owner.

While every reasonable effort has been made to
ensure that the information compiled in this atlas
is accurate, complete and up-to-date at the time
of publication, some of this information is subject
to change and the Publisher cannot guarantee its
correctness or completeness.

The information in this atlas is provided without
any representation or warranty, express or
implied and the Publisher cannot be held liable
for any loss or damage due to any use or reliance
on the information in this atlas, nor for any
errors, omissions or subsequent changes in such
information.

The representation in this atlas of a road, track
or path is no evidence of the existence of a right
of way.

Ordnance Survey and the OS Symbol are registered
trademarks of Ordnance Survey, the national
mapping agency of Great Britain.

Speed camera data provided by
PocketGPSWorld.com Ltd

Post Office is a trade mark of Post Office Ltd in the
UK and other countries.

Printed in China

Contents

III Mobile safety cameras

IV **Key to map pages**

VI **Route planning**

X Major administrative and Postcode boundaries

1 **Key to map symbols**

2 **Street maps** at 1⅓ inches to 1 mile

104 **Street maps** at 2⅔ inches to 1 mile

148 **Street map of Plymouth city centre**
at 5⅓ inches to 1 mile

150 **Index** of towns, villages, streets, hospitals, industrial
estates, railway stations, schools, shopping centres,
universities and places of interest

Digital Data

The exceptionally high-quality mapping found in this atlas is available as digital data in TIFF format,
which is easily convertible to other bitmapped (raster) image formats.

The index is also available in digital form as a standard database table. It contains all the details
found in the printed index together with the National Grid reference for the map square in which each
entry is named.

For further information and to discuss your requirements, please contact
philips@mapsinternational.co.uk

Mobile safety cameras

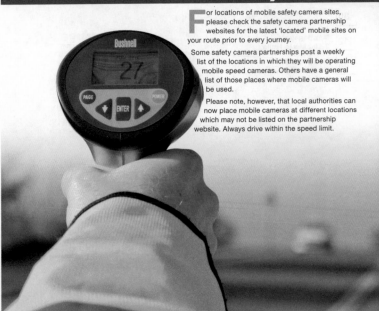

For locations of mobile safety camera sites, please check the safety camera partnership websites for the latest 'located' mobile sites on your route prior to every journey.

Some safety camera partnerships post a weekly list of the locations in which they will be operating mobile speed cameras. Others have a general list of those places where mobile cameras will be used.

Please note, however, that local authorities can now place mobile cameras at different locations which may not be listed on the partnership website. Always drive within the speed limit.

Mike Harrington / Alamy

Useful websites

Devon and Cornwall Safety Camera Partnership
www.dcsafetycameras.org

Further information
www.dvla.gov.uk
www.thinkroadsafety.gov.uk
www.dft.gov.uk
www.road-safe.org

IV

80	Map pages at 1⅓ inches to 1 mile
112	Map pages at 2⅔ inches to 1 mile
148	Map pages at 5⅓ inches to 1 mile

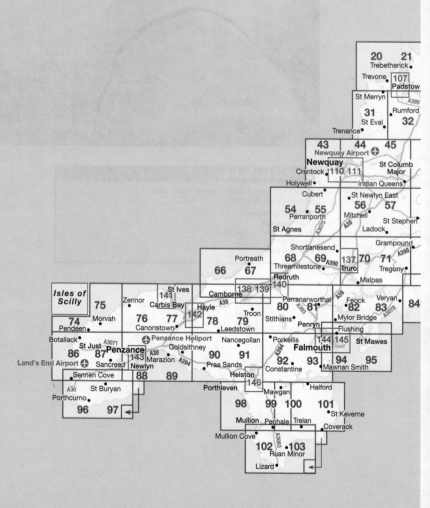

20 21
Trebetherick
Trevone 107
Padstow
A389
St Merryn
31 Rumford
St Eval 32
Trenance

43 44 45
Newquay Airport
Newquay
Crantock 110 111 St Columb Major
Holywell Indian Queens
Cubert
St Newlyn East
54 55 56 57
Mitchell
Perranporth St Stephen
St Agnes Ladock

Grampound
Shortlanesend
68 69 137 70 71
Threemilestone Truro Tregony
Redruth Malpas
66 67 140
Portreath Perranarworthal Veryan
138 139 80 81 82 83 84
Camborne Feock Mylor Bridge
St Ives 141 Troon Stithians Penryn Flushing
Zennor Carbis Bay 142 78 79 Leedstown Porkellis 144 145 St Mawes
Isles of Scilly 75 Hayle Mylor Bridge
74 Morvah 76 77 Nancegollan Falmouth
Pendeen Canonstown 90 91 92 93 94 95
Botallack Penzance Heliport Praa Sands Constantine Mawnan Smith
St Just A3071 87 Goldsithney Helston
86 Penzance 143 Marazion 146
Land's End Airport Sancreed Newlyn 88 89 Porthleven Helford
Sennen Cove St Buryan 98 99 100 101 St Keverne
Porthcurno 96 97 Mullion Penhale Trelan Coverack
Mullion Cove 102 103
Ruan Minor
Lizard

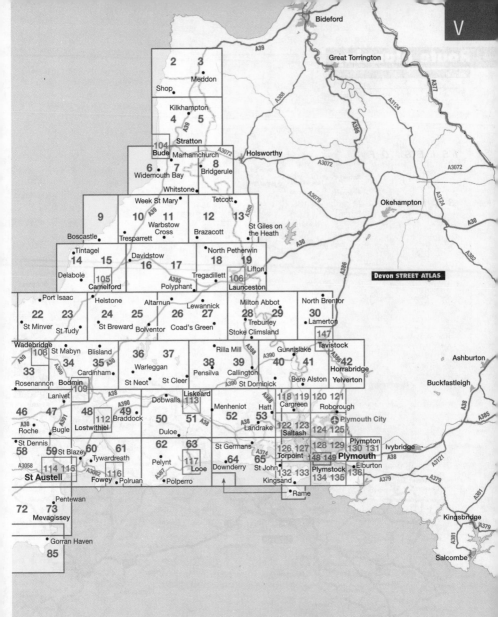

V

Bideford

Great Torrington

A39

A388

A3124

A386

A377

2 3
Meddon
Shop

Kilkhampton
4 5
Stratton
104
Bude Marhamchurch
Bridgerule
8
A3072 Holsworthy

A3072

A3072

Okehampton

A388

A386

A3124

A30

A382

6 7
Widemouth Bay
Whitstone

A3079

9 Week St Mary
10 11 Tetcott
Warbstow 12 13
Cross Brazacott St Giles on
Boscastle the Heath
Tresparrett

Devon STREET ATLAS

14 15 Tintagel North Petherwin
Davidstow 18 19
Delabole 16 17 Lifton
105 Tregadillett 106
Camelford Polyphant Launceston
A395

Port Isaac Helstone Altarnun Milton Abbot North Brentor
22 23 24 25 26 27 28 29 30
St Minver St Breward Lewannick Treburley Lamerton
St Tudy Bolventor Coad's Green Stoke Climsland
147

Wadebridge Rilla Mill Tavistock
108 St Mabyn Blisland 36 37 38 39 Gunnislake 42
34 35 Warleggan Pensilva Callington 40 41 Horrabridge
33 Cardinham St Neot St Cleer Bere Alston Yelverton
Rosenannon Bodmin St Dominick
109 Liskeard Ashburton
Lanivet Dobwalls 113 118 119 120 121
46 47 48 49 50 51 52 Menheniot Hatt 53 Cargreen Roborough Buckfastleigh
Roche Bugle Lostwithiel Braddock Duloe Landrake 122 123 Plymouth City
St Dennis Saltash 124 125
58 59 St Blazey 60 61 62 63 St Germans 126 127 128 129 Plympton
Tywardreath 64 65 Torpoint 130 131 Ivybridge
114 115 Pelynt 117 Downderry St John 148 149 Plymouth
St Austell 116 Looe Kingsand 132 133 134 135 136 Elburton
Fowey Polruan Polperro Rame

Pentewan
72 73
Mevagissey

Gorran Haven
85

Kingsbridge

Salcombe

A39 A30 A390 A391 A3058 A3082 A387 A374 A38 A388 A390 A386 A390 A388 A30 A38 A385 A38 A3121 A381 A379 A379 A381

Scale
0 5 10 15 20 25 km
0 5 10 15 miles

Route planning

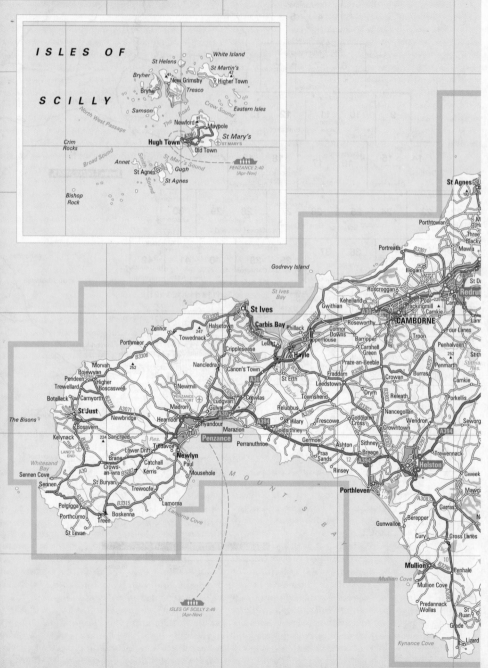

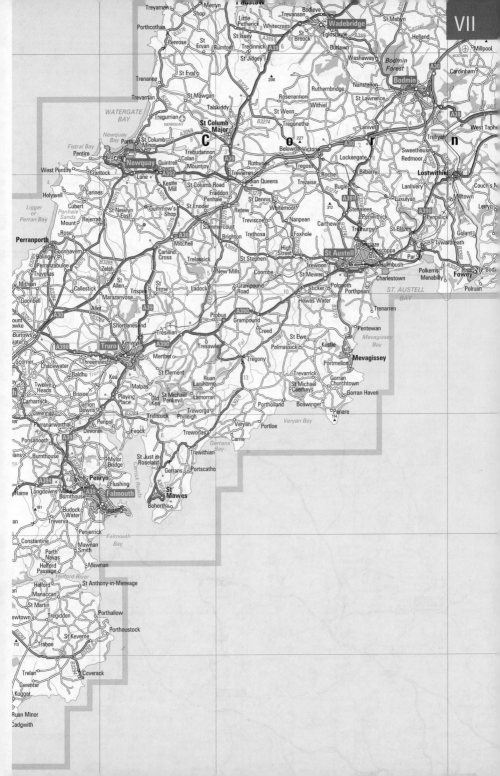

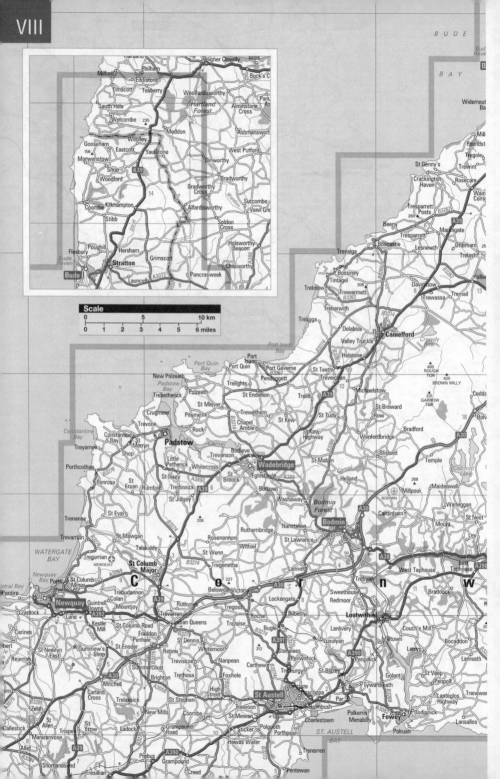

Major administrative and Postcode boundaries

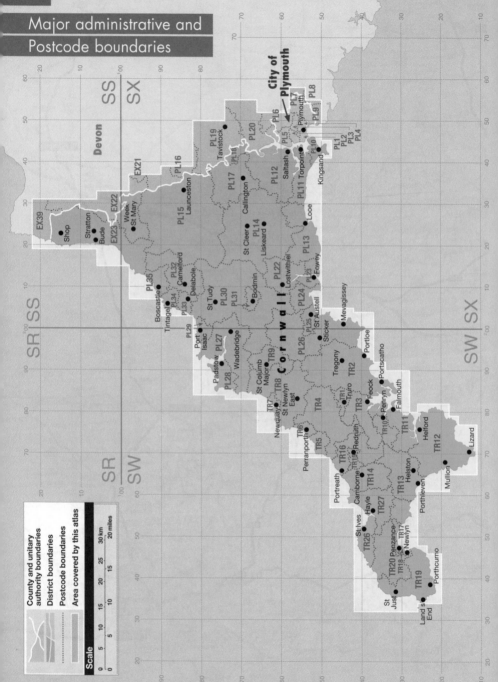

Key to map symbols

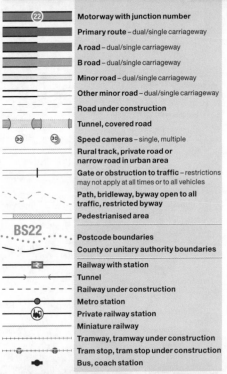

	Motorway with junction number
	Primary route – dual/single carriageway
	A road – dual/single carriageway
	B road – dual/single carriageway
	Minor road – dual/single carriageway
	Other minor road – dual/single carriageway
	Road under construction
	Tunnel, covered road
	Speed cameras – single, multiple
	Rural track, private road or narrow road in urban area
	Gate or obstruction to traffic – restrictions may not apply at all times or to all vehicles
	Path, bridleway, byway open to all traffic, restricted byway
	Pedestrianised area
BS22	Postcode boundaries
	County or unitary authority boundaries
	Railway with station
	Tunnel
	Railway under construction
	Metro station
	Private railway station
	Miniature railway
	Tramway, tramway under construction
	Tram stop, tram stop under construction
	Bus, coach station

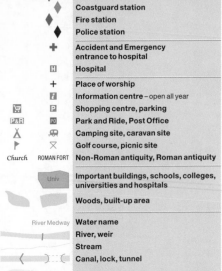

	Ambulance station
	Coastguard station
	Fire station
	Police station
	Accident and Emergency entrance to hospital
H	Hospital
+	Place of worship
i	Information centre – open all year
	Shopping centre, parking
P&R	Park and Ride, Post Office
	Camping site, caravan site
	Golf course, picnic site
Church ROMAN FORT	Non-Roman antiquity, Roman antiquity
Univ	Important buildings, schools, colleges, universities and hospitals
	Woods, built-up area
River Medway	Water name
	River, weir
	Stream
	Canal, lock, tunnel
	Water
	Tidal water

Adjoining page indicators and overlap bands – the colour of the arrow and band indicates the scale of the adjoining or overlapping page (see scales below)

The dark grey border on the inside edge of some pages indicates that the mapping does not continue onto the adjacent page

The small numbers around the edges of the maps identify the 1-kilometre National Grid lines

Abbreviations

Acad	Academy	Meml	Memorial
Allot Gdns	Allotments	Mon	Monument
Cemy	Cemetery	Mus	Museum
C Ctr	Civic centre	Obsy	Observatory
CH	Club house	Pal	Royal palace
Coll	College	PH	Public house
Crem	Crematorium	Recn Gd	Recreation ground
Ent	Enterprise		
Ex H	Exhibition hall	Resr	Reservoir
Ind Est	Industrial Estate	Ret Pk	Retail park
IRB Sta	Inshore rescue boat station	Sch	School
		Sh Ctr	Shopping centre
Inst	Institute	TH	Town hall / house
Ct	Law court	Trad Est	Trading estate
L Ctr	Leisure centre	Univ	University
LC	Level crossing	W Twr	Water tower
Liby	Library	Wks	Works
Mkt	Market	YH	Youth hostel

Enlarged maps only

	Railway or bus station building
	Place of interest
	Parkland

The map scale on the pages numbered in green is 1⅓ inches to 1 mile
2.1 cm to 1 km • 1 : 47 620

| 0 | ½ mile | 1 mile | 1½ miles | 2 miles |
| 0 | 500m | 1km | 1½km | 2km |

The map scale on the pages numbered in blue is 2⅔ inches to 1 mile
4.2 cm to 1 km • 1 : 23 810

| 0 | ¼ mile | ½ mile | ¾ mile | 1 mile |
| 0 | 250m | 500m | 750m | 1km |

The map scale on the pages numbered in red is 5⅓ inches to 1 mile
8.4 cm to 1 km • 1 : 11 900

| 0 | 220yds | 440yds | 660yds | ½ mile |
| 0 | 125m | 250m | 375m | 500m |

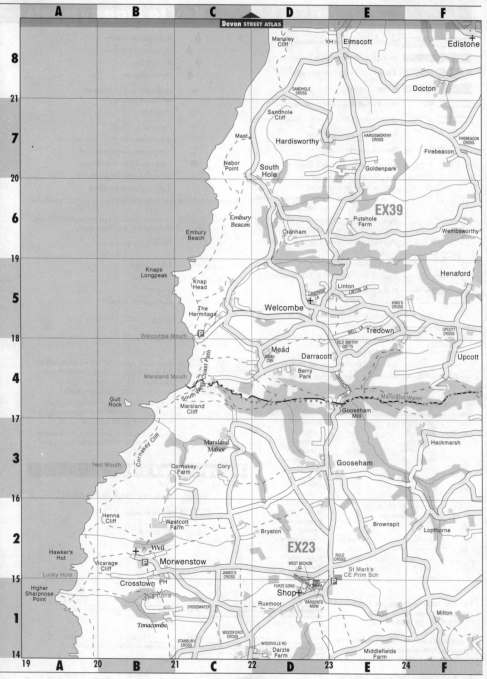

Mansley Cliff
YH
Elmscott
Edistone

SANDHOLE CROSS
Docton

Sandhole Cliff
HARDISWORTHY CROSS
FIREBEACON CROSS

Mast
Hardisworthy
Firebeacon

Nabor Point
South Hole
Goldenpark

EX39

Embury Beacon
Cranham
Putshole Farm
Wembsworthy

Embury Beach

Knaps Longpeak
Henaford

Knap Head
Linton
LINTON LA
KING'S CROSS

The Hermitage
Welcombe
LANEPARK LA

UPCOTT CROSS

Welcombe Mouth
P
WELL LA
Tredown

Mead
Darracott
OLD SMITHY COTTS
Upcott

MEAD CNR

Marsland Mouth
Berry Park

South West Coast Path
Marsland Water

Gull Rock
Marsland Cliff
Gooseham Mill

Cornakey Cliff
Hackmarsh

Yeol Mouth
Marsland Manor
Gooseham

Cornakey Farm
Cory

Henna Cliff
Westcott Farm
Brownspit
Lopthorne

Hawker's Hut
Well
Bryaton
EX23

Vicarage Cliff
P
Morwenstow
WEST BECKON CL
RULE CROSS
St Mark's CE Prim Sch

Lucky Hole
Crosstown
PH
JAMES'S CROSS
P

Higher Sharpnose Point
The Tidna
Shop
SARGENTS MOW

CROSSWATER
Ruxmoor

Tonacombe
STANBURY CROSS
WOODFORD CROSS
WOODVILLE RD
Milton

Darzle Farm
Middlefields Farm

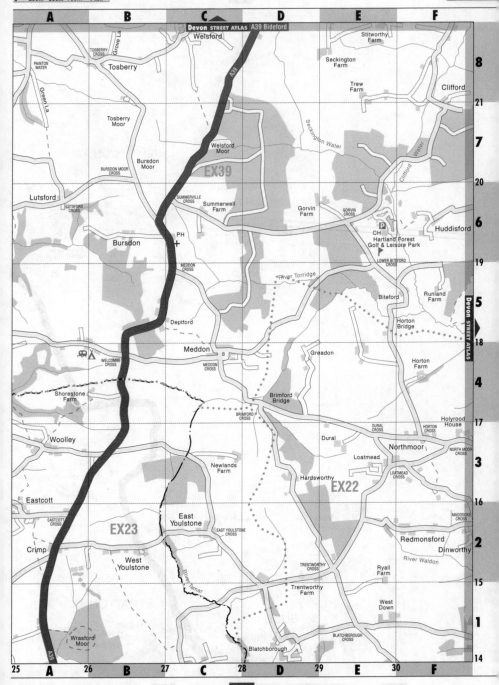

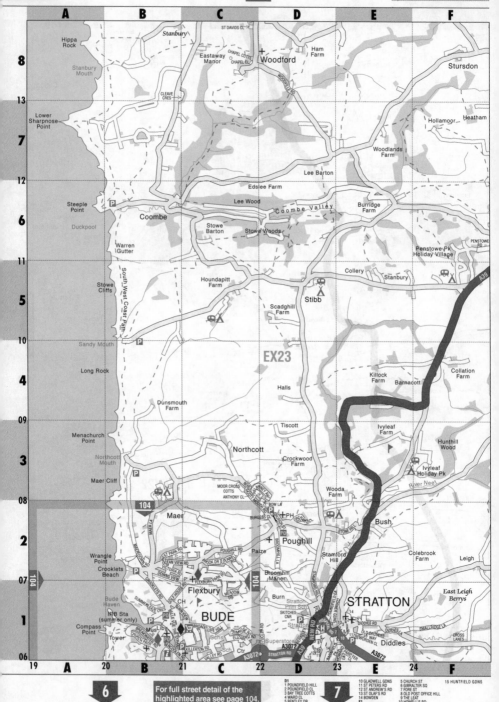

Scale: 1½ inches to 1 mile

0   ¼   ½ mile
0   250m   500m   750m   1 km

For full street detail of the highlighted area see page 104.

D1
1 POUNDFIELD HILL
2 POUNDFIELD CL
3 BAY TREE COTTS
4 WARD CL
5 BENTLEY DR
6 UNION HILL
7 BRIDGE ST
8 WOODLEY CL
9 ST MICHAEL'S RD

10 GLADWELL GDNS
11 ST PETERS RD
12 ST ANDREW'S RD
13 ST OLAF'S RD
14 BOWDEN
E1
1 MAIDEN ST
2 COT HILL
3 MARKET ST
4 CHURCH SQ

5 CHURCH ST
6 GIBRALTAR SQ
7 FORE ST
8 OLD POST OFFICE HILL
9 THE LEAT
10 HOWELL'S RD
11 SPICERS LA
12 SANCTUARY LA
13 BIDEFORD MEWS
14 TOWNSEND

15 HUNTFIELD GDNS

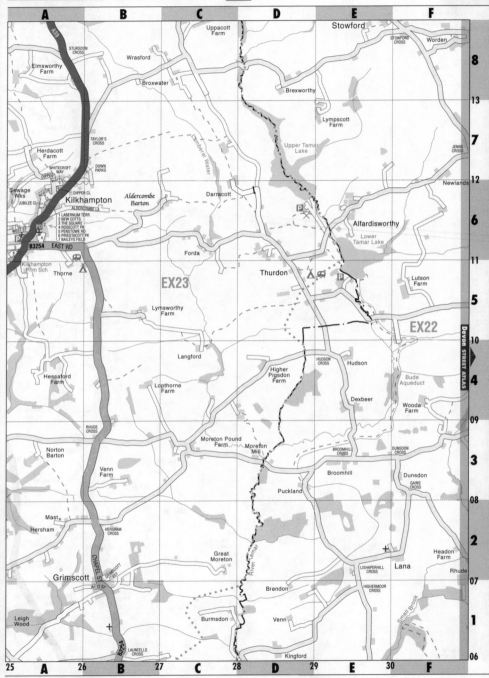

For full street detail of the highlighted area see page 104.

Scale: 1⅓ inches to 1 mile

0   ¼   ½ mile
0   250m 500m 750m 1 km

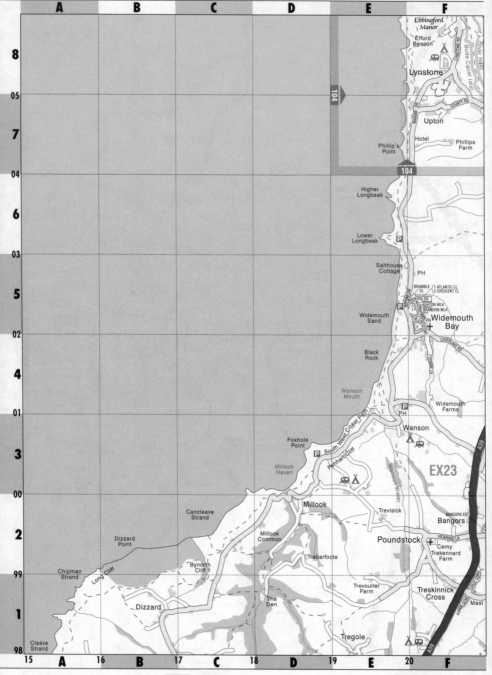

Ebbingford Manor
Efford Beacon
Lynstone
Upton
Hotel
Phillips Farm
Phillip's Point
Higher Longbeak
Lower Longbeak
Salthouse Cottage
PH
BRAMBLE CL
1 ATLANTIC CL
2 CRESCENT CL
MADEIRA DR
ASHTON WLK
BRANDON WLK
Widemouth Sand
Widemouth Bay
Black Rock
Wanson Mouth
Widemouth Farms
Foxhole Point
South West Coast Path
Penhalt Cliff
Wanson
PH
Millook Haven
Cancleave Strand
Millook
Trevisick
EX23
Bangors
BANGORS EST
Poundstock
VICARAGE LA
Dizzard Point
Millook Common
Trebarfoote
Cemy
Trekennard Farm
Chipman Strand
Long Cliff
Bynorth Cliff
Trevoulter Farm
Treskinnick Cross
Mast
Dizzard
The Den
Tregole
Cleave Strand
River Neet
Bude Canal (dis)
COUNTY RD
LEVEN LAKE RD
Wanson Water

8
05
7
04
6
03
5
02
4
01
3
00
2
99
1
98

15   A   16   B   17   C   18   D   19   E   20   F

A   B   C   D   E   F

104

10   11

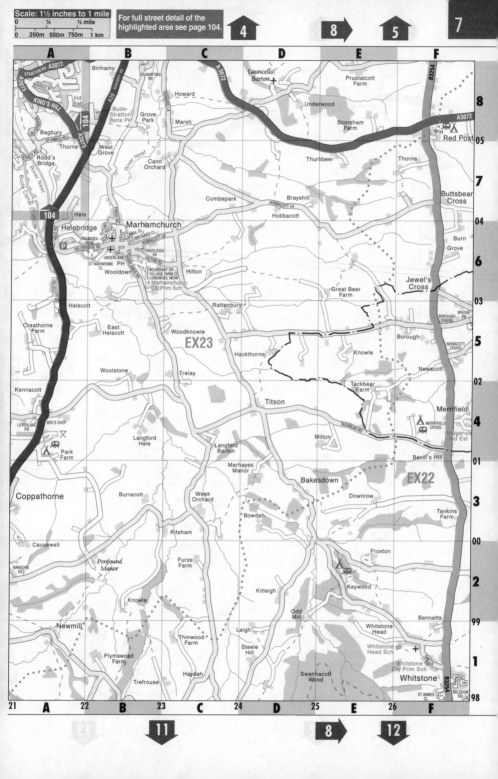

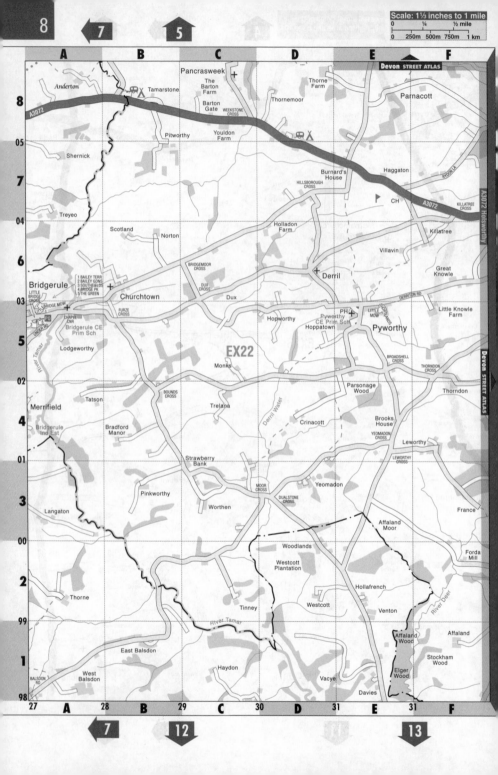

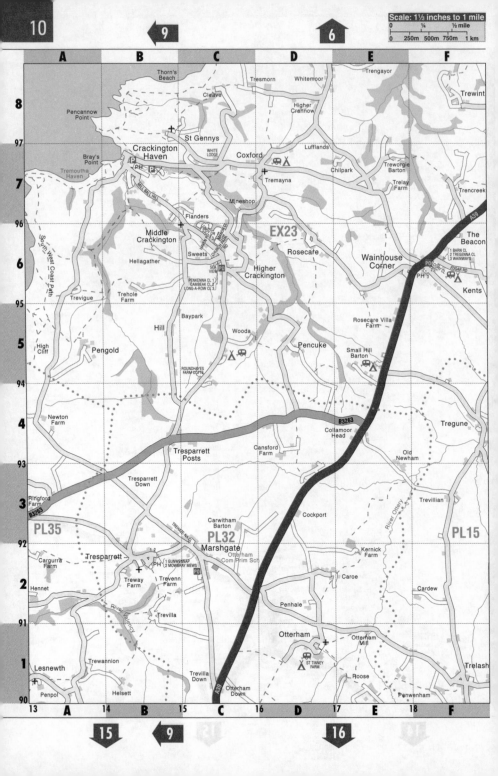

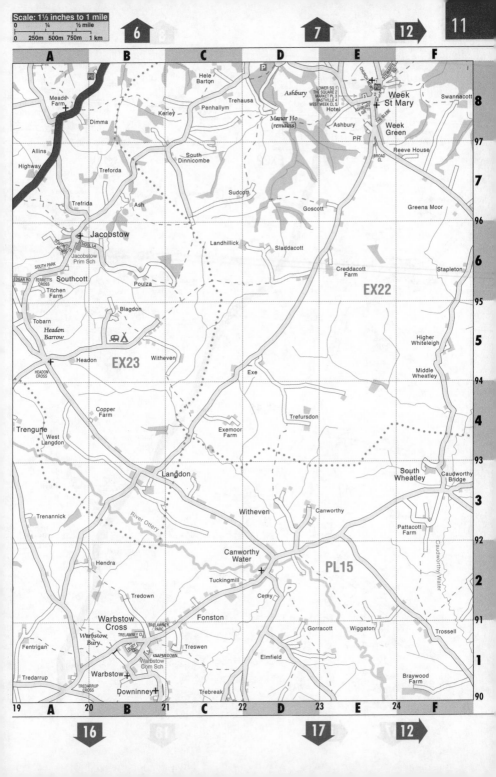

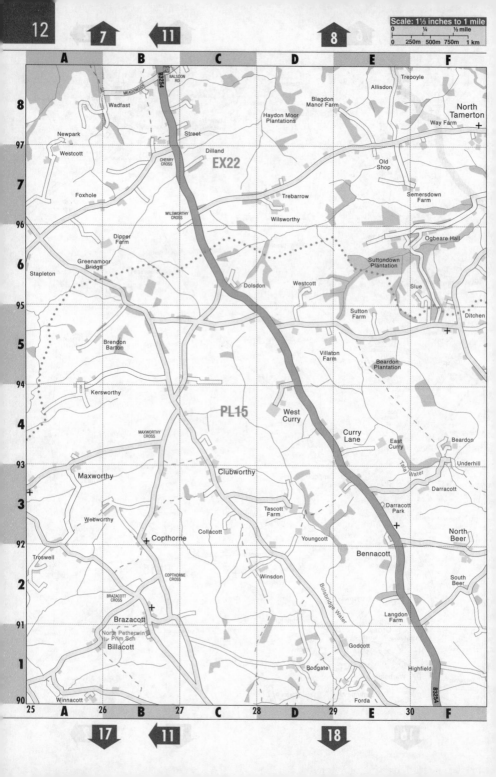

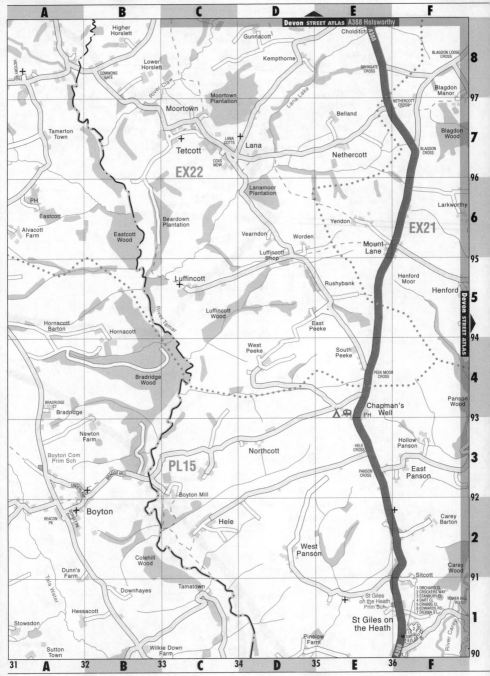

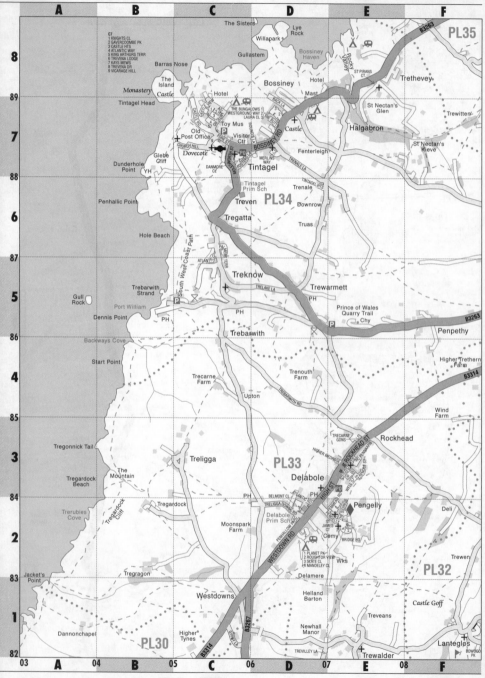

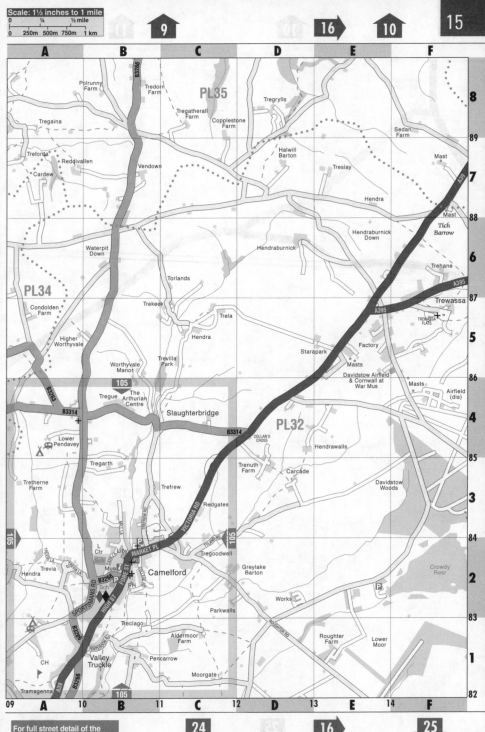

A   B   C   D   E   F

8

89

PL35

Polrunny Farm
Tredorn Farm
Tregatherall Farm
Copplestone Farm
Tregrylls

Tregaina

Treforda
Reddivallen
Vendown
Halwill Barton
Treslay
Sedan Farm

Mast

7

Cardew

Hendra

Mast

Tich Barrow

88

Waterpit Down

Hendraburnick Down

Trehane

A395

PL34

Condolden Farm

Hendraburnick

Trewassa

87

Higher Worthyvale

Trekeek

Trela

Starapark

Factory

TREWASSA FLATS

A395

6

Torlands

5

Hendra

Worthyvale Manor

Trevilla Park

Masts

Davidstow Airfield & Cornwall at War Mus

Masts

Airfield (dis)

86

105

B3263

Tregue

The Arthurian Centre

Slaughterbridge

B3314

COLLAN'S CROSS

PL32

4

B3314

B3314

Lower Pendavey

Tregarth

Trefrew

Trenuth Farm

Hendrawalls

Carcade

Davidstow Woods

85

Tretherne Farm

Redgates

3

Trevia

Hendra

Trefrew

VICTORIA RD

TYLANS RD

Tregoodwell

Greylake Barton

84

105

L Ctr
Sch
Liby
Mus
PO

MARKET PL

Camelford

Works

P

2

Trevia

B3266

Sch

FORE ST

HIGH ST

PH

Parkwalls

ROUGHTON RD

Crowdy Resr

83

SPORTSMANS RD

Treclago

Aldermoor Farm

Pencarrow

Roughter Farm

Lower Moor

1

CH

Valley Truckle

Moorgate

Tramagenna

A39

B3266

105

82

09   A   10   B   11   C   12   D   13   E   14   F

For full street detail of the highlighted area see page 105.

24

16

25

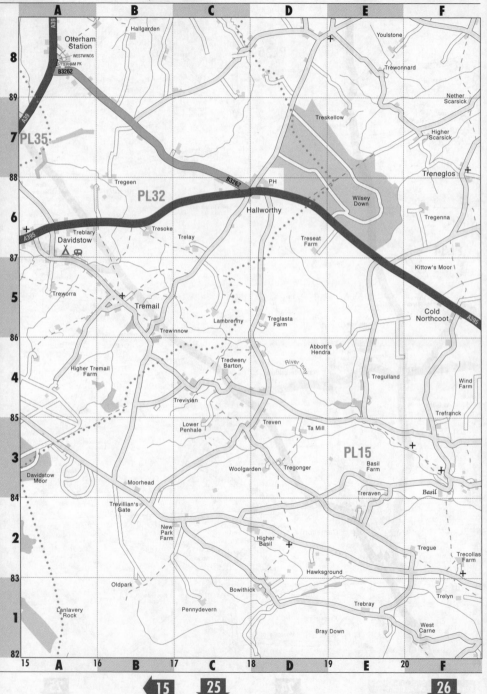

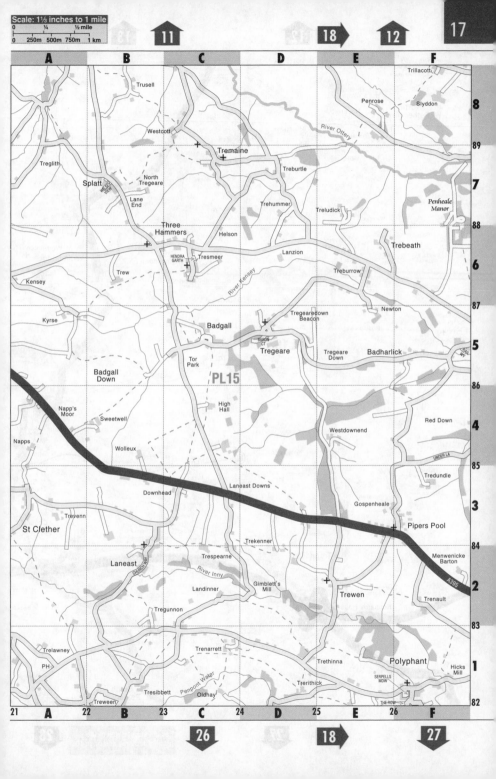

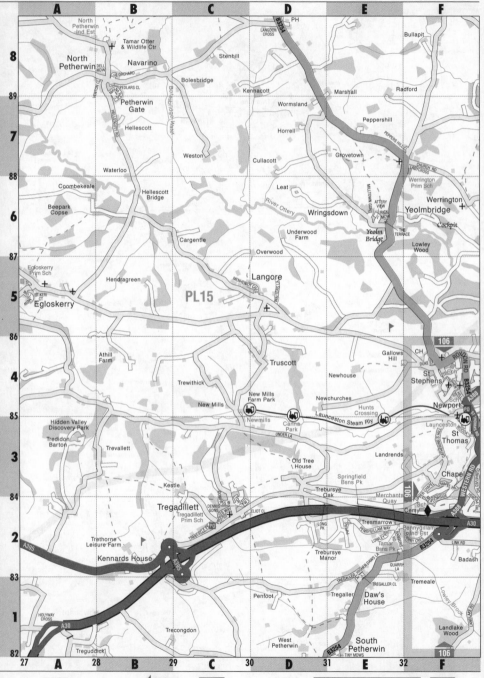

Scale: 1⅓ inches to 1 mile

0   ¼   ½ mile
0   250m 500m 750m 1 km

A **B** **C** **D** **E** **F**

B3254
LANGDON CROSS
PH
North Petherwin Ind Est
Tamar Otter & Wildlife Ctr
Bullapit
8
North Petherwin
DELL MDW
Navarino
Stenhill
Radford
KYE ORCHARD
Bolesbridge
Marshall
Wormsland
PEDLARS CL
89
Petherwin Gate
Kennacott
Peppershill
Hellescott
Horrell
Grovetown
CHURCH RD
LADYCROSS
7
HELLESCOTT RD
BOLESBRIDGE WATER
Weston
Cullacott
PEPPERS HILL RD
Werrington Prim Sch
Waterloo
88
Coombekeale
Hellescott Bridge
Leat
Werrington
Beepark Copse
River Ottery
Wringsdown
ATTERY VIEW
RIGN MDW
Yeolmbridge
6
Cargentle
Underwood Farm
Yeolm Bridge
THE TERRACE
Cockpit
Lowley Wood
87
Overwood
Egloskerry Prim Sch
MENHENIOT GDNS
Langore
5
ST KERI CT
PL15
WALTERSLADE
Egloskerry
Hendragreen
106
CH
DUKE ST
ROYDON RD
B3254
86
Gallows Hill
St Stephens
Athill Farm
Truscott
Newhouse
Sch
4
Trewithick
Newchurches
Newport
New Mills Farm Park
Hunts Crossing
St Thomas
New Mills
Launceston Steam Rly
Launceston
85
Newmills
Canna Park
UNDER LA
Hidden Valley Discovery Park
Old Tree House
Landrends
Chapel
3
Tredidon Barton
Trevallett
Springfield Bsns Pk
CHAPEL LA
A388
106
Merchants Quay
Trebursye Oak
WESTERN RD
Kestle
Tresmarrow
Cemy
PENNYGILLAM WAY
TREBURSYE RD
Pennygillam Ind Est
ELIOT CL
LONG PK
A388
2
A395
DENNIS GDNS
Treburse Manor
Tamar Bsns Pk
LINK RD
B3254
Trethorne Leisure Farm
Tregadillett Prim Sch
Badash
TRERITHICK RD
QUARRY LA
Kennards House
A395
Penfoot
TREGALLER LA
TIGER DOWNS LA
Tremeale
83
Tregaller
TREGALLER CL
Daw's House
Lowley Brook
HOLYWAY CROSS
1
A30
Trecongdon
LANDLAKE RD
Landlake Wood
West Petherwin
B3254
South Petherwin
106
82
Treguddick
TINY MDWS

A **B** **C** **D** **E** **F**
27   28   29   30   31   32

For full street detail of the highlighted area see page 106.

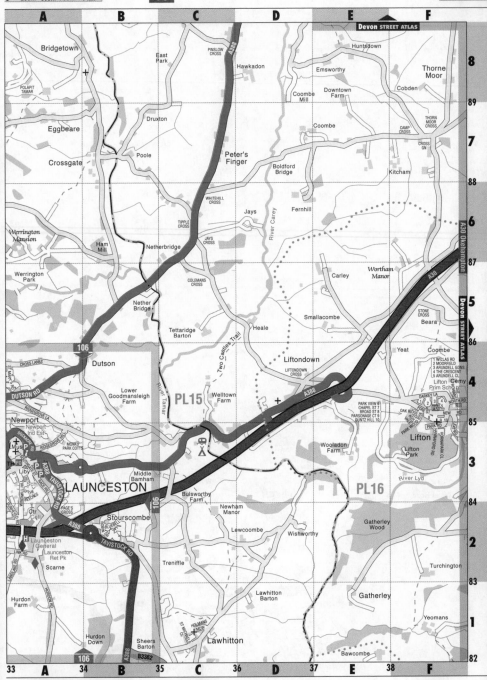

Scale: 1⅓ inches to 1 mile

13

Bridgetown

Huntsdown

East
Park

Pinslow
Cross

Hawkadon

Emsworthy

Thorne
Moor

POLAPIT
TAMAR

Coombe
Mill

Downtown
Farm

Cobden

89

Eggbeare

Druxton

Coombe

CAMP
CROSS

THORN
MOOR
CROSS

7

Crossgate

Poole

Peter's
Finger

Boldford
Bridge

Kitcham

CROSS
GN

88

Werrington
Mansion

WHITEHILL
CROSS

Jays

Fernhill

River Carey

A30 Okehampton

6

TIPPLE
CROSS

Ham
Mill

Netherbridge

JAYS
CROSS

Carley

Wortham
Manor

A30

Devon STREET ATLAS

87

Werrington
Park

Nether
Bridge

COLEMANS
CROSS

Smallacombe

STONE
CROSS

Beara

5

106

Dutson

Tettaridge
Barton

Heale

Two Castles Trail

Liftondown

Yeat

Coombe

86

CROSS LANES

Lower
Goodmansleigh
Farm

River Tamar

PL15

Welltown
Farm

LIFTONDOWN
CROSS

1 WILLAS RD
2 MOORFIELD
3 ARUNDELL GDNS
4 THE CRESCENT
5 ARUNDELL CL

Lifton Cemy

Lifton
Prim Sch

DUTSON RD

RIDGEGROVE LA

Newport
Newport
Ind Est

MONKS
PARK COTTS

PARK VIEW 6
CHAPEL ST 7
BROAD ST 8
PARSONAGE CT 9
QUINTZ HILL 10

OAK RIDGE

Lifton
Park

85

RIDGEGROVE

Mus

Liby

Middle
Bamham

Wooladon
Farm

Lifton

River Lyd

PL16

3

LAUNCESTON

106

Bulsworthy
Farm

Newham
Manor

84

Ctr
Cell

Stourscombe

TAVISTOCK RD

A388

Lewcoombe

Wishworthy

Gatherley
Wood

2

H

Launceston
General

Launceston
Ret Pk

Treniffle

Lawhitton
Barton

Gatherley

Turchington

83

Scarne

Hurdon
Farm

ST MICHAELS CL

HOLMANS
MOOR

Lawhitton

Yeomans

1

Hurdon
Down

Sheers
Barton

B3362

Bawcombe

82

33

34

35

36

37

38

For full street detail of the
highlighted area see page 106.

28

29

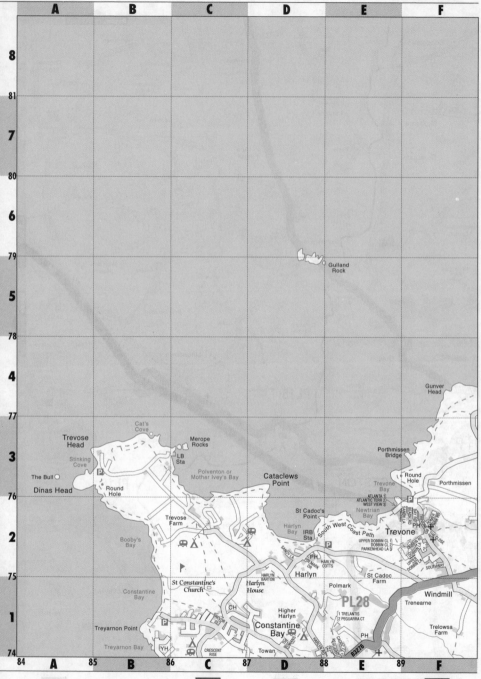

8
81
7
80
6
79
5
78
4
77
3
76
2
75
1
74

A   85   B   86   C   87   D   88   E   89   F

84   A   85   B   86   C   87   D   88   E   89   F

Gunver
Head

Trevose
Head

Cat's
Cove

Merope
Rocks

LB
Sta

Stinking
Cove

The Bull

Dinas Head

Round
Hole

Polventon or
Mother Ivey's Bay

Cataclews
Point

Porthmissen
Bridge

Round
Hole

Porthmissen

Trevone
Bay

ATLANTA 1
ATLANTIC TERR 2
WEST VIEW 3

Newtrain
Bay

Trevone

Trevose
Farm

St Cadoc's
Point

Harlyn
Bay

South West Coast Path

IRB
Sta

UPPER DOBBIN CL 1
DOBBIN CL 2
PARKENHEAD LA 3

Booby's
Bay

PH

Harlyn
Cotts

Harlyn

St Cadoc
Farm

SMELTA

St Constantine's
Church

Harlyn
Barton

Harlyn
House

Polmark

Windmill

Constantine
Bay

CH

Higher
Harlyn

PL28

Trenearne

Trelowsa
Farm

Treyarnon Point

1 TRELANTIS
2 PEGUARRA CT

Treyarnon Bay

YH

CRESCENT
RISE

Towan

Constantine
Bay

PH

B3276

Gulland
Rock

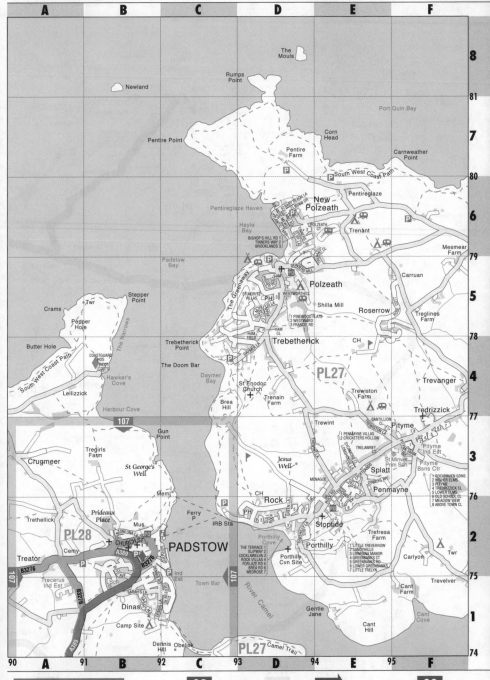

22

Scale: 1⅓ inches to 1 mile

0   ¼   ½ mile
0   250m 500m 750m 1 km

The Mouls

Newland

Rumps Point

Port Quin Bay

Pentire Point

Corn Head

Pentire Farm

Carnweather Point

South West Coast Path

Pentireglaze

New Polzeath

BEACH DR
BEVAN DR

Trenant

Mesmear Farm

Hayle Bay

BISHOP'S HILL RD 1
TINNERS WAY 2
BROOKLANDS 3

POLZEATH CT

Carruan

Padstow Bay

The Greenaway

ST MORITZ VILLAS

WENTWORTH CL

PH

Polzeath

Shilla Mill

Roserrow

Treglines Farm

Crams

Twr

Stepper Point

HAM
CL

1 PINEWOOD FLATS
2 WESTWARD
3 FRANCIS RD

Pepper Hole

HAM FIELD

Trebetherick

PL27

Trevanger

Butter Hole

The Narrows

Trebetherick Point

The Doom Bar

Daymer Bay

St Enodoc Church

Trenain Farm

Trewiston Farm

Tredrizzick

South West Coast Path

Hawker's Cave

COASTGUARD HOS
PILOT COTTS

Brea Hill

CANTILLION CL

Pityme

Lellizzick

Harbour Cove

Trewint

1 PENMAYNE VILLAS
2 CRICKETERS HOLLOW

Pityme Ind Est

107

Gun Point

TRELAWNEY

St Minver Prim Sch

Pityme Bsns Ctr

Tregirls Farm

MENAGUE

Splatt

1 ROCKHAVEN GDNS
2 HIGHER ELMS
3 PITYME
4 TREDRIZZICK CL
5 LOWER ELMS
6 OLD SCHOOL CL
7 MEADOW VIEW
8 ABOVE TOWN CL

Crugmeer

St George's Well

Jesus Well

DINAS LEY

Penmayne

Mem

CH

Rock

Stoptide

Trefresa Farm

Trethellick

Prideaux Place

Ferry P

PH

Porthilly

Carlyon

Twr

PL28

SONLUNA LA

Mus

IRB Sta

THE TERRACE 1
SLIPWAY 2
COCKLAWELLA 3
ROCK VILLAS 4
FORLAZE RD 5
BREA RD 6
MEDROSE 7

Porthilly Cove

1 LITTLE TREVERROW
2 SANDYHILLS
3 LOWENNA MANOR
4 GREENBANKS CL
5 GREENBANKS RD
6 LOWER GREENBANKS
7 LITTLE TRELYN

Trevelver

Treator

CHURCH ST

A389

PADSTOW

Porthilly Cvn Site

Cant Farm

Cemy

P

B3276

Town Bar

107

Cant Cove

107

Trecerus Ind Est

B3276

Sch

Ind Est

River Camel

Gentle Jane

Cant Hill

Dinas

SARAH'S LA

Camp Site

Obelisk

PL27

Camel Trail

Dennis Hill

A389

32

22

33

For full street detail of the highlighted area see page 107.

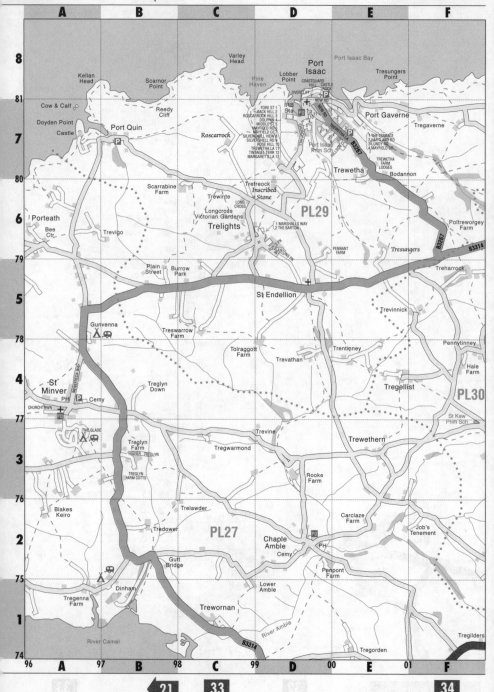

Scale: 1⅓ inches to 1 mile

| 0 | ¼ | ½ mile |
| 0 | 250m | 500m | 750m | 1 km |

A   **B**   **C**   **D**   **E**   **F**

8

Varley Head

Port Isaac Bay

Port Isaac

Tresungers Point

81

Kellan Head

Scarnor Point

Pine Haven

Lobber Point

COASTGUARD HILL

CASTLE ROCK

Cow & Calf

Reedy Cliff

OVERCLIFF

NEW RD

FORE ST 1
BACK HILL 2
ROSCARROCK HILL 3
DOLPHIN 4
MIDDLE ST 5
MAYFIELD RD 6
SILVERSHELL VIEW 8
SILVERSHELL RD 9
ROSE HILL 10
TREWETHA LA 11
TINTAGEL TERR 12
MARGARET'S LA 13

Port Gaverne

Doyden Point

Castle

Port Quin

Roscarrock

Port Isaac Prim Sch

Tregaverne

7

1 THE TERRACE
2 HAZELAND RD
3 LUNDY RD
4 MAYFIELD DR

Trewetha

TREWETHA FARM LODGES

Bodannon

80

Scarrabine Farm

Tretreock Inscribed Stone

PL29

Trewinte

Poltreworgey Farm

6

Porteath

Bee Ctr.

Longcross Victorian Gardens

LONG CROSS

Trelights

1 MARSHALLS WAY
2 THE BARTON

Tresungers

B3267

B3314

Trevigo

PENNANT FARM

79

Plain Street

Burrow Park

Treharrock

5

St Endellion

Trevinnick

Gunvenna

Treswarrow Farm

Trentinney

Pennytinney

78

Tolraggott Farm

Trevathan

Hale Farm

4

St Minver

PH

Cemy

Treglyn Down

Tregellist

PL30

St Kew Prim Sch

CHURCHTOWN

77

THE GLADE

Trevine

Trewethern

3

Treglyn Farm

HIGHER TREGLYN

Tregwarmond

TREGLYN FARM COTTS

Rooke Farm

Carclaze Farm

76

Blakes Keiro

Trelawder

Job's Tenement

2

Tredower

PL27

Chaple Amble

Cemy

Penpont Farm

Gutt Bridge

75

Dinham

Lower Amble

Tregenna Farm

Trewornan

1

River Camel

River Amble

Tregilders

74

Tregorden

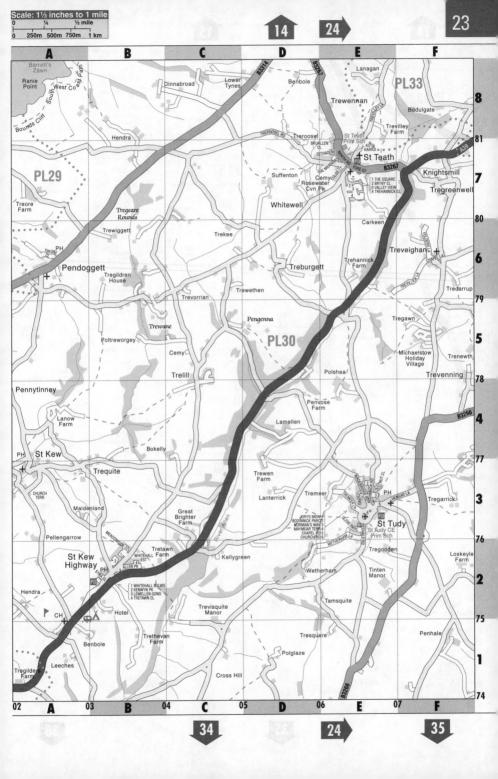

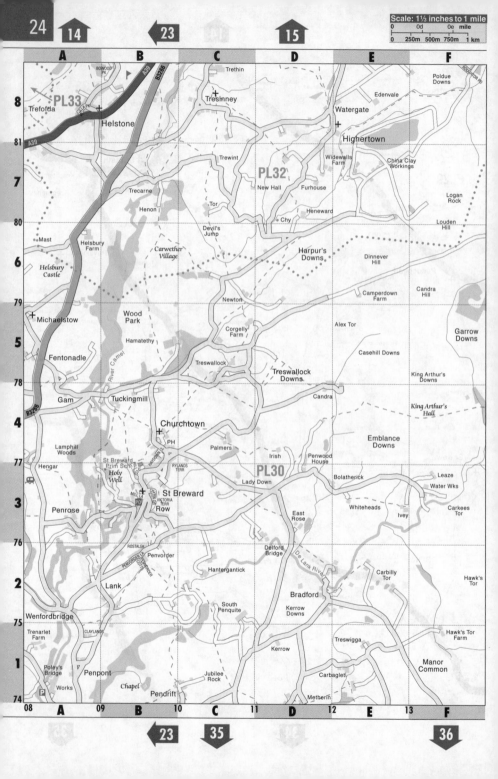

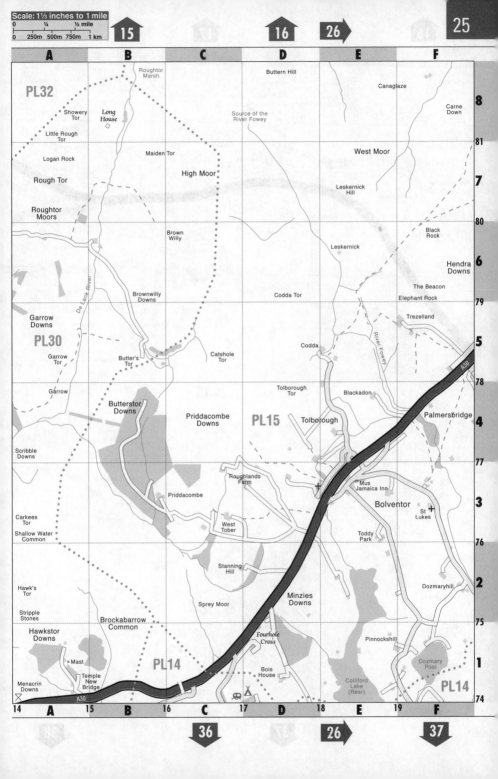

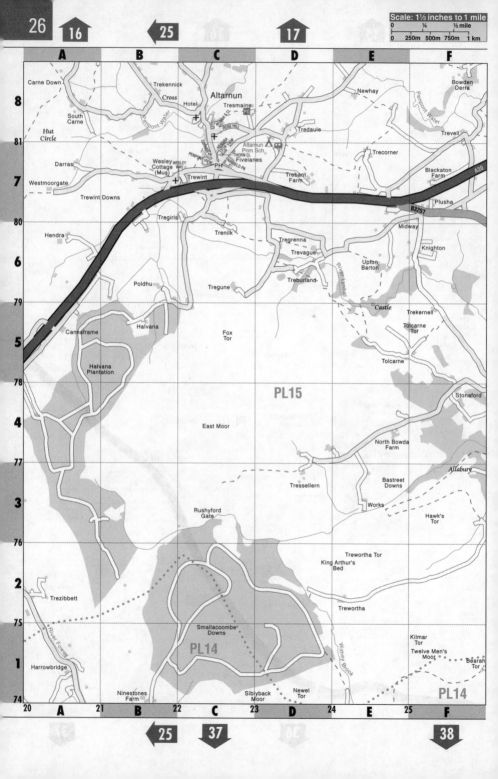

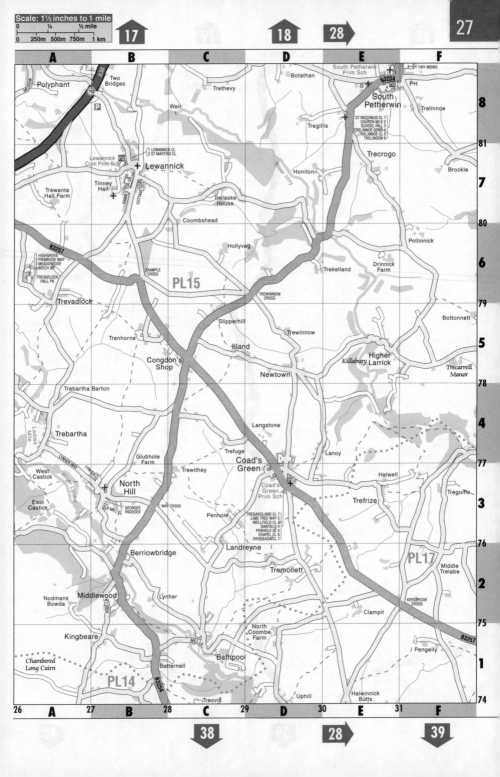

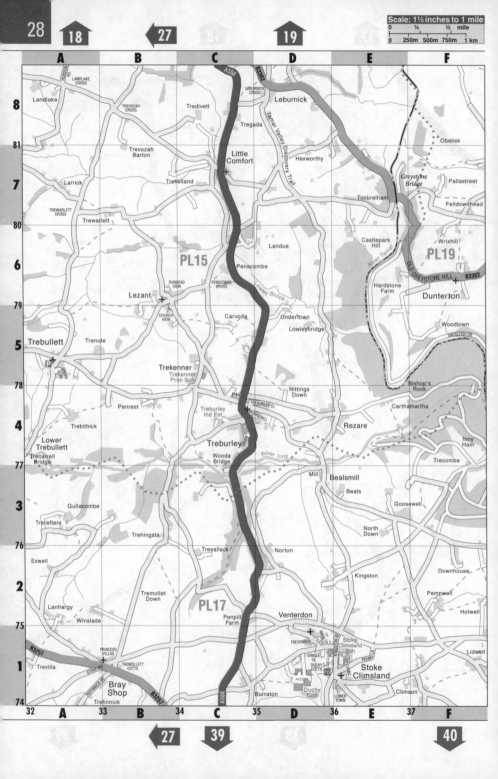

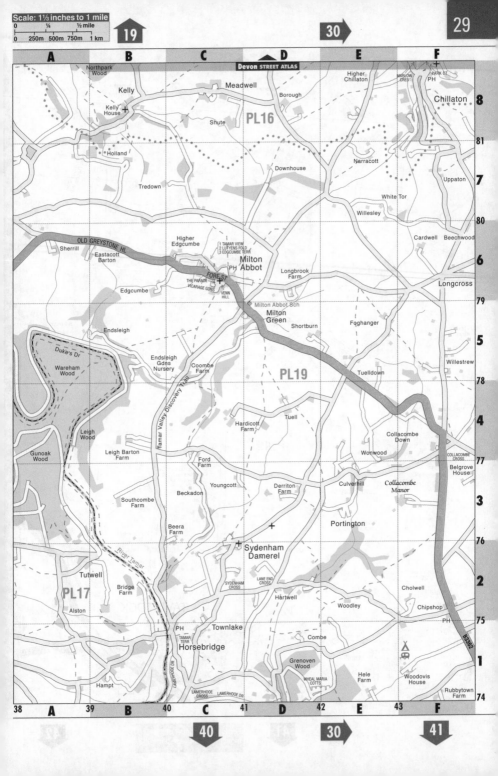

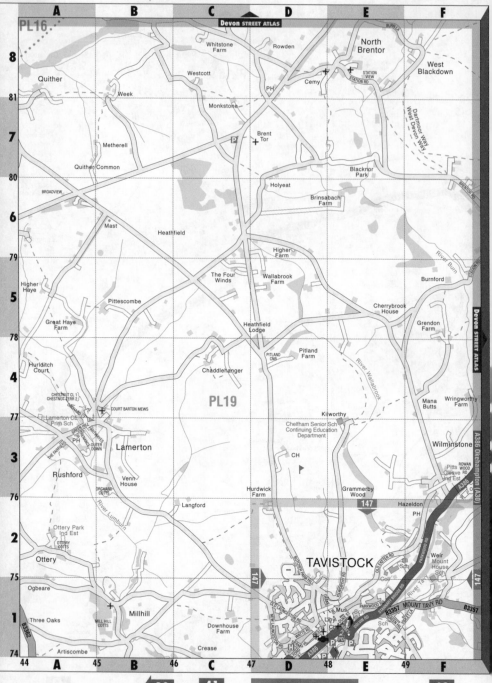

Scale: 1⅓ inches to 1 mile
0   ¼   ½ mile
0   250m 500m 750m   1 km

PL16

Devon STREET ATLAS

Whitstone Farm

Rowden

North Brentor

West Blackdown

Quither

Westcott

PH

Cemy

STATION VIEW

STATION RD

Week

Monkstone

Darmoor Way West Devon WW?

Metherell

Brent Tor

P

Blacknor Park

Quither Common

BROADVIEW

Holyeat

Brinsabach Farm

River Burn

Mast

Heathfield

Higher Farm

Higher Haye

The Four Winds

Wallabrook Farm

Burnford

Great Haye Farm

Pittescombe

Heathfield Lodge

Cherrybrook House

Grendon Farm

Hurlditch Court

PITLAND CNR

Pitland Farm

PITLAND

River Wallabrook

Mana Butts

Wringworthy Farm

CHESTNUT CL 1
CHESTNUT TERR 2

COURT BARTON MEWS

Chaddlehanger

PL19

Kilworthy

Cheltham Senior Sch
Continuing Education
Department

Wilminstone

ORCHARD

GREEN HILL

Lamerton CE
Prim Sch

PH

OUTER DOWN

CH

Rushford

Venn House

Hurdwick Farm

Grammerby Wood

Pitts Cleave Ind Est

ROWAN WOOD RD

A386 Okehampton (A30)

Hazeldon

PH

ORCHARD COTTS

River Lumburn

Langford

147

TAVISTOCK

Weir Mount House Sch

Ottery Park Ind Est

OTTERY COTTS

Ogbeare

Ottery

River Tavy

MOUNT TAVY RD

B3357

Three Oaks

MILL HILL COTTS

Millhill

Downhouse Farm

Mus
Lib
Ctr

B3362

Crease

Artiscombe

44   45   46   47   48   49

29   41

42

For full street detail of the
highlighted area see page 147.

20
32

Scale: 1⅓ inches to 1 mile

0   ¼   ½ mile
0   250m 500m 750m 1 km

	A	B	C	D	E	F

Trethias Island

Treyarnon

Trevear

St Merryn

Hotel

Cemy

PH

JOWAN CT

B3276

DUNES PK

St Merryn Prim Sch

1 TREVITHICK CL
2 PARC FIGLOS
3 HARLYN RD
4 TRELATIS EST
5 WARWICK CL
6 CROSSROADS CL

8

Pepper Cove

Trethias Farm

Shop

Warren Cove

Trehemborne

Kerketh Farm

Higher Trevorgus

Fox Cove

Carnevas

JASMINE WAY
PARC TRENANCE
ST. CADOCS
PENDARVES
PARC TRETHIAS
GUNVER
TRESCORE
LILY WAY
MARIBOU CT
FOXGLOVE CRES 10
DAISYMOUNT DR 11
PRIMROSE DR 12
TAMARISK CL 13

73

Minnows Islands

PL28

Trevoyan

Will's Rock

Trevorrick

Trevean

Tregolds

BAY RETREAT

7

Porthcothan Bay

Trescore Islands

Furze Park

ST MERRYN AIRFIELD

72

Porth Mear

Porthcothan

P PH

Trevethian

Trevio

Airfield (disused)

6

High Cove

Trevemedar

Lewidden

71

Park Head

Pentire Farm

P

Treburrick

Penrose

Cow & Calf

Pentire Steps

Efflins

Trevorgey

5

Diggory's Island

Tregona

Trethewell Farm

Cemy

70

Queen Bess Rock

Engollan

Trerair Farm

Trembleathe Barton

Pendarves Island

Redcliff Castle

PL27

Trevisker Farm

4

Carnewas Island

P

Bedruthan Steps

Hotel

Carnewas

Trerathick Point

P

Downhill

St Eval Airfield (disused)

St Eval

Trevisker Prim Sch

High Cove

Masts

3

Trenance Point

Higher Lanherne

68

Trenance Rock

GWEL-AN-MOR 1
TREDRAGON CL 2
SANDY CT 3
EUROPA CT 4

Trenance

Hotel

CH

Lower Lanherne

Trevilledor

Dayman's Farm

2

Berryl's Point

Mawgan Porth

P

PH

Merlin Farm

TR8

Lower Denzell

67

Beacon Cove

The Beacon

Gluvian Farm

Retorrick Mill

Trevedras

1

Griffin's Point

Trevarrian

Vale of Mawgan or Lanherne

Stem Point

PH

Tolcarne Merock

Polgreen

Bolingey

B3276

83	A	84	B	85	C	86	D	87	E	88	F	66

44
32
45

F3
1 BOTHA RD
2 WELLINGTON RD
3 MOSQUITO CRES
4 LIBERATOR ROW
5 WARWICK CRES
6 LINCOLN ROW
7 WILDEBEEST RD
8 BEAUFORT AVE
9 SHACKLETON CRES

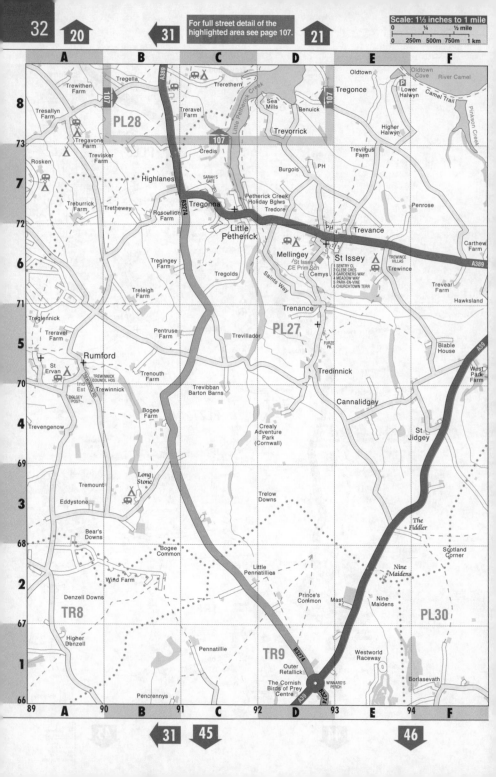

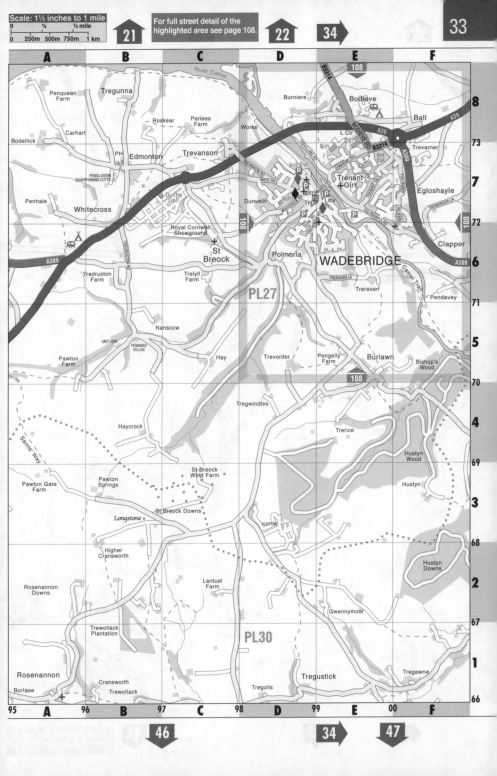

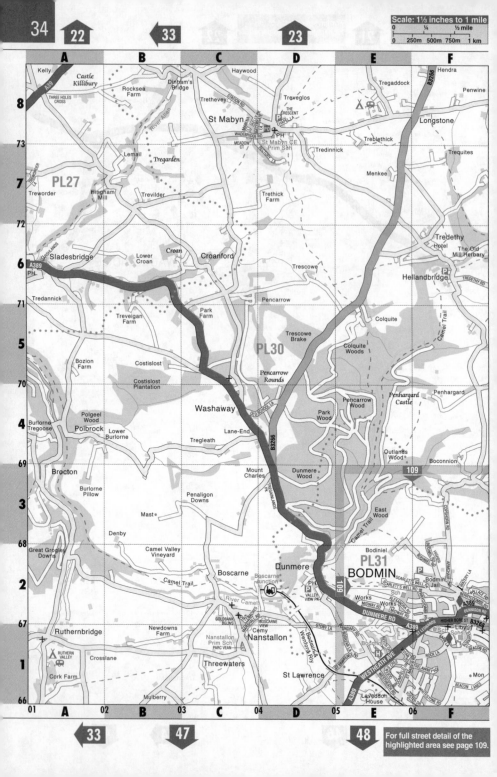

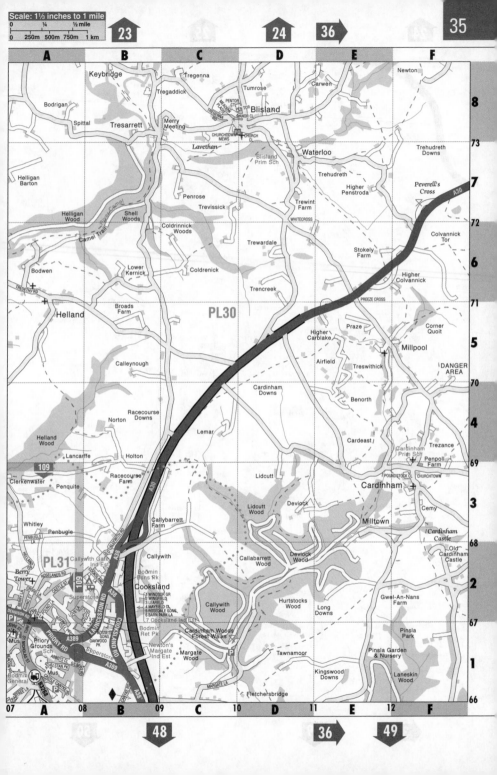

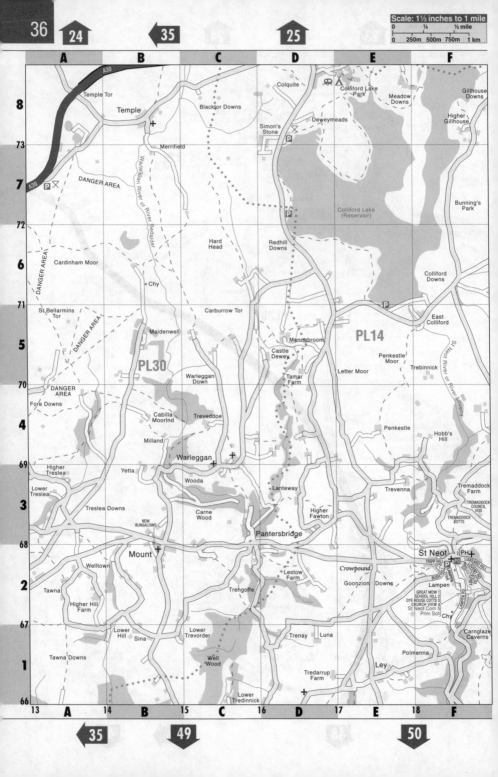

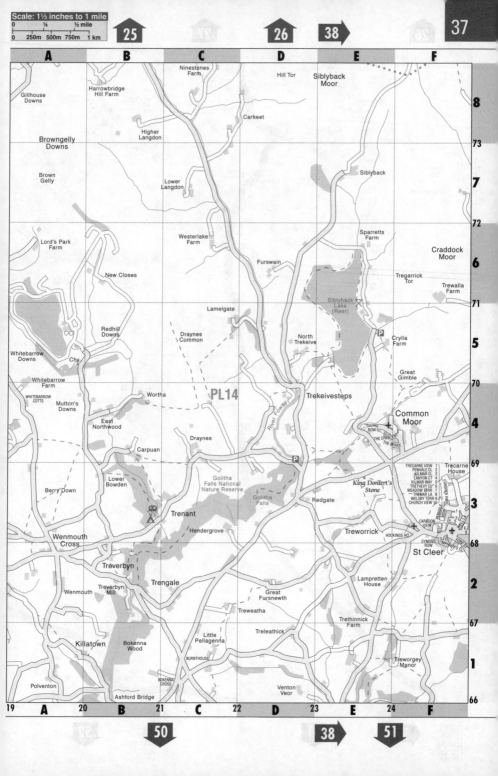

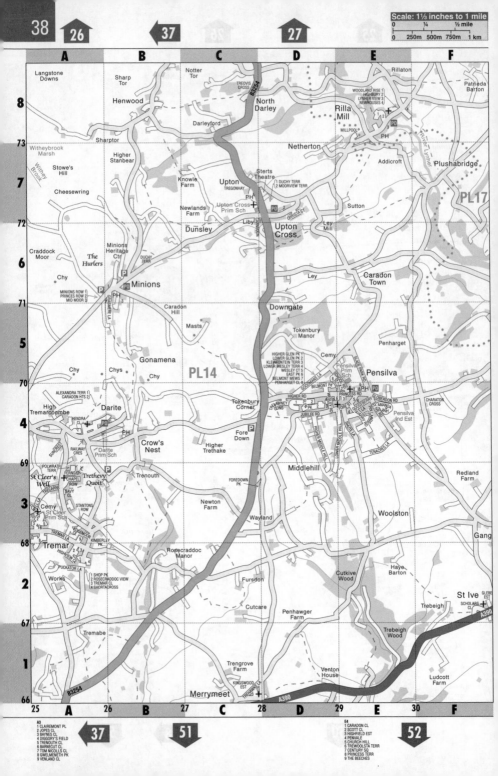

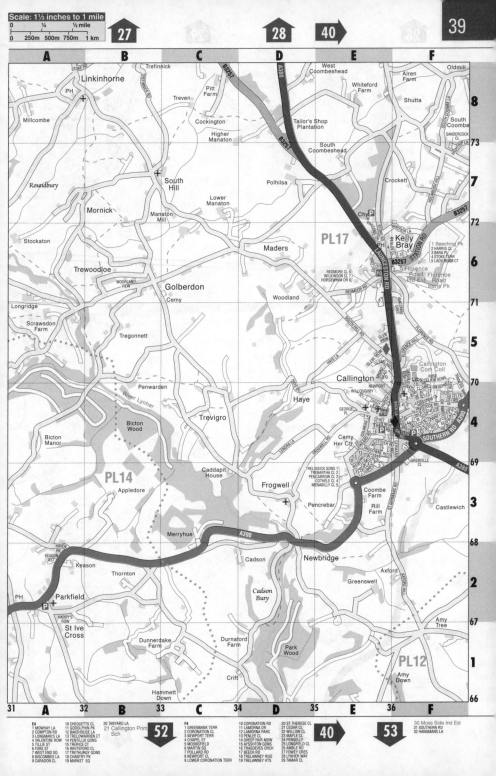

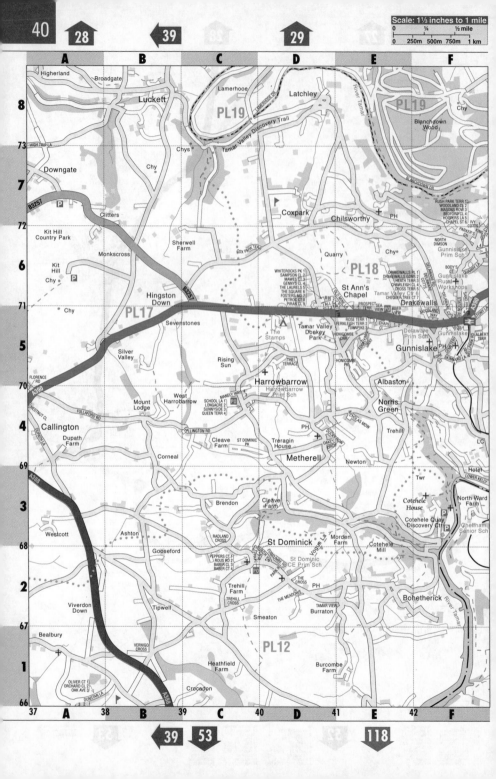

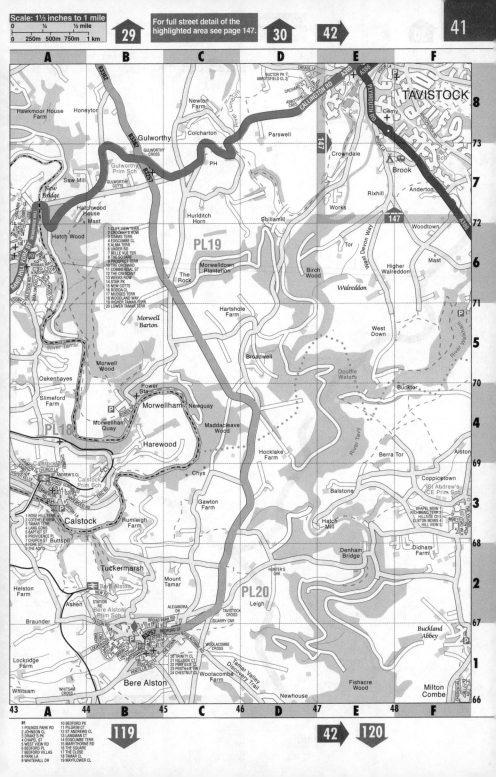

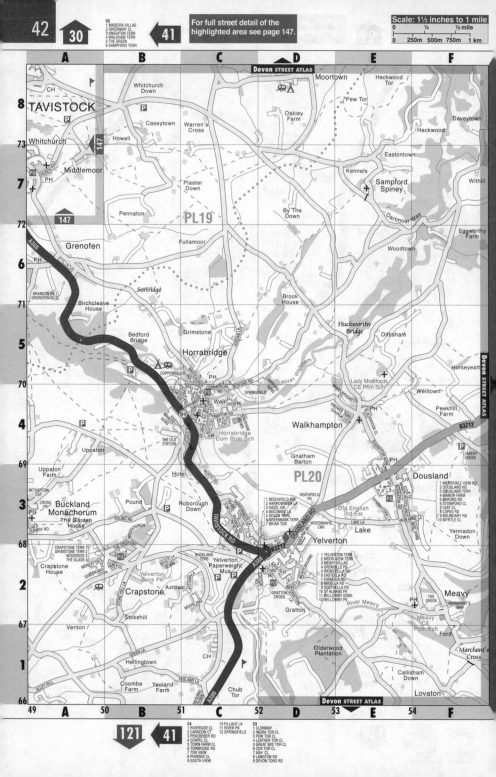

Scale: 1½ inches to 1 mile
0   ¼   ½ mile
0   250m 500m 750m 1 km

A   B   C   D   E   F

8

65

7

64

6

Towan Head

110

63

Gazzle

Fistral
Bay

Hotel

Fistral
Beach

5

HEADLAND RD

DANE RD

NEWQUAY

TR7

CH

L.B.
Sta

62

Cemy

CRANTOCK ST

The
Goose

Pentire
Point East

PH

ESPLANADE
RD

ESPLANADE RD

South West
Coast Path

MOUNT WISE

Pentire

Pentire
Point West

PENTIRE RD

PENTIRE AVE

PENTIRE CRES

PEMMERE RD

GANNEL RD

TREVEAN WAY

A3075

4

Ferry P
(summer only)

The
Chick

Vugga
Cove

Crantock
Beach

110

61

Kelsey
Head

Porth
Joke

Hotel

West
Pentire

Crantock

BEACH RD

Penpol

The
Gannel

GREEN LA

South West Coast Path

PENPOL HILL

3

WEST PENTIRE RD

GUSTORY RD

ST
CARANTOC
WAY

PENTIRE RD

KOSGARTH WAY

PO

PENPOL RD

TRELEAVER RD

Trevella

Treringey

Cave

Treago
Farm

Trevella
Park

60

Holywell
Bay

South West Coast Path

The
Kelseys

HALWYN RD

Wheelgate
House Sch

Trevowah

2

Holywell
Beach

Cubert
Common

TR8

Trevowah

Carters or
Gull Rocks

Dunes

Lewannick

Carines

110

59

Penhale
Point

Holywell

Treworgans

Carevick

Treworthal

TREGUTH
CL

RHUBARB HILL

GOLDEN DR

CH

Penhale
Camp

OURLEWS

Trevornick

Tresean

Cemy

Trenissick

Cave

Holywell Bay
Fun Park

TREVALGA
COTTS

Trevail

Cubert
Sch

Hoblyn's
Cove

CHYNOWEN
PARC

HOLYWELL RD

CHYNOWEN LA

PH

Ligger
Point

DANGER
AREA

58

For full street detail of the
highlighted area see page
110.

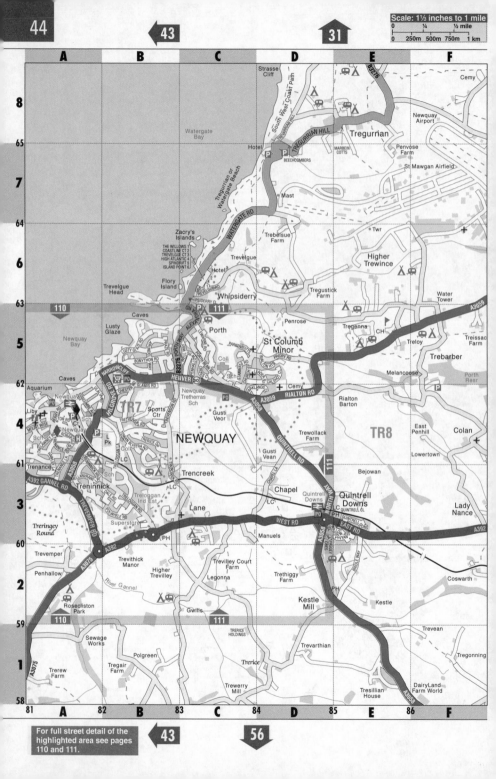

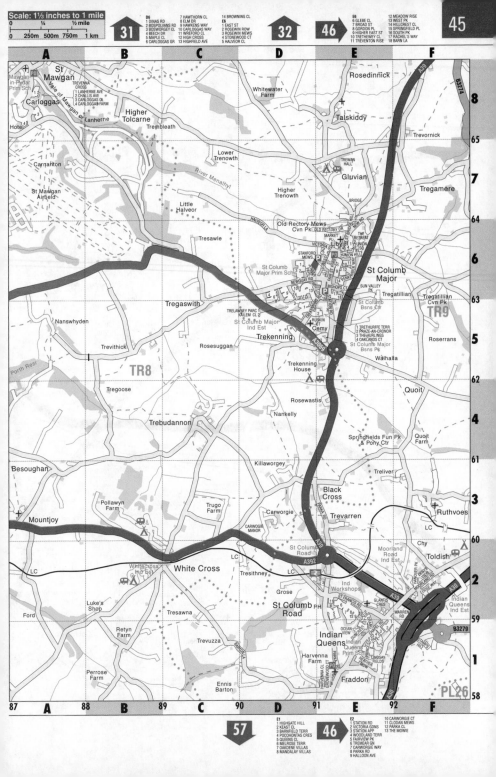

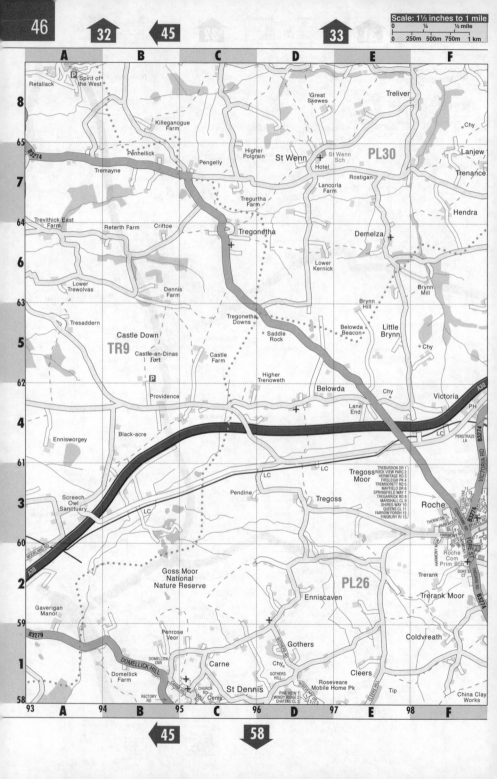

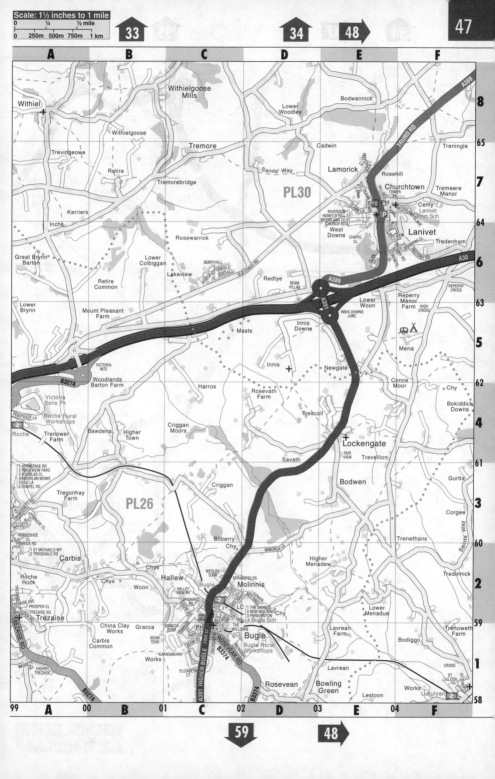

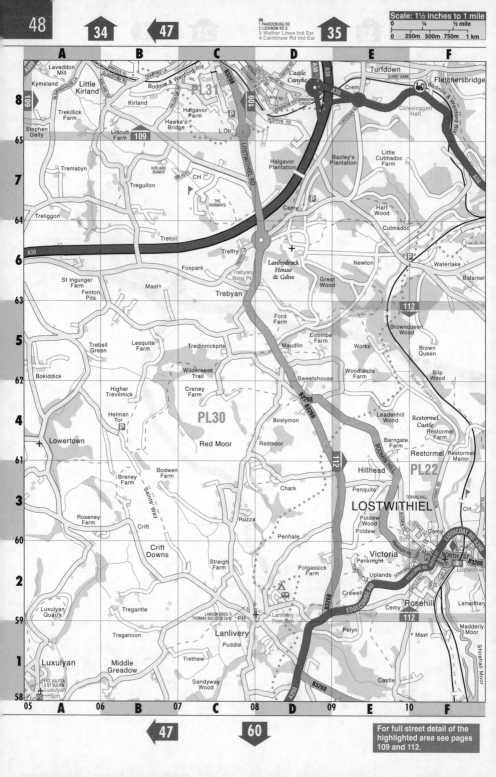

48

34

47

DB
1 PAARDEBURG RD
2 LUCKNOW RD S
3 Walker Lines Ind Est
4 Carminow Rd Ind Est

35

Scale: 1⅓ inches to 1 mile
0   ¼   ½ mile
0   250m 500m 750m 1 km

47

60

For full street detail of the
highlighted area see pages
109 and 112.

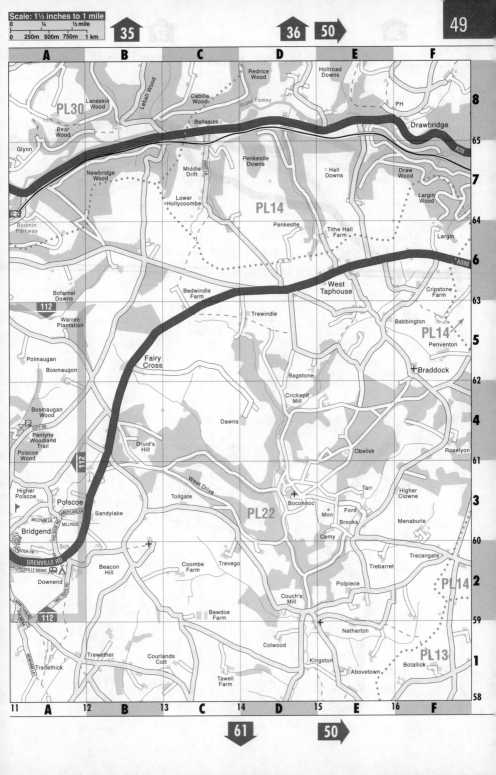

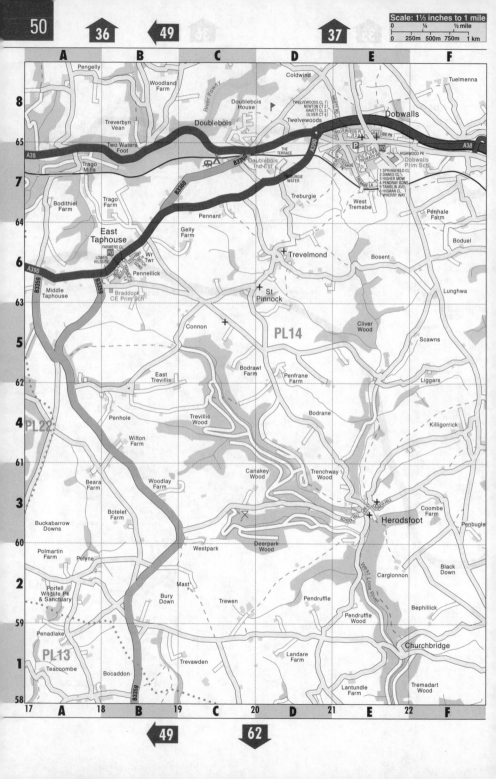

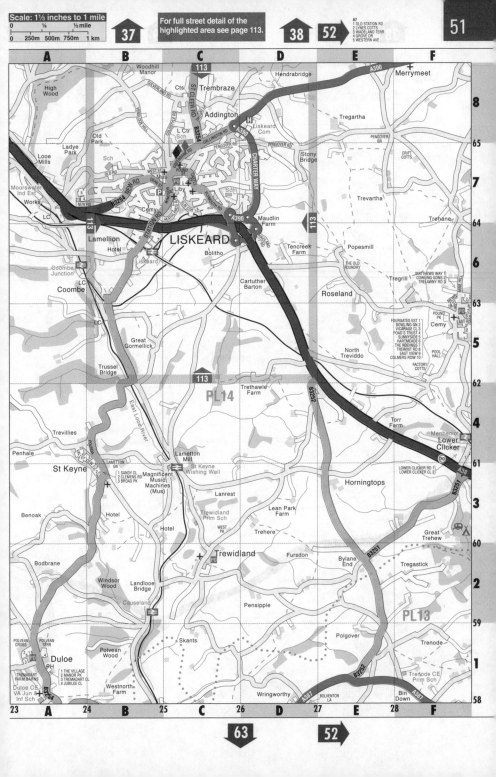

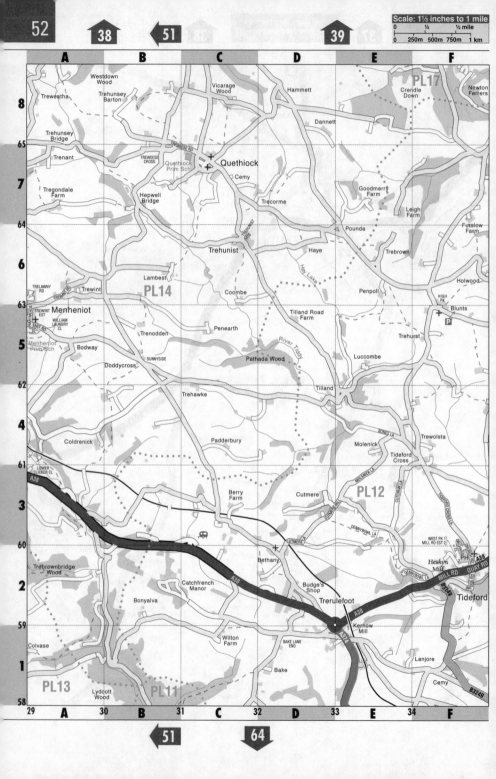

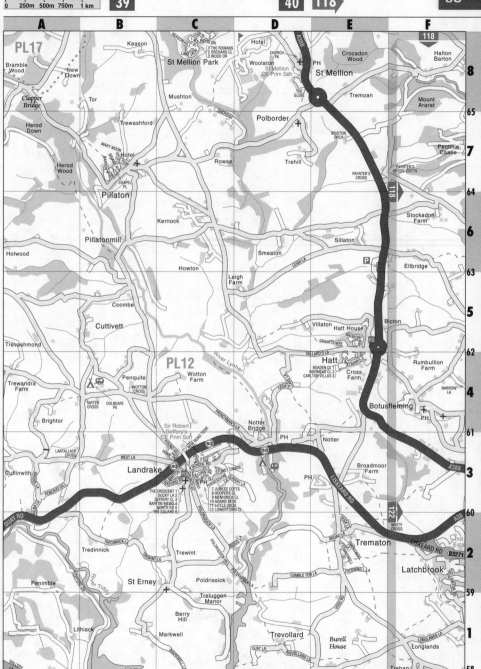

PL17

Bramble Wood

New Down

Clapper Bridge

Keason

St Mellion Park

WOOD DR
KEASON VIEW

1 THE ROWANS
2 ORCHARD CL
3 WOOD DR

Hotel

Woolaton

Church PK

Crocadon Wood

Halton Barton

8

Herod Down

Tor

Mushton

St Mellion CE Prim Sch

St Mellion

Mount Ararat

65

Herod Wood

Trewashford

OAKRIDGE

Polborder

Tremoan

7

Mary Moon Cl Hotel
THE ROW
BARTON CL
CHAPEL PL

Rowse

Trehill

BRISTON ORCH

Pentillie Castle

PAYNTER'S CROSS COTTS

Pillaton

Trewashmond

Kernock

PAYNTER'S CROSS

118

64

Pillatonmill

Holwood

Howton

Leigh Farm

Smeaton

LEIGH LA

Sillaton

Stockadon Farm

6

Coombe

Ellbridge

63

Cuttivett

PL12

Villaton

Hatt House

Bicton

5

Trevashmond

River Lynher

Wotton Farm

ST HARTS WAY
ANCHORSWAY

Hatt

Rumbullion Farm

62

Penquite

WOTTON CROSS

VALLARD'S LA

SYBANKS
BOADEN CL
FAIRMEAD CL
CARLTON VILLAS

Cross Farm

NARROW LA

Trewandra Farm

TARTEN CROSS

DOLBEARE PK

TRENCHMAN'S LA

Botusfleming

PH

4

Brighton

Sir Robert Geffery's CE Prim Sch

Notter Bridge

COCKS

PH

61

LANTALLACK CROSS

WEST LA

NEW ROAD TERR

PH

Notter

Broadmoor Farm

A388

Cutlinwith

Landrake

HOME PK
SCHOOL RD

Cutlinwith

LISKEARD RD

3

PENCARD HILL

QUARRY LA
STONEY LANDS

PH

PH

Treforda

QUAY RD

THE CRESCENT
DUCKY LA
GEFFERY CL
BARTON MEWS
NORTH RD
TRE SQUARE

7 JUBILEE COTTS
8 HOOPERS CL
9 MENHINICK CL
10 ADAMS BECK
11 LITTLE ORCH
12 LOWERTOWN CL

DUCKS LA

Trematon

WHITY CROSS

122

A38

60

Tredinnick

TREDINNICK LA

TREWINT LA

Trewint

POLDRISSICK HILL
POLDRISSICK LA

BROAD LA

TOWN MEAD

THORNWELL LA

B3271

Latchbrook

End Ests

2

Penimble

River Tiddy

St Erney

Poldrissick

CROSS RD

CUMBLE TOR LA

Trehan

59

RICHMOND DR

Treluggan Manor

Trevollard

Burell House

LONGLANDS LA

Longlands

1

Lithiack

GALLERY LA

Berry Hill

Markwell

MARKWELL LA

QUAY LA

TREVOLLARD LA

Trehan

58

35   36   37   38   39   40

65

122

For full street detail of the highlighted area see pages 118 and 122.

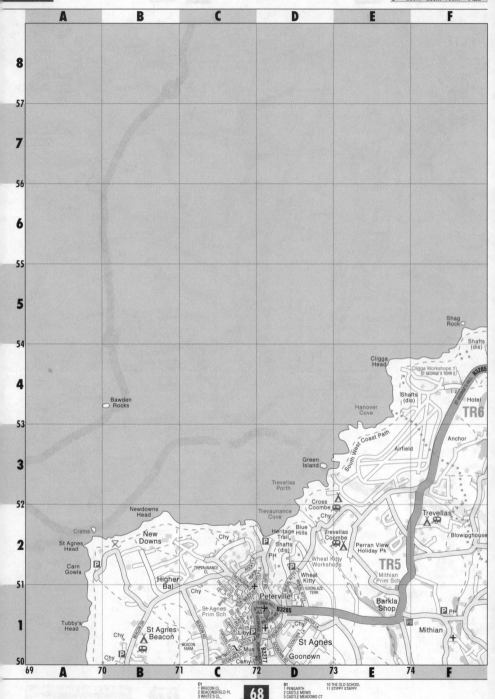

Scale: 1⅓ inches to 1 mile

| 0 | ¼ | ½ mile |
| 0 | 250m | 500m | 750m | 1 km |

8
57
7
56
6
55
5
54
4
53
3
52
2
51
1
50

A   B   C   D   E   F

Shag Rock
Shafts (dis)
Cligga Head
Cligga Workshops 1
ST GEORGE'S TERR 2
Shafts (dis)
Hotel
TR6
Hanover Cove
Anchor
South West Coast Path
Airfield
Green Island
Trevellas Porth
Trevellas
Blowinghouse
Cross Coombe
Chy
Newdowns Head
Trevaunance Cove
Blue Hills
Trevellas Coombe
Perran View Holiday Pk
TR5
Crams
New Downs
Chy
Heritage Trail
Shafts (dis)
PH
Wheal Kitty Workshops
St Agnes Head
Carn Gowla
Wheal Kitty
GOONLAZE TERR
Mithian Prim Sch
Higher Bal
Chy
Peterville
Barkla Shop
Tubby's Head
Chy
St Agnes Beacon
St Agnes Prim Sch
TOWN HILL
B3285
Chy
PO
PH
Mithian
BEACON FARM
Liby
Mus
St Agnes
Goonown
B3277
Cemy

69   70   71   72   73   74

68

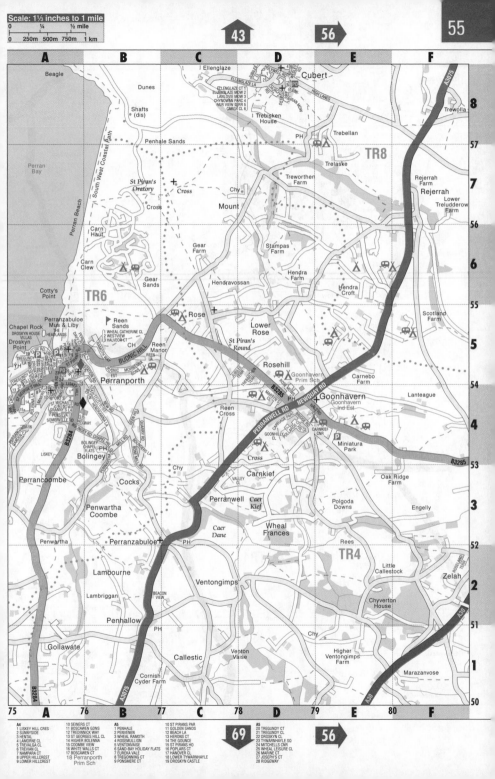

Scale: 1½ inches to 1 mile
0   ¼   ½ mile
0   250m 500m 750m 1 km

Beagle

Dunes

Shafts
(dis)

Penhale Sands

Perran
Bay

8

57

St Piran's
Oratory
Cross
Cross

Cross

Mount

Perran Beach

Carn
Haut

Carn
Clew

Gear
Farm

7

56

Cotty's
Point

TR6

Gear
Sands

Gear
Sands

Hendravossan

Hendra
Farm

Hendra
Croft

6

55

Perranzabuloe
Mus & Liby

THE
HEADLANDS

Reen
Sands
1 WHEAL CATHERINE CL
2 WESTVIEW
3 HALVEOR CT

Rose

Lower
Rose

St Piran's
Round

Scotland
Farm

Chapel Rock
DROSKYN HOUSE
VILLAS
Droskyn
Point
YH
TREGUNDA
P

CH

Reen
Manor

Rosehill

Goonhavern
Prim Sch

Carnebo
Farm

5

54

Perranporth

BUDNIC HILL

Reen
Cross

Goonhavern
Ind Est

Goonhavern

PERRANWELL RD

NEWQUAY RD

Lanteague

ST MICHAELS
GRANNY'S LA
PENGLAZE
SOMERVILLE RD

WE WAY

Chy

GOONHILLY
CL

CARNKIEF
CNR

Miniatura
Park

4

53

LISKEY

BOLINGEY
CHAPEL
FLATS
PH
Bolingey

Cross

Carnkief

VALLEY
CL

Oak Ridge
Farm

B3285

Perrancoombe

Cocks

Chy

Perranwell

Caer
Kief

Polgoda
Downs

Engelly

3

52

Penwartha
Coombe

Caer
Dane

Wheal
Frances

Rees

TR4

Penwartha

Perranzabuloe

PH

Little
Callestock

Zelah

2

51

Lambourne

Ventongimps

Lambriggan

BEACON
VIEW

Chyverton
House

Penhallow

PH

Chy

Higher
Ventongimps
Farm

Gollawate

Callestic

Venton
Vaise

Marazanvose

1

50

Cornish
Cyder Farm

A4
1 LISKEY HILL CRES
2 SUNNYSIDE
3 HENTAL
4 LAMORNE CL
5 TREVALGA CL
6 TREVIAN CL
7 NAMPARA CT
8 UPPER HILLCREST
9 LOWER HILLCREST

10 SEINERS CT
11 BOSCAWEN GDNS
12 TREDINNICK WAY
13 ST GEORGES HILL CL
14 HIGHER BOLENNA
15 COOMBE VIEW
16 WHITE WALLS CT
17 BOSCAWEN CT
18 Perranporth
Prim Sch

A5
1 PENHALE
2 PENVENEN
3 WHEAL RAMOTH
4 ROSEMULLION
5 VENTONVAISE
6 SAND-BAY HOLIDAY FLATS
7 EUREKA VALE
8 TREGONNING CT
9 PONSMERE CT

10 ST PIRANS PAR
11 GOLDEN SANDS
12 BEACH LA
13 HERONS CT
14 THE GOUNCE
15 ST PIRANS HO
16 POPLARS CT
17 HANOVER CL
18 LOWER TYWARNHAYLE
19 DROSKYN CASTLE

A5
20 TREGUNDY CT
21 TREGUNDY CL
22 DROSKYN CL
23 TYWARNHAYLE SQ
24 MITCHELLS CNR
25 WHEAL LEISURE CL
26 MARINE CT
27 JOSEPH'S CT
28 RIDGEWAY

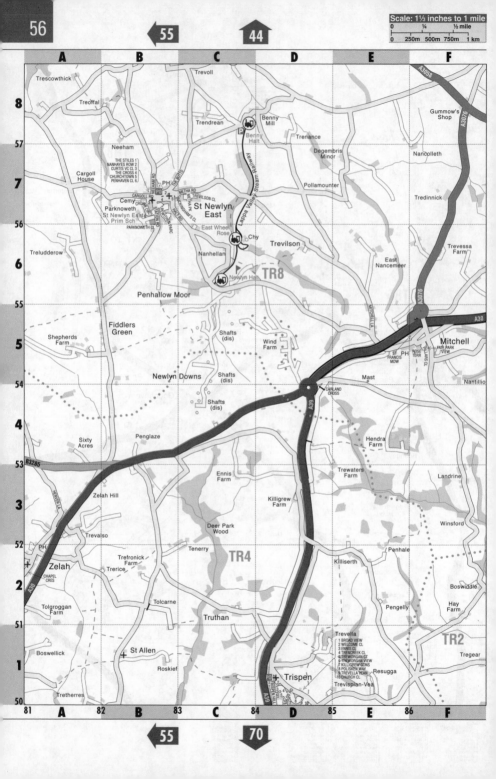

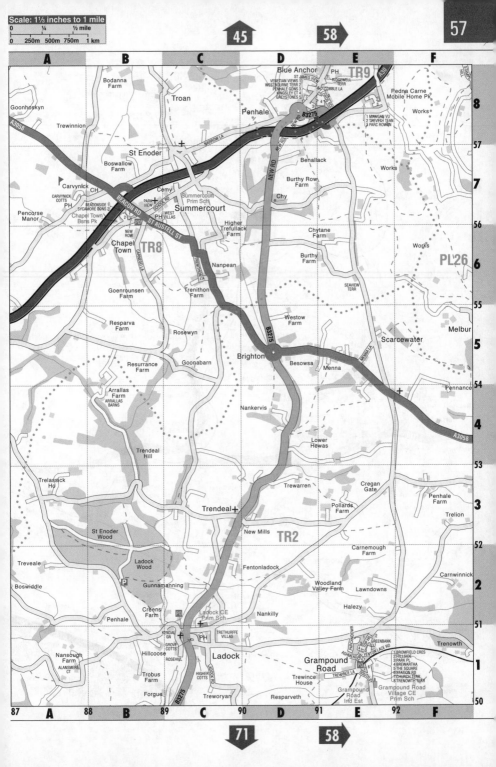

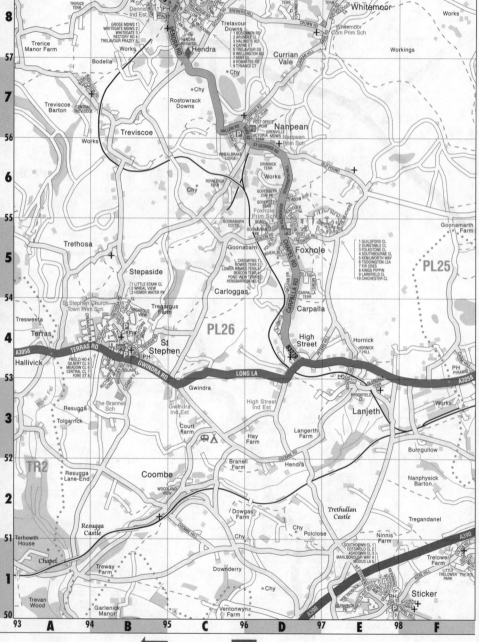

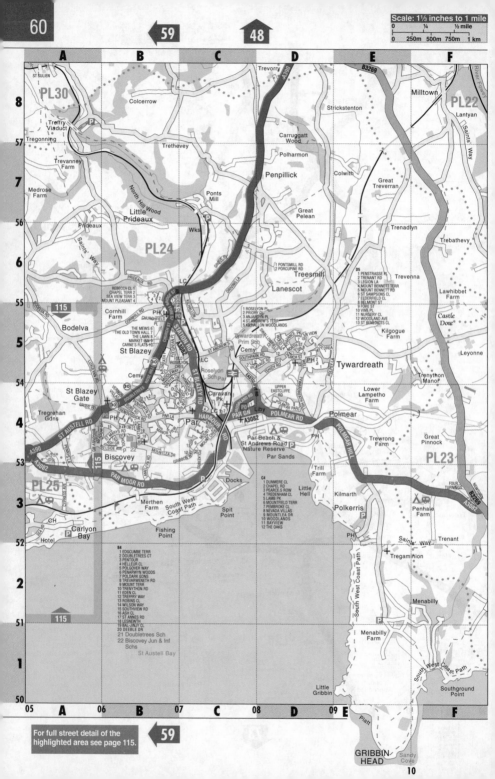

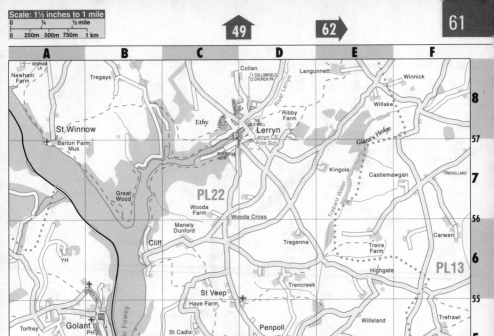

A   B   C   D   E   F

Newham
Farm
Newham
NEWHAM
LA

Tregays

Collan
1 COLLONFIELD
2 CHURCH PK

Langunnett

Winnick

St Winnow

Ethy

Lerryn
THE OLD MILL
Lerryn CE
Prim Sch

River Lerryn

Ribby
Farm

Willake

Willake

Barton Farm
Mus

RIVER
VIEW

Giant's Hedge

PL22

Great
Wood

Wooda
Farm

Wooda Cross

Kingole

Castlemawgan

TREVOLLARD

7

57

8

Manely
Dunford

Carwen

56

Cliff

Tregenna

Treire
Farm

PL13

6

YH

St Veep

Highgate

Trencreek

Willsland

Trefrawl

55

Torfrey

Golant
PH

Haye Farm

St Cadix

Penpoll

Trevelyan

Peakswater

5

SCHOOL HILL 1
WATER LA 2
FORE ST 3
ST-SAMPSON'S TERR 4

Saints' Way

Penpoll Creek

54

Trezare

116

Lanteglos
Highway

Polveithan
Farm

Lanlawren

4

Penventinue
Farm

PL23

Colvithick
Wood

Dorset
Farm

Lombard
Farm

Trevedda
Farm

53

Lescrow

Mixtow

Yeate
Farm

Trethake

Tremeer
Farm

3

B3269

PASSAGE LA

Liby

Bodinnick

Lamellyon
Hall
Farm

Pont

Tredudwell
Manor

Carneggan
Farm

Trevarder

52

Tristan
Stone

TAVERN BABR

Cemy
PARK

PH

LB
Sta

PH

Pendower
House

Frogmore
Farm

116

FOWEY

NEW ROAD HILL

Mus

Mon

Triggabrowne

West
Coombe

2

Readymoney

Ferry (P)

Essa

Churchtown
Farm

51

St Catherine's Castle
(remains of)

Polruan

South West Coast Path

Lantivet Bay

1

SWCP

Coombe
Haven

Washing
Rocks

Lantic Bay

Blackbottle
Rock

Pencarrow
Head

50

11   A   12   B   13   C   14   D   15   E   16   F

116

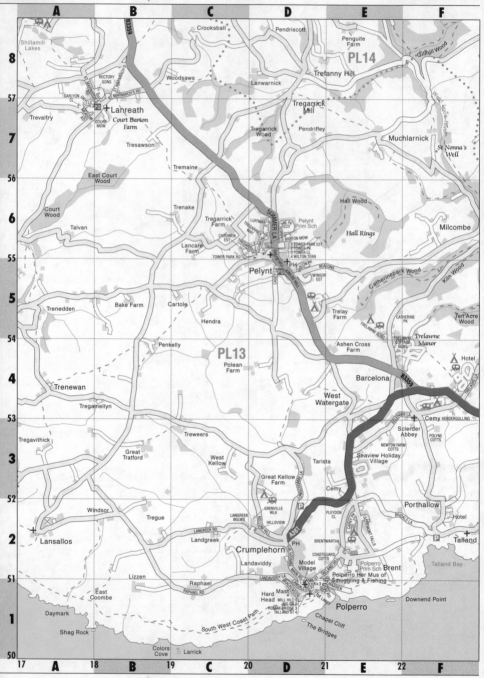

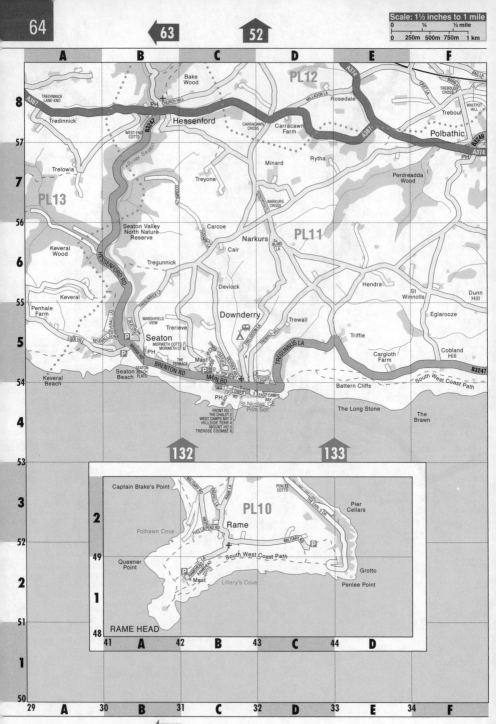

Scale: 1⅓ inches to 1 mile

53 · 126

For full street detail of the highlighted area see pages 126 and 132.

132

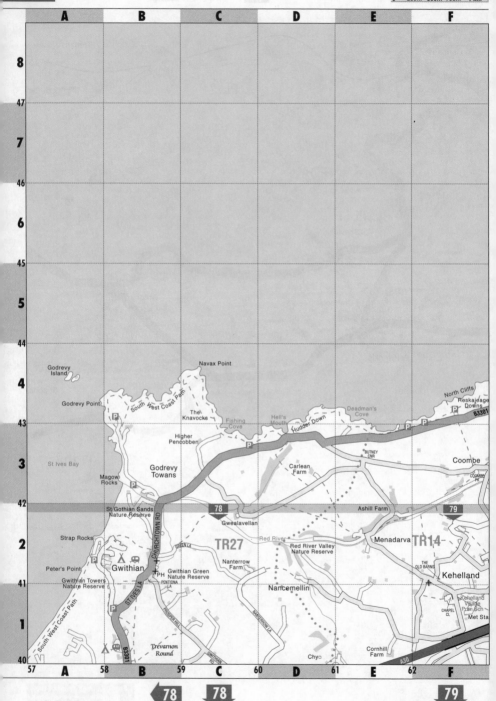

Scale: 1⅓ inches to 1 mile

Scale: 1½ inches to 1 mile

0	¼	½ mile
0	250m 500m 750m	1 km

E4
1 CORONATION RD
2 VENTONRAIZE TERR
3 ROBARTES TERR
4 HARMONY TERR
5 ALEXANDRA CL
6 TREFORTHLAN CL

7 TREFORTHLAN
8 ILLOGAN PK
9 SUNNYSIDE PARC
10 KESTRAL WAY
11 BOSVEAN GDNS
12 POLDARK RD
13 PENCARROW RD

14 PENWARTHA VEAN
15 PENWARTHA RD
16 LAMANVA CL
17 LAMANVA RD
18 TREVELTHAN RD
19 VALLEY VIEW
20 VALLEY GDNS

21 FORTH DALL
22 LOWER MERRITTS HILL
23 BEACON VIEW PK

68

TR4

Tobban Horse
Chy
Factory Farm

Gullyn Rock

Sheep Rock
South West Coast Path
Nancekuke Common
Diamond
Airfield (dis)

FORTHVEAN RD

1 GREENFIELD TERR
2 LAMORNA CT
3 BASSETT TERR

Horse Rock Portreath
Landmark
Gull Rock
TR16
Cambrose

HARBOUR TERR 1
KINGSLEY TERR 2
CAYFORTH FLATS 3
FORTH-AN-NANCE 4
CLIFF TERR 5
HARBOUR CT 6
THE SQUARE 7
GLENFEADON TERR 8
BAINES HILL 9
SUNNYVALE CL 10
CHAPEL TERR 11

Pier
PH
PH
PENBERTHY RD
B3300
NEW PORTREATH RD
B3300

Ralph's Cupboard
Cvn Pk
TREGEA HILL
Portreath Com Prim Sch
Trad Est

B3301
FORTHVEAN
COLLETTS CT
Sunland Holiday Est
PH
Bridge
Cornish Goldsmiths

Samphire Island

Crane Islands
Basset's Cove
Carnanter Downs
Tehidy Barton
Nance Farm Churchtown
Illogan Prim Sch
Redruth Tin Old Cornwall Soc Mus

Crane Castle
Tehidy Ctry Pk
ALEXANDRA RD
Illogan
Sparnon Gate

Reskajeage Downs
Tehidy Copse
THE STABLES
CH
PRIMROSE GDNS 1
WOODBINE LA 2
COLDRINE AVE 3
WARWICK AVE 4
THE MEADOW 5
Paynter's Lane End
Bassett RD
PH

Oak Wood
Old Merrose Farm

138 Home Farm
139 West Tolgus
Tolgus Mount

South Tehidy
Halgoss
Park Bottom
WEST TOLGUS
Chys
A30

TR14
MOUNT WHISTLE RD
PH

Roscroggan
Tolvaddon Downs
TR15
Chy
80
A3047

79 Chy
Mast
Coll
Illogan Highway
Tolskithy

Reskadinnick
Roskear Croft
Coll
AGAR RD
Camborne Redruth Com
H

138
Chys
TREVENSON RD FORE ST
Pool
Mus Pool Ind Est
Carn Brea Village
Cambria Castle

Magor Farm
TA Ctr
Mine (dis)
L Ctr
Carn Brea
Tregajorran

Race Farm
Bosewarne
PENDARVES ST
Tuckingmill
Brea
Penhallick
TR16

Treswithian
A3047
CAMBORNE
DOLCOATH AVE
Carn Arthen
Bosleake

79
80
80

For full street detail of the highlighted area see pages 138 and 139.

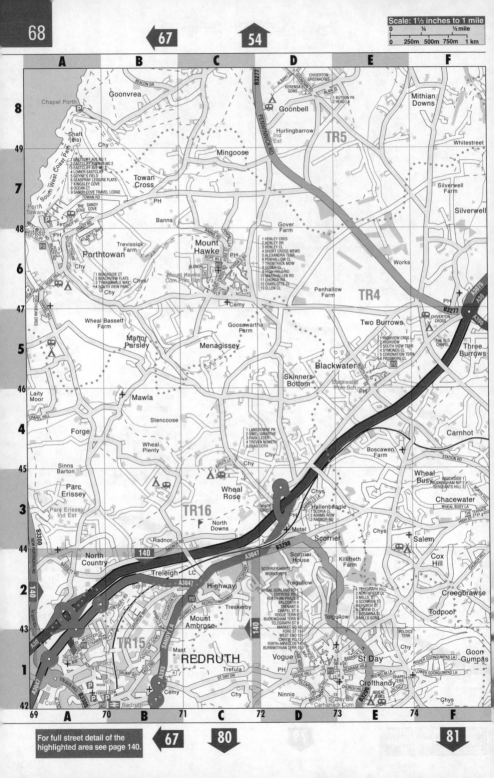

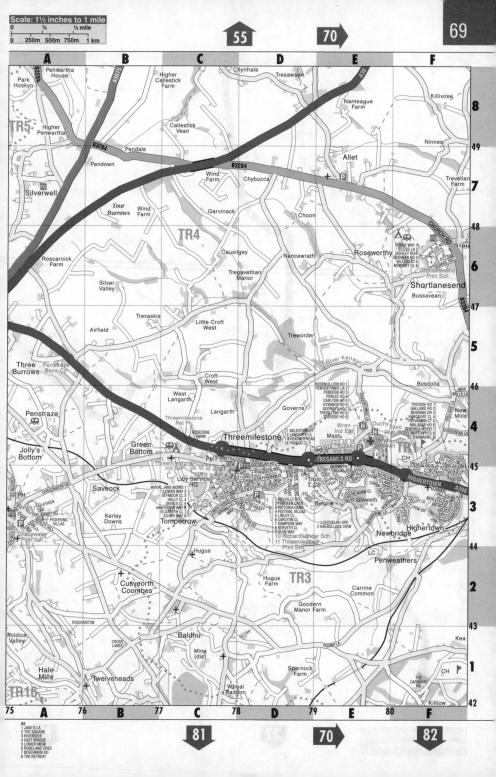

69
56

Scale: 1½ inches to 1 mile

| 0 | | ¼ | | ½ mile |
| 0 | 250m | 500m | 750m | 1 km |

A **B** **C** **D** **E** **F**

8

St Erme
St Erme
Prim Sch

1 KILLIGREW GDNS
2 POLGLASE WLK
3 TREVELLA VEAN
4 TOWER RD
5 CHANCERY CL
6 ALLIUM CT
7 FOREST HOS

Lanner
Barton

Treworgan

Tresithick

Great
Tregassow
Wood

Trehane
Vean

49

Pennare

Gwarnick

Tregassow

Trehane
Wood

Nankilly

7

Trevellan

Garras

St Clement,
Woods

TR4

Laniley

Bodrean Manor
Farm

Frogmore

Trehane
Barton

48

Idless Wood
Forest Walk

COURTYARD
COTTS

Calerick

Pencoose

6

Carvinack

Idless

Penmount
(Crem)

Polwhele
House
Sch

Polwhele

Trevella Stream

Nansmerrow

Polperrow

Tregeagle

47

137

Treheveras

Killagerden

Buckshead

Tregurra

Tregoninny

Works

TR2
Tresillian

Cemy

B3284

5

Featherbeds

Nancemere

Potsue Manor
Farm

RIVER
VIEW

1 CARNE MDWS
2 PRIMROSE TERR
3 BONE CELLAR ROW
4 PENDARVES

46

KENWYN RD

KENWYN PK

NEW MILLS LA

A39
A390

Penair

Pencalenick

Treffry

4

Kenwyn

KENWYN RD

Sch

CHELLEW RD

Penair
Sch

Penair

Pencalenick

Pencalenick
Sped Sch

Merther

45

137

A390

Cty Hall

Bosvigo
Gdns

Truro
Sch

Mus

Cath

Cemy

THELANDER HIGHWAY

St Clement's Hill

Cemy

Lambesso

TR1

3

Treyew
Mills

Sch

DANIELL ST

BARRACK LA

Newham
Ind Est

Sch

Mast

Trennick

TRURO

Menadews
Farm

St
Clement

44

Nansavallan

ROSEWICK RD

137

Higher
Newham

Calenick

Works

Park
Farm

Park Farm

Tresawson

2

TR3

MALPAS RD

Malpas

BAR MDWS 1
RIVIERA EST 2
TRENHAILE TERR 3
SCOBLE'S TERR 4
VICTORIA QUAY 5

Fentongollan

TR2

Merther
Lane

43

Kea
Com Prim
Sch

Trethowell

Ferry P
(summer only)

PARK
TERR

Tregonian

1

Carlyon

Porth
Kea

Woodbury

Ferries P

St Michael
Penkevil

42

A 82 **B** 83 **C** 84 **D** 85 **E** 86 **F**

69
82
83

For full street detail of the
highlighted area see page 137.

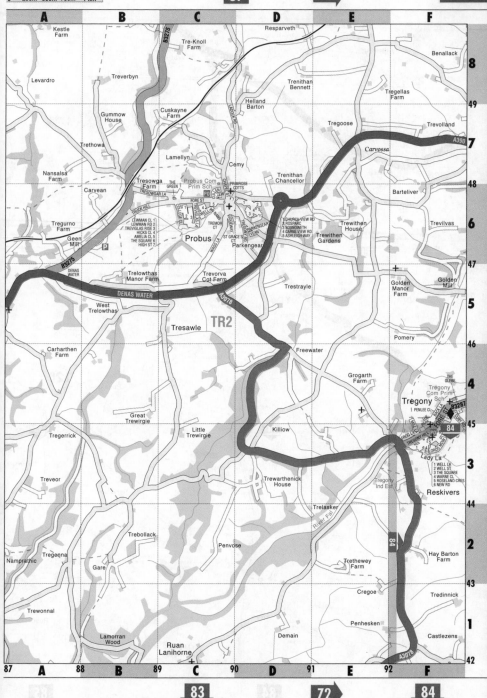

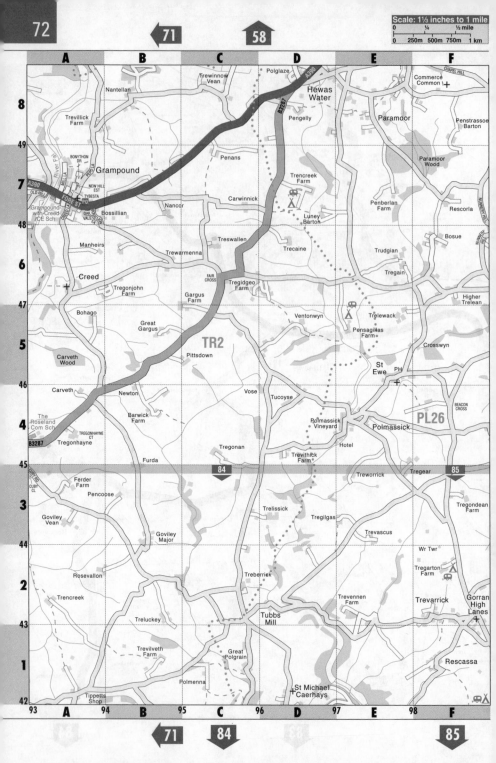

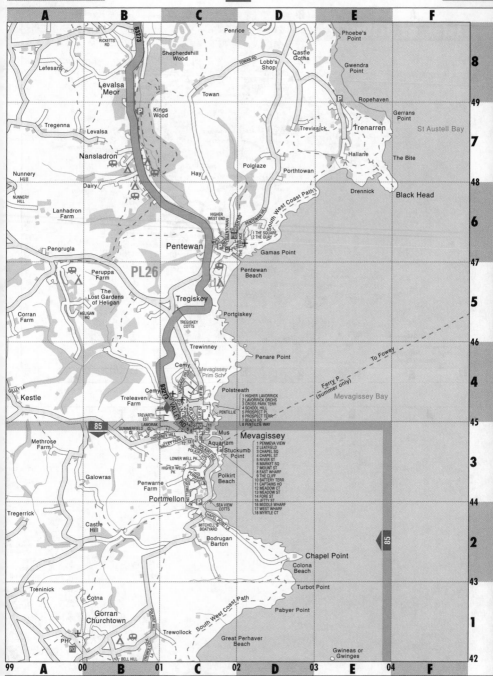

Scale: 1½ inches to 1 mile

0   ¼   ½ mile
0   250m 500m 750m 1 km

8

Penrice

Phoebe's Point

Shepherdshill Wood

Lobb's Shop

Castle Gotha

Gwendra Point

Lefesant

49

Levalsa Meor

Kings Wood

Towan

RICKETTS RD

B3273

TOWAN RD

Ropehaven

Gerrans Point

St Austell Bay

Tregenna

Levalsa

Trevissick

Trenarren

7

Nansladron

Dairy

Hay

Polglaze

Hallane

The Bite

Nunnery Hill

NUNNERY HILL

Porthtowan

Drennick

Black Head

48

Lanhadron Farm

Pengrugla

Peruppa Farm

Higher West End

Pentewan

Gamas Point

6

PL26

The Lost Gardens of Heligan

HELIGAN HO

Tregiskey

Pentewan Beach

47

Corran Farm

Portgiskey

TREGISKEY COTTS

5

Kestle

Trewinney

Penare Point

To Fowey

46

GILLEY LA

Cemy

Mevagissey Prim Sch

1 HIGHER LAVORRICK
2 LAVORRICK ORCHS
3 CROSS PARK TERR
4 SCHOOL HILL
5 PROSPECT PL
6 PROSPECT TERR
7 BEACH RD
8 PENTILLIE WAY

Ferry P. (summer only)

Mevagissey Bay

4

Cemy

Treleaven Farm

B3273

VALLEY RD

Polstreath

PENTILLIE

45

TREVARTH EST

LAMORAK CL

Mevagissey

1 PENMEVA VIEW
2 LEATFIELD
3 CHAPEL SQ
4 CHAPEL ST
5 RIVER ST
6 MARKET SQ
7 MOUNT ST
8 EAST WHARF
9 THE CLIFF
10 BATTERY TERR
11 CAPTAINS HO
12 MEADOW CT
13 MEADOW ST
14 FORE ST
15 JETTY ST
16 MIDDLE WHARF
17 WEST WHARF
18 MYRTLE CT

Methrose Farm

SUMMERFIELD CL

THEGNEY HILL

VALLEY PARK LA

Mus

Aquarium

Stuckumb Point

3

Galowras

HIGHER WELL PK

LOWER WELL PK

Penwarne Farm

Polkirt Beach

Portmellon

PORTMELLON PK

SEA VIEW COTTS

44

Tregerrick

Castle Hill

CHAPEL POINT LA

Mitchell's Boatyard

Bodrugan Barton

85

2

Chapel Point

Colona Beach

Treninick

Cotna

Turbot Point

43

Gorran Churchtown

PH

PO

South West Coast Path

Trewollock

Pabyer Point

Great Perhaver Beach

Gwineas or Gwinges

1

BELL HILL

42

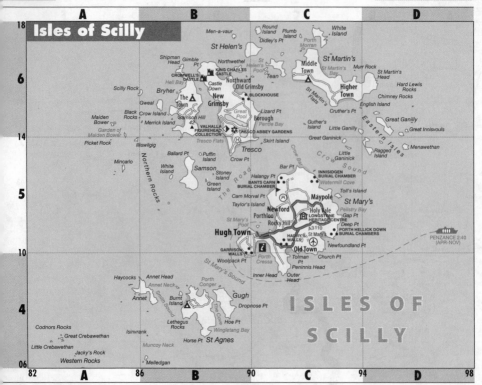

Isles of Scilly

A   B   C   D

18

Men-a-vaur
Round Island
Plumb Island
White Island
St Helen's
Didley's Pt
Porth Morran
6
Shipman Head
Gimble Pt
Northwethel
St Helen's Pool
St Martin's
Middle Town
St Martin's Bay
Murr Rock
St Martin's Head
Hard Lewis Rocks
CROMWELL'S CASTLE
KING CHARLES CASTLE
Castle Down
Northward
Tean
Higher Town
Scilly Rock
Bryher
Heli Bay
The Town
New Grimsby
Old Grimsby
BLOCKHOUSE
Chimney Rocks
English Island
Gweal
Crow Island
Samson Hill
Great Pool
Lizard Pt
St Martin's Flats
Great Ganilly
14
Black Rocks
Merrick Island
Pentle Bay
Borough
Cruther's Pt
Great Innisvouls
Maiden Bower
Garden of Maiden Bower
VALHALLA FIGUREHEAD COLLECTION
TRESCO ABBEY GARDENS
Guther's Island
Little Ganilly
Ragged Island
Menawethan
Picket Rock
Illiswilgig
Tresco Flats
Skirt Island
Great Ganinick
Little Ganinick
Tresco
Crow Pt
Crow Bar
Crow Sound
Eastern Isles
5
Mincarlo
Northern Rocks
Puffin Island
White Island
Samson
Stoney Island
Bar Pt
Halangy Pt
INNISIDGEN BURIAL CHAMBER
Watermill Cove
Ballard Pt
BANTS CARN BURIAL CHAMBER
Green Island
Carn Morval Pt
Maypole
Toll's Island
St Mary's
Taylor's Island
Holy Vale
Pelistry Bay
The Road
Newford
Porthloo
LONGSTONE HERITAGE CENTRE
Gap Pt
Deep Pt
St Mary's Pool
Rocky Hill
A3110
St Mary's
PORTH HELLICK DOWN BURIAL CHAMBERS
Hugh Town
HARRY'S WALLS
Old Town
Newfoundland Pt
PENZANCE 2:40 (APR-NOV)
10
GARRISON WALLS
Woolpack Pt
Porth Cressa
Tolman
Church Pt
St Mary's Sound
Peninnis Head
Inner Head
Outer Head
Haycocks
Annet Head
Annet Neck
Porth Conger
I S L E S   O F
4
Annet
Swan Sound
Burnt Island
Gugh
Dropnose Pt
S C I L L Y
Isinvrank
Lethegus Rocks
The Cove
Hoe Pt
Wingletang Bay
Codnors Rocks
Great Crebawethan
Muncoy Neck
Horse Pt
St Agnes
Little Crebawethan
Jacky's Rock
06
Western Rocks
Melledgan

82   A   86   B   90   C   94   D   98

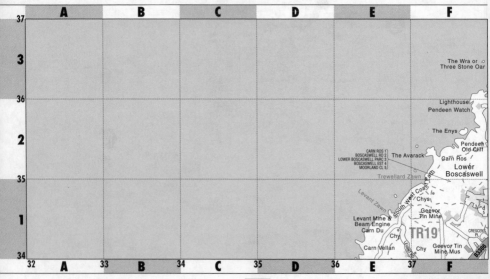

A   B   C   D   E   F

37

3
The Wra or Three Stone Oar

36
Lighthouse Pendeen Watch

2
The Enys

CARN ROS 1)
BOSCASWELL RD 2)
LOWER BOSCASWELL PARC 3)
BOSCASWELL EST 4)
MOORLAND CL 5)
The Avarack
Pendeen Old Cliff
Carn Ros
Lower Boscaswell

35
Trewellard Zawn

Levant Zawn
South West Coast Path
Chys
1
Levant Mine & Beam Engine
Carn Du
Geevor Tin Mine
TR19
CRESCENT PL
Carn Vellan
Chy
Geevor Tin Mine Mus
Chy
B3306

34
32   A   33   B   34   C   35   D   36   E   37   F

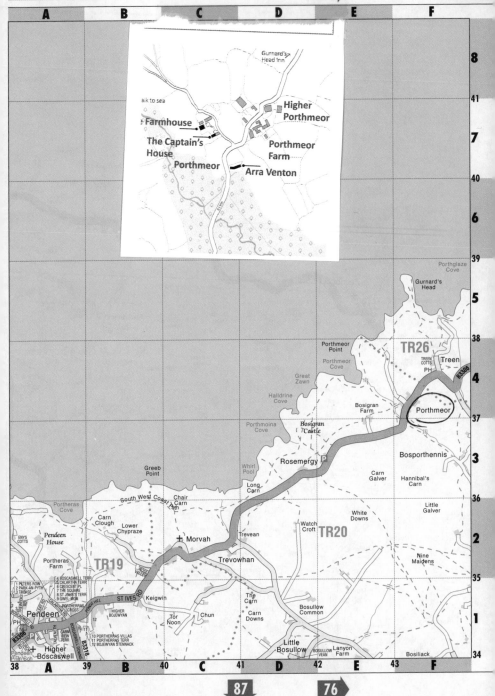

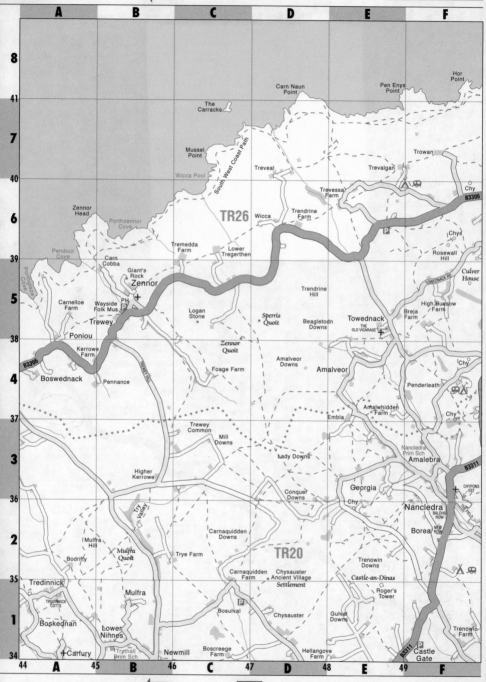

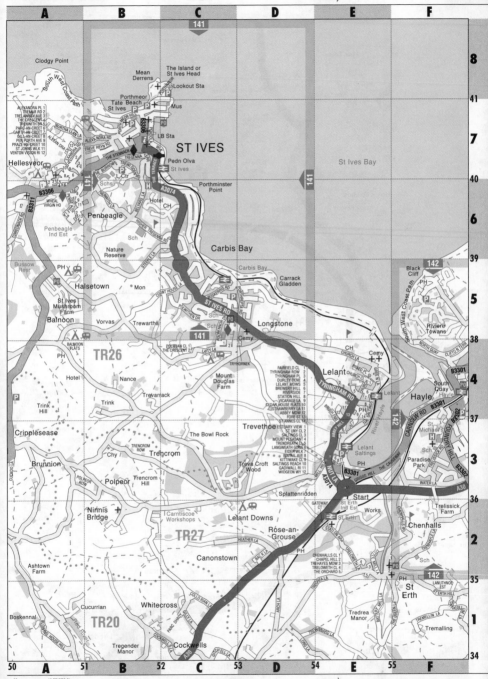

89

78

For full street detail of the highlighted area see pages 141 and 142.

A6
1 CHYANDOUR CL
2 HELLESVEAN
3 HELLESVEAN CL
4 PARC-AN-STAMPS
5 CROWS-AN-EGLOS
6 PARC-AN-FORTH
7 PENBEAGLE TERR
8 PENBEAGLE CRES
9 CORVA RD
10 PRIORS CL
11 CORVA CL
12 PORTHIA RD
13 CARNSTABBA RD
14 ALAN HARVEY CL
15 JUBILEE CT
16 TINNERS WAY
17 PENBEAGLE CL

77
66

Scale: 1⅓ inches to 1 mile

0   ¼   ½ mile
0   250m 500m 750m 1 km

A   B   C   D   E   F

8
41
7
40
6
39
5
38
4
37
3
36
2
35
1
34

St Gothian Sands Nature Reserve
Ashill Farm
Menadarva
Strap Rocks
Gwealavellan
Red River
Red River Valley Nature Reserve
Peter's Point
Gwithian
PH Gwithian Green Nature Reserve
Nanterrow Farm
Nancemellin
Gwithian Towers Nature Reserve
St Ives Bay
Pentiona La
Trevarnon Round
Cornhill Farm
Chyo
A30
Trevarnon
Cemy
66
Upton Towers
Chy
Treeve La Ind Est
Connor Downs Prim Sch
Roseworthy
TR14
Upton Towers Nature Reserve
Pulsack Manor
Gwinear Rd
Lowenac Cres
Roseworthy Barton
Ventonleague Row
Loggans Moor
Turnpike Rd
Arundell Rd
10 Clemens Way
11 Colver Cl
12 Rosewithian Cl
13 Kensa Way
Mexico Towans
142
Trevere Cl 1
Sampson's Ct 2
Telcarne Cl 3
Chapel Cl 4
Angarrack La
Trenawin La
Rosewarne Manor Holiday Village
Carwin Rise
Connor Downs
5 Arundel Pk
6 Trevarnon Cl
7 Barn Crtyd
8 Prout's La
9 Tresdale Parc
Cemy
Phillack
Carwin Farm
LC
LC
Motel
Trenawin
LC
Ventonleague
Works
1 Vellan Parc Ave
2 Hillside Ct
3 Angarrack Mews
4 Vellan Vrane
PH
Copperhouse
Riverside Mews
Angarrack
TR27
Lanyon
Gwinear
Carnhell Green
Hayle
Harvey's Way
High Lanes
Coll
Nanpusker Farm
Gwinear Prim Sch
PH
Gwinear La
Rosewarne
St George's Rd
Penpol Prim Sch
142
Wheal Alfred
Shafts (dis)
Wall Vean
Wall
Rosewarne
Tregilleson Rural Workshops
Bezurrel
Cober Cres
1 Wall Gdns
Gear
Higher Treglisson Farm
Joppa
Trewoone Rd
Reawla
1 Menadue Ct
2 Henver Cl
Trethingey Farm
Lemin Parc
A30
Trenhayle La
Bosparva
Trenhayle Farm
Tolroy Farm
Castle Kayle
Tregotha Farm
Trenerth
Howe Downs
Tolroy Rd
St Erth Praze
PH
Deveral
Calloose
B3280
142
Steppy Downs Rd
Calais Rd
Hayle Rd
Fraddam
Gwinear Downs
St Erth Hill
Trelean Farm
Fraddam Rd
Praze Rd
Tregenhorne Barton
Woodridge Cl 1
St Crewenna Terr 2
The Square 3
Roomill Cl 4
Leedstown
Horsedowns
Porthcollum La
Treven Farm
Leedstown Prim Sch
Carzise

56   57   58   59   60   61
A   B   C   D   E   F

77   90

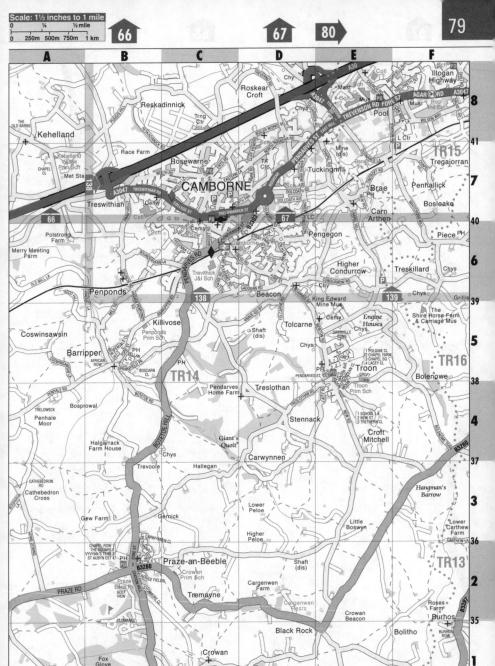

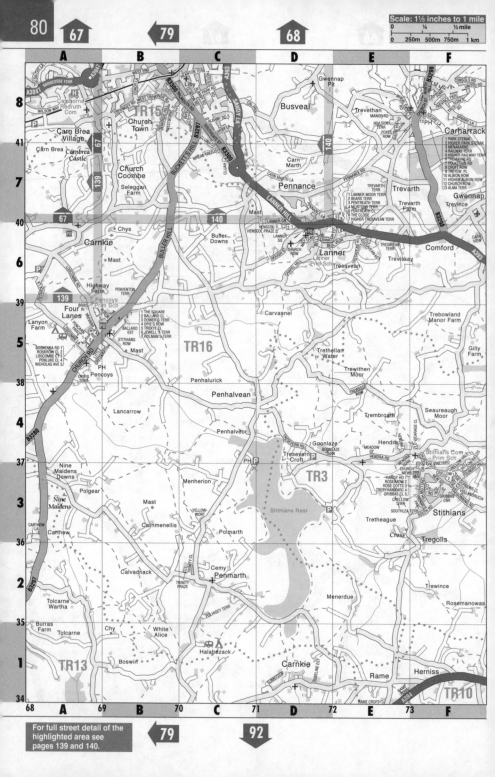

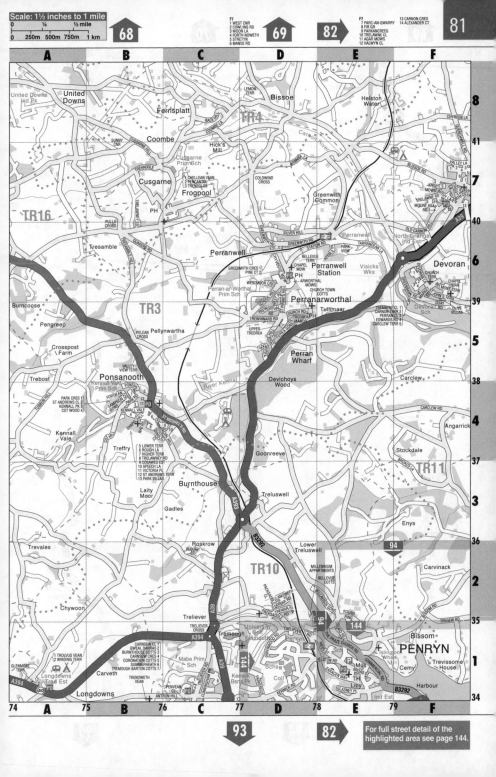

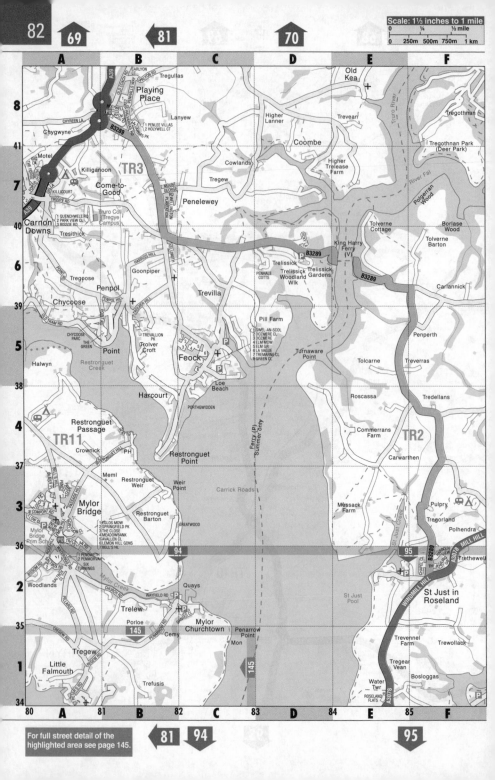

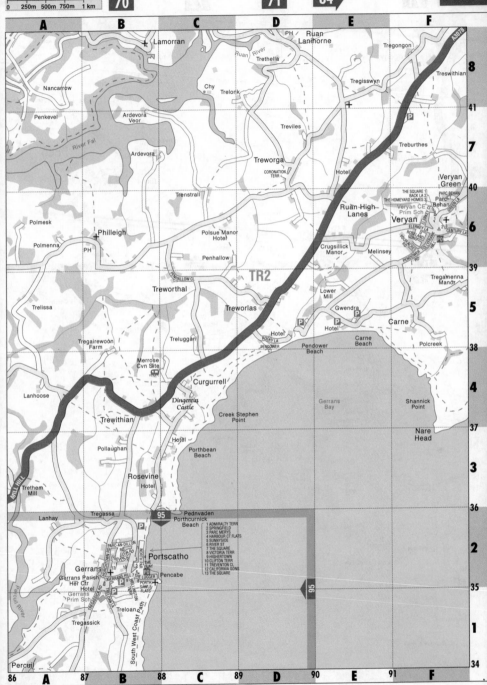

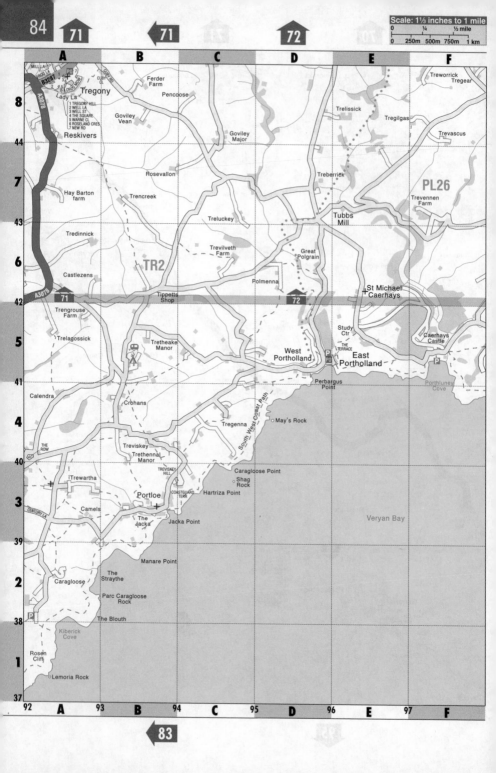

Scale: 1½ inches to 1 mile
0   ¼   ½ mile
0   250m 500m 750m 1 km

A **B** **C** **D** **E** **F**

MILL LA
ENOS LA
B3287
A3078
Tregony
1 TREGONY HILL
2 WELL LA
3 WELL ST
4 THE SQUARE
5 WARNE CL
6 ROSELAND CRES
7 NEW RD
Lady La
CUBY RD
LORD

Ferder
Farm
Pencoose

Reskivers
Goviley
Vean

Goviley
Major

Trelissick

Tregilgas

Treworrick
Tregear

Trevascus

44

Rosevallon

Treberrick

PL26

7

Hay Barton
farm

Trencreek

Treluckey

Tubbs
Mill

Trevennen
Farm

43

Tredinnick

TR2

Trevilveth
Farm

Great
Polgrain

6

Castlezens

Polmenna

St Michael
Caerhays

42

A3078
71

Tippetts
Shop

72

5

Trengrouse
Farm

Trelagossick

Tretheake
Manor

West
Portholland

Study
Ctr

THE
TERRACE
P

East
Portholland

Caerhays
Castle

P

Porthluney
Cove

41

Calendra

Crbhans

Perbargus
Point

South West Coast Path

4

Tregenna

May's Rock

THE
ROW

Treviskey

Trethennal
Manor

TREVISKEY
HILL

Caragloose Point

Shag
Rock

40

Trewartha

Portloe

COASTGUARD
TERR

Hartriza Point

Veryan Bay

3

Camels

The
Jacka

Jacka Point

39

Manare Point

2

Caragloose

The
Straythe

Parc Caragloose
Rock

P

The Blouth

38

Kiberick
Cove

1

Rosen
Cliff

Lemoria Rock

37

A **92** **B** **93** **C** **94** **D** **95** **E** **96** **F** **97**

CENTURY LA

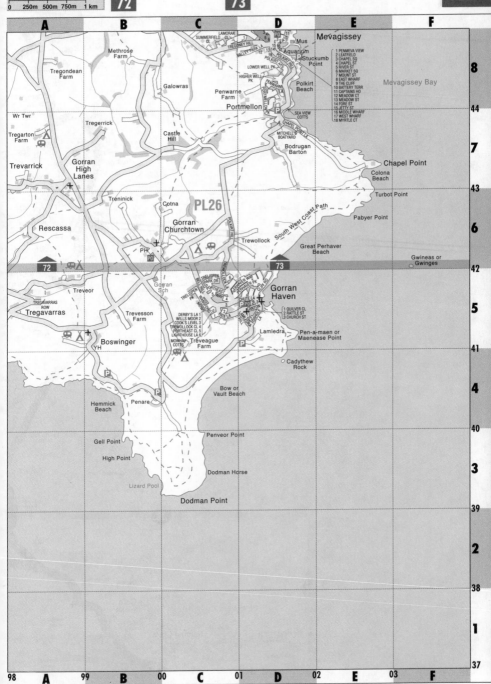

A   B   C   D   E   F

8

Methrose Farm

Tregondean Farm

Galowras

SUMMERFIELD CL
LAMORAK CL
TREGONEY HILL
VALLEY PARK LA
POLKIRT HILL
LOWER WELL PK
HIGHER WELL PK

Mevagissey

1 PENMEVA VIEW
2 LEATFIELD
3 CHAPEL SQ
4 CHAPEL ST
5 RIVER ST
6 MARKET SQ
7 MOUNT ST
8 EAST WHARF
9 THE CLIFF
10 BATTERY TERR
11 CAPTAINS HO
12 MEADOW CT
13 MEADOW ST
14 FORE ST
15 JETTY ST
16 MIDDLE WHARF
17 WEST WHARF
18 MYRTLE CT

Mus
Aquarium
Stuckumb Point

Mevagissey Bay

44

Wr Twr

Tregerrick

Penwarne Farm

Portmellon

Polkirt Beach

SEA VIEW COTTS

7

Tregarton Farm

Castle Hill

MITCHELL'S BOATYARD

CHAPEL POINT LA

Bodrugan Barton

Chapel Point

Colona Beach

Trevarrick

Gorran High Lanes

Treninick

Cotna

PL26

Trewollock

South West Coast Path

Turbot Point

43

Pabyer Point

Gorran Churchtown

Great Perhaver Beach

6

Rescassa

PH
PO

72   73

Gwineas or Gwinges

42

Treveor

Gorran Sch

TRELISPEN PARK DR
PRETHEAST PK
WARD LA

KERSELAND
SKIVERICK WAY
CHUTE LA

Gorran Haven

1 QUIVER CL
2 RATTLE ST
3 CHURCH ST

5

TREGAVARRAS ROW
Tregavarras

Trevesson Farm

DERBY'S LA 1
WILLS MOOR 2
COOK'S LEVEL 3
TREWOLLOCK CL 4
PORTHEAST CL 5
LIGHTHOUSE LA 6

Lamledra

Pen-a-maen or Maenease Point

41

Boswinger

YH

MOWHAY COTTS

Tréveague Farm

Cadythew Rock

4

Hemmick Beach

Penare

Bow or Vault Beach

40

Gell Point

Penveor Point

High Point

3

Dodman Horse

Lizard Pool

Dodman Point

39

2

38

1

37

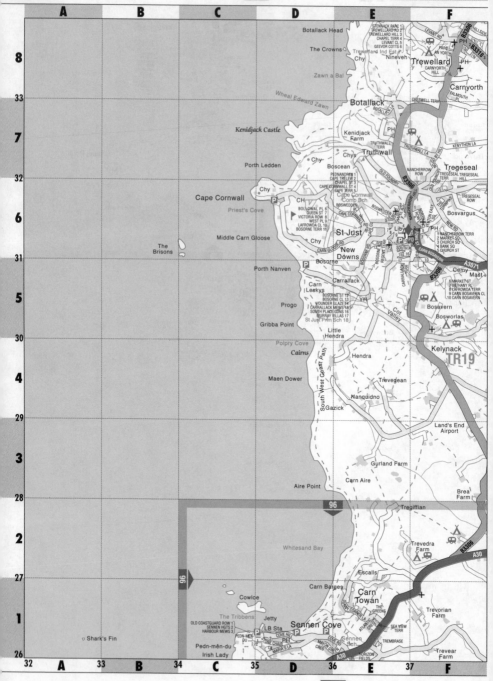

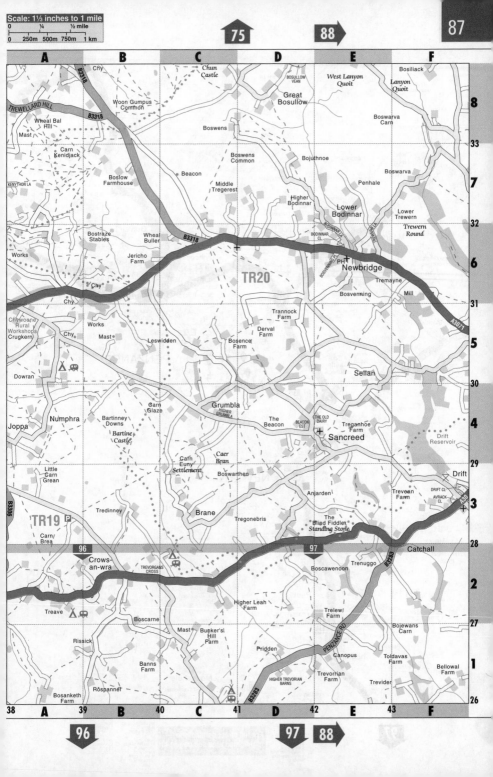

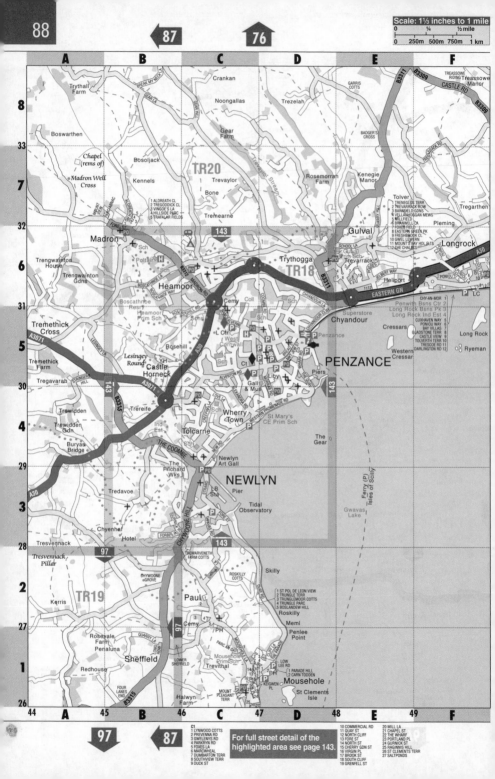

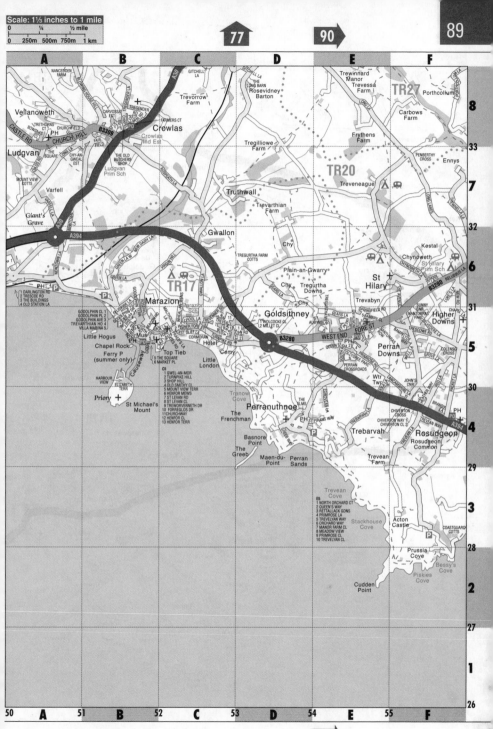

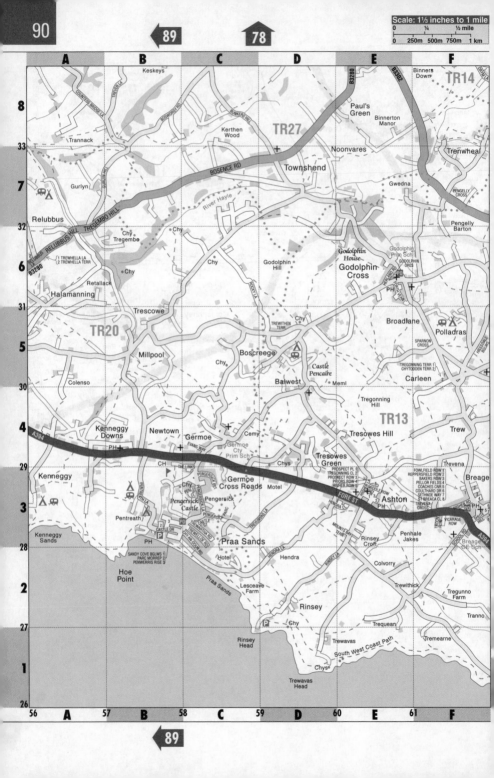

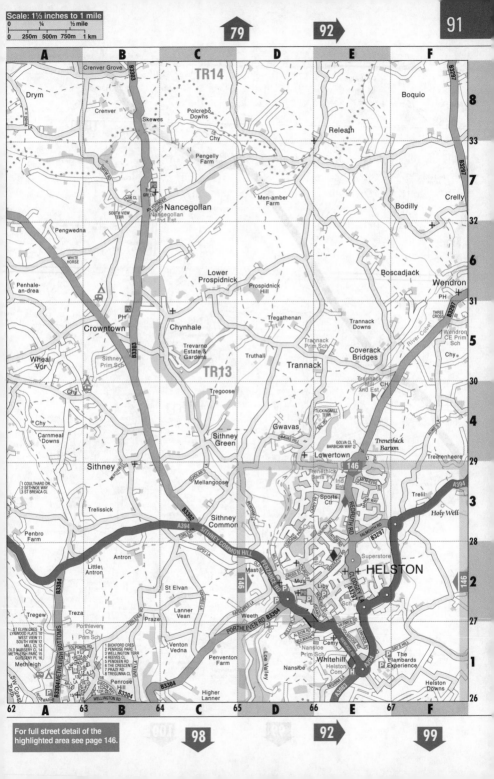

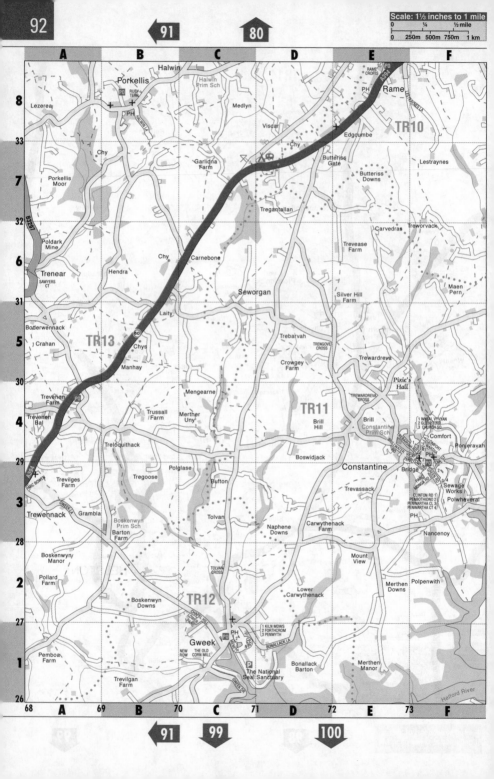

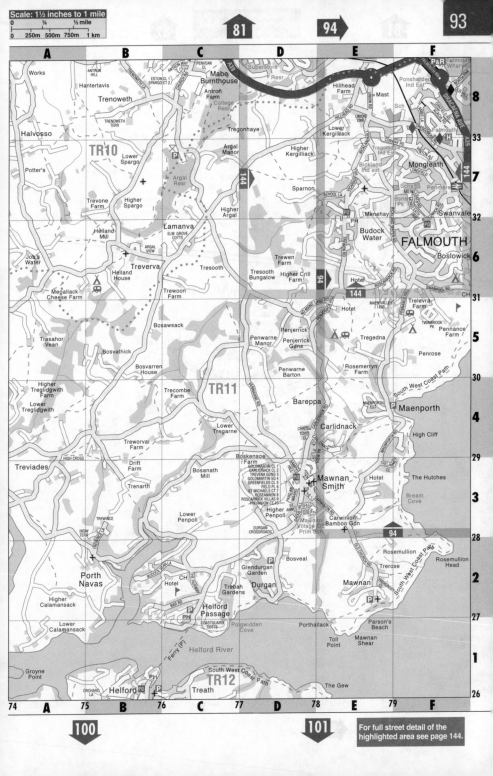

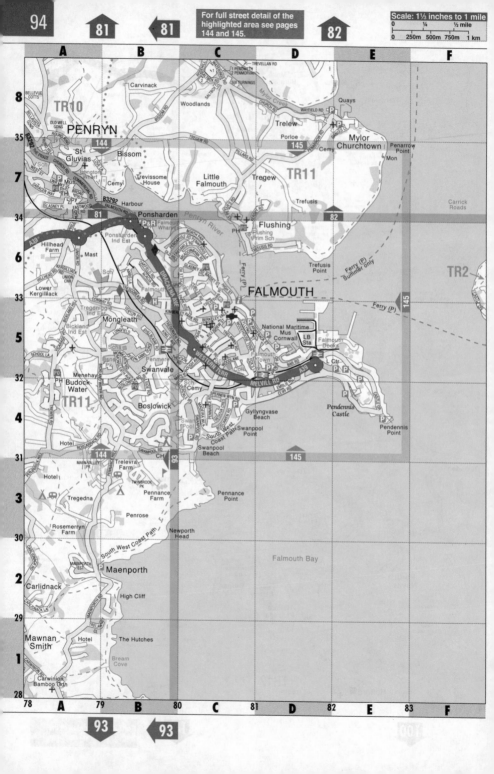

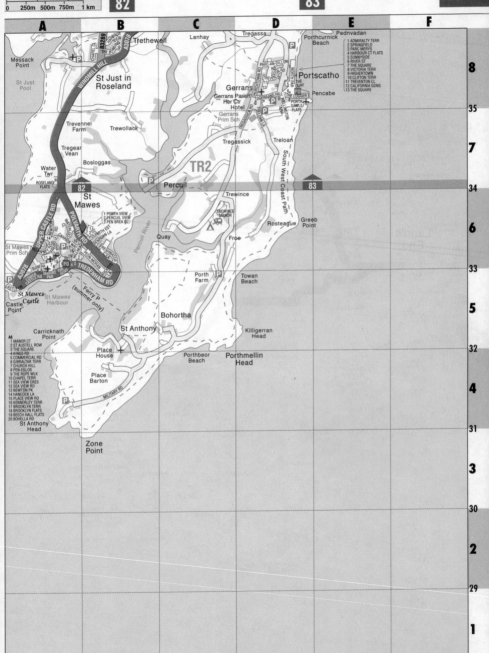

Scale: 1⅓ inches to 1 mile

0 ¼ ½ mile
0 250m 500m 750m 1 km

Messack Point

St Just Pool

Trethewell

Lanhay

Tregassa

Pednvadan

Porthcurnick Beach

Portscatho

1 ADMIRALTY TERR
2 SPRINGFIELD
3 PARC MERYS
4 HARBOUR CT FLATS
5 SUNNYSIDE
6 RIVER ST
7 THE SQUARE
8 VICTORIA TERR
9 HIGHERTOWN
10 CLIFTON TERR
11 TREVENTON CL
12 CALIFORNIA GDNS
13 THE SQUARE

St Just in Roseland

Gerrans

Gerrans Parish Her Ctr
Hotel

Parc-an-Dillon

Pencabe

Trevennel Farm

Trewollack

Gerrans Prim Sch

Tregear Vean

Bosloggas

Tregassick

Treloan

Water Twr

ROSELAND FLATS

TR2

St Mawes

Percuil

Trewince

South West Coast Path

1 PORTH VIEW
2 PERCUIL VIEW
3 PEN BREA CL

Quay

Froe

Rosteague

Greeb Point

St Mawes Prim Sch

St Mawes Castle

Castle Point

St Mawes Harbour

Ferry P (summer only)

Bohortha

Porth Farm

Towan Beach

Killigerran Head

Carricknath Point

St Anthony

A6
1 MANOR CT
2 ST AUSTELL ROW
3 THE SQUARE
4 KINGS RD
5 COMMERCIAL RD
6 GIBRALTAR TERR
7 CHURCH HILL
8 PEN-EGLOS
9 THE ROPE WLK
10 CHAPEL TERR
11 SEA VIEW CRES
12 SEA VIEW RD
13 NEWTON PK
14 HANCOCK LA
15 PLACE VIEW RD
16 KENNERLEY TERR
17 BROOKLYN TERR
18 BROOKLYN FLATS
19 BEECH HALL FLATS
20 BOHELLA RD

Place House

Porthbeor Beach

Porthmellin Head

Place Barton

MILITARY RD

St Anthony Head

Zone Point

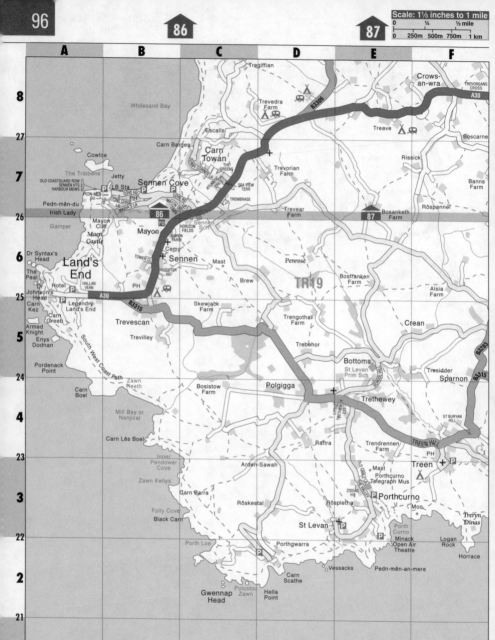

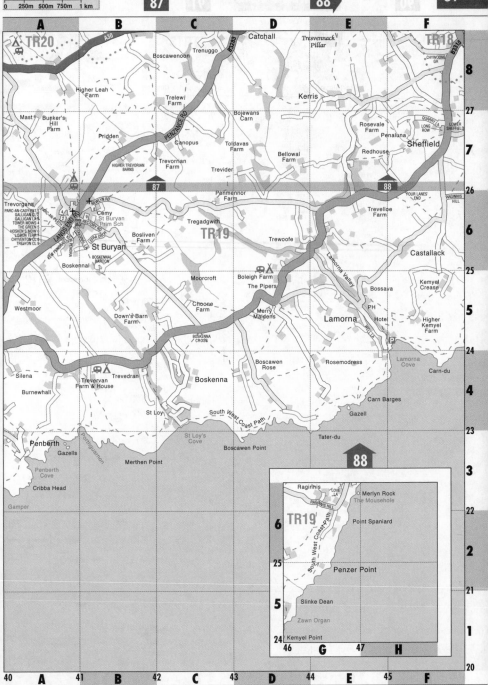

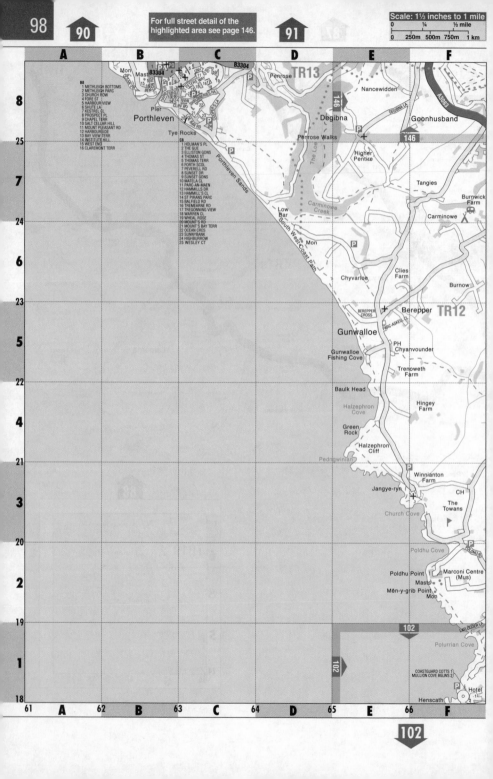

For full street detail of the highlighted area see page 146.

Scale: 1⅓ inches to 1 mile
0   ¼   ½ mile
0   250m 500m 750m 1 km

B8
1 METHLEIGH BOTTOMS
2 METHLEIGH PARC
3 CHURCH ROW
4 FORE ST
5 HARBOUR VIEW
6 SHUTE LA
7 KESTREL CL
8 PROSPECT PL
9 CHAPEL TERR
10 SALT CELLAR HILL
11 MOUNT PLEASANT RD
12 HARBOURSIDE
13 BAY VIEW TERR
14 INSTITUTE HILL
15 WEST END
16 CLAREMONT TERR

C8
1 HOLMAN'S PL
2 THE GUE
3 ELLISTON GDNS
4 THOMAS ST
5 THOMAS TERR
6 FORTH SCOL
7 PEVERELL RD
8 SUNSET DR
9 SUNSET GDNS
10 MATELA CL
11 PARC-AN-MAEN
12 HAMMILLS DR
13 HAMMILL'S CL
14 ST PIRANS PARC
15 BALFIELD RD
16 TREMEARNE RD
17 TREGONNING VIEW
18 WARREN CL
19 WHEAL ROSE
20 MOUNT'S RD
21 MOUNT'S BAY TERR
22 OCEAN CRES
23 SUNNYBANK
24 HIGHBURROW
25 WESLEY CT

TR13
Nancewidden
Penrose
Degibna
Goonhusband
Porthleven
Pier
Mast
Mon
B3304
B3304
Tye Rocks
Penrose Walks
Higher Pentire
Tangies
Burnwick Farm
Carminowe
The Loe
Carminowe Creek
Porthleven Sands
Low Bar
Mon
South West Coast Path
Chyvarloe
Clies Farm
Burnow
Berepper
BEREPPER CROSS
PARC-AN-KELL
TR12
Gunwalloe
PH
Chyanvounder
Gunwalloe Fishing Cove
Trenoweth Farm
Baulk Head
Halzephron Cove
Hingey Farm
Green Rock
Halzephron Cliff
Pedngwinian
Winnianton Farm
Jangye-ryn
CH
The Towans
Church Cove
Poldhu Cove
Poldhu Point
Marconi Centre (Mus)
Masts
Mên-y-grib Point
Mon
146
146
146
102
102
102
Polurrian Cove
COASTGUARD COTTS 1;
MULLION COVE BGLWS 2
Hotel
Henscath

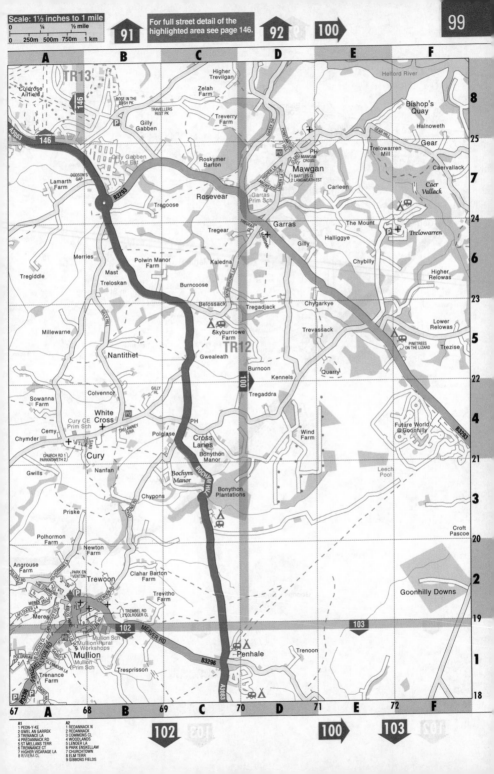

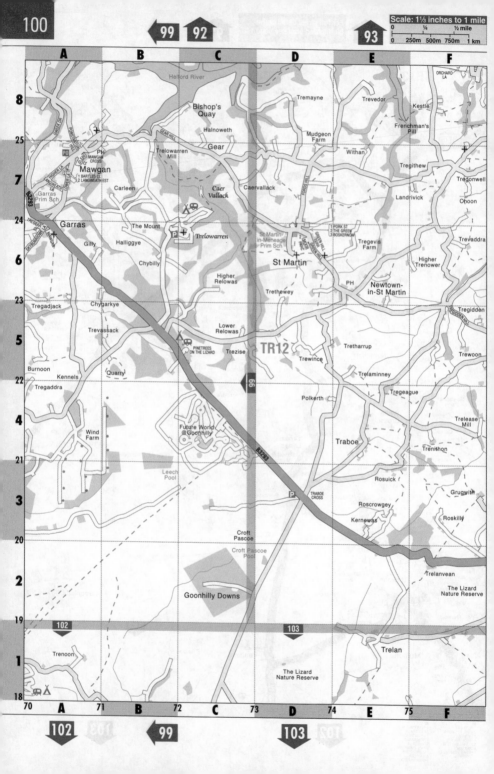

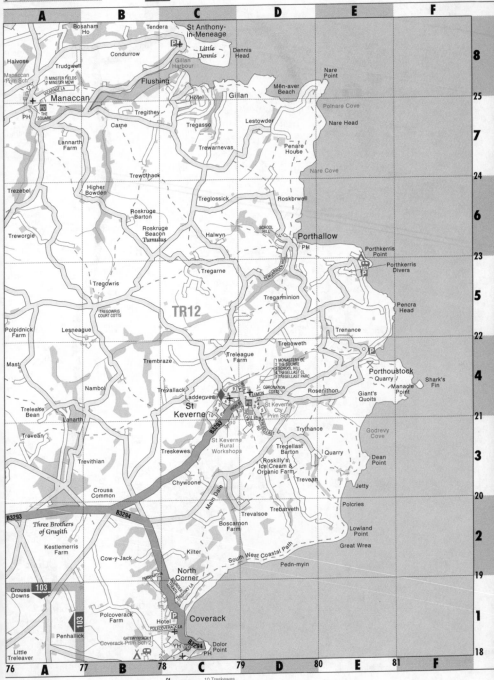

Scale: 1½ inches to 1 mile

0   ¼   ½ mile

0   250m 500m 750m 1 km

93

103

A   B   C   D   E   F

Bosaham Ho
Tendera
St Anthony-in-Meneage
Little Dennis
Dennis Head

Halvose
Trudgwell
Condurrow
Gillan Harbour

Manaccan Prim Sch
1 MINSTER FIELDS
2 MINSTER MDW
Flushing

8

Nare Point

Manaccan
Hotel
Gillan
Mên-aver Beach

PH
THE SQUARE
P
VICARAGE LA

25

Tregithey
Carne
Lestowder
Polnare Cove

Nare Head

Lannarth Farm
Tregasso
Penare House

7

Trewarnevas

Trezebel
Higher Bowden
Trewothack

Nare Cove

24

Treworgie
Roskruge Barton
Treglossick
Roskbrwell

Roskruge Beacon Tumulus
Halwyn
SCHOOL HILL
Porthallow

6

Tregowris
Tregarne
PH
Porthkerris Point

Polpidnick Farm
Lesneague
TR12

PEMGARROCK HILL

Porthkerris Divers

23

Tregowris Court Cotts
Tregarminion

Mast
Trembraze
Trenoweth
Trenance

Pencra Head

5

Nambol
Treleague Farm
1 MONASTERY CL
2 THE SQUARE
3 SCHOOL HILL
4 TREGELLAST CL
5 TREGELLAST PARC
Rosenithon

Porthoustock
Quarry

22

Treleague Bean
Trevallack
Laddenvean
CORONATION
TERR
LEMON

Giant's Quoits
Manacle Point

Shark's Fin

Lanarth
St Keverne
St Keverne City Prim Sch
4

Trevean
Treskewes
St Keverne Rural Workshops
Liby
Trythance

Godrevy Cove

21

Trevithian
Chywoone
Tregellast Barton
Quarry

Dean Point

3

Crousa Common
Main Dale
Roskilly's Ice Cream & Organic Farm
Trevean

Jetty

B3293
B3294
Three Brothers of Grugith
Boscarnon Farm
Trevalsoe
Trebarveth
Polcries

20

Kestlemerris Farm
Cow-y-Jack
Kilter
South West Coastal Path
Pedn-myin
Great Wrea
Lowland Point

2

Crousa Downs
103
North Corner

19

Penhallick
Polcoverack Farm
Hotel
Coverack

1

Little Treleaver
Coverack Prim Sch
GATEWYNYACK
POLECOVERACK LA
YH
B3294
Dolor Point
PH

18

76   A   77   B   78   C   79   D   80   E   81   F

103

C4
1 TRESKEWES EST
2 TREVALLACK VIEW
3 TREVALLACK PARC
4 LANHEVERNE PARC
5 DOCTORS HILL
6 POLVENTON PARC
7 PENMENNER EST
8 COMMERCIAL RD
9 TREGONNING PARC

10 Treskewes Ind Est

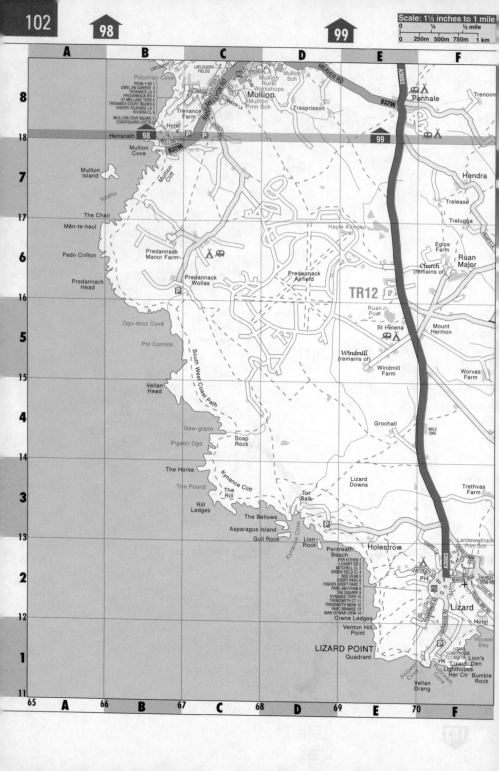

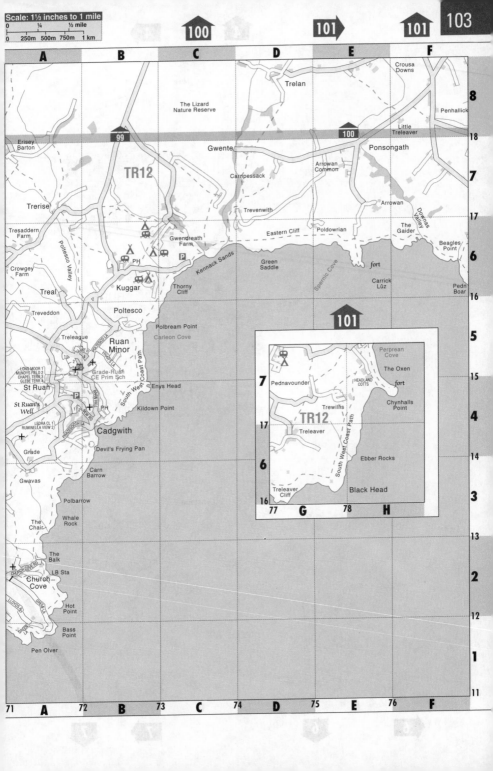

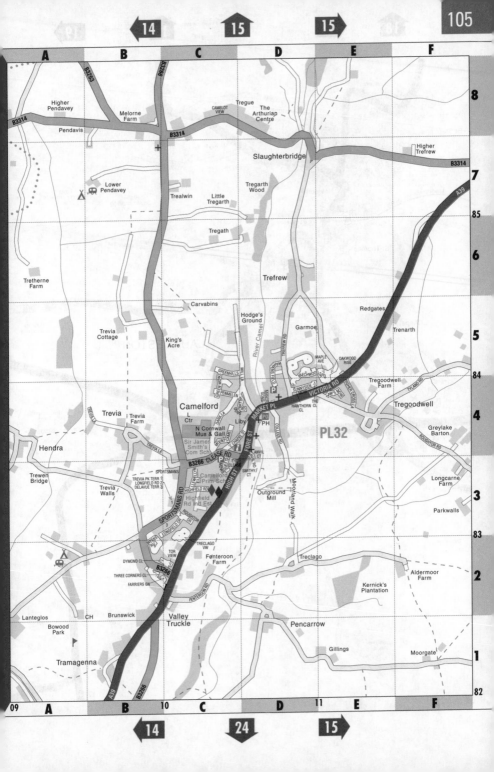

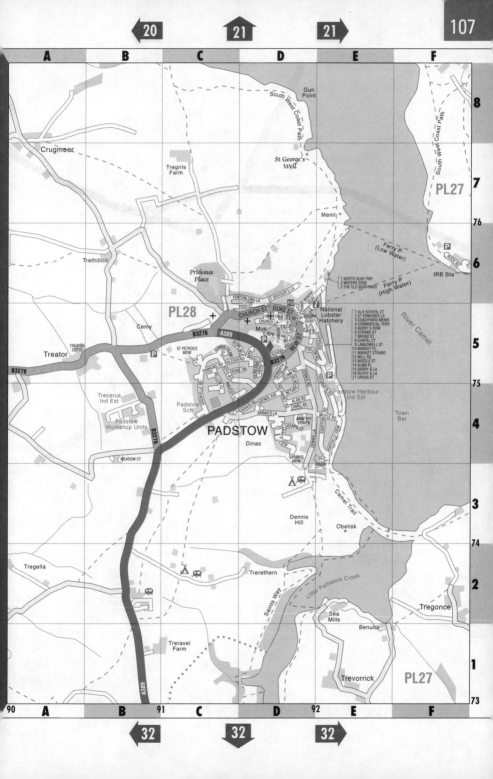

A   B   C   D   E   F

8

Gun Point

South West Coast Path

St George's Well

7
PL27

76

Crugmeer

Tregirls Farm

Meml

Ferry P (Low Water)

P
ROCK RD
IRB Sta

6

Trethillick

Prideaux Place

1 NORTH QUAY PAR
2 WATERS EDGE
3 THE OLD BOAT-YARD

Ferry P (High Water)

PL28

Gemy

FENTONLUNA LA
ST SAVIOUR'S LA
HIGH ST
CHURCH ST
DUKE ST

Mus
Liby
P

National Lobster Hatchery

1 OLD SCHOOL CT
2 ST EDMUNDS LA
3 COACHYARD MEWS
4 COMMERCIAL TERR
5 AVERY S ROW
6 STRAND ST
7 BROAD ST
8 CHAPEL ST
9 LANADWELL ST
10 MARKET PL
11 MARKET STRAND
12 MILL SQ
13 MIDDLE ST
14 ALMA PL
15 BARRY S LA
16 RUTHY S LA
17 CROSS ST

River Camel

Treator

TREATOR COTTS
B3276

B3276   A389

ST PETROCS MDW

DOWNS HILL
P

HAWKINS RD
RALEIGH RD
DRAKE RD
TUDOR PL
RALEGH DR

B3276

STATION RD

P

Padstow Harbour Ind Est

5

75

Trecerus Ind Est

Padstow Workshop Units

Padstow Sch

SARAH'S CL
DENEX AVE
SARAH'S LA

ALAN RD
CAMEL CL

Town Bar

4

MEADOW CT

PADSTOW

Dinas

ANNETHY LOWEN

SARAH'S MDW

MOYLE RD

Camel Trail

3

Dennis Hill

Obelisk

74

Tregella

Trerethern

Saints Way

Little Petherick Creek

Tregonce

2

Sea Mills

Benuick

Treravel Farm

Trevorrick

PL27

1

73

90   A   B   91   C   D   92   E   F

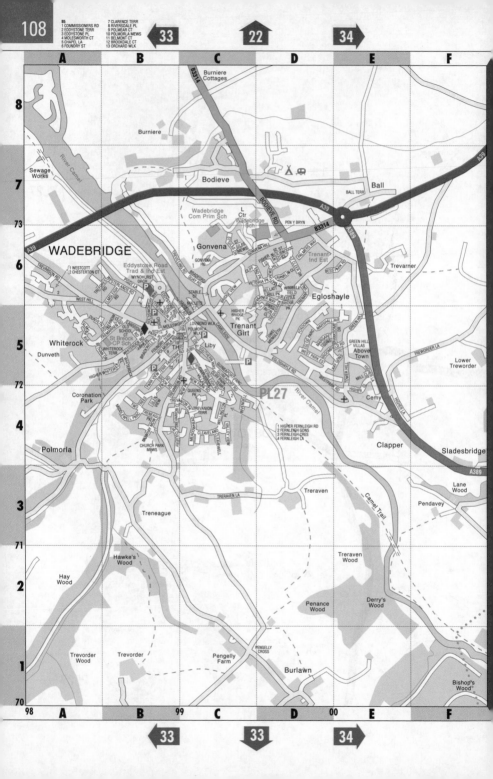

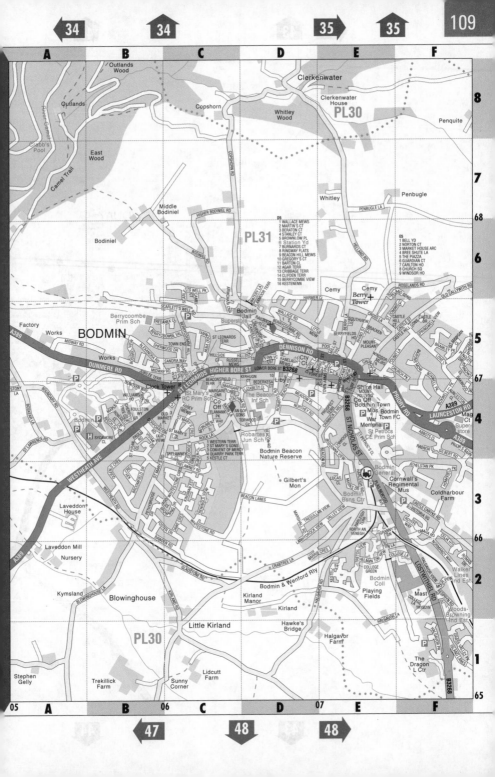

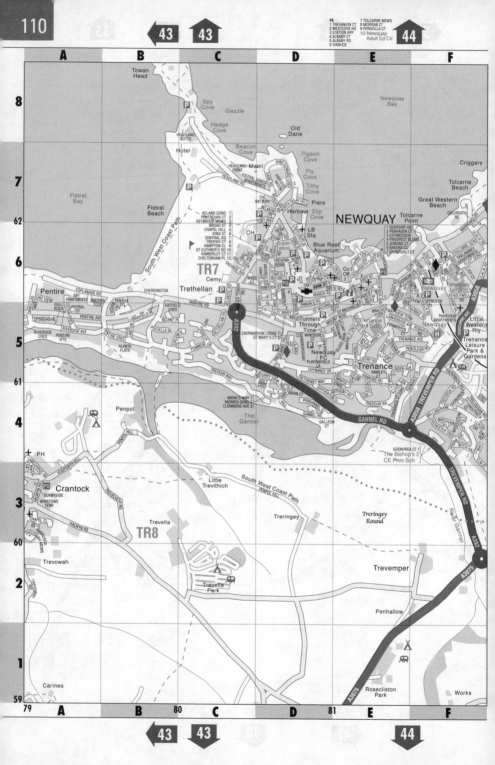

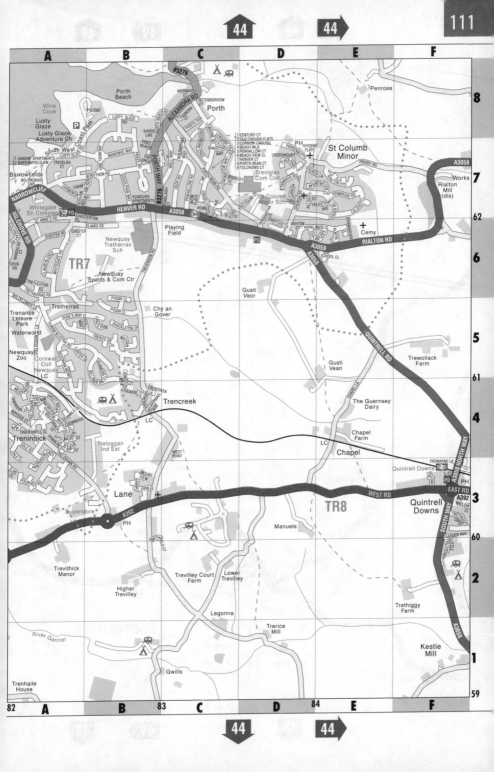

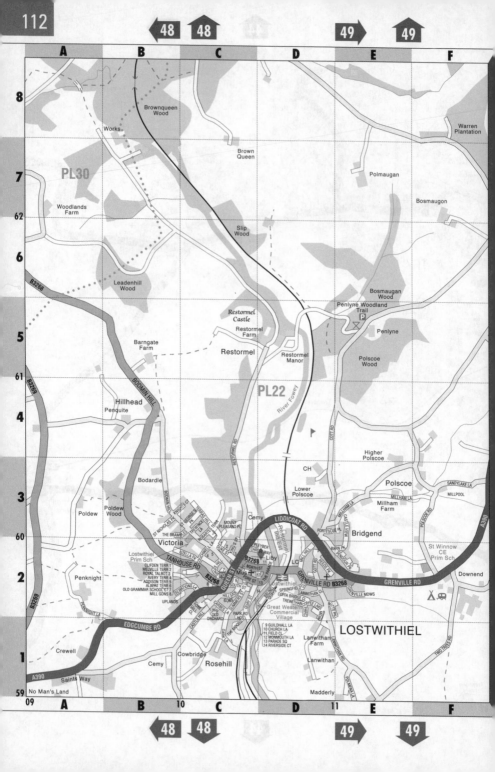

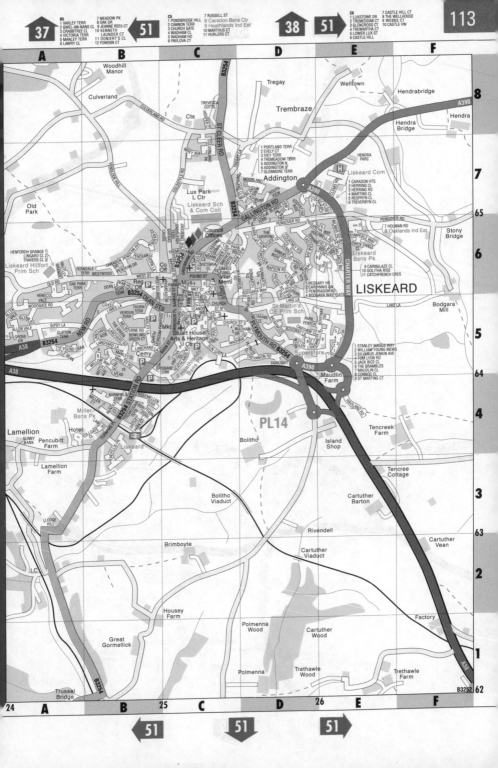

59 59

| A | B | C | D | E | F |

8
Trenance Downs
Lansalson Farm
Colchester House
Drummer's Hill
Scredda
Clay Pit
Carclaze Downs

PL26

B3274

7
Sunny Corner
Works (dis)
Palace Close Farm
Bojea Ind Est
Mount Stamper Farm
Carclaze Ind Est

54
Bojea Farm
Mast
Carwollen
Carclaze
Carclaze Com Inf Sch
PENDILLY DR 1
LAMORNA PK 2
GWITHIAN CL 3
OCEAN VW 4
PENTILLIE GDNS
CHYNON GDNS
CENTURY CL

6
Trethowel
PH
PL25
John Keay House
Cornwall College
JERYON CL 1
ROPEHAVEN CL 2
PRIDMOUTH RD 3
SYLVAN CL 4
TREGONISSY LA END 5
Carclaze Com Jun Sch
EMLYN
MEADOW

Trenance Farm
Mast
Menacuddle Well
Menacuddle Farm

5
ST AUSTELL
Resr
WATERSEDGE CL 1
TRENANCE PL 2
BLOWING HOUSE LA 3
TRENANCE PL 4
BLOWING HOUSE CL 5
PRINCE CHARLES RD
PRINCE CHARLES PK
Sandy Hill Prim Sch
Sandy Bottom

53
TURNAVEAN RD
TREMBEAR RD
1 BLOWING HOUSE HILL
2 MARKET HILL
3 ELM TREE
4 TREVARTHIAN RD
5 THE SYCAMORES
Poltair Sports Coll
St Austell Brewery (Visitors Ctr)
ROBARTES GDNS

4
A3058
EDGCUMBE RD
St Austell
Poltair Park
Liby & Performing Arts
Polkyth L Ctr
Mount Charles

3
TRURO RD
B3274
B3398
Army's Air Cadet Training Ctr
White River Place Sh Ctr
Cornwall Ho
East Hill
Cemy
Mount Charles Sch
Benan Chy
Meryon Trad Est
POLMEAR RD

52
PENWINNICK RD
DITHMARSCHEN WAY
Pondhu Prim Sch
Council Offices
Trewhiddle Farm
TREVANION RD
SOUTHBOURNE RD
CHARLES CL 1
BOSCARNE CRES 2
DUCHY CL 3
Long Stone
Superstore

2
A390
TRURO RD
B3273
1 BEECH LA
2 CHERRY TREE MEWS
3 CARVATH HO
4 CHISHOLME CL
5 CHISHOLME CT
6 HORSLEY RISE
7 BOURNESIDE
Gewans Farm

1
Trewhiddle House
THE COPSE
White House Cottage
Tregorrick
Tregorrick Farm
TREGORRICK RD
PL26
Tregorrick Park (St Austell RFC)
St Austell Com

51
St Austell River
PENTEWAN RD
B3273
PORTHPEAN BEACH RD

| 00 | A | B | 01 | C | D | 02 | E | F |

59 59

C3
1 MOORLAND CT
2 GRENVILLE CT
3 SAVOY BLDG
4 GRANT'S WLK
5 BIDDICK'S CT
6 MARKET ST
7 CROSS LA
8 CHURCH ST
9 VICTORIA PL
10 VICARAGE HILL
11 OLD VICARAGE PL
12 CHANDOS PL
13 AYLMER PL
14 AYLMER SQ
15 BURTON HO
16 WEST HILL CT

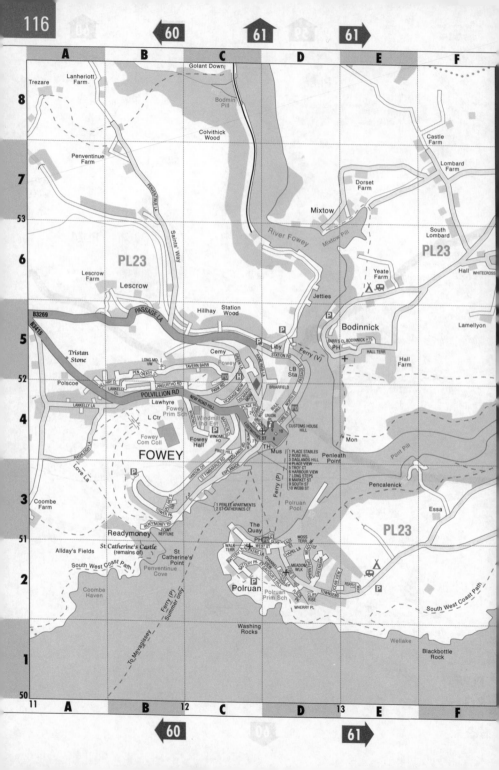

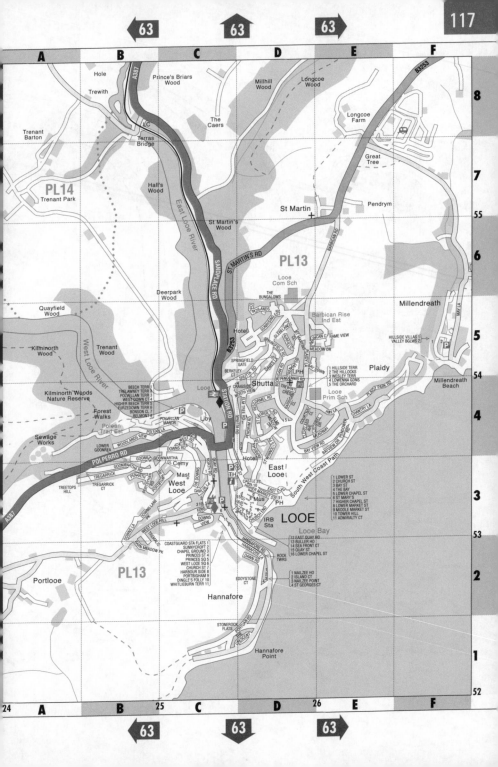

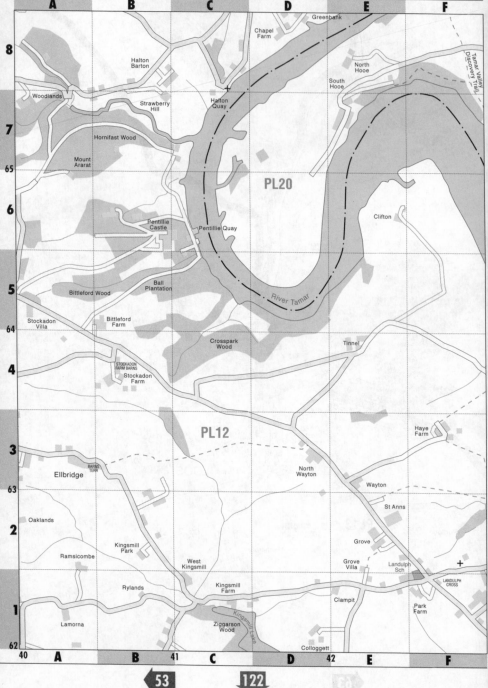

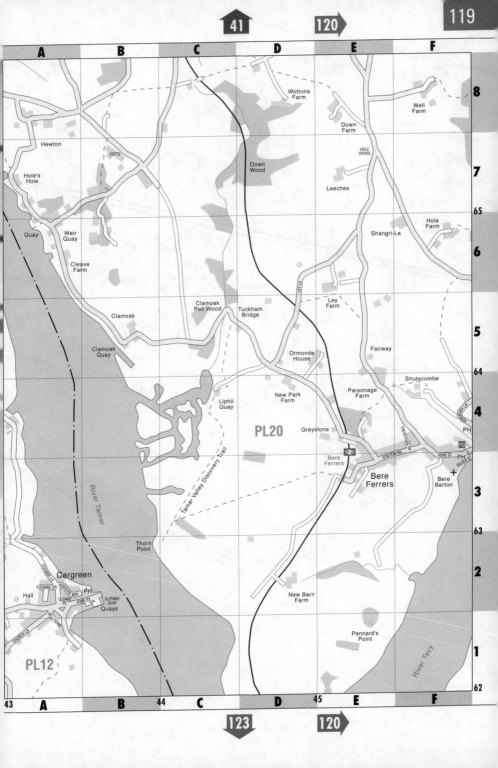

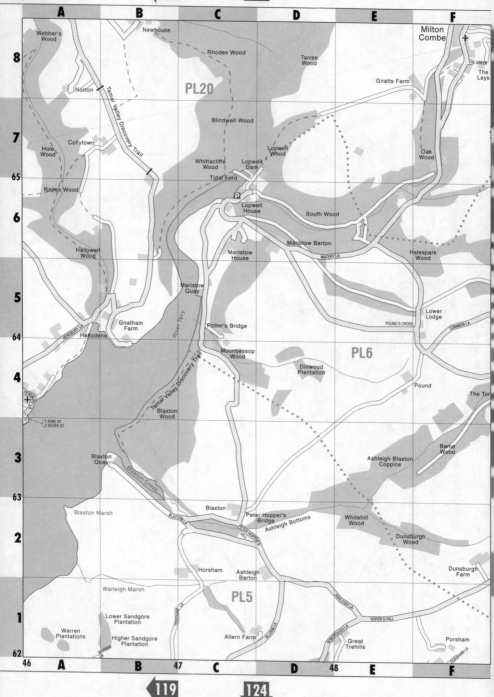

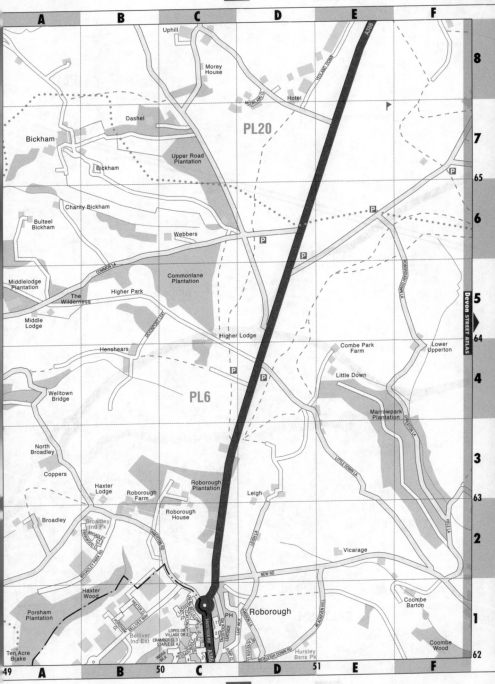

A B C D E F

8
7
65
6
5
64
4
3
63
2
1
62

Devon STREET ATLAS

Uphill
Morey House
Hotel

PL20

Bickham
Dashel
Upper Road Plantation
Bickham
Charity Bickham
Bulteel Bickham
Webbers

Middlelodge Plantation
The Wilderness
Higher Park
Commonlane Plantation
COMMON LA

Middle Lodge

Henshears
Higher Lodge

PL6

Welltown Bridge

Combe Park Farm
Lower Upperton
Little Down

Marrowpark Plantation

North Broadley
Coppers
Broadley

Haxter Lodge
Roborough Farm
Roborough House
Roborough Plantation
Leigh

Vicarage

Coombe Barton

Haxter Wood
Broadley Ind Pk

NEW RD

Roborough

Coombe Wood

Porsham Plantation
Belliver Ind Est

Hursley Bsns Pk

Ten Acre Brake

A B C D E F
49 50 51

53
118

A B C D E F

8

Cross Park Farm
Rumbullion Farm
Sladeland
Marraborough
Colloggett Hill
PL12

7
Botusfleming
PH
Clark's Lake
Smallacombe
Marsh Farm
Holy Well
The Marsh
Moditonham Quay
Moditonham House
South Down

61
A388
East Town Farm
The Marsh
Burrhills Farm
Burrhills Quay
Kingsmill Lake

6
Woodside Racing Stables
Atuba
PINKHAMS COTTS
Carkeel
Hole Wood
Skinham Creek
Chine Fleet Country Club

Broadmoor Wood
DIRTY LA
CARKEEL BARNS
Carkeel Farm
Motel
RIVER CT
Tamar View Ind Est
Quarryfield Coppice

5
Saltash Service Area
LIBBY CT
AVERY WAY
Carkeel Ind Est
PL12
Tamar Park

60
Peninsula Pk
Gwel Avon Bsns Pk
Saltash Ind Est
Pill Farm
Pill LA
Mill Park
BEAUMONT TERR

WHITY CROSS
Saltash Bsns Pk
B3271
Saltash Moorlands Trad Est
GILSTON
Saltmill Creek

4
A38 LISKEARD RD
B3271
Saltash Parkway Ind Est
BURRATON RD
CALLINGTON RD
Burraton
NEW RD
P
B3271

LISKEARD RD
PH
PLOUGH GN
ASHTON WAY
South Pill

3
Latchbrook
BARROW DOWN
Burraton Prim Sch
GRENFELL GDNS
WARRATON LA
St Stephens Prim Sch
Saltash Library
Saltash Leisure Ctr
Brunel Terr Prim Sch

59
FOXGLOVE WAY
THE HEDGEROWS
OAKLANDS DR
TOP OF THE TOWN
GREENWICH PL
MARISTOW LA
WINDMILL
St Barnabas

2
Wadgeworthy Farm
TOWER CT
CASTLE CT
YELLOW TOR CT
POLLARD CL
Burraton Coombe
St Andrews
St Stephens Saltash
Cornwall Coll Saltash
HIGHER PORT VIEW
Wearde

Longlands
St Stephens
PARKESWAY
Bishop Cornish CE Prim Sch

1
SALTASH
Forder
CHURCHILL WLK
COURTLANDS
House on the Hill

58
Trehan
Little Trehan Farm
Cross
FAYRE VIEW
GERALDINE TERR
RIVERSIDE COTTS
Saltash Com Sch

40 A B 41 C D 42 E F

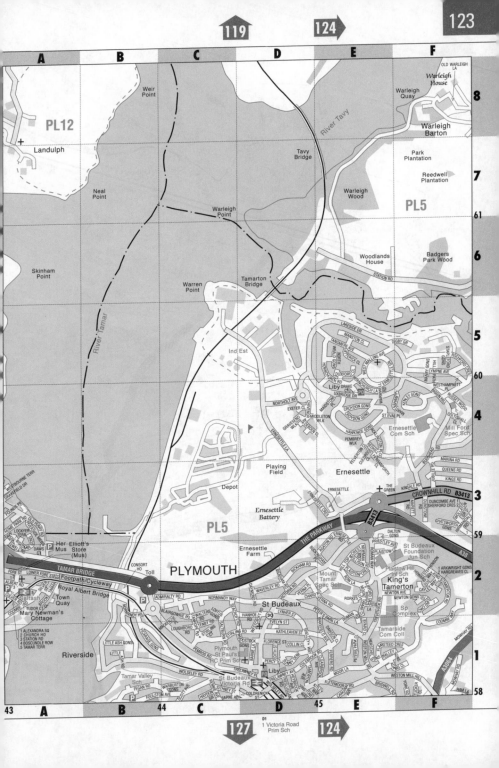

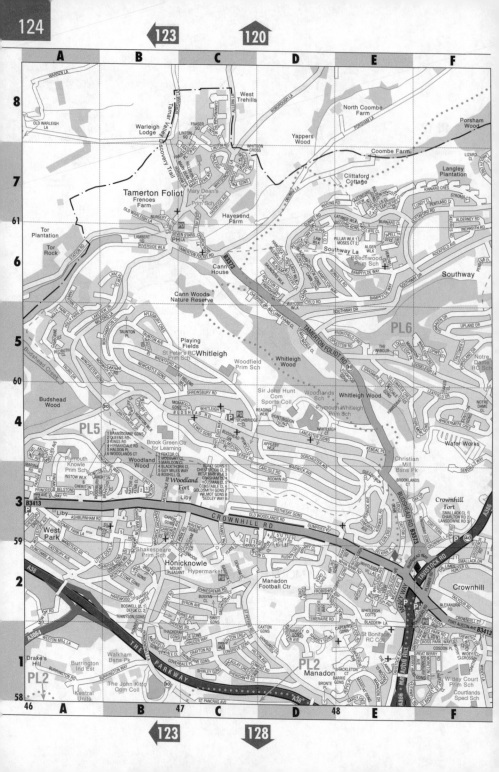

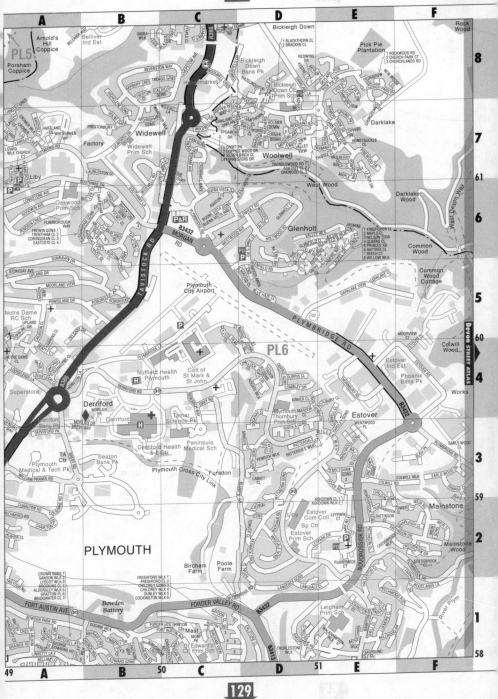

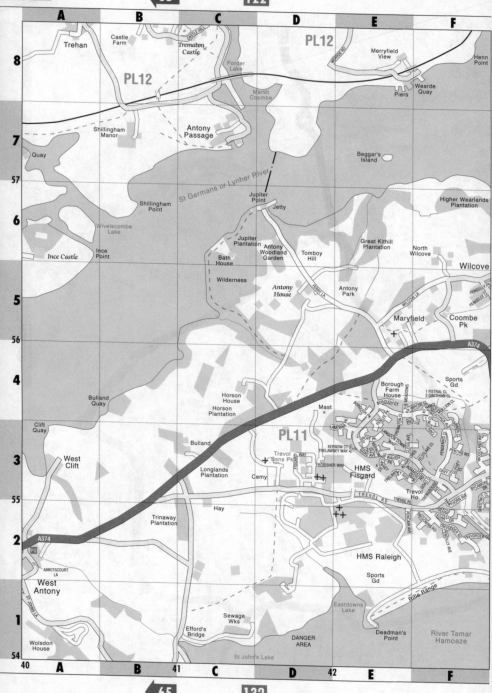

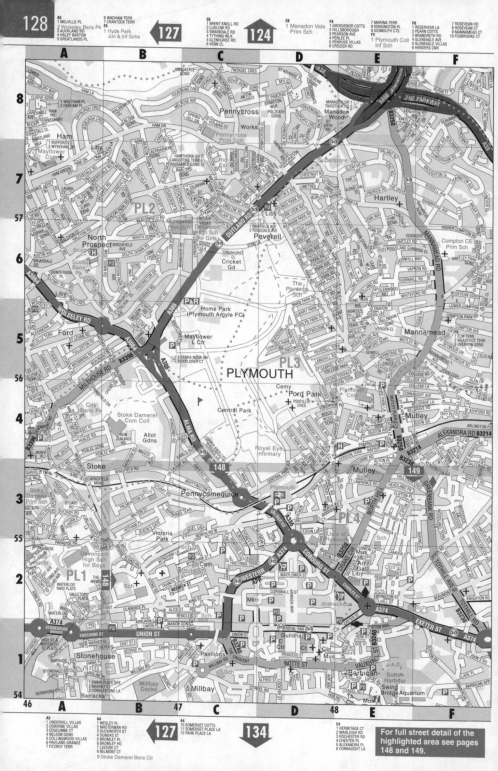

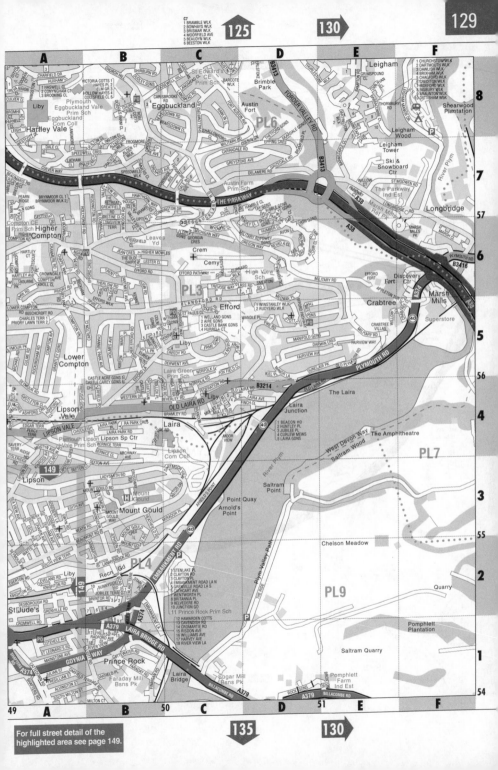

E7
1 PERSEVERANCE COTTS
2 BLANCHARD PL

Devon STREET ATLAS

A B C D E F

8

Triumphal Arch
China Clay Works
Hilltops
Boringdon Hall
The Croft
Brockhole Wood
Elfordleigh Wood
Binicliff Wood
Boringdon Cottages

7

57

Marsh Mills
P&R
LC
Triumphal Cres
Woodford
Hele's Sch
Woodford Jun & Inf Schs
Ashcombe Cl
Cranfield
South View
Long Mdw
Meadow Way
Crossway
The Mead
Courtland Cres
Fairfield
Boringdon Prim Sch
Elford Cres
Brett Wlk
Devonia
Deeble Cl
Perryman Cl
Waddon Cl
Colebrook La
Clifton Cl
Colebrook
Newnham Ind Est
Huxley Cl
Newnham
Boringdon Mill Bsns Ct

6

B3416
Marsh Mills
LC
Cot Hill Trad Est
Trad Est
Plymouth Rd
Molesworth Rd
Seymour Rd
Woodland
Ind & Trad Est
Emp Ret Pk
Lucas La
Hemerdon Way
Treverbyn Rd
Chamberlayne
1 Tory Brook Ave
2 Tory Brook Ct
3 Whitewater Ct
Glen Rd
B3417
Boringdon Terr
Harewood
Plympton
Ridgeway Sp Sch
B3416
Westfield

5

Sewage Works
Valley Rd
Underwood
Chantry Ct
Dudley Rd
Plympton St Mary CE Inf Sch
Old Priory Jun Sch
The Priory
Liby
Geasons La
Highbridge
Elm Gr
Green Cross
Mallard Cl
Downfield Way

56

Morley Cl
Robert Adams Cl
Merafield Rd
Maple Gr
Lane End
Woodland Dr
Amados Cl
Merafield Rise
Merafield Dr
Amados Cl
Kennel Hill Cl
Rock Terr
Underwood Rd
Walton
Colebrook Barton
Plympton St Maurice
Manor Park Cl
Longcause Special Sch

4

Saltram House
Saltram Park
P
Merafield Farm Cotts
Grantham
Amados Cl
Amados Rise
Amados Dr
Amados Hill
Hardwick Wood Mast
PL7
Dorsmouth Rock
Castlehayes Gdns
Castle Barbican
School La
Fore St
Castle La
St Maurice
Cotton Cl
Hele Gdns
Buller Cl

3

Stable House
P
Television Relay Sta
Telegraph Cottage
The Gables
Hardwick Farm
PLYMOUTH
New Rd
Ridge Rd
Wolverwood La
Plympton St Maurice Prim Sch
Magdalen Gdns

55

The Belt
Vinery La
Heather Grange
A38

2

Sellar Acres
Wixenford Brake
P
Cemy
New Barne Farm
Vealeholme
Furze Park

1

Wixenford Farm
Colebrook Hill
Haye Farm
PL9
Moorcroft Quarry
Haye Road Nurseries
Priors Park Nursery
Higher Sherford

54
Third Ave
Second Ave

52 A 53 B C 54 D E F

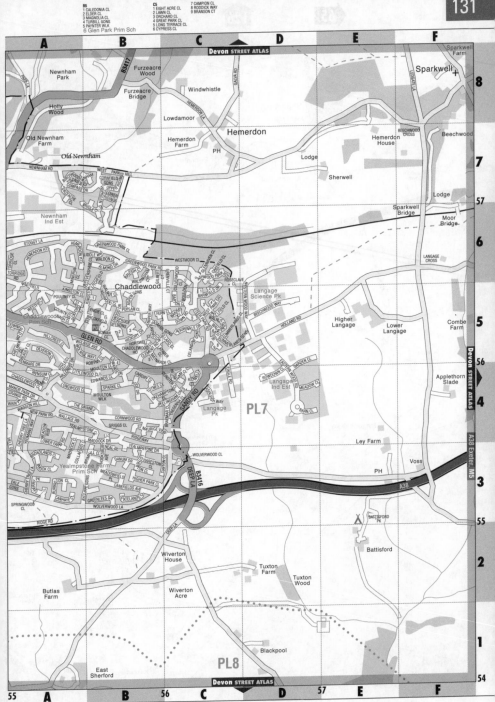

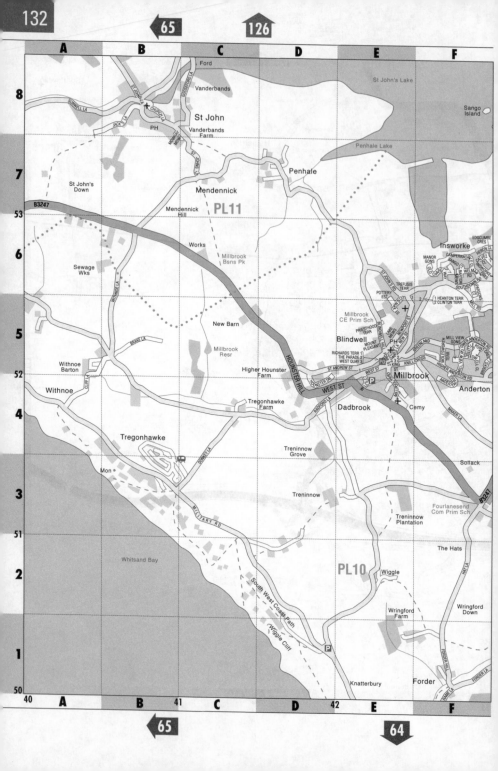

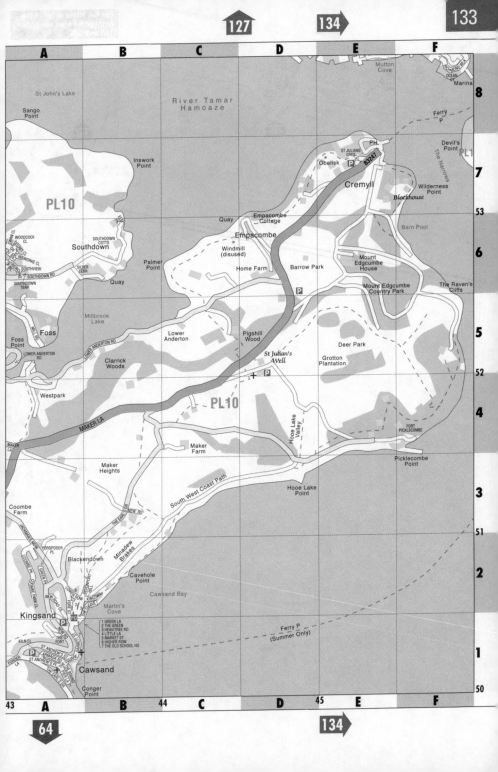

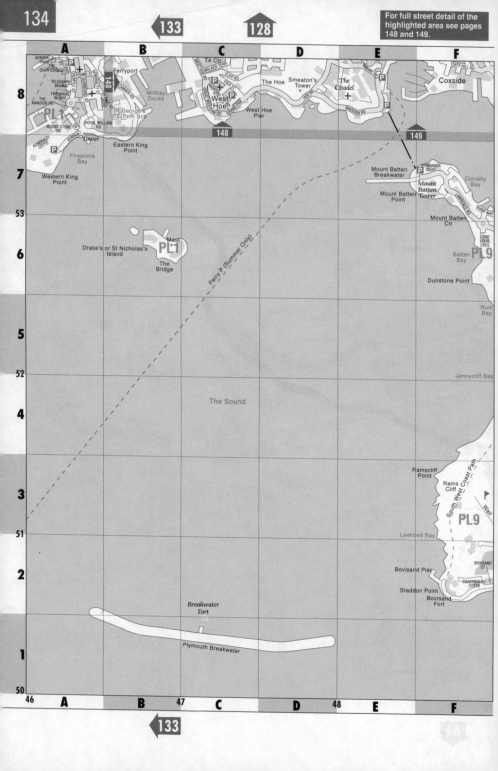

133
128
For full street detail of the highlighted area see pages 148 and 149.
148
149
133

A B C D E F

8

7

53

6

5

52

4

3

51

2

50

Admiral's Hard
THE QUARTERDECK
STRAND
PROVINCE ST
Telegraph Wharf
FREEMANS WHARF
THE MANSION HO
PL1
MOUNT STONE RD
ADMIRALTY COTTS
Tower
Firestone Bay
Western King Point

Ferryport
Millbay Docks
St George's CE Prim Sch
ROYAL WILLIAM RD
Eastern King Point

TA Ctr
WALKER TERR
CLIFF RD
West Hoe
WEST HOE RD
GRAND PDE
West Hoe Pier

The Hoe
Smeaton's Tower
HOE RD
The Citadel
MADEIRA RD

Coxside
TEATS HILL RD

Mount Batten Breakwater
SPINNAKER QUAY
Mount Batten Tower
Mount Batten Point
Clovelly Bay
Mount Batten Ctr
LAWRENCE RD
LORD LOUIS CRES
Batten Bay
PL9
Dunstone Point
Rum Bay

Drake's or St Nicholas's Island
Mast
PL1
The Bridge

Ferry P (Summer Only)

The Sound

Jennycliff Bay

Ramscliff Point
Rams Cliff
South West Coast Path
PL9
Wall
Leekbed Bay
BOVISAND CT
Bovisand Pier
Staddon Point
Bovisand Fort
COASTGUARD COTTS

Breakwater Fort

Plymouth Breakwater

46 A B 47 C D 48 E F

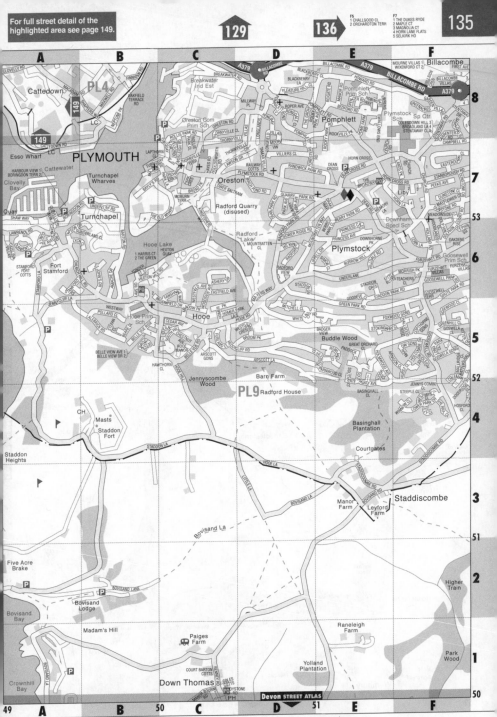

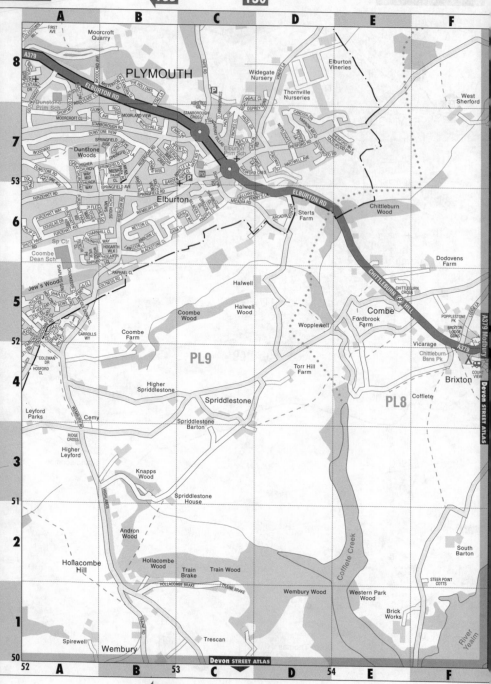

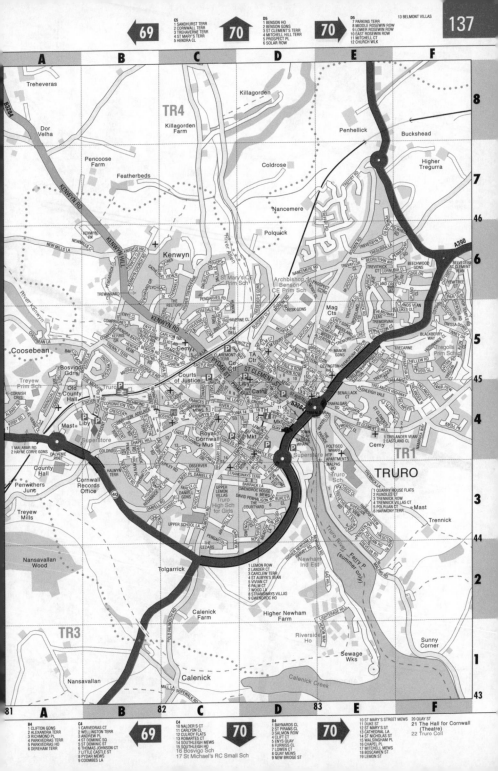

69

70

70

C5
1 SANDHURST TERR
2 CORNWALL TERR
3 TREHAVERNE TERR
4 ST MARY'S TERR
5 HENDRA CL

D5
1 BENSON HO
2 BENSON GDNS
3 ST CLEMENT'S TERR
4 MITCHELL HILL TERR
5 PROSPECT PL
6 SOLAR ROW

D5
7 PARKINS TERR
8 MIDDLE ROSEWIN ROW
9 LOWER ROSEWIN ROW
10 EAST ROSEWIN ROW
11 MITCHELL CT
12 CHURCH WLK

TR4

Treheveras
Dor Velha
Killagorden
Killagorden Farm
Penhellick
Buckshead
Pencoose Farm
Featherbeds
Coldrose
Higher Tregurra
Nancemere
Polquick
Kenwyn
St Mary's CE Prim Sch
Archbishop Benson CE Prim Sch
Coosebean
Bosvigo Gdns
Old County Hall
Treyew Prim Sch
Tregolls Prim Sch
Courts of Justice
Royal Cornwall Mus
Truro
Mast
Superstore
County Hall
Penwithers Junc
Cornwall Records Office
Truro High Sch for Girls
TRURO
TR1
Cemy
Mast
Trennick
Treyew Mills
Nansavallan Wood
Tolgarrick
Truro High Sch
Newham Ind Est
TR3
Calenick Farm
Higher Newham Farm
Riverside Ho
Sunny Corner
Nansavallan
Calenick
Sewage Wks
Calenick Creek

1 MALABAR RD
2 HAYNE CORFE GDNS

1 QUARRY HOUSE FLATS
2 RUNDLES CT
3 TRENNICK ROW
4 TRENNICK VILLAS CT
5 POLRUAN CT
6 HARMONY TERR

1 LEMON ROW
2 LANDER CT
3 CARCLEW TERR
4 ST AUBYN'S VEAN
5 VIVIAN CT
6 PALM CT
7 WOOD LN
8 STRANGWAYS VILLAS
9 GWENDROC HO

B4
1 CLIFTON GDNS
2 ALEXANDRA TERR
3 RICHMOND PL
4 PARKVEDRAS TERR
5 PARKVEDRAS HO
6 DEREHAM TERR

C4
1 CARVEDRAS CT
2 WELLINGTON TERR
3 ANDREW PL
4 ST AUBYN'S SQ
5 ST DOMINIC ST
7 LITTLE CASTLE TERR
8 PYDAR MEWS
9 COOMBES LA

C4
10 NALDER'S CT
11 CARLYON CL
12 CULROY FLATS
13 ROBARTES CT
14 SOUTHLEIGH MEWS
15 SOUTHLEIGH HO
16 Bosvigo Sch
17 St Michael's RC Small Sch

D4
1 BAYNARDS CL
2 ST PIRANS CL
3 SALMON ROW
4 CLIFT CT
5 ENYS QUAY
6 FURNISS CL
7 LOWEN CT
8 QUAY MEWS
9 NEW BRIDGE ST

10 ST MARY'S STREET MEWS
11 DUKE ST
12 ST MARY'S ST
13 CATHEDRAL LA
14 ST NICHOLAS ST
15 WALSINGHAM PL
16 CHAPEL PL
17 MITCHELL MEWS
18 BOSCAWEN ST
19 LEMON ST
20 QUAY ST
21 The Hall for Cornwall (Theatre)
22 Truro Coll

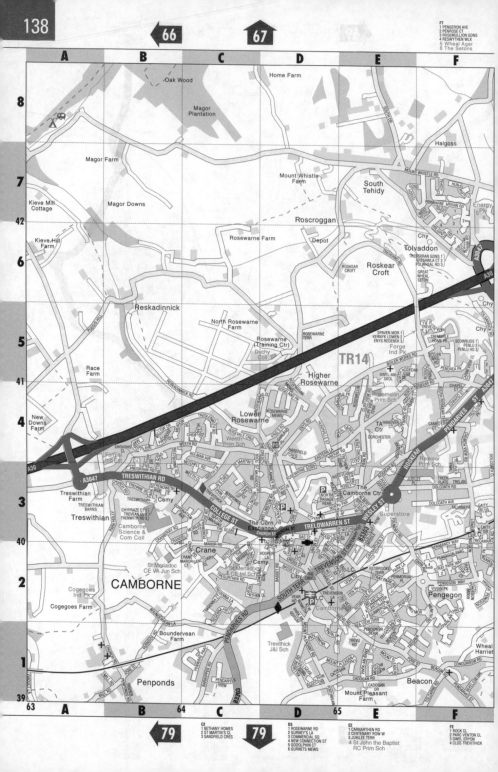

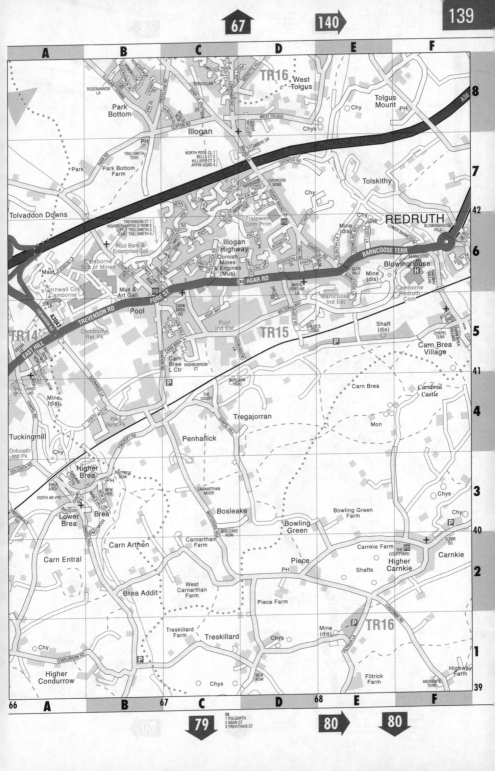

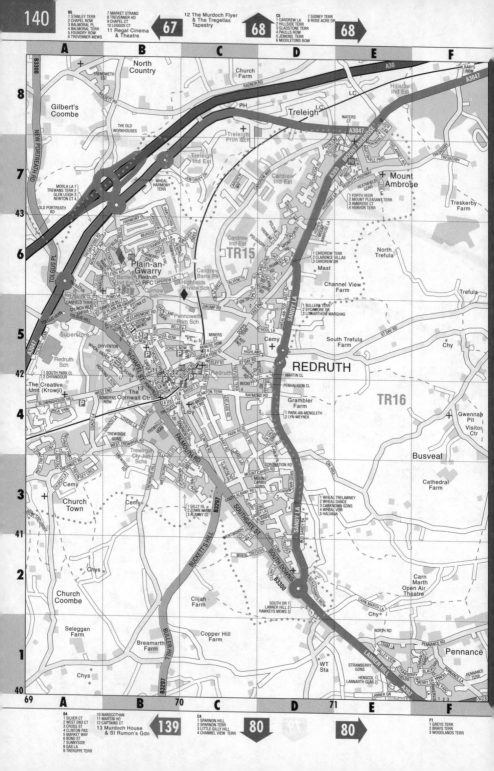

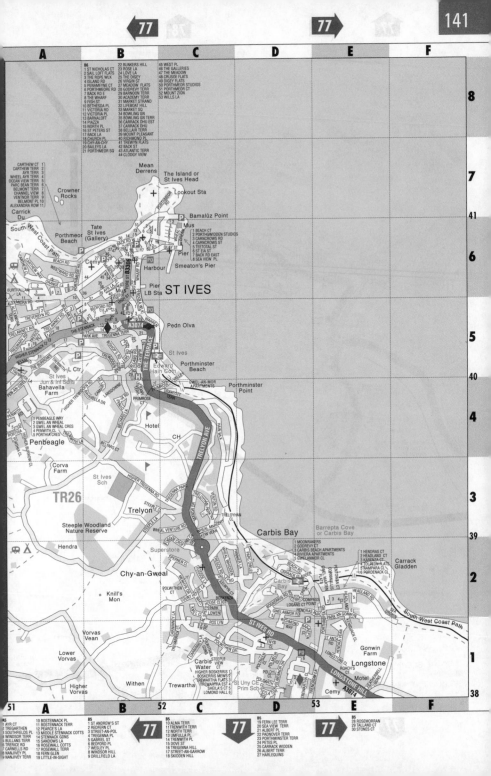

B6
1 ST NICHOLAS CT
2 SAIL LOFT FLATS
3 THE ROPE WLK
4 ISLAND RD
5 PENAMEYNE CT
6 PORTHMEOR RD E
7 BACK RD E
8 THE WHARF
9 FISH ST
10 BETHESDA PL
11 VICTORIA RD
12 VICTORIA PL
13 BARNALOFT
14 PIAZZA
15 NORTH PL
16 ST PETERS ST
17 BACK LA
18 CHURCH PL
19 CHY-AN-CHY
20 BAILEYS LA
21 PORTHMEOR SQ

22 BUNKERS HILL
23 ROSE LA
24 LOVE LA
25 THE DIGEY
26 VIRGIN ST
27 MEADOW FLATS
28 GODREVY TERR
29 BARNOON TERR
30 ACADEMY TERR
31 MARKET STRAND
32 LIFEBOAT HILL
33 MARKET SQ
34 BOWLING GN
35 BOWLING GN TERR
36 CARRACK DHU EST
37 CARRACK DHU
38 BELLAIR TERR
39 MOUNT PLEASANT
40 RICHMOND PL
41 TREWYN FLATS
42 BACK ST
43 ATLANTIC TERR
44 CLODGY VIEW

45 WEST PL
46 THE GALLERIES
47 THE MEADOW
48 CRUSOE FLATS
49 DIGEY FLATS
50 PORTHMEOR STUDIOS
51 PORTHMEOR CT
52 MOUNT ZION
53 WILLS LA

CARTHEW CT 1
CARTHEW TERR 2
AYR TERR 3
WHEEL AYR TERR 4
OCEAN VIEW TERR 5
PARC BEAN TERR 6
BELMONT TERR 7
CHANNEL VIEW 8
VENTNOR TERR 9
BELMONT PL 10
ALEXANDRA ROW 11

1 BEACH CT
2 PORTHGWIDDEN STUDIOS
3 CARNCROWS ST
4 CARNCROWS ST
5 TEETOTAL ST
6 ST EIA ST
7 BACK RD EAST
8 SEA VIEW PL

1 PENBEAGLE WAY
2 GWEL AN WHEAL
3 GWEL AN WHEAL CRES
4 PENWITH CL
5 PORTHIA CRES

1 MOONRAKERS
2 GODREVY CT
3 CARBIS BEACH APARTMENTS
4 RIVIERA APARTMENTS
5 GWELANMOR CL

1 HENDRAS CT
2 HEADLAND CT
3 KARENZA CT
4 TOLROON FLATS
5 STAMPARA CL
6 PURDENACK CL

Mean Derrens

The Island or St Ives Head

Crowner Rocks

Lookout Sta

Carrick Du

South West Coast Path

Porthmeor Beach

Tate St Ives (Gallery)

Bamalûz Point

Mus

Pier

Harbour

Quay St

Smeaton's Pier

ST IVES

Pier LB Sta

Pedn Olva

St Ives

Park Ave

Tregenna Ave

L Ctr

St Ives Jun & Inf Schs

Bahavella Farm

Higher Trenwith

St Ives

Edward Hain Court

Porthminster Beach

Gwel-an-Mor Apartments

Porthminster Point

Primrose Valley

Hotel

Penbeagle

Corva Farm

St Ives Sch

TR26

Trelyon

Steeple Woodland Nature Reserve

Hendra

Superstore

Carbis Bay

Barrepta Cove or Carbis Bay

Chy-an-Gweal

Knill's Mon

Carbis Bay

Compass

Logans Point

Carrack Gladden

Vorvas Vean

Lower Vorvas

Withen

Trewartha

St Uny CE Prim Sch

Gonwin Farm

Longstone

Longstone Motel

South West Coast Path

Higher Vorvas

Carbis Water

Roach's

Cemy

A3074

LONGSTONE HILL

A5
1 AYR CT
2 TREGARTHEN
3 SOUTHFIELDS PL
4 WINDSOR TERR
5 BULLANS TERR
6 TRERICE RD
7 CARNELLIS RD
8 NANJIVEY PL
9 NANJIVEY TERR
10 BOSTENNACK PL
11 BOSTENNACK TERR
12 PEARCE LA
13 MIDDLE STENNACK COTTS
14 STENNACK GDNS
15 SANDOWS LA
16 ROSEWALL COTTS
17 ROSEWALL TERR
18 FERN GLEN
19 LITTLE-IN-SIGHT

B5
1 ST ANDREW'S ST
2 REDFERN CT
3 STREET-AN-POL
4 TREGENNA PL
5 GABRIEL ST
6 BEDFORD PL
7 WESLEY PL
8 WINDSOR HILL
9 DRILLFIELD LA
10 ALMA TERR
11 TRENWITH TERR
12 NORTH TERR
13 UMFULLA PL
14 TRENWITH PL
15 DOVE ST
16 TREGENNA HILL
17 STREET-AN-GARROW
18 SKIDDEN HILL

B5
19 FERN LEE TERR
20 SEA VIEW TERR
21 ALBERT PL
22 PADNOVER TERR
23 PORTHMINSTER TERR
24 PETES PL
25 CARRACK WIDDEN
26 ALBERT TERR
27 HARLEQUINS

B5
28 ROSEMORRAN
29 TALLAND CT
30 STONES CT

← 77   77   77 →

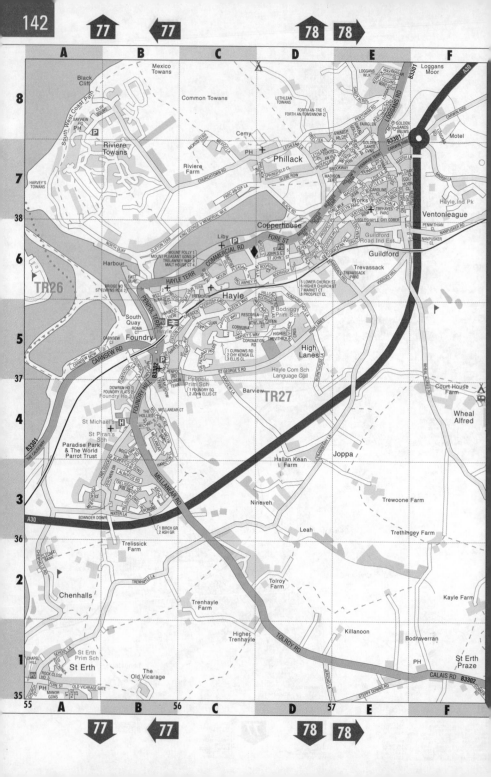

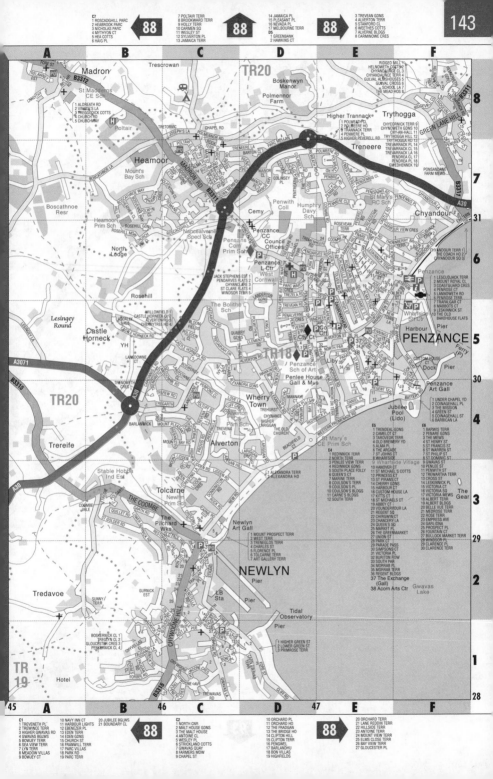

C7
1 ROSCADGHILL PARC
2 HEABROOK PARC
3 NICHOLAS GATE
4 MYTHYON CT
5 HEA COTTS
6 HAIG PL
7 POLTAIR TERR
8 BROOKWARD TERR
9 HOLLY TERR
10 CARMEL SQ
11 WESLEY ST
12 SYLVERTON PL
13 JAMAICA TERR
14 JAMAICA PL
15 PLEASANT PL
16 NEVADA PL
17 MELBOURNE TERR

D5
1 GREENBANK
2 HAWKINS CT

3 TREVEAN GDNS
4 ALVERTON TERR
5 STANFORD CL
6 WEETHES COTTS
7 ALVERNE BLDGS
8 CARMINOWE CRES

C1
1 TREVENETH PL
2 TREWINCE TERR
3 HIGHER GWAVAS RD
4 GWAVAS BGLWS
5 BOWJEY TERR
6 SEA VIEW TERR
7 LYN TERR
8 MEADOW VILLAS
9 BOWJEY CT
10 NAVY INN CT
11 HARBOUR LIGHTS
12 EBENEZER PL
13 EDEN TERR
14 EDEN GDNS
15 CHURCH ST
16 FRANWILL TERR
17 PARC VILLAS
18 PARK RD
19 PARC TERR
20 JUBILEE BGLWS
21 BOUNDARY CL

C2
1 NORTH CNR
2 MALT HOUSE GDNS
3 THE MALT HOUSE
4 ANTOINE CL
5 WESLEY PL
6 STRICKLAND COTTS
7 GWAVAS QUAY
8 FARMERS MDW
9 CHAPEL ST
10 ORCHARD PL
11 ORCHARD HO
12 THE FRADGAN
13 THE BRIDGE HO
14 CLIFTON TERR
15 CLIFTON TERR
16 PENJOWL
17 BARLANDHU
18 BON VILLAS
19 HIGHFIELDS
20 ORCHARD TERR
21 LANE REDOIN TERR
22 HILLSIDE TERR
23 ANTOINE TERR
24 MOUNT VIEW TERR
25 ELMS CLOSE TERR
26 BAY VIEW TERR
27 GLOUCESTER PL

← 81

C7
1 HARRIS CT
2 SLADES LA
3 BENNETTS COTTS
4 RUSSELL WAY
5 SARACEN HO
6 BANK COTTS

↑ 81

C8
1 Three Bridges Specl Sch

A B C D E F

8

University Coll Falmouth (Tremough Campus)

TREMOUGHDALE

THE PRAZE
CHURCH RD

St Gluvias

1 ST GLUVIAS PARC
12 BOHELLAND RISE

Bissom

Bissom Farm

Trevissome Farm

TR11

Penryn CE Inf Sch

Penryn Jun Sch

Penryn Coll

7

TR10

PENRYN

Penryn CE Inf Sch

COMMERCIAL RD

Gorran Gorras

Cemy

TH Mus

1 CHARTER CT
2 BOHILL CT
3 SUMMERCOURT
4 SOUTH HARBOUR
5 DANIELS SAIL LOFT
6 FOXS
7 FOXSTANTON DR
8 CARN ROCK
9 TRESOOTH TERR
10 TRESOOTH CT
11 THE BAKEHOUSE

Quay Harbour

Penryn River

Trevissome House

34

FALMOUTH RD B3292

Ponsharden

6

A39

Superstore

Kernick Ind Est

Kernick Gdns

Kernick House

Resr

Hillhead Farm

Mast

Ponsharden Ind Est

Ponsharden Cotts

P+R

Homestead Ct

Falmouth Wharves

Trevissome Ut

North Park

Penwerris Farm

5

College Resr

Tregonhaye

HILLHEAD RD

KERGILLIACK RD

Higher Kergilliack

Lower Kergilliack

UNION CNR

Falmouth Com Sch

Dracaena View

Grenville Rd

33

Bickland Water

Tregoniggie Ind Est

Mongleath

H

Falmouth

Highfield Rd

Kimberley Park Rd

4

TR11

Nangitha Farm

Bickland Ind Est

St Francis CE Sch

CHURCH WAY

St Mary's RC Prim Sch

MOUNT STEPHENS LA
MEARWOOD LA

Longfield

Penmere

Swanvale

3

Sparnon

CORONATION COTTS

NANGITHA CL

SCHOOL LA

VICTORIA COTTS

VICARAGE RD

Eglos Farm

St Francis CE Sch

Falmouth Bsns Pk

SHELBURNE CT

Penmere Hill

32

MERRY MIT MOW

MENHAY VIEW

PH

Menehay

BOSMEAR RD

Boslowick

MARLBOROUGH AVE

CROSSWAYS

2

Budock Water

Trewen House

ROSE EGLOS

CONDOR COTTS

Roscarrack House

Boslowick Ct

TUNWARE RD

Boslowick

SPEAR'S TERR

1

Tresooth Bungalow

Trewen Farm

Higher Crill Farm

BAY VIEW TERR

CRILL CNR

Hotel

Higher Roscarrack Farm

MAEN VALLEY PK

GOLDEN BANK PK

SWANPOOL RD

Trelevra Farm

CH

TREMORVAH CT

31

77 A B 78 C D 79 E F

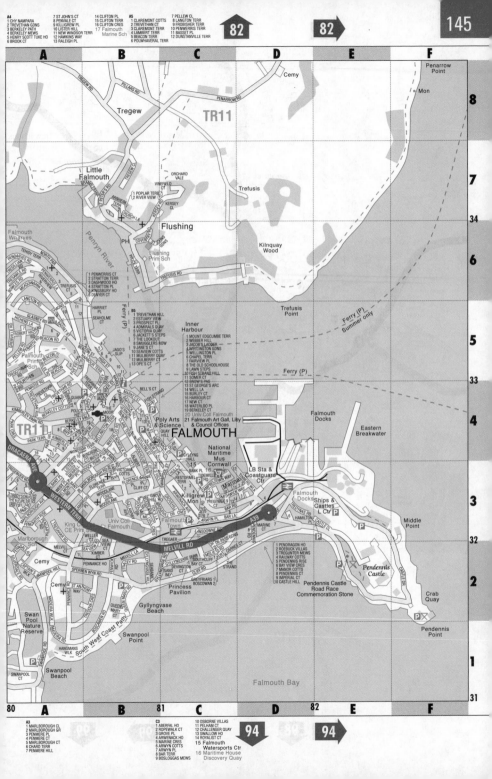

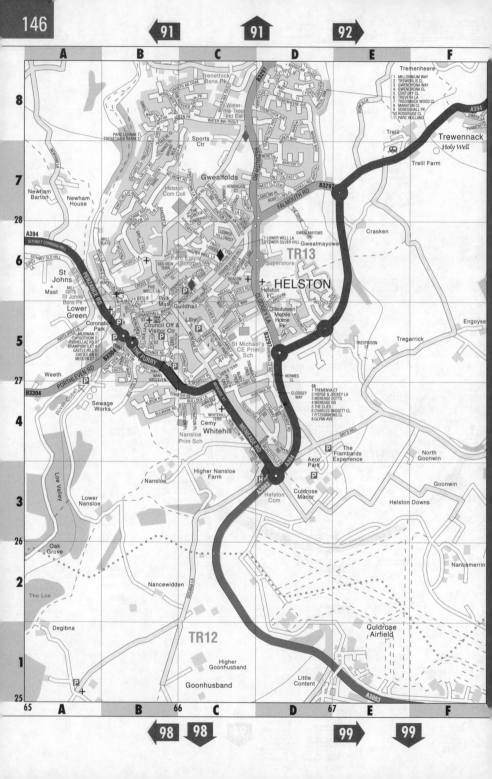

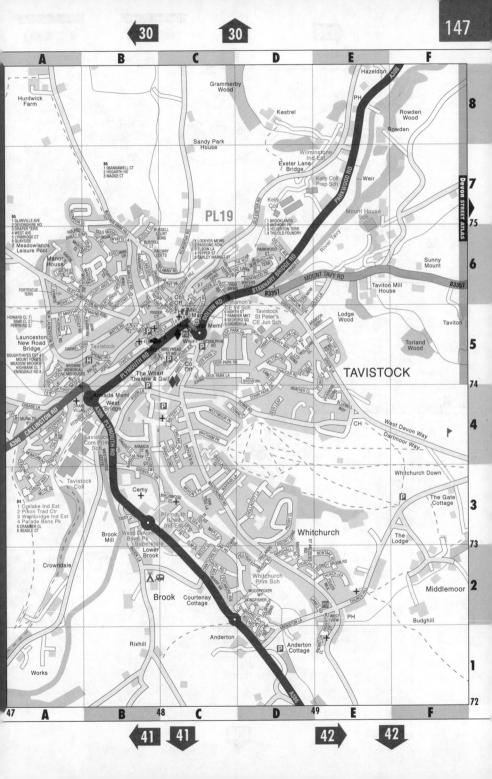

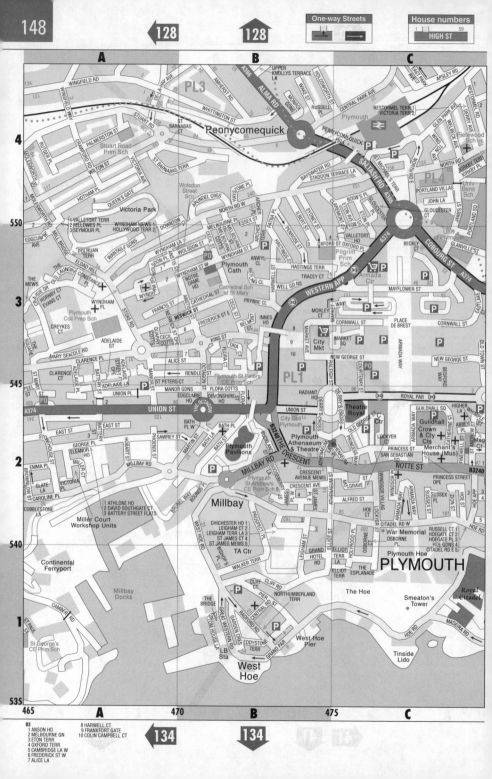

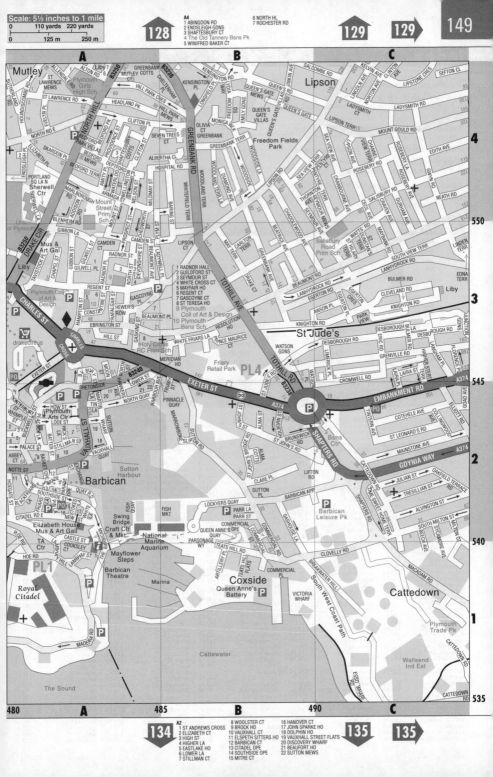

Index

Place name May be abbreviated on the map

Location number Present when a number indicates the place's position in a crowded area of mapping

Locality, town or village Shown when more than one place has the same name

Postcode district District for the indexed place

Page and grid square Page number and grid reference for the standard mapping

Church Rd **6** Beckenham BR2..........**53** C6

Cities, towns and villages are listed in CAPITAL LETTERS

Public and commercial buildings are highlighted in magenta **Places of interest** are highlighted in blue with a star★

Abbreviations used in the index

Acad	Academy	Comm	Common	Gd	Ground	L	Leisure	Prom	Promenade
App	Approach	Cott	Cottage	Gdn	Garden	La	Lane	Rd	Road
Arc	Arcade	Cres	Crescent	Gn	Green	Liby	Library	Recn	Recreation
Ave	Avenue	Cswy	Causeway	Gr	Grove	Mdw	Meadow	Ret	Retail
Bglw	Bungalow	Ct	Court	H	Hall	Meml	Memorial	Sh	Shopping
Bldg	Building	Ctr	Centre	Ho	House	Mkt	Market	Sq	Square
Bsns, Bus	Business	Ctry	Country	Hospl	Hospital	Mus	Museum	St	Street
Bvd	Boulevard	Cty	County	HQ	Headquarters	Orch	Orchard	Sta	Station
Cath	Cathedral	Dr	Drive	Hts	Heights	Pal	Palace	Terr	Terrace
Cir	Circus	Dro	Drove	Ind	Industrial	Par	Parade	TH	Town Hall
Cl	Close	Ed	Education	Inst	Institute	Pas	Passage	Univ	University
Cnr	Corner	Emb	Embankment	Int	International	Pk	Park	Wk, Wlk	Walk
Coll	College	Est	Estate	Intc	Interchange	Pl	Place	Wr	Water
Com	Community	Ex	Exhibition	Junc	Junction	Prec	Precinct	Yd	Yard

Index of towns, villages, streets, hospitals, industrial estates, railway stations, schools, shopping centres, universities and places of interest

Abb–AND

A

Abbey Cl PL20 . . . . **42** B2
Abbey Ct
　19 Penzance TR18 . . . . **143** E5
　Plymouth PL1 . . . . **149** A2
Abbey Hill TR26 . . . . **77** E3
Abbey Mdw TR26 . . . . . . **77** E4
Abbeymead Mews PL19 **147** C5
Abbey Mews PL31 . . . . . **109** C4
Abbey Pl
　Plymouth PL1 . . . . **148** C2
　Tavistock PL19 . . . . . . **147** C5
Abbey Rise PL19 . . . . . . **147** C5
Abbey St TR18 . . . . **143** E5
Abbotsbury Way PL2 . . **127** F8
Abbots Cl PL31 . . . . **109** F4
Abbotscourt La PL11 . . . **126** A2
Abbotsfield Cl PL20 . . . . **41** D8
Abbotsfield Cres PL19 . . **41** D8
Abbots Rd PL3 . . . . **128** E6
Aberdeen Ave PL5 . . . . . **124** D1
Aberfal Ho **1** TR11 . . . . **145** C3
Abingdon Rd **1** PL4 . . . . **149** A4
Abney Cres PL6 . . . . **125** B6
Above Town Cl PL27 . . . . **21** F3
Abscott La PL9 . . . . **135** C5
Acacia Rd TR11 . . . . **144** F5
Academy Terr **20** TR26 . **141** B6
Acklington Pl PL5 . . . . . **123** E4
Acland Cl EX23 . . . . **104** E7
Acland Gdns TR7 . . . . . . **110** D6
Acorn Arts Ctr **31** TR18 **143** E5
Acorn Dr PL25 . . . . **115** A3
Acre Cotts PL1 . . . . **127** F3
Acre Pl PL1 . . . . **127** F3
Adams Cl
　Plymouth PL5 . . . . **123** F1
　Torpoint PL11 . . . . **126** F3
Adams Cres PL11 . . . . . **126** E3
Adams Row TR16 . . . . . . **68** D3
ADDINGTON **113** D7
Addington S PL14 . . . . . **113** D6
Addison Rd PL4 . . . . **149** A4
Addison Terr PL22 . . . . . **112** C2
Adelaide La PL1 . . . . **148** A2

Adelaide Pl PL1 . . . . **148** A3
Adelaide Rd TR15 . . . . . **140** C4
Adelaide St
　Camborne TR14 . . . . . **138** E3
　Penzance TR18 . . . . . . **143** E6
　2 Plymouth, Ford PL2 . **127** F5
　Plymouth PL1 . . . . **148** A3
Adelaide Street Ope PL1 **148** A3
Adelaide Terr TR1 . . . . . **137** B4
Adela Rd PL11 . . . . **127** A3
Adit La
　Newlyn TR18 . . . . **143** C1
　Saltash PL12 . . . . **122** E3
Adits The PL18 . . . . **41** A3
Admiral's Hard PL1 . . . . **134** A8
Admirals Quay **4** TR11 . **145** B5
Admiralty Cotts PL1 . . . . **134** A7
Admiralty Ct PL13 . . . . . **117** D3
Admiralty Rd
　Plymouth, Millbay PL1 . **134** A8
　Plymouth, St Budeaux PL5 **123** C2
Admiralty St
　Plymouth, Keyham PL2 . **127** E6
　Plymouth, Millbay PL1 . **134** A8
Admiralty Terr TR2 . . . . . **83** B2
African Row TR14 . . . . . . **79** B5
Agar Cres TR15 . . . . **139** D6
Agar Ct
　2 Camborne TR15 . . . **139** C6
　Truro TR1 . . . . **137** D5
Agar Mdws **11** TR3 . . . . . **81** F7
Agar Rd
　Camborne TR15 . . . . . **139** D6
　Newquay TR7 . . . . **110** E5
　St Austell PL25 . . . . . . **114** E6
　Truro TR1 . . . . **137** E5
Agar Terr **12** PL31 . . . . . **109** D5
Agar Way TR15 . . . . **139** C5
Agaton Rd PL5 . . . . **123** E3
Agnes Cl EX23 . . . . **104** F4
Ainslie Terr PL2 . . . . **127** E7
Aire Gdns PL3 . . . . **129** B5
Alamein Ct PL12 . . . . . . **122** E2
Alamein Rd PL12 . . . . . . **122** D2
Alan Harvey Cl **14** TR26 . **77** A6
Alan Rd PL28 . . . . **107** D4
Alansmere Ct TR2 . . . . . . **57** A1
Alanta Flats TR7 . . . . . . **110** B5
Albany Cl
　Redruth TR15 . . . . **140** C3
　Redruth TR15 . . . . **140** C3
　St Agnes TR5 . . . . **68** D8

Albany Ct
　4 Newquay TR7 . . . . . **110** F6
　Redruth TR15 . . . . **140** D3
Albany Gdns TR15 . . . . . **140** C3
Albany La TR15 . . . . **140** C4
Albany Pl TR11 . . . . **145** A3
Albany Rd
　Falmouth TR11 . . . . . . **145** A3
　5 Newquay TR7 . . . . . **110** F6
　Redruth TR15 . . . . **140** C4
Albany St PL1 . . . . **127** E2
Albany Terr TR26 . . . . . . **141** B4
ALBASTON **40** E5
Albemarle Villas PL1 . . . **127** F3
Albert Bldgs **19** TR18 . . . **143** E6
Albert Cotts TR11 . . . . . **145** B4
Albertha Cl PL4 . . . . **149** B4
Albert Pl
　Camborne TR14 . . . . . **138** E3
　21 St Ives TR26 . . . . . **141** B5
　Truro TR1 . . . . **137** C3
Albert Rd
　Plymouth PL2 . . . . **127** F3
　Saltash PL12 . . . . **123** A2
　St Ives TR26 . . . . **114** D3
　St Ives TR26 . . . . **141** B5
Albert St
　Camborne TR14 . . . . . **138** E3
　Penzance TR18 . . . . . . **143** F6
Albert Terr
　Gunnislake PL18 . . . . . **40** F5
　Lostwithiel PL22 . . . . . **112** C2
　12 Penzance TR18 . . . **143** E6
　28 St Ives TR26 . . . . . **141** B5
Albertus Dr TR27 . . . . . . **142** B3
Albertus Gdns TR27 . . . . **142** B3
Albertus Rd TR27 . . . . . . **142** B3
Albert Villas PL2 . . . . . . **127** E4
Albion Ct PL11 . . . . **127** B3
Albion Dr PL2 . . . . **128** B7
Albion Rd
　Helston TR13 . . . . **146** B4
　Torpoint PL11 . . . . **127** B3
Albion Row TR16 . . . . . . **80** F8
Alcester Cl PL2 . . . . **127** E4
Alcester St PL2 . . . . **127** F4
Alden Wlk PL6 . . . . **129** B7
Aldercombe La EX23 . . . . **5** A6
Alderney Rd PL6 . . . . . . **124** F7
Alder Rd PL19 . . . . **147** C3
Aldersley Wlk PL6 . . . . . **125** A1
Aldreath Cl TR20 . . . . . . **88** B7

Aldreath Rd TR20 . . . . . . **88** B7
Alexander Ct
　14 Carnon Downs TR3 . **81** F7
　Gorran Haven PL26 . . . . **85** D5
Alexandra Cl
　5 Illogan TR16 . . . . . . **67** E4
　Plymouth PL9 . . . . **136** B8
　St Ives TR26 . . . . **77** A7
Alexandra Ct TR7 . . . . . **111** C8
Alexandra Dr PL20 . . . . . **41** C1
Alexandra Gdns TR18 . . . **143** D4
Alexandra Ho TR18 . . . . **143** D3
Alexandra Pl
　Penzance TR18 . . . . . . **143** D4
　5 Plymouth PL4 . . . . . **128** E4
　St Ives TR26 . . . . **77** A7
Alexandra Rd
　Bodmin PL31 . . . . **109** B5
　Newquay TR7 . . . . **111** C8
　Penzance TR18 . . . . . . **143** D4
　Plymouth, Crownhill PL6 **124** F2
　Plymouth, Ford PL2 . . . **127** F5
　Plymouth, Mutley PL4 . . **128** E4
　St Austell PL25 . . . . . . **114** E3
　St Ives TR26 . . . . **77** A7
Alexandra Sq PL12 . . . . . **123** A2
Alexandra Terr
　Mount Hawke TR4 . . . . **68** C6
　Penzance TR18 . . . . . . **143** D3
　Plymouth PL2 . . . . **127** F5
　St Ives TR26 . . . . **141** A5
　Tremar PL14 . . . . **38** A4
　2 Truro TR1 . . . . **137** B4
ALFARDISWORTHY **5** E6
Alford Cl EX23 . . . . **104** F5
Alfred Pl PL2 . . . . **127** F5
Alfred Rd PL2 . . . . **127** F5
Alfred St PL1 . . . . **148** C2
Alger Wlk PL6 . . . . **124** E6
Alice La **7** PL1 . . . . **148** B3
Alice St PL1 . . . . **148** A3
Allanfield Ct TR7 . . . . . . **111** D7
Allenby Rd PL2 . . . . **128** A6
Allendale PL26 . . . . **58** E8
Allendale Rd PL4 . . . . . . **149** A4
Allen Pk PL30 . . . . **23** B2
Allen Vale PL14 . . . . **113** A5
Allern La PL5 . . . . **120** D1
Allerton Wlk PL6 . . . . . . **129** B7
Alley Hill PL20 . . . . **42** A1
Alleyn Gdns PL3 . . . . . . **128** E8
Allium Ct TR4 . . . . **70** D8

All Saints Pk PL18 . . . . . **40** E5
Alma Cl TR5 . . . . **68** D8
Alma Cotts PL4 . . . . **149** B2
Alma Pl
　Heamoor TR18 . . . . . . **143** C7
　Newquay TR7 . . . . **110** D6
　Padstow PL28 . . . . **107** D5
　5 Penzance TR18 . . . . **143** E5
　Redruth TR15 . . . . **140** B5
Alma Rd
　Plymouth PL3 . . . . **128** C4
　Truro TR1 . . . . **69** F3
Alma St PL4 . . . . **149** B2
Alma Terr
　Carharrack TR16 . . . . . **80** F8
　Gunnislake PL18 . . . . . **41** A6
　Penzance TR18 . . . . . . **143** E5
　10 St Ives TR26 . . . . . **141** B5
Almond Dr PL7 . . . . **131** B6
Almshouse Hill TR13 . . . **146** B5
ALTARNUN **26** C8
Altarnun Prim Sch PL15 . **26** C7
Alton Pl PL4 . . . . **128** E4
Alton Rd PL4 . . . . **149** A4
Alverne Bldgs **7** TR18 . . **143** C5
ALVERTON **143** C4
Alverton Ct TR1 . . . . **137** E5
Alverton Cty Prim Sch
　TR18 . . . . **143** C4
Alverton Rd TR18 . . . . . . **143** C5
Alverton St TR18 . . . . . . **143** D4
Alverton St TR18 . . . . . . **143** E5
Alverton Terr
　4 Penzance TR18 . . . . **143** D5
　Truro TR1 . . . . **137** E5
Alvington St PL4 . . . . . . **149** C2
Alwin Pk PL6 . . . . **125** A5
Alwyn Cl TR7 . . . . **111** C6
Amacre Dr PL9 . . . . **135** B6
Amados Cl PL7 . . . . **130** B4
Amados Dr PL7 . . . . **130** C4
Amados Rise PL7 . . . . . . **130** C4
Amber Ct TR27 . . . . **142** E7
Amelia An Avon TR27 . . . **142** E7
AMALEBRA **76** E4
AMALVEOR **76** E4
Amanda Way PL14 . . . . . **38** E4
Amble Rd **26** PL17 . . . . . **39** F4
Ambrose Ct TR15 . . . . . **140** E7
Amelia Cl TR2 . . . . **71** C6
Amherst Rd PL3 . . . . **148** B4
Amity Pl PL4 . . . . **149** A4
ANDERTON **132** F4

Anderton Cl PL19 ...... 147 E1
Anderton Ct PL19 ...... 147 E2
Anderton La PL19 ...... 147 D2
Anderton Rise PL10 ... 132 F4
Andrewartha Rd TR10 . 144 A8
Andrew Pl **3** TR1 ...... 137 C4
Andrew's Terr TR16 .... 139 F1
Andrews Way PL12..... 53 E5
Andurn Cl PL9 .... 136 B6
Aneray Rd TR14........ 138 D4
ANGARRACK........... 78 C5
Angarrack La TR27 ..... 78 D5
Angarrack Mews TR27 . 78 C5
Angavran Mdw TR8 .... 55 D8
Angel Hill **7** PL5 ...... 106 C6
An Gof Gdns PL31...... 109 C4
Angwin Ave **4** TR5.... 54 C1
Anjardyn Pl PL24....... 60 D5
Ankervis La TR16 .... 140 F1
Anmear Rd TR10........ 144 A6
Ann's Pl PL3............ 128 A4
Anson Ho **1** PL1....... 148 B3
Anson Pl
  Plymouth, Devonport
   PL2................... 127 F4
  Plymouth, St Jude's PL4. 149 C3
Anson Rd PL27......... 31 F3
Anson Way TR11 .... 146 D4
Anstis St PL1 .... 148 A3
Anthony Cl EX23 .... 4 C3
Anthony Lowen PL28... 107 D4
Anthony Pk PL19....... 147 D6
Anthony Rd TR7 .... 110 E4
Antoine Cl **4** TR18 .... 143 C2
Antoine Terr **2** TR18... 143 C2
ANTONY................ 65 E5
Antony CE Prim Sch PL11 65 E5
Antony Gdns PL22...... 128 C8
Antony Hill PL11........ 65 E5
Antony House* PL11...126 D5
Antony Rd PL11........ 65 E5
Antony Woodland Gdn*
  PL11..................126 D6
Antron Hill TR10........ 81 B1
Antron La TR10 .... 93 C8
Antron Way TR10 ...... 93 C8
Anvil Ct
  Camelford PL32.......105 D3
  Venterdon PL17....... 28 D1
Anvil Rd PL8 .... 149 A2
An Vownder Goth TR13.. 91 B7
Anwyl Cl PL1........... 148 B3
Anzac Ave PL5 .... 124 A4
Appin Gdns TR15....... 139 C7
Appleby Wlk PL5 ...... 124 D4
Appleton Tor Cl PL3.... 129 F5
Appletree La PL25 ..... 115 D3
Apsley Rd PL4.......... 149 B4
Arbour The PL6......... 124 E5
Arcade The **6** TR18.... 143 E5
Arcadia PL9 .... 136 D6
Arcadia Rd PL9 .... 136 D6
Archbishop Benson CE Prim
  Sch TR1...............137 D6
Archer Pl PL1.......... 148 B4
Archer Terr PL1 .... 148 B3
Arch Hill TR1........... 137 C2
Arch La TR27 .... 77 D1
Archway Ave PL4 ...... 129 B3
Arden Gr PL2 .... 128 C8
Arena Cres PL25 ...... 115 B4
Argal View PL10 .... 93 B6
Arimore Gdns PL19 .... 147 E5
Ark Royal Cl PL5....... 127 D8
Arkwright Gdns PL5.... 123 F2
Arley Cl PL6 .... 125 B6
Arlington Rd PL4 ...... 128 F4
Armada Ct PL19........ 147 B4
Armada Ctr PL1........ 148 C3
Armada Rd PL10 ...... 133 A1
Armada Way PL1....... 148 C3
Armchair Cnr PL31..... 109 C5
Arnheim Terr TR11 .... 145 B7
Arnison Cl PL9 .... 135 F5
Arnold's Point PL4 .... 129 C3
Arnside Cl PL6......... 125 D3
Arrallas Barns TR2 .... 57 B4
Arscott Gdns PL9...... 135 C5
Arscott La PL9......... 135 C5
Art Gallery Terr TR18... 143 E4
Arthurian Ctr The*
  PL32..................105 D8
Arthur Terr PL11....... 127 B2
Artillery Pl PL4 .... 149 B1
Arun Cl PL3............ 129 C5
Arundel Cres PL1 ..... 148 B4
Arundel Ct TR27 ...... 78 D6
Arundel Dr PL16....... 19 F4
Arundel Gdns
  Falmouth TR11........ 144 E6
  Lifton PL16........... 19 F4
Arundel Hill TR1....... 137 C3
Arundel Pk TR27 ...... 78 D6
Arundel Terr
  Bude EX23............104 D4
  Plymouth PL2..........127 F4
Arundel Way
  Connor Downs TR27 .. 78 D6
  Plymouth PL27........111 B7
Arundle Cl PL26........ 58 C8
Arwenack Ave TR11 ... 145 C3
Arwenack Ho **4** TR11.. 145 C3
Arwenack St TR11 ..... 145 C4
Arworthal Mdws TR3... 81 D6
Arwyn Cotts **3** TR11.. 145 C3
Arwyn Pl **7** TR11...... 145 C3
Asdally Vale TR18...... 143 B5

Ashburgh Parc PL12 ... 122 B3
Ashburnham Rd PL5 ... 124 A3
Ashbury Cl PL14 .... 113 D7
Ashbury Gr EX22....... 11 E8
Ash Cl
  16 Par PL24.......... 60 B4
  7 Yelverton PL20..... 42 C3
Ashcombe Cl PL7 ...... 130 C7
Ashdown Cl
  Plymouth PL6.......... 125 E3
  Sticker PL26........... 58 E1
Ashdown Wlk PL6...... 125 E3
Ash Dr TR27 .... 142 B3
Ashery Dr PL9 .... 135 C6
Ashfield Gdns TR11 .... 144 E6
Ashfield Rd TR11....... 144 F6
Ashfield Villas TR11.... 144 F6
Ashford Cl PL3......... 129 A4
Ashford Cres PL3 ...... 129 A4
Ash Gr
  Hayle TR27............142 B3
  Par PL24.............. 60 B4
  Plymouth PL2..........127 F7
Ashleigh Cl PL5........ 124 C7
Ashleigh La PL5 .... 120 D1
Ashleigh Way
  Plymouth PL7..........131 C4
  Probus TR2............ 71 D6
Ashley Cl **9** PL26 ..... 59 D7
Ashley Rd
  Shortlanesend TR4.... 69 F6
  Truro TR1.............137 C4
Ashmead TR2........... 57 E1
Ashridge Gdns PL5..... 124 B2
ASHTON................ 90 E3
Ashton Cl PL6......... 125 C6
Ashton Ct TR7 .... 111 D6
Ashton Way PL12 ..... 122 D3
Ashton Wlk EX23....... 6 F5
Ashtree Cl PL5......... 123 D7
Ashtree Gr PL9 .... 136 C8
Ash Vale TR16 .... 19 F4
Ashwood Cl PL7 ...... 131 B5
Ashwood Park Rd PL7.. 131 C6
Aspen Cl PL19 .... 147 C3
Aspen Gdns PL7 ...... 131 B5
Astor Dr PL4........... 129 C3
Astwood Developments
  PL13..................148 B3
Atheistan Pk PL13...... 109 F3
Athenaeum La PL1 .... 148 B2
Athenaeum Pl PL1 .... 148 C2
Athenaeum St PL1 .... 148 B2
Atherton Pl PL2........ 127 E4
Athlone Ho PL1 .... 148 A2
Atlanta PL28........... 20 E2
Atlantic Cl
  Camborne TR14....... 138 E2
  Treknow PL34......... 14 C5
  Widemouth Bay EX23 .. 6 F5
Atlantic Cres TR19 .... 96 C7
Atlantic Mews
  New Polzeath PL27 ... 21 C6
  4 St Agnes TR5 ..... 54 D1
Atlantic Rd
  Delabole PL34.........14 D2
  Newquay TR7..........110 C6
  Tintagel PL34......... 14 C7
Atlantic Terr
  Camborne TR14....... 138 E2
  New Polzeath PL27 ... 21 D6
  Trevone PL28.......... 20 E2
Atlantic Way
  Porthtowan TR4....... 68 A6
  4 Tintagel PL34 ..... 14 C7
Attenborrow Ct TR7.... 111 C8
Attery View PL15....... 18 E6
Auckland Rd **3** PL2... 128 A5
Aud House La PL26 .... 59 C7
Austin Ave PL12 ...... 122 D3
Austin Cres PL6........ 125 C1
Austin Farm Prim Sch
  PL6...................129 C7
Ava PL26.............. 73 C4
Avallen Cl TR11........ 82 A3
Avent Wlk PL7......... 130 F7
Avenue Rd TR11 ...... 145 C3
Avenue The
  St Hilary TR20........ 89 F6
  Truro TR1.............137 D5
Avery's Row PL15...... 107 D5
Avery Terr PL22........ 112 C2
Avery Way PL12........ 122 C5
Avon Cl
  Plymouth PL3..........129 D6
  St Austell PL25........115 A5
Avondale Rd TR1 ...... 137 B4
Avon Flats TR7......... 111 C7
Avrack Cl TR19 .... 87 F3
Axe Cl PL3............. 129 D6
Axford Hill PL17 .... 39 F2
Axtown La PL20........ 42 C2
Aycliffe Gdns PL7 ..... 131 A5
Aylesbury Cres PL5.... 124 B5
Aylmer Pl **3** PL5...... 114 C3
Aylmer Sq **14** PL25... 114 C3
Aylwin Cl PL7.......... 130 E6
Ayr Cl **1** TR26........ 141 A5
Ayreville Rd PL2....... 128 B7
Ayr La TR26............ 141 B6
Ayr Terr TR26.......... 141 A6
Aysshton Gdns **18** PL17.. 39 F4

B

Babbacombe Cl PL6.... 129 E8
Baber Cl PL12.......... 40 C2
Baber Ct PL12.......... 40 D2
Babis Farm Cl PL12 .... 122 F1
Babis Farm Ct PL12 .... 122 F1
Babis Farm Mews PL12.. 122 F1
Babis Farm Row PL12... 122 F1
Babis Farm Way PL12... 122 F2
Babis La PL12.......... 122 F1
Baby Beach La PL27.... 21 D6
Back Hill
  Port Isaac PL29........22 D7
  Saltash PL12.......... 122 D7
Back La
  Angarrack TR27....... 78 C5
  Callington PL17....... 39 F4
  Marazion TR17........ 89 B5
  Plymouth PL7..........130 E4
  St Erth TR27...........77 D2
  17 St Ives TR26...... 141 B6
  Tintagel PL34......... 14 D7
  Tregony TR2...........71 F4
  Veryan TR2............ 83 F6
Back Lane W TR15 ..... 140 B4
Back Quay TR1 .... 137 D4
Back Rd PL18 .... 41 A3
Back Road E **7** TR26... 141 B6
Back Road W TR26..... 141 B6
Back St **8** TR26....... 141 B6
BADGALL.............. 17 C5
Badger's Cross TR20 ... 88 E8
Badgers Wlk PL12 ..... 122 D4
Badger View PL9 ...... 135 E5
BADHARLICK........... 17 E5
Bagbury Rd EX23 ..... 104 E3
Bag La
  Polbathic PL12........ 64 F8
  St Germans PL12...... 65 A8
Bahavella Dr TR26 ..... 141 B4
Bailey Gdns EX22 ...... 8 A5
Baileys Field EX23 ..... 5 A6
Baileys La **20** TR26 ... 141 B6
Bailey Terr EX22........ 8 A5
Bainbridge Ave PL2 ... 128 F7
Bainbridge Ct PL7 ..... 130 E7
Baines Hill TR16 .... 67 C6
Bakehouse La **7** PL17... 39 E4
Bakehouse The PL10... 144 D7
Bake Lane End PL12.... 52 D1
Bakers Cl PL7.......... 131 C5
Bakers Ct TR7 .... 110 E6
Bakers Gn PL25........ 115 B4
Bakers Pl PL1.......... 127 F1
Bakers Row TR13 ...... 90 F3
Bakesdown EX23....... 7 B6
Balcoath TR16.......... 68 D1
BALDHU................ 69 C1
Baldhu Row TR 20...... 76 F2
Balfield Rd **15** TR13... 98 C8
Balfour Terr PL2 .... 127 E4
Bal-Jinjy Cl **10** PL24... 60 B4
Balkin Way PL5........ 139 D7
BALL.................. 108 B7
Ballard Cl TR16......... 80 B5
Ballard Est TR16........ 80 B5
Ball Terr PL27.......... 108 E7
Balmoral Ave PL2 ..... 127 F5
Balmoral Pl **3** TR15... 140 B5
Balmoral Terr **4** TR15.. 140 B5
BALNOON.............. 77 A5
Balnoon Flats TR26 .... 77 A4
Bal Rd TR13............ 91 E4
BALWEST.............. 90 D5
Bambry Cl TR20........ 89 E5
Bampfylde Way
  Goldsithney TR20..... 89 F5
  Plymouth PL6..........124 D6
Bampton Rd PL6 ...... 125 E1
Band House La PL26 ... 59 C7
BANGORS.............. 7 E2
Bangors Est EX23 ..... 6 F2
Bangors Rd **6** PL15... 18 E2
Bank Cotts **6** TR10 ... 144 C7
Bank Pl TR11........... 145 C3
Bank Sq TR19.......... 86 F6
Bank St
  Newquay TR7..........110 D6
  St Columb Major TR9.. 45 E6
Bannawell St **1** PL15.. 147 B6
Bannawell St PL19 ..... 147 B6
Banns Rd TR4.......... 68 C6
Baptist Hill TR27 ...... 142 C6
Baptist St PL17 .... 41 A3
Bara Pl PL17........... 39 F6
Barbara Hepworth Mus &
  Sculpture Gdn* TR26.. 141 B6
BARBICAN............. 149 A2
Barbican App PL4...... 149 B2
Barbican Cl
  Helston TR13..........146 D8
  Looe PL13............ 117 D4
Barbican Ct
  Looe PL13............ 117 D5
  Plymouth PL7..........149 A2
Barbican Hill PL13 ..... 117 D4
Barbican La TR18 ...... 143 F4
Barbican Leisure Pk PL4 149 C2
Barbican Rd
  Looe PL13............ 117 E6
  Plymouth PL7..........130 E4
Barbican Rise Ind Est
  PL13..................117 E5
Barbican The PL1 ...... 149 A2
Barbican Theatre PL1 .. 149 A1
Barbican Way TR13 .... 91 E4

Barbury Cres PL6 ...... 125 B8
BARCELONA............ 62 E4
Barcote Wlk PL6 .... 129 C8
Bardsey Cl PL6......... 125 A7
BAREPPA............... 93 D4
Baring St PL4........... 149 B4
Barker's Hill PL12...... 122 C1
Barkhouse La PL25..... 115 B2
BARKLA SHOP 54 E1
Bar La
  Connor Downs TR27 .. 78 C6
  Falmouth TR11........ 145 C3
Barlandhu **17** TR18.... 143 C2
Barlanwick TR18........ 143 C2
Barley Market St PL19.. 147 C6
Barlowena TR14 .... 138 D1
Barlow Gdns PL22 ..... 128 B7
Bar Mdws TR1.......... 70 D2
Barnaloft PL25 .... 141 B6
Barn Cl
  Plymouth PL7..........131 C5
  Wainhouse Corner EX23.. 10 F6
Barncoose Ave TR15 ... 139 E5
Barncoose Ind Est TR15 139 E5
Barncoose La TR15 .... 139 E6
Barncoose Terr TR15 ... 139 D6
Barn Courtyard TR27... 78 D6
Barndale Cres PL6 ..... 125 B6
BARNE BARTON........ 127 C8
Barne Cl PL5 .... 127 C8
Barnecut Cl **2** PL14... 38 A3
Barne La PL5........... 123 D1
Barne Rd PL5.......... 127 C8
Barnfield Dr PL7 ...... 131 C5
Barnfield Gdns PL18.... 88 E6
Barnfield Pk EX23 ..... 4 E1
Barnfield Terr
  3 Indian Queens TR9.. 45 E1
  Liskeard PL14..........113 B4
Barn Hill
  Cadgwith TR12........ 103 B4
  Polbathic PL12........ 64 F8
  Tideford PL12......... 52 F1
Barningham Gdns PL6 . 125 B6
Barn La
  Bodmin PL31..........109 C4
  18 St Columb Major TR9. 45 E6
Barn Meadow Pk PL13 . 117 B2
Barnoon Hill TR26 ..... 141 B6
Barnoon Terr **2** TR26.. 141 B6
Barn Park La PL31...... 35 B2
Barnpark Rd PL35...... 9 C1
Barn Park Rd PL3 ..... 128 D6
Barn Pk
  Lostwithiel PL22....... 112 E2
  Saltash PL12.......... 122 F3
Barns Terr PL12........ 118 A3
Barnwood Cl PL9 ..... 135 E5
Baron Ct PL15......... 17 D5
Barons Mdw PL31...... 109 F5
Barons Rd PL20........ 42 E3
Barossa Rd PL11....... 127 B3
Barrack La TR1 .... 137 C4
Barrack Pl PL1......... 128 A1
Barrack's La TR16...... 68 E1
Barrack St PL1......... 127 E2
Barras Cross PL14 .... 113 C6
Barras Pl PL14......... 113 C6
Barras St PL14......... 113 C6
BARRIPPER............ 79 B5
Barripper Rd
  Camborne TR14....... 138 C1
  9 St Austell PL25.... 115 C3
Barrowfield View TR7... 111 A7
Barr's Ct PL23......... 116 D5
Barry's La PL28........ 107 D5
Bartholomew Rd PL2... 128 B5
Bartles Cl TR12 .... 99 D7
Bartles Ind Est TR15... 140 B6
Bartles Row TR15 ..... 139 A5
Barton Ave EX23 ...... 104 F5
Barton Ave PL2 .... 128 A5
Barton Cl
  11 Bodmin PL31..... 109 D5
  Heamoor TR18........ 143 D7
  Helston TR13..........146 D7
  Landrake PL12........ 53 C3
  Plymouth PL7..........131 C5
Barton Ct PL26........ 58 A7
Barton La TR9 .... 45 D1
Barton Mdw
  Pelynt PL13........... 62 D6
  Truro TR1.............137 A5
Barton Mdws PL12..... 53 B7
Barton Mews
  Landrake PL12........ 53 C3
  Millbrook PL10........132 F6
Barton Rd
  Plymouth PL3..........135 B6
  St Dennis PL26........ 58 A7
Barton The PL20....... 22 D6
Barview La TR27 .... 142 C4
Barwis Hill TR18 ...... 143 E6
Barwis Terr **1** TR18... 143 E6
Basghall Cl PL9........ 135 F5
Basket Ope PL4........ 149 A2
Basset Rd TR14........ 138 D2
Basset St
  Camborne TR14....... 138 D2

Basset St continued
  Falmouth TR11........ 145 A5
  Redruth TR15......... 140 C4
Bassett Cl PL26 .... 47 A1
Bassett Ct **11** TR11... 145 A5
Bassett Rd
  Illogan TR16.......... 67 E4
  Redruth TR15......... 140 B8
Bassett Terr TR16...... 67 D6
Bastville EX22......... 11 E8
Bath La PL1............ 148 B2
Bath Pl PL1............ 148 B2
Bath Place W PL1...... 148 B2
BATHPOOL............ 27 C1
Bath St PL1............ 148 B2
Battershall Ct PL9...... 135 F5
Batter St PL4........... 149 A2
Battery Hill TR16....... 67 C6
Battery La
  Polruan PL23..........116 C2
  Tavistock PL19........ 147 C4
Battery Mill La TR27.... 77 E1
Battery Pk PL23........ 116 C2
Battery Rd TR18 ...... 143 F4
Battery St PL1......... 148 A3
Battery Terr PL26 ..... 73 C3
Battery The TR7 ...... 110 D7
Battisford Rd PL7 ..... 131 E3
Bawden Rd PL31....... 109 B3
Bay Apartments TR7... 110 A6
Bay Ct TR11........... 145 C2
Baydon Cl PL6......... 125 C1
Bay Down PL13 .... 117 D5
Bayly's Rd PL9......... 135 B7
Baynards Ct **1** TR1.... 137 D4
Baynes Cl **3** PL14..... 38 A3
Bay Rd PL28........... 20 F2
Bay Retreat PL28...... 31 F7
Bay St PL13........... 117 D3
Bayswater Rd PL1..... 148 B4
Bay The PL13.......... 117 D3
Baytree Cl PL6......... 125 D6
Bay Tree Cotts **3** EX23.. 4 D1
Baytree Gdns PL2 ..... 128 A7
Baytree Hill PL14 ..... 113 C5
Bayview **1** PL24...... 60 C4
Bay View Cres TR11 ... 145 D3
Bayview Dr PL13....... 117 E4
Bayview Ho TR27 ..... 142 A8
Bay View Pk PL25 .... 114 F6
Bay View Rd
  Looe PL13............ 117 D4
  St Austell PL26........ 115 A1
Bay View Terr
  Budock Water TR11.... 144 A5
  Hayle TR27............142 C6
  15 Newlyn TR18..... 143 C2
  Newquay TR7..........110 E5
  Penzance TR18........ 143 D4
  18 Porthleven TR13.. 98 B8
  3 Porthleven TR13... 98 B8
Bay Villas TR26 .... 141 C6
Beachfield Ave TR7 .... 110 D6
Beachfield Ct TR7 ..... 111 C7
Beachview Flats TR14 . 68 A6
Beach Wlk TR7 .... 111 C7
BEACON................ 138 F1
Beach Cl
  Carbis Bay TR26...... 141 D2
  Crantock TR8......... 43 D3
  Mevagissey PL26...... 73 C2
  Newquay TR7..........110 D6
  Perranporth TR6....... 55 A5
  Porthtowan TR4....... 68 A6
  St Austell PL25........ 115 D3
  St Ives TR26.......... 141 A6
Beacon Cl
  Falmouth TR11........ 145 A5
  St Austell PL25........ 115 A5
Beacon Cross PL26 .... 72 F4
Beacon Down Ave PL12 128 B7
Beacon Dr TR5 .... 54 B1
Beacon Est TR20....... 87 D4
Beacon Farm TR5 ..... 54 C1
Beaconfield Rd PL2 .... 128 B7
Beacon Fields TR14 ... 138 E2
Beacon Hill PL11....... 109 D4
Beacon Hill Mews **2**
  PL31..................109 D5
Beacon Ho PL31 ...... 129 D4
Beacon Inf Sch The
  PL31..................109 D5
Beacon Lanes PL31 .... 109 D3
Beacon Parc TR13 .... 146 C6
Beacon Park Rd PL2 ... 128 B7
Beacon Pk
  Boyton PL15.......... 13 A2
  Pelynt PL13........... 62 D5
Beacon Rd
  Bodmin PL31..........109 E3
  Falmouth TR15........ 145 A5
  Foxhole PL26......... 58 D5
  Marazion TR17........ 89 B5
  Newquay TR7..........110 D7
  St Dennis PL26........ 58 A5
  2 St Helens TR8..... 98 B8
  St James TR18........ 57 B7
  Summercourt TR8..... 57 B7
Beacons PL13.......... 62 E5
Beaconsfield Pl **2** TR5.. 54 C1

Beaconsfield Terr PL31 109 C5
Beaconside
Foxhole PL26 58 D5
Summercourt TR8 57 B7
Beacon Sq TR14 138 F1
Beacon St TR11 145 B5
Beacon Terr
Camborne TR14 138 E1
5 Falmouth TR11 145 A5
Foxhole PL26 58 D5
Helston TR13 146 C6
Lizard TR12 102 F2
Beacon The TR11 145 A5
Beacon View TR4 55 B2
Beacon View Pk 23 TR16 67 E4
Beadle Ct 6 PL19 147 B4
BEALSMILL 28 E3
Bealswood Cl PL18 41 A6
Bealswood Rd PL18 41 A6
Beam Rd PL26 47 C1
Beam Terr PL26 47 B1
Beam Villas PL30 47 D5
Beare Cl PL9 135 B5
Bearsdown Cl PL6 129 C8
Bearsdown Rd PL6 129 C8
Bears Terr TR16 80 E7
Beatrice Ave
Plymouth, Keyham PL2 127 E5
Plymouth, St Jude's PL4 149 B3
Saltash PL12 122 E2
Beatrice Gdns PL12 122 E1
Beatrice Rd PL31 48 D8
Beatrice Terr TR27 142 D7
Beattie Rd PL5 127 B8
Beatty Cl PL6 125 A4
Beauchamp Cres PL2 128 C7
Beauchamp Rd PL2 128 C7
Beauchamps Mdw TR15 140 D2
Beaudyn Wlk 5 PL6 129 C7
Beaufighter Ave PL27 31 F3
Beaufort Ave 8 PL27 31 F3
Beaufort Ho 21 PL4 149 A2
Beauly Cl PL7 131 A5
Beaumaris Gdns PL3 128 F8
Beaumaris Rd PL3 128 F7
Beaumont Ave PL4 149 A3
Beaumont Pl PL4 149 A3
Beaumont Rd PL4 149 B3
Beaumont St PL2 128 A5
Beaumont Terr PL12 122 F4
Beck Adams PL12 53 C3
Beckett Cl TR15 140 C4
Beckford Cl PL7 131 A5
Beckham Pl PL3 129 A6
Beckly Ct PL1 148 C3
Bede Gdns PL5 124 C1
Bede Haven Cl EX23 104 E4
Bederkesa Ct PL31 109 D4
Bedford Cl PL18 40 F6
Bedford Mews PL4 149 A4
Bedford Park Villas PL4 149 A4
Bedford Pk
10 Bere Alston PL20 41 B1
Plymouth PL4 149 A4
Bedford Pl
6 Bere Alston PL20 41 B1
6 St Ives TR26 141 B5
Bedford Rd
Horrabridge PL20 42 C4
Plymouth PL9 135 E8
St Ives TR26 141 B5
Bedford Sq PL19 147 C5
Bedford St
Bere Alston PL20 41 B1
Plymouth PL2 127 F5
Bedford Terr PL4 149 A4
Bedford Units PL18 40 F5
Bedford Villas 7 PL20 41 B1
Bedford Way PL1 148 C3
Bedowan Mdws TR7 111 A4
Bedruthan Ave TR1 137 E6
Bedruthan Steps★ PL27 31 B4
Beech Ave
Liskeard PL14 113 B5
Plymouth PL4 149 C2
Beech Cl
Falmouth TR11 144 F5
Tavistock PL19 147 C2
Torpoint PL11 127 A3
Beechcombers TR8 44 D7
Beechcroft Rd
Plymouth, Lower Compton PL3 129 A6
Plymouth, North Prospect PL2 128 B7
Beech Ct PL6 125 D5
Beech Dr
Bodmin PL31 109 B4
Lewannick PL15 27 A6
4 St Columb Major TR9 45 D6
Beeches The
Launceston PL15 106 C5
9 Pensilva PL14 38 E4
Beechfield Ave PL20 42 D3
Beechfield Gr PL3 128 E6
Beech Hall Flats 19 TR2 95 A6
Beeching Pk PL17 39 F6
Beech La PL25 114 D3
Beech Rd
17 Callington PL17 39 F4
Falmouth TR11 144 F5
St Austell PL25 114 D3
Beech Terr PL13 117 C4
Beechwood Ave PL4 128 D4
Beechwood Cross PL7 131 F7
Beechwood Dr PL32 105 D5
Beechwood Gdns TR1 137 E6
Beechwood Prim Sch PL6 124 E6
Beechwood Rise PL6 125 E1
Beechwood Terr PL4 128 D4
Beechwood Way PL7 131 D5
Beehive Workshops TR10 144 A7
BEENY 9 E3
Beeston Wlk 6 PL6 129 C7
Behenna Dr TR1 69 F3
Bekelege Dr TR14 138 F1
Belair Rd PL2 128 C7
Belair Villas PL2 128 C7
Belerion Rd TR16 67 C5
Belgrave La PL4 128 F4
Belgrave Rd PL4 128 F4
Belgrave Terr PL14 113 D6
Belgravia St TR18 143 E5
Belhay TR10 144 C8
Bellair Rd TR20 143 A8
Bellair Terr 38 TR26 141 B6
Bellamy Cl PL6 125 A1
Bellatt PL27 108 D6
Bella Vista Gdns TR10 81 E2
Bell Cl PL7 130 F6
Belle Acre Cl PL3 128 F6
Bellever Parc TR14 138 F4
Bellevue TR15 140 C5
Belle Vue
Bude EX23 104 D6
Newlyn TR18 143 C1
Belle Vue Ave
Bude EX23 104 D6
Plymouth PL9 135 B5
Bellevue Cotts TR10 81 E2
Belle Vue Dr PL9 135 B5
Belle Vue La EX23 104 D6
Belle Vue Rd
Plymouth PL9 135 C5
Saltash PL12 122 F2
Belle Vue Rise PL9 135 B5
Bellevue Sq PL11 127 B2
Bellevue Terr TR3 81 D6
Belle Vue Terr
Gunnislake PL18 41 A6
20 Penzance TR18 143 E6
Bellflower Cl PL6 121 C1
Bell Hill PL26 85 C5
Belliers La TR26 141 B5
Bellingham Cres PL7 131 C4
Belliver Ind Est PL6 121 B1
Belliver Way PL6 121 B1
Bell La
Bodmin PL31 109 E5
Lanner TR16 80 D6
Bells Ct TR15 139 C7
Bell's Ct TR11 145 B4
Bell's Hill
Falmouth TR11 82 A3
Mylor Bridge TR11 82 A3
Bell Veor TR16 80 E6
Bell Yd 1 PL31 109 E5
Belmont PL13 117 C4
Belmont Cl PL33 14 D2
Belmont Ct
8 Plymouth PL3 128 A4
11 Wadebridge PL27 108 B5
Belmont Mews PL14 38 D4
Belmont Pk PL14 38 D4
Belmont Pl
Newquay TR7 110 D7
Plymouth PL3 128 A4
St Ives TR26 141 A6
Belmont Rd
Falmouth TR11 145 A3
Helston TR13 146 B7
St Austell PL25 114 D3
Belmont St
Plymouth PL1 148 B3
8 Tywardreath PL24 60 D5
Belmont Terr
Devoran TR3 81 F6
St Ives TR26 141 A6
Belmont Villas 13 TR1 137 D5
BELOWDA 46 D4
Belstone Cl PL5 124 A3
Belvedere TR1 137 F6
Belvedere La TR20 89 F5
Belvedere Rd PL4 129 B2
Belyars Ct TR26 141 B4
Belyars La TR26 141 B4
Benallack Ct TR1 137 E4
Benan Chy PL25 114 F3
Benbow St PL2 127 F4
Bencoolen Rd EX23 104 D5
Beneathway PL14 50 E7
BENNACOTT 12 E2
Bennets La PL12 122 F3
Bennetts Cotts 3 TR10 144 C7
Bennett St PL1 127 E1
Benny Halt Sta★ TR8 56 C8
Benson Gdns 2 TR1 137 D5
Benson Ho 1 TR1 137 D5
Benson Rd TR1 137 B5
Bentley Dr 5 EX23 4 D1
Beramic Cl TR27 78 D6
Beraton Ct 3 PL31 109 D5
BERE ALSTON 41 B1
Bere Alston Prim Sch PL20 41 B1
Bere Alston Sta PL20 41 B2
BERE FERRERS 119 E3
Bere Ferrers Sta PL20 119 E3
BEREPPER 98 F5
Berepper Cross TR12 98 E5
Beresford St PL2 128 A4
Berkeley Cl EX23 4 D1
Berkeley Cotts TR11 145 A4
Berkeley Ct
Falmouth TR11 145 B4
Looe PL13 117 C5
Berkeley Hill TR11 145 A4
Berkeley Mews 4 TR11 145 A4
Berkeley Path 3 TR11 145 A4
Berkeley Vale TR11 145 A4
Berkshire Dr PL2 127 F5
Bernice Cl PL4 129 B4
Bernice Terr PL4 129 B4
Berries Ave EX23 104 E4
Berries Mount EX23 104 F4
BERRIOWBRIDGE 27 B2
Berrow Park Rd PL3 128 E6
Berrycombe View 15 PL31 109 D5
Berrycoombe Hill PL31 109 C5
Berrycoombe Prim Sch PL31 109 B5
Berrycoombe Rd PL31 109 D5
Berrycoombe Vale PL31 109 C5
Berryfields Ho PL31 109 E5
Berry Head Gdns PL6 124 E1
Berryhill PL30 47 C6
Berry La PL31 109 E5
Berryman Cres TR11 144 F3
Berry Park Cl PL9 135 E6
Berry Park Rd PL9 135 E7
Berry Pk PL12 122 D4
Berry Rd TR7 110 E6
Berthon Rd PL5 127 C8
Berveth Cl TR3 69 D3
Berwick Ave PL5 124 E3
BESOUGHAN 45 A3
Bess Park Rd PL27 108 E6
Bethan Dr PL27 108 B5
Bethany Homes 1 TR14 138 C2
Bethany Pl TR19 86 F6
BETHEL 115 A5
Bethel Rd PL25 115 A4
Bethesda Pl 10 TR26 141 B6
Betjeman Wlk PL5 124 C3
Beverley Cres TR27 142 E7
Beverley Rd PL3 129 C4
Beverston Way PL6 125 B8
Beweys Pk PL12 122 C2
Beyrout Pl 6 PL1 127 F3
Bezant Pl TR7 110 B5
Bickern Rd PL11 127 B3
Bickford Cres TR13 91 B1
Bickford Rd PL15 106 B8
BICKHAM 121 A7
Bickham Park Rd PL3 128 D7
Bickham Rd PL5 123 D2
Bickland Hill TR11 144 D4
Bickland Ind Est TR11 144 D4
Bickland Water Rd TR11 144 D2
Bickland Wlk TR11 144 D4
Bickleigh Cl PL6 125 A1
Bickleigh Down Bsns Pk PL6 125 D8
Bickleigh Down CE Prim Sch PL6 125 D7
Bickleigh Down Rd PL6 121 D1
Bicton Cl PL6 125 D1
Biddick Dr PL2 127 F6
Biddick's Ct 5 PL25 114 C3
Bideford Mews 13 EX23 4 E1
Bideford Wlk PL6 129 E8
Bigbury Wlk PL6 129 E8
Biggin Hill PL5 123 F4
Big Gn PL13 62 D1
Bilbury St PL4 149 A3
BILLACOMBE 135 F8
Billacombe Rd PL9 129 E1
Billacombe Villas PL9 135 F8
BILLACOTT 12 B1
Billings Cl PL6 124 D6
Billings Dr TR7 111 B5
Billington Cl PL6 129 B7
Bindown Ct PL13 63 E8
Binhamy Cl EX23 104 F4
Binhamy Rd EX23 7 B8
Binkham Hill PL20 42 D3
Bircham View PL6 125 C1
Birch Cl PL6 125 E7
Birches The PL6 125 D6
Birchfield Ave PL2 128 B6
Birch Gr TR27 142 B3
Birchill PL30 47 C6
Birch Pond Rd PL9 135 D7
Birchwood Cl PL19 147 C3
Birchwood Gdns PL7 131 A7
Birkbeck Cl PL7 130 E7
Birkdale Cl PL12 122 C2
Biscombe Gdns PL12 123 A2
Biscombes La 8 PL17 39 E4
BISCOVEY 60 B4
Biscovey Jun & Inf Schs 22 PL24 60 B4
Biscovey Rd PL24 115 F5
Bishop Bronescombe CE Prim Sch PL25 115 B5
Bishop Cornish CE Prim Sch PL12 122 F1
Bishop's CE Prim Sch The TR7 110 F4
Bishops Cl
Saltash PL12 122 E3
Truro TR1 137 C6
Bishops Ct TR9 45 E6
Bishop's Hill Rd PL27 21 D6
Bishop's Pl PL1 148 B1
BISHOP'S QUAY 99 F8
Bishop's Rd TR26 141 B5
Bishop Temple Rd TR1 137 F6
BISSOE 81 D8
BISSOM 144 E8
Bissom Rd TR10 81 F2
Blackberry Cl PL9 135 E8
Blackberry La PL9 135 E8
Blackberry Way TR1 137 F5
Blackbird Cres PL15 106 E4
Blackbrook Cl PL20 42 E4
BLACK CROSS 45 E3
Blackerry Cl TR16 140 F1
Blackeven Cl PL6 121 D1
Blackeven Hill PL6 121 E1
Blackfriars La PL1 149 A2
Blackhall Gdns PL6 124 D6
Blackmore Cres PL6 124 D6
Black Rd TR27 142 D7
BLACK ROCK 79 D1
Blacksmith La TR27 78 D6
Blackstone Cl PL9 136 B6
Blackthorn Cl
Plymouth, Honicknowle PL5 124 B3
Plymouth, Woolwell PL6 125 D8
BLACKWATER 68 D5
Blackwater Prim Sch TR4 68 E5
Bladder La PL5 124 E2
Blagdon Cross EX21 13 F7
Blagdon Lodge Cross EX21 13 F8
Blairgowrie Rd PL5 123 C2
Blake Gdns PL5 124 C3
Blakes Pk PL14 113 D7
Blanchard Pl 2 PL7 130 E7
Blanchdown Dr PL18 40 F7
Blanchminster Rd EX23 104 E5
Blandford Rd PL3 129 C6
Blatchborough Cross EX22 3 E1
Blaxton La PL5 120 C2
Blenheim Rd PL4 149 A4
Bligh Cres TR13 146 C5
Blight's Row TR15 140 B5
Blindhole 8 PL15 106 C6
Blind La PL11 64 D6
BLINDWELL 132 E5
Blindwell Hill PL10 132 E5
BLISLAND 35 D8
Blisland Prim Sch PL30 35 D7
Blissoe Rd TR3 81 F7
Bloomball Cl PL3 129 B6
Bloom Fields TR18 143 C5
BLOWINGHOUSE
Bodmin 109 B2
Redruth 139 F6
Blowing House Cl PL25 114 B4
Blowinghouse Hill TR15 140 A4
Blowing House Hill
Crowlas TR20 89 B8
Hayle TR20 77 A1
St Austell PL25 114 C4
Blowinghouse La PL30 109 B2
Blowing House La PL25 114 B4
BLUE ANCHOR 57 D8
Bluebell Cl PL12 122 D4
Bluebell Way
Launceston PL15 106 E4
Tavistock PL19 147 E4
Blue Haze Cl PL6 125 D5
Blue Reef Aquarium★ TR7 110 D6
Blunt's La PL6 125 C3
Boaden Cl PL12 53 E5
Boase St TR18 143 C1
Bobs Rd PL24 60 B4
Bochym Hill TR12 99 C3
Boconnic La PL20 42 D3
Boconnoc Ave PL17 39 F3
Boconnoc Rd PL25 114 D2
BODELVA 115 F8
Bodelva Rd PL24 115 E8
Bodgara Way PL14 113 D6
Bodgara Way Flats PL14 113 D6
BODIEVE 108 C7
Bodieve Rd PL27 108 D7
BODILLY 91 F7
Bodinar Rd TR10 81 D2
Bodiniel Rd PL31 109 C6
Bodiniel View PL31 109 B5
Bodinnar Cl TR20 87 E6
Bodinnar La TR20 87 E6
BODINNICK 116 E5
Bodinnick Hts PL23 116 E5
Bodinnick Parc PL30 23 E3
Bodinnick Rd PL30 23 E3
BODMIN 109 B5
Bodmin Beacon Nature Reserve★ PL31 109 D4
Bodmin Bsns Ctr PL31 109 E3
Bodmin Bsns Pk PL31 35 B2
Bodmin Coll PL31 109 F2
Bodmin General Sta★ PL31 109 E3
Bodmin Hill PL22 112 B4
Bodmin Hospl PL31 109 B4
Bodmin Jail★ PL31 109 D5
Bodmin Parkway Sta PL30 49 A7
Bodmin Rd
Plymouth PL5 124 D3
St Austell PL25 114 C6
Truro TR1 137 E6
Bodmin Ret Pk PL31 35 B1
Bodmin Town Mus★ PL31 109 E4
Bodmin & Wenford Rly★ PL30 109 D2
Bodrigan Rd PL13 117 D5
Bodriggy Cres TR27 142 C5
Bodriggy Ct TR27 142 D6
Bodriggy Prim Sch TR27 142 D5
Bodriggy St TR27 142 D6
Bodriggy Villas TR27 142 D6
BODWEN 47 E3
Body's Ct PL18 40 F6
Bohelland Rd TR10 144 D8
Bohelland Rise TR10 144 D8
Bohelland Way TR10 144 D8
Bohella Rd 20 TR2 95 A6
BOHETHERICK 40 F2
Bohill TR10 144 D7
Bohill Ct TR10 144 D7
BOHORTHA 95 C5
Boiler Works Rd TR14 138 E5
Bojea Ind Est PL25 114 C7
Bojea Terr PL25 114 C6
Bojewyan Stennack TR19 75 B1
Bokenna Cross PL14 37 C1
Boldventure Ave PL25 115 B5
Boldventure Cl PL25 115 B5
Boldventure Rd PL25 115 B5
Bolenna La TR6 55 A4
BOLENOWE 79 F5
Bolenowe Terr TR14 79 F4
BOLINGEY 55 B4
Bolingey Chapel Flats TR6 55 B4
Bolingey Rd TR6 55 A4
BOLITHO 79 F1
Bolitho Rd TR18 143 C7
Bolitho Sch The TR18 143 C5
Bollowal Pl TR19 86 E6
Bolowthas Cnr TR7 111 A7
Bolowthas Way TR7 111 C7
Bolster Cl 8 TR5 54 C1
Boltern Rd TR17 89 C5
Bolt House Cl PL19 147 A5
BOLVENTOR 25 E3
Bolventor La PL13 63 E8
Bonallack La TR12 92 D1
Bon Cot Rd TR18 143 C2
Bond St
Plymouth PL6 124 E6
6 Redruth TR15 140 B4
Bone Cellar Row TR2 70 F5
Bone Mill Rd TR6 55 B4
Bones La PL12 52 E4
Bonson Cl PL13 117 C4
Bon Villas 18 TR18 143 C2
Bonville Rd PL6 124 E6
Bonython Cl TR11 82 A3
Bonython Dr TR2 72 A7
Bonython Rd TR7 111 B7
Bonython Terr PL14 113 B4
Boon's Pl PL1 148 C4
BOQUIO 91 F8
BOREA 76 F2
Borgwitha TR16 80 B5
Boringdon Ave PL5 127 D8
Boringdon Cl PL7 130 D7
Boringdon Hill PL7 130 E7
Boringdon Mill Bsns Ctr PL7 130 F6
Boringdon Prim Sch PL7 130 D7
Boringdon Rd
Plymouth, Plympton PL7 130 D6
Plymouth, Turnchapel PL9 135 A7
Boringdon Terr
Plymouth, Plympton PL7 130 D6
Plymouth, Turnchapel PL9 135 A7
Boringdon Villas PL7 130 D6
Borlase Cl TR13 146 B5
Borough Cross EX22 7 F5
Borough Ct PL11 126 E4
Borough Pk PL11 126 E4
Borrowdale Cl PL6 124 D5
Boscawna Cl TR16 68 E1
BOSCADJACK 91 F6
Boscarn Cl TR14 79 B5
BOSCARNE 34 C2
Boscarne Cres PL25 114 F3
Boscarne Junction Sta★ PL30 34 D2
Boscarnek TR27 142 A1
Boscarne View PL30 34 D2
Boscarn Parc TR15 139 C4
Boscarn Rd TR15 140 D6
BOSCASTLE 9 C1
Boscastle Com Prim Sch PL35 9 C1
Boscastle Gdns PL2 128 C8
Boscastle Visitor Ctr★ PL35 9 D2
Boscaswell Downs TR19 75 A1
Boscaswell Est TR19 74 F1
Boscaswell Rd TR19 75 A1
Boscaswell Terr TR19 75 A1
Boscathnoe La TR18 143 B7
Boscathnoe Way TR18 143 B7
Boscawen Ct 17 TR6 55 A4
Boscawen Gdns 11 TR6 55 A4
Boscawen Pk PL26 58 B8
Boscawen Pl PL2 127 E4
Boscawen Rd
7 Chacewater TR4 69 A3
Falmouth TR11 145 B2
Helston TR13 146 D4
Perranporth TR6 55 A4
St Dennis PL26 58 C8
Boscawen St 18 TR1 137 D4
Boscean Cl TR14 79 E4
BOSCOPPA 115 A6
Boscoppa Cl TR15 140 D7
Boscoppa Rd
St Austell, Bethel PL25 115 A5
St Austell, Boscoppa PL25 115 B5
Boscowan TR11 145 C2

BOSCREEGE 90 C5
Boscundle Ave TR11 . . . . 144 F1
Boscundle Cl PL25 . . . . . 115 D5
Boscundle Row PL12 . . . 123 A2
Bosence Rd TR27 . . . . 90 C7
Bosillion La TR2 . . . . 72 A7
Bosinney Rd PL25 . . . . . 114 D3
Bosinver La PL26 . . . . 59 A1
Boskear La PL31 . . . . . . 109 A4
BOSKEDNAN 76 A1
BOSKENNA 97 C4
Boskenna Cross TR19 . . . 97 C5
Boskennal Barton TR19 . . 97 B6
Boskennal La TR19 . . . . . 97 B6
Boskenna Rd TR16 . . . . . . 80 A5
Boskennel Dr TR27 . . . . 142 B4
Boskenwyn Prim Sch
  TR13 . . . . 92 B3
Boskenza Ct TR26 . . . . . 141 C2
Boskernick Ct TR13 . . . . 143 B1
Boskernow TR12 . . . . . . 100 D6
Boskerris Cres TR26 . . . 141 D1
Boskerris Mews TR26 . . 141 D1
Boskerris Rd TR26 . . . . . 141 D2
Boslandew Hill TR19 . . . . 88 C2
BOSLEAKE 139 C3
Bosleake Row TR11 . . . . 139 C3
Bosloggas Mews [9]
  TR11 . . . . 145 C3
BOSLOWICK 144 F2
Boslowick Cl TR11 . . . . . 144 F3
Boslowick Ct TR11 . . . . . 144 E2
Boslowick Rd TR11 . . . . 144 E2
Bosmeor Cl TR11 . . . . . . 144 E2
Bosmeor Pk TR15 . . . . . 139 D6
Bosmeor Rd TR11 . . . . . 144 E3
Bosnoweth
  Helston TR13 . . . . 146 D5
  Probus TR2 . . . . 71 D6
Bosorne Cl TR19 . . . . 86 E6
Bosorne Rd TR19 . . . . . . 86 E6
Bosorne St TR19 . . . . 86 E6
Bosorne Terr TR19 . . . . . 86 E6
Bosparva La
  [8] Illogan TR16 . . . . . . 67 E4
  Truro TR19 . . . . 137 B5
Bosvean Rd TR4 . . . . 69 F6
Bosvenna View TR3 . . . . 109 E4
Bosvenna Way TR18 . . . 143 B7
Bosvenning PI TR20 . . . . . 87 E6
Bosvigo La TR1 . . . . 137 B5
Bosvigo Rd TR1 . . . . 137 B5
Bosvigo Sch TR1 . . . . . . 137 C4
Boswedden PI TR19 . . . . 86 E6
Boswedden Rd TR19 . . . . 86 E6
BOSWEDNACK 76 A4
Boswell Cl PL5 . . . . 124 B2
Boswergy TR18 . . . . 143 C5
BOSWINGER 73 F3
Boswithian Rd TR14 . . . 138 F6
Bosworgey Cl [3] TR9 . . . 45 D6
Bosworgy Rd TR20, TR27 . 90 B8
Bosworgy Rd TR20 . . . . . 90 B8
BOTALLACK 86 E7
Botallack La TR19 . . . . . . 86 E7
Botetoe Hill TR14 . . . . . . 79 C4
Botetoe Rd TR14 . . . . 79 B4
Botha Rd [1] PL27 . . . . . . 31 F3
Bothwicks Rd PL6 . . . . . 129 E8
BOTTOMS 96 E5
BOTUSFLEMING 122 B7
Boughthayes Est PL19 . . 147 A5
Boulden Cl PL7 . . . . 131 C5
Boulter Cl PL6 . . . . 121 C1
Boundary Ct [21] TR18 . . 143 C1
Boundary Dr EX23 . . . . 7 B6
Boundary Rd
  Bodmin PL31 . . . . 109 A4
  Dousland PL20 . . . . 42 E3
Bounders La TR6 . . . . 55 B4
Bounder Treath TR12 . . . 101 C1
Boundervean La TR14 . . 138 B2
Bounds Cross EX22 . . . . . . 8 A4
Bounds Pl PL11 . . . . 133 A1
Bound The PL10 . . . . 133 A1
Bounsalls Ct [3] PL15 . . . 106 C5
Bounsall's La PL15 . . . . . 106 C5
Bourne Cl PL3 . . . . 129 D6
Bourneside PL25 . . . . . . 114 D3
Boveway Dr PL14 . . . . . . 113 C5
Boveway La PL14 . . . . . . 113 D5
Boville La PL9 . . . . 136 C7
Bovisand Cl PL9 . . . . 136 C7
Bovisand La
  Down Thomas PL9 . . . . 135 B2
  Staddiscombe PL9 . . . . 135 D3
Bovisand Pk PL9 . . . . . . 135 A1
Bovisand Rd PL9 . . . . . . 135 E3
Bowden [14] EX23 . . . . . . 4 D1
Bowden Bank Rd PL6 . . . 125 A1
Bowdens Row TR15 . . . . 140 A4
Bowers Park Dr PL6 . . . . 125 E7
Bowers Rd PL2 . . . . 128 B5
Bowglas Cl TR20 . . . . 89 A8

Bowhays Wlk [2] PL6 . . . 129 C7
Bowjey Ct [2] TR18 . . . . 143 C1
Bowjey Hill TR18 . . . . . . 143 C1
Bowjey Terr [3] TR18 . . . 143 C1
Bow La EX23 . . . . 4 D2
Bowles Rd TR11 . . . . 145 A6
Bowling Gn
  Menheniot PL14 . . . . . . 51 E5
  [34] St Ives TR26 . . . . 141 B6
Bowling Gn The TR2 . . . . 82 F2
BOWLING GREEN
  Bugle 47 E1
  Redruth 139 D3
Bowling Green Ct
  Hayle TR27 . . . . 142 D5
  Liskeard PL14 . . . . . . 113 B5
Bowling Green Rd TR11 . . 92 F3
Bowling Green Terr [38]
  TR26 . . . . 141 A5
Bownder Dowr TR27 . . . 142 B3
Bownder Vean PL25 . . . . 115 A5
Bowood Pk
  Delabole PL33 . . . . 14 F1
  Helstone PL32 . . . . 24 B8
Boxhill Cl PL5 . . . . 124 B3
Boxhill Gdns PL2 . . . . . . 128 C8
Box's Shop EX23 . . . . 7 A4
Boxwell Pk PL31 . . . . . . 109 F4
Boyd Ave PL28 . . . . 107 C5
BOYTON 13 B2
Boyton Com Prim Sch
  PL15 . . . . 13 A3
Bracken Cl
  Bodmin PL31 . . . . 109 E5
  Plymouth PL6 . . . . . . 125 D8
Brackenside PL13 . . . . . . 62 D1
Bracken Terr TR7 . . . . . 110 E5
Brackwell Pl PL27 . . . . . 108 B5
Bramble Cl
  Newquay TR7 . . . . 111 A4
  Plymouth PL3 . . . . . . 129 B7
  Widemouth Bay EX23 . . . 6 F5
Brambles The
  Liskeard PL14 . . . . . . 113 C5
  Lostwithiel PL22 . . . . . 112 C3
Bramble Wlk [1] PL6 . . . 129 C7
Bramfield PL6 . . . . 129 D7
Bramley Cl PL25 . . . . . . 114 E4
Bramley Pk PL31 . . . . . . 109 F5
Bramley Rd PL3 . . . . 129 C4
Brancker Rd PL2 . . . . . . 128 C6
Brandon Rd PL3 . . . . 129 C4
Brandon Wlk EX23 . . . . . . 7 B8
Brandreth Rd [3] PL3 . . . 128 F6
Brandy La TR20 . . . . 89 F4
BRANE 87 C3
Branksome Pk PL2 . . . . . 128 C6
Brannel Sch The PL26 . . . 58 B3
Branscombe Gdns PL5 . . 124 A3
Branson Ct TR14 . . . . . . 138 D3
Branson Ct [9] TR7 . . . . 131 C5
Branson Pk PL19 . . . . . . 42 A8
Branwell La TR18 . . . . . . 88 E6
Braunton Wlk PL6 . . . . . 129 E8
Bray Cl PL25 . . . . 147 A5
Brayford Cl PL5 . . . . 124 B3
Bray Rise TR16 . . . . 80 A5
BRAY SHOP 28 B1
Bray's Pl PL25 . . . . 114 F4
Brays Terr [2] TR16 . . . . 140 F1
BRAZACOTT 12 B2
Brazacott Cross PL15 . . . 12 B2
BREA 139 B3
BREA ADDIT 139 B3
Brea Arch TR14 . . . . 139 A3
Bread St TR18 . . . . 143 E5
BREAGE 90 F3
Breage CE Sch TR13 . . . . 90 F3
Break My Neck La TR20 . . 88 A8
Breakwater Hill PL4 . . . . 149 C1
Breakwater Ind PL9 . . . . 135 C8
Breakwater Rd
  Bude EX23 . . . . 104 D5
  Plymouth PL9 . . . . . . 135 C8
Brean Down Cl PL3 . . . . 128 E6
Brean Down Rd PL3 . . . . 128 E7
Breanside TR12 . . . . 21 D2
Breaside TR14 . . . . 139 A3
Brecon Cl
  Plymouth PL3 . . . . . . 129 A7
  [1] St Agnes TR5 . . . . . 54 C1
Bredon Ct TR7 . . . . 110 C6
Bree Shute La [4] PL31 . . 109 E5
BRENT 62 E2
Brentford Ave PL5 . . . . . 124 B5
Brent Knoll Rd [1] PL3 . . 128 E6
Brenton Rd PL11 . . . . . . 64 B5
Brentons Pk PL29 . . . . . . 22 D6

Brentor Rd
  Mary Tavy PL19 . . . . . . 30 F6
  Plymouth PL4 . . . . . . 129 B2
Brent Tor★ PL19 . . . . . . 30 D7
Brentwartha PL13 . . . . . . 62 E2
Brest Rd PL6 . . . . 125 A3
Brest Way PL6 . . . . 125 A3
Bretonside PL4 . . . . 149 A2
Brett Wlk PL7 . . . . 130 F7
Brewartha TR2 . . . . 57 E1
Brewers Cl PL30 . . . . 47 F6
Brewers Hill PL26 . . . . . . 58 C8
Brewers Rd TR1 . . . . 137 F5
Brewery Hill TR26 . . . . . . 77 E4
Brewery La TR13 . . . . . . 146 B6
Briansway PL12 . . . . 122 D2
Briardale Rd PL2 . . . . . . 127 F6
Briarfield Rd PL2 . . . . . . 116 D4
Briarleigh Cl PL6 . . . . . . 125 F2
Briar Rd
  Bude EX23 . . . . 104 E4
  Plymouth PL3 . . . . . . 128 F7
Briars Row PL12 . . . . . . 122 D4
Briars Ryn PL12 . . . . 53 B7
Briar Tor PL20 . . . . 42 D3
Briarwood PL14 . . . . 113 D5
Brickfields Sp Ctr PL2 . . 127 F2
Brickworks Hill TR16 . . . 68 D1
Bridals La PL13 . . . . 62 E2
BRIDGE 67 E5
Bridge TR9 . . . . 45 E7
Bridge Cl TR7 . . . . 111 A4
Bridge Cl PL25 . . . . 114 F4
Bridge Hill
  Helston TR13 . . . . 67 E5
  St Columb Major TR9 . . 45 E6
Bridge Ho
  Delabole PL33 . . . . 14 E2
  Hayle TR27 . . . . 142 B6
Bridge Ho The [18] TR18 . 143 C2
Bridge La PL12 . . . . 53 A3
Bridgemead Cl PL26 . . . 114 C1
Bridgemoor Cross EX22 . . 8 C6
BRIDGEND 112 E3
Bridge Pk EX22 . . . . 8 A5
Bridge Rd
  Goonhavern TR4 . . . . . . 55 D4
  Illogan TR16 . . . . 67 E4
  Seaton PL11 . . . . 64 B5
  St Austell PL25 . . . . . . 114 B3
  Tideford PL12 . . . . 52 F2
Bridge Row TR16 . . . . . . 67 E5
BRIDGERULE 8 A6
Bridgerule CE Prim Sch
  EX22 . . . . 8 A5
Bridgerule Ind Est EX22 . . 7 F4
BRIDGES 59 F8
Bridge St
  Par PL24 . . . . 60 B6
  [17] Stratton EX23 . . . . . 4 D1
Bridges The PL11 . . . . . 122 C1
Bridge The PL11 . . . . . . 148 B1
BRIDGETOWN 19 B8
Bridge View PL27 . . . . . 108 C6
Bridge Wlk [2] PL35 . . . . . 9 C2
Bridgwater Cl PL6 . . . . . 125 C1
Bridle Cl PL7 . . . . 131 B7
Bridle Way
  Quintrell Downs TR8 . . . 44 E3
  Saltash PL12 . . . . 122 D4
Bridwell Cl PL5 . . . . 127 E8
Bridwell Lane N PL5 . . . 127 E8
Bridwell Rd PL5 . . . . . . 127 E8
BRIGHTON 57 D5
Brilliant Terr TR11 . . . . . 92 E4
Brimford Cross EX22 . . . . 3 D4
Brimhill Cl PL7 . . . . 131 B3
Brisbane Terr PL14 . . . . 113 C5
Brismar Wlk [3] PL6 . . . 129 C7
Briston Orch PL12 . . . . . . 53 E7
Britannia Pl PL4 . . . . . . 149 C3
Britticheston Cl PL9 . . . 136 A5
British Rd PL5 . . . . 54 D1
Briton's Hill PL14 . . . . . 143 F6
Brixham Wlk PL6 . . . . . . 129 E8
BRIXTON 136 F4
Brixton Lodge Gdns PL8 . 136 F5
Brixton Terr PL13 . . . . . 146 C6
Broad Cl EX22 . . . . 11 E7
Broadclose Hill EX23 . . . 104 E5
Broad La
  Illogan TR15 . . . . 139 D7
  Trematon PL12 . . . . 53 E2
Broadland Gdns PL9 . . . 136 A8
Broadland La PL9 . . . . . . 135 F8
Broadlands Cl PL7 . . . . . 131 A3
BROADLANE 90 E5
Broadley Cl PL6 . . . . 121 B2
Broadley Ind Pk PL6 . . . 121 B2
Broadley Park Rd PL6 . . 121 B2
Broad Mead PL7 . . . . 39 E5
Broad Park Rd
  Bere Alston PL20 . . . . . 41 B2
  Plymouth PL3 . . . . . . 128 D6
Broad Pk
  Launceston PL15 . . . . 106 B7
  Plymouth PL9 . . . . . . 135 C7
  St Keyne PL14 . . . . 51 B3
Broadshell Cross EX22 . . . 8 E1
Broads La TR11 . . . . 81 F3
Broad St
  [12] Launceston PL15 . . 106 C6
  Lifton PL16 . . . . 19 F4
  Newquay TR7 . . . . . . 110 D6
  Padstow PL28 . . . . . . 107 D5
  Penryn TR10 . . . . 144 D7
  [7] St Columb Major TR9 . 45 E6
  Truro TR1 . . . . 137 E5

Broads Yd PL11 . . . . 64 C5
Broadview PL19 . . . . 30 A6
Broad View TR4 . . . . 56 D1
Broadway The PL9 . . . . . 135 E7
Broad Wlk
  Helston TR13 . . . . 146 B7
  Saltash PL12 . . . . 122 E1
Brock Ho [9] PL4 . . . . . . 149 C3
Brockhole La PL7 . . . . . 130 E8
Brockley Rd PL3 . . . . . . 129 C4
Brocks La PL10 . . . . 132 F5
Brockstone Rd PL25 . . . 115 A5
Brockton Gdns PL6 . . . . 125 B6
BROCTON 34 A3
Bromfield Cres TR2 . . . . . 57 E1
Bromhead Ct PL6 . . . . . 129 A8
Bromley Ho [6] PL2 . . . . 127 F4
Bromley PI [5] PL2 . . . . . 128 A4
Bromscombe Cl TR10 . . 144 D7
Bronte PI PL5 . . . . 124 D1
BROOK 147 B2
Brook Cl
  Helston TR13 . . . . 146 B7
  Plymouth PL7 . . . . . . 131 A3
Brook Ct [6] TR11 . . . . . 145 A4
Brookdale Cl [8] PL27 . . 108 B5
Brookdown Terr PL12 . . 122 E3
Brookdown Villas PL12 . . 122 E3
Brook Dr EX23 . . . . 104 E7
Brooke Cl PL12 . . . . 123 A2
Brookfield Cl
  Lanjeth PL26 . . . . 58 E3
  Plymouth PL7 . . . . . . 131 B5
Brookfields Cl PL11 . . . . 127 F1
Brook Green Ctr for Learning
  PL5 . . . . 124 B4
Brooking Cl PL7 . . . . 131 B5
Brookingfield Cl PL7 . . . 130 C5
Brooking Way PL12 . . . . 122 C3
Brook La PL19 . . . . 147 B2
Brooklands
  New Polzeath PL27 . . . . 21 D6
  Tavistock PL19 . . . . . . 147 D6
Brooklands Ct PL6 . . . . . 124 E3
Brooklyn Flats [18] PL4 . . 95 A6
Brooklyn Terr [17] TR2 . . 95 A6
Brook Pl
  Falmouth TR11 . . . . . . 145 A4
  Penryn TR10 . . . . 144 C7
Brook Rd
  Falmouth TR11 . . . . . . 144 F3
  Wadebridge PL27 . . . . 108 B5
Brooks PL22 . . . . 49 E3
Brookside
  Chacewater TR4 . . . . . . 68 F3
  St Austell PL25 . . . . . . 114 F4
Brookside Cl PL15 . . . . . 106 B8
Brook St
  Falmouth TR11 . . . . . . 145 A4
  [17] Mousehole TR19 . . . 88 C1
  Tavistock PL19 . . . . . . 147 C6
Brook The PL12 . . . . 122 E2
Brookway TR27 . . . . 142 E7
Brookwood Rd PL9 . . . . 136 D7
Broom Hill PL12 . . . . . . 122 D2
Broomhill Cross EX22 . . . . 5 E3
Broomhill La EX23 . . . . . . 4 B2
Broom Pk PL9 . . . . 135 D5
Broughton Cl PL7 . . . . . 128 F7
Browne Memorial
  Almshouses PL19 . . . . 147 A5
Browning Cl [14] TR7 . . . 45 D6
Browning Dr PL31 . . . . . 109 C3
Browning Rd PL2 . . . . . . 128 A5
Brownlow PI [5] PL31 . . 109 D5
Browns Hill PL23 . . . . . . 116 C4
Brown's Hill TR10 . . . . . 144 C8
Broxton Dr PL9 . . . . 129 E1
Bruallen Cl PL30 . . . . 23 E7
Brunel Ave PL2 . . . . 127 F5
Brunel Prim Sch PL12 . . 122 E2
Brunel Quays PL22 . . . . 112 C2
Brunel Rd PL12 . . . . 122 C4
Brunel Terr [8] PL2 . . . . 127 F5
Brunel Way PL1 . . . . 148 A2
BRUNNION 141 B6
Brunswick PI [10] PL2 . . 127 F4
Brunswick Rd PL4 . . . . . 149 B2
Brush End TR26 . . . . 77 E4
Brynmoor Cl PL3 . . . . . . 129 A6
Brynmoor Pk PL3 . . . . . 129 A6
Brynmoor Wlk PL3 . . . . 129 A6
Bryny Cl PL30 . . . . 23 E7
Buckett's Hill TR15 . . . . 140 C2
Buckeys La PL14 . . . . 92 B6
Buckfast Cl PL2 . . . . 128 A8
Buckingham Cl PL5 . . . . 124 B5
Buckingham Nip TR4 . . . 66 F5
Buckingham PI PL5 . . . . 123 E2
Buckingham's Cl TR8 . . . 56 B7
Buckingham Terr TR16 . . 68 C5
Buckland Abbey★ PL20 . . 41 F1
Buckland Cl PL7 . . . . . . 130 D7
BUCKLAND
  MONACHORUM 42 A3
Buckland St PL4 . . . . . . 148 B2
Buckland Terr PL20 . . . . . 42 C2
Bucklawren Rd PL13 . . . . 63 E7
Bucklers Ho PL25 . . . . . 115 B4
Bucklers La PL25 . . . . . . 115 B4
Buckler Village (Mobile
  Homes Pk) PL25 . . . . . 115 B4

Buctor Pk PL19 . . . . 41 D8
Buddle Cl
  Plymouth PL9 . . . . . . 136 A5
  Tavistock PL19 . . . . . . 147 B6
BUDE 104 E6
Budehaven Com Sch
  EX23 . . . . 104 F5
Budehaven L Ctr EX23 . . 104 F5
Bude Ind Est EX23 . . . . 104 F4
Bude Inf Sch EX23 . . . . 104 E5
Bude Jun Sch EX23 . . . . 104 E5
Bude Marshes Nature
  Reserve★ EX23 . . . . . 104 D4
Bude-Stratton Bsns Pk
  EX23 . . . . 7 B8
Bude-Stratton Mus★
  EX23 . . . . 104 D5
Budge Mdws PL15 . . . . . 28 C4
Budleigh Cl PL9 . . . . 135 F5
Budnic Est TR6 . . . . 55 B5
Budnic Hill TR6 . . . . 55 B5
Budock PI PL11 . . . . 145 B4
Budock Vean La TR11 . . . 93 B2
BUDOCK WATER 144 C2
Budshead Gn PL5 . . . . . 124 C4
Budshead Rd PL5 . . . . . . 124 C4
Budshead Way PL5 . . . . 124 E2
Buena Vista Cl PL6 . . . . 125 C6
Buena Vista Dr PL6 . . . . 125 C6
Buena Vista Gdns PL6 . . 125 C6
Buena Vista Way PL6 . . . 125 C6
BUGLE 47 D1
Bugle Rural Workshops
  PL26 . . . . 47 C1
Bugle Sch PL26 . . . . 47 C1
Bugle Sta PL26 . . . . 47 C2
Buildings The TR20 . . . . . 89 A6
Bullan's La TR16 . . . . . . 141 A5
Bullans Terr [3] TR26 . . 141 A5
Bulleid Cl PL2 . . . . 127 F7
Bulleid Way EX23 . . . . . 104 E4
Buller Cl
  Plymouth PL7 . . . . . . 130 F4
  Torpoint PL11 . . . . . . 127 A3
Buller Ho TR16 . . . . 80 B6
Buller Ho PL13 . . . . 117 D3
Buller Pk
  Liskeard PL14 . . . . . . 113 C5
  Saltash PL12 . . . . 122 D3
Buller Rd PL11 . . . . 127 B3
Buller St PL13 . . . . 117 C3
Bullers Terr TR15 . . . . . 140 D5
Bull Hill PL23 . . . . 116 C4
Bullock La
  Helston, Lower Green
    TR13 . . . . 146 B5
  Helston, Whitehill TR13 . 146 C4
Bullock Market Terr [27]
  TR18 . . . . 143 E6
Bulmer Rd PL4 . . . . 149 C3
Bulteel Gdns PL6 . . . . . 124 E7
Bulwark Rd PL13 . . . . . . 146 B4
Bungalows The
  Looe PL13 . . . . 117 D6
  Tintagel PL34 . . . . 14 D7
Bunkers Hill
  [22] St Ives TR26 . . . . 141 B6
  Townshend TR27 . . . . . 90 C8
Bunyan Cl PL5 . . . . 124 C2
Burden Cl PL31 . . . . 109 C4
Burgess Cl EX23 . . . . 4 D2
BURHOS 79 F2
Buriton Row [32] TR18 . . 143 E5
BURLAWN 108 D1
Burleigh La PL3 . . . . 128 D7
Burleigh Manor PL3 . . . . 128 D7
Burleigh Park Rd PL3 . . . 128 D6
Burley Cl TR11 . . . . 137 D3
Burley Ct TR11 . . . . 145 B4
Burnard Cl PL6 . . . . 124 E7
Burnards La [7] PL31 . . . 109 D5
Burnett Cl PL12 . . . . 122 D2
Burnett Rd PL6 . . . . 124 E6
Burnham Park Rd PL3 . . 128 D6
Burniston Cl PL7 . . . . . . 131 A3
Burnistone Cl PL7 . . . . . 131 A3
Burn La PL19 . . . . 30 E8
Burns Ave PL5 . . . . 124 C2
Burns View PL11 . . . . 65 B5
Burnthouse Cotts TR10 . . 81 C1
Burnthouse La TR27 . . . 142 D5
Burn View PL15 . . . . 104 D6
Burnwithian Terr TR16 . . 68 D1
BURRATON 122 D4
BURRATON COOMBE . . . 122 C2
Burraton Rd PL12 . . . . . 122 C4
Burrator Rd PL20 . . . . . . 42 E3
Burrington Ind Est PL5 . . 123 E1
Burrington Rd PL5 . . . . . 124 A1
Burrington Way PL5 . . . . 124 B1
Burrow Hill PL9 . . . . 135 E6
Burrows The PL26 . . . . . 141 A6
BURSDON 3 B7
Bursdon Moor Cross EX39 . 3 A7
Burthallan La TR26 . . . . . 77 A7
Burton Ho PL26 . . . . 125 B6
Burton Ho [8] PL25 . . . . 114 C3
Burwell Cl PL6 . . . . 125 E4
Bury Cl PL15 . . . . 11 B1
Bush Hill PL14 . . . . 36 F2

Bush Pk
Launceston PL15 . . . . 106 D5
Plymouth PL6 . . . . 125 F3
BUSVEAL 140 F4
Butcher Park Hill PL19 . 147 B7
Bute Rd PL4 . . . . 129 A4
Butler Cl PL6 . . . . 125 B6
Butney Cnr TR14 . . . . 66 E3
Butson Pk TR5 . . . . 68 D8
Buttercup Mdw PL15 . . . 106 E4
Butterdown PL12 . . . . . . 122 B3
Buttlegate PL11 . . . . 64 D5
Butt Park Rd PL5 . . . . . . 124 B3
BUTTSBEAR CROSS 7 F7
Butts La PL35 . . . . 9 D1
Butts Pk PL22 . . . . 112 D2
Butts The
  St Newlyn East TR8 . . . . 56 B7
  Tintagel PL34 . . . . 14 D7
Buzzard Rd PL19 . . . . . . 147 D2
Byard Cl PL5 . . . . 123 E1
Byland Rd PL3 . . . . 129 A6
Byron Ave PL5 . . . . 124 C2

C

Cabot Cl PL12 . . . . 122 E2
Cades Parc TR13 . . . . . . 146 C6
CADGWITH 103 B4
Cadoc Cl PL28 . . . . 20 E1
Cadogan Cl TR14 . . . . . . 138 E1
Cadogan Rd TR14 . . . . . 138 E1
Cadover Cl PL6 . . . . 125 A1
Caernarvon Gdns PL2 . . 128 B7
Caernarvon Lodge TR7 . 110 D5
Calais Rd TR27 . . . . 78 C2
Calartha Rd TR19 . . . . . . 75 A1
Calartha Terr TR19 . . . . . 75 A1
Calder Cl PL3 . . . . 129 B6
Caldicot Gdns PL6 . . . . . 125 C8
Caldwells Rd TR18 . . . . . 143 E6
Caledonia Cl ☐ PL7 . . . 131 B5
CALENICK 137 C1
Calenick St TR1 . . . . 137 C4
Cal Hill TR16 . . . . 140 D3
California Gdns
  Plymouth PL3 . . . . 129 D6
  Portscatho TR2 . . . . 83 B2
CALLESTICK 55 C1
CALLINGTON 39 F4
Callington Com Coll PL17 39 E5
Callington Inr Ctr* PL17 39 E4
Callington Prim Sch ☐
  PL17 . . . . 39 E4
Callington Rd
  Harrowbarrow PL17 . . . . 40 C4
  Liskeard PL14 . . . . 113 D7
  Saltash PL12 . . . . 122 E3
  Tavistock PL19 . . . . 147 A4
CALLOOSE 78 D2
Calloose Lane E TR27 . . . 78 D1
Calloose Lane W TR27 . . 78 D1
Callywith Gate Ind Est
  PL31 . . . . 35 B2
Calshot Cl TR7 . . . . 111 E7
CALSTOCK 41 A3
Calstock Prim Sch PL18 . 41 A3
Calstock Rd PL18 . . . . . . 41 A6
Calstock Sta PL17 . . . . . . 41 A3
Calver Cl TR10 . . . . 144 C8
Calvez Cl PL10 . . . . 132 F6
Camaret Dr TR26 . . . . . . 141 B4
Cambeak PL35 . . . . 9 C1
Cambeak Cl EX23 . . . . . 148 A1
Camber Rd PL4 . . . . 148 A1
CAMBORNE 138 E2
Camborne Cl PL5 . . . . . . 124 A5
Camborne Ctr The* . . . . . .
  TR14 . . . . 138 E3
Camborne Geological Mus &
  Art Gal* TR15 . . . . . . 139 B6
Camborne Redruth Com
  Hospl TR15 . . . . 139 F6
Camborne Ret PkTR15 . . 139 B5
Camborne Sch of Mines
  TR15 . . . . 139 B6
Camborne Science & Com
  CollTR14 . . . . 138 B3
Camborne StaTR14 . . . . 138 D2
Cambridge La W ☐ PL1 . 148 B3
Cambridge Pl PL11 . . . . 145 A3
Cambridge Rd PL2 . . . . . 127 F5
CAMBROSE 67 F6
Camden Cl PL4 . . . . 149 A3
Camden St PL4 . . . . 149 A3
Camel Cl PL28 . . . . 109 D7
Camel Ct PL30 . . . . 109 C6
CAMELFORD 105 C4
Camelford L Ctr PL32 . . 105 C4
Camelford Prim Sch
  PL32 . . . . 105 C3
Camelot Ct ☐ PL18 . . . . 143 E5
Camelot View PL32 . . . . 105 C8
CAMELS HEAD 127 E7
Camelside PL27 . . . . 108 C5
Camel Valley Vineyard* . . .
  PL30 . . . . 34 B2
Cameo Ct TR14 . . . . 138 F4
Cameron Cl EX23 . . . . . 104 D7
Cameron Way PL6 . . . . . 125 B1
Camilla Terr PL2 . . . . . . 128 D7
Campbell Rd PL9 . . . . . . 135 F7
Campbeltown Way PL11 . 145 C3

Camp Cross PL15 . . . . . . 19 F7
Camperdown St PL2 . . . 127 E2
Camperknowle Cl PL10 . 132 F6
Campfield Hill TR1 . . . . . 137 D5
Camp Hall Rd TR8 . . . . . . 43 B1
Campion Cl
  ☐ Plymouth PL7 . . . . . 131 C5
  Saltash PL12 . . . . 122 D4
Campion Rise PL19 . . . . 147 D6
Campion View PL6 . . . . . 125 D8
Camullas Way TR7 . . . . . 110 A5
Canal Rd PL19 . . . . 147 B5
Candish Dr PL9 . . . . 136 D7
Canefields Ave PL7 . . . . 131 B3
Canfield Pl TR15 . . . . . . 140 A5
Canfield Terr TR15 . . . . 140 A5
Canhaye Cl PL7 . . . . 131 A3
CANNALIDGEY 32 E4
Cannamanning Rd ☐
  PL26 . . . . 59 D7
Canna Park Sta* PL15 . . 18 D3
Cann Gdns PL6 . . . . 124 D6
Cannis Rd PL25 . . . . 114 E6
Cannon Hill TR14 . . . . . 113 C5
Cannons Pl TR13 . . . . . . 146 D7
Cannon St PL1 . . . . 127 D2
Cannon Terr ☐ PL14 . . . 113 C5
Cann Woods Nature
  Reserve* PL6 . . . . 124 C6
Cann Wood View PL6 . . 125 E7
CANONSTOWN 77 C2
Canons Way PL19 . . . . . 147 A3
Canterbury Dr PL5 . . . . 124 B3
Cantillion Cl PL27 . . . . . 21 E3
Canton PL26 . . . . 85 D5
CANWORTHY WATER . . . 11 D2
Canyke Rd PL31 . . . . 48 D8
Cape Cl TR19 . . . . 86 E6
Cape Cornwall Comp Sch
  TR19 . . . . 86 E6
Cape Cornwall Rd TR19 . 86 E6
Cape Cornwall St TR19 . 86 E6
Cape Terr TR19 . . . . 86 E6
Cape Trelew TR19 . . . . . 86 E6
Captains Gdns PL15 . . . 124 E1
Captains Ho PL26 . . . . . . 73 C3
Captain's Wlk TR11 . . . 145 A2
Caradon Bsns Ctr ☐
  PL14 . . . . 113 C5
Caradon Cl
  ☐ Callington PL17 . . . . 39 E4
  ☐ Pensilva PL14 . . . . . . 38 E4
  Plymouth PL6 . . . . 125 A5
Caradon Ct ☐ PL20 . . . . 42 C4
Caradon Dr PL14 . . . . . . 113 B6
Caradon Hts
  Liskeard PL14 . . . . 113 D7
  Tremar PL14 . . . . 38 B4
Caradon Terr PL12 . . . . 122 E3
CARADON TOWN 37 F3
Caradon View PL14 . . . . 37 F3
Carbeile Jnr Sch PL11 . . 127 A3
Carbeile Rd PL11 . . . . . 127 A2
Carbes La PL22 . . . . 112 C2
CARBIS 47 A2
CARBIS BAY 141 D3
Carbis Bay StaTR26 . . . 141 D2
Carbis Ct TR15 . . . . 140 A5
Carboth La PL15 . . . . . . 106 B5
CARCLAZE 114 E6
Carclaze Com Inf Sch
  PL25 . . . . 114 E6
Carclaze Com Jun Sch
  PL25 . . . . 114 E6
Carclaze Ind Est PL25 . . 114 E7
Carclaze Rd PL25 . . . . . 114 E7
Carclew Ave TR7 . . . . . . 110 E6
Carclew Rd TR11 . . . . . . 81 F4
Carclew St TR1 . . . . 137 D3
Carclew Terr
  Devoran TR3 . . . . 81 F6
  Truro TR1 . . . . 137 D3
Cardell Rd PL31 . . . . 109 D5
Cardell Way TR7 . . . . . . 111 A5
Cardiff Cl PL7 . . . . 131 B4
Cardigan Rd PL5 . . . . . . 125 C1
Cardinal Ave PL5 . . . . . . 127 D8
CARDINHAM 35 E3
Cardinham Prim Sch
  PL30 . . . . 35 F3
Cardinham Woods Forest
  Walks* PL30 . . . . 35 C1
Cardinnis Cl PL14 . . . . . 113 D6
Cardinnis Rd TR18 . . . . 143 B5
Cardrew Bsns PkTR15 . . 140 C6
Cardrew Dr TR15 . . . . . 140 B6
Cardrew Ind EstTR15 . . 140 D7
Cardrew La ☐ TR15 . . . . 140 D7
Cardrew Terr TR15 . . . . 140 D6
Cardrew Way TR15 . . . . 140 D7
Cardwen Est PL13 . . . . . 62 C6
Careswell Ave PL2 . . . . . 127 F8
Carew Ave PL5 . . . . 124 B3
Carew Cl
  Crafthole PL11 . . . . 65 B5
  St Day TR16 . . . . 68 E1
Carew Gdns
  Plymouth PL5 . . . . 124 B3
  Saltash PL12 . . . . 122 D3
Carew Gr PL5 . . . . 124 B3
Carew-Pole Cl TR1 . . . . 137 E3
Carew Rd
  St Day TR16 . . . . 68 D1
  Truro TR1 . . . . 137 C5
Carew Terr PL11 . . . . . . 127 B2
Carew Wharf PL11 . . . . 127 C2

Carew Wharf Bsns Ctr
  PL11 . . . . 127 C2
Carey Ct PL12 . . . . 122 E3
Carey Pk
  Helston TR13 . . . . 146 B7
  Polperro PL13 . . . . 62 E2
  Truro TR1 . . . . 137 C4
CARFURY 76 A1
Cargoll Rd TR8 . . . . 56 B7
CARGREEN 119 A2
Cargwyn PL26 . . . . 59 D6
Cargy Cl TR8 . . . . 55 D8
CARHARRACK 80 F8
Carisbrooke Rd PL6 . . . 125 C1
Carkeek's Cl PL26 . . . . . 58 B3
CARKEEL 122 C6
Carkeel Barns PL12 . . . . 122 C5
Carkeel Ind Est PL12 . . 122 D5
Carknown Gdns TR15 . . 140 D3
Carland Cross TR8 . . . . . 56 D4
Carland Cross TR8 . . . . . 56 D4
CARLEEN 90 F5
CARLIDNACK 93 D3
Carlidnack La TR11 . . . . . 93 D4
Carlidnack Rd TR11 . . . . 93 E4
Carlisle Rd PL5 . . . . 124 D3
CARLOGGAS
  Foxhole 58 C5
  Penwithick 59 D7
  St Mawgan 45 A8
Carloggas Cl TR8 . . . . . . 45 A8
Carloggas Farm TR8 . . . 45 A8
Carloggas Gr ☐ TR8 . . . 45 D6
Carloggas Way ☐ TR9 . . 45 D6
Carlton Cl PL3 . . . . 129 B5
Carlton Ho ☐ PL31 . . . . 109 E5
Carlton Terr
  Plymouth, Lipson PL4 . . 149 B3
  Plymouth, Weston Mill PL5 127 E8
Carlton Vills PL12 . . . . . . 53 E4
CARLUDDON 59 D6
CARLYON BAY 115 E3
Carlyon Cl
  Looe PL13 . . . . 62 A7
  Threemilestone TR3 . . . 69 D3
  Torpoint PL11 . . . . 126 F4
  ☐ Truro TR1 . . . . 137 C4
Carlyon Ct TR3 . . . . 82 B8
Carlyon Ho ☐ TR1 . . . . . 69 E4
Carlyon Rd
  Playing Place TR3 . . . . . 82 B8
  St Austell PL25 . . . . . . 114 E4
  Truro TR1 . . . . 137 C5
Carmarthen Rd PL4 . . . 129 B2
Carmel Gdns PL14 . . . . 147 A5
Carminow Cross PL30 . . 48 D8
Carminowe Cres ☐
  TR18 . . . . 143 D5
Carminowe Rd PL31 . . . . 48 D8
Carminow Way TR7 . . . 111 A7
Carmython Ct TR7 . . . . 111 A3
Carnanton Moor TR15 . 139 C3
CARN ARTHEN 139 B2
Carn Arthen Rd ☐ TR14 . 138 E2
Carnarthen St TR14 . . . 138 E2
Carn Ave TR14 . . . . 138 D3
Carn Bargus PL26 . . . . . 58 B8
Carn Bosavern TR19 . . . . 86 F6
Carn Bosavern Cl TR19 . . 86 F6
Carn Brae L CtrTR15 . . 139 C5
Carn Brea Ave TR15 . . . 139 C5
Carn Brea Ho TR15 . . . . 139 C5
Carn Brea Rd TR15 . . . . 139 C5
CARN BREA VILLAGE . . . 139 F5
Carn Brea Village TR15 . 139 F5
Carn Cl TR27 . . . . 78 E1
Carncrows Rd TR26 . . . . 141 C6
Carncrows St TR26 . . . . 141 C6
CARNE
  St Dennis 46 C1
  Veryan 83 F5
Carne Cross PL24 . . . . . . 59 F7
Carne Cl PL26 . . . . 58 C8
Carnedon PL14 . . . . 38 C7
Carnego La TR8 . . . . 57 B6
Carne Hill
  St Dennis PL26 . . . . 46 C1
  Trewoon PL25 . . . . 58 F4
Carnellis Rd ☐ TR26 . . . 141 A5
Carne Mdws TR2 . . . . 70 F5
CARN ENTRAL 139 A2
Carne Rd TR18 . . . . 143 C3
Carne's Bldgs ☐ TR18 . . 143 E4
Carnes St PL11 . . . . 145 C2
Carne's Flats PL24 . . . . . 60 B5
Carneton Cl ☐ TR8 . . . . 43 D3
Carn Euny Settlement* . . .
  TR20 . . . . 87 C3
Carne View Cl TR14 . . . 138 F5
Carne View Rd TR2 . . . . 71 D6
Carnglaze Caverns* PL14 36 F1
Carn Gloose Rd TR19 . . . 86 D6
Carn Gwaves Terr TR18 . 143 D1
CARNHELL GREEN 78 F4
Carnhell Rd TR14, TR27 . 78 F4
CARNHOT 80 C3
Carninney La TR26 . . . . 141 C1
CARNKIE 139 F2
CARNKIEF 55 C5
Carnkief Cnr TR4 . . . . . . 55 D4
Carn Marth La TR16 . . . 140 E2
Carnock Rd PL2 . . . . 128 D8
Carnon Cres ☐ TR3 . . . . 81 F7
CARNON DOWNS 82 A7

Carnon Terr TR3 . . . . . . 81 F6
Carnoustie Dr PL12 . . . 122 C2
Carn Rock TR10 . . . . 144 D7
Carn Ros TR19 . . . . 74 F1
Carnsew Cres TR10 . . . . 81 C1
Carnsew Cres TR10 . . . . 81 C1
Carnsew Mdw TR27 . . . 142 A5
Carnsew Rd TR27 . . . . . 142 A5
Carnsew Mdw TR27 . . . 142 A5
Carnsew Rd TR27 . . . . . 142 A5
Carnsmerry PL26 . . . . . . 47 C1
Carnsmerry Cres PL25 . . 114 E4
Carnstabba Rd ☐ TR26 . 77 A6
Carnthorne PL27 . . . .
  PL25 . . . . 77 C2
Carn Todden TR19 . . . . . 88 D1
CARN TOWAN 96 C7
Carn View TR16 . . . . 80 F6
Carn View Terr TR19 . . . 75 A1
CARNYORTH 86 F8
Carnyorth Hill TR19 . . . 86 F8
Carnyorth Terr TR19 . . . 86 F8
Carolina Gdns PL2 . . . . 127 F7
Caroline Cl TR27 . . . . . . 142 E7
Caroline Row TR27 . . . . 142 E7
CARPALLA 58 D4
Carpalla Rd PL26 . . . . . . 58 D5
Carpalla Terr PL26 . . . . . 58 D5
Carpenter Rd PL9 . . . . . 135 F8
Carpmael Ave TR18 . . . 111 B4
Carraccawn Cross PL12 . 64 D8
Carrack Dhu TR26 . . . . . 141 B6
Carrack Dhu Est ☐ TR26 141 B6
Carrack Gladden TR26 . 141 D2
Carrack Widden ☐ TR26 141 B5
Carradale Rd PL6 . . . . . 129 C7
Carrallack Mews TR19 . . 86 E6
Carrallack Terr TR19 . . . 86 E5
Carriage Ho The TR19 . . 69 F1
Carriage Parc TR4 . . . . . 55 D4
Carrickowel Cres ☐
  PL25 . . . . 115 A5
Carrick Rd TR11 . . . . . . 144 E2
Carrick Way TR27 . . . . . . 95 A6
Carrine Rd TR1 . . . . 69 F3
Carrisbrooke Way PL12 . 122 B2
Carrnown Gdns TR15 . . 140 D3
Carroll Rd PL5 . . . . 124 C2
Carrolls Way PL7 . . . . . 136 A5
Carron La PL6 . . . . 121 D1
Carsize La TR27 . . . . 78 E1
Carter Cl TR7 . . . . 111 A5
Carteret Rd EX23 . . . . . 104 E5
CARTHEW 59 B6
Carthew La
  Four Lanes TR13 . . . . . . 80 A3
  Praze-an-Beeble TR13 . . 79 F2
Carthew Terr TR26 . . . . 141 A6
Carthew Way TR26 . . . . 141 A6
Carvath Ho TR3 . . . . 114 D3
Carvedras Ct ☐ TR1 . . . 137 C4
Carvossa Est TR20 . . . . . 89 B8
Carvoza Rd TR1 . . . . 137 D5
Carvynick Cotts TR8 . . . . 57 A7
Carwinard Cl TR27 . . . . . 78 C5
Carwinion Bamboo Gdn*
  TR11 . . . . 93 E3
Carwinion Rd TR11 . . . . . 93 E3
Carwin La TR27 . . . . 78 C5
Carwin Rise
  Angarrack TR27 . . . . . . 78 C5
  Hayle TR27 . . . . 142 E7
Carwollen Rd PL25 . . . . 114 E7
Carworgie Cl ☐ TR9 . . . . 45 E2
Carworgie Manor TR8 . . 45 D3
Carworgie Way ☐ TR9 . . 45 E2
CARWYNNEN 79 D4
CARZISE 78 D1
Casey La PL13 . . . . 62 D5
CASTALLACK 97 F6
Castel Wary Cl TR13 . . . 146 B5
Casterills Rd TR13 . . . . 146 D4
Castle Acre Gdns PL3 . . 129 B5
Castle Bank Gdns PL3 . . 129 B5
Castle Barbican PL7 . . . 130 E4
Castle Canyke Rd PL31 . 109 F3
Castle Carey Gdns PL3 . 129 B5
Castle Cl TR11 . . . . 145 E3
Castle Ct
  Praa Sands TR20 . . . . . 90 C3
  Saltash PL12 . . . . 122 C2
Castle Dr
  Bodmin PL31 . . . . 109 F5
  Falmouth TR11 . . . . . . 145 F2
  Praa Sands TR20 . . . . . 90 B3
  St Mawes TR2 . . . . 94 F5
Castle Dyke PL15 . . . . . 106 C6
CASTLE GATE 76 F1
Castle Gdns PL14 . . . . . 113 C6
Castle Gn PL13 . . . . 146 B5
Castlehayes Gdns PL7 . . 130 E4
Castle Hill
  Falmouth TR11 . . . . . . 145 D3
  Helston TR13 . . . . 146 B5
  ☐ Liskeard PL14 . . . . . 113 C6
  Lostwithiel PL22 . . . . . 112 C2
  Saltash PL12 . . . . 122 C1
Castle Hill Ct
  Bodmin PL31 . . . . 109 E5
  ☐ Liskeard PL14 . . . . . 113 C6
Castle Hill Gdns PL31 . . 109 F5
CASTLE HORNECK 143 B5
Castle Horneck Cl TR18 . 143 C5

Castle Horneck Rd TR18 . 143 C5
Castle Hts ☐ PL34 . . . . . 14 C7
Castle La
  Liskeard PL14 . . . . 113 C6
  Plymouth PL7 . . . . 130 E4
Castle Mdws
  Launceston PL15 . . . . . 106 A4
  ☐ St Agnes TR5 . . . . . . 54 D1
Castlemead Cl PL12 . . . 122 D3
Castlemead Dr PL12 . . . 122 D3
Castle Meadows Ct ☐
  TR5 . . . . 54 D1
Castle Rd
  Longrock TR20 . . . . 88 F8
  Ludgvan TR20 . . . . 89 A8
  Penzance TR18 . . . . . . 143 E7
  Tintagel PL34 . . . . 14 C7
Castle Rise
  Plymouth PL3 . . . . 129 B4
  Saltash PL12 . . . . 122 D1
  Truro TR1 . . . . 137 C5
Castle Rock PL29 . . . . . . 22 D8
Castle St
  Bodmin PL31 . . . . 109 F5
  Launceston PL15 . . . . . 106 C6
  Liskeard PL14 . . . . 113 C6
  Looe PL13 . . . . 117 D3
  Plymouth PL1 . . . . 149 A2
  Truro TR1 . . . . 137 C4
Castleton Cl PL3 . . . . . . 129 A4
Castle View
  ☐ Liskeard PL14 . . . . . 113 C6
  Longrock TR20 . . . . 88 F6
  Lostwithiel PL22 . . . . . 112 E3
  Saltash PL12 . . . . 122 D1
  Tintagel PL34 . . . . 14 C7
Castle View TR15 . . . . . 140 B6
Castle View PkTR11 . . . . 93 D3
Caswarth Terr PL25 . . . 107 D5
Catalina Row PL27 . . . . . 31 F3
Catalina Villas PL9 . . . . 135 A6
CATCHALL 97 D8
Catchfrench Cres PL14 . 113 E6
Cathcart Ave PL4 . . . . . 129 B2
Cathedron Rd
  Carnhell Green TR14 . . . 78 F1
  Praze-an-Beeble TR14 . . 79 A3
Cathedral Church of the
  Blessed Virgin Mary*
  TR1 . . . . 137 D4
Cathedral La ☐ TR1 . . . 137 D4
Cathedral of St Mary & St
  Boniface PL1 . . . . 148 B3
Cathedral School of St Mary
  PL1 . . . . 148 B3
Cathedral St PL1 . . . . . . 148 B3
Cathedral View TR1 . . . 137 C6
Catherine Ct EX23 . . . . 104 F4
Catherine Pk PL13 . . . . . 62 E5
Catherine's Hill PL15 . . 106 A6
Catherine St TR7 . . . . . . 148 C2
CATTEDOWN 149 C1
Catterick Cl PL5 . . . . . . 123 E5
Cattewater Rd PL4 . . . . 149 C1
Caudledown La PL26 . . . 59 C8
Caunter Rd PL14 . . . . . . 113 D6
Causeland Sta PL14 . . . . 51 B2
Causewayhead TR18 . . . 143 E5
Causeway The
  Falmouth TR11 . . . . . . 144 F4
  Hayle TR27 . . . . 142 A4
Causley Cl PL15 . . . . . . 106 C7
Cavendish Rd PL4 . . . . . 129 B1
CAWSAND 133 B1
Caxton Gdns PL5 . . . . . . 124 C1
Cayforth Flats TR15 . . . . 67 C6
Cecil Ave PL4 . . . . 129 C6
Cecil Cl PL4 . . . . 129 C6
Cecil Cotts PL1 . . . . 148 A3
Cecil St PL1 . . . . 148 B3
Cedar Ave PL9 . . . . 135 C5
Cedar Cl
  ☐ Callington PL17 . . . . 39 F4
  Torpoint PL11 . . . . 126 F2
Cedarcroft Rd PL2 . . . . 128 B7
Cedar Ct
  Camborne TR14 . . . . . 139 A5
  Saltash PL12 . . . . 122 F2
Cedar Dr PL11 . . . . 126 F2
Cedar Gr EX23 . . . . 104 E7
Cedar House Flats TR26 . 77 C4
Cedars The TR15 . . . . . 137 C2
Celandine Gdns PL7 . . . 131 C5
Celia Hts PL31 . . . . 109 F2
Celtic Rd PL12 . . . . 39 F4
Cemetery Rd PL18 . . . . . 40 F5
Centenary Row Middle
  TR14 . . . . 138 E3
Centenary Row W ☐
  TR14 . . . . 138 E2
Centenary St TR14 . . . . 138 E3
Central Ave PL25 . . . . . 114 C5
Central Cl PL26 . . . . 58 B4
Central Park Ave PL4 . . 148 C4
Central Rd
  Holywell TR8 . . . . 43 B1
  Plymouth PL1 . . . . 148 B1
Central Sq TR7 . . . . 110 D6
Central Treviscoe PL26 . . 58 A7
Century Cl
  Helston TR13 . . . . 146 D8
  St Austell PL25 . . . . . . 114 F6
Century Ct TR7 . . . . 111 C7
Century La TR2 . . . . 71 B6
Century Sq ☐ PL14 . . . . 38 E4
Ceres Ct EX23 . . . . 104 E4
CHACEWATER 68 F3
Chacewater La TR4 . . . . . 69 A3

Chacewater Prim Sch
TR4 . . . . 69 A3
CHADDLEWOOD 131 B6
Chaddlewood Ave PL4 . . 149 B3
Chaddlewood Cl PL7 . . . 131 A4
Chaddlewood Ho PL7 . . . 131 B5
Chaddlewood Prim Sch
PL7 . . . . 131 A5
Chagford Wlk PL6 . . . . . . 129 E8
Chainwalk Dr TR1 . . . . . . 137 C6
Chalets The TR18 . . . . 88 E6
Chalet The PL11 . . . . 64 C4
Challacombe Gdns PL10 . 144 C8
Challenger Quay 12
TR11 . . . . 145 C3
Challgood Cl 1 PL9 . . . . 135 F5
Challgood Rise PL9 . . . . 135 F5
Challis Ave TR8 . . . . 45 A8
Challock Cl PL6 . . . . 125 D4
Chamberlayne Dr PL7 . 130 E6
Champion's Ct TR13 . . . . 146 B6
Chancery Cl TR4 . . . . 70 D8
Chancery La 2 TR18 . . . . 143 E5
Chandlers Wlk PL25 . . . . 115 A3
Chandos Pl 12 PL25 . . . . 114 C3
Channel Park Ave PL3 . . 129 B5
Channel View
Polruan PL23 . . . . 116 D2
St Austell PL25 . . . . 115 A6
St Ives TR26 . . . . 141 C6
Channel View Terr
Plymouth PL4 . . . . 149 C4
4 Redruth TR15 . . . . . . 140 C4
Channon Rd PL12 . . . . . . 122 C4
Chantry Ct PL7 . . . . 130 B5
Chantry La PL13 . . . . 117 E4
Chantry Pk 18 PL17 . . . . . 39 E4
CHAPEL
Launceston 106 A5
Quintrell Downs 111 E4
Chapel Cl
Camborne, Kehelland
TR14 . . . . 66 F1
Camborne, Tuckingmill
TR14 . . . . 139 A4
Coad's Green PL15 . . . . . . 27 D3
Connor Downs TR27 . . . . 78 D6
Crantock TR8 . . . . 110 A3
Gunnislake PL18 . . . . 40 E5
4 Horrabridge PL20 . . . 42 C4
Lanivet PL30 . . . . 47 E6
St Just in Roseland TR2 . . 82 F2
Chapel Cnr EX22 . . . . 8 A5
Chapel Cotts EX23 . . . . . . 4 C8
Chapel Cres TR4 . . . . 56 A2
Chapel Ct
Camborne TR14 . . . . 138 F4
Padstow PL28 . . . . 107 D5
9 Redruth TR15 . . . . . . 140 B5
Chapeldown Rd PL11 . . 127 A2
Chapel Farm TR14 . . . . . . 79 E5
Chapel Field PL25 . . . . . . 115 B5
Chapel Gn PL26 . . . . 59 A1
Chapel Ground PL13 . . . 117 C3
Chapel Hill
Camborne, Brea TR14 . . 139 A3
Camborne, Tregajorran
TR15 . . . . 139 C4
Gweek TR12 . . . . 92 C2
Hayle TR27 . . . . 142 C6
Lanner TR16 . . . . 80 D6
Launceston PL15 . . . . . . 106 D6
Newquay TR7 . . . . 110 D6
Perranporth TR6 . . . . 55 B4
Polgooth PL26 . . . . 59 A1
Ponsanooth TR3 . . . . 81 B4
Porthtowan TR4 . . . . 68 A4
Redruth TR16 . . . . 68 A4
St Erth TR27 . . . . 142 A1
Sticker PL26 . . . . 58 F1
Truro TR1 . . . . 137 B4
Chapel Mdw
Buckland Monachorum
PL20 . . . . 41 F3
Perranarworthal TR3 . . . . 81 D6
Chapel Park Terr PL15 . 106 B5
Chapel Pk PL15 . . . . 106 B5
Chapel Pl
Pillaton PL12 . . . . 53 B7
18 Truro TR1 . . . . 137 D4
Chapel Point La PL26 . . . 73 C2
Chapel Rd
Camborne TR14 . . . . 139 A4
Foxhole PL26 . . . . 58 D5
Heamoor TR18 . . . . 143 C8
Indian Queens TR9 . . . . . 45 E1
Leedstown TR27 . . . . 78 E1
2 Par PL24 . . . . 60 C4
Roche PL26 . . . . 46 F3
Saltash PL12 . . . . 122 B3
St Just TR19 . . . . 86 E6
St Tudy PL30 . . . . 23 E3
Chapel Row
Praze-an-Beeble TR14 . . 79 B2
2 Redruth TR15 . . . . . . 140 B5
Tremar PL14 . . . . 38 A3

Chapel Row continued
Truro TR1 . . . . 137 D4
Widegates PL13 . . . . 63 F8
Chapel Sq
Crowlas PL25 . . . . 89 B8
Mevagissey PL26 . . . . 73 C3
Troon TR14 . . . . 79 E5
Chapel St
4 Bere Alston PL20 . . . 41 B1
4 Callington PL17 . . . . 39 F4
Camborne TR14 . . . . 138 D2
Camelford PL32 . . . . 105 C4
Grimscott EX23 . . . . 5 B2
Gunnislake PL18 . . . . 40 F6
Lifton PL16 . . . . 19 F4
Marazion TR17 . . . . 89 B5
Mevagissey PL26 . . . . 73 C3
2 Mousehole TR19 . . . 88 C1
9 Newlyn TR18 . . . . . . 143 C2
Penzance TR18 . . . . 143 E5
Plymouth, Mount Wise PL1 127 E2
Plymouth PL4 . . . . 149 A3
Probus TR2 . . . . 71 C6
Redruth TR15 . . . . 140 B5
St Day TR16 . . . . 68 D1
St Ives TR26 . . . . 141 B5
St Just TR19 . . . . 86 E6
Tavistock PL19 . . . . 147 B5
Chapel Terr
Camborne TR15 . . . . 139 D6
Devoran TR3 . . . . 81 F6
Falmouth TR11 . . . . 145 B4
Hayle TR27 . . . . 142 B2
Par PL24 . . . . 60 B6
9 Porthleven TR13 . . . 98 B8
Portreath TR16 . . . . 67 C6
Redruth, Carn Brea Village
TR15 . . . . 139 F5
Redruth TR15 . . . . 140 D2
Ruan Minor TR12 . . . . . 103 A3
St Day TR16 . . . . 68 E1
10 St Mawes TR2 . . . . . 95 A6
Trevelland TR19 . . . . 86 F8
CHAPEL TOWN 45 E1
Chapel Town Bsns Pk
TR8 . . . . 57 B7
Chapel Town Cl TR11 . . . 93 D4
Chapel Way PL3 . . . . 129 A6
CHAPLE AMBLE 22 D2
Chapman Cr PL12 . . . . . 122 B3
Chapmans Ope PL11 . . . 127 D2
CHAPMAN'S WELL 13 E4
Charaton Cross PL14 . . . 38 F4
Chard Barton PL5 . . . . . . 124 B3
Chard Rd PL5 . . . . 123 D2
Chard Terr 6 TR11 . . . . 145 B4
Charfield Dr PL6 . . . . 129 A8
Chariot Rd TR15 . . . . . . 139 E6
Charles Ave TR11 . . . . . . 144 E2
Charles Bassett Cl 6
TR13 . . . . 146 C5
Charles Cl PL25 . . . . 114 F3
Charles Cross PL4 . . . . . . 149 A3
Charles St
Bugle PL26 . . . . 47 C1
Newlyn TR18 . . . . 143 C3
Plymouth PL4 . . . . 149 A3
Truro TR1 . . . . 137 C4
Charles Terr PL3 . . . . 129 A6
CHARLESTOWN 115 B2
Charlestown Prim Sch
PL25 . . . . 115 B3
Charlestown Rd PL25 . . 115 B3
Charlestown Shipwreck &
Heritage Ctr★ PL25 . . 115 B2
Charlotte Cl TR14 . . . . . . 68 C6
Charlotte St PL2 . . . . 127 E4
Charlton Cres PL6 . . . . . 125 A2
Charlton Rd PL6 . . . . 125 A3
Charnhill Cl PL7 . . . . 136 A6
Charnhill Way PL9 . . . . . 136 A6
Charter Cl TR13 . . . . 146 C4
Charter Ct TR10 . . . . 144 D7
Charter Way PL14 . . . . . 113 E6
Chateau Cl PL6 . . . . 124 E1
Chatsworth Gdns PL5 . . 123 F3
Chatsworth Way PL25 . 115 C2
Chaucer Rd PL19 . . . . . . 147 D5
Chaucer Way PL5 . . . . . . 124 C1
Chawleigh Cl PL18 . . . . . 40 F5
Chedworth St PL4 . . . . . 149 A3
Chegwin Gdns TR7 . . . . . 110 E5
Chegwins Hill PL26 . . . . . 58 D5
Chegwyn Gdns 5 TR5 . . 54 C1
Chegwyns PL26 . . . . 58 D5
Chelfham Senior Sch
PL20 . . . . 40 F3
Chelfham Senior Sch
Continuing Ed Department
PL19 . . . . 30 E3
Chellean Vean TR14 . . . . 81 C7
Chellew Rd TR1 . . . . 137 F5
Chelmer Cl PL7 . . . . 131 A5
Chelmsford Pl PL5 . . . . . 124 C4
Chelson Gdns PL6 . . . . . 125 E3
Cheltenham Pl
Newquay TR7 . . . . 110 D6
Plymouth PL4 . . . . 149 B4
Chelwood Gr PL7 . . . . . . 130 F5
CHENHALLS 142 A2
Chenhalls Cl TR27 . . . . . . 77 E2
Chenhalls Rd TR27 . . . . . 142 A2
Chenoweth Cl TR14 . . . . 81 C7
Chepstow Ave PL6 . . . . . 125 C8
Chequer Tree Ct PL18 . . 40 F5
Chequetts Cl 10 PL17 . . . 39 E4
Cheriton Cl PL25 . . . . 124 A3
Cherrill Gdns EX23 . . . . . 104 D7

Cherrington TR7 . . . . 110 B5
Cherry Cross EX22 . . . . . . 12 B7
Cherry Gdns 14 TR18 . . 143 E5
Cherry Gdn St 15 TR19 . . 88 C1
Cherry Pk PL7 . . . . 131 A3
Cherry Tree Cl PL31 . . . . 109 B4
Cherrytree Ho TR18 . . . . 143 C5
Cherry Tree La PL7 . . . . 131 A4
Cherry Tree Mews PL25 . 114 D3
Cheshire Dr PL6 . . . . 124 D6
Chesnut Cl PL12 . . . . 122 D4
Chester Ct TR7 . . . . 111 A6
Chesterfield Rd PL3 . . . . 129 B4
Chester Pl 4 PL4 . . . . . . 128 E4
Chester Rd TR7 . . . . 111 A6
Chesterton Cl PL5 . . . . . 126 C8
Chesterton Ct PL27 . . . . 108 A6
Chesterton Pl TR7 . . . . . 111 A7
Chestnut Ave PL9 . . . . . . 135 C5
Chestnut Cl
Callington PL17 . . . . 40 A4
Falmouth TR11 . . . . 144 F5
Lamerton PL19 . . . . 30 A4
St Tudy PL30 . . . . 23 E3
Torpoint PL11 . . . . 126 F3
24 Yelverton PL20 . . . . . 41 B1
Chestnut Gr PL31 . . . . . . 109 B4
Chestnut Rd PL3 . . . . 128 D7
Chestnut Terr PL19 . . . . . 30 A4
Cheviot Rd TR7 . . . . 110 E4
Chichester Cl PL26 . . . . . 58 E5
Chichester Cres
Newquay TR7 . . . . 110 F4
Saltash PL12 . . . . 122 E1
Chichester Ct PL20 . . . . . 42 C4
Chichester Ho PL1 . . . . . 148 B2
Childrey Gdns PL6 . . . . . 125 C1
Childrey Wlk PL6 . . . . . . 125 C1
Chili Rd TR15 . . . . 140 A6
CHILLATON 29 F8
CHILSWORTHY 40 E7
Chilton Cl PL6 . . . . 129 B7
China Clay Ctry Pk★ PL26 59 A7
Chings Alley TR15 . . . . . 106 C6
Chipponds Dr PL25 . . . . 114 A3
Chirgwin Ct 22 TR18 . . 143 E5
Chisholme Cl PL25 . . . . . 114 D3
Chisholme Pl PL25 . . . . . 114 D3
Chittleburn Bsns Pk PL8 136 F6
Chittleburn Cross PL8 . . 136 E5
Chittleburn Hill PL8 . . . . 136 E5
Chivenor Ave PL5 . . . . . . 123 D4
Chiverton Cl PL20 . . . . . . 89 F4
Chiverton Cross
Blackwater TR4 . . . . 68 F5
Rosudgeon TR20 . . . . 89 F4
Chiverton Greenacres
TR5 . . . . 68 D8
Chiverton Way PL20 . . . . 89 F4
Chollacott Cl PL19 . . . . . 147 C4
Chollacott La PL19 . . . . . 147 D3
Chough Cl
Falmouth TR11 . . . . 144 E4
Launceston PL15 . . . . . . 106 E4
Chough Cres PL15 . . . . . 114 F4
Choughs Cl TR14 . . . . . . 138 B3
Christa Cl PL14 . . . . 113 C6
Christian Mill Bsns Pk
PL6 . . . . 124 E4
Christian Way TR7 . . . . . 111 C7
Chubb Dr PL3 . . . . 128 B4
Chudleigh Rd PL4 . . . . . . 129 A4
Chun Castle★ TR20 . . . . . 87 C8
CHURCHBRIDGE 50 F1
Church Cl
Blisland PL30 . . . . 35 D8
Lelant TR26 . . . . 77 E4
Plymouth PL7 . . . . 130 F4
Trispen TR4 . . . . 56 D1
CHURCH COMBE 140 A2
CHURCH COVE 103 A2
Church Cove Rd TR12 . . 103 A2
Church End PL13 . . . . 117 D3
Churchfield Cl TR20 . . . . 89 A8
Churchfield Pl PL4 . . . . . 60 B5
Churchfields Rd TR8 . . . . 55 D8
Church Gate 8 PL14 . . . 113 C5
Church Hill
Calstock PL18 . . . . 41 A3
Chacewater TR4 . . . . 68 F2
Golant PL23 . . . . 61 B6
Helston TR13 . . . . 146 C7
Herodsfoot PL14 . . . . 50 E3
Hessenford PL11, PL12 . . 64 B8
Ludgvan TR20 . . . . 89 A8
Milton Combe PL20 . . . . . 41 F1
Penryn TR10 . . . . 144 D8
9 Pensilva PL14 . . . . . . 38 E4
Plymouth PL6 . . . . 125 B1
Port Isaac PL29 . . . . 22 D7
Sticker PL26 . . . . 58 F1
5 St Mawes TR2 . . . . . . 95 A6
Tavistock PL19 . . . . 147 E2
Tintagel PL34 . . . . 14 C7
Church Hill Rd PL9 . . . . . 135 A6
Church Ho PL12 . . . . 123 A2
Churchill Rd PL19 . . . . . 147 D2
Churchill Way
10 Penwithick PL26 . . . 59 D7
Plymouth PL3 . . . . 128 E6
Churchill Wlk PL12 . . . . 122 E1
Church La
Bodmin PL31 . . . . 109 E5
Bude EX23 . . . . 104 D5

Church La continued
Calstock PL18 . . . . 41 A3
Camborne TR14 . . . . 138 D3
Cargreen PL12 . . . . 119 A1
Flushing TR11 . . . . 145 B7
Helston TR13 . . . . 146 B6
Lelant TR26 . . . . 77 E4
Lostwithiel PL22 . . . . 112 C2
Mevagissey PL26 . . . . 73 C4
Padstow PL28 . . . . 107 D5
Redruth TR15 . . . . 140 A3
St Columb Minor TR7 . . 111 E7
St John PL11 . . . . 132 B8
Tavistock PL19 . . . . 147 C5
Churchlands PL13 . . . . . 117 D5
Churchlands Rd PL6 . . . 125 E7
Church Lea
Launceston PL15 . . . . . . 106 A7
Tavistock PL19 . . . . 147 E2
Church Mews
Stithians TR3 . . . . 80 F3
Week St Mary EX22 . . . . 11 E8
Church Park Ct PL6 . . . . 125 E8
Church Park Mews PL27 . 108 B6
Church Path EX23 . . . . . 104 C5
Church Pk
Bodmin PL31 . . . . 109 F5
Horrabridge PL20 . . . . . . 42 C4
Lerryn PL22 . . . . 61 D8
St Mellion PL12 . . . . 53 D8
Church Pl
Liskeard PL14 . . . . 113 C5
18 St Ives TR26 . . . . . . 141 B6
Church Rd
Camborne TR15 . . . . 139 B6
Cury TR12 . . . . 99 A4
Four Lanes TR16 . . . . 80 A5
Heamoor TR18 . . . . 143 C7
Illogan TR16 . . . . 67 E4
Lanivet PL30 . . . . 47 E7
Launceston PL15 . . . . 18 F6
Lelant TR26 . . . . 77 E4
Mabe Burnthouse TR10 . . 93 D7
Madron TR20 . . . . 143 A8
Mount Hawke TR4 . . . . . . 68 C6
Mylor Bridge TR11 . . . . . . 82 B2
Pendeen TR19 . . . . 75 A1
Penponds TR14 . . . . 138 B1
Penryn TR10 . . . . 144 C8
Perranarworthal TR3 . . . . 81 D5
Plymouth, Plymstock PL9 135 F7
Plymouth, Plymstock PL9 . 135 F7
Saltash PL12 . . . . 122 D2
Shortlanesend TR4 . . . . . . 69 F6
St Austell PL25 . . . . 115 B3
St Dennis PL26 . . . . 46 C1
St Day TR16 . . . . 80 F4
St Tudy PL30 . . . . 23 E3
Tideford PL12 . . . . 52 F2
Church Row La PL5 . . . . 124 C6
Church Sq
8 Bodmin PL31 . . . . . . 109 E5
St Just TR19 . . . . 86 F6
4 Stratton EX23 . . . . 4 E1
Church St
Callington PL17 . . . . 39 E4
Calstock PL18 . . . . 41 A3
Camborne TR14 . . . . 138 D3
Carharrack TR16 . . . . 80 F8
Falmouth TR11 . . . . 145 B4
Gorran Haven PL26 . . . . . 85 D5
Helston TR13 . . . . 146 B6
Landrake PL12 . . . . 53 C3
Launceston PL15 . . . . . . 106 C6
Liskeard PL14 . . . . 113 C5
Looe, East Looe PL13 . . 117 D3
Looe, West Looe PL13 . . 117 C3
Mevagissey PL26 . . . . 73 C3
15 Newlyn TR18 . . . . . 143 C1
Padstow PL28 . . . . 107 D5
Par PL24 . . . . 60 B5
Plymouth PL3 . . . . 128 A4
Poughill EX23 . . . . 4 D2
8 St Austell PL25 . . . . 114 C3
St Columb Minor TR7 . . 111 D7
St Day TR16 . . . . 68 E1
St Erth TR27 . . . . 142 A1
St Germans PL12 . . . . 65 A8
St Just TR19 . . . . 86 F6
5 Stratton EX23 . . . . 4 E1
Tywardreath PL24 . . . . . . 60 D5
Churchstow Wlk PL6 . . . 129 E8
Church Street N PL14 . . 113 C5
Church Street S PL14 . . 113 C5
Church Terr
Devoran TR3 . . . . 81 F6
Grampound Road TR2 . . . 57 E1
St Kew PL30 . . . . 23 A3
CHURCHTOWN
Bridgerule 8 B6
Camborne 139 A4
Lanivet 47 E7
St Breward 24 B6
CHURCH TOWN 140 A3
Churchtown
Cardinham PL30 . . . . 35 F3
Gwinear TR27 . . . . 78 D4
7 Mullion TR12 . . . . 99 A2

Churchtown continued
5 St Agnes TR5 . . . . 54 C1
St Minver PL27 . . . . 22 A4
St Newlyn East TR8 . . . . . 56 B7
Church Town TR11 . . . . . 144 D3
Church Town Cotts TR3 . 81 D5
Churchtown Mdws PL16 . 19 E3
Churchtown Mews PL30 . 35 C8
Churchtown Rd
Gwithian TR27 . . . . 66 B2
Illogan TR16 . . . . 67 E5
Phillack TR27 . . . . 142 C7
Portscatho TR2 . . . . 83 B2
St Stephen PL26 . . . . 58 B4
Churchtown Terr PL27 . . 32 D6
Churchtown Vale PL12 . 122 D1
Church View
St Cleer PL14 . . . . 37 F3
St Dominick PL12 . . . . 40 D2
St Neot PL14 . . . . 36 F2
Treburley PL15 . . . . 28 B5
Walkhampton PL20 . . . . . 42 E4
Church View TR18 . . . . . 143 B6
Church View Rd
Camborne TR14 . . . . 138 F4
Probus TR2 . . . . 71 D6
Churchway
Madron TR20 . . . . 143 A8
Madron TR17 . . . . 89 C5
Church Way
Falmouth TR11 . . . . 144 E3
Plymouth PL5 . . . . 127 E8
St Clether PL15 . . . . 17 B2
Church Wlk
Redruth TR15 . . . . 140 A5
South Petherwin PL15 . . . 27 E8
17 Truro TR1 . . . . 137 D5
Chute La PL26 . . . . 85 D5
Chy-an-Chy 19 TR26 . . . 141 B6
Chyanclare TR18 . . . . 143 D6
Chyandaunce Cl TR18 . . 143 F8
Chyandaunce Terr TR18 . 143 F8
Chyandor Cl PL24 . . . . . . 60 C4
CHYANDOUR 143 F7
Chyandour TR15 . . . . 140 A4
Chyandour Cl 1 TR18 . . . 77 A4
Chyandour Cliff TR18 . . 143 F6
Chyandour La TR18 . . . . 143 F7
Chy-an-Dour Rd TR20 . . 90 C3
Chyandour Sq TR18 . . . 143 F7
Chyandour Terr TR18 . . 143 F7
Chy an Dowr TR22 . . . . . 142 E7
Chy-an-Gweal TR18 . . . 143 B2
CHY-AN-GWEAL 141 B2
Chy-an-Gweal Est TR20 . 89 A7
Chy-an-Hall TR18 . . . . . . 143 B6
Chy-an-Mor TR20 . . . . . . 88 F6
Chy Cober TR27 . . . . 142 E7
CHYCOOSE 82 A6
Chycoose Parc TR3 . . . . . 82 A5
Chycornick Terr TR18 . . 143 F8
Chygothow TR13 . . . . . . 146 B6
Chy Hwel TR1 . . . . 137 F6
Chy Kensa Cl TR27 . . . . 142 C5
Chylan Cres TR7 . . . . 111 E6
Chymeddon TR7 . . . . 110 E6
Chy Nampara 1 TR11 . . 145 A4
Chynance
Penzance TR18 . . . . 143 D4
Portreath TR16 . . . . 67 C6
Chynance Dr TR7 . . . . . . 110 D5
CHYNHALE 91 C5
Chynoon Gdns PL25 . . . 114 F6
Chynowen La TR8 . . . . . . 43 D1
Chynowen Parc TR8 . . . . 43 D1
Chynoweth PL26 . . . . 59 C8
Chynoweth Gdns TR18 . 143 F8
Chynoweth La TR20 . . . . 89 F6
Chy Pons PL25 . . . . 114 A4
Chynoweth Mews TR18 . 143 D1
Chywoone Ave TR18 . . . 143 C1
Chywoone Cres TR18 . . 143 C1
Chywoone Cres TR18 . . . 97 F8
Chywoone Hill TR18 . . . 143 C1
Chywoone Pl TR18 . . . . 143 C1
Chywoone Rural Workshops
TR19 . . . . 87 A5
Chywoon Gdns TR15 . . 139 D6
Citadel Ope 18 PL1 . . . . 149 A2
Citadel Rd E PL1 . . . . . . 149 A2
Citadel Road E PL1 . . . . 148 C2
Citadel Rd W PL1 . . . . . 148 C2
Citadel The★ PL1 . . . . . . 149 A1
City Bsns Pk PL3 . . . . . . 128 A4
City Coll Plymouth (Kings
Road Ctr) PL1 . . . . 128 A2
City Coll Plymouth (Learning
Warehouse) PL1 . . . . . 148 B2

City Rd TR1. . . . . 137 C4
Clairemont Pl **1** PL14. . . . 38 A3
Clampet La PL11. . . . . 65 E4
Clann Hl PL30. . . . . 47 E7
Clann La PL30. . . . . 47 E7
Clann Mdws PL30. . . . . . . 47 E7
CLAPPER. 108 E4
Claremont Cotts **1**
  TR11. . . . . 145 A5
Claremont Falls PL13 . . . 62 E2
Claremont Mews TR15. . . 140 B5
Claremont Rd TR15 . . . . . 140 B5
Claremont St PL1. . . . . . . 148 C4
Claremont Terr
  3 Falmouth TR11. . . . . 145 A4
  10 Porthleven TR13. . . . 98 B8
  Truro TR1. . . . . 137 C5
Clarence Ct PL1. . . . . 148 A3
Clarence Pl
  20 Penzance TR18. . . . . 143 E6
  Plymouth, Morice Town
    PL2. . . . . 127 E4
  Plymouth, Stonehouse PL1 148 A3
Clarence Rd
  St Austell PL25 . . . . 114 B4
  Torpoint PL11 . . . . 127 B3
Clarence St TR18 . . . . 143 E5
Clarence Terr
  Penzance TR18. . . . . 143 E6
  17 Wadebridge PL27. . . 108 B5
Clarence Villas TR15. . . . 140 D6
Clarendon Ho **1** PL1 . . . 127 F3
Clarendon La **11** PL13 . . . 127 F3
Clare Pl PL4 . . . . 149 B2
Clare Terr TR11. . . . . 145 B4
Claybourne Cl PL25. . . . . 114 F6
Claylands PL30 . . . . 24 A1
Claytonia Cl PL6. . . . . 121 C1
Clayton Pl PL4. . . . . 129 B2
Clayton Rd PL4. . . . . 129 B2
Clearbrook Ave PL5. . . . . 123 E1
Clear View PL12 . . . . 122 E3
Clease Mdws PL32 . . . . . 105 C3
Clease Rd PL32 . . . . 105 C4
Clease The PL32 . . . . 105 C3
Cleave Cres EX23 . . . . . . 4 D8
Cleaveland PL27 . . . . 108 C4
Cleaverfield Mews PL15. 106 C7
Cleave The PL10 . . . . 133 B2
Cleavewell PL27 . . . . 108 C4
Cledma Bank TR27 . . . . . 142 A2
CLEERS 46 E1
Cleers Hill
  St Dennis PL26 . . . . 46 E1
  Whitemoor PL26 . . . . 58 E8
Cleeve Gdns PL2. . . . . . . 128 A8
Clegg Ave PL11 . . . . 126 E3
Clemens Cl TR7 . . . . 111 B5
Clemens Rd PL14 . . . . 51 B3
Clemens Way TR27. . . . . . 78 D6
Clement Rd PL17. . . . . . . 131 B5
Clements Rd TR18. . . . . . 143 D5
Clemmens Ave TR7 . . . . . 110 D4
Clemo Rd PL14 . . . . 113 E7
CLERKENWATER 109 D8
Clevedon Park Ave PL2. 128 B6
Clevedon Rd TR7 . . . . 110 D5
Cleveland Ave PL13. . . . . 117 D4
Cleveland Rd PL4 . . . . . . 149 C3
Clies The **5** TR13 . . . . . . 146 C5
Clifden Cl
  Mullion TR12 . . . . 99 A1
  Newquay TR7. . . . . 110 E5
Clifden Dr PL27 . . . . 21 D6
Clifden Rd PL25. . . . . 114 F4
Cobbett Rd PL5. . . . . 124 B2
Clifden Terr
  14 Bodmin PL31 . . . . . . 109 D5
  Lostwithiel PL22 . . . . 112 C2
CLIFF 61 B6
Cliff Bglws TR27 . . . . 142 A8
Cliff Ct
  Falmouth TR11. . . . . 145 B3
  Plymouth PL1. . . . . 148 B1
Cliff End Pk PL27 . . . . . . 108 D6
Cliff La
  Millbrook PL10. . . . . 132 A4
  Mousehole TR19 . . . . 88 D1
  New Polzeath PL27. . . . . 21 D6
CLIFFORD. 3 F8
Clifford Cl PL5. . . . . 123 E2
Cliff Park Terr PL27 . . . . 108 C5
Cliff Rd
  Falmouth TR11. . . . . 145 C2
  Gorran Haven PL26. . . . . 85 D5
  Mevagissey PL26. . . . . . . 73 C4
  Mousehole TR19 . . . . 88 D2
  Newlyn TR18 . . . . 143 D1
  Newquay TR7. . . . . 110 F6
  Perranporth TR6 . . . . 55 A5
  Plymouth PL1. . . . . 148 B1
  Porthleven TR13 . . . . 98 B8
Cliff Rise PL23 . . . . 116 D2
Cliff St PL26 . . . . 73 C4
Cliff Terr TR16. . . . . 67 C6
Cliff The PL26 . . . . 73 C3
Cliff View Rd TR14 . . . . . . 138 E4
Cliff View Terr TR14. . . . . 138 E4
Clift Ct **8** TR1. . . . . 137 D4
Clifton Ave PL7 . . . . 130 E7
Clifton Cl PL7. . . . . 130 E7
Clifton Cres **10** TR11 . . . 145 A4
Clifton Gdns **1** TR1 . . . . 137 B4
Clifton Hill **14** TR18 . . . . 143 C2

Clifton Pl
  14 Falmouth TR11. . . . . 145 A4
  Plymouth PL4. . . . . 149 A4
Clifton Rd TR15. . . . . 139 C8
Clifton St PL4. . . . . 149 A4
Clifton Terr
  15 Falmouth TR11. . . . . 145 A4
  Hayle TR27. . . . . 142 B6
  Liskeard PL14 . . . . 113 A5
  10 Newlyn TR18 . . . . . . 143 C2
  Portscatho TR2 . . . . 83 B2
Cligga Workshops TR6 . . 54 F4
Clijah Cl TR15 . . . . 140 C2
Clijah La TR15 . . . . 140 D2
Clinton Ave PL4. . . . . 129 A4
Clinton Cl
  Bude EX23. . . . . 104 E4
  Redruth TR15. . . . . 140 C4
Clinton Dr PL25. . . . . 114 B3
Clinton Pas **4** TR15 . . . . 140 B4
Clinton Rd
  Constantine TR11. . . . . . 92 F3
  Redruth TR15. . . . . 140 C4
Clinton Terr PL10 . . . . 132 F6
Clittaford Rd PL6 . . . . 124 F7
Clittaford View PL6 . . . . . 124 E7
Cloake Pl PL12. . . . . 119 A2
Clodan Mews **11** TR9 . . . 45 E2
Clodgey La TR13 . . . . 146 D5
Clodgey Way TR11. . . . . . 146 D4
Clodgey View **14** TR26 . . 141 B6
Clonway **1** PL20. . . . . . . 42 C3
Close Hill TR15 . . . . 140 B6
Close The
  17 Bere Alston PL20. . . . 41 B8
  Lanner TR16. . . . . 80 E6
  Mylor Bridge TR11. . . . . . 82 A3
  Penzance TR18. . . . . 143 D7
  Saltash PL12 . . . . 122 C3
  Trevone PL28 . . . . 20 F2
  Truro TR1. . . . . 137 F6
Clos Trevithick **4** TR14 . 138 F2
Clovelly Rd PL4 . . . . 149 C1
Clovelly View PL9. . . . . . . 135 A7
Clover Lane Cl **6** PL35. . 9 C1
Clover Rise PL6. . . . . 125 E8
Clover Wlk PL6 . . . . 122 C3
Clowance TR14. . . . . 79 B2
Clowance La PL1. . . . . 127 F1
Clowance La PL1. . . . . 127 E1
Clowance St PL1. . . . . 127 F1
CLOWANCE WOOD 79 A1
CLUBWORTHY 12 C3
Clyde St PL2. . . . . 127 F5
Coaches Cnr TR13 . . . . . . 90 F3
Coach Ho The
  Penryn TR10. . . . . 144 D7
  Penzance TR18. . . . . 143 F7
Coach House La PL25 . . . 114 C4
Coach House Mews PL9 . 136 B6
Coach La TR15. . . . . 140 A4
Coachyard Mews PL28 . . 107 D5
COAD'S GREEN. 27 D4
Coad's Green Prim Sch
  PL15. . . . . 27 D3
Coastguard Cotts
  Down Thomas PL9 . . . . . 134 F2
  Mawnan Smith TR11 . . . . 93 C1
  Mullion TR12 . . . . 99 B1
  Polperro PL13 . . . . 62 E2
  Rosudgeon PL20 . . . . . . 89 F3
Coastguard Cres TR18. . . 143 F6
Coastguard Hill PL29 . . . 22 D8
Coastguard Rds PL28 . . . 21 B4
Coastguard Sta Flats
  PL13. . . . . 117 C3
Coastguard Terr TR2 . . . . 84 B3
Coastline Ct TR18 . . . . . . 44 C6
Coast Rd TR4 . . . . 68 A7
Cobbett Rd PL5. . . . . 124 B2
Cobb La PL9. . . . . 135 F6
Cobble La TR9 . . . . 57 E8
Cobblestone La PL1. . . . . 128 A1
Cobbs Well PL23. . . . . . . 116 C4
Cober Cres TR7 . . . . 78 E3
Cobourg St PL1. . . . . 148 C3
Cockington Cl PL6 . . . . . . 21 D2
Cockington Wlk PL6 . . . . 125 C1
Cocklawelva PL27. . . . . . . 21 D2
COCKS. 55 B3
Cock's Lake La PL12 . . . . 53 D4
COCKWELLS 77 C1
Cockwells La TR26. . . . . . 77 C1
Codiford Cres TR14 . . . . . 138 E4
Coffa Bridge Cl PL22 . . . 112 D2
Coffee Lake Mdw PL22 . . 112 D2
Cogegoes Ind Pk TR14 . . 138 A2
Cogos Pk TR11 . . . . 82 A3
Coinaghall Pl TR18. . . . . . 143 F4
Coinagehall St
  Helston TR13. . . . . 146 B5
  Penzance TR18. . . . . 143 F4
COLAN 44 F4
Colborne Ave TR15 . . . . . 67 D4
Colborne Rd PL6. . . . . . . 125 E2
COLD NORTHCOTT 16 F5
Coldrenick St PL5. . . . . . . 123 D1
Coldrose Ct TR1 . . . . 137 B4
Coldstyle Rd PL14. . . . . . 113 C7
COLDVREATH 46 F1
Coldwind Cross TR3. . . . . 81 D7
COLEBROOK. 36 B3
Colebrook Cl PL15 . . . . . 140 A5
Colebrook La PL7 . . . . 130 E7
Colebrook Rd
  Plymouth, Plympton PL7 . . 130 E6
  Plymouth, St Budeaux PL5 123 D1
Coleman Dr PL9 . . . . 135 F4

Colemans Cross PL15 . . . 19 C5
Cole Moore Mdw PL19 . . 147 B6
Colenso Cross PL20. . . . . 89 F5
Colenso Pl PL25 . . . . 114 D3
Coleridge Ave PL6 . . . . . . 124 F2
Coleridge Rd PL4 . . . . 129 A4
Coles Cotts PL9 . . . . 135 C1
Cole's Cotts PL7 . . . . 130 E6
Colesdown Hill PL9 . . . . . 130 D1
Coleswoggett Halt Sta*
  PL30. . . . . 48 F8
Colin Campbell Ct **10**
  PL1. . . . . 148 B3
Colinsey Pl TR18. . . . . . . 143 D7
Colinsey Rd TR18 . . . . . . 143 D7
Coliza Hill PL26. . . . . 59 A2
Collacombe Cross PL19 . 29 F4
Collaford Cl PL7 . . . . 131 A4
Collan's Cross PL32 . . . . 15 D4
College Ave
  Plymouth PL3. . . . . 128 E5
  Tavistock PL19 . . . . 147 D6
College Cl TR2. . . . . 71 C6
College Dean Cl PL6 . . . . 125 C5
College Gn
  Bodmin PL31. . . . . 109 E2
  St Austell PL25 . . . . 114 C3
College Hill TR10 . . . . 144 C7
College La
  Bodmin PL31. . . . . 109 F2
  Plymouth PL4. . . . . 128 F4
  Redruth TR15. . . . . 140 E7
College Ope TR10. . . . . . . 144 D7
College Park Pl PL3 . . . . . 128 E5
College Rd
  Camelford PL32. . . . . . . 105 D4
  Plymouth PL2. . . . . 127 E6
College Road Prim Sch
  PL2. . . . . 127 E6
College St TR14. . . . . 138 C3
College View PL4 . . . . 128 F4
College Way TR1. . . . . 69 E3
Colletts Ct TR16 . . . . 67 C5
Collford Lake Pk* PL14. . 36 E8
Collin Cl PL5. . . . . 123 D1
Collingwood Ave PL4 . . . 149 C2
Collingwood Rd PL1 . . . . 128 A3
Collingwood Villas **5**
  PL1. . . . . 128 A3
Collins Parc TR3. . . . . 80 F3
Coll of St Mark & St John
  PL6. . . . . 125 C4
Collon Field PL12. . . . . . . 61 D8
Colloian La TR26. . . . . 77 C1
Collygree Parc TR20. . . . . 89 E5
Colmers Row PL14 . . . . . . 51 F5
Colmers Row PL14 . . . . . . 51 F5
Col-Moor Cl TR27 . . . . . . 142 E7
Colne Gdns PL21 . . . . . . 129 B5
Cologer Cl TR12. . . . . 99 B2
Colston Cl PL6 . . . . 125 B6
Coltishall Cl PL5. . . . . 123 F4
Coltness Rd PL9. . . . . 136 B5
Coltsfield Cl PL6 . . . . 129 B8
Colver Cl TR27 . . . . 78 B6
Colveath Rd TR7 . . . . 110 F6
Colwill Rd PL6 . . . . 125 C3
Colwill Wlk PL6 . . . . 125 F3
Colworth Ave TR11 . . . . . 144 F3
Colwyn Rd PL11. . . . . 127 A3
COMBE. 136 E5
Combe La EX23 . . . . 6 F4
Combley Dr PL6 . . . . 125 D4
COME-TO-GOOD 82 B7
COMFORD. 80 F6
Comfort Rd TR11 . . . . 82 A3
Comfort Wartha TR11 . . . 92 F4
Commercial Hill TR3. . . . . 81 B4
Commercial Ope PL4 . . . . 149 B2
Commercial Pl PL4 . . . . . 149 B1
Commercial Rd
  Calstock PL18 . . . . 41 A3
  Hayle TR27. . . . . 142 C6
  Horrabridge PL20. . . . . . 42 C4
  10 Mousehole TR19. . . 88 C1
  Penryn TR10. . . . . 144 D7
  Plymouth PL4. . . . . 149 B2
  8 St Keverne TR12. . . . 101 C4
  3 St Mawes TR2. . . . . . 95 A6
Commercial Sq **3** TR14 . 138 D3
Commercial St
  Camborne TR14. . . . . . . 138 D3
  Gunnislake PL18 . . . . 41 A6
  Plymouth PL4. . . . . 149 B2
Commercial Terr PL28 . . . 107 D5
Commissioners Rd **1**
  PL26. . . . . 121 B5
Common La PL14 . . . . 121 B5
COMMON MOOR 37 F4
Commons Cl **3** TR12. . . . 99 A2
Commons Gate EX22 . . . 13 B8
Commons The TR12. . . . . 99 A2
Compass Dr PL7 . . . . 131 A7
Compass Point TR26 . . . . 141 D2
Compass W PL15. . . . . . . 18 C2
Compringey Cl TR1 . . . . . 137 B5
Compringey Hill TR1. . . . 137 B5
Compton Ave PL3. . . . . . . 129 A5
Compton CE Prim Sch
  PL3. . . . . 129 A5
Compton Knoll Cl PL3. . . 129 A6
Compton Leigh PL3 . . . . . 129 A6
Compton Park Rd PL3. . . 128 F5
Compton Rd **3** PL17 . . . 39 E4
Compton Vale PL3 . . . . . . 129 A5
CONDON'S SHOP 27 B5
Condor Cotts TR11. . . . . . 144 C2
Condurrow Rd TR14. . . . . 139 A1

Congreve Gdns PL5 . . . . 124 C1
Coniston Gdns PL6. . . . . 124 F4
Conker Rd TR27. . . . . 78 C1
Connaught Ave PL4 . . . . 128 F4
Connaught La **6** PL4. . . 128 E4
Connoc Cl PL14. . . . . 113 D5
CONNOR DOWNS 78 D5
Connor Downs Prim Sch
  TR27. . . . . 78 D6
Connor Hill TR27. . . . . . . 78 D6
Conqueror Dr PL5 . . . . . . 124 E1
Conrad Rd PL5. . . . . 124 D1
Consols Rd TR16. . . . . . . 80 F8
Consort Cl PL3. . . . . 128 E7
Consort Ho PL5. . . . . 123 B2
Constable Cl PL5. . . . . . . 124 D3
Constance Pl PL1. . . . . . . 148 A3
CONSTANTINE 92 E3
CONSTANTINE BAY 20 D1
Constantine Prim Sch
  TR11. . . . . 92 E4
Constantine St PL4. . . . . 149 A3
Convent Cl PL12 . . . . 122 E3
Convent of Mercy PL31. . 109 C4
Conway Cl TR11. . . . . 144 E4
Conway Gdns
  Falmouth TR11. . . . . 144 D4
  Plymouth PL2. . . . . 128 B7
Conway Rd TR11 . . . . 144 D4
Conyngham Ct PL6. . . . . 129 A8
Cooban Ct PL6 . . . . 129 A8
Cook Ct PL12 . . . . 122 B3
COOKSLAND 35 B2
Cooksland Ind Est PL31 . 35 B2
Cooksland La PL31. . . . . . 35 B2
Cooksland Rd PL31. . . . . 35 B1
Cook's Level PL26. . . . . . 85 C5
Cooksley Ct PL1 . . . . 149 A1
Cookworthy Rd PL2 . . . . 127 F6
COOMBE
  Camborne. 66 F3
  Perranarworthal. 81 B8
  Playing Place. 82 D8
  St Stephen. 58 B2
Coombe Dean Sch PL9 . 136 A6
Coombe Dean Sp Ctr
  PL9. . . . . 136 A6
Coombe Dr PL12 . . . . 119 A2
Coombe Hill PL26 . . . . . . 58 C2
Coombe Junction Halt
  PL14 . . . . 51 A6
Coombe La
  Cargreen PL12 . . . . 119 A2
  Crafthole PL11. . . . . 65 B5
  Penzance TR18. . . . . 143 D7
  Plymouth PL5. . . . . 124 D7
  Seaton PL11 . . . . 64 B3
  Truro TR4. . . . . 81 C8
Coombe Park Cl PL10 . . 133 A2
Coombe Park La PL5 . . . 124 A3
Coombe Pk
  Camborne TR14. . . . . . . 66 F3
  Kingsand PL10. . . . . 133 A2
  Penzance TR18. . . . . 143 E6
  Saltash PL12 . . . . 122 F2
Coombe Rd
  Callington PL17 . . . . 39 F4
  Lanjeth PL26 . . . . 58 D3
  Penzance TR18. . . . . 143 E7
  Saltash PL12 . . . . 123 A2
Coombes La **9** TR1 . . . . 137 C4
Coombe The
  Crumplehorn PL13. . . . . . 62 D2
  Newlyn TR18 . . . . 143 B3
Coombe Vale TR18. . . . . . 143 B3
Coombe View
  18 Perranporth TR6. . . . 55 A4
  Plymouth PL2. . . . . 127 F7
Coombe Way PL5 . . . . . . 123 F1
Cooperage Gdns **8** PL25 59 A3
Cooperage Rd PL25 . . . . 59 A3
Cooper Rd TR13. . . . . 98 C8
COOSEBEAN 137 A5
Coosebean La TR4 . . . . . 137 A5
Copes Gdns TR1 . . . . 137 C5
Copleston Rd PL6. . . . . . 124 E5
Coppard Mdws PL7. . . . . 130 B6
COPPATHORNE 7 A3
Copper Beech Way PL6 . 125 C7
Copperfields PL20 . . . . . . 42 B5
Copper Hill PL27. . . . . . . 142 D6
COPPERHOUSE 142 D6
Copper Pl PL1. . . . . 148 A3
Coppers Pk PL6. . . . . 125 E7
Copper Terr PL27 . . . . . . 142 D7
Coppice Gdns PL5. . . . . . 124 E2
Coppice Wood Dr PL6. . . 125 C7
Copse Cl PL7 . . . . 130 D4
Copse Rd PL7 . . . . 130 D4
Copse The
  St Austell, Sandy Bottom
    PL25 . . . . 114 F5
  St Austell, Tregorrick PL26 114 B1
Copshorn Rd PL31 . . . . . 109 C7
COPTHORNE 12 B3
Copthorne Cross PL15. . . 12 B2
Copthorne Gdns PL6 . . . 135 F5
Corea Terr PL1 . . . . 128 A2
Corfe Ave PL3 . . . . 128 F8
Coringdean Cl PL6 . . . . . 125 B6
Cormac Ct TR17 . . . . 89 C5
Cormorant Dr PL25. . . . . 115 A4
Corner Brake PL6. . . . . . . 125 D7
Corner Gdns EX23. . . . . . 4 D1
Corner Pk PL15 . . . . 26 C7
Cornerstone Ct PL11 . . . 127 B3
Cornfield Gdns PL7 . . . . . 131 B7
Cornflower Cres PL15. . . 106 E4

Cornhill Rd PL24. . . . . 60 B5
Cornish Birds of Prey Ctr
  The* TR9 . . . . 32 D1
Cornish Chough TR7 . . . . 111 B7
Cornish Cider Farm* TR4 55 B1
Cornish Cres TR1 . . . . . . 69 F4
Cornish Goldsmiths*
  TR16. . . . . 67 F5
Cornish Mines & Engines
  (Mus)* TR15 . . . . 139 C6
Cornubia Cl
  Hayle TR27. . . . . 142 C5
  Truro TR1. . . . . 137 F6
Cornwall Beach PL1. . . . . 127 D2
Cornwall Coll Camborne
  TR15. . . . . 139 B4
Cornwall Coll Newquay
  TR7. . . . . 111 A5
Cornwall Coll St Austell
  PL25 . . . . 114 D5
Cornwall Coll Saltash
  PL12 . . . . 122 D2
Cornwall Ctr* TR15. . . . . 140 B4
Cornwall Ho PL25. . . . . . 114 C3
Cornwallis TR26 . . . . 141 E2
Cornwall's Regimental Mus
  (Duke of Cornwall's Light
   Infantry Mus)* PL31. . . 109 F3
Cornwall St
  Bere Alston PL20. . . . . . . 41 B1
  Plymouth, Morice Town
    PL1 . . . . 127 D4
  Plymouth PL1. . . . . 148 C3
Cornwall Terr
  Penzance TR18. . . . . 143 E4
  2 Truro TR1. . . . . 137 C5
Cornwood Rd PL7. . . . . . 131 B4
Cornworthy Cl PL2. . . . . . 128 A7
Coronation Ave TR14. . . . 138 C3
Coronation Cl **2** PL17. . . 39 F4
Coronation Cotts
  Budock Water TR11 . . . . 144 C3
  Mabe Burnthouse TR10 . 81 C1
  St Keverne TR12 . . . . . . 101 D4
Coronation Pl
  Helston TR13 . . . . 146 C4
  Plymouth PL5. . . . . 127 E8
Coronation Rd
  16 Callington PL17 . . . . 39 F4
  Hayle TR27. . . . . 142 D5
  1 Illogan TR16. . . . . . . 67 E4
  Redruth TR15. . . . . 140 D4
Coronation Terr
  Blackwater TR4 . . . . 68 E5
  Truro TR1. . . . . 137 B4
  Veryan TR2. . . . . 83 D7
Coronation Way TR7 . . . . 111 C7
Corondale Rd PL2. . . . . . 128 B7
Corporation Rd
  Bodmin PL31. . . . . 109 B4
  Plymouth PL2. . . . . 128 D7
Corsham Cl PL5. . . . . 125 B6
Cort Simmons TR15. . . . . 139 C6
Cort Treloweth TR15 . . . . 139 B6
Corva Cl **11** TR26. . . . . . 77 A6
Corva Rd **3** TR26 . . . . . . 77 A6
Cory Cl EX23. . . . . 10 F6
Coswees Est TR3. . . . . . . 81 B4
Cosdon Pl PL6 . . . . 124 F1
COSWINSAWSIN 79 A5
Coswinsawsin La TR14 . . 79 A5
Cotehele Ave
  Plymouth, Keyham PL2 . . 127 F5
  Plymouth, Prince Rock PL4 149 C2
Cotehele Ho* PL12 . . . . . 40 F3
Cotehele Quay Discovery
  Ctr* PL12. . . . . 40 F3
Cotehele View PL18 . . . . . 41 A3
Cothele Cl PL17. . . . . 39 E3
Cot Hill
  Plymouth PL7. . . . . 130 B5
  Poundstock TR3. . . . . . . 81 B4
  2 Stratton EX23 . . . . . . 4 E1
Cot Hill Trad Est PL7 . . . 130 B6
Cot Rd TR15, TR16 . . . . . 67 D4
Cotsland Rd TR1 . . . . 137 F5
Cotswold Ave PL26. . . . . 58 E1
Cotswold Cl PL26 . . . . . . 58 E1
Cottage Gdns PL15 . . . . . 27 B7
Cottage Mews PL7 . . . . . 130 E4
Cotton Cl PL7 . . . . 130 F4
Cott Rd
  Lostwithiel PL22 . . . . 112 D2
  Lostwithiel, Polscoe PL22 112 D2
Cotts PL20. . . . . 119 B7
Cot Wood TR3 . . . . 81 B4
Couchwell La PL22. . . . . . 112 C2
Coulson's Bldgs **10** TR18 143 E4
Coulson's Pl **9** TR18. . . . 143 E4
Coulson's Terr **8** TR18. . 143 E4
Coulthard Dr TR3 . . . . . . 81 B4
Countess Bridge La TR27 90 A8
Count House La TR26 . . . 141 C2
County Cl PL7 . . . . 131 A5
County Rd EX23. . . . . 104 E2
Court Barton Cross PL9 . 135 C1
Court Barton Mews PL9. . 30 B4
Courtenay Rd PL19. . . . . 147 B6
Courtenay St PL1. . . . . . . 148 C3
Courtfield Rd PL3. . . . . . . 128 F5
Court Gdns PL25 . . . . 114 C3
Courtland Cres PL7. . . . . 130 D7
Courtlands PL12. . . . . 122 E1
Courtlands Cres **4** PL25. 115 A5
Courtlands Rd PL19 . . . . 147 B6
Courtlands Specl Sch
  PL6. . . . . 124 F1

Court Mdw PL13 . . . . 62 B7
Courtnay Cl PL13 . . . . 117 D4
Courtney Ho PL5 . . . . 124 B2
Courtney Rd
  Liskeard PL14 . . . . 113 D6
  St Austell PL25 . . . . 114 F5
  Truro TR1 . . . . 137 B5
Court The
  Camborne TR15 . . . . 139 C4
  Plymouth PL6 . . . . 125 C7
  Saltash PL12 . . . . 122 C2
Court View PL4 . . . . 136 F4
Courtyard Cotts TR4 . . . . 70 C6
Courtyard The
  Redruth TR16 . . . . 139 F2
  Truro TR1 . . . . 137 D3
Cove Hill
  Perranarworthal TR3 . . . . 81 D5
  Sennen Cove TR19 . . . . 96 B7
Cove Mdw PL11 . . . . 127 A6
Coventry Rd TR11 . . . . 145 B4
COVERACK 101 C1
COVERACK BRIDGES 91 E5
Coverack Prim Sch TR12 101 C1
Cove Rd TR19 . . . . 96 C7
Coverdale Pl PL5 . . . . 124 C1
Cove The TR4 . . . . 68 A7
Cowdray Cl PL12 . . . . 122 E2
Cowdray Terr PL12 . . . . 122 E1
Cow Lard Cl PL15 . . . . 106 A4
Cowley Rd PL5 . . . . 124 D3
Cowling Gdns PL14 . . . . 51 F6
Cowling Rd 2 TR3 . . . . 81 D7
COXFORD 10 D7
COX HILL 68 F2
COXPARK 40 D7
Cox Park Terr PL18 . . . . 40 C6
Cox's Cl PL6 . . . . 125 B1
COXSIDE 149 B1
Coxs Mdw EX22 . . . . 13 C7
Cox Tor Cl 6 PL20 . . . . 42 C3
Cox Tor Rd PL19 . . . . 147 E5
Coypool Rd PL7 . . . . 130 A6
Crabbs Cl PL15 . . . . 13 F1
Crabtree Cl 3 PL14 . . . . 113 B5
CRABTREE 129 E5
Crabtree Cl PL3 . . . . 129 F5
Crabtree La PL30, PL31 . . . . 109 D2
Crabtree Villas PL3 . . . . 129 E5
CRACKINGTON HAVEN 10 B7
Crackston Cl PL6 . . . . 129 B7
CRAFTHOLE 65 B5
Craigie Dr PL1 . . . . 148 A3
Craigmore Ave PL2 . . . . 127 F5
Craigside PL13 . . . . 117 D4
Cramber Cl
  6 Tavistock PL19 . . . . 147 B4
Cranberry Rd TR14 . . . . 138 B3
Cranbourne Ave PL4 . . . . 149 C4
CRANE 138 C2
Crane Manor Ct TR14 . . . . 138 C2
Crane Rd TR14 . . . . 138 C2
Cranfield PL7 . . . . 130 C7
Cranfield Rd TR14 . . . . 138 B3
Crammere Rd PL3 . . . . 129 A6
CRANTOCK 43 D3
Crantock St TR7 . . . . 110 D6
Crantock Terr 7 PL12 . . . . 128 A5
CRAPSTONE 42 B2
Crapstone Terr PL20 . . . . 42 B2
Crashaw Cl PL3 . . . . 124 D3
Craven Ave PL4 . . . . 149 C4
Crawford Rd PL1 . . . . 148 A4
Creakavose PL26 . . . . 58 B4
Creakavose Pk PL26 . . . . 58 A4
Crealy Adventure Park
(Cornwall)* PL27 . . . . 32 C4
CREAN 96 F5
Crease La PL19 . . . . 147 A4
Creathorne Rd EX23 . . . . 104 E7
Creative Unit (Krowji)*
  TR15 . . . . 140 A4
Creaz-an-Bre PL26 . . . . 58 D5
Crediton Wlk PL6 . . . . 129 E8
CREED 72 A6
Creed La TR2 . . . . 72 A7
Creedy Rd PL3 . . . . 129 C5
CREEGBRAWSE 68 F2
Creekside View TR2 . . . . 70 F4
Creeping La
  Newlyn TR18 . . . . 143 C3
  Penzance TR18 . . . . 143 C4
Crelake Cl PL19 . . . . 147 C4
Crelake Ind Est 1 PL19 147 B4
Crelake Pk PL19 . . . . 147 C4
Crellow Fields TR3 . . . . 80 F3
Crellow Hill TR3 . . . . 80 F3
Crellow La TR3 . . . . 80 F3
Crellow Terr TR3 . . . . 80 F3
Crellow Vale TR3 . . . . 80 F3
CRELLY 91 F7
Crembling Well TR15 . . . . 139 E6
CREMYLL 133 E7
Cremyll Rd PL11 . . . . 127 B2
Cremyll St PL1 . . . . 134 A8
Crescent Ave PL2 . . . . 148 B2
Crescent Avenue Mews
  PL1 . . . . 148 B2
Crescent Cl
  Hayle TR27 . . . . 142 C5
  Widemouth Bay EX23 . . . . 6 F5
Crescent Gdns TR1 . . . . 137 B4
Crescent Pl TR19 . . . . 74 F1
Crescent Rd
  Bugle PL26 . . . . 47 C1
  Truro TR1 . . . . 137 B4

Crescent Rise
  Constantine Bay PL28 . . . . 20 C1
  Truro TR1 . . . . 137 B4
Crescent The
  Bude EX23 . . . . 104 C5
  Camborne TR14 . . . . 138 D4
  Carbis Bay TR26 . . . . 77 C4
  Common Moor PL14 . . . . 37 F4
  Crapstone PL20 . . . . 42 B3
  Gunnislake PL18 . . . . 41 A6
  Landrake PL12 . . . . 53 C3
  Lifton PL16 . . . . 19 F4
  Liskeard PL14 . . . . 113 C6
  Looe PL13 . . . . 117 D1
  Newquay TR7 . . . . 110 E6
  Plymouth PL12 . . . . 148 B2
  Porthleven TR13 . . . . 91 B3
  St Austell PL25 . . . . 115 B5
  St Ives TR26 . . . . 77 A7
  St Mabyn PL30 . . . . 34 D8
  Truro TR1 . . . . 137 B4
  Widemouth Bay EX23 . . . . 6 F5
Cressbrook Cl PL6 . . . . 125 F2
Cressbrook Dr PL6 . . . . 125 F2
Cressbrook Wlk PL6 . . . . 125 F2
Cresthill Rd PL2 . . . . 128 B7
Creswell Terr TR19 . . . . 86 F7
Creykes Ct PL1 . . . . 148 A3
Cribbage Terr 13 PL31 . . . . 109 D5
Cricketers Hollow PL27 . . . . 21 E3
Cricket Pk EX23 . . . . 7 B6
Crift Cotts PL14 . . . . 51 F7
Crift La PL12 . . . . 64 F8
Crift Cnr TR11 . . . . 144 C1
CRIMP 3 A2
Crinnick's Hill PL31 . . . . 109 E4
Crinnis Cl PL25 . . . . 115 E3
Crinnis Rd PL25 . . . . 115 B3
Crinnis Wood PL25 . . . . 115 B3
Crinnis Wood Ave PL25 . . 115 D3
CRIPPLESEASE 77 A3
CRONFORD 34 C6
Crocker's Row PL18 . . . . 41 A6
Crockers Way PL15 . . . . 13 F1
Crockwell St PL31 . . . . 109 E5
Croft Cl TR14 . . . . 79 E5
CROFTHANDY 68 E1
Croftlands PL7 . . . . 21 E3
CROFT MITCHELL 79 E4
Croft Parc PL12 . . . . 102 F2
Croft Pk PL6 . . . . 125 C7
Croft Rd TR18 . . . . 143 C4
Croft Row TR16 . . . . 80 F8
Crofty Cl TR15 . . . . 139 C5
Cromartie Rd PL4 . . . . 149 C4
Cromer Cl PL6 . . . . 129 B1
Cromer Wlk PL6 . . . . 125 A7
Cromwell Gate PL6 . . . . 125 C7
Cromwell Rd
  Plymouth PL4 . . . . 149 C3
  St Austell PL25 . . . . 114 F3
Crookeder Cl PL9 . . . . 136 A5
Crookedor La PL11 . . . . 65 D5
Crooklets PL23 . . . . 104 C7
Crooklets Rd EX23 . . . . 104 D6
Cross PL30 . . . . 47 F1
Cross Cl TR1 . . . . 111 C7
Cross Comm PL12 . . . . 102 F2
CROSSGATE 19 A7
Cross Gn PL5 . . . . 19 F7
Cross Hill PL2 . . . . 127 E4
Cross La
  Camborne TR14 . . . . 138 D2
  Cross Lanes TR12 . . . . 99 C4
  Launceston PL15 . . . . 106 C8
  Stratton EX23 . . . . 4 F1
  Constantine TR7 . . . . 111 D7
Cross Park Ave PL6 . . . . 124 F1
Cross Park Rd PL6 . . . . 124 F1
Cross Park Terr PL26 . . . . 73 C4
Cross Park Way PL6 . . . . 124 F1
Cross Pk
  Buckland Monachorum
  PL20 . . . . 42 A3
  Crafthole PL11 . . . . 65 B5
Crossroads Cl PL28 . . . . 31 B8
Cross St
  Camborne TR14 . . . . 138 D2
  Hayle TR27 . . . . 142 D6
  Helston TR13 . . . . 146 B6
  Padstow PL28 . . . . 107 D5
  13 Penzance TR18 . . . . 143 E6
  13 Redruth TR15 . . . . 140 B4
  Wadebridge PL27 . . . . 108 B5
Cross Terr PL18 . . . . 40 F5
Cross The
  Camborne TR14 . . . . 138 D2
  St Dominick PL12 . . . . 40 D2
  St Newlyn East TR8 . . . . 56 B7
CROSSTOWN 2 B1
Crosswalla Fields TR13 . . 146 C2
Crosswater EX23 . . . . 4 F1
Crossway PL21 . . . . 130 C7
Crossway Ave PL4 . . . . 129 B3
Crossways TR11 . . . . 144 F2
CROWAN 79 C1
Crowan Prim Sch TR14 . . 79 C2
CROWLAS 89 C8
Crowlas Ind Est TR20 . . . . 89 B8
Crown Cl TR7 . . . . 111 A4
Crown Cres TR8 . . . . 56 B7
Crowndale Ave PL3 . . . . 129 A6
Crown Gdns PL6 . . . . 125 A1
CROWNHILL 124 F2

Crownhill Ct PL6 . . . . 124 F2
Crownhill Fort* PL6 . . . . 124 F3
Crownhill Fort Rd PL6 . . . . 124 F3
Crownhill Rd PL5 . . . . 124 C3
Crown Rd PL26 . . . . 58 D8
Crown Terr PL26 . . . . 58 D8
CROWNTOWN 91 B5
Crow Pk PL3 . . . . 128 F5
Crows-an-Eglos 5 PL26 . . 77 A6
CROWS-AN-WRA 96 F8
CROW'S NEST 38 B4
Croydon Gdns PL5 . . . . 123 E4
Crozier Rd 6 PL4 . . . . 128 F4
CRUGMEER 107 A7
CRUMPLEHORN 62 D2
Crum-Melyn Parc TR27 . . 142 B4
Crusoe Flats 4 PL26 . . . . 141 B6
Cryben PL12 . . . . 92 C1
Cryon View TR1 . . . . 69 E3
CUBERT 55 D8
Cubert Sch TR8 . . . . 43 D1
Cuby Ct TR2 . . . . 72 A3
Cuby Rd TR2 . . . . 71 F4
Cuckoo La TR10 . . . . 93 E2
Cuddenbeake Terr PL12 . . 65 B8
Cuffe Rd PL3 . . . . 128 C4
Culdrose Airfield TR12 . . 146 E1
Culdrose Cl TR15 . . . . 123 E4
Cullen View TR2 . . . . 71 C6
Culme Rd PL3 . . . . 129 A6
Culrose Cl PL3 . . . . 58 D7
Culroy Flats 12 TR1 . . . . 137 C4
Culver Cl PL6 . . . . 129 A8
Culver Ct PL12 . . . . 122 F2
Culverland Pk PL14 . . . . 113 C7
Culverland Rd PL14 . . . . 113 B8
Culver Rd PL12 . . . . 122 F2
Culvers Mdw PL15 . . . . 106 B6
Culver Way PL6 . . . . 129 A7
Culverwood Cl PL7 . . . . 131 C6
Culvery The PL27 . . . . 108 B4
Cumberland Rd PL1 . . . . 127 F1
Cumberland St PL1 . . . . 127 E2
Cumble Tor La PL12 . . . . 53 D2
Cundy Cl PL7 . . . . 130 A7
Cundy's La TR7 . . . . 58 D4
Cunliffe Ave PL9 . . . . 135 A6
Cunnack Cl TR13 . . . . 146 C7
Cunningham Pk TR10 . . . . 81 C1
Cunningham Rd PL5 . . . . 124 C8
Cunningham Way PL12 . . 122 D3
CURGURRELL 83 C4
Curlew Cl TR7 . . . . 110 B5
Curlew Mews PL3 . . . . 129 C4
Curlew Pk Ind Est TR4 . . 69 C3
Curlows TR8 . . . . 43 B1
Curnow Sch TR15 . . . . 140 B6
Curnows Rd TR27 . . . . 142 C5
Currian Hill PL26 . . . . 58 D8
Currian Rd PL26 . . . . 58 D7
CURRIAN VALE 58 D8
Curry La TR27 . . . . 12 E4
Curtis St PL1 . . . . 127 E1
Curtis VC Cl TR8 . . . . 56 B7
CURY 99 B4
Cury CE Prim Sch TR12 . . 99 A4
CUSGARNE 81 B7
Cusgarne Hill TR4, TR16 . . 81 B8
Cusgarne Prim Sch TR4 . . 81 C7
Custom House Ct TR18 . . 143 F5
Custom House La
  18 Penzance TR18 . . . . 143 E5
  Plymouth PL1 . . . . 148 B1
Customs House Hill
  TR23 . . . . 116 D4
CUSVEORTH COOMBES . . 69 B2
Cutcrew La PL12 . . . . 52 E3
Cuth Avallon TR1 . . . . 137 C4
Cutmere Hill PL12 . . . . 52 D3
Cutmere La PL12 . . . . 52 D3
CUTTIVETT 53 B5
Cuxhaven Way PL9 . . . . 88 F6
Cuxton Mdws PL20 . . . . 41 F3
Cypress Ave PL25 . . . . 115 F4
Cypress Cl 6 PL7 . . . . 131 C5
Cyril Rd TR1 . . . . 137 C5

D

Dabryn Way PL26 . . . . 58 B4
DADBROOK 132 E4
Daglands Hill PL23 . . . . 116 C4
Daglands Rd PL23 . . . . 116 C4
DairyLand Farm World*
  TR8 . . . . 44 F1
Daisymount Dr PL7 . . . . 31 F7
Dale Ave PL6 . . . . 129 C7
Dale Cl TR7 . . . . 111 A4
Dale Gdns PL4 . . . . 128 D4
Dale Rd
  Newquay TR7 . . . . 111 A4
  Plymouth PL4 . . . . 128 D4
Daleswood Rd PL19 . . . . 147 A4
Dalton Gdns PL5 . . . . 123 E3
Damerel Cl PL1 . . . . 127 F2
Dandre Apartments PL7 . . 111 A7
Dane Rd TR7 . . . . 110 D7
Daniell Ct TR1 . . . . 137 C3
Daniell Gdns TR1 . . . . 137 C3
Daniell Rd TR1 . . . . 137 B3
Daniell St TR1 . . . . 137 C3
Daniel Pl TR18 . . . . 143 E4
Daniels La PL25 . . . . 115 B4
Daniels Sail Loft 10 PL14 . . 117 D3
Danmore Cl PL34 . . . . 14 C7

Danum Dr PL7 . . . . 131 B3
DARITE 38 B4
Darite Prim Sch PL14 . . . . 38 A4
Darkey La PL16 . . . . 19 F4
Dark La
  Camelford PL32 . . . . 105 C4
  Liskeard PL14 . . . . 113 D6
  Lostwithiel PL22 . . . . 112 C1
Darklake Cl PL6 . . . . 125 E5
Darklake La PL6 . . . . 125 D8
Darklake View PL6 . . . . 125 E5
Dark Street La PL7 . . . . 130 F6
Darlington Rd TR20 . . . . 88 F6
Darloe La PL13 . . . . 117 C3
DARRACOTT 2 E4
Dart Cl
  Plymouth PL3 . . . . 129 D7
  St Giles on the Heath PL15 . . 13 F1
Dartington Wlk PL6 . . . . 129 E8
Dartmeet Ave PL3 . . . . 129 B6
Dartmoor View
  Plymouth PL4 . . . . 129 C3
  Saltash PL12 . . . . 122 E4
Dartmouth Wlk PL6 . . . . 129 E8
Darwin Cres PL3 . . . . 129 C3
Dashwood Ho TR11 . . . . 145 A6
Daubuz Cl TR1 . . . . 137 C6
Daubuz Cl TR1 . . . . 137 D5
Daucus Cl PL19 . . . . 147 B4
Davenham Cl PL6 . . . . 125 B6
Davey's Cl TR1 . . . . 144 E1
David Cl PL7 . . . . 130 F6
David Penhaligon Way
  TR1 . . . . 137 B4
David Southgate Ct PL1 . . 148 A2
DAVIDSTOW 16 A4
Davidstow Airfield &
  Cornwall at War Mus*
  P132 . . . . 15 F5
Davy Cl
  Torpoint PL11 . . . . 126 F3
  Tremar PL14 . . . . 38 A3
Davy Rd PL6 . . . . 125 C4
Davys Row PL14 . . . . 37 E4
Dawe Cres PL3 . . . . 109 C3
Dawes Cl PL14 . . . . 50 E7
Dawes La
  Looe PL11 . . . . 117 D5
  Millbrook PL10 . . . . 132 E5
  Plymouth PL9 . . . . 136 D7
Dawlish Wlk PL6 . . . . 129 E8
Dawney Terr PL11 . . . . 65 B5
Dawn Rd PL3 . . . . 117 D2
Daws Cl PL12 . . . . 123 A2
DAW'S HOUSE 18 E1
Daw's Mdw PL7 . . . . 105 E4
Dawson Cl PL3 . . . . 123 E1
Daymer La PL27 . . . . 21 C4
Daymond Rd PL5 . . . . 123 D2
Dayton Cl PL6 . . . . 124 E3
Deacon Dr PL12 . . . . 122 F1
Deacons Gn PL19 . . . . 147 A3
Dean Cross Rd PL9 . . . . 135 E7
Dean Cross Rd PL9 . . . . 135 E7
Dean Hill
  Liskeard PL14 . . . . 113 B6
  Plymouth PL9 . . . . 135 E7
Dean La PL14 . . . . 113 B6
Dean Park Rd PL9 . . . . 135 D7
Dean Rd PL14 . . . . 113 B6
Dean St PL14 . . . . 113 B5
Dean Terr PL14 . . . . 113 B6
Debden Cl PL6 . . . . 123 D4
Deeble Cl
  Plymouth PL7 . . . . 130 E7
  Threemilestone TR3 . . . . 69 C3
Deeble Dr 20 PL24 . . . . 60 B4
Deep La PL7 . . . . 131 C3
Deep Lane PL19 . . . . 147 D4
Deer Park Cl PL19 . . . . 147 C5
Deer Park La PL19 . . . . 147 C5
Deer Park Cres PL19 . . . . 147 C5
Deer Park Rd PL19 . . . . 147 C5
Deerpark Forest Trail*
  PL14 . . . . 50 C3
Deer Park La PL14 . . . . 147 C5
Deer Park Rd PL19 . . . . 147 C5
Deer Pk
  Newquay TR7 . . . . 110 D6
  Saltash PL12 . . . . 122 F3
Defoe Cl PL5 . . . . 124 C1
Degibna La TR12, TR13 . . 146 C2
DELABOLE 14 D3
Delabole Prim Sch PL33 . . 14 D2
Delacombe Cl PL7 . . . . 130 F7
De-la-Hay Ave PL3 . . . . 148 A4
Delamere Rd PL6 . . . . 129 D7
Delavue Terr PL32 . . . . 105 C3
Delaware Cotts PL18 . . . . 40 F6
Delaware Gdns PL12 . . . . 127 F2
Delaware Prim Sch PL18 . . 40 F5
Delaware Rd PL18 . . . . 40 F6
Delgany Dr PL14 . . . . 125 A5
Dell Cl TR18 . . . . 143 C3
Dell Mdw PL18 . . . . 18 B8
Dell The
  Plymouth PL2 . . . . 130 B6
  Tavistock PL19 . . . . 147 B6
  Truro TR1 . . . . 137 A4
DEMELZA 46 E6
Denas Water TR2 . . . . 71 A5
Dengie Cl PL7 . . . . 131 B5
Denham Ct PL6 . . . . 124 C2
Dennis Cl PL5 . . . . 124 D3
Dennis Gdns PL15 . . . . 18 C2
Dennis La PL28 . . . . 107 D4
Dennison Ave PL25 . . . . 115 A4

Dennison Rd PL31 . . . . 109 D5
Dennis Rd
  Liskeard PL14 . . . . 113 D6
  Padstow PL28 . . . . 107 D5
Dennybowl La PL12 . . . . 52 E3
Denyer Ct TR11 . . . . 145 A6
Denys View TR9 . . . . 45 F2
De Pass Gdns TR11 . . . . 145 C3
De Pass Rd TR11 . . . . 145 C2
Deptford Pl PL4 . . . . 149 A4
Derby Rd PL5 . . . . 85 C5
Derby's La PL26 . . . . 85 C5
Dereham Terr 6 TR1 . . . . 137 B4
Derowen Dr TR27 . . . . 142 B3
DERRIFORD 125 B4
Derriford Bsns Pk PL6 . . . . 125 A4
Derriford Health & Ctr
  PL6 . . . . 125 B3
Derriford Hospl PL6 . . . . 125 B3
Derriford Pk PL6 . . . . 125 A3
Derriford Rd PL6 . . . . 125 B4
DERRIL 8 D6
Derriton Rd EX22 . . . . 8 F6
Derry Ave PL4 . . . . 148 A4
Derry's Cross PL1 . . . . 148 B2
Derwent Ave PL3 . . . . 129 C5
Desborough La PL4 . . . . 149 C3
Desborough Rd PL4 . . . . 149 C3
Deva Ho TR7 . . . . 111 A6
DEVERAL 78 D2
Deveral Rd TR27 . . . . 78 D2
Deveron Ct PL7 . . . . 131 A5
Devington Ct TR11 . . . . 145 C4
Devington Hall TR1 . . . . 137 E5
Deviock Hill PL11 . . . . 64 C5
Devonia Cl PL7 . . . . 130 E7
DEVONPORT 127 D4
Devonport High Sch for Boys
  PL1 . . . . 128 A4
Devonport High Sch for Girls
  PL2 . . . . 128 C6
Devonport Hill
  Kingsand PL10 . . . . 133 A2
  Plymouth PL1 . . . . 127 F1
Devonport Leat PL6 . . . . 121 B5
Devonport Rd PL3 . . . . 127 F3
Devonport Sta PL1 . . . . 127 F3
Devonshire Ct PL11 . . . . 127 B3
Devonshire Ho
  Plymouth PL1 . . . . 148 B2
  2 Tavistock PL19 . . . . 147 B5
Devonshire St PL4 . . . . 149 A3
Devon Terr PL3 . . . . 128 E5
Devon Tors PL20 . . . . 42 D3
Devon Tors Rd 9 PL20 . . 42 C3
DEVORAN 81 F6
Devoran La TR3 . . . . 81 F6
Devoran Sch TR3 . . . . 81 F6
Diamond Ave PL4 . . . . 149 B4
Dickens Rd PL5 . . . . 124 B1
Dickiemoor La PL5 . . . . 124 C2
Dickna St PL15 . . . . 13 F1
Dicky La TR3 . . . . 82 D6
Diddies Rd EX23 . . . . 4 E1
Diddies Rd EX23 . . . . 4 E1
Dieppe Cl PL1 . . . . 127 F2
Digby Gr PL5 . . . . 123 D3
Digey Flats 19 TR26 . . . . 141 B6
Digey The 28 TR26 . . . . 141 B6
Diggory's Field 4 PL14 . . 38 A3
Dinas Ct PL11 . . . . 64 C5
Dinas Rd 1 TR9 . . . . 45 D6
Dingle Cl PL17 . . . . 28 D1
Dingle Rd
  Plymouth, North Prospect
  PL2 . . . . 128 A6
  Plymouth, Plympton PL7 . . 130 C6
Dingles Cl TR3 . . . . 81 B4
Dingle's Folly PL13 . . . . 117 C3
Dingles Way PL27 . . . . 21 E3
Dingwall Ave PL5 . . . . 124 E3
DINWORTHY 3 F2
Dipper Cl EX23 . . . . 5 A6
Dipper La EX23 . . . . 5 A7
Discovery Wharf 20 PL4 . . 149 A2
Distine Cl PL3 . . . . 129 B7
Dithmarschen Way PL25. . 114 B2
Dittisham Wlk PL6 . . . . 129 E8
Ditton Ct PL6 . . . . 129 A8
Dixon Pl PL12 . . . . 127 F4
DIZZARD 6 B1
Dobbin Cl PL28 . . . . 20 F2
Dobbin La PL28 . . . . 20 F2
Dobbin Rd PL28 . . . . 20 F2
Dobbs La TR1 . . . . 137 A4
Dobell Rd PL25 . . . . 114 E4
DOBWALLS 50 E8
Dobwalls Prim Sch PL14 . . 50 F7
Dockacre Rd PL15 . . . . 106 C6
Dockey 1 PL15 . . . . 106 C5
Dock La TR18 . . . . 143 F5
Dockray Cl PL6 . . . . 125 D4
Dockyard Sta PL2 . . . . 127 E4
DOCTON 2 E1
Doctors Hill
  6 Boscastle PL35 . . . . 9 C1
  St Keverne TR12 . . . . 101 C4
Doctors La PL12 . . . . 65 A8
Doctor's La PL14 . . . . 113 C6
Doddridge Cl PL9 . . . . 135 F4
Dodson's Gap TR12 . . . . 99 B3
Doidges Farm Cl PL6 . . . . 129 B8
Dola La TR20 . . . . 89 E5

Dolcoath Ave TR14...... 138 F3
Dolcoath Cl TR14...... 138 F3
Dolcoath Ind Pk TR14 ... 139 A4
Dolcoath Rd TR14 ...... 138 F3
Dolgey Post PL27 ...... 32 A4
Dolphin PL29 .... 22 D7
Dolphin Cl PL9.......... 135 D5
Dolphin Court Rd PL9 .. 135 F6
Dolphin Ho 15 PL4 ..... 149 A2
Dolphin Sq PL9 .... 135 F6
Dolvin Rd PL19 .... 147 C5
Domellick Cnr PL26 ..... 46 B1
Domellick Hill PL26 .... 46 B1
Domiert's Cl 11 PL14.. 113 B5
Donkey La
 Millbrook PL10........ 132 C4
 Portwrinkle PL11...... 65 A4
Donkey Pk PL28 .... 31 F8
Donnington Dr PL3 ..... 129 C7
Donnington Rd TR18 ... 143 C3
Donovan Way PL31...... 109 B4
Dopps Terr TR15........ 140 C5
Dorchester Ave PL5 .... 124 D4
Dorchester Cl PL14..... 138 E4
Doreena Rd PL9 .... 136 C7
Dorminack Cl PL26...... 58 D8
Dormy Ave PL3 .... 128 F5
Dorset Pk PL15 .... 13 A2
Dorsmouth Terr PL7 .... 130 E4
DOUBLEBOIS 50 C8
Doublebois Ind Est PL14. 50 D7
Doubletrees PL24....... 60 B4
Doubletrees Ct 2 PL24 .. 60 B4
Doubletrees Sch 21 PL24. 60 B4
Douglas Cl PL2 .... 47 A3
Douglas Dr PL3 .... 136 A6
Douglass Rd PL3 .... 129 C6
Doulton Rd PL25........ 115 A4
DOUSLAND 42 F3
Dousland Ho PL20 .... 42 E3
Dousland Rd PL20 ...... 42 D3
Dousland Terr PL20 .... 42 E3
Dovedale Rd PL2........ 128 A7
Dove Gdns PL3 .... 129 D7
Dover Rd PL6............ 125 E3
Dove St 15 TR26 .... 141 B5
Dower's Terr TR16...... 80 B5
Down Cl PL12............ 122 C2
DOWNDERRY 64 C5
Downfield Dr PL7........ 130 F5
Downfield Way PL7...... 130 F5
Downfield Wlk PL7...... 130 F5
DOWNGATE
 Kelly Bray 40 A7
 Pensilva 38 D5
Downgate Gdns PL2 .... 128 D8
Downham Gdns PL5..... 124 C7
Downham Specl Sch
 PL9 .... 135 F7
Downhorne Pk PL9 ..... 135 F6
DOWNINNEY 11 B1
Downlea PL19 .... 147 D4
Down Park Dr PL19 .... 147 D4
Down Parks EX23 .... 5 B7
Down Rd
 Plymouth PL7.......... 131 C5
 Tavistock PL19........ 147 D4
Downs Cl PL26.......... 58 C8
Downside Ave PL6 ...... 129 C7
Downside Cl TR7........ 111 A4
Downs La PL13 .... 117 B3
Downs Lane Pk PL13 ... 117 B3
Downs Rd PL13 .... 117 C4
Downs The PL13 .... 117 C3
Downstream Cl PL28.... 107 C5
Downs View
 Bude EX23 .... 104 D7
 Looe PL13 .... 117 D3
Down The PL20 .... 41 C1
DOWN THOMAS 135 C1
Downton Cl PL1 .... 148 A4
Dowren Ho PL27........ 142 B5
Dozmere TR3 .... 82 C5
Dozmere Cl TR3......... 82 C5
Dracaena Ave
 Falmouth TR11........ 144 F5
 Hayle TR27............ 142 E6
Dracaena Cres TR27 ... 142 E6
Dracaena Pl TR11...... 144 F4
Dracaena View TR11 ... 144 F5
Dragon L Ctr The TR1.. 109 F1
Drake Cl PL1, PL4..... 149 A3
Drakecircus Sh Ctr PL1 . 149 A3
Drake Ct
 Plymouth, Ernesettle
  PL5.................. 123 E4
 Plymouth, St Jude's PL4. 149 B3
Drakefield Dr PL23 ..... 123 A3
Drake Gdns PL19....... 147 C4
Drake Pk
 Padstow PL28 .... 107 C5
 Tavistock PL19........ 147 D5
Drakes Cl PL6.......... 124 F4
Drake's Pk 3 PL20...... 41 B1
Drake Villas PL19 ...... 147 A4
Drakewalls Gdns PL18.. 40 F5
Drakewalls Pk PL18 .... 40 F5
Drake Way PL9 .... 135 E2
Drang The TR9 .... 45 E1
Drannack La TR27....... 78 D4
Draper Terr 8 PL19.... 147 B5
DRAWBRIDGE 49 F8
Drax Gdns PL6.......... 128 E8
Draycott Terr TR26..... 141 C4

Drayton Rd PL5......... 124 C1
Dreysen Cl TR15 .... 139 C8
DRIFT.................... 87 F3
Drift La PL14 .... 49 C7
Drillfield La 9 TR26.... 141 B5
Drinnick Terr PL26..... 58 D6
Drive The
 Helston TR13 .... 146 D7
 Plymouth PL3.......... 128 E7
Driving La PL24......... 60 C6
Drogeada Cl PL15....... 27 D3
Droskyn Castle 19 TR6. 55 A5
Droskyn Cl 22 TR6..... 55 A5
Droskyn House Villas TR6 55 A5
Droskyn Way TR6....... 55 A5
Druckham Pl PL15 ..... 106 D5
Druckham Terr PL15 ... 106 D5
Druid's Lodge PL15 ... 139 D5
Druid's Rd
 Camborne TR15....... 139 D5
 Redruth TR15......... 139 D6
Drummer's Hill PL26 .. 114 C8
Drummond Cl PL2...... 127 F7
Drummond Pl PL1 ..... 127 F3
Drump Rd TR15........ 140 C5
Drunken Bridge Hill PL7. 130 D4
Dryburgh Cres PL2..... 128 A8
Dryden Ave PL15....... 124 C1
Dye House Cotts PL14 .. 36 F2
Dymond Cl PL32....... 105 B2
Dymond Ct (Kingdom Pl)
 PL12.................. 122 F2
Dynas-la Rd TR26...... 141 B4
Dynevor Cl PL12 .... 128 F7

DUNTERTON 28 F6
Duntz Hill PL16 .... 19 F4
Dunvegan Rd PL14...... 144 B8
Dunveth Rd PL27....... 108 A5
Dupath La PL17 .... 40 A4
DUPORTH 115 A1
Duporth Bay PL26..... 115 A1
Duporth Rd PL24, PL26.. 115 A2
Dural Cross EX22 .... 3 E3
Durban Rd PL3 .... 128 D5
DURGAN 93 D2
Durgan Crossroads TR11. 93 D3
Durgan La TR10........ 144 C8
Durham Ave PL4....... 149 C4
Durley Dene TR26....... 77 E4
Durnford St PL1 .... 128 A1
Durning Rd TR5........ 54 C1
Durrant Cl PL7......... 127 E3
Durris Cl PL6 .... 125 D4
Durris Gdns PL6 .... 125 D4
Durston Rd EX23...... 104 E7
Durwent Cl PL25....... 135 A6
DUTSON 106 E8
Dutson Rd PL15........ 106 C7
Dutson Terr PL15 ..... 106 C7
Dux Cross EX22 .... 8 C6
Duxford Cl PL5 .... 123 E5

Eagle Rd PL7 .... 131 C4
Earle's Retreat TR11 .. 145 B3
Earl's Acre PL3 .... 128 C4
Earl's Dr The
 Cawsand PL10........ 133 A1
 Kingsand PL10........ 133 B3
Earls Mill Rd PL7...... 130 E6
Earls Wood Cl PL6 .... 125 F3
Earls Wood Dr PL6 .... 125 F3
Eastbourne Cl PL25 ... 114 E3
Eastbourne Rd PL25... 114 E3
East Bridge 4 TR4...... 69 A3
Eastbury Ave PL5 ..... 124 A2
East Camps Bay PL11.. 64 D4
East Charles St TR14 . 138 E2
East Cl TR13 .... 146 D7
East Cliff PL13 .... 117 D3
Eastcliff Ave TR4...... 68 A7
Eastcliff Avenue No 2
 TR4 .... 68 A7
Eastcliffe Rd PL24..... 60 C5
East Cliff La TR17 ..... 89 C5
Eastcote Cl PL6 ...... 125 B6
EASTCOTT 3 A3
Eastcott Cross EX23 .... 3 A2
Estella Rd PL20 .... 42 D2
East End TR15......... 140 C5
Easterdown Cl PL9.... 135 F7
Eastern Ave PL14 ..... 113 D6
Eastern Gn
 Gulval TR18........... 88 E6
 Penzance TR18....... 143 F7
Eastern Green Pk TR18.. 88 E6
Eastern La TR14 ...... 138 D4
Eastern Wood Rd PL7. 131 D4
East Fairholme Rd EX23. 104 F7
Eastfield Ave PL9 ..... 135 C6
Eastfield Cres PL3 .... 129 A6
Eastfield Way PL25.... 114 F5
East Hill
 Camborne TR14....... 139 A5
 St Austell PL25....... 114 D3
Eastlake Ho 6 PL1..... 149 A2
Eastlake St PL4........ 148 C3
Eastlake La TR14 ..... 137 F4
East Park Ave PL4..... 148 C4
East Pk
 Pensilva PL14......... 38 D4
 Redruth TR15......... 140 D6
East Pool Pk TR15 .... 139 D6
East Quay TR27 .... 142 B6
East Quay Ho PL13 ... 117 D3
East Rd
 Kilkhampton EX23 ..... 5 A6
 Menheniot PL14....... 52 A5
 Quintrell Downs TR8 . 44 E3
 Stithians TR3......... 80 F5
East Rise TR11........ 144 F3
East Rosewin Row 10
 TR1................... 137 D5
East St
 Newquay TR7......... 110 E6
 Plymouth PL1......... 148 A2
 St Columb Major TR9 . 45 E6
 St Erme TR4........... 70 D8
Eastville 2 PL35 .... 9 C1
EGLOSHAYLE 108 D6
Egret Cl PL10 .... 133 A6
Eight Acre Cl 1 PL7 .. 131 C5
Elaine Cl PL30 .... 130 B5
Elbow La PL19......... 147 C6
ELBURTON 136 B6
Elburton Prim Sch PL9 . 136 A7
Elburton Rd PL9 ...... 136 B8
Eldad Hill PL1 .... 148 A3

East Youlstone Cross EX23 3 C2
Ebenezer Pl 11 TR18 ... 143 E5
Ebrington St PL4...... 149 A3
Echo Cres PL5 .... 124 D2
Eddystone Ct PL13 .... 117 D2
Eddystone Pl 3 PL27 .. 108 B5
Eddystone Rd
 Down Thomas PL9 .... 135 C1
 St Austell PL25....... 114 E5
 Wadebridge PL27 .... 108 B6
Eddystone Rise PL14 .. 113 D7
Eddystone Road Trad &
 Ind Est PL27.......... 108 B6
Eddystone Terr
 Plymouth PL1......... 148 B1
 2 Wadebridge PL27... 108 B5
Eden Cl 11 PL4....... 60 B4
Eden Gdns 14 TR18... 143 C1
Eden Project* PL24,
 PL26.................. 115 D8
Edenside PL3 .... 128 D7
Eden Terr 15 TR18 .... 143 C1
Edgar Rd
 Jacobstow EX23 ...... 11 A6
 Wainhouse Corner EX23. 10 F6
Edgar Terr PL4 .... 129 A4
Edgcumbe Ave
 Newquay TR7.......... 110 F5
 Plymouth PL1......... 148 A3
Edgcumbe Cl PL18 .... 41 A6
Edgcumbe Cres PL10 .. 132 F6
Edgcumbe Ct 3 PL3 .. 128 A3
Edgcumbe Dr PL19.... 147 B6
Edgcumbe Gdns TR7 .. 110 F6
Edgcumbe Grn PL25 .. 114 A3
Edgcumbe Ho PL1 .... 148 B2
Edgcumbe Park Rd PL3. 128 D6
Edgcumbe Terr
 Lostwithiel PL22 ...... 112 B1
 Roche PL26 .... 46 F3
 Saltash PL12.......... 122 C5
 St Austell PL25....... 114 A3
 St Dominick PL12..... 40 D2
Edgcumbe St PL1 ..... 128 A1
Edgcumbe Terr
 Milton Abbot PL19 .... 29 C6
 1 Par PL24............ 60 B4
Edgecombe Way PL18.. 40 E5
Edgecumbe Terr 14 PL20. 41 B1
Edgemoor Cl PL14 .... 38 A3
Edinburgh Cl PL25 .... 115 C3
Edinburgh St PL1..... 127 E1
EDISTONE 2 F8
Edith Ave PL4......... 149 C4
Edith St PL5 .... 123 D1
EDMONTON 33 B7
Edmund Rd TR15...... 140 B6
Edna Terr PL4 .... 149 C3
Edovean La TR20 ...... 89 E4
Edward Hain Com Hospl
 TR26.................. 141 B5
Edwards Cl PL7........ 131 B4
Edwards Cres PL12.... 122 C2
Edwards Dr PL7........ 131 B5
Edwards Rd
 Devoran TR3 .... 81 F6
 St Giles on the Heath PL15. 13 F1
Edward St
 Camborne TR14....... 138 F4
 Truro TR1............. 137 C4
Edymeade Ct PL15 .... 106 C5
Edymeade Gdn 9 PL15. 106 C5
Effingham Cres PL3.... 128 D7
EFFORD 129 C5
Efford Cres PL3........ 129 B6
Efford Down Pk EX23 .. 104 C5
Efford Farm Bsns Pk
 EX23.................. 104 C4
Efford Farm Cotts EX23. 104 C4
Efford Fort PL3........ 129 E6
Efford La PL3.......... 129 B5
Efford Pathway PL3 ... 129 C6
Efford Rd PL3.......... 129 B6
Efford Wlk PL3 .... 129 B6
Egerton Cres PL4 ..... 149 C3
Egerton Rd
 Padstow PL28 .... 107 E4
 Plymouth PL4......... 149 C3
EGGBEARE 21 A7
EGGBUCKLAND 129 C8
Eggbuckland Rd PL3 .. 129 C7
Eglos Ct PL30.......... 23 E7
Egloshayle Rd
 Wadebridge PL27 .... 108 D5
EGLOSKERRY 18 A5
Egloskerry Prim Sch PL15 18 A5
Eglos Mdw TR11....... 82 A3
Eglos Pdoc
 Mullion TR12.......... 99 A2
 Wadebridge PL27 .... 108 D5
Eglos Rd
 Ludgvan TR20 .... 89 A7
 Shortlanesend TR4.... 69 F6

Elder Cl 2 PL7......... 131 B5
Elderfield Cl 7 PL24 .. 60 D5
Eleanor Ho PL1........ 148 A2
Elerkey Cl TR2......... 83 F6
Elerkey La TR2......... 83 F6
Eleven Doors PL25 .... 115 B2
Elford Cres PL7........ 130 E7
Elford Pk PL20........ 42 D2
Elgin Cres PL5 .... 124 E3
Elim Cl PL3........... 128 E5
Elim Terr PL3.......... 128 E5
Eliot Cl PL15.......... 18 C2
Eliot Ct TR7 .... 110 F6
Eliot Dr PL12 .... 65 B8
Eliot Gdns TR7........ 110 F6
Eliot Rd
 St Austell PL25....... 114 E4
 Truro TR1............. 137 C5
 St Ives PL5........... 127 E8
Elizabeth Cl
 Bodmin PL31......... 109 D4
 Threemilestone TR3... 69 C3
Elizabeth Ct
 Bugle PL26............ 47 C1
 2 Plymouth PL1....... 149 A2
Elizabeth House Mus & Arts
 Gall* PL4............. 149 A2
Elizabeth Pl PL4....... 149 A4
Elizabeth Rd
 Bude EX23 .... 104 F5
 St Austell PL25....... 114 E3
Elizabeth Terr TR17 .... 89 B5
Ellen Cl TR4........... 68 C6
Ellenglaze Ct TR8 ..... 55 D8
Ellenglaze La TR8..... 55 D8
Ellenglaze Mdw TR8 .. 55 D8
Elliot Sq PL11......... 127 B3
Elliot St PL1.......... 148 B1
Elliott Cl PL12........ 122 D2
Elliot Terr PL1........ 148 C1
Elliot Terrace La PL1.. 148 C1
Ellis Cl PL7........... 131 B4
Ellison Gdns 3 TR13 .. 98 B5
Elliss Way TR7........ 142 C5
Elm Cl
 Callington PL17....... 39 F4
 Camborne TR15....... 139 D6
 Newquay TR7.......... 110 F5
 Tavistock PL19........ 147 C3
Elm Cotts PL12........ 122 C3
Elm Court Gdns PL14.. 137 D5
Elm Cres PL3, PL4 .... 129 A4
Elm Croft PL12........ 128 B7
Elm Ct TR1............ 137 D5
Elm Dr
 Bude EX23 .... 104 F5
 3 St Columb Major TR9. 45 D6
Elmgate Crossways PL12. 65 E8
Elm Gr
 Feock TR3............. 82 C5
 Plymouth, Eggbuckland
  PL6.................. 129 B8
 Plymouth, Plympton PL7. 130 E5
Elm Grove Cotts TR10 . 93 C6
Elmlea EX23 .... 104 F5
Elm Mdw TR3.......... 82 C5
Elm Meadow Dr PL13 . 117 D4
Elm Pk PL10........... 133 B6
Elm Rd
 Plymouth, Glenholt PL6.. 125 D6
 Plymouth, Mannamead PL4. 128 F4
 Elms Close Terr 25 TR18. 143 C2
 St Austell PL25....... 114 C4
Elm Tree Rd PL13 .... 117 D4
Elmwood Cl PL6....... 125 D5
Elowen Cl TR11........ 144 E2
Elphinstone Rd PL2 ... 128 C7
Elspeth Sitters Ho 11
 PL4................... 149 A2
Elwell Rd PL12 .... 123 A2
Elwick Gdns PL3 ...... 129 B5
Embankment La PL4... 129 B2
Embankment Rd PL4.. 129 B2
Embankment Road Lane N
 PL4................... 129 B2
Emily Gdns PL4 .... 149 B4
Emlyn Fields PL25 .... 114 F6
Emma Cl PL4.......... 129 B1
Emma Place Ope PL1 . 128 A1
EMPACOMBE 133 D6
Empire Way PL11...... 127 B3
Empress Ave 22 TR18.. 143 E6
Emslie Rd TR11........ 145 C2
Endeavour Ct PL1 .... 128 A3
Endsleigh Dr PL15, PL19. 29 F5
Endsleigh Gdns 2 PL4. 149 A4
Endsleigh Gardens Nursery*
 PL19.................. 29 B8
Endsleigh Park Rd PL3. 128 D6
Endsleigh Pk EX23 .... 77 F2
Endsleigh Rd PL4...... 149 A4
Endsleigh Rd PL5...... 123 D1
Endsleigh Terr PL14... 113 C6
Eningdale Rd PL9 ..... 147 A4
Ennerdale Gdns PL6 .. 124 E5
ENNISCAVEN 46 D2

Ennis CI TR4....56 D1
Ennor's Rd TR7....110 D6
Enys CI
  Carbis Bay TR26....141 D1
  Truro TR1....137 B5
Enys Cotts TR19....75 A2
Enys Quay 5 TR1....137 D4
Enys Rd
  Camborne TR14....138 D4
  Truro TR1....137 B5
Enys Redenek TR14....138 F5
Epping Cres PL6....129 D7
Epworth CI TR1....137 E4
Epworth Terr 4 PL2....127 F5
Erddiston Ct EX23....104 D6
Ergue-Gaberic Way EX23....104 D5
Eric Rd
  Calstock PL18....41 B3
  Plymouth PL4....149 C3
Erisey Terr TR11....145 B4
Erith Ave PL2....127 E7
Erle Gdns PL7....130 F3
Erlstoke CI PL6....125 D1
Erme Gdns PL3....129 C5
Ermington Terr PL4....128 E4
ERNESETTLE....123 E3
Ernesettle Cres PL5....123 E3
Ernesettle Gn PL5....123 E4
Ernesettle La PL5....123 E4
Ernesettle Prim Sch PL5 123 E4
Ernesettle Rd PL5....123 E3
Erow Glas TR10....144 C8
Esmonde Gdns PL5....127 B8
Esmonde Rd TR13....146 D4
Esperanza Ct TR11....144 F6
Esplanade PL23....116 C3
Esplanade Rd TR7....110 A6
Esplanade The PL1....148 C1
Essa Rd PL12....122 F2
Essex Dr TR15....139 B8
Essex St PL1....148 B4
Esso Wharf Rd PL4....149 C1
Eston CI TR10....93 C8
ESTOVER....125 E4
Estover CI PL6....125 F5
Estover Com Coll PL6....125 D2
Estover Ind Est PL6....125 E4
Estover Prim Sch PL6....125 D2
Estover Rd PL6....125 F4
Estuary View
  5 Falmouth TR11....145 B5
  Lelant TR26....77 E3
  Newquay TR7....110 D5
Eton Ave PL1....148 C4
Eton CI PL1....148 C4
Eton St PL1....148 C4
Eton Terr 3 PL1....148 B3
Eury Ct TR15....140 A4
Eureka Vale 7 TR6....55 A5
Europa Ct TR8....31 C2
Evans Ct PL1....148 A3
Evans PI PL2....128 B5
Evans Way TR20....90 C4
Evea CI TR1....69 F3
Evely Ct PL4....113 D7
Evelyn PI PL4....149 A4
Evelyn St PL5....123 D1
Evenden Ct PL11....127 A3
Example Cross PL15....27 B6
Exchange (Gall) The* 37 TR18....143 E5
Exchange St PL4....149 A2
Exe Gdns PL3....129 C7
Exeter CI PL5....123 D4
Exeter Ct 8 PL15....106 C6
Exeter St
  Launceston PL15....106 C6
  Plymouth, Barbican PL4....149 A3
  Plymouth, St Jude's PL4....149 B2
Exmouth Ct PL1....127 F3
Exmouth Rd PL1....127 F3
Explorer Ct PL2....128 B5

F

Factory Cotts PL14....51 F5
Fairbourne Rd PL25....114 F4
Fair Cross TR2....72 C6
Fairfax Terr 6 PL2....70 F5
Fairfax Terr 6 PL2....127 F4
Fairfield
  Plymouth PL7....130 E7
  St Germans PL12....65 A8
Fair Field TR20....89 B8
Fairfield Ave PL2....128 C7
Fairfield CI
  Lelant TR26....77 E4
  St Austell PL25....115 A4
Fairfield Pk PL15....26 C7
Fairfield Rd
  Bude EX23....104 E5
  Falmouth TR11....144 F4
Fairfields PL13....117 D5
Fairlight Rd TR1....137 D4
Fairmead CI PL12....53 E4
Fairmead Ct PL12....122 C3
Fairmead Mews PL12....122 C3
Fairmeadow TR10....144 B7
Fairmead Rd PL12....122 C2
Fairpark Rd
  Liskeard PL14....113 C5
  Wadebridge PL27....108 B5
Fair Pk CI 10 PL15....106 C5
Fair St TR9....45 E6

Fair View
  Bodmin PL31....109 B4
  Lanivet PL26....47 E4
Fairview Ave PL3....129 C5
Fairview Pk 5 TR9....45 E2
Fairview PI TR11....145 B4
Fairview Terr TR7....110 E6
Fair View Terr TR4....55 D8
Fairview Way PL3....129 E5
Fairway
  Saltash PL12....122 C2
  St Austell PL25....115 D3
Fairways The PL30....48 C7
Fairway The TR11....93 C2
FAIRY CROSS....49 B5
Falcon Terr EX23....104 C4
FALMOUTH....145 C4
Falmouth Art Gall* TR11....145 A4
Falmouth Bsns Pk TR11....144 E3
Falmouth Com Sch TR11....144 D3
Falmouth Docks Sta TR11....145 A4
Falmouth Hospl TR11....144 F4
Falmouth Marine Sch 17 TR11....145 A4
Falmouth PI TR11....86 F8
Falmouth Prim Sch TR11....145 A5
Falmouth Rd
  Helston TR13....146 D7
  Penryn TR10....144 E7
  Redruth TR15....140 C4
  Truro TR1....137 C3
Falmouth Town Sta TR11....145 B4
Falmouth Watersports Ctr 18 TR11....145 A5
Falmouth Wharves TR11 145 A6
Fanshawe Way PL9....135 C6
Faraday Mill Bsns Pk PL4....129 B1
Faraday Rd PL4....129 B1
Farfield PI TR7....110 B5
Faringdon Rd PL4....129 B3
Farley CI TR1....137 C3
Farm CI PL7....130 C7
Farmers CI PL14....50 B6
Farmers CI TR20....89 B8
Farmer's La PL14....50 B6
Farmers Mdw 8 TR13....143 C2
Farm La
  Plymouth PL5....124 B2
  Saltash PL12....122 D1
FARMS COMMON....79 F1
Farm Town TR15....140 C3
Farnley CI PL6....125 N6
Farrar CI TR27....142 E8
Farriers Cotts PL7....130 E7
Farriers Gn PL32....105 B2
Farriers The PL19....30 A3
Farrow Fordh PL26....46 F3
Faugan La PL14....143 B1
Faugan Rd TR18....143 B1
Faukener CI PL14....114 E1
Fayre View PL12....122 B1
Fearnside Way PL12....122 C3
Federation Rd PL3....129 C4
Fegan Rd PL5....123 B1
Feliskirk La TR17....89 B6
Felixstowe Ave TR7....111 E7
Fellowes PI PL1....128 A2
Fenten Pk PL12....122 F3
Fenteroon Rd PL32....105 C2
FENTONADLE....24 A5
Fentonluna La PL28....107 D6
Fenwick Rd TR11....145 B2
FEOCK....82 C5
Fern CI PL4....131 C5
Ferndale Ave PL2....127 E7
Ferndale CI PL6....125 D8
Ferndale Rd
  Falmouth TR11....145 A2
  Plymouth PL2....127 F7
Ferndale Terr PL14....113 B6
Fern Glen 18 TR18....143 A5
Fern Lee Terr 10 TR6....141 B5
Fernleigh Cres PL27....108 C4
Fernleigh Gdns PL27....108 C4
Fernleigh La PL27....108 C4
Fernleigh Rd
  Plymouth PL3....128 F5
  Wadebridge PL27....108 C5
Fernleigh Terr
  Gunnislake PL18....40 E5
  Nanpean PL26....58 C6
Fern Mdw PL19....147 D6
Fernside Pk PL14....38 A3
Fernside Rd TR14....138 B1
FERNSPLATT....81 B8
Ferrers Rd PL5....123 E1
Ferrets Cross EX23....11 A6
Ferris Town TR1....137 C4
Ferris Way PL23....116 D5
Ferry La PL11....126 D5
Ferry Rd PL11....127 E3
Ferry St PL11....127 C3
Festival Villas TR3....69 D3
Feversham CI PL7....131 B6
FIDDLERS GREEN....56 B5
Field CI PL22....112 D2
Field PI TR11....93 D3
Field The TR20....76 F2
Fifield Ho PL26....58 B4
Fillace La 10 PL26....42 C4
Fillace Pk PL20....42 C4

Filtrick La TR16....139 E1
Finch CI PL3....129 D4
Finches CI PL9....136 C7
Findon Gdns PL6....125 D4
Finewell St PL1....148 C2
Finnigan Rd PL4....129 B1
Finn VC Est PL31....109 D5
Finnygook La PL11....65 A4
Finsbury Rise PL26....46 F3
Fir CI
  Goonhavern TR4....55 D4
  Helston TR13....146 B7
  St Austell PL25....114 B3
Fir Cres PL26....58 D5
Fircroft Rd PL2....128 C6
Firebeacon Cross EX39....2 F7
Fir Gr 6 PL25....114 B3
Firsleigh Pk PL26....46 F3
First Ave
  Plymouth, Billacombe PL9....135 F8
  Plymouth, Stoke PL1....128 A2
Firs The PL26....58 E8
Fisgard Way PL11....126 D3
Fisher CI PL27....108 D6
Fisher Rd PL2....128 A5
Fish Mkt PL4....149 B2
Fish Quay PL4....149 A2
Fish St 9 TR26....141 B6
Fish Strand Hill TR11....145 B4
Fish Strand Quay TR11....145 B4
Fistral Cres PL11....126 F4
Fistral Cres TR7....110 A5
Fistral Ct TR7....110 A5
Fistral Sands Apartments TR7....110 D7
Fitzford Cotts PL19....147 B4
Fitzroy Rd PL3....128 A3
Fitzroy Terr 7 PL3....128 A3
Fitzsimmons Ct 7 TR13 146 C5
Five Fields La TR11....145 A5
Five Wells La TR13....146 B5
Flamank Pk PL31....109 C4
Flambards Experience The* TR13....146 E4
Flamborough Rd PL6....125 A7
Flamborough Way PL6....125 A6
Flamsteed Cres PL5....123 E1
Flaxmoor Terr PL13....109 D5
Fleet St PL7....127 E6
Fletcher Cres PL9....136 B6
FLETCHERSBRIDGE....48 F8
Fletcher Way PL9....136 A6
Fletemoor Rd PL5....123 E1
Fletewood Sch PL4....148 C4
FLEXBURY....104 E6
Flexbury Ave EX23....104 E7
Flexbury Mews EX23....104 E7
Flexbury Park Ct EX23....104 E7
Flexbury Pk EX23....104 E7
Flora Cotts PL1....148 B2
Flora CI PL1....148 B3
Flora St PL1....148 B2
Florence Hill PL17....39 F5
Florence PI
  Falmouth TR11....145 B3
  Newlyn TR18....143 C3
  Plymouth PL4....149 C3
Florence Rd PL17....39 F5
Florence Road Bsns Pk PL17....39 F6
Florence Road Ind Est PL17....39 F6
Florence St PL5....123 D1
Florence Terr TR11....145 B3
Florida Gdns PL26....59 C6
Floyd CI PL7....127 F7
FLUSHING
  Manaccan....101 B8
  Penryn....145 C6
Flushing Prim Sch TR11..145 B6
Folders La PL30....23 F6
Foliot Ave PL2....128 A6
Foliot Rd PL2....128 A6
Folkstone CI PL26....58 E6
FONSTON....11 C2
Forbes CI TR18....143 B1
Forbes Rd TR18....143 B1
FORD....128 A5
Ford PL22....49 E3
FORDER
  Cawsand....132 F1
  Saltash....122 C1
Forder Hill PL10....132 F1
Forder Hts PL6....125 C1
Forder La PL10....132 F1
Forder Valley Rd PL6....125 D3
Ford Hill PL7....130 E8
Ford Park La PL4....128 D4
Ford Park Rd PL4....128 D4
FORD PARK....128 D4
Ford Prim Sch PL2....127 F5
Ford's Hill TR12....146 C5
Ford's Row PL13....118 B5
Ford St PL19....147 B5
Foredown Pk PL14....38 C3
Fore St
  Ashton TR13....90 E3
  Barripper TR14....79 B5
  Bere Alston PL20....41 B1
  Bere Ferrers PL20....119 D5
  Boscastle PL35....9 C1
  Bugle PL26....47 C1
  6 Callington PL17....39 E4
  Calstock PL18....41 A3

Fore St continued
  Camborne TR15....139 B6
  Camelford PL32....105 D4
  Cargreen PL12....119 A2
  Carharrack TR16....80 F8
  Chacewater TR4....69 A3
  Constantine TR11....93 D1
  Crumpleton PL13....62 D1
  Fowey PL23....116 D4
  Golant PL23....61 B5
  Goldsithney TR20....89 E5
  Grampound Road TR2....72 A7
  Grampound PL12....72 A7
  Gunnislake PL18....40 F5
  Hayle TR27....142 D6
  Herodsfoot PL14....50 E3
  Kingsand PL10....133 A2
  Lelant TR26....77 E4
  Lerryn PL22....61 C7
  Lifton PL16....19 F4
  Liskeard PL14....113 C6
  Looe PL13....117 C3
  Lostwithiel PL22....112 C2
  Madron TR20....88 B7
  Marazion TR17....89 C5
  Mevagissey PL26....73 C3
  Millbrook PL10....132 E5
  Milton Abbot PL19....29 C6
  Mount Hawke TR4....68 C6
  13 Mousehole TR19....88 C1
  Nanpean PL26....58 D7
  Newlyn TR18....143 C1
  Newquay TR7....110 D6
  Par PL24....60 B5
  Penponds TR14....138 B1
  Pensilva PL14....38 E4
  Plymouth, Devonport PL1....127 F2
  Plymouth, Plympton PL7....130 C4
  Plymouth, Tamerton Foliot PL5....124 B6
  Polgooth PL26....59 A1
  Polruan PL23....116 E2
  4 Porthleven TR13....98 B8
  Port Isaac PL29....79 B2
  Praze-an-Beeble TR14....79 B2
  Probus TR2....71 C6
  Redruth TR15....140 B5
  Roche PL26....46 F2
  Saltash PL12....122 F2
  St Austell PL25....114 C3
  St Cleer PL14....37 E3
  St Columb Major TR9....45 E6
  St Day TR16....68 D1
  St Dennis PL26....58 C8
  St Erth TR27....142 A1
  St Germans PL12....65 A8
  Sticker PL26....58 E1
  St Ives TR26....141 B6
  St Just TR19....86 F6
  7 Stratton EX23....4 E1
  St Stephen PL26....58 D8
  St Teath PL30....23 E7
  Tintagel PL34....14 C7
  Torpoint PL11....127 B3
  Tregony TR2....71 F3
  Troon TR14....79 E5
  20 Tywardreath PL24....60 D5
Forest Ave PL2....128 C7
Foresters Rd PL9....135 D7
Forest Hos TR4....70 D8
Forest View PL6....125 D7
FORGE....68 A4
Forge Gdns EX23....6 F1
Forge Ind Pk TR14....138 E5
Forge La PL12....122 F4
Forge The TR3....82 A7
Forge Way PL6....69 F6
Forlaze Rd PL27....108 C3
Formal Ind Pk TR14....138 B4
FORRABURY....9 C2
Forrabury Hill 5 PL35....9 C1
Forregios Dr TR7....89 C5
Forresters Dr PL6....125 D7
Forsythia Dr PL12....122 C3
Fort Austin Ave PL6....125 C1
Fortescue CI PL26....58 D5
Fortescue PI
  Lostwithiel PL22....112 D3
  Plymouth PL3....129 A6
Fortescue Terr PL19....147 A6
Forth an Cos TR3....81 B4
Forth-an-Eglas TR3....68 D1
Forth-an-Nance TR16....67 C6
Forth-an-Praze
  Illogan TR15....139 D8
  St Day TR16....68 D1
Forth-an-Ryn TR15....140 D4
Forth an Streth TR27....142 D7
Forth an Tewennow TR27....142 D7
Forth-an-Tre TR27....142 D7
Forth an Ula TR27....142 E7
Forth an Veneth PL31....109 F7
Forth an Yre TR14....139 A3
Forth Coth TR3....82 A7
Forthcrom TR12....92 C1
Forth Dall 21 TR6....67 E4
Forth Gdns PL3....129 A6
Forth Gwedhen TR13....146 D8
Forth Kegyn TR15....139 B4
Forth Noweth 4 TR3....81 F7
Forth Scol
  Camborne TR15....139 D7
  6 Porthleven TR13....98 C8
Forthvean
  Camborne TR14....138 D1
  Portreath TR16....67 C5

Forth Vean TR13....90 E6
Forthvean Cres TR4....68 A4
Forthvean Rd TR4....146 E7
Forth Veor TR13....140 E7
Forthwras TR15....139 B8
Fort Picklecombe PL10...133 F4
Fosbrooke Ct 10 PL3....128 F6
Fort Terr PL6....124 F3
Fort The PL10....133 A1
FOSS....133 A5
Foster Dr PL31....109 C3
Fosters La PL14....14 C7
Fosters Mdw PL18....40 E6
Fosters Way EX23....104 F6
Foulston Ave PL5....127 B8
Foulston Way PL31....109 B4
FOUNDRY....142 E5
Foundry Dr PL25....115 B3
Foundry Flats TR27....142 B5
Foundry Gdns PL15....106 B6
Foundry Hill
  Hayle TR27....142 B4
  Stithians TR3....80 F3
Foundry Ho 3 TR27....142 B5
Foundry La
  Hayle TR27....142 B4
  Newlyn TR18....143 C2
Foundry Rd TR14....138 E3
Foundry Row
  Marhamchurch EX23....7 B6
  5 Redruth TR15....140 B5
Foundry Sq TR27....142 B5
Foundry Terr 6 PL27....108 B5
Foundry Terr PL27....108 B5
Fountain Ct 22 TR18....143 E6
Fountains Cres PL2....128 C8
Four Acres Rd PL2....83 F6
Fourgates Est PL14....51 F5
FOUR LANES....80 A5
Four Lanes' End TR19....97 F6
Fourlanesend Com Prim Sch PL10....132 F3
Four Turnings PL23....60 F3
Fowen Ct 2 PL14....113 B6
FOWEY....116 B4
Fowey Com Coll PL23....116 B4
Fowey Com L Ctr PL23....116 B4
Fowey Cres 27 PL17....39 F4
Fowey Gdns PL3....129 D6
Fowey Hospl PL23....116 C5
Fowey Prim Sch PL23....116 C4
Fowfield Row TR13....90 F3
Foxdown PL27....108 D5
Foxes La PL18....88 E6
Foxes La 5 TR19....88 C1
Foxes Row TR16....80 E8
Fox Field CI PL25....129 C5
Foxglove CI PL15....106 E4
Foxglove Way PL12....122 B3
FOXHOLE....58 D5
Foxhole Prim Sch PL26....58 D5
Fox's La PL1....145 B3
Foxstanton Dr TR10....144 D7
Foxs Yd PL31....109 C3
Foxtor Ct PL5....124 B3
Foxwood Gdns
  Plymouth, Plymstock PL9....135 F5
  Plymouth, Southway PL6....124 E5
Foyle CI PL7....131 A5
FRADDAM....78 D1
Fraddam Rd TR27....78 D1
Fradgan PI TR18....143 C2
Fradgan The 8 TR18....143 C2
Frances St TR1....137 C4
Francis Rd PL27....21 D5
Francis St PL1....148 A3
Frankfort Gate 9 PL1....148 B3
Frankland CI TR11....144 F3
Franklin CI PL27....108 D6
Franklyn CI PL25....114 F5
Franklyns Cl PL6....125 A4
Franklyns Cl PL6....125 A4
Franwell Terr 18 TR18....143 C1
Fraser PL15....124 C7
Fraser Rd PL5....124 C3
Fraser Sq PL5....124 C2
FREATHY....65 E3
Frederick Street E PL1....148 B3
Frederick Street W PL1....148 B3
Fredington Gr PL2....128 B6
Freedom Sq PL4....149 B4
Freeman Collins Dr TR11....144 F4
Freemans Wharf PL1....134 A8
Fremantle Gdns 4 PL2....127 F4
Fremantle PI PL2....127 F4
Frenchman's La PL12....53 C4
Frensham Ave PL6....125 C7
Frensham Gdns PL6....125 C7
Freshbrook Ct TR18....88 E6
Freshford CI PL6....125 C1
Freshford La TR16....125 C1
Friars' La TR12....102 F6
Friars' La PL1....149 A2
Friars' La TR12....103 B5
Friars Wlk PL19....147 E2
Friary Pk PL4....149 B3

Friary St PL4 . . . . 149 B3
Frith Rd PL12 . . . . 122 D3
Frobisher App PL5 . . . . . 124 D2
Frobisher Dr PL12 . . . . . 122 E2
Frobisher Terr **9** TR11 . . 145 A5
Frobisher Way
Tavistock PL19 . . . . 147 B5
Torpoint PL11 . . . . 126 D3
Frog La TR2 . . . . 71 F3
Frogmore Ave PL6 . . . . . 129 B7
Frogmore Ct PL6 . . . . . . 129 B7
FROGPOOL 81 C7
FROGWELL 39 D3
Frogwell Rd PL17 . . . . . . 39 E4
Frome Cl PL7 . . . . 131 A4
Frontfield Cres PL6 . . . . 124 E5
Front Rd PL11 . . . . 64 C4
Frost Ct TR11 . . . . 144 E5
Fuggoe Croft TR26 . . . . . 141 C3
Fuggoe La TR26 . . . . 141 C3
Fullaford Rd PL17 . . . . . . 40 A4
Fuller Rd TR6 . . . . 55 A5
Fullerton Rd PL2 . . . . . . 128 A5
Fuller-Tre Cl PL26 . . . . . . 46 F3
Furland Cl PL9 . . . . 135 C5
Furneaux Ave PL2 . . . . . 128 B5
Furneaux Rd PL2 . . . . . . 128 B6
Furniss Cl **6** TR1 . . . . . 137 D4
Furry The TR13 . . . . 146 B5
Furry Way TR13 . . . . 146 B5
Fursdon Cl PL9 . . . . 136 C6
Furse Pk PL5 . . . . 127 C7
Furzeacre Cl PL7 . . . . . . 131 A7
Furze Cross EX23 . . . . 8 B5
Furzehatt Ave PL9 . . . . . 136 A6
Furzehatt Park Rd PL9 . . 136 A6
Furzehatt Rd PL9 . . . . . . 135 F6
Furzehatt Rise PL9 . . . . . 136 A6
Furzehatt Villas PL9 . . . . 135 F6
Furzehill Rd PL4 . . . . 128 F4
Furze Pk
Polruan PL23 . . . . 116 D2
St Issey PL27 . . . . 32 D5
Trelights PL29 . . . . 22 D6
FutureWorld@Goonhilly
TR12 . . . . 99 F4

G

Gabriel St **5** TR26 . . . . . 141 B5
Gadiwall Rise TR27 . . . . . 77 E3
Gainsborough Cl PL7 . . . 110 D5
Gainsborough Ho PL19 . . 147 B6
Gains Cross EX22 . . . . 5 F3
Galileo Cl PL7 . . . . 130 E6
Gallacher Way PL12 . . . . 122 D3
Galland Rd TR1 . . . . 69 F4
Gallant's Dr PL23 . . . . . . 116 B3
Galleon Ct TR7 . . . . 110 D4
Galleries The **46** TR26 . . 141 B6
Gallery La
Landrake PL12 . . . . 53 A1
St Germans PL12 . . . . 65 A8
Galligan Cl TR19 . . . . 97 A6
Galligan La TR19 . . . . 97 A6
Gallops The PL12 . . . . . . 122 D4
Galsworthy Cl PL5 . . . . . 124 C2
Galva Rd PL7 . . . . 131 C8
GAM 24 A4
Gander La TR13 . . . . 146 B6
GANG 38 F3
Ganges Cl TR11 . . . . 82 C2
Ganges Rd PL2 . . . . 128 A5
Ganna Park Rd PL3 . . . . 128 D6
Gannel Rd TR7 . . . . 110 E4
Gannel View Cl TR8 . . . . 111 B3
Gannet Dr PL25 . . . . 114 F4
Gara Cl PL9 . . . . 136 B6
Garby La TR15 . . . . 140 C3
Garcia Terr PL15 . . . . 106 D4
Garden Cl PL7 . . . . 131 D5
Garden Cres PL1 . . . . 148 B1
Gardeners Way PL27 . . . . 32 E6
Garden House The * PL20 42 A3
Garden La PL19 . . . . 147 B5
Garden Park Cl PL7 . . . . 136 C7
Garden St PL2 . . . . 127 E4
Garden Village PL9 . . . . 135 F8
Garden Way TR8 . . . . 111 F3
Gards La PL5 . . . . 123 E2
Garfield Terr PL1, PL3 . . 128 A3
Garland Pl TR14 . . . . 138 D4
Garlidna **24** TR18 . . . . . 143 E6
GARRAS 99 D6
Garras Prim Sch TR12 . . 99 D7
Garrett St PL10 . . . . 253 A1
Garrick Cl PL5 . . . . 124 C2
Garris Cotts TR20 . . . . . . 88 E8
Garrison Cl PL1 . . . . 127 E1
Garro La TR12 . . . . 99 A1
Garston Cl PL9 . . . . 136 A8
Garth-an-Creet TR26 . . . 77 A7
Garth Marhas TR14 . . . . 138 C3
Garth Morcom PL14 . . . . 113 B5
Garth Rd TR18 . . . . 143 B3
Gascoyne Cl PL4 . . . . . . 149 A3
Gascoyne Pl PL4 . . . . 149 A3
Gas Hill TR1 . . . . 137 E2
Gashouse La PL4 . . . . . . 149 B2
Gasking St PL4 . . . . 149 A3

Gas La **8** TR15 . . . . 140 B4
Gas St TR14 . . . . 138 D3
Gateway Ct TR27 . . . . 77 E2
Gatewynyack TR12 . . . . . 101 C1
GATHERLEY 19 E1
Gavercoombe Pk **2** PL34. 14 C7
Gay's Hill TR12, TR13. . . 146 E4
Gays La PL12 . . . . 65 A8
Gdynia Way PL4 . . . . 149 C2
GEAR 99 F7
Gear Hill
Madron TR20 . . . . 88 C8
Mawgan TR12 . . . . 99 E8
Gear La TR20 . . . . 88 D8
Gears La TR17, TR20 . . . . 89 D6
Geasons La PL7 . . . . 130 E5
Geevor Cotts TR19 . . . . . 86 F8
Geevor Tin Mine Mus *
TR19 . . . . 74 F1
Geffery Cl PL12 . . . . 53 C3
Gendalls Way PL15. . . . . 106 B8
Gennys Cl PL18 . . . . 40 E6
George Ave PL7 . . . . 130 F6
George Cross PL7 . . . . . . 130 F5
George Downing Ho
PL6. . . . . 125 A1
George Fox Cl PL15 . . . . 106 A4
George La PL7 . . . . 130 F5
George Pl
Callington PL17 . . . . 39 E4
Plymouth PL1. . . . . 148 A2
Georges Paddock PL15. . 27 B3
George Sq PL1. . . . . 127 F1
George St
Plymouth PL1. . . . . 127 F1
Truro TR1. . . . . 137 C4
GEORGIA 76 E3
Georgia Cres PL3 . . . . . . 129 C6
Geraldine Terr PL12. . . . 122 C1
GERMOE 90 C4
GERMOE CROSS ROADS. . 90 C3
Germoe Cty Prim Sch
TR20. . . . . 90 C4
GERRANS 83 B2
Gerrans Cl PL25. . . . . 115 B5
Gerrans Hill TR2 . . . . 83 B2
Gerrans Parish Her Ctr *
TR2. . . . . 83 B2
Gerrans Prim Sch TR2. . 83 B1
Gerrans Sq TR2 . . . . 83 B2
Gewans Mdw PL25. . . . . 114 E2
Ghost Hill TR12 . . . . 99 A1
Gibbon La PL4. . . . . 149 A3
Gibbons Fields **9** TR12. . 99 A2
Gibbon St PL4 . . . . 149 A3
Gibbs La PL35 . . . . 9 C1
Gibraltar Terr **6** EX23 . . . 95 A6
Gibralter Sq **6** EX23 . . . . 4 E1
Gibson Way TR13 . . . . . . 91 B1
Gifford Pl PL3 . . . . 128 D4
Gifford Terrace Rd PL3. . 128 D5
Gig La TR3 . . . . 82 A7
Gilbert Cl PL26. . . . . 58 B4
Gilbert Ct PL7 . . . . 131 B6
Gilbert La PL7 . . . . 128 C5
Gilbert Rd PL31. . . . . . . 109 F4
GILBERT'S COOMBE 140 A8
GILLAN 101 C8
Gill-an-Creet TR26 . . . . . 77 A7
Gillard Centenary Flats
PL15. . . . . 106 B5
Gillbard Centenary Homes
PL15. . . . . 106 B5
Gilley La PL26 . . . . 73 A4
Gill Pk PL3 . . . . 129 B5
Gills Cl TR10 . . . . 144 B6
Gilly Fields TR11 . . . . 144 B6
Gilly Gabben Ind Est TR12 99 B7
Gilly Hill
Curry TR12 . . . . 99 B5
Redruth TR15 . . . . 140 C3
Gilly La TR26 . . . . 77 C1
Gilston Rd PL12 . . . . 122 D4
Gilwell Ave PL9 . . . . 136 B7
Gilwell Pl PL4 . . . . 149 A3
Gilwell St PL4 . . . . 149 A3
Gipsy La
Liskeard PL14 . . . . 113 A5
Sithney TR13 . . . . 91 C2
Gitchell La
Crowlas TR20. . . . . 89 C8
St Erth TR26. . . . . 77 C1
Glade Cl PL6. . . . . 125 A4
Glade The
Crapstone PL20 . . . . 42 B2
St Minver PL27 . . . . 22 A3
Gladstone Rd PL30. . . . . 109 C2
Gladstone Terr
Longrock TR20 . . . . 88 F6
3 Redruth TR15 . . . . . 140 C5
Gladwell Gdns **10** EX23 . 4 D1
Glamis Rd TR7 . . . . 111 B6
Glantis Cres TR9 . . . . 45 E2
Glanville Ave **11** PL19. . 147 B5
Glanville Rd PL19 . . . . . . 147 B6
Glanville St PL1, PL4. . . . 148 C3
Glanville Terr PL12. . . . . 122 F3
Glasney Pl TR10 . . . . 144 C2
Glasney Rd TR11. . . . . . . 145 A5
Glasney Terr TR10 . . . . . 144 D7
Glebe Ave PL12 . . . . 122 F3
Glebe Cl
Mawgan TR12 . . . . 99 D7
Pelynt PL13 . . . . 62 D5
6 St Columb Major TR9 . 45 E6
Glebe Cres PL27 . . . . 32 D6
Glebe Dr PL26 . . . . 46 F3

Glebe Est PL14 . . . . 38 F2
Glebelands
Callington PL17 . . . . 39 E5
Looe PL13 . . . . 117 D5
Glebe Mdw PL17 . . . . 39 E5
Glebe Parc PL30 . . . . 23 E3
Glebe Pl TR12 . . . . 103 B5
Glebe Row TR27 . . . . . . 142 D7
Glebe Terr
Constantine TR11. . . . . . 92 F4
Ruan Minor TR12 . . . . . 103 B5
Glebe The
Camborne TR14 . . . . . . 138 C3
Cubert TR8. . . . . 55 D8
St Mellion PL12 . . . . 53 D8
Tregony TR2 . . . . 71 F4
Week St Mary EX22. . . . 11 E8
Glenavon Rd PL3 . . . . . . 128 E5
Glenburn Cl PL3 . . . . . . 128 E7
Glencross Cl **3** PL14 . . 113 C6
Glen-Dale Cl **3** PL25. . . 115 A5
Glendale Cres TR4 . . . . . . 68 C6
Glen Dale Cres TR15 . . . 140 D4
Glen Dale Cres PL25 . . . 115 A5
Glendale Terr PL26 . . . . . 58 E3
Glendower Rd PL3 . . . . . 128 E5
Glendurgan Gdn * TR11 . 93 D2
Gleneagle Ave **4** PL3 . . 128 F6
Gleneagle Rd **4** PL3 . . . 128 F6
Gleneagle Villas **5** PL3 . 128 F6
Glenfeadon Terr TR16. . . 67 C6
Glenfield Cl PL6 . . . . . . 125 D6
Glenfield Rd PL6 . . . . . . 125 D5
Glenfield Way PL6 . . . . . 125 E6
GLENHOLT 125 D6
Glenholt Cl PL6 . . . . 125 D6
Glenholt Rd PL6 . . . . . . 125 D6
Glenhurst Rd **5** PL3 . . 128 E6
Glen Leigh TR15 . . . . . . 140 A6
Glenleigh Pk PL26 . . . . . . 58 E1
Glenmoor La TR12 . . . . . 99 A1
Glenmore Ave PL12 . . . . 127 F5
Glenmore Terr
Liskeard PL14 . . . . 113 D6
Mabe Burnthouse TR10. . 81 A1
Glen Park Ave TR15 . . . . 148 C4
Glen Park Prim Sch **6**
PL7 . . . . 131 B5
Glen Pk PL14 . . . . 38 D4
Glen Rd
Plymouth, Mannamead
PL3 . . . . 128 F5
Plymouth, Plympton PL7 . . 130 F6
Wadebridge PL27 . . . . . 108 B5
Glenside Rise PL7 . . . . . 130 E6
Glenthorne Rd TR3 . . . . 69 D3
Glentor Rd PL3 . . . . 128 E7
Glentowan Rd PL26 . . . . . 73 C6
Glen Vale TR15 . . . . 139 E6
Glenview PL25 . . . . 114 B3
Glen View
Callington PL17 . . . . 39 E5
Penryn TR10. . . . . 144 B8
Tywardreath PL24 . . . . . . 60 D5
Wadebridge PL27 . . . . . 108 B4
Glenwood Rd PL3 . . . . . 128 E6
Globerdon Rd PL14 . . . . 38 E4
Globe Sq TR16 . . . . 139 F2
Gloucester Ave PL25 . . . 115 C3
Gloucester Cres PL1 . . . 143 B1
Gloucester Ct PL1. . . . . 148 C4
Gloucester Pl
27 Newlyn TR18 . . . . . 143 C2
Plymouth PL1. . . . . 148 C4
Gloucester Rd TR18 . . . . 143 C2
GLOWETH 69 E3
Gloweth View TR1 . . . . . 69 E3
Gloweth Villas TR1. . . . . 69 E3
GLUVIAN 45 E7
Gluyas The TR11 . . . . . . 144 E1
Glynn Ave **8** TR13 . . . . 146 C5
Glynn Rd
Liskeard PL14 . . . . 113 A5
Padstow PL28 . . . . 107 D5
Glyn Way TR3 . . . . 69 D3
Goad Ave
Plymouth PL4. . . . . 149 C2
Torpoint PL11 . . . . 126 E3
Goad Cl PL11 . . . . 126 F3
Godding Gdns PL6 . . . . . 124 E6
Godolphin Ave TR17 . . . . 89 B5
Godolphin Cl TR17 . . . . . 89 B6
Godolphin Cres TR13. . . 90 E6
GODOLPHIN CROSS. 90 E6
Godolphin Ct **5** TR14 . . 138 D3
Godolphin Dr TR17 . . . . 89 B5
Godolphin Ho * TR13. . . 90 E6
Godolphin Ho PL19 . . . . 147 C5
Godolphin Pk **11** PL17 . . 39 E4
Godolphin Pl TR17 . . . . . 89 B5
Godolphin Prim Sch TR13 90 E6
Godolphin Rd
Falmouth TR11. . . . . . . 144 F5
Helston TR13 . . . . 146 C6
Longrock TR20 . . . . 88 F6
Godolphin Terr TR17. . . . 89 B5
Godolphin View TR14 . . 138 D1
Godolphin Way TR7 . . . . 111 B7
Godrevy Ct TR26 . . . . . . 141 D2
Godrevy Ho TR11 . . . . . . 69 E4
Godrevy Terr **28** TR26 . 141 B6
GODREVY TOWANS 66 B3
GOLANT 61 A5
GOLBERDON 39 C6
Goldbank Bglws PL30 . . . 34 C2
Golden Bank Pk TR11 . . 144 E1
Golden Sands **3** TR6. . . 55 A5

Goldfinch Cl PL15. . . . . . 106 E4
Goldfinch Gdns PL19 . . . 147 D2
Goldfinch Gr PL12 . . . . . 122 D4
Goldmartin Cl TR11 . . . . 93 D3
Goldmartin Sq TR11. . . . 93 D3
GOLDSITHNEY 89 D5
Goldsmith Gdns PL5 . . . 124 D3
Goldsworthy Way PL27. . 108 B5
Golf House Rd EX23. . . . 104 D6
Golf Terr TR7 . . . . 110 C6
Golf View TR14 . . . . 79 B2
Golitha Falls National Nature
Reserve * PL14 . . . . 37 D3
Golitha Rise PL14 . . . . . . 113 E6
GOLLAWATER. 55 A1
Golva Cl TR13. . . . . 91 E4
GONAMENA 37 F5
GONVENA 108 C6
Gonvena Hill PL27 . . . . . 108 D6
Gonvena Ho PL27 . . . . . 108 C6
Goodeve Cl PL9 . . . . 135 E6
Goodmans La PL14 . . . . . 38 D4
Goodwin Ave PL6 . . . . . . 125 A6
Goodwin Cres PL2 . . . . . 128 A6
Goonabarn Cotts PL26 . . 58 C5
Goonavean Pk PL26 . . . . 58 D5
GOONBELL 68 D8
GOON GUMPAS 68 F1
Goongumpas La TR16 . . . 68 E1
GOONHAVERN 55 E4
Goonhavern Ind Est TR4 . 55 D4
Goonhavern Prim Sch
TR4. . . . . 55 D4
Goonhilly Cl TR4 . . . . 55 D4
GOONHUSBAND 146 C1
Goonlaze Terr
St Agnes TR5 . . . . 54 D1
Stithians TR3 . . . . 80 D4
GOONOWN 54 D1
Goonown La TR5. . . . . . . 54 D1
Goonown Rd
Goonbell TR5 . . . . 68 D8
St Agnes TR5 . . . . 54 D1
Goonrea PL13 . . . . 117 B4
GOONVREA 68 B8
Goonvrea TR3 . . . . 81 D5
Goonvrea Cl TR7 . . . . . . 110 F4
Goonvrea Ct TR7 . . . . . . 110 F4
Goonvrea Rd TR5 . . . . . . 54 C1
Goonwartha Cl PL13 . . . 117 C4
Goonwartha Rd PL13. . . 117 B3
Gooseberry La
Pensilva PL14 . . . . 38 E4
Plymouth PL1. . . . . 148 B2
Gooseford La PL11. . . . . 132 C8
GOOSEHAM 2 E3
Goosewell Hill PL6 . . . . . 124 F2
Goosewell Park Rd PL9. . 135 F6
Goosewell Prim Sch PL9 135 F6
Goosewell Rd PL9 . . . . . 135 F5
Goosewell Terr PL9 . . . . 135 F6
Gordon Cl PL21. . . . . 122 D2
Gordon Pl **8** TR9. . . . . . 45 E6
Gordons Cl TR3 . . . . 80 F3
Gordon Terr PL4. . . . . . . 128 F4
GORRAN CHURCHTOWN. . 73 B1
Gorran Haven Rd PL14. . 38 E4
GORRAN HAVEN 85 D5
GORRAN HIGH LANES . . . 72 F2
Gorran Sch PL26. . . . . . . 85 B5
Gorse Cl TR7 . . . . 111 A4
Gorsey Cl PL5. . . . . 124 E2
Gorvin Cross EX39 . . . . 3 A6
Goss Moor National Nature
Reserve * PL26 . . . . 46 B2
Goswela Cl PL9 . . . . 135 F5
Goswela Gdns PL9 . . . . . 135 F5
Gotch Gdns PL14. . . . . . . 50 B6
GOTHERS 46 D1
Gothers Hill PL26 . . . . . . 46 D1
Gothers Rd
St Dennis, Gothers PL26. . 46 D1
St Dennis, Hendra PL26 . . 58 C8
Goudges La PL26 . . . . 58 E8
Gounce The **14** TR6 . . . . 55 A5
Gover Cl TR4 . . . . 68 C6
Gover La TR7 . . . . 110 D6
Gover Rd PL25 . . . . 114 B4
Goverseth Hill PL26 . . . . 58 D6
Goverseth Rd PL26. . . . . 58 D6
Goverseth Terr PL26. . . . 58 D6
GOVER VALLEY. 59 A4
Gower Ridge Rd PL9 . . . 135 D6
Goyne's Field TR4. . . . . . 68 A7
Gracca Terr PL26 . . . . . . 47 C1
Grade-Ruan CE Prim Sch
TR12. . . . . 103 B5
Grafton Rd PL4 . . . . 128 E4
Graham Ave PL25 . . . . . 114 E4
Graham Rd TR15. . . . . . 140 C5
Grainge Rd PL6 . . . . 125 A1
GRAMPOUND 72 B7
GRAMPOUND ROAD 57 E1
Grampound Road Ind Est
TR2. . . . . 57 E1
Grampound Road Village CE
Prim Sch TR2. . . . . 57 E1
Grampound-with-Creed CE
Sch TR2 . . . . 72 A7
Granby Cl PL1 . . . . 127 E2
Granby Gn PL1 . . . . 127 E2
Granby Pl PL1 . . . . 127 E2
Granby St PL1 . . . . 127 E2
Granby Way PL1. . . . . . . 127 E2
Grand Hotel Rd PL1 . . . 148 B1
Grand Par PL1 . . . . 148 B1
Grange Rd
Helston TR13 . . . . 146 B5

Grange Rd *continued*
Plymouth PL7. . . . . 131 A4
Yelverton PL20. . . . . 42 C3
Grange The TR14 . . . . . . 138 C2
Granite Way PL17 . . . . . . 39 F4
Grannery Ct EX23 . . . . . 104 D5
Granny's Gn PL31. . . . . . 109 E3
Granny's La TR6 . . . . 55 A4
Grantham Cl PL7 . . . . . . 130 B4
Grantley Gdns PL3 . . . . . 129 A5
Grant's Cl PL25. . . . . 114 C3
Grant's Wlk **4** PL25. . . . 114 C3
Granville Terr EX23 . . . . 104 D5
Grasmere Cl PL6. . . . . . . 124 E5
Grasmere La PL14. . . . . . 38 B5
Grassendale Ave PL2. . . 127 F7
Grass La PL2 . . . . 128 C6
Grassmere Way PL12. . . 122 D4
Grass Valley Pk PL31. . . 109 F1
Gratton Cross PL20 . . . . 42 D2
Gratton La PL20. . . . . 42 D2
Gratton Pl PL14 . . . . 125 A1
Gravesend Gdns PL11 . . 127 B3
Gravesend Wlk PL5 . . . . 123 D4
Graybridge Rd PL20 . . . . 42 C4
Gray Cres PL5 . . . . 127 C8
Great Berry Rd PL6 . . . . 124 F1
GREAT BOSULLOW. 87 D8
Great Charles Cl PL26 . . 58 B4
Great Churchway PL9 . . 136 A7
Greatfield Rd PL3. . . . . . 129 B7
Greatlands Cres PL2 . . . 128 A5
Greatlands Pl **5** PL2 . . . 128 A5
Great Mdw PL14 . . . . 36 F2
Great Mills Ind Parc
PL25. . . . . 115 E4
Great Mis Tor Cl **5** PL20. 42 C3
Great Orchard Cl PL9. . . 135 E5
Great Park Cl **4** PL7 . . . 131 C5
Great Western Commercial
Village PL22. . . . . 112 D2
Great Western Rd PL1. . . 148 B1
Great Wheal Seton TR14 138 F6
Greatwood TR11 . . . . 82 C3
Great Woodford Dr PL7 . 130 B6
Grebe Cl PL7 . . . . 130 F5
Greeb Way TR20 . . . . 89 D4
Green Acre PL15 . . . . 28 A5
Greenacres
Bodmin PL30 . . . . 34 C2
Plymouth PL9. . . . . 135 F8
Greenbank
Connor Downs TR27 . . . . 78 D6
1 Penzance TR18 . . . . 143 D5
Plymouth PL4. . . . . 149 A4
Polruan PL23. . . . . 116 D2
Greenbank Ave PL4 . . . . 149 B3
Greenbank Cl TR2 . . . . . . 57 E1
Greenbank Cottages
PL4. . . . . 149 B4
Greenbank Cres TR7 . . . 111 C7
Greenbank La PL14 . . . . 113 C6
Greenbank Rd
Devoran TR3 . . . . 81 F6
Liskeard PL14 . . . . 113 C6
Plymouth PL4. . . . . 149 B4
Greenbanks Ct PL7 . . . . . 21 E2
Greenbanks Rd PL27 . . . 21 C2
Greenbank Terr
1 Callington PL17 . . . . 39 F4
Plymouth PL4. . . . . 149 B4
Yelverton PL20. . . . . 42 D3
GREEN BOTTOM 69 B4
Green Cl
Feock TR3 . . . . 82 C5
Truro TR1. . . . . 137 B3
Green Cres TR13 . . . . . . 146 D7
Greendale Rd PL2 . . . . . 128 A7
Green Field Cl TR12 . . . . 102 F2
Greenfield Rd PL12 . . . . 122 D2
Greenfield Terr TR16. . . . 67 D6
Greenfinch Cres PL12 . . 122 E4
Green Hill
Lamerton PL19 . . . . 30 A3
St Martin TR12. . . . . . . 100 D6
Tavistock PL19. . . . . 147 D5
Wadebridge PL27 . . . . . 108 C5
Greenhill Cl PL9 . . . . 135 F5
Greenhill Rd PL6 . . . . . . 136 A5
Greenhills PL32. . . . . 105 C5
Green Hill Terr TR12 . . . 100 D6
Green Hill Villas PL27 . . 108 C5
Green La
Bodmin PL31 . . . . 109 F2
Boscastle PL35 . . . . 9 C1
Crantock TR8 . . . . 43 D3
Fowey PL23 . . . . 116 C5
Gwithian TR27 . . . . 66 B2
Kingsand PL10. . . . . 133 A2
Lelant TR26 . . . . 141 B2
Lizard TR12 . . . . 103 A2
Marazion TR17 . . . . 89 B6
Penryn TR10. . . . . 144 B8
Porthleven TR13 . . . . . . 91 B1
Portreath TR16 . . . . 67 C6
Redruth, Plain-an-Gwarry
TR15. . . . . 140 C5
Redruth, Wheal Rose TR16 . 68 C4
Rock PL27 . . . . 21 D2
Tavistock PL19. . . . . 147 E5
Truro TR1. . . . . 137 B3
Veryan TR2 . . . . 83 F6
Yelverton PL20. . . . . 42 C1
Greenland PL10 . . . . 132 F5
Greenlands Est PL19 . . . 147 D5
Green Lane Cl TR10 . . . . 144 B8
Green Lane Hill TR18. . . 143 F6

Green Lane Vean TR15 . . . . 140 B5
Green Lane W TR17 . . . . 89 B6
Green La The TR27 . . . . 77 F1
Greenlees Dr PL7 . . . . 131 B3
Greenmarket The 26
 TR18 . . . . 143 E5
Green Mdws PL32 . . . . 105 C4
Green Park Rd TR27 . . . . . . 142 D5
Green Park Ave PL4 . . . . . . 128 D4
Green Park Rd PL9 . . . . 135 E5
Green Pk PL10 . . . . 133 A2
GREENSPLAT 59 A6
Greensplat Rd PL25 . . . . . . 114 A6
Green St
 Penzance TR18 . . . . 143 F4
 Truro TR1 . . . . 137 D4
Greens The TR19 . . . . 96 C7
Greensway Rd PL19 . . . . . . 147 A4
Green The
 Bridgerule EX22 . . . . 8 A5
 Carnon Downs TR3 . . . . . . 82 A5
 5 Horrabridge PL20 . . . . . . 42 C5
 Kingsand PL10 . . . . 133 A2
 Liskeard PL14 . . . . 113 B5
 Mxwy PL20 . . . . 42 F2
 Milton Combe PL20 . . . . . 120 F8
 Nancegollan TR13 . . . . 91 B7
 Plymouth, Ernesettle PL5 . 123 E3
 Plymouth, Hooe PL9 . . . . 135 B6
 Probus TR2 . . . . 71 C6
 Saltash PL12 . . . . 122 C3
 St Buryan TR19 . . . . 97 A6
 St Martin TR12 . . . . 100 D6
 5 Trewoon PL25 . . . . 59 A3
Greenway Ave PL7 . . . . 130 B6
Greenway CI 2 PL20 . . . . . . 42 C5
Greenwich PI PL12 . . . . 122 F3
Greenwich Rd TR1 . . . . 137 B3
Greenwith Cres TR3 . . . . . . 81 D6
Greenwith Hill TR3 . . . . 81 D6
Greenwith Rd TR3 . . . . 81 D6
Greenwood Cres TR10 . . . . 144 A8
Greenwood Park CI PL7 . . . 131 A6
Greenwood Park Rd PL7 . . 131 B6
Greenwood Rd TR10 . . . . . . 144 A8
Gregor Rd TR1 . . . . 137 F5
Gregory's CI 10 PL31 . . . . 109 D5
Gregory's Mdw PL15 . . . . . 106 F3
Grenfell Ave PL12 . . . . 122 D3
Grenfell Gdns PL12 . . . . . . 122 C3
Grenfell St 15 TR19 . . . . . . 88 C1
Grenifer Rd TR15 . . . . 139 D7
Grenna La TR3 . . . . 81 D7
GRENOFEN 42 A6
Grenofen CI PL19 . . . . 42 A6
Grenville CI PL17 . . . . 39 F4
Grenville Cres TR11 . . . . . . 144 F5
Grenville CI
 Plymouth PL7 . . . . 131 C6
 2 St Austell PL25 . . . . . . 114 C3
Grenville Dr
 6 St Agnes TR5 . . . . 54 D1
 Tavistock PL19 . . . . 147 B3
Grenville Gdns TR14 . . . . . . 79 E5
Grenville Mdws
 Lostwithiel PL22 . . . . 112 E2
 St Austell PL25 . . . . 58 D7
Grenville Pk PL20 . . . . 42 D2
Grenville Rd
 Falmouth TR11 . . . . 145 A5
 Helston TR13 . . . . 146 D5
 Lostwithiel PL22 . . . . 112 E2
 Padstow PL28 . . . . 107 C4
 Plymouth PL4 . . . . 149 C3
 Truro TR1 . . . . 137 B5
Grenville Road Lane S
 PL4 . . . . 129 B2
Grenville Wlk PL13 . . . . 62 D2
Gresham CI
 Newquay TR7 . . . . 110 F4
 Plymouth PL5 . . . . 124 C7
Greyfriars TR11 . . . . 145 C2
Greys Terr TR13 . . . . 140 F1
Greystone Ave PL26 . . . . . . 58 E5
Greystones TR9 . . . . 57 E8
Gribbas CI TR3 . . . . 80 F3
Gribbas Cnr TR3 . . . . 80 F3
Gribben CI PL25 . . . . 114 E6
Gribben Rd PL25 . . . . 114 E6
Gribbon Way PL24 . . . . 60 C4
Griffins The PL14 . . . . 113 D6
Griffin Way PL9 . . . . 136 C6
Griggs CI PL7 . . . . 131 B4
Griggs Hill TR27 . . . . 77 E3
GRIMSCOTT 5 A2
Grimscott Est EX23 . . . . . . 5 B2
Grimspound CI PL6 . . . . . . 129 E8
Grimstone Terr PL20 . . . . . 42 B2
Grist La TR27 . . . . 78 C5
Grizedale Rd PL6 . . . . 129 D7
Grose Hill Cres 11 PL26 . . 59 D7
Grose Mdws PL26 . . . . 58 B8
Grosvenor Ave TR1 . . . . . . 137 B4
Grosvenor Cotts 1 PL14 . . 128 F4
Grosvenor PI PL25 . . . . 114 B4
Grosvenor Rd PL6 . . . . 124 F2
Grove Cotts TR9 . . . . 57 C1
Grove Dr 4 PL14 . . . . 51 A7
Grove Hill
 Mawnan Smith TR11 . . . . . 93 D3
 St Mawes TR2 . . . . 95 A6
Grovehill Cres TR11 . . . . . . 145 C3
Grovehill Rd TR11 . . . . 145 C3
Grovehill Ho TR11 . . . . 145 B3
Grove La TR19 . . . . 89 F5
Grove Park Ct PL14 . . . . . . 113 B4

Grove Pk
 Par PL24 . . . . 60 C6
 Tavistock PL19 . . . . 147 D5
 Torpoint PL11 . . . . 126 E3
Grove PI 3 TR11 . . . . 145 C3
Grove Rd
 Par PL24 . . . . 115 F6
 St Austell PL25 . . . . 114 B4
Grove The
 Plymouth, Plymstock
 PL9 . . . . 135 D8
 Plymouth, Stoke PL3 . . . . 128 A4
Grovewood Ct TR9 . . . . 45 E1
GRUMBLA 87 C4
Grylls Parc TR13 . . . . 146 B6
Grylls Pk PL13 . . . . 62 A7
Guardian Ct 6 PL31 . . . . . 109 E5
Gue The 2 TR13 . . . . 98 C8
GUILDFORD 142 E6
Guildford CI
 Foxhole PL26 . . . . 58 D6
 Plymouth PL5 . . . . 124 E3
Guildford Rd Ind Est
 TR27 . . . . 142 E6
Guildford St 4 TR27 . . . . . 143 A3
Guildhall La PL22 . . . . 112 C2
Guildhall Sq PL1 . . . . 148 C2
Guineaport Parc PL27 . . . . 108 C5
Guineaport Rd PL27 . . . . . 108 C5
Guipavas Rd PL17 . . . . 39 F4
Guissney PI TR13 . . . . 91 B1
Guiland Rd PL27 . . . . 21 D6
Gull Rock
 Newquay TR7 . . . . 110 A5
 Wadebridge PL27 . . . . 21 D2
GULVAL 88 E3
Gulval Almshouses TR18 . 143 F8
Gulval Cross TR18 . . . . . . 143 F8
Gulval Prim Sch TR18 . . . . . 88 E6
GULWORTHY 41 B8
Gulworthy Cotts PL19 . . . . . 41 B7
Gulworthy Cross PL19 . . . . 41 B7
Gulworthy Prim Sch PL19 . 41 B7
Gun Hill Rd TR8 . . . . 43 B1
GUNNISLAKE 40 F6
Gunnislake Prim Sch
 PL18 . . . . 40 F6
Gunnislake Rural Workshops
 PL18 . . . . 40 F6
Gunnislake Sta PL18 . . . . . 40 F5
Gunpool La 9 PL35 . . . . 9 C1
Gunver PL28 . . . . 31 F7
GUNWALLOE 98 E5
Gunwennap PL32 . . . . 10 B2
Gurlyn Hill TR20 . . . . 90 A7
Gurnard Wlk PL3 . . . . 129 C6
Gurney CI
 Bude EX23 . . . . 104 E7
 Torpoint PL11 . . . . 126 F3
Gurney's La 2 TR14 . . . . . 138 D3
Gurneys Mews 6 TR14 . . . 138 D3
Gurnick Est TR18 . . . . 143 B2
Gurnick Rd TR18 . . . . 143 B1
Gurnick St 2 TR18 . . . . 88 C1
Gustavus Rd TR14 . . . . . . 138 D3
Gustory Rd TR8 . . . . 43 D3
Guy Miles Way PL5 . . . . . . 124 B3
GWALLON 89 C6
Gwallon La TR17 . . . . 89 C6
Gwallon Rd PL25 . . . . 114 F5
Gwarnick Rd TR1 . . . . 137 B4
Gwarth an Drae TR13 . . . . 146 C3
Gwarth an Dre TR27 . . . . . 142 E8
GWAVAS 91 D4
Gwavas Bglws 4 TR18 . . . 143 C1
Gwavas La TR18 . . . . 88 C2
Gwavas Quay 7 TR18 . . . . 143 C2
Gwavas Rd TR18 . . . . 143 C1
Gwavas St 9 TR18 . . . . 143 E6
Gweal-an-Top TR15 . . . . . 140 D5
Gweal Darras TR10 . . . . 81 C1
Gwealdues TR13 . . . . 146 D7
GWEALFOLDS 146 C2
Gweal Gollas TR27 . . . . . . 142 E8
Gwealhellis Warren
 TR13 . . . . 146 B7
Gwealmayowe Pk TR13 . . 146 D6
Gweal Pawl TR15 . . . . 140 A4
Gweal Wartha TR13 . . . . . 146 B8
Gwedhennek TR18 . . . . . . 143 F7
GWEEK 92 C1
Gweek Dr
 Gweek TR12 . . . . 92 D1
 Mawgan TR12 . . . . 99 D8
Gweek La TR13 . . . . 92 A3
Gwel an Garrek 2 TR12 . . . 99 A1
Gwel-an-mor
 1 Marazion TR17 . . . . 89 C5
 St Austell PL25 . . . . 115 A5
 Trenance TR8 . . . . 31 C2
Gwel-an-mor Apartments
 TR26 . . . . 141 C4
Gwelannor CI TR26 . . . . . . 141 D2
Gwelannor Rd TR26 . . . . . 141 D2
Gwel-an-Nans CI 2
 PL14 . . . . 113 B5
Gwel-an-Scol TR3 . . . . 82 C5
Gwel-an-Skol TR14 . . . . . 138 C5
Gwel an Wheal TR26 . . . . 141 A4
Gwel an Wheal Cres
 TR26 . . . . 141 A4
Gwel Avon Bsns Pk PL12 122 D4
Gwelavon CI PL27 . . . . . . 108 D5
Gwelenys Rd 3 TR19 . . . . . 88 C1
Gwel Eryon 3 TR14 . . . . . 138 F2
Gwel Gwarthe TR16 . . . . . . 68 C3

Gwell-an-Nans TR2 . . . . . . 71 C6
Gwel Lewern TR18 . . . . 88 E6
Gwel Marten Flats TR26 . 141 E2
Gwelmeneth Pk 8 PL14 . . 38 A3
Gwel Mengleth PL27 . . . . . 108 D5
Gwelmor TR14 . . . . 138 E2
Gwel-Mor TR19 . . . . 75 A1
Gwel-Tek TR27 . . . . 142 D8
Gwel Trencrom TR27 . . . . 142 B3
Gwendra La PL26 . . . . 58 E8
Gwendroc CI TR1 . . . . 137 D3
Gwendroc Ho TR1 . . . . . . 137 D3
Gwendroc House Mews
 TR1 . . . . 137 D3
Gwendrock Villas PL17 . . 108 C5
Gwendrona CI TR13 . . . . . 146 D8
Gwendrona Way TR13 . . . 146 D8
GWENNAP 80 F7
Gwennap Pit ★ TR16 . . . . 140 F4
Gwindra Ind Est PL26 . . . . 58 C3
Gwindra Rd PL26 . . . . 58 B4
GWINEAR 78 E4
Gwinear TR27 . . . . 78 E4
Gwinear Prim Sch TR27 . . 78 E4
Gwinear Rd TR27 . . . . 78 E5
GWITHIAN 66 B2
Gwithian CI
 St Austell PL25 . . . . 114 E7
 Torpoint PL11 . . . . 126 F4
Gwithian Green Nature
 Reserve ★ TR27 . . . . 78 C8
Gwithian Rd TR27 . . . . 78 D6
Gwithian Sands Chalet Pk
 TR27 . . . . 66 B1
GWITHIAN TOWANS 66 A2
Gwithian Towers Nature
 Reserve ★ TR27 . . . . 78 B8
Gwyn Rd PL4 . . . . 149 C4
Gwithian Way TR6 . . . . 55 A4
Gyllyng Hall TR11 . . . . 145 B3
Gyllyng St TR11 . . . . 145 B4
Gyllyngvase Hill TR11 . . . 145 B2
Gyllyngvase Rd TR11 . . . . 145 C2
Gyllyngvase Terr TR11 . . . 145 C2
Gypsy La PL33 . . . . 14 C1

H

Haddington Rd PL2 . . . . . 127 F4
Haddon Way PL25 . . . . . . 115 D3
Haddy's Row PL14 . . . . 39 A2
Haig PI 6 TR18 . . . . 143 C7
Hain Wlk TR26 . . . . 141 C4
HALAMANNING 90 A6
Halbullock View TR1 . . . . . 69 E3
Halcyon Ct PL2 . . . . 128 A6
Halcyon Rd PL2 . . . . 128 A6
Haldon PI PL5 . . . . 124 A3
HALE MILLS 69 A1
Haley Barton 2 PL2 . . . . . 128 A5
HALGABRON 14 E7
Halgavor La PL31 . . . . . . 109 E2
Halgavor Pk PL31 . . . . . . 109 D1
Halgavor Rd PL30, PL31 . 109 D2
Halgavor View PL31 . . . . . 109 F2
Halifax Rd PL27 . . . . 31 F3
Halimote Rd PL26 . . . . 58 C8
Hallane Rd PL25 . . . . 115 A6
Hallan Vean TR19 . . . . 96 A4
Hallaze Rd PL26 . . . . 59 D7
Hallerton CI PL6 . . . . 125 E2
Hallett CI PL12 . . . . 122 B3
Hallett Way EX23 . . . . 104 F7
HALLEW 47 C2
Hallew Rd PL26 . . . . 58 C7
Halley Gdns PL5 . . . . 123 E1
Hall for Cornwall (Theatre)
 The ★ 18 TR1 . . . . 137 D4
HALLIVICK 58 A4
Halloon Ave 8 TR9 . . . . . . 45 E2
Hall Pk PL26 . . . . 58 C8
Hall Terr PL23 . . . . 116 E5
HALLWORTHY 16 D6
HALSETOWN 77 A5
Halt Rd
 Goonhavern TR4 . . . . 55 D4
 St Newlyn East TR8 . . . . . 56 B7
Halvana TR15 . . . . 140 D3
Halvarras Pk TR3 . . . . 82 B8
Halvarras Rd TR3 . . . . 82 B8
Halveor Ct 5 TR6 . . . . 45 E6
Halveor La TR6 . . . . 45 D6
HALVOSSO 80 F3
HALWIN 92 B8
Halwin La TR13 . . . . 92 B8
Halwin Prim Sch TR13 . . . . 92 C8
Halwyn CI 12 TR3 . . . . 81 F7
Halwyn Hill TR8 . . . . 110 A3
Halwyn PI TR1 . . . . 137 B4
Halwyn Rd TR8 . . . . 110 A3
Halwyn Terr TR1 . . . . 137 B3
HAM 128 A8
Hamble CI PL3 . . . . 129 D7
Ham Dr PL2 . . . . 128 B8
Ham Field PL27 . . . . 21 D5
Ham Gn PL2 . . . . 128 A7
Ham Green Ct PL2 . . . . . . 128 A7
Ham Green La PL2 . . . . . . 128 A7
Ham Ho PL2 . . . . 128 A8
Hamilton Ct TR7 . . . . 110 D6
Hamilton Gdns PL4 . . . . . 128 D4
Hamilton PI TR11 . . . . 145 D3
Ham La PL2 . . . . 128 A8

Hammill's CI 13 TR13 . . . . 98 C8
Hammills Dr 12 TR13 . . . . . 98 C8
Hamoaze Ave PL5 . . . . . . 127 D8
Hamoaze PI PL1 . . . . 127 D2
Hamoaze Rd PL11 . . . . . . 127 B2
Hampton CI TR1 . . . . 110 D6
Hampton St PL4 . . . . 149 A3
Hancock CI PL6 . . . . 124 D6
Hancock La 14 TR2 . . . . 95 A6
Hangmans La 32 PL17 . . . 39 F4
Hangmans Wlk TR11 . . . . 145 A1
Hannaford Rd PL16 . . . . . . 19 F3
HANNAFORE 117 C2
Hannafore La PL13 . . . . . . 117 C3
Hannafore La PL13 . . . . . . 117 C3
Hannafore Rd PL13 . . . . . 117 D2
Hanover CI
 17 Perranporth TR6 . . . . . 55 A5
 Plymouth PL3 . . . . 129 B5
Hanover Ct
 Camborne TR14 . . . . 138 E4
 18 Penzance TR18 . . . . . 143 E5
 6 Plymouth PL1 . . . . 149 A2
Hanover Ho EX23 . . . . 4 D4
Hanover Pk TR9 . . . . 45 F2
Hanover Rd PL3 . . . . 129 C4
Hanson Dr PL23 . . . . 116 C3
Hanson Rd PL14 . . . . 113 D6
Harbour Ave
 Plymouth, Camels Head
 PL5 . . . . 127 E8
 Plymouth PL4 . . . . 149 A2
Harbour Ct
 Falmouth TR11 . . . . 145 B4
 19 Penzance TR18 . . . . . 143 E5
 Portreath TR16 . . . . 67 C6
Harbour Ct Flats TR2 . . . . . 95 B5
Harbour Lights 11 TR18 . 143 C1
Harbour Mews TR19 . . . . . 96 B7
Harbour Rd
 Par PL24 . . . . 60 C4
 Porthleven TR13 . . . . 98 B8
 Wadebridge PL27 . . . . . . 108 C5
Harbourside 12 TR13 . . . . . 98 B8
Harbour Side PL13 . . . . . . 117 C3
Harbour St PL11 . . . . 127 B3
Harbour Terr
 Falmouth TR11 . . . . 145 B5
 Portreath TR16 . . . . 67 C6
Harbour View
 Fowey PL23 . . . . 116 C4
 Hayle TR27 . . . . 142 B5
 Marazion TR17 . . . . 89 B5
 Penryn TR10 . . . . 144 B8
 Plymouth PL5 . . . . 135 A7
 5 Porthleven TR13 . . . . . . 98 B8
 Saltash PL12 . . . . 122 E2
 Truro TR1 . . . . 137 D4
Harbour View Cres TR18 143 E6
HARCOURT 82 B4
Harcourt Ct TR1 . . . . 69 F3
Harding Mdw PL13 . . . . 63 F8
Hardings CI PL12 . . . . 122 E3
HARDISWORTHY 2 D7
Hardiswrthy Cross EX39 . . . 2 E7
Hardwick Farm PL7 . . . . . 130 C3
Hardy Cres PL5 . . . . 124 B3
Hardy Ho TR3 . . . . 80 F3
Harebell CI PL12 . . . . 122 D4
Harefield Cres TR14 . . . . . 138 D4
Hareston CI PL7 . . . . 131 B3
Harewood CI PL7 . . . . 130 E5
Harewood Cres PL5 . . . . . 124 B2
Harewood Rd PL18 . . . . 41 A3
Hargood Terr 6 PL2 . . . . . 127 F4
Hargreaves CI PL5 . . . . . . 123 F2
Harlech CI PL3 . . . . 129 A7
Harleigh Rd PL31 . . . . 109 E3
Harleigh Terr PL31 . . . . . . 109 E3
Harlequins 27 TR26 . . . . . 141 B5
HARLYN 20 D2
Harlyn Barton PL28 . . . . . . 20 D2
Harlyn Cotts PL28 . . . . 20 D2
Harlyn Rd PL28 . . . . 20 D1
Harmer CI PL31 . . . . 109 D6
Harris CI
 Redruth TR15 . . . . 140 B6
 Roche PL26 . . . . 46 F3
Harmony Mdw PL26 . . . . . 46 F3
Harmony Rd PL26 . . . . 46 F3
Harmony Terr
 4 Illogan TR16 . . . . 67 E4
 Truro TR1 . . . . 137 E2
Harronhen Rd PL22 . . . . . 128 D7
Haroldsleigh Ave PL5 . . . 124 E2
Harriet Gdns PL7 . . . . 130 B6
Harriet PI TR11 . . . . 145 A5
Harris CI
 1 Penryn TR10 . . . . 144 C7
 Plymouth PL5 . . . . 135 B6
Harrison Gdns TR15 . . . . . 139 D7
Harrison St 8 PL2 . . . . . . 127 F4
Harrison Terr TR1 . . . . . . 137 B4
Harriss Hill PL3 . . . . 82 A7
HARROWBARROW 40 D5
Harrowbarrow Prim Sch
 PL17 . . . . 40 D4
Harrowber La PL20 . . . . . . 42 C3
Hartland CI PL6 . . . . 125 A7
Hartland Forest Golf &
 Leisure Parc EX39 . . . . . . 3 E6
Hartland Rd PL29 . . . . 22 F7
Hartland Terr EX23 . . . . . 104 D6
HARTLEY 128 F5
Hartley Ave PL3 . . . . 129 A6
Hartley Ct PL3 . . . . 129 A6
Hartley Park Gdns PL3 . . 128 F6

Hartley Rd PL3 . . . . 128 E6
HARTLEY VALE 129 A8
Hartmeade PL14 . . . . 52 A5
Hartwell Ave PL9 . . . . 136 D7
Harvenna CI TR9 . . . . 45 E1
Harvest Moon TR7 . . . . . . 110 D7
Harvey Ave PL4 . . . . 129 B1
Harvey Rd TR1 . . . . 137 D2
Harvey St PL11 . . . . 127 B3
Harvey's Towans TR27 . . . 142 A7
Harvey's Way TR27 . . . . . 142 C5
Harwell CI 8 PL11 . . . . . . 148 B3
Harwell St PL1 . . . . 148 B3
Harwood Ave PL5 . . . . 124 C7
Hastings St PL1 . . . . 148 B3
Hastings Terr PL1 . . . . 148 B3
Haswell CI PL6 . . . . 129 A8
Hatch's Hill TR27 . . . . 78 C5
Hatfield Cres TR7 . . . . 110 B5
Hat La PL10 . . . . 132 F2
HATT 53 E4
Havelock Terr PL2 . . . . . . 127 F3
Haven Ct TR27 . . . . 142 C5
Haven Pk PL14 . . . . 39 A2
Haven Rd EX23 . . . . 10 C6
Havett CI PL14 . . . . 50 E8
Havett Rd PL14 . . . . 50 E8
Haviland Rd PL4 . . . . 113 E4
Hawarden Cotts PL4 . . . . 129 B1
Haweswater CI PL6 . . . . . 124 E4
Hawke CI PL7 . . . . 110 D6
Hawkens Way 9 TR9 . . . . . 45 D6
Hawke Rd TR13 . . . . 146 D4
Hawkers Ave PL4 . . . . 149 A2
Hawkers CI EX23 . . . . 104 D7
Hawkers La PL3 . . . . 128 E5
Hawkeys Mews TR15 . . . . 140 D2
Hawkinge Gdns PL5 . . . . . 123 E4
Hawkins CI PL6 . . . . 125 A5
Hawkins Ct 2 PL13 . . . . . 143 D5
Hawkins Rd
 Plymouth PL6 . . . . 125 C5
 Padstow PL28 . . . . 107 C5
 Penzance TR18 . . . . 143 D5
Hawkins Way 12 TR11 . . . 145 A4
Hawks Pk PL12 . . . . 122 C2
Hawk's Tor Dr PL15 . . . . . . 27 B7
Hawthorn Ave
 Bude EX23 . . . . 104 E4
 Torpoint PL11 . . . . 126 F3
Hawthorn CI
 Bude EX23 . . . . 104 E4
 Camelford PL32 . . . . 105 D4
 Plymouth, Hooe PL9 . . . . 135 C5
 Plymouth, Woolwell PL6 . 125 D7
 Redruth TR15 . . . . 140 B6
 St Columb Major TR9 . . . 45 E2
Hawthorn Dr PL2 . . . . 128 C7
Hawthorn Rd PL19 . . . . . . 147 C2
Hawthorns PL12 . . . . 122 D2
Hawthorn Way
 Plymouth PL3 . . . . 129 B7
 Threemilestone TR3 . . . . . 69 C3
Haxter CI PL6 . . . . 121 B1
Haydon Gr PL5 . . . . 123 C1
Haydon Cr PL30 . . . . 2 F4
HAYE 39 D4
Haye La PL17 . . . . 39 E5
Haye Rd
 Callington PL17 . . . . 39 D4
 Plymouth PL7, PL9 . . . . . 130 C1
Hayes Pk PL6 . . . . 136 C7
Hayes R SI PL9 . . . . 129 B8
Hayes Rd PL9 . . . . 135 C7
Hay La
 Looe PL13 . . . . 117 E4
 Sheviock PL11 . . . . 65 B6
HAYLE 142 C6
Hayle Com Sch Lang Coll
 TR27 . . . . 142 D5
Hayle Ind Pk TR27 . . . . . . 142 F7
Hayle Rd TR27 . . . . 78 C1
Hayle Sta TR27 . . . . 142 B5
Hayle Terr TR27 . . . . 142 C6
Hayman Way TR11 . . . . . . 144 E5
Hayne Corfe Gdns TR1 . . 137 A4
Haystone PI PL1 . . . . 148 B4
Haytor CI PL5 . . . . 124 B3
Hazel CI
 Plymouth PL6 . . . . 125 B6
 St Austell PL25 . . . . 115 A6
Hazel Dr PL9 . . . . 136 C7
Hazel Gr
 Plymouth PL9 . . . . 136 C7
 Yelverton PL20 . . . . 42 D3
Hazelmead PL14 . . . . 113 B5
Hazelmead Rd PL25 . . . . 115 B4
Hazel Rd PL19 . . . . 147 C2
Hazelwood Cres PL9 . . . . 136 D7
Hazelwood Dr PL6 . . . . . . 125 D8
Hazelwood Rd PL17 . . . . . 39 F4
Hazelbrook Parc 2 TR18 . 143 C2
Hea CI TR1 . . . . 143 C7
Hea Cotts 5 TR18 . . . . . . 143 C7
Head La TR15 . . . . 68 D8
Headland Cl TR26 . . . . . . 141 E2
Headland Cotts
 Coverack TR12 . . . . 103 H7
 Newquay TR7 . . . . 110 C8
Headland Ct TR26 . . . . . . 141 E2
Headland Pk PL4 . . . . 149 A4
Headland Point TR7 . . . . . 110 C7
Headland Rd
 Carbis Bay TR26 . . . . 141 E2

Headland Rd continued
Newquay TR7..............110 C5
Headlands The TR6 .... 55 A5
Headleigh Rd TR7.......110 F5
Headon Cross EX23 ..... 11 A5
Healy Ct **9** PL2...........127 F4
Healy Pl PL2..............127 F4
HEAMOOR..................143 B7
Heamoor Prim Sch TR18 143 B6
Heanton Terr
  Millbrook PL10...........132 E6
  Redruth TR15............140 C4
Heanton Villas TR15.....140 C4
Hea Rd TR18...............143 C7
Hearl Rd PL12.............122 B3
Heatherbell Gdns TR26.. 141 E1
Heather Cl
  Heamoor TR18...........143 B7
  Tavistock PL19...........147 D4
Heather Ct TR27 ....77 D2
Heather Mdw TR9.........45 E1
Heathers The
  Foxhole PL26.............58 E5
  Plymouth PL6............125 D7
Heather Vean TR3.........69 D4
Heather Way TR20........89 F4
Heathfield Gdns TR15 ...140 E7
Heathfield Pk PL20........42 D3
Heathfield Rd PL4........129 B3
Heathlands Bsns Pk
  PL14....................113 C5
Heathlands Ind Est **9**
  PL14....................113 C5
Heathlands Rd PL14......113 C5
Heath Terr PL18...........40 F5
Heavitree Rd PL10........133 A2
Hedgerow Cl PL6..........123 E6
Hedgerows The PL12.....122 B3
Hedingham Cl PL7........131 C4
Hedingham Gdns PL6....125 B7
Helca Dr TR26............141 C3
HELE....................13 C2
HELEBRIDGE..............7 A6
Helebridge Rd EX23......7 B6
Hele Cross PL15..........13 C3
Hele Gdns PL7...........131 A4
Hele La PL6..............121 F2
Helena Ct **7** PL26.........59 D7
Hele Rd
  Bude EX23...............104 F1
  Marhamchurch EX23.....7 A6
Hele's Sch PL7............130 C6
Hele's Terr PL4...........129 D7
HELFORD..................93 B1
HELFORD PASSAGE.......93 C2
Heligan Ho PL26..........73 A5
HELLAND..................35 A5
HELLANDBRIDGE..........34 F6
Helland Rd PL31..........109 E6
Hellandrew Way TR13....146 D8
Hellescott Rd PL15........11 A5
Hellesvean **2** TR26.......77 A6
Hellesvean Cl **3** TR26....77 A6
HELLESVEOR...............77 A7
Helleur Cl **4** PL24.........60 B4
Hellis Wartha TR11........55 A4
Helman Tor View PL31 ...109 E2
Helnoweth Cotts TR18....143 F8
Helnoweth Gdns TR18....143 F8
Helnoweth Hill TR18......143 F8
Helscott Rd EX23.........7 A6
HELSTON..................146 D6
Helston Com Coll TR13 ..146 C7
  TR13....................146 D3
HELSTONE..................24 B8
Helston Folk Mus*
  TR13....................146 B5
Helston Rd TR10..........144 C8
Helston Sp Ctr TR13......146 C7
Hembal Cl **5** PL25.........59 A3
Hembal La PL25...........59 A3
Hembal Rd **4** PL25.........59 A3
HEMERDON................131 D7
Hemerdon House* PL7 ..131 E7
Hemerdon Hts PL7........131 A6
Hemerdon La PL7.........131 C8
Hemerdon Way PL7.......130 D6
HENAFORD..................2 F5
Hendergulling PL13.......62 F4
Henders Cnr **6** PL3........128 F6
Henderson Pl PL2.........127 F6
HENDRA
  Bodmin..................46 F7
  Camelford...............105 A4
  Mullion.................102 F7
  St Dennis...............58 C8
Hendra Barton TR1.......137 B5
Hendra Cl
  Ashton TR13.............90 E3
  Liskeard PL14...........38 A4
  Stithians TR3............90 E4
  5 Truro TR1............137 C5
Hendra Garth PL15.......17 C6
Hendra Gdns PL15.......106 B5
Hendra Hts PL15.........58 C8
Hendra La
  Ashton TR13.............90 D2
  Truro TR3...............137 C5
Hendra Parc PL14........113 E7
Hendra Pk PL15.........106 B5
Hendra Prazey PL26......58 B8
Hendra Rd
  St Dennis PL26..........58 C8
  Stithians TR3............80 E4

Hendra Rd continued
  Truro TR1...............137 C5
Hendras Ct TR26..........141 E1
Hendras Parc TR26.......141 D2
Hendra Terr TR3..........80 E4
Hendra Vale PL15........106 B4
Hendra Vean
  Carbis Bay TR26.........141 E1
  Truro TR1...............137 B5
Hendrawna La TR6........55 B4
Hendwell Cl PL6..........124 E6
Henfor Cl **12** TR17........89 C5
Henfor Mews **9** TR17.....89 C5
Henfor Terr **8** TR17.......89 C5
Hengar La PL30...........23 F3
Henley Cl TR4............68 C6
Henley Cres TR4..........68 C6
Henley Dr
  Mount Hawke TR4.......68 C6
  Penzance TR18..........144 C4
Henliston Dr TR13........146 C4
Henry Scott Tuke Ho **13**
  TR11...................145 A4
Hensbarrow Mdws PL26.. 58 D5
Hensbury La PL20........119 F4
Henscol TR16.............80 D6
Henscol Praze TR16......80 D6
Henscol Vale PL14.......113 A6
Henshorn Ct TR13........146 C7
Hental **5** TR6.............55 A4
Henver Cl TR27..........78 E3
Henver Ct TR7...........111 C7
Henver Gdns TR27.......78 E3
Henver La TR4...........56 A3
Henver Rd TR7..........111 B7
Henvor Cl TR15..........140 D6
Henvor Terr TR15........140 E7
HENWOOD..................38 B8
Henwood Cres TR7.......111 D7
Hen Wythva TR14........138 E2
Herbert Pl PL2...........127 E4
Herbert St PL2...........127 E4
Hereford Rd PL5.........124 B5
Heritage Cl PL12.........122 C3
Heritage Pk PL19........147 D6
Herland Hill TR27........78 D4
Herland Rd TR13.........90 E6
Hermes Cl TR13..........146 D5
Hermes Rd TR13.........146 C4
Hermitage Ct **1** PL4.....128 E4
Hermitage Rd
  Plymouth PL3............128 E5
  Roche PL26..............46 F3
HERNISS..................80 F1
HERODSFOOT..............50 E3
Heron Cl
  Millbrook PL10..........132 F6
  Tresillian TR2...........70 F5
Herons Ct **15** TR6.........55 A5
Heron Way TR1..........137 E1
Herring Cl PL14...........113 D7
Herring Rd PL14..........113 D7
Herschel Gdns PL5.......123 E1
Hersham Cross EX23 ....5 B2
Hertland Wlk PL2.........128 A7
Hessary Dr PL6...........121 C1
Hessary Ho PL14.........113 D6
Hessary View
  Saltash PL12............122 E4
  Tavistock PL19..........147 B6
HESSENFORD..............64 C8
Hessenford Rd PL13, PL11.64 B6
Hetling Cl PL1...........148 B3
HEWAS WATER............72 D8
Hewer's Row PL14.......149 A3
Hewitt Cl PL12...........122 C1
Hexham Pl PL2...........128 A8
Hexton Hill Rd PL9.......135 B6
Hexton Quay PL9........135 C6
Heybrook Ave PL5.......123 D1
Heybrook Mews TR7.....110 D6
Hibernia Rd TR13.........146 D4
Hibernia Terr PL5.........127 E8
Hichens La TR11.........145 A5
Hichens Rd TR13.........146 D4
Hickory Dr PL7...........131 B5
Hicks Cl TR2.............71 C6
Hick's La PL4............149 A2
Hidden Valley Discovery Pk*
  PL15....................18 A3
High Atlantic TR8.........44 C6
Highbank Cl PL19.........147 A4
Highbridge Ct PL7........130 E5
Highburrow **24** TR13......98 C8
Highburrow Ct TR15......139 C5
Highburrow La TR15......139 C5
Highbury PL17............38 E8
Highbury Cres PL7........130 D7
Highclere Gdns PL6......125 B8
Highcliffe PL27...........71 C6
High Cross
  Lanivet PL30............47 F5
  Porth Navas TR11.......93 A4
  12 St Columb Major TR9..45 D6
  Truro TR1...............137 C5
High Cross St PL25.......114 D4
Higher Albion Row TR16..80 F8
Higher Anderton Rd
  PL10....................132 F5
HIGHER BAL..............54 B2
Higher Beech Terr PL13..117 C4
Higher Besore Rd TR3 ...69 D4
Higher Bodiniel Rd PL31.109 C7
Higher Bojewyan TR19...75 B1
Higher Bolenna **14** TR6...55 A4

Higher Bore St PL31.....109 C5
HIGHER BOSCASWELL....75 A1
Higher Bosporthennis TR26.75 A1
HIGHER BREA............139 B3
Higher Bridge Pk PL27 ..108 D5
Higher Broad La TR15....139 D7
Higher Bugle
  Bugle PL26..............47 C1
  Stenalees PL26..........59 C8
Higher Burrow Cl TR26..141 A4
HIGHER CARNKIE.........139 F2
Higher Chapel St TR13 ..117 D3
Higher Church St TR27...142 D6
Higher Churchway PL9...136 A7
Higher Cl PL27...........108 E4
Higher Cleaverfield
  PL15....................106 C7
HIGHER COMPTON.......129 A6
Higher Compton Rd PL3..128 F6
HIGHER CONDURROW....139 A1
Higher Cotts TR2.........57 C1
Higher Cross La PL32....105 C4
Higher Daws La PL15.....18 E2
HIGHER DOWNS..........89 F5
Higher East St **9** TR9.....45 E1
Higher Efford Rd PL3.....129 B5
Higher Elms PL27.........21 F3
Higher Fernleigh Rd
  PL27....................108 C4
Higher Fore St
  Marazion TR17..........89 C5
  Redruth TR15...........140 C4
Higher Glen Pk PL14.....38 D4
Higher Goongumpas La
  TR16....................68 F1
Higher Green St TR18 ...143 D1
Higher Grumbla TR20....87 C4
Higher Gwavas Rd **3**
  TR18....................143 C1
Higher Kelly PL18........41 A3
Higher La
  Ashton TR13.............90 E3
  Mawgan TR12...........99 D7
  Plymouth PL1............148 C2
  Wadebridge PL27........108 E4
Higher Larrigan TR18....143 D4
HIGHER LARRICK.........27 E5
Higher Lavorrick PL26 ...73 C4
Higher Lidden Rd TR18..143 C3
Higher Lux St PL14......113 C6
Higher Market St
  Looe PL13...............117 D3
  Penryn TR10.............144 C7
Higher Mdw PL14.........50 E7
Higher Medrose PL33....14 F3
Higher Middle Hill PL14..38 D4
Higher Moors Cross EX22..5 E1
Higher Mount Ambrose La
  TR15....................140 D6
Higher Mowles PL3......129 B6
Higher Newham La TR1..137 D2
Higher Park Cl PL7........131 B3
Higher Park Stenak TR16.80 F8
Higher Pengegon TR14 ..138 F2
Higher Penpords Rd
  TR14....................79 B5
Higher Peverell Rd PL3..143 E7
Higher Polsue Way TR2..70 F5
HIGHER PORTHPEAN.....59 D1
Higher Port View PL12 ..122 F2
Higher Pumpfield Row
  TR15....................139 B6
Higher Railway Terr TR16 80 F8
Higher Rd
  Breage TR13.............90 F3
  Pensilva PL14............38 D4
  Redannick TR1..........137 B3
HIGHER ROSEWARNE....138 D5
Higher Row
  Ashton TR13.............90 E3
  Kingsand PL10..........133 A2
Higher Silver Hill TR13 ..146 C6
Higher Stennack TR26...141 A5
Higher Stert Terr PL4 ....149 C3
Higher Tamar Terr PL18..41 A7
Higher Terr TR3..........81 B4
HIGHER TOLCARNE.......45 B8
Higher Tower Rd TR7 ...110 C6
HIGHERTOWN
  Camelford...............24 E8
  Truro...................69 F3
Hightertown
  Portscatho TR2..........83 B2
  Truro TR1...............69 F3
Highertown Pk PL12.....53 C3
Higher Tregenna Rd
  TR26....................141 B3
Higher Treglyn PL27......22 B3
Higher Trehaverne TR1..137 C6
Higher Tremena PL25....114 B3
Higher Tresavean Terr
  TR16....................80 E6
Higher Trevithick TR27...142 D5
Higher Trevorian Barns
  TR19....................97 B7
Higher Trewidden Rd
  TR26....................141 B4
HIGHER TREWINCE.......44 E6
Higher Trezaise PL26....47 A1
Higher Tristram PL27....21 D5
Higher Vicarage La **7**
  TR12....................99 A1
Higherwell Cl TR7........111 A4
Higher Well La TR13.....146 C6
Higher Well Pk PL26.....73 C3

Higher West End PL26....73 C6
Higher Whiterock PL27..108 B5
Higher Woodford La
  PL7....................130 C7
Higher Woodside PL25 ..114 A4
Highfield Ave
  St Austell PL25..........114 D3
  18 St Columb Major TR9 ..45 D6
Highfield Cl
  Plymouth PL3............129 C5
  St Austell PL25..........114 D3
Highfield Est **3** PL14.....38 E4
Highfield Park Rd PL15...106 A5
Highfield Pk PL12........122 B3
Highfield Rd
  Camelford PL32.........105 C3
  Falmouth TR11.........144 F4
  Mount Hawke TR4.......68 C6
Highfield Rd Ind Est
  PL32....................105 C3
Highfields **19** PL18.......143 C2
Highfields Private Sch
  TR15....................140 B6
Highgate Hill **1** TR9.....45 E1
Highglen Dr PL7.........131 B7
Highgrove PL15...........27 A6
Highland Pk
  Penryn TR10............144 B8
  Redruth TR15...........140 C5
Highlands PL9............136 B3
HIGHLANES................32 B7
HIGH LANES..............142 D5
High Lanes
  Cubert TR8.............55 E8
  Hayle TR27.............142 D5
High Pk PL12.............52 F6
High St
  Boscastle PL35...........9 D1
  Camelford PL32.........105 C3
  Chacewater TR4.........68 F3
  Delabole PL33..........14 D3
  Falmouth TR11.........145 B5
  Launceston PL15........106 C6
  Padstow PL28...........107 D5
  Penzance TR18..........143 E5
  3 Plymouth PL1.........149 A2
  Plymouth, Stonehouse PL1 128 A2
  Probus TR2.............71 C6
  St Ives TR26............141 B6
  St Keverne TR12........101 C4
HIGH STREET............58 D4
High Street Ind Est PL26.58 D3
High Street Prim Sch
  PL1....................128 A2
High Street & Waterloo
  Street Flats PL1........128 A1
Hightrip La PL17.........39 F7
Hightrip La PL17.........40 A8
Highview TR4............68 E5
Highview Cl PL14........38 A2
Highview Cres TR4.......68 E5
Highview Prim Sch PL3 129 D6
Highway PL14...........50 B6
Highway La TR15........140 D7
Highwood Pk PL14.......50 E7
Higman Cl PL14..........50 E7
Hilgrove Rd TR7.........111 A6
HILL....................10 B5
Hill Church TR4..........68 F2
Hill Cl
  Heamoor TR18..........143 B7
  Plymouth PL7...........130 D4
  St Breward PL30........24 B3
Hillcrest
  Helston TR13............146 C7
  Shortlanesend TR4......69 F6
Hill Crest PL3............128 E5
Hillcrest Ave TR1........137 A5
Hillcrest Cl
  Plymouth PL7............131 A5
  16 St Columb Major TR9..45 D6
Hillcrest Dr PL7..........131 A4
Hillcrest Rd PL27........142 D6
Hilldale Rd PL9..........135 E6
Hilldean Cl PL5...........124 C7
Hill Gdns PL12...........119 A2
Hill Hay Cl PL23.........116 A4
Hillhead PL30............24 C1
Hillhead Gdns PL32......105 D4
Hillhead Rd TR11........144 C5
Hill La PL3...............128 F7
Hillocks The PL13.......117 D4
Hillpark Cotts PL15......106 D6
Hill Park Cres
  Plymouth PL4...........149 A4
  St Austell PL25..........114 A2
Hill Park Mews PL4......149 B4
Hill Path PL5.............123 F5
Hill Pk PL27.............108 D6
Hill Rd PL27.............108 C5
Hillsborough **2** PL4......128 D4
Hillsborough Cross EX22..8 D7
Hillsdale Bglws TR15....90 F5
Hillsdunne Rd PL3.......128 E6
Hillside
  Grampound Road TR2...57 L1
  Lanivet PL30............47 F7
  Portreath TR16..........67 C6
  St Austell PL25..........115 B3
  Trewalllard TR19........86 F8
Hillside Ave
  Par PL24...............60 B4
  Plymouth PL4...........128 D4
  Saltash PL12............122 F3
Hillside Cl PL20..........41 F3
Hillside Cres PL9.........135 F8

Hillside Ct
  Angarrack TR27.........78 C5
  Bodmin PL31...........109 C5
  20 Velverton PL20......41 B1
Hillside Gdns PL22......112 C2
Hillside Ind Est TR16....140 E8
Hillside Mdw TR10......144 D7
Hillside Mdws PL26......58 D5
Hillside Parc TR20.......88 B7
Hillside Pk PL31.........109 C5
Hillside Rd
  Falmouth TR11.........144 F2
  Saltash PL25............122 E3
  St Austell PL25..........114 D5
Hillside Terr
  Carharrack TR16........80 E8
  Downderry PL11........64 C5
  Looe PL13..............117 D4
  22 Newlyn TR18........143 C2
  2 Redruth TR15.........140 C5
Hillside Villas PL13......117 F5
Hillson Cl PL29..........22 E7
Hill St
  Padstow PL28...........107 D5
  Plymouth PL4...........149 A3
Hillsview PL13...........62 D2
Hill Top Crest PL5.......123 E2
Hill View PL20...........41 F3
Hilton Ave PL5...........124 D1
Hilton Rd EX23...........7 B6
Hingston Ct PL6.........129 A8
HINGSTON DOWN.........40 B6
Hinton Ct PL6............125 C1
Hirmandale Rd PL5......123 F3
Hirst Ho TR14...........139 A4
Hobart St PL1...........148 A2
Hobbacott La EX23.......7 B6
Hobbs Cres PL12........122 C3
Hockens La PL23.........116 C2
Hockings Ho PL14.......37 F3
Hodders Way PL12......119 A2
Hodge Cl PL12...........122 C2
Hoe App PL1.............148 C2
Hoe Ct PL1..............148 C2
Hoegate Ct PL1..........148 C2
Hoegate Pl PL1..........148 C2
Hoegate St PL1..........149 A2
Hoe Gdns PL1...........148 C1
Hoe Rd PL1.............148 C1
Hoe St PL1..............148 C2
Hoe The PL1............148 C1
Hogarth Cl PL0..........136 B6
Hogarth Ho **2** PL19.....147 B6
Hogarth Wlk PL9........136 B6
Holborn Pl PL7..........130 E6
Holborn St PL4..........149 B2
Holcombe Dr PL9........135 F5
Holcroft Cl PL12.........122 D2
Holdsworth St PL4.......148 B4
Holebay Cl PL0..........136 A5
Hole Cross PL20.........119 F7
HOLESTOW...............102 E2
Hollabury Rd EX23.......104 F7
Hollacombe Brake PL9 ..136 C1
HOLLACOMBE HILL......136 A2
Holland Rd
  Plymouth, Chaddlewood
  PL7....................131 D5
  Plymouth, Peverell PL3..128 E6
  Widegates PL13.........63 E7
Hollies Cl PL15..........106 B7
Hollies Rd PL15..........106 A7
Hollies The TR27........142 B4
Hollong Pk PL11.........65 E5
Holloway Gdns PL9......136 A5
Hollowell Ho **1** PL35.....9 C2
Hollow Hayes PL6.......129 B8
Hollow's Terr TR27......142 E7
Hollows The PL9.........136 B8
Holly Cl TR3............69 C3
Hollycroft Rd PL3........129 A7
Holly Ct PL6............129 C7
Holly Park Cl PL5........124 A5
Holly Park Dr PL5........124 A5
Holly Terr **9** TR18........143 C7
Hollywood Terr PL1......148 A3
Holman Ave TR14.......138 C4
Holman Ct PL2...........128 C8
Holman Rd PL14........113 E6
Holmans Bldg PL6.......127 D2
Holmans Mdw PL15.....19 C1
Holman's Pl **8** TR13.....98 C8
Holman's Terr TR16.....80 B5
HOLMBUSH...............115 B4
Holmbush Arch Rd PL25.115 B3
Holmbush Hill PL17......39 F7
Holmbush Ind Est PL25..115 B4
Holmbush Rd PL25.......115 C4
Holmer Down PL6........125 D7
Holmes Ave PL3.........129 B5
Holmwood Ave PL9......135 E5
Holne Chase PL6.........125 B7
Holnicote Rd EX23.......104 E5
Holt Cres TR7...........110 D5
Holtwood Rd PL6........125 D6
Holwell Cl PL9...........136 B6
Holy Cross RC Prim Sch
  PL4....................149 A3
Holyrood Pl PL1.........148 C2
Holway Cross PL15......18 A1
HOLYWELL...............43 B2
Holywell Bay Fun Pk*
  TR8....................43 C1
Holywell Ct TR3.........82 B8
Holywell Rd
  Cubert TR8.............55 D8
  Playing Place TR3......43 C1

Holywell Rd continued
Liskeard PL14 . . . . 113 E6
Newquay TR7 . . . . 110 F6
Playing Place TR3 . . . . . . 82 B8
Home Farm Rd PL9 . . . . 135 E8
Homefield Pk PL31 . . . . 109 F3
Home Park Ave PL3 . . . . 128 E6
Home Park (Plymouth Argyle FC) PL2 . . . . 128 C5
Home Park Rd PL12 . . . . 123 A3
Home Pk
Landrake PL12 . . . . 53 C3
Plymouth PL2 . . . . 127 F4
Homer Park Lane S PL9 . 135 C5
Homer Park Rd PL28 . . . . 20 F2
Homer Pk
Plymouth PL9 . . . . 135 C5
Saltash PL12 . . . . 122 D3
Homer Rise PL9 . . . . 136 B7
Homer Water Pk PL26 . . . 58 B4
Homestead Ct TR11 . . . . 144 F6
Home Sweet Home Terr
PL4 . . . . 149 C2
Homeyard Homes The
TR2 . . . . 83 F6
Honcray PL9 . . . . 135 D8
Honey's Hill PL30 . . . . . . 47 E7
Honey St PL31 . . . . 109 E4
Honeysuckle Cl
Plymouth PL6 . . . . 125 D7
Saltash PL12 . . . . 122 D4
Honeysuckle Gdns PL15 . 106 E4
HONICKNOWLE 124 B2
Honicknowle Ho PL5 . . . 124 B2
Honicknowle Gn PL5 . . . 124 B2
Honicknowle La PL5 . . . . 124 B1
Honicombe Cnr PL17 . . . . 40 E5
Honicombe Pk PL17 . . . . . 40 E5
Honiton Cl PL5 . . . . 124 B3
Honiton Wlk PL5 . . . . 124 B4
Hood Hill TR14 . . . . 79 A6
HOOE 135 C5
Hooe Hill PL9 . . . . 135 C5
Hooe La PL9 . . . . 135 C5
Hooe Manor PL9 . . . . 135 C5
Hooe Prim Sch PL9 . . . . 135 B5
Hooe Rd PL9 . . . . 135 C5
Hooksbury Ave PL7 . . . . 131 B3
Hooper Ct PL14 . . . . 113 C8
Hooper La TR14 . . . . 138 C2
Hoopers Cl PL12 . . . . 53 C3
Hoopers La PL18 . . . . 40 F6
Hooper St PL11 . . . . 127 C3
Hope Terr TR7 . . . . 110 D6
Hopton Cl
Bude EX23 . . . . 104 F5
Plymouth PL6 . . . . 128 F8
Hornapark Cl PL16 . . . . . . 19 F3
Hornbrook Gdns PL6 . . . 124 D6
Hornby Ct PL1 . . . . 148 A3
Hornby St PL2 . . . . 127 F4
Hornchurch La PL5 . . . . . 123 E4
Hornchurch Rd PL5 . . . . 123 E5
Horn Cross PL9 . . . . 135 E7
Horn Cross Rd PL9 . . . . 135 F7
Hornick Hill PL26 . . . . . . 58 E4
HORNINGTOPS 51 E3
Horn La
Liskeard PL14 . . . . 113 B6
Plymouth PL9 . . . . 135 F7
Horn Lane Flats 4 PL9 . 135 F7
HORRABRIDGE 42 C5
Horrabridge Com Prim Sch
PL20 . . . . 42 C4
HORSEBRIDGE 29 C1
HORSEDOWNS 78 F1
Horse & Jockey La 2
TR13 . . . . 146 C5
Horsepool La PL11 . . . . . . 65 B6
Horsepool Rd
Connor Downs TR27 . . . . 78 E6
Sheviock PL11 . . . . 65 B6
Horseshoe Cl PL26 . . . . . 47 A3
Horsewhim Dr PL17 . . . . . 39 E6
Horse Whim Dr PL25 . . . 115 B5
Horsham La
Plymouth, Honicknowle PL5 . . . . 124 C2
Plymouth, Tamerton Foliot PL5 . . . . 124 C7
Horsley Rise PL25 . . . . . 114 D3
Horswell Cl PL7 . . . . 131 B5
Horton Cross EX22 . . . . . . 3 F3
Hosford Cl PL9 . . . . 136 A4
Hosken's Mdw TR19 . . . . . 97 A6
Hosking's Row TR15 . . . . 140 B4
Hospital Rd
Plymouth PL4 . . . . 149 B4
Stratton EX23 . . . . 4 D1
Hotham Pl PL1 . . . . 148 A4
Houldsworth Rd PL9 . . . 135 C7
Houndiscombe Rd PL4 . . 128 E4
Hounster Dr PL10 . . . . . 132 D4
Hounster Hill PL10 . . . . . 132 D4
Housel Bay Rd TR12 . . . 102 F2
Housman Cl PL3 . . . . 124 D3
Howard Cl
Plymouth PL5 . . . . 123 F2
Saltash PL12 . . . . 122 D3
Tavistock PL19 . . . . 147 A5
Howard La
EX23 . . . . 7 C8
Howard Rd PL9 . . . . 135 E8
Howards Way EX23 . . . . 104 D5
Howe Downs TR14 . . . . . . 79 A2
Howell's Rd 6 EX23 . . . . . 4 E1
Howeson La PL6 . . . . 125 A4
How St PL4 . . . . 149 A2
HTP Apartments TR1 . . . 137 E4

Hts The PL19 . . . . 147 A6
HUDDISFORD 3 F6
Hudson Cross EX22 . . . . . . 5 E4
Hudson Rd PL27 . . . . 31 F3
Hughville St TR14 . . . . . 138 D4
Hugus Rd TR3 . . . . 69 D3
Hull's La TR11 . . . . 145 C3
Humber Cl PL3 . . . . 129 D6
Humphrey's Cl PL14 . . . . 37 F3
Humphry Davy La PL27 . 142 D5
Humphry Davy Sch TR18 143 E6
Hungerford Rd PL2 . . . . 128 B5
Hunkin Cl TR1 . . . . 137 C5
Hunter Cl PL4 . . . . 124 F2
Huntersfield TR14 . . . . . 138 F7
Hunter's Oak PL20 . . . . . 41 D2
Huntfield Gdns 18 EX23 . . 4 E1
Huntingdon Ave PL5 . . . 124 D4
Huntley Pl PL3 . . . . 129 C4
Hunts Crossing Sta ★
PL15 . . . . 18 E4
Hurdon Rd PL15 . . . . . . 106 D2
Hurdon Way PL15 . . . . . 106 C3
Hurdwick Rd PL19 . . . . . 147 A5
Hurland Rd TR1 . . . . 137 D3
Hurlers Cl 11 PL14 . . . . 113 C5
Hurlers The ★ PL14 . . . . . 38 A6
Hurlings The TR9 . . . . . . 45 E5
Hurrabrook Cl PL6 . . . . . 125 E2
Hurrabrook Gdns PL6 . . 125 E2
Hurrell Cl PL6 . . . . 124 D6
Hurrell Ct PL3 . . . . 129 C5
Hursley Bsns Pk PL6 . . . 121 D1
Hurst Cl PL9 . . . . 135 F5
Hustyns PL27 . . . . 33 D3
Hutchings Cl PL6 . . . . . . 124 D6
Huthnance Cl TR1 . . . . . 137 F5
Hutton Hts TR1 . . . . 69 F3
Huxham Cl PL6 . . . . 129 A8
Huxley Cl PL7 . . . . 130 F7
Hyde Park Jun & Inf Sch 3
PL3 . . . . 128 E5
Hyde Park Rd PL3 . . . . . 128 E5

I

IDLESS 70 B6
Idless La TR4 . . . . 69 F6
Idless Wood Forest Walk ★
TR4 . . . . 70 B6
Ilbert Cotts PL7 . . . . 130 E4
Ilbert St PL1 . . . . 148 B4
ILLOGAN 67 E4
Illogan Downs TR15 . . . . 139 B8
ILLOGAN HIGHWAY 139 C6
Illogan Pk 8 TR16 . . . . . . 67 E4
Illogan Prim Sch TR16 . . 67 D5
Imperial Ct TR11 . . . . . . 145 D3
Ince Cl PL11 . . . . 126 F4
Inchkeith Rd PL6 . . . . . . 124 F7
INDIAN QUEENS 45 E2
Indian Queens Ind Est
TR9 . . . . 45 F2
Indian Queens Prim Sch
TR9 . . . . 45 E1
Industrial Est The TR6 . . 55 B4
Infirmary Hill TR1 . . . . . 137 C4
Ingra Pl PL3 . . . . 129 A6
Ingra Tor Cl 2 PL20 . . . . 42 C3
Ingra Wlk PL6 . . . . 125 B8
Innes Ho PL1 . . . . 148 B3
Inney Cl PL15 . . . . 39 F4
Inow Terr TR11 . . . . 93 A2
Institute Hill TR13 . . . . . . 98 B8
Instow Wlk PL5 . . . . 124 A3
Inswell Ct PL19 . . . . 147 A6
INSWORKE 132 F6
Insworke Cl PL10 . . . . . 133 A6
Insworke Cres PL10 . . . 132 F6
Insworke Pl PL10 . . . . . 133 A6
Inverdene PL3 . . . . 128 D5
Ipswich Cl PL5 . . . . 124 C4
Iron Mine La PL20 . . . . . 42 E3
Isacombe Oaks PL17 . . . 39 F6
Island Cres TR7 . . . . 110 E6
Island Cl PL13 . . . . 117 D2
Island Lanes PL31 . . . . . 109 F1
Island Point TR8 . . . . 44 C6
Island Rd 4 TR26 . . . . . 141 B6
Island Sq 8 TR26 . . . . . 141 B6
Islington Wharf TR10 . . . 144 D8
Ivanhoe 6 TR7 . . . . 110 F6
Ivanhoe Rd PL5 . . . . 123 D2
Ivey Terr PL14 . . . . 113 D7
Ivy Cotts PL18 . . . . 40 F6
Ivydale PL15 . . . . 106 B6
Ivydale Rd PL4 . . . . 128 F4
Ivydene Flats TR7 . . . . . 111 D7
Ivy La TR18 . . . . 143 C5
Ivyleaf Holiday Pk EX23 . . 4 F3

J

Jack Bice Cl PL14 . . . . . 113 E5
Jackett's Steps 6 TR11 . 145 B5
Jack La TR10 . . . . 144 D7
Jackman's Mdw PL10 . . 133 A3
Jacks Cl TR10 . . . . 144 D7
Jackson Cl PL5 . . . . 127 F8
Jackson Pl PL2 . . . . 127 F4
Jackson Way PL12 . . . . . 122 E3
Jack Stephens Est TR18 143 D6
Jacob's Ladder PL31 . . . 145 B4
JACOBSTOW 11 B6

Jacobstow Prim Sch
EX23 . . . . 11 A6
Jago Ave PL11 . . . . 127 B3
Jago Cl PL31 . . . . 109 B3
Jago's Slip TR11 . . . . . . 145 B5
Jake's La 1 TR4 . . . . 69 A3
Jamaica Inn Mus ★ PL15 . 25 C3
Jamaica Pl 14 TR18 . . . . 143 C7
Jamaica Terr 13 TR18 . . 143 C7
Jamaica Cl PL9 . . . . 136 B6
James Pl TR1 . . . . 137 D4
James Rd PL19 . . . . 147 E2
James's Cross EX23 . . . . 2 C2
James St
Plymouth, Mount Wise PL1 . . . . 127 E1
Plymouth PL4 . . . . 148 C4
Jane's Ct 9 TR11 . . . . . . 145 B5
Jasmine Gdns
Plymouth, Chaddlewood PL7 . . . . 131 B5
Plymouth, Glenholt PL6 . 125 E6
Jasmine Way PL28 . . . . . 31 F7
Jasper Parc PL14 . . . . . . 37 F3
Jays Cross PL15 . . . . 19 C6
Jean Cres PL3 . . . . 129 B6
Jeanne Rees Ct 9 PL14 . 113 B5
Jedburgh Cres PL2 . . . . 128 A8
Jeffery Cl PL6 . . . . 124 D6
Jelbert Way TR18 . . . . . . 88 E6
Jellicoe Rd PL5 . . . . 124 E1
Jenkins Cl PL9 . . . . 136 A5
Jenkins Cl PL6 . . . . 110 E6
Jenkins Terr 6 TR15 . . . 140 C5
Jenner Parc TR9 . . . . 45 D6
Jennings Rd TR10 . . . . . 144 A6
Jennings St TR18 . . . . . 143 E5
Jenns Cross EX22 . . . . . . 5 F7
Jennycliff La PL9 . . . . . . 135 A6
Jennys Combe Cl PL9 . . 135 E4
Jephson Rd PL4 . . . . 129 B3
Jericho La TR17 . . . . 142 D1
Jeryon Cl PL25 . . . . 114 E6
Jessops PL7 . . . . 130 D7
Jethan Dr TR14 . . . . 138 B4
Jetty St PL26 . . . . 73 C3
Jewell's Terr TR16 . . . . . . 80 B5
JEWEL'S CROSS 7 F6
Jinkin Ave PL4 . . . . 149 B4
John Ellis Ct TR27 . . . . . 142 C5
John Kitto Com Coll The
PL5 . . . . 124 B1
John La PL4 . . . . 148 C4
John's Cnr PL20 . . . . 89 F5
Johnson Cl 2 PL20 . . . . . 41 B1
Johnson Pk PL18 . . . . . . 41 A2
John Sparke Ho 17 PL1 . 149 A2
Johns Pk TR15 . . . . 140 B6
John St
Plymouth PL1 . . . . 127 E3
Truro TR1 . . . . 137 C4
JOLLY'S BOTTOM 69 A4
Jon Davey Dr TR16 . . . . 140 C7
Jopes Cl 2 PL14 . . . . 38 A3
JOPPA 142 E4
Jordan La PL20 . . . . 42 C5
Jorys Mdw PL30 . . . . 23 E3
Joseph's Ct 2 TR5 . . . . . 55 A5
Joseph's La PL18 . . . . . . 143 C8
Jubilee Cl TR1 . . . . 137 B6
Jubilee Bglws 20 TR18 . 143 C1
Jubilee Cl
Cubert TR4 . . . . 55 D8
Duloe PL14 . . . . 51 A1
Kilkhampton EX23 . . . . . . 5 A6
Saltash PL12 . . . . 122 D2
Jubilee Cotts
Landrake PL12 . . . . 53 C3
Plymouth PL3 . . . . 128 C4
Saltash PL12 . . . . 122 C1
Jubilee Ct 18 PL23 . . . . . 77 A6
Jubilee Hill PL13 . . . . . . 62 D5
Jubilee Mdw PL25 . . . . . 115 C5
Jubilee Pl
Camborne TR14 . . . . . . 138 E3
Plymouth PL3 . . . . 129 C4
Torpoint PL18 . . . . 143 F4
Jubilee Rd
Falmouth TR11 . . . . 145 A5
Pensilva PL14 . . . . 38 D4
Plymouth PL5 . . . . 123 F3
Threemilestone TR3 . . . . 69 C3
Wadebridge PL27 . . . . . 108 C5
Jubilee St TR7 . . . . 110 D6
Jubilee Terr
Bodmin PL31 . . . . 109 B5
3 Camborne TR14 . . . . 138 E2
Goonhavern TR4 . . . . 55 D5
Helston TR13 . . . . 146 C4
Plymouth PL4 . . . . 129 B2
Julian St PL4 . . . . 149 C2
Julian Wlk PL6 . . . . 125 E6
Jump Cl PL6 . . . . 121 C1
Junction Gdns PL4 . . . . 149 C3
Juniper Way PL7 . . . . . . 131 B5

Keason Hill PL12 . . . . 53 C8
Keast Cl 2 TR9 . . . . 45 E1
Keat St PL2 . . . . 127 F4
Kedlestone Ave PL5 . . . 124 A3
Keeble Pk TR3 . . . . 81 E6
Keep The PL12 . . . . 122 C2
Kehelland Village Prim Sch
TR14 . . . . 66 F1
Keigwen Pl TR19 . . . . . . 88 C1
Kel Avon Cl TR1 . . . . . . 137 F5
Kellaway Rd TR13 . . . . . 146 D6
Kelley Rd TR11 . . . . 144 E5
Kellwith TR3 . . . . 82 B6
Kellow Hill PL13 . . . . 62 D2
Kellow Pk PL11 . . . . 65 A7
Kellow Rd PL26 . . . . 58 C8
KELLY 29 B8
KELLY BRAY 39 F6
Kelly Cl PL5 . . . . 127 C7
Kelly Coll PL19 . . . . 147 D7
Kelly Coll Prep Sch
PL19 . . . . 147 D7
Kelly Pk PL30 . . . . 34 C8
Kelvin Ave PL4 . . . . 149 C4
Kelwyn Ct TR26 . . . . 141 C2
KELYNACK 86 F4
Kemp Cl TR1 . . . . 137 D4
Kempe Cl PL2 . . . . 127 F6
Kemp's Cl 7 TR5 . . . . 54 C1
Kempton Terr PL11 . . . . 127 B2
Kemyel Pl PL2 . . . . 127 E4
Kendal Gn TR2 . . . . 57 C1
Kendal Pl PL5 . . . . 124 E4
Kenidjack Cl TR26 . . . . . 141 E1
Kenilworth Rd PL2 . . . . 128 B7
Kenilworth Way PL26 . . . 58 E8
Kenley Gdns PL5 . . . . . . 123 F4
Kenmare Dr PL7 . . . . . . 131 A5
Kennall Vale 3 TR3 . . . . . 81 B4
Kennall Vale TR3 . . . . . . 81 B4
Kennall Vale Prim Sch
TR3 . . . . 81 B4
Kenna Pk TR1 . . . . 69 F3
KENNARDS HOUSE 18 B2
Kenn Cl PL5 . . . . 124 B3
Kennedy Ct TR15 . . . . . 139 B8
Kennedy Dr PL5 . . . . . . 124 A3
KENNEGGY 90 A3
KENNEGGY DOWNS 90 A4
Kennel Hill PL7 . . . . 130 D4
Kennel Hill Cl PL7 . . . . . 130 D4
Kennerley Terr 18 TR2 . . 95 A6
Kennet Cl PL3 . . . . 129 B6
Kenneth Launder Ct 10
PL14 . . . . 113 B5
Kensa Way TR27 . . . . 78 E6
Kensey Pl 3 PL15 . . . . . 106 C6
Kensey Valley Mdw
PL15 . . . . 106 D6
Kensey View PL15 . . . . . 106 D6
Kensington Pl 8 PL4 . . . 128 F4
Kensington Rd PL4 . . . . 149 B4
Kenstella Rd TR18 . . . . . 143 C2
Kent Ave PL25 . . . . 115 D3
Kent Cl PL26 . . . . 58 C8
Kent Rd PL2 . . . . 127 F5
KENTS 10 F6
KENWYN 137 C6
Kenwyn Church Rd TR1 . 137 B6
Kenwyn Cl
Bude EX23 . . . . 104 D7
Truro TR1 . . . . 137 B6
Kenwyn Hill TR1 . . . . . . 137 B6
Kenwyn Mews TR1 . . . . 137 C4
Kenwyn Pk
St Kew Highway PL30 . . 23 B2
Truro TR1 . . . . 137 B6
Kenwyn Rd TR1 . . . . 137 C5
Kenwyn St TR1 . . . . 137 C4
Kenython La TR19 . . . . . . 86 F7
Keppel Pl PL2 . . . . 127 F4
Keppel St PL2 . . . . 127 F4
Keppel Terr 8 PL2 . . . . . 127 F4
Kerensa Gdns TR5 . . . . . 68 D8
Kerensa Gn TR11 . . . . . 144 E5
Kergilliack Rd TR11 . . . . 144 D5
Kerhuon Ct PL31 . . . . . . 109 D5
Kerler Gr TR1 . . . . 69 F3
Kerley Hill TR4 . . . . 69 A3
Kerley Vale TR4 . . . . 69 A3
Kernick Bsns Pk TR10 . . 144 A6
Kernick Gdns TR10 . . . . 144 A6
Kernick Ind Est TR10 . . . 144 A7
Kernick Rd TR10 . . . . . . 144 A6
Kernick Way TR27 . . . . . 142 B7
Kernou Cl
Bodmin PL31 . . . . 109 F5
Torpoint PL11 . . . . 126 E3
Wadebridge PL27 . . . . . 108 B5
Kernow Cres EX23 . . . . 104 E4
Kernow Ct
Newquay TR7 . . . . 110 E6
Torpoint PL11 . . . . 126 E3
Kernow Mill ★ PL12 . . . . . 52 E1
Kernyk Lowen TR14 . . . . 138 F5
KERRIS 97 E8
Kerris Gr TR11 . . . . 137 E8
Kerrow Moor PL9 . . . . . . 59 D8
Ker St Ope PL1 . . . . 127 E2
Kersbrook Cross PL17 . . 27 F2
Kersey Cl TR11 . . . . 144 E5
Kersey Rd TR11 . . . . 144 E5
Ker St PL1 . . . . 127 E2
Keryor Cl PL25 . . . . 114 F3
Kestell Pk PL13 . . . . 117 D4
Kestenenn 18 PL31 . . . . 109 D5
KESTLE 73 A4
Kestle Ct PL31 . . . . 109 C5

Kestle Dr TR1 . . . . 69 F3
KESTLE MILL 111 F1
Kestral Units PL5 . . . . . 124 A1
Kestral Way 10 TR16 . . . 67 E4
Kestrel Cl
Plymouth PL6 . . . . 125 D8
7 Porthleven TR13 . . . . 98 B8
Kestrel Pk TR19 . . . . 147 D2
Keswick Cres PL6 . . . . . 125 D2
Keveral Gdns PL6 . . . . . . 64 B5
Keveral La PL11 . . . . 64 B5
Kew Cl TR2 . . . . 111 A4
Kew Noweth TR14 . . . . . 138 D2
Kew Pendra TR19 . . . . . . 97 A6
Kew Pendra Cl TR19 . . . 97 A6
Kew Vean TR26 . . . . 141 C3
KEYBRIDGE 35 B8
Keyes Cl PL1 . . . . 127 F2
KEYHAM 127 E6
Keyham Ct PL2 . . . . 127 E6
Keyham Rd PL2 . . . . 127 E4
Keyham St PL5 . . . . 127 E8
Keyham Sta PL2 . . . . . . 127 E6
Khyber Cl PL11 . . . . 127 A3
Kibbiscombe Terr PL14 . . 63 A8
Kidwelly Cl PL7 . . . . 131 C4
Kiel Pl PL3 . . . . 129 D5
Kilhallon PL24 . . . . 60 C5
Kilhallon Woodlands
PL24 . . . . 60 C5
KILKHAMPTON 5 A6
Kilkhampton Prim Sch
EX23 . . . . 5 A6
KILLATOWN 37 B1
Killatree Cross EX22 . . . . 8 F7
Kilberton Rd EX23 . . . . . 104 E5
Kilicourt TR3 . . . . 82 A7
Killiers Ct TR15 . . . . 139 C7
Killiersfield TR15 . . . . . . 139 C6
Killigrew Ave PL12 . . . . 122 D1
Killigrew St TR14 . . . . . . 70 D8
Killigrew Pl 9 TR11 . . . . 145 A4
Killigrew Rd TR11 . . . . . 113 D6
KILLIVOSE 79 C5
Killivose Gdns TR14 . . . 138 D1
Killivose Rd TR14 . . . . . 138 D1
Killyvarder Way PL25 . . 115 B6
Kilmar Cl PL14 . . . . 37 F3
Kilmar Rd PL14 . . . . 113 E6
Kilmar Way PL14 . . . . . . 37 F3
Kilminorth Woods Nature Reserve ★ PL13 . . . . 117 A4
Kilna La PL12 . . . . 53 A2
Kiln Cl
Cawsand PL10 . . . . 133 A1
Mevagissey PL26 . . . . . . 73 C4
Plymouth PL5 . . . . 127 C8
Kiln Mews PL12 . . . . 92 C1
Kilworthy Hill PL19 . . . . 147 C6
Kilworthy Rd PL19 . . . . 147 C6
Kimber Ct TR11 . . . . 145 B2
Kimberley Ct TR7 . . . . . 110 D6
Kimberley Foster Cl PL11 . 65 B5
Kimberley Park Rd TR11 . 145 A4
Kimberley Pk PL14 . . . . . 38 A3
Kimberley Pl TR11 . . . . . 145 A4
Kimberley Rd TR7 . . . . . 110 D6
Kimberly Dr PL6 . . . . . . 125 B1
Kiming EX23 . . . . 104 E4
King Arthurs Terr 5 PL34 114 C7
KINGBEARE 27 A1
King Charles Prim Sch
TR11 . . . . 145 A3
King Edward Cres PL7 . . 130 E6
King Edward Mine Mus ★
TR14 . . . . 79 E5
King Edward Rd PL12 . . 122 F2
Kingfisher Cl
Plymouth PL6 . . . . 125 E6
Tavistock PL19 . . . . 147 D2
Kingfisher Dr PL25 . . . . 115 A4
Kingfisher Way PL9 . . . . 135 C5
King George V Memorial Wlk
TR27 . . . . 142 C6
KINGSAND 133 A2
King's Ave
Falmouth TR11 . . . . 144 F4
St Austell PL25 . . . . 114 D3
Kingsbury Ho TR11 . . . . 145 A6
Kings Cl PL6 . . . . 125 E6
Kings Cross EX39 . . . . . . 2 E3
Kings Ct PL1 . . . . 128 A3
King's Hill EX23 . . . . 104 E3
King's Hill Cl EX23 . . . . 104 E4
King's Hill Ind Est EX23 . 104 F3
King's Hill Mdw EX23 . . 104 E3
Kingsland Gardens Cl
PL3 . . . . 128 E6
Kingsley Ave PL11 . . . . . 127 B2
Kingsley Cl TR1 . . . . 69 E3
Kingsley Cove TR4 . . . . . 68 A7
Kingsley Ct TR9 . . . . 57 E8
Kingsley Meade TR8 . . . 111 B8
Kingsley Rd PL4 . . . . . . 128 E4
Kingsley Terr TR16 . . . . . 67 C6
Kingsley Way TR13 . . . . 146 C5
Kingsmill Rd PL12 . . . . . 122 C5
Kingspark PL26 . . . . 58 E5
Kings Rd
Marazion TR17 . . . . 89 B5
Plymouth, Devonport PL1 127 F3
Plymouth, West Park PL5 123 F3
4 St Mawes TR2 . . . . . . 95 A6

King's Rd
Camborne TR14 ....138 D4
Penzance TR18 ....143 D5
Plymouth PL1 ....128 A2
Kings Sch PL3 ....128 E6
King's St PL12 ....112 C2
King St
Bude EX23 ....104 E5
Gunnislake PL18 ....41 A6
Millbrook PL10 ....132 E5
Newquay TR7 ....110 D6
Plymouth PL1 ....148 B3
Redruth TR15 ....140 B5
Tavistock PL19 ....147 B6
Torpoint PL11 ....127 C3
Truro TR1 ....137 D4
KING'S TAMERTON 123 F2
King's Tamerton Rd PL5 .123 F2
Kingston Cl PL7 ....131 A5
Kingston Dr PL7 ....131 B5
Kingston Rd PL17 ......28 E1
Kingsway PL10 ....133 B2
Kingsway Gdns PL6 ....124 F3
Kingswear Cres PL6 ...125 B1
Kings Wood* PL26 .....73 B7
Kingswood Est PL14 ...38 C1
Kingswood Park Ave
PL3 ....128 D6
Kingswood Rd PL18 ....41 A6
Kinnard Cres PL6 .....124 F7
Kinross Ave PL4 ......129 A4
Kinsale Rd PL5 ....123 E3
Kinsman Est PL31 ....109 C3
Kinterbury Rd PL5 ...128 B8
Kinterbury St PL1 ...149 A2
Kinterbury Terr PL5 .127 B8
Kinver Cl PL4 ....125 D4
Kipling Gdns PL5 ....124 D2
Kirby Rd TR1 ....137 A4
Kirby Pl PL4 ....148 C4
Kirby Terr PL4 ....148 C4
Kirkdale Gdns PL2 ...128 B7
Kirkella Rd PL20 ....42 D2
Kirkland Cl PL6 .....125 C7
Kirkstall Cl PL2 ....128 A8
Kirkwall Rd PL5 .....124 E3
Kirland Bower PL30 ..48 B7
Kirland Rd PL30 .....109 D2
Kirton Pl PL3 ....129 B5
Kit Hill Cres PL5 ...127 C8
Kit Hill Ctry Pk* PL17 .40 A6
Kitley Way PL5 ......123 D1
Kitter Dr PL9 ....136 A5
Kittiwake Cl TR27 ...77 E3
Kitts St **17** TR18 .143 E5
Kleinfontein Terr PL14 .38 D4
Knapmedown PL15 ...11 B1
Knapps Cl PL9 ......136 C6
Knave-Go-By TR14 ...79 D5
Kneele Gdns PL3 ....128 E8
Knighton Rd PL4 ....149 C3
Knighton Terr **3** PL2 .42 C5
Knightor Cl PL26 ...59 E6
Knights Ct PL12 ....112 B3
Knights Hill TR1 ...137 B6
Knight's Mdws TR3 ..81 F7
KNIGHTSMILL 23 F7
Knights Way TR15 ..140 D7
Knill Cl TR26 ......141 C2
Knill Cross PL10 ...132 E5
Knill Cross Cotts PL10 .132 E5
Knoll Pk TR1 ....137 F4
Knoll The PL7 ......130 B6
Knowland Cl PL1 ...127 F3
Knowle Ave PL2 ....122 E6
Knowle Terr PL20 ..42 E4
Koth Karrji PL30 ..23 E7
KUGGAR 103 B6
Kyl Cober Parc PL17 .28 E1
Kynance Cl PL11 ...126 F4
Kynance Ho TR1 ....69 E4
Kynance Terr TR12 .102 F2

L

Labatt Cl PL6 ......125 D3
Labernum Terr EX23 ..5 A6
Laburnum Cl TR11 ..144 F5
Laburnum Cotts PL19 .147 C6
Laburnum Dr TR11 ..144 F5
Lacey Cl TR14 ......79 E5
LADOCK 57 C1
Ladock Ce Prim Sch TR2 .57 C2
Ladock Rd
Ladock TR2 ....57 C1
Probus TR2 ....71 C7
Lady Beam Ct PL17 .39 F6
Ladycross PL15 ....18 F7
Ladyfern Rd PL6 ...121 C1
Lady Modifords CE Prim Sch
PL20 ....42 E4
LADY NANCE 44 F3
Ladysmith Ct PL4 .149 C4
Ladysmith Rd PL4 .149 C4
Lady St TR13 ......146 B5
Ladywell PL28 .....107 D5
Ladywell Rd PL4 ..149 B3
Laflouder Fields TR12 .99 A2
Laflouder La TR12 .99 A2
Lafrowda Cl TR19 .86 E6
Lafrowda Terr TR19 .86 F6
Laguna Ct TR15 ...140 B5
LAIRA 129 C4

Laira Ave PL3 ....129 D4
Laira Bridge Rd PL4 .129 B1
Laira Gdns PL3 .....129 C4
Laira Green Prim Sch
PL3 ....129 C4
Laira Park Cres PL4 .129 C4
Laira Park Pl PL4 ..129 B4
Laira Park Rd PL4 ..129 B4
Laira Pl PL4 ....149 C2
Laira St PL4 ....149 C3
Laity Dr TR14 ......138 F3
Laity Fields PL14 ..138 F3
Laity La TR26 ......77 C4
Laity Rd TR4 ....79 E4
Laity Wlk PL6 ......124 D6
LAKE 42 E3
Lake La
Dousland PL20 ......42 E3
Liskeard PL14 ......113 D5
Lake Mews PL10 ...132 E5
Lake Rd PL9 ....135 B6
Lakeside PL19 .....147 B6
Lakeside Dr PL5 ...123 E5
Lake View PL12 ....53 C8
Lake View Cl PL5 ..124 B6
Lakeview Dr PL5 ...124 B5
Lalebrick Rd PL9 ..135 B5
LAMANVA 93 C6
Lamanva Cl **10** TR16 .67 E4
Lamanva Rd **17** TR16 .67 E4
Lambert Rd PL5 ....124 B6
Lambert Terr **4** TR11 .145 A5
Lambhay Hill PL1 ..149 A1
Lambhay St PL1 ....149 A1
LAMBOURNE 55 B2
Lambourne Ave **7** TR5 .54 D1
Lamb Pk **6** PL24 ..60 C4
Lambs La TR11 .....144 E5
LAMELLION 113 A4
Lamellyn Dr TR1 ...69 F3
Lamellyn Rd PL14 ..29 C1
Lamerhooe Cross PL19 .29 C1
Lamerhooe Dr
Horsebridge PL19 ..29 C1
Luckett PL19 ....40 C8
LAMERTON 30 B3
Lamerton CE Prim Sch
PL19 ....30 B3
Lamerton Cl PL5 ...124 B3
Lametton Gn PL14 ..51 B4
Lamledra Hill PL26 .55 B5
Lamorak Ct PL26 ...73 B3
LAMORICK 47 E7
LAMORNA 97 E5
Lamorna Ct TR16 ..67 E4
Lamorna Dr **11** PL17 .39 F4
Lamorna Parc **2** PL7 .39 F4
Lamorna Pk
St Austell PL25 ....114 E7
Torpoint PL11 ......126 E4
Lamorne Cl **4** TR6 .55 A4
LAMORRAN 83 C8
Lampen Rd PL14 ...36 F2
Lampen Terr PL14 .36 F2
LANA 13 D7
Lana Cotts EX22 ...13 D7
Lanadwell St PL28 .107 D5
Lanaton Rd PL10 ..144 A8
Lancashire La PL30 .89 F5
Lancaster Cres PL27 .31 F3
Lancaster Gdns PL5 .124 D4
Lanchard La PL14 ..113 A5
Lanchard Rd PL14 ..113 B5
Lanchard Rise PL14 .113 B5
Landaviddy La PL13 .62 D2
Lander Ct TR1 .....137 D3
Lander Rd PL12 ....122 F3
Landeryon Gdns PL13 .143 D5
Landewednack Prim Sch
TR12 ....102 F2
Landithy TR20 .....143 A8
Landlake Cross PL15 .28 A8
Landlake Rd PL15 ..106 B2
LANDRAKE 53 B3
Landrake Cl PL5 ...127 C8
Landreath Pl PL24 .60 B5
Landrew Rd PL25 ..114 F6
LANDREYNE 27 C2
Land's End Airport TR19 .97 A6
Lands Pk PL9 ......135 F7
LANDULPH 123 A7
Landulph Cross PL12 .118 F1
Landulph Gdns PL5 .122 E8
Landulph Sch PL12 .118 F1
LANE 111 B3
LANEAST 17 B2
Lane End Cross PL14 .29 D2
Lanepark La EX39 ..2 D5
Lane Reddin Terr **2**
TR18 ....143 C2
LANESCOT 60 D6
Lane The PL7 ......130 D6
Langage Cross PL7 .131 F4
Langage Ind Est PL7 .131 E4
Langage Pk PL7 ....131 C4
Langage Science Pk
PL7 ....131 D5
Langarth PL13 .....69 D4
Langdale Cl PL6 ...125 D1
Langdale Gdns PL6 .125 D1
LANGDON 111 B4
Langdon Cross PL15 .18 D8
Langdon Ct PL9 ...136 B6
Langdon Down Way
PL18 ....126 C3
Langerwell Cl PL12 .122 C3
Langerwell La PL12 .122 C3

Langfords Mdw **4** PL35 ..9 C1
Lang Gr PL18 ......41 A3
Lang Gr
Plymouth PL9 ......136 C7
Torpoint PL19 .....147 D5
Langham Pl PL4 ...149 C3
Langhill Rd PL3 ...128 D5
Langley Cl PL6 ....125 A4
Langley Cres PL6 .124 F7
Langman Ct **13** PL20 ..41 B1
Langmead Cl PL6 ..129 C8
Langmead Rd PL6 .129 C8
Langmore Cl PL4 ..129 A7
LANGORE 18 D5
Langorran Rd TR14 .138 B3
Lang Rd PL14 .....113 B4
Langreek Bglws PL13 .62 C2
Langreek Rd PL13 .62 C2
Langstone Rd PL2 .128 C7
Langstone Terr PL2 .128 C7
Langton Rd
Falmouth TR11 ....145 A6
8 Yelverton PL20 ..42 C3
Langton Terr **8** TR11 .145 A5
Langurroc Rd TR8 .110 A3
Langurtho Rd PL23 .116 B4
Langweath Est PL12 .99 D7
Langweath Gdns TR27 .77 E3
Langweath La TR12 .99 D7
Langwedh TR11 ....67 D4
Lanhenvor Ave TR7 .110 E5
Lanherne Ave TR8 .45 A8
Lanheverne Parc **4**
TR12 ....101 C4
Lanhydrock Ho & Gdns*
PL30 ....48 D6
Lanhydrock Rd PL4 .129 B2
Lanhydrock View PL31 .109 D3
LANIVET 47 E7
Lanivet Prim Sch PL30 .47 E7
LANJETH 58 E3
LANJEW 46 F7
Lanjowan TR13 ....146 B6
LANK 24 C2
Lankelly Cl PL23 .116 B4
Lankelly La PL23 .116 A4
LANLIVERY 48 C1
Lanlivery Prim Sch PL30 .48 D2
Lanlovie Mdw PL13 .55 D8
Lanmoor Est TR16 .80 D6
Lannarth Glas TR13 .140 E1
LANNER 80 D6
Lanner Gn TR16 ...140 E1
Lanner Hill
Redruth, Pennance TR16 .140 E1
Redruth TR15 .....140 D2
Lanner Moor Terr TR16 ..80 D6
Lanner Prim Sch TR16 .80 D6
Lanner Sq TR16 ...80 D6
Lannoweth Rd TR18 .143 F6
Lanoweth TR10 ....81 D2
LANREATH 62 A2
LANSALLOS 62 D1
Lansallos St PL13 .62 D1
Lansdown Cl EX23 .104 D5
Lansdowne TR26 ..141 B4
Lansdowne Cl TR18 .143 C5
Lansdowne Ct TR18 .143 B5
Lansdowne Pk TR16 .68 C3
Lansdowne Pl TR18 .143 C4
Lansdowne Rd
Callington PL17 ...39 E4
Falmouth TR11 ....145 C3
Penzance TR18 ....143 C5
Plymouth PL6 .....124 F2
Lansdown Rd
Bude EX23 ....104 D5
Wadebridge PL27 .108 B5
LANSTEPHAN 106 C8
Lantallack Cross PL12 .53 A3
LANTEGLOS 14 F1
LANTEGLOS HIGHWAY .61 E4
Lanuthnoe Est TR27 .77 F1
Lanwithan Cl PL22 .112 D2
Lanwithan Rd PL22 .112 D2
Lanxon Cres PL30 .48 C2
Lanyon Cl PL14 ...37 F3
Lanyon Rd TR3 ....82 B8
Lappa Valley Steam
Railway* TR8 .....56 C7
Lapthorn Cl PL9 ..135 C7
Larch Cl PL12 .....122 C3
Larch Dr PL6 ......122 F7
Larcombe Rd PL25 .115 A6
Laregan Hill TR18 .143 C3
Lariggan Cres TR18 .143 D4
Lariggan Rd TR18 .143 D4
Larkfield Cl PL26 .58 E5
Larkhall Rise PL3 .129 B5
Larkham Cl PL7 ...130 C6
Larkham La PL7 ...130 C6
Lark Hill PL2 .....128 A6
LATCHLEY 40 D8
Latham Cl PL7 ....129 A7
Latimer Cl PL7 ...131 B5
Latimer Wlk PL6 ..124 E7
Launcells Cross PL15 ..5 B1
Launceston Castle*
PL15 ....106 C6

Launceston Rd
Bodmin PL31 ......35 B1
Kelly Bray PL17 ...39 E6
Launceston Ret Pk PL15 .106 C4
Launceston Sta* PL15 .106 B6
Launceston Steam Rly*
PL15 ....18 E3
Laura Cl PL34 .....14 D7
Laura Dr PL25 ....115 A5
Laurel Cl PL2 .....128 A7
Laurel Dene PL2 ..128 A7
Laurel Dr PL6 ....125 E5
Laurel Rd PL12 ...128 A7
Laurels The PL18 .40 E6
La Vague TR3 .....82 C5
Lavington Cl PL7 .131 B5
Lavinia Dr PL7 ...130 C5
Lavorrick Orchs PL26 ..73 C4
LAWHITTON 19 C1
Lawn Cl **2** PL7 ..131 C5
Lawn Steps TR11 .145 B4
Lawns The
Plymouth PL5 .....124 E1
Torpoint PL11 ....127 A4
Lawn The
Par PL24 ....60 B5
Tavistock PL19 ...147 D6
Lawrence House Mus* PL15 .106 C6
Lawrence Rd
Plymouth PL3 .....135 A6
St Agnes TR5 .....54 C1
Lawry Cl **6** PL4 .113 B5
Lawson Gr PL9 ...135 C7
Lawton Cl TR7 ....110 B5
Law Wlk PL6 .....124 D6
Leader Rd TR1 ....111 E7
Leafield PL31 .....35 B2
Leander Way PL5 .124 D2
Leanway PL12 ....122 E2
Leap Pk TR3 .....69 C3
Leas The TR1 ....137 E5
Leat Cl PL20 .....42 E3
Leatfield Dr PL6 .124 F4
Leatherby Cl PL6 .124 F7
Leather Tor Cl **4** PL20 ..42 C3
Leat Rd
Lifton PL16 ......19 F3
Pendeen TR19 ....75 A1
Leatside PL6 .....121 C1
Leats The TR1 ...137 C4
Leat View PL12 ..122 B3
Leat View **7** EX23 ..4 E1
Leat Wlk
Plymouth PL3 ....128 E6
Roborough PL6 ..121 D1
Saltash PL12 ....122 D4
Leaves Yd PL3 ...122 D4
Le Way EX23 .....104 F6
LEBURNICK 28 D8
Leburnick Cross PL15 .28 D8
Ledgate La PL7 ...131 F8
Ledra Cl TR12 ....103 A4
Ledrah Gdns PL25 .114 B3
Ledrah Rd PL25 ..114 B3
LEEDSTOWN 78 E1
Leedstown Prim Sch
TR27 ....78 E1
Leeside Ct **7** PL2 .128 A4
Lefra Orch TR19 ..97 B6
Legendry Land's End*
TR19 ....96 A5
Leggos Ct **10** TR15 .140 B5
Legion La **3** PL24 ..60 D5
Legis Wlk PL5 ...125 B8
LEIGHAM 124 E7
Leigham Ct PL4 ..148 B2
Leigham Manor Dr PL6 .129 F8
Leigham Prim Sch PL6 .125 E1
Leigham Terrace La PL1 .148 B2
Leigh Ct PL6 .....129 A8
Leigh La
Hatt PL12 ....53 D6
Roborough PL6 ..121 D5
Leighton Rd PL3 .128 F8
LELANT 77 E4
LELANT DOWNS ...77 D2
Lelant Mdws TR26 .77 E3
Lelant Saltings Sta TR26 ..77 E3
Lelant Stn PL30 ..23 B2
Lemellen Gdns PL30 .23 B2
Lemin Parc TR27 .78 E3
Lemin's Ct TR15 .140 B5
Lemon Hill TR11 .82 A3
Lemon Hill Gdns TR11 ..82 A3
Lemon Mews Rd TR1 .137 D4
Lemon Quay TR1 .137 D4
Lemon Row TR1 ..137 D4
Lemon St
St Keverne TR12 .101 D4
10 Truro TR1 ...137 D4
Lemon Terr TR4 ..81 D8
Lender La **5** TR12 .99 A2
Lendra Cl PL7 ....39 D4
LERRYN 61 D8
Lerryn CE Prim Sch PL22 .61 D8
Lerryn View PL22 .61 C8
Lerwick Rd PL17 .31 F3
LESCROW 116 B6
Lescudjack Cres TR18 .143 F6
Lescudjack Rd TR18 .143 E6
Lescudjack Terr TR18 .143 E6
Lesingey La TR20 .88 A5
Leskinnick Pl **14** TR18 .143 E6
Leskinnick St TR18 .143 E6
Leskinnick Terr TR18 .143 E6

Leslie Ct TR13 ....146 B6
LESNEWTH 10 A1
Lesnewth **18** PL24 ..60 B4
Lester Cl PL3 .....129 B6
Lestraynes La TR10 .92 E8
Lethlean Cl TR27 .142 D7
Lethlean La TR27 .142 D7
Lethlean Towans TR27 ..142 D8
LEVALSA MEOR ...73 B8
Levant Cl TR19 ...86 F8
Levant Mine & Beam
Engine* TR19 .....74 E1
Levant Rd TR19 ..86 F8
Leven Cotts EX23 .104 D5
Leverlake Rd EX23 ..6 F4
Levine View TR11 .144 E1
LEWANNICK 27 B7
Lewannick Cl PL15 ..27 B7
Lewannick Com Prim Sch
PL15 ....27 B7
Lewarne Barton TR18 .43 D1
Lewarne Cres TR7 .111 C7
Lewarne Rd TR7 .111 C8
Lewes Gdns PL5 .124 C4
Lewis Way PL25 ..114 E6
Lewman Rd TR2 ..71 C6
Lewman Rd TR2 ..71 C6
Leworthy Cross EX22 ..8 E4
LEY 126 E1
Ley La PL20 .....119 D6
Leypark Ct PL6 ..125 E2
Leypark Dr PL6 ..125 E2
Leypark Wlk PL6 .125 E2
Leys La TR17 .....89 B5
LEZANT 28 B6
Libby Ct PL12 ....122 C5
Liberator Row **4** PL27 ..31 F3
Lidden Cl TR18 ..143 C3
Lidden Cres TR18 .143 C3
Lidden Rd PL23 ..143 C3
Liddicoat Rd PL22 .112 D3
Liddle Way PL7 ..131 B6
Lifeboat Hill **22** TR26 .141 B6
LIFTON 19 F3
LIFTONDOWN 19 F3
Liftondown Cross PL16 ..19 F4
Lifton Prim Sch PL16 ..19 F4
Lighterage Hill TR1 .137 E2
Lighthouse Hill TR11 ..67 C6
Lighthouse La PL26 ..85 C5
Lighthouse Rd TR12 .102 F2
Lilac Cl PL9 .....135 C5
Lillicrap Ct TR1 .137 C4
Limerick Pl PL4 ..149 C3
Limes La
Liskeard PL14 ....113 B5
Tavistock PL19 ...147 A6
Limes The PL6 ...124 F2
Limetree Rd PL3 .128 D7
Line Tree Way PL15 ..27 D4
Lincoln Ave PL4 .149 C4
Lincoln Row **9** PL27 ..31 D3
Linden Ave TR7 ..110 E5
Linden Cres TR7 .110 E5
Linden Terr PL14 .149 C3
Lindsay Fields TR9 ..45 E1
Lingard Cl PL14 ..113 A6
Lingfield Ave PL26 ..58 E1
Linhay Cl PL25 ..115 D6
Linkadells PL7 ...130 C6
Link Cl TR11 .....144 F4
Linketty La PL7 ..130 C5
Linketty Lane E PL6 .125 A1
Linketty Lane W PL6 .128 F8
LINKINHORNE 39 B8
Link Rd PL5 .....106 B3
Links The
Falmouth TR11 ...144 F1
Praa Sands TR20 ..90 C4
Links View EX23 .104 F6
Linley Cl TR3 ....69 D3
Linnet Ct PL12 ..122 C2
Linton Cl PL5 ....124 C8
Linton La EX39 ...2 E5
Linton Rd PL5 ...124 C7
Linton Sq PL5 ...124 C8
Lippall Dr PL9 ..135 E6
LIPSON 149 C4
Lipson Ave PL4 ..149 C4
Lipson Com Coll PL4 .129 C4
Lipson Ct PL4 ...149 B3
Lipson Rd PL4 ...149 B4
Lipson Sp Ctr PL4 .129 B4
Lipson Terr PL4 .149 C4
LIPSON VALE 129 A4
Lipson Vale PL4 .129 A4
Lipstone Cres PL4 .149 C4
Lisbon Terr TR19 .97 A6
Liscawn Terr PL11 .127 B3
Liscombe Cl PL18 .41 A7
Lishaperhill Cross EX22 ..5 E4
LISKEARD 113 E6
Liskeard Bsns Pk PL14 .113 E6
Liskeard Com Hospl
PL14 ....113 E7
Liskeard & District Mus*
PL14 ....113 C6
Liskeard Hill PL14 ..36 F2
Liskeard Hillfort Prim Sch
PL14 ....113 A6
Liskeard Rd
Callington PL17 ...39 E4
Saltash PL12 .....122 B3
Trematon PL12 ...53 E3
Liskeard Sch & Com Coll
PL14 ....113 C7
Liskeard Sta PL14 .113 B4
Liskerrett Rd PL14 .113 D5

Liskey TR6. . . . . 55 A4
Liskey Hill TR6. . . . . 55 A4
Liskey Hill Est TR6 **1**. . . 55 A4
Liskey Tourist Pk TR3 . . . 69 C6
Lisson Gr PL4. . . . . 128 F4
Lister Cl PL7. . . . . 130 F6
Lister Hill **10** TR11 . . . . 145 A4
Lister St TR11. . . . . 145 A3
Listowel Dr PL13. . . . . . . 117 D4
Listry Rd TR7. . . . . 110 E5
Litchaton Cres PL7. . . . . 130 B7
Litchaton Way PL7. . . . . 130 B7
Litchfield Cl PL7 . . . . 131 B6
Little Ash Gdns PL5 . . . . 123 B1
Little Ash Rd PL5 . . . . . . 123 B1
LITTLE BOSULLOW 75 D1
Little Bridge Cross EX22. . 8 A5
Littlebridge Mdw EX22. . . 8 A5
Little Bridge Pk PL27. . . 108 D6
LITTLE BRYNN 46 E5
Little Butts PL9 . . . . 135 E6
Little Castle St **7** TR1 . . 137 C4
LITTLE COMFORT. 28 C7
Little Dean PL14 . . . . 113 A5
Little Dinas PL28. . . . . . . 107 E4
Little Dock La PL5 . . . . . 124 B2
Little Down La PL5 . . . . . 121 E3
Little Down Pk TR7 . . . . 111 A4
LITTLE FALMOUTH 145 B7
Little Fancy Cl PL6 . . . . . 125 C7
Little Gilly Hill **3** TR15 . 140 C4
Little Gregwartha PL14. . 80 A5
Little-in-sight **10** TR26 . 141 A5
LITTLE KIRLAND. 109 C1
Little La
  Hayle TR27. . . . . 142 E7
  Kingsand PL10. . . . . . 133 A2
  Staddiscombe PL9 . . . 135 D3
Little Laney PL13. . . . . 62 E1
Little Mdw
  Bodmin PL31. . . . . 109 D5
  Pyworthy EX22 . . . . 8 E5
Little Mill La PL27 . . . . . . 77 E2
Little Oaks TR10 . . . . 144 B6
Little Orch PL12. . . . . 53 C3
LITTLE PETHERICK 32 C6
Little Point Cres PL10 . . 132 F5
LITTLE PRIDEAUX 60 B7
Little Stark Cl PL26. . . . . 58 B4
Littleton Pl PL7 . . . . 127 F4
Little Trelower Pk PL26 . 58 F1
Little Treloweth TR15 . . 139 B6
Little Tregullas Est PL27 . . 21 E2
Little Trethew PL27 . . . . . 21 E2
Little Trethewey Est TR19 96 E4
Little Trethiggey TR8. . . 111 F2
Little Treverrow PL27. . . . 21 E2
Little Western Ry★ TR7 110 E5
Little Woburn Cl PL15 . . 106 C4
Littlewood Cl PL7. . . . . . 131 A4
LIZARD. 102 F2
Lizard Cl PL6 . . . . 124 F7
Lizard Lighthouse Her Ctr★
  TR12. . . . . 102 F1
Lizard Nature Reserve The★
  . . . . 100 F2
Lizard Wlk PL6. . . . . 125 A7
Llantillio Dr PL2 . . . . 128 B8
Llawnroc Cl TR14 . . . . . . 138 E2
Llewellyn Cl PL32. . . . . . 105 C3
Lloyds Rd TR12 . . . . 103 A2
Loatmead Cross EX22 . . . . 3 E3
LOCKENGATE 47 E4
Lockeridge Rd PL20. . . . . 41 B1
Lockington Ave PL3. . . . 128 F7
Locks Wlk PL1 . . . . 127 E1
Lockyer Ct PL1 . . . . 148 C2
Lockyer Mews PL19 . . . . 147 C6
Lockyer Rd PL3 . . . . 128 E5
Lockyers Quay PL4. . . . . 149 B2
Lockyer St PL1. . . . . 148 C2
Lockyer Terr PL12 . . . . . 123 A3
Lodenek Ave PL28 . . . . . 107 D4
Lodge Dr TR1. . . . . 137 F6
Lodge Gdns PL6 . . . . 124 E3
Lodge Hill PL14 . . . . 113 A3
Lodge La PL8 . . . . 136 F5
Lodge Way TR9 . . . . 45 F2
Loe Bar Rd TR13 . . . . 98 C8
Loe Valley Rd TR13. . . . . 146 A7
Lofoten Cl PL1. . . . . 127 E2
Loftus Gdns PL5 . . . . 123 C2
Logans Ct TR14. . . . . 141 D2
Loggans Cl TR27 . . . . . . 142 E8
Loggans Rd TR27 . . . . . . 142 F8
Loggans Way TR27. . . . . 142 E8
Loggans Wlk TR27 . . . . . 142 E8
Lollabury Rd PL12. . . . . . 122 E3
Lomond Hall TR26 . . . . . 141 D1
LONDON APPRENTICE . . 59 B1
Longcarne
  Harrowbarrow PL17 . . . 40 C4
  Plymouth PL7. . . . . . . 130 B7
Long Acre PL12 . . . . 122 B4
Long-A-Row Ct EX23. . . . 10 C6
Long Barn The TR20. . . . . 89 D8
LONGBRIDGE 129 F7
Longbridge Cl PL6 . . . . . 129 F6
Longbridge Rd
  Plymouth, Laira PL3. . . 129 F7
  Plymouth, Longbridge PL6. 129 E7
Longbrook Barton PL7 . 130 D5
Longbrook St PL7. . . . . . 130 F4
Longcause PL7 . . . . 130 F4
Longcause Specl Sch
  . . . . 130 F4
Longcombe La PL13 . . . . . 62 D3
LONGCROSS 29 F6
Long Cross PL29 . . . . 22 C6
Longcross Victorian Gdns★
  PL29. . . . . 22 C6
Long Downs PL6 . . . . . . 125 E3
LONGDOWNS 81 A1
Longdowns Trad EstTR10. 81 A1
Longfield TR11 . . . . 144 E4
Longfield Cl **23** PL17 . . . 39 F4
Longfield Dr PL32. . . . . . 105 C3
Longfield Pl PL4 . . . . 149 B4
Longfield Rd PL32 . . . . . 105 C3
Longfield Villas PL5 . . . . 135 D8
Longhouse La PL27 . . . . . 21 E3
Long La
  High Street PL26. . . . . . 58 C4
  Ludgvan TR20 . . . . 89 A7
  St Erth TR20, TR27. . . . 89 F8
LONGLANDS 122 A1
Longlands PL9. . . . . 135 D8
Longlands La PL22 . . . . . . 89 F7
Long Lanes TR20. . . . . . . 89 F7
Long Ley PL3 . . . . 129 B6
Longman's La **3** PL14 . . 39 E4
Long Mdw PL30 . . . . 107 D7
Long Mdw View PL23 . . . 116 B5
Longmeadow PL23 . . . . 130 E7
Longmeadow Rd PL2. . . 122 E3
Long Moor TR12 . . . . 103 A5
Long Orch PL20 . . . . 41 B1
Long Park Cl PL9. . . . . . . 135 F5
Longpark Dr EX23. . . . . . . 4 D5
Long Park Dr PL6 . . . . . . 125 D7
Long Park Rd PL12 . . . . . 122 D2
Longpark Way PL25 . . . . 114 F5
Long Pk PL15 . . . . 18 D2
Long Rd PL12 . . . . 122 B4
LONGROCK 88 F6
Longrock Bsns PkTR20 . . 88 F6
Longrock Ind EstTR20 . . 88 F6
Long Row PL3 . . . . 97 F7
Long Rowden PL3. . . . . . 128 E6
Long Steps PL23 . . . . . . 116 C4
LONGSTONE
  Carbis Bay 141 E1
  St Mabyn 34 F8
Longstone Ave PL6. . . . . 125 A6
Longstone Cl TR26. . . . . 141 E1
Longstone Hill TR26. . . . 141 E1
Long Terrace Cl PL7. . . . 131 C5
Longview Rd PL12 . . . . . 122 D2
Longview Terr PL3 . . . . . 129 B7
Longwood Cl PL7 . . . . . . 131 A4
Longwool Mdw EX23 . . . . 7 B6
LOOE 117 D3
Looe Com Sch PL13. . . . 117 D6
Looe Hill
  Looe PL13 . . . . 63 F5
  Seaton PL13, PL11. . . . 64 A5
Looe Prim Sch PL11 . . . 117 D4
Looe St PL4 . . . . 149 A2
Looe Sta PL13. . . . . 117 C4
Lookout The **7** TR11. . . . 145 B5
Looseleigh Cl PL6. . . . . . 125 A4
Looseleigh La PL6 . . . . . 124 F5
Looseleigh Pk PL6 . . . . . 124 E5
Lopes Ct PL26 . . . . 121 C1
Lopes Rd
  Dousland PL20. . . . . . . 42 E3
  Plymouth PL2. . . . . . . 128 B6
Lopwell Cl PL6 . . . . 124 F5
Lord Louis Cres PL9 . . . . 134 F6
Lords Mdw TR2 . . . . 71 F3
Lorrimore Ave PL2. . . . . 127 F7
Loscombe Cl TR16 . . . . . 80 A5
Loscombe La PL6 . . . . . . 80 A5
Loscombe Rd TR16 . . . . 139 E1
Lost Gdns of Heligan The★
  PL26. . . . . 73 B5
LOSTWITHIEL 117 C3
Lostwithiel Mus★ PL22. 112 C2
Lostwithiel Prim Sch
  . . . . 112 C2
Lostwithiel Rd PL30, PL31. 48 C7
Lostwithiel St PL23. . . . . 116 C4
Lostwithiel Sta PL22 . . . 112 D2
Lostwood Rd PL25 . . . . . 114 E4
Lotherton Cl PL7. . . . . . . 131 B3
Loughborough Rd PL5 . . 123 C1
LOVATON 42 F1
Love La
  Bodmin PL31. . . . . 109 F5
  Hayle TR27. . . . . 142 E7
  Mousehole TR19 . . . . . 88 C1
  Penryn TR10. . . . . 144 D8
  Penzance TR18. . . . . . 143 C4
  Saltash PL12 . . . . 122 E2
  24 St Ives TR26. . . . . 141 B6
Lovell Rd PL3 . . . . 128 D6
Loveny Cl PL14 . . . . 36 F2
Loveny Rd PL14 . . . . 36 F2
Lovibond Wlk PL7. . . . . . 108 C5
Lowarth Cl TR13 . . . . . . 146 B6
Lowarthan Marghas
  TR15 . . . . 140 D5
Lowenac Ct **2** PL3. . . . 128 E6
Lowenac Gdns TR14 . . . 138 C2
Lowena Ct **1** TR1 . . . . . 137 D4
Lowenek Ct TR11. . . . . . 144 E5
Lowenna Gdns PL13. . . . 117 C4
Lowenna Manor PL27 . . . 21 E3
Lowen Way TR3. . . . . 69 C3
Lower Anderton Rd PL10 132 F5
Lower Barncoose TR15. . 139 F6
Lower Biteford Cross EX39 . 3 A6
LOWER BODINNAR 87 D5
Lower Bore St PL31 . . . . 109 D5
LOWER BOSCASWELL . . . 74 E2

Lower Boscaswell Parc
  TR19 . . . . 74 F1
LOWER BREA 139 A3
Lower Broad La TR15,
  TR16 . . . . 139 C8
Lower Cardrew La TR15 . 140 B6
Lower Castle Rd TR2. . . . 95 A5
Lower Chapel St PL13 . . 117 D3
Lower Church St TR2 . . . 142 D6
Lower Cleaverfield PL15. 106 C7
Lower Compton Rd PL3 . 128 F5
LOWER CLICKER 51 F4
Lower Clicker Rd PL14 . . 51 F4
LOWER COMPTON 129 A5
Lower Coronation Terr **9**
  PL17. . . . . 39 F4
Lower Eastcliff TR4 . . . . . 68 A7
Lower Elms PL7. . . . . 21 F3
Lower Fairfield PL12 . . . . 65 A8
Lower Farm Rd PL7 . . . . 131 A4
Lower Fore St PL12 . . . . 123 A2
Lower Glen Pk PL14. . . . . 38 C4
Lower Goongumpas La
  . . . . 68 F1
Lower Goonrea PL13 . . . 117 B4
LOWER GREEN 146 A5
Lower Greenbanks PL7. . 21 E2
Lower Green St TR18. . . 143 D1
Lower Gurnick Rd PL18 . 143 B3
Lower Hill TR13 . . . . 146 C6
Lower Hillcrest
  Helston TR13 . . . . 146 C6
  6 Perranporth TR6. . . . 55 A4
Lower Hillside PL14. . . . . 50 B6
Lower Hugus Rd TR3 . . . 69 C3
Lower Kelly PL18 . . . . 41 A3
Lower La
  Mawgan TR12. . . . . 99 D7
  6 Plymouth PL1. . . . . 149 A2
Lower Lux St **5** PL14 . . 113 C6
Lower Market St
  Looe PL13 . . . . 117 D3
  Penryn TR10. . . . . 144 C7
Lower Mdw **5** TR4 . . . . . 69 A3
Lower Merritts Hill
  TR16 . . . . 67 E4
Lower Middle Hill PL14. . 38 E4
Lower Moors Rd TR15 . . 140 B6
LOWER NINNES 76 B1
Lower Parc PL9 . . . . 135 F4
Lower Pengegon TR14 . . 138 F3
Lower Peverell Rd PL18. 143 E7
Lower Pk TR2. . . . . 70 F5
Lower Polstain Rd TR3 . . 69 D3
LOWER PORTHPEAN 59 E1
Lower Port View PL12 . . 122 F2
LOWER PROSPIDNICK . . . 91 C6
Lower Pumpfield Row
  TR15 . . . . 139 B6
Lower Rd PL11 . . . . 64 C4
Lower Redannick TR1 . . 137 C4
Lower Ridings PL7. . . . . . 131 B7
LOWER ROSE 55 D5
LOWER ROSEWARNE . . . 138 C4
Lower Rosewin Row **9**
  TR1 . . . . 137 D5
Lower Row PL10 . . . . 133 A2
Lower Rowes Terr PL26. . 58 D5
Lower Saltram PL9. . . . . 135 C7
Lower Sheffield TR19 . . . 97 F7
Lowerside PL2. . . . . 128 A8
Lower St EX22. . . . . 11 E8
Lower St
  Looe PL13 . . . . 117 D3
  Plymouth PL4. . . . . . . 149 A3
Lower Tamar Terr **18** PL18 41 A7
Lower Terr TR3 . . . . 81 B4
LOWERTOWN
  Helston 91 E4
  Lostwithiel. 48 A4
Lower Town PL17 . . . . 28 E1
Lowertown Cl PL12 . . . . . 53 C3
Lowertown La TR13 . . . . 146 C7
LOWER TREBULLETT 28 A4
Lower Tregosteeves
  PL26. . . . . 59 A1
Lower Tywarnhayle **10**
  TR6 . . . . 55 A5
Lower Well La TR15 . . . . 146 C6
Lower Well Pk PL26. . . . . 73 C3
Lower Wesley Terr PL14. . 38 D4
Lower Woodside PL25. . . 114 A4
Lowery Cross PL20. . . . . . 42 F4
Low Lee Rd TR19 . . . . 88 D1
Lowley Rd PL15 . . . . 18 E2
Lucas Cl PL31. . . . . 109 E3
Lucas La PL7 . . . . 130 D6
Lucas Terr PL4 . . . . 129 B2
LUCKETT. 40 B8
Lucknow Rd PL31 . . . . . . 48 D8
Lucknow Road S **2** PL31. 48 D8
LUDGVAN 89 A7
Ludgvan Prim SchTR20. . 89 B8
Ludwell Rd **2** PL3 . . . . 128 E6
LUFFINCOTT 13 C5
Luffman Cl PL25 . . . . 62 D6
Lugger The PL2 . . . . 83 B2
Lukes Cl TR1 . . . . 137 F5
Luke's La TR10. . . . . 89 F6
Lulworth Dr PL6 . . . . 125 B7
Lundy Cl PL6 . . . . 124 F7
Lundy Dr EX23 . . . . 10 C6
Lundy Rd PL29 . . . . 22 E7
Lusart Dr PL31 . . . . 102 F2
Lusty Glaze Adventure Ctr
  TR7 . . . . 111 A8
Lusty Glaze Rd TR7 . . . . 111 A7

LUTSFORD 3 A6
Lutsford Cross EX39. . . . . 3 A6
Lutyens Fold PL19 . . . . . . 29 C6
Luxmore Cl PL6. . . . . 125 E1
Luxon Dr TR7. . . . . 110 F4
Lux Park L Ctr PL14 . . . . 113 C7
Luxstowe Dr TR11 . . . . . 113 C6
Luxstowe Gdns PL14 . . . 113 C6
LUXULYAN 48 A1
Luxulyan Rd PL24 . . . . . 115 F7
Luxulyan Sch PL30 . . . . . 48 A1
Luxulyan Sta PL30 . . . . . 47 F1
Lych Cl PL9 . . . . 135 A6
Lychgate Dr TR1 . . . . . . 137 C6
Lydcott Cres PL14. . . . . . 63 F8
Lydcott Cres PL13. . . . . . 63 F8
Lydcot Wlk PL6 . . . . 124 F7
Lyford Park Rd PL3 . . . . 128 D5
Lyd Gdns PL19 . . . . 147 D5
Lydia Way PL3 . . . . 149 B4
Lympne Ave PL5 . . . . . . 123 E5
Lynbridge Ct **5** PL19. . . 147 B5
Lyndhurst Ave PL2 . . . . . 128 A5
Lyndhurst Cl PL2 . . . . . . 128 C6
Lyndhurst Rd PL2. . . . . . 128 C6
Lyndon Ct PL12 . . . . 122 D4
Lyndrick Rd PL3. . . . . . . 128 E7
Lynes Cotts **2** PL14. . . 51 A7
Lyngrove Terr TR2 . . . . . 27 B3
Lynher Ct PL12 . . . . 122 F1
Lynher Dr PL12 . . . . 122 F1
Lynher St PL5. . . . . 123 D2
Lynher Way PL17 . . . . . . 38 E8
Lynher Way
  28 Callington PL17 . . . 39 F4
  North Hill PL15 . . . . . . 27 A4
Lyn-Meynek TR15 . . . . . 140 D4
Lynmouth Cl PL7 . . . . . . 130 C7
LYNSTONE 104 D3
Lynstone Cotts EX23 . . . 104 D3
Lynstone Rd EX23 . . . . . 104 D3
Lyn Terr **8** TR18 . . . . . . 143 C1
Lynwood Ave PL7 . . . . . 130 B6
Lynwood Cl PL31. . . . . . 109 A4
Lynwood Cotts **1** TR19. 88 C1
Lynwood Flats 91 A1
Lyons Rd PL25 . . . . 115 B4
Lytton Pl PL7 . . . . 114 F4

M

Mabbots Ct TR18. . . . . . 143 F6
MABE BURNTHOUSE 93 C8
Mabena Cl PL30. . . . . 34 C8
Mabe Prim SchTR10 . . . . 81 C1
MacAdam Rd PL4. . . . . . 149 C1
MacAulay Cres PL5 . . . . 124 C1
Macey St PL11 . . . . 127 C3
Mackenzie Pl PL5 . . . . . 123 C2
McLean Dr PL26 . . . . 58 D5
Madden Rd PL1 . . . . 127 F2
Maddever Cres PL14 . . . 113 C5
Maddock Cl PL3 . . . . 131 A4
Maddock Dr PL7 . . . . 131 B4
Maddocks Cross EX22 . . . 3 F2
Madeira Dr EX23. . . . . 6 F5
Madeira Rd
  Falmouth TR11. . . . . . 145 A1
  Plymouth PL1 . . . . 149 A1
Madeira Villas **1** PL20 . . 42 C5
Madeira Wlk TR11 . . . . . 145 A2
MADERS 39 D6
Madford La PL15. . . . . . . 106 C5
Madge Ct **3** PL19 . . . . . 147 B6
Madge La PL19 . . . . 147 B6
Madison Terr PL14 . . . . . 142 E7
Madison Vean TR27 . . . . 142 E7
MADRON 143 B8
Madron Rd TR18 . . . . . . 143 C7
MAENPORTH 93 F4
Maenporth Est TR11 . . . . 93 E4
Maenporth Rd TR11. . . . . 93 E4
Maen Valley Pk TR11. . . . 93 E5
MAER 104 C3
Maer Down Rd EX23 . . . 104 C3
Maer La EX23 . . . . 104 C3
Magdalen Gdns PL7. . . . 130 F3
Magnificent Music Machines
  Mus★ PL14 . . . . 51 C3
Magnolia Cl **3** PL31 . . . 131 B5
Magnolia **3** PL9 . . . . . . 135 F7
Magor Ave TR14 . . . . 79 E5
Maida Vale Terr PL4. . . . 128 F4
Maiden St **1** EX23 . . . . . . 4 E1
Maidenwell Rd PL7 . . . . 130 C5
Maidstone Pl PL5. . . . . . 123 E4
Maine Gdns PL2 . . . . 127 F7
Main Rd
  Crumplehorn PL13. . . . 62 D2
  Downderry PL11 . . . . . . 64 C5
Main St TR18 . . . . 143 C7
MAINSTONE 104 C3
Mainstone Ave PL4. . . . . 149 C2
Maitland Dr PL3 . . . . 128 F8
Majorca Rd PL14. . . . . . 133 B4
Maker La PL11 . . . . 133 B4
Maker Rd PL11 . . . . 127 A2
Maker View PL3 . . . . 128 B4
Malabar Ho TR1 . . . . 69 F3
Malabar Rd TR1. . . . . . . 137 D4
Mallard Cl PL7. . . . . 130 F5
Mallard Cl PL6 . . . . 108 C6
Malmesbury Cl PL2 . . . . 128 B8
Malory Cl PL5. . . . . 124 D2
MALPAS. 70 D2
Malpas Ho TR1 . . . . 137 E4
Malpas Rd TR1. . . . . 137 D4
Malt House Cl **3** TR3. . . 68 D6
Malt House Rd TR27 . . . 142 D6

Malt House Gdns **2**
  TR18 . . . . 143 C2
Malthouse La TR17. . . . . 89 C5
Malt House **3** TR18. . . 143 C2
MANACCAN 101 A8
Manaccan Prim Sch
  TR12 . . . . 101 A8
MANADON 124 D3
Manadon Cl PL5. . . . . . . 124 E1
Manadon Dr PL5. . . . . . . 124 E1
Manadon Football Ctr
  PL2 . . . . 124 D2
Manadon Hill PL5, PL6. . 124 E1
Manadon Vale Prim Sch **1**
  PL5. . . . . 128 E8
Manaton Cl TR13. . . . . . 146 D8
Manby Gdns PL5 . . . . . . 123 F5
Mandalay Villas **3** TR9 . . 45 E1
Mandeley Cl PL33. . . . . . 14 D2
Manely Way PL7 . . . . 131 A4
Manewas Way TR7 . . . . . 111 B7
Manfield Way PL5 . . . . . 115 C4
Manifold Gdns PL3. . . . . 129 D5
Manley Cl PL14 . . . . 113 B5
Manley Rd PL14 . . . . 113 B5
Manley Terr **5** PL14 . . . 113 B5
MANNAMEAD 128 F5
Mannamead Ave PL3 . . . 128 F5
Mannamead Ct **9** PL3 . 128 F6
Mannamead Rd PL3. . . . 128 F6
Man of War View PL7 . . 102 F2
Manor Bourne Rd PL9. . 135 C1
Manor Cl
  Blisland PL30. . . . . 35 D8
  Crackington Haven EX23 . 10 C6
  Falmouth TR11. . . . . . 144 E5
  Heamoor TR18 . . . . . . 143 D7
  Helston TR13 . . . . 146 D8
  St Austell PL25 . . . . . . 114 F5
  Tavistock PL19 . . . . . . 147 A6
Manor Cotts TR11 . . . . . 145 D3
Manor Cres TR11 . . . . . . 144 E5
Manor Dr TR26 . . . . 141 C3
Manor Farm PL20 . . . . . . 42 E3
Manor Farm Rd PL26. . . 115 A1
Manor Gdns
  Camelford PL32. . . . . . 105 D4
  Horrabridge PL20 . . . . 42 B4
  Millbrook PL10. . . . . . 132 F6
  Plymouth PL6. . . . . . . 128 B2
  Redruth TR15 . . . . 140 B6
  St Erth TR27. . . . . 142 A1
  Truro TR1 . . . . 137 E5
Manor La PL3. . . . . 129 D5
Manor Park Cl PL7 . . . . . 130 F5
Manor Park Dr PL7. . . . . 131 A4
MANOR PARSLEY 68 B5
Manor Pk
  Dousland PL20. . . . . . . 42 E3
  Duloe PL14 . . . . 51 A1
  Saltash PL12 . . . . 122 D2
Manor Pl TR18. . . . . 143 D7
Manor Rd
  Bude EX23 . . . . 104 C4
  Camborne TR14. . . . . 138 C2
  Carharrack TR16 . . . . . 80 E8
  Falmouth TR11. . . . . . 144 E5
  Newquay TR7. . . . . . . 110 D6
  Plymouth PL9. . . . . . . 135 E8
  Tavistock PL19 . . . . . . 147 B6
  Torpoint PL11 . . . . . . 127 A2
Manor St PL1 . . . . 148 A3
Manor View PL24 . . . . . . 60 B4
Manor Way
  Heamoor TR18 . . . . . . 143 D7
  Helston TR13 . . . . 146 D8
  Tavistock PL19 . . . . . . 147 B6
Manse Rd **6** TR3 . . . . . . 81 F7
Mansion Ho The PL1 . . . 134 A8
Manson Pl PL26 . . . . 58 C8
Manston Ct PL5 . . . . 123 E5
Mantle Gdns PL5. . . . . . 127 D8
Maple Ave
  Camelford PL32. . . . . . 105 C5
  Torpoint PL11 . . . . . . 127 A3
Maple Cl
  Bodmin PL31. . . . . 109 A4
  23 Callington PL17 . . . 39 F4
  Plymouth PL6. . . . . . . 125 E6
  5 St Columb Major TR9 . 45 D6
  St Dennis PL26 . . . . . . 58 C8
  Tavistock PL19 . . . . . . 147 D3
Maple Ct **2** PL9 . . . . . . 135 F7
Maple Gr
  Plymouth, Mutley PL4 . 128 D4
  Plymouth PL6. . . . . . . 130 B5
Maple Way PL6. . . . . 125 E7
MARAZION 89 B6
Marazion Mus★ TR17 . . . 89 B5
Marazion SchTR17. . . . . 89 C6
Marchant's Cross PL20. . . 42 F1
Marchant's Way PL20 . . . 42 F2
Marconi Centre (Mus)★
  TR13 . . . . 98 F2
Marconi St PL13 . . . . . . 146 B6
Marcus Hill TR7 . . . . 110 E6
Marcwheal **3** TR19 . . . . 88 C1
Mardon Cl PL6. . . . . 125 D4
Marett Rd PL5 . . . . 123 F3
Margaret Ave PL25 . . . . 114 E3
Margaret Cl PL31 . . . . . . 109 C4
Margaret Cres PL31. . . . 109 C4
Margaret Gdns PL27. . . . 108 D5
Margaret Pk PL3 . . . . . . 128 E8

Margaret Pl TR11 . . . . 144 F3
Margaret's La PL29 . . . . . 22 D7
Margate La PL30 . . . . 35 C1
MARHAMCHURCH
EX23 . . . . 7 B6
Marhamchurch CE Prim Sch
EX23 . . . . 7 B6
Maria's La TR19 . . . . 96 B7
Maribou Ct PL28 . . . . 31 F7
Marina Ct TR16 . . . . 67 C5
Marina Rd PL5 . . . . 123 F3
Marina Terr **7** PL4 . . . . 128 F4
Marine Cres **5** TR11 . . . 145 C3
Marine Ct
Falmouth TR11 . . . . 145 D3
22 Perranporth TR6 . . . . 55 A5
Torpoint PL11 . . . . 127 B2
Marine Dr
Looe PL13 . . . . 117 D1
Torpoint PL11 . . . . 127 B2
Widemouth Bay EX23 . . . . 6 E5
Marine Par 95 A5
Marine Rd PL9 . . . . 135 B7
Marine Terr
Boscastle PL35 . . . . 9 C2
7 Penzance TR18 . . . . . 143 E4
Maristow Ave PL2 . . . . . . 127 F5
Maristow Cl PL6 . . . . 124 F5
Maristow La PL12 . . . . . . 122 F3
Maritime House Discovery
Quay **10** TR11 . . . . 145 C3
Marjorie Ct PL12 . . . . 122 C4
Market Ave PL1 . . . . 148 B3
Market Cl PL1 . . . . 128 A1
Market Ct
Hayle TR27 . . . . 142 D6
9 Launceston PL15 . . . 106 C6
Market Hill PL25 . . . . 114 C4
Market House Arc
6 Bodmin PL31 . . . . . . 109 E5
10 Launceston PL15 . . 106 C6
Market Inn PL24 . . . . 60 B5
Market Jew St TR18 . . . . 143 E5
Market Pl
Camelford PL32 . . . . 105 D4
Helston TR13 . . . . 146 B5
Marazion TR17 . . . . 89 B5
Padstow PL28 . . . . 107 D5
28 Penzance TR18 . . . . 143 E5
St Columb Major TR9 . . . 45 E6
33 St Ives TR26 . . . . . 141 B6
Week St Mary EX22 . . . . . 11 E8
Market Rd
Plymouth PL4 . . . . 130 D5
Tavistock PL19 . . . . 147 C5
Market Sq
16 Callington PL17 . . . 39 E4
Hayle TR27 . . . . 142 D6
Plymouth PL1 . . . . 148 C3
St Day TR16 . . . . 68 D1
St Just TR19 . . . . 86 F6
Market St
Bodmin PL31 . . . . 109 E5
Devoran TR3 . . . . 81 F6
Falmouth TR11 . . . . 145 B4
Fowey PL23 . . . . 116 D4
Hayle TR27 . . . . 142 D6
Kingsand PL10 . . . . 133 A1
11 Launceston PL15 . . 106 C6
Liskeard PL14 . . . . 113 C6
Plymouth PL1 . . . . 128 A1
61 St Austell PL25 . . . . 114 C3
St Just TR19 . . . . 86 F6
1 Stratton EX23 . . . . . . 4 E3
Tavistock PL19 . . . . 147 C5
Market Strand
Falmouth TR11 . . . . 145 B4
Padstow PL28 . . . . 107 D5
7 Redruth TR15 . . . . . . 140 B5
31 St Ives TR26 . . . . . 141 B6
Market Way
Plymouth PL1 . . . . 148 C3
5 Redruth TR15 . . . . . . 140 B4
Marks Dr PL31 . . . . 109 E3
Mark's Way TR7 . . . . 110 D4
Marlborough Cl
1 Falmouth TR11 . . . . 145 A3
Saltash PL12 . . . . 122 F1
Marlborough Cres TR11 . 145 A3
Marlborough Ct **5** TR11 . 145 A3
Marlborough Gr **2** TR11 145 A3
Marlborough Prim Sch
PL1 . . . . 127 E2
Marlborough Rd
Falmouth TR11 . . . . 145 B3
Plymouth PL4 . . . . 149 A4
Marlborough Row PL1 . . 127 E2
Marlborough Sch TR11 . . 145 A3
Marlborough St PL1 . . . . 127 E2
Marlborough Way PL26 . 58 E1
Marldon Cl PL5 . . . . 124 B3
Marlow Cres PL16 . . . . . . 29 F8
Marlow Gdns PL9 . . . . . . 135 F5
Marriotts Ave TR14 . . . . . 138 B4
Marrowbone Slip PL4 . . . 149 B2
Marryat Gdns PL5 . . . . . 124 E1
Marshall Ave PL27 . . . . . 108 D5
Marshall Cl
Roche PL26 . . . . 46 F3
Tavistock PL19 . . . . 147 D2
Marshallen Rd TR4 . . . . . 68 C6
Marshall Rd
Bodmin, Nanstallon PL30 . 34 C2
Bodmin PL31 . . . . 109 D3

Marshall Rd continued
Plymouth PL7 . . . . 130 A5
Tavistock PL19 . . . . 147 D2
Marshalls Way PL29 . . . . 22 D6
Marsh Cl PL4 . . . . 149 B2
Marshfield View PL11 . . . 64 B5
MARSHGATE 10 C2
Marsh La
Angarrack TR27 . . . . 142 F7
Calstock PL18 . . . . 41 A3
Hayle TR27 . . . . 142 E7
Marshlands PL27 . . . . 34 A6
MARSH MILLS 130 A6
Marsh Mills PL6 . . . . 129 F7
Marsh Mills Pk PL6 . . . . 129 F6
Marsh Mills Ret Pk PL6 . 129 E7
Marsh Mills Sta* PL7 . . 130 A7
Martin Cl TR15 . . . . 140 D5
Martin Ct TR15 . . . . 140 D5
Martin Ho **11** TR15 . . . 140 B4
Martin La PL4 . . . . 149 A2
Martins Cl PL14 . . . . 113 E7
Martin's Ct **2** PL31 . . . 109 D5
Martin's La TR15 . . . . . . 139 C8
Martin Sq **6** PL17 . . . . 39 F4
Martinvale Ave TR15 . . . 140 E2
Martinvale Parc TR15 . . 140 E7
Martlesham Pl PL5 . . . . . 123 F4
Martyn's Cl TR15 . . . . . . 55 D4
Mary Dean Ave PL5 . . . . 124 C7
Mary Dean Cl PL5 . . . . . . 124 C7
Mary Dean's CE Prim Sch
PL5 . . . . 124 C7
Maryland Gdns PL2 . . . . 127 F7
Mary Moon Cl PL12 . . . . 53 B7
Mary Newman's Cottage*
PL12 . . . . 123 A2
Mary Seacole Rd PL1 . . 148 A3
Marythorne Rd **16** PL20 . 41 B1
Masefield Gdns PL5 . . . . 124 B1
Masons Row PL18 . . . . . . 40 F6
Masterman Rd PL2 . . . . . 127 F4
Matela Cl **10** TR13 . . . . 98 C8
Matthews Way PL14 . . . . 51 F6
Maudlin Cl PL14 . . . . 113 D5
Maudlins La PL19 . . . . . . 147 A5
Maunsell Cl PL2 . . . . 127 F7
Mavisdale PL2 . . . . 127 F6
Mawes Ct PL18 . . . . 40 D5
MAWGAN 99 D7
Mawgan PL21 . . . . 99 D6
Mawgan Cross TR12 . . . . 99 D7
Mawgan-in-Pydar Com Prim
Sch TR8 . . . . 45 A8
MAWGAN PORTH 31 B2
Mawgan Vu TR9 . . . . 57 E8
MAWLA 68 B4
MAWNAN 93 E2
MAWNAN SMITH 93 C3
Mawnan Village CE Prim Sch
TR11 . . . . 93 D3
Maxwell Rd PL4 . . . . 135 B8
MAXWORTHY 12 A3
Maxworthy Cross PL15 . 12 B4
Maybank Rd PL4 . . . . 135 C1
Maybrook Dr PL12 . . . . . 122 D2
Mayers Way PL9 . . . . 135 D6
Mayfair Cres PL25 . . . . . 125 B1
Mayfair Ho PL4 . . . . 149 A3
Mayfield Cl
Bodmin PL31 . . . . 35 B2
Port Isaac PL29 . . . . 22 D7
St Austell PL25 . . . . 115 A4
Mayfield Cres TR7 . . . . . 110 E5
Mayfield Dr
Port Isaac PL29 . . . . 22 E7
Roche PL26 . . . . 47 A3
Mayfield Rd
Falmouth TR11 . . . . 144 F4
Newquay TR7 . . . . 110 E5
Port Isaac PL29 . . . . 22 D7
Mayflower Cl
6 Bere Alston PL20 . . . 41 B1
Plymouth PL9 . . . . 135 F7
Mayflower Com Sch PL2 128 A7
Mayflower Dr PL2 . . . . . . 128 B5
Mayflower L Ctr PL2 . . . . 128 C5
Mayflower St PL1 . . . . . . 148 C3
May Gdns PL16 . . . . 80 D6
May La PL13 . . . . 117 F5
Maymear Terr PL30 . . . . 23 E3
Mayna Parc PL15 . . . . . . 18 B8
Maynarde Cl PL7 . . . . . . 131 B5
Maynard Pk PL20 . . . . . . 41 B1
Mayne Cl PL15 . . . . 106 B7
Maynes Row PL4 . . . . . . 139 A5
MAYON 96 B6
Mayon Farm TR19 . . . . . . 96 B6
Mayon Green Cres TR19 . 96 B7
May Terr PL4 . . . . 149 B3
MEAD 2 D4
Mead Cnr EX39 . . . . 2 D4
Meadfoot Terr **2** PL4 . . 128 F5
Mead Hos The TR18 . . . . 143 F8
Meadowbank TR11 . . . . . 82 A3
Meadow Brook PL9 . . . . 147 A4
Meadow Cl
Gloweth TR1 . . . . 69 E3
Newquay TR7 . . . . 111 A4
Plymouth PL7 . . . . 131 D4
Polruan PL23 . . . . 116 D2
Saltash PL12 . . . . 122 F3
St Austell PL25 . . . . 114 F6
St Stephen PL26 . . . . 58 B4
Meadow Crt
Mevagissey PL26 . . . . . . 73 C3

Meadow Ct continued
Padstow PL28 . . . . 107 B4
Stithians TR3 . . . . 80 E4
St Mabyn PL30 . . . . 34 C8
Meadow Dr
Bude EX23 . . . . 104 F6
Camborne TR14 . . . . 138 C4
Looe PL13 . . . . 117 D5
Par PL24 . . . . 115 F5
Saltash PL12 . . . . 122 D4
Meadowfield Pl PL7 . . . 131 B3
Meadow Flats **27** TR26 . 141 B6
Meadowhead PL27 . . . . . 108 C4
Meadow La TR1 . . . . 137 D3
Meadowlands PL6 . . . . . . 125 D7
Meadowlands Leisure Pool
PL19 . . . . 147 B5
Meadow Pk
7 Liskeard PL14 . . . . . 113 B5
Plymouth PL9 . . . . 135 C5
Trewoon PL25 . . . . 59 A3
Meadow Pl PL31 . . . . 109 D4
Meadow Plash PL30 . . . . 35 C8
Meadow Rd PL13 . . . . . . 62 A7
Meadow Rise
Foxhole PL26 . . . . 58 D6
7 Penwithick PL26 . . . . 59 D7
Plymouth PL7 . . . . 131 A4
12 St Columb Major TR9 . 45 E6
Meadowside
Launceston PL15 . . . . . . 106 A4
Lewannick PL15 . . . . 27 A6
Newquay TR7 . . . . 111 A4
Plymouth PL9 . . . . 135 F7
St Austell PL25 . . . . 115 C6
Whitstone EX22 . . . . 12 B8
Meadowside Cl
Hayle TR27 . . . . 142 A3
St Kew Highway PL30 . . . 23 B2
Meadowside Rd TR11 . . 144 F2
Meadow St PL26 . . . . 73 C3
Meadows The
St Dennis PL26 . . . . 58 C8
St Dominick PL12 . . . . . . 40 D2
St Teath PL30 . . . . 23 E7
Torpoint PL11 . . . . 126 F2
Meadowsweet Pk PL12 . 122 C2
Meadow Terr PL14 . . . . . . 37 F3
Meadow The
Illogan TR16 . . . . 67 D4
Polgooth PL26 . . . . 59 A1
47 St Ives TR26 . . . . . 141 B6
Truro PL7 . . . . 137 B5
Meadow View
Camborne TR14 . . . . 138 E1
8 Goldsithney TR20 . . . 89 E5
St Minver PL27 . . . . 21 F3
Meadow View Rd PL7 . . 130 D5
Meadow Villas **8** TR18 . 143 C1
Meadow Way
Plymouth PL7 . . . . 130 D7
St Issey PL27 . . . . 32 E6
Meadow Wlk PL23 . . . . . 116 D2
Mead The PL7 . . . . 130 D7
Meadway
Looe PL13 . . . . 117 E4
Saltash PL12 . . . . 122 E1
St Austell PL25 . . . . 114 F5
MEADWELL 29 C8
Mearwood La TR11 . . . . 144 F4
Meaver Rd TR12 . . . . 99 B1
MEAVY 42 F2
Meavy Ave PL5 . . . . 124 E2
Meavy Bourne PL20 . . . . 42 D2
Meavy CE Prim Sch PL20 . 42 F2
Meavy La PL20 . . . . 42 D2
Meavy Villas PL20 . . . . . 42 D2
Meavy Way
Plymouth PL5 . . . . 124 E2
Tavistock PL19 . . . . 147 D5
MEDDON 3 C4
Meddon Cross
Edistone EX39 . . . . 3 C5
Welcombe EX39 . . . . 3 C4
Medland Cres PL6 . . . . . 124 D6
Medland Gdns PL25 . . . . 114 C4
Medlyn Ct TR13 . . . . 146 B5
Medrose PL27 . . . . 21 D2
Medrose St PL33 . . . . 14 E6
Medrose Terr **21** TR18 . 143 E6
Medway PL13 . . . . 117 E5
Medway Pl PL3 . . . . 129 D6
Melbourne Cotts PL1 . . 148 B3
Melbourne Gn **2** PL1 . . 148 B3
Melbourne Pl **1** PL1 . . . 148 B4
Melbourne Rd PL14 . . . . 113 B5
Melbourne St **3** PL1 . . 148 B3
Melbourne Terr **17** TR18 . 143 C7
MELBUR 57 F5
Mellanear Cl TR27 . . . . . 142 B4
Mellanear Ct TR27 . . . . . 142 B4
Mellanear Rd TR27 . . . . . 142 B3
Mellanvrane La TR7 . . . . 110 F4
Melliars Way EX23 . . . . . 104 F6
MELLINGEY 32 D6
Melrose Ave PL25 . . . . . 128 C8
Melrose Terr **6** TR9 . . . 45 E1
Melvill Cres TR11 . . . . . . 145 C4
Melvill Ct TR11 . . . . 145 B2
Melville Pl **1** PL1 . . . . 128 A5
Melville Rd
Plymouth PL2 . . . . 128 A5
Threemilestone TR3 . . . . 69 D3
Melville Terr PL12 . . . . . 122 C2
Melville Terrace La PL12 128 A5
Melvill La TR11 . . . . 145 B2
Melvill Rd TR11 . . . . 145 C2
Melyn Cl TR27 . . . . 142 E8

Memory La PL9 . . . . 135 E7
Menabilly Cl PL17 . . . . . . 39 E3
Menacken Rd PL25 . . . . 114 C6
Menacuddle Hill PL25 . . 114 C4
Menacuddle La PL25 . . . 114 C4
MENADARVA 66 E2
Menadue Ct TR27 . . . . . . 78 E3
Menage St TR13 . . . . 146 C5
MENAGISSEY 68 C5
Menague PL27 . . . . 21 E3
Menakarne TR16 . . . . . . 68 D3
Menallack Cheese Farm*
TR10 . . . . 93 A6
Mena Park Cl PL9 . . . . . 136 B7
Mena Park Rd PL9 . . . . . 136 B7
MENDENNICK 132 C7
Meneage Cotts **5** TR13 . 146 C5
Meneage Ho **4** TR13 . . 146 C5
Meneage Parc TR13 . . . 146 C5
Meneage Rd TR13 . . . . . 146 C4
Meneage St TR13 . . . . . . 146 C5
Meneage Villas PL25 . . 114 B3
Menear Rd PL25 . . . . 115 A6
Menefreda Way PL27 . . . 22 A4
Meneth TR22 . . . . 92 C1
Meneth Rd TR14 . . . . 138 F2
Menhay Gdns TR15 . . . . 139 D7
Menhay View TR11 . . . . . 144 C3
Menheniot Cres PL15 . . . 18 D5
Menheniot Prim Sch
PL14 . . . . 52 A5
Menheniot Sta PL14 . . . . 51 F4
Menhinick Cl PL12 . . . . . 53 C8
Menhyr Dr TR26 . . . . 141 C2
Menna La TR2 . . . . 57 E5
Mennaye Ct TR18 . . . . . 143 D4
Mennaye Rd TR18 . . . . . 143 D4
Merafield Cl PL7 . . . . . . 130 B5
Merafield Dr PL7 . . . . . . 130 C4
Merafield Farm Cotts
PL7 . . . . 130 B4
Merafield Rd PL7 . . . . . . 130 C4
Merbein Cotts TR8 . . . . . 44 E8
Merchant's House (Mus)*
PL1 . . . . 148 C2
Merchants Quay PL15 . . 18 E2
Meredith Rd PL2 . . . . . . 128 C6
Meres Valley TR12 . . . . . 99 A2
Meridian Ho PL4 . . . . . . 149 A3
Merlin Cl PL6 . . . . 125 E8
Merlins Way PL34 . . . . . . 14 D7
Mermaid Ct TR7 . . . . 111 C8
Merrick Ave TR1 . . . . 137 E6
MERRIFIELD 7 F4
Merrifield Cl TR1 . . . . . . 137 B5
Merrifield Cross EX22 . . . 7 F4
Merritt Pl PL11 . . . . 145 A5
Merritts Hill TR16 . . . . . . 67 E4
Merritts Way TR15 . . . . . 139 C7
Merrivale Rd
Plymouth, Ham PL2 . . . . 127 B7
Plymouth, Honicknowle
PL5 . . . . 124 B3
Merrivale View Rd PL20 . 42 E3
MERRYMEET 38 C1
Merry Mit Mdw TR11 . . . 144 C3
Mersey Cl PL3 . . . . 129 D6
MERTHER 70 F3
Merther Cl TR13 . . . . 91 B3
Merther Ct TR11 . . . . 144 E2
Messack Cl TR11 . . . . . . 144 E2
Metha Pk TR8 . . . . 56 C7
Metha Rd TR8 . . . . 56 C7
METHERELL 40 D4
Methleigh Bottoms TR13 . 91 A1
Methleigh Parc TR13 . . . 91 A1
MEVAGISSEY 73 D3
Mevagissey Aquarium*
PL26 . . . . 73 C3
Mevagissey Ho TR1 . . . . 69 E4
Mevagissey Mus* PL26 . 73 C3
Mevagissey Prim Sch
PL26 . . . . 73 C4
Mews Ct PL14 . . . . 51 F6
Mews The
Launceston PL15 . . . . . . 106 A8
Par PL24 . . . . 60 B5
3 Penzance TR18 . . . . 143 E6
Plymouth, Devonport PL1 . 128 A3
Plymouth, Stonehouse PL1 148 A3
Mexico La TR27 . . . . 142 C7
Mexico Terr TR27 . . . . . . 142 C8
Michael Rd PL3 . . . . 129 A5
Michaelstow 24 A5
Michell Ave TR14 . . . . . . 110 E6
Michell Ct TR7 . . . . 110 D6
Michigan Way PL3 . . . . . 129 C6
Mid Churchway PL9 . . . . 136 A7
Mid Cornwall Bsns Ctr
PL25 . . . . 115 E4
MIDDLE CRACKINGTON . 10 B6
Middle Down Cl PL9 . . . 136 A5
Middlefield Rd PL6 . . . . 124 D6
Middlefield Cl PL12 . . . . 122 B2
Middlegates **5** TR5 . . . 54 D1
MIDDLE GREADOW 48 B3
MIDDLEHILL 38 D3
Middle Market St PL13 . 117 D3
MIDDLEMOOR 147 F2
Middle Rd TR15 . . . . 140 E7
Middle Rosewin Row **8**
TR1 . . . . 137 D5
Middle Row TR13 . . . . . . 90 E3
Middle St
Padstow PL28 . . . . 107 D5
Port Isaac PL29 . . . . 22 D7

Middle Stennack Cotts **13**
TR26 . . . . 141 A5
Middleton Cres TR7 . . . . 110 F4
Middletons Row **6** TR15 140 C5
Middleton Wlk PL5 . . . . . 123 D4
Middleway PL24 . . . . 60 B5
Middlewell Parc PL27 . . 108 B4
Middle Wharf PL26 . . . . . 73 C3
Middle Wlk **1** PL26 . . . 115 A1
MIDDLEWOOD 27 B2
Midland Rd PL20 . . . . 42 D2
Mid Moor PL14 . . . . 38 B6
Midway Dr TR1 . . . . 137 E5
Midway Rd PL31 . . . . 109 A5
Miers Cl PL5 . . . . 127 C8
Miers Ct PL5 . . . . 127 C8
Milch Pk PL12 . . . . 122 C2
MILCOMBE 62 F6
Mildmay St PL4 . . . . 149 A4
Mile End TR12 . . . . 102 F4
Milehouse Rd PL2 . . . . . 128 A5
Miles Mitchell Ave PL6 . 125 A1
Milestone Ct TR3 . . . . . . 69 D4
Milford La PL5 . . . . 124 B5
Military Rd
Millbrook PL10 . . . . 132 C3
Plymouth PL3 . . . . 129 C6
Rame PL10 . . . . 64 C2
St Mawes TR2 . . . . 95 B4
Mill Ball Hill EX23 . . . . . . 10 E7
Millbank Mdw TR27 . . . . 78 E1
MILLBAY 148 B2
Millbay Rd PL1 . . . . 148 A2
Mill Bridge PL1 . . . . 148 A3
MILLBROOK 132 E5
Millbrook Bsns Ctr PL11 132 C6
Millbrook CE Prim Sch
PL10 . . . . 132 E5
Mill Cl
Porthleven TR13 . . . . 91 A1
Wadebridge PL27 . . . . . . 108 C5
Mill Ct TR15 . . . . 146 A6
MILLENDREATH 117 F5
Millennium Appartments
TR10 . . . . 81 D2
Millennium Way TR13 . . 146 D8
Miller Bsns Pk PL14 . . . 113 B4
Miller Ct
Liskeard PL14 . . . . 113 B4
Plymouth PL4 . . . . 148 A2
Miller Way PL6 . . . . 125 E3
Millet Cl TR17 . . . . 89 C5
Millfield TR18 . . . . 88 E6
Mill Flats TR13 . . . . 146 B6
Mill Ford Specl Sch PL5 . 123 F4
Mill Gdns PL22 . . . . 112 C2
Milham La PL22 . . . . 112 E3
MILLHILL 30 B1
Mill Hill
Crumplehorn PL13 . . . . . . 62 D1
Lelant TR27 . . . . 77 E3
Lostwithiel PL22 . . . . 112 D2
St Just in Roseland TR2 . . 82 F3
Mill Hill Cotts PL19 . . . . . 30 B1
Millhouse Pk PL11 . . . . . 127 A2
Mill La
Camelford PL32 . . . . 105 D5
Coad's Green PL15 . . . . . . 27 C1
Grampound TR2 . . . . 72 A7
Helston TR13 . . . . 146 C5
20 Mousehole TR19 . . . 88 C1
Porthleven TR13 . . . . 91 A1
St Breward PL30 . . . . 24 B3
St Germans PL12 . . . . . . 65 A8
Torpoint PL11 . . . . 127 A2
Tregony TR2 . . . . 71 F3
Truro TR1 . . . . 137 C1
MILLOOK 6 D2
Millpond Ave TR27 . . . . 142 B4
MILLPOOL
Cardinham 35 F5
Praa Sands 90 B5
Millpool
Lostwithiel PL22 . . . . 112 F3
Rilla Mill PL14 . . . . 38 E8
Millpool Head PL10 . . . . 132 E4
Mill Pool PL10 . . . . 133 A6
Mill Rd
Millbrook PL10 . . . . 133 A5
Padstow PL28 . . . . 107 D5
Penponds TR14 . . . . 79 B5
Perranporth TR6 . . . . 55 B4
Tideford PL12 . . . . 52 F2
Mill Rd Est PL12 . . . . 52 F2
Mills Gdns TR16 . . . . 68 E1
Mill Sq PL28 . . . . 107 D5
Mills Rd PL1 . . . . 127 F2
Mill St St PL31 . . . . 109 E5
MILLTOWN
Cardinham 35 E3
Lostwithiel 60 F8
Milltown Gdns PL16 . . . . 18 E6
Mill View Gdns PL10 . . . 132 F5
Mill View Rd PL10 . . . . . 132 F5
Millway PL9 . . . . 135 D8
Millwood Dr PL6 . . . . . . 125 E3
Milne Pl PL1 . . . . 127 F1
MILTON ABBOT 29 D5
Milton Abbot Sch PL19 . 29 D5
Milton Cl PL5 . . . . 124 D2
MILTON COMBE 120 F8
Milton Cres PL19 . . . . . . 147 D5
Milton Ct
Plymouth, Cattedown
PL4 . . . . 149 C2
Plymouth, Prince Rock PL4 129 B1

MILTON GREEN 29 D5
Minack Open Air Theatre★
TR19................... 96 E2
Mine Hill PL14 .... 51 F6
Mine La PL30 .... 47 E7
Miners Ct
  Perranporth TR6 .... 55 A4
  Redruth TR15 .... 140 C5
Miners Row TR15 .... 140 C5
Miners Way PL14 .... 113 D7
Minerva Cl PL7 .... 131 A6
MINGOOSE 68 C7
Miniatura Park★ TR4. .. 55 E4
MINIONS 38 B6
Minions Heritage Ctr★
  PL14................... 38 B6
Minions Row PL14 .... 38 B6
Minnie Pl TR11 .... 145 B3
Minorca La PL26 .... 47 D2
Minses Cl PL9 .... 136 C7
Minster Ave EX23 .... 104 F4
Minster Mdw TR12 .... 101 A8
Minster Terr TR12 .... 101 A8
Minton Cl PL25 .... 115 A4
Mirador Pl PL4 .... 129 C3
Mission The TR18 .... 143 C4
Misterton Cl PL9 .... 136 B8
MITCHELL 56 F5
Mitchell Cl
  Lizard TR12 .... 102 F2
  Plymouth PL9 .... 135 D5
Mitchell Ct 🔢 TR1 .... 137 D5
Mitchell Hill TR1 .... 137 D5
Mitchell Hill Terr 🔢
  TR1................... 137 D5
Mitchell La
  Camborne TR14 .... 138 E3
  Mitchell TR8 .... 56 E5
Mitchell Mews 🔢 TR1 ... 137 D4
Mitchell Rd
  Camborne TR14 .... 138 C3
  St Austell PL25 .... 114 F4
Mitchell's Boatyard PL2. 73 C2
Mitchells Cnr 🔢 TR6 ... 55 A5
MITHIAN 54 F1
MITHIAN DOWNS 68 F8
Mithian Prim Sch TR5 ... 54 E1
Mitre Cl PL3 .... 147 A3
Mitre Ct 🔢 PL1 .... 149 A2
MIXTOW 116 D7
Moat Pk PL6 .... 125 C5
Modbury Cl PL5 .... 124 B3
Modus La PL26 .... 58 D5
Modyford Wlk PL20 .... 41 F3
Mohun's Cl PL3 .... 147 C4
Mohun's Ct PL11 .... 147 C4
Mohun's Pk PL19 .... 147 C3
Molenick La PL12 .... 52 E3
Molesworth Cl 🔢 PL27 . 108 B5
Molesworth Rd
  Plymouth, Plympton PL7. 130 C6
  Plymouth, Stoke PL1, PL3 . 128 A3
Molesworth St
  Tintagel PL34............ 14 C7
  Wadebridge PL27 .... 108 B5
Molesworth Terr PL10. .. 132 F5
MOLINNIS 47 C2
Molinnis PL26 .... 47 C2
Molinnis Rd PL26 .... 47 C2
Mollison Rd PL5 .... 123 E2
Molyneaux Pl 🔢 PL1 .. 127 F3
Monastery Cl TR12 .... 101 C6
MONGLEATH 144 E4
Mongleath Ave TR11 ... 144 E3
Mongleath Cl TR11 .... 144 E3
Mongleath Rd TR11 .... 144 E3
Monica Wlk PL4 .... 149 B4
Monkey Sanctuary The★
  PL13................... 63 F5
Monks Hill PL15 .... 28 C4
Monkswood PL19 .... 147 A4
Monks Park Cotts PL15. 106 D6
Monmouth Gdns PL5 ... 124 C4
Monmouth La PL22 .... 112 D2
Monroe Gdns PL4 .... 148 B4
Montacute Ave PL5 .... 124 B2
Montague Ave TR15..... 140 A6
Monterey Cl EX23 .... 104 E4
Monterey Gdns TR1 ..... 137 E5
Montgomery Cl PL12 ... 122 D3
Montgomery Dr PL3.. .. 147 A6
Montgomery Rd 🔢 PL26. 59 D7
Montpelier Prim Sch
  PL2................... 128 B6
Montpelier Rd PL2 .... 128 B6
Monument Rd TR13 ... 146 B5
Monument Pl PL1 .... 127 E1
Monument Way PL31. .. 109 C4
Moonrakers TR26 .... 141 D2
Moonsfield 🔢 PL17 ..... 39 F4
Moon St PL4 .... 149 A3
Moorcroft Cl PL9 .... 136 A7
Moor Cross EX22. .... 8 D3
Moor Cross Cotts EX23. .. 4 C3
Moorfield PL16 .... 19 F4
Moorfield Ave 🔢 PL6 .. 129 C7
Moorfield Rd
  Camborne TR15 .... 139 C6
  St Giles on the Heath PL15. 13 F1
Moor La PL5................ 123 E1
Moorland Ave PL7 .... 130 F6
Moorland Cl
  Liskeard PL14 .... 113 D7
  Pendeen TR19 .... 74 F1
  Yelverton PL20....... 121 D8
Moorland Ct
  🔢 St Austell PL25. ..... 114 C3
  Yelverton PL20....... 42 C2
Moorland Dr PL7 .... 130 C6

Moorland Gdns PL7 .... 130 F6
Moorland Rd
  Indian Queens TR9 .... 45 F2
  Launceston PL15 .... 106 A4
  Plymouth PL7............ 130 E5
  St Austell PL25 .... 114 C3
  Tywardreath PL24. ...... 60 C4
Moorland Road Ind Est
  TR9................... 45 F2
Moorlands La PL12 .... 122 C4
Moorlands Trad Est
  PL12................... 122 C4
Moorland View
  Golberdon PL17......... 39 B6
  Liskeard PL14 .... 113 D7
  Plymouth, Derriford PL6 .. 125 A5
  Plymouth, Plymstock PL9 . 136 B7
  Saltash PL12............ 122 F4
Moorland Way PL18..... 40 F5
Moorlan Mdws PL26 .... 47 A3
Moor Parc TR12 .... 100 D6
Moor St TR14............ 138 C3
Moors The PL22 .... 112 C1
Mooreswater Ind Est PL14. 51 A7
Moor The PL11 .... 145 B4
MOORTOWN
  Tavistock 42 D8
  Tetcott 13 C7
Moor View
  Bodmin PL31 .... 109 F2
  Plymouth, Keyham PL2 .. 127 F5
  Plymouth, Laira PL3..... 129 C4
  Plymouth PL9.. .... 135 D7
  Torpoint PL11 .... 127 B3
  🔢 St Ives TR26 .... 141 B6
Moor View Terr
  Plymouth PL4............ 128 E4
  Yelverton PL20......... 42 D2
Morcom PL25 .... 115 A5
Moresk Cl TR1 .... 137 D5
Moresk Gdns TR1 .... 137 D5
Moresk Rd TR1 .... 137 D5
Moreton Ave PL6 .... 124 F1
Morice Sq PL1 .... 127 E2
Morice St PL1 .... 127 E2
MORICE TOWN 127 D3
Morice Town Prim Sch
  PL2................... 127 E4
Morlaix Ave TR1 .... 137 D3
Morlaix Dr PL6........... 125 B4
Morla La TR15 .... 140 A6
Morleigh Cl PL25 .... 114 F3
Morley Cl PL7 .... 130 A5
Morley Ct PL1 .... 148 B3
Morley Dr PL20 .... 42 A2
Morley View Rd PL7 ... 130 C6
MORNICK 39 B7
Morrab Ct 🔢 TR7 .... 110 F6
Morrab Pl 🔢 TR18 ..... 143 E5
Morrab Rd
  Camborne TR14 .... 138 C3
  Penzance TR18. .... 143 E5
Morrab Terr 🔢 TR18 .. 143 E5
Morris Gdns TR1 .... 110 D4
Morrish Pk PL9 .... 135 F6
Morshead Rd PL6 .... 124 F2
Mortain Rd PL12 .... 122 D4
Mortimore Cl PL12. ..... 122 D2
MORVAH 75 C2
MORVAL 63 D7
Morval Trad Est PL25. .. 114 F3
Morven Rd PL25 .... 114 F3
Morview Rd PL13 .... 63 F8
Morwell Gdns PL2 .... 128 A6
MORWELLHAM 41 A4
Morwellham Quay★ PL19. 41 B4
Morwenna Gdns PL2 ... 128 A6
Morwenna Rd TR26 ..... 55 B5
Morwenna Terr EX23 ... 2 D1
MORWENSTOW 2 B2
Morweth Cotts PL11 .... 64 C5
Morweth Ct PL11 .... 64 C5
Moses Cl PL6 .... 124 E7
Moses Ct PL6 .... 124 E7
Mosquito Cres 🔢 PL27 . 31 F3
Moss Side Ind Est 🔢 PL17 39 F4
Moss Terr PL23 .... 116 D3
Mostyn Ave PL4 .... 129 A4
Mote Pk PL12 .... 122 C4
Mothecombe Wlk PL6. .. 125 E1
Moulton Cl PL7 .... 131 B5
Moulton Wlk PL7 .... 131 B4
MOUNT
  Cardinham 36 B2
  Cubert 55 C7
Mount Agar Rd TR3. .... 81 F7
MOUNT AMBROSE 140 E7
Mount Ambrose TR15 ... 140 E7
Mountbatten Cl
  Plymouth PL9........... 135 D6
  St Columb Minor TR7 ... 111 E7
Mount Batten Ctr★ PL9 . 134 F7
Mountbatten Rd 🔢 PL26. 59 D7
Mountbatten Way PL9 . 135 E6
Mount Bennett Rd 🔢
  PL24................... 60 D5
Mount Bennett Terr 🔢
  PL24................... 60 D5
Mount Camel PL32. ..... 105 C4
Mount Carbis Gdns
  TR15................... 140 C3
Mount Carbis Rd TR15. . 140 D3
MOUNT CHARLES 114 E4
Mount Charles Rd PL25 . 114 F3
Mount Cres PL24....... 60 C4

Mount Edgcumbe House &
  Country Pk★ PL10....... 133 E6
Mount Edgcumbe Terr
  TR11................... 145 B4
Mountfield Terr 🔢 PL24. 60 C4
Mount Folly TR27 .... 142 C6
Mount Folly Sq PL31 ... 109 C4
Mount Ford PL19 .... 147 A5
Mount George Rd TR3. . 82 B7
MOUNT GOULD 129 B3
Mount Gould Ave PL4 .. 129 B2
Mount Gould Cres PL4 . 129 B2
Mount Gould Hospl PL4. 129 B3
Mount Gould Rd PL4 ... 129 B3
Mount Gould Way PL4. . 129 B3
MOUNT HAWKE 68 C6
Mount Hawke Com Prim Sch
  TR4................... 68 C6
Mount Ho PL11 .... 64 C5
Mount House Sch PL19. . 147 E7
MOUNTJOY 45 A3
MOUNT LANE 13 E6
Mount Ho 🔢 PL24 ..... 60 C4
Mount Lidden TR18 .... 143 C4
Mount Pleasant
  Bodmin PL31 .... 109 E5
  Boscastle PL35. .... 9 D1
  Falmouth TR11. .... 144 E1
  Hayle TR27............ 142 C6
  Lelant TR26............ 77 E3
  Millbrook PL10. .... 132 E5
  Newlyn TR18 .... 143 C4
  Par PL24................ 60 B6
  Plymouth PL5. .... 124 B2
  🔢 St Ives TR26 .... 141 B6
Mount Pleasant Cl TR14. 138 C1
Mount Pleasant Gdns
  TR27................... 142 C6
Mount Pleasant Pl TR22. 112 C3
Mount Pleasant Rd
  Camborne TR14 .... 138 D1
  🔢 Porthleven TR13 .... 98 B8
  Threemilestone TR3..... 69 D3
Mount Pleasant Terr
  TR18................... 143 C3
  Mousehole TR19 .... 88 C1
  Redruth TR15. .... 140 E7
Mount Prospect Terr
  TR18................... 143 C3
Mount Rd PL24 .... 60 C4
Mount Royal Cl TR18 .. 143 F6
Mounts Bay Sch TR18. . 143 B7
Mount's Bay Terr TR13. . 90 E3
Mount's Bay Terr 🔢 TR13 98 C8
Mount's Rd 🔢 TR18 ... 143 C3
Mount St
  Mevagissey PL26. .... 73 C3
  Penzance TR18. .... 143 E6
  Plymouth, Mount Wise PL1. 127 E1
  Plymouth, Mutley PL4 .. 149 A4
Mount Stamper Rd PL25. 114 D7
Mount Stephen Cl PL25. . 114 B3
Mount Stephens La
  TR11................... 144 F4
Mount Stone Rd 🔢 PL1. 134 A8
Mount Street Prim Sch
  PL4................... 149 A4
Mount Tamar Cl TR1 ... 123 E2
Mount Tamar Specl Sch
  PL5................... 123 E2
Mount Tavy Rd PL19 ... 147 E6
Mount Terr 🔢 PL20 ... 60 B4
Mount View
  Lane TR8................ 111 B3
  Madron TR20............ 88 A7
Mount View Cotts TR20. . 89 A7
Mount View Terr
  🔢 Maraston TR17 ..... 89 C5
  🔢 Newlyn TR18........ 143 C2
Mount Whistle Rd TR14. 138 F7
MOUNT WISE 127 F1
Mount Wise
  Launceston PL15 .... 106 C5
  Newquay TR7............ 110 D5
Mount Wise Cotts TR7 . 110 E5
Mount Wise Ct PL1...... 127 F1
Mount Wise Prim Sch
  PL1................... 127 E1
Mount Zion 🔢 TR26 ... 141 B6
Mourne Villas PL9 .... 135 F8
MOUSEHOLE 88 D1
Mousehole La TR19 .... 88 C1
Mousehole Prim Sch
  TR19................... 88 C1
Mowbray Mews PL32. ... 10 B2
Mowhay Cl TR7 .... 111 A4
Mowhay Cotts PL26 .... 85 C5
Mowhay La 🔢 PL17 ... 39 E4
Mowhay Mdw
  St John PL11 .... 132 B8
  Wadebridge PL27 .... 108 B4
Mowhay Rd PL5 .... 124 A2
Mowie The 🔢 TR9 ..... 45 E2
Moyle Rd PL28 .... 107 E4
MUCHLARNICK 62 E7
Mudges Terr PL18 .... 41 A6
Mudge Way PL7 .... 130 E5
Mulberry Cl PL25 .... 125 E7
Mulberry Ct 🔢 PL11 .. 145 B5
Mulberry Gr PL19 .... 147 C2
Mulberry Quay 🔢 TR11. 145 B5
Mulberry Rd PL12 .... 122 E1
MULFRA 76 B1
Mulgrave St 🔢 PL1 ... 148 C2
Mullet Ave PL3 .... 129 C4
Mullet Cl PL3 .... 129 C4
Mullet Rd PL3 .... 129 C4

MULLION 99 A1
Mullion Cl PL11 .... 126 F4
Mullion Cove TR12 .... 102 B7
Mullion Cove Bglws TR12. 98 F1
Mullion Gdns PM TR12. . 99 A1
Mullion Rural Workshops
  TR12................... 99 A1
Mullion Sch TR12 .... 99 B1
Mundys Field TR12 ..... 103 A5
Muralto Ho PL19 .... 147 A4
Murdoch Cl
  Redruth TR15. .... 140 B6
  Truro TR1................ 137 E6
Murdoch Flyer The★ 🔢
  TR15................... 140 B4
Murdoch House & St
  Rumon's Gdn★ 🔢
  TR15................... 140 B4
Murdock Rd PL11 .... 126 F3
Murray Villas TR19 ..... 86 E6
Murtons Terr TR16 ..... 80 E7
Mus of Witchcraft★ PL35.. 9 C2
MUTLEY 128 F4
Mutley Ct PL4 .... 149 A4
Mutley Plain PL4 .... 128 E4
Mutley Plain La PL4 .... 128 E4
Mutley Rd PL3 .... 128 E5
Mutton Hill TR27 .... 78 D6
Mutton Row TR10 .... 144 C8
MYLOR BRIDGE 82 A3
Mylor Cl PL2 .... 128 D8
Mylor Bridge Prim Sch
  TR11................... 82 A3
My Lords Rd TR19 .... 57 E8
Myrtle Cl PL20 .... 42 E3
Myrtle Ct PL26 .... 73 C3
Myrtle Ct PL12 .... 122 D4
Myrtleville PL2 .... 128 A6
Mython Ct 🔢 TR18 .... 143 C4

N

Nailzee Ho PL13 .... 117 D2
Nailzee Point PL13 .... 117 D2
Nalder's Ct 🔢 TR1 ..... 137 C4
Nampara Cl TR26 .... 141 E2
Nampara Ct 🔢 TR6 ... 55 A4
Nampara Way TR1 ..... 137 F4
Nancarrows PL22 .... 122 C2
Nanceddan Farm TR20 . 89 A8
NANCEGOLLAN 91 C7
Nancegollan Ind Est TR13 91 B7
NANCEMELLIN 66 D1
Nancemere Rd TR1 ..... 137 D6
Nancevallon TR14 .... 66 A6
Nancherrow Hill TR19 . 86 F6
NANCLEDRA 76 F2
Nancledra Prim Sch TR
  26................... 76 F3
Nangitha Cl TR11 .... 144 C3
Nangitha Terr TR11 .... 144 C3
Nanhayes Row TR8 ..... 56 B7
Nanjivey Pl TR1 .... 137 A6
Nanjivey Terr 🔢 TR26. . 141 A5
NANPEAN 58 D7
Nanpean Prim Sch PL26. 58 D6
Nanpusker Cl TR27. .... 142 E6
Nanpusker Rd TR27 .... 78 C4
Nansalsa Ct TR7 .... 111 A6
Nansavallon Rd TR1. ... 69 F3
Nanscober Pl TR13 ..... 146 B8
Nanscobe 🔢 TR15 ..... 140 B4
Nans Kestate TR13 ..... 146 B5
NANSLADRON 73 B7
Nansloe Cl TR13 .... 146 A4
Nansloe Prim Sch TR13 . 146 C4
Nansmellyon Rd TR12 ... 99 A1
NANSTALLON 34 C1
Nanstallon Prim Sch
  PL30................... 34 C1
Nanterrow La TR27 ..... 66 D1
NANTITHET 99 B5
Nanturras Parc TR20 ... 89 F5
Nanturras Row TR20 ... 89 F5
Napier St PL1 .... 127 F3
Napier Terr PL4......... 128 E4
Narkurs Cross PL11 .... 64 D7
Narrowcliff TR7 .... 111 A7
Narrow La
  Botusfleming PL12 ...... 122 C7
  Summercourt TR8 .... 57 C8
Nash Cl PL7 .... 131 A5
Nathan St TR7 .... 111 B5
National Lobster Hatchery★
  PL28................... 107 D5
National Marine Aquarium★
  PL4................... 149 A2
National Maritime Mus
  Cornwall★ TR11 .... 145 C3
National Seal Sanctuary
  The★ TR12 .... 92 C1
NAVARINO 18 B8
Navy Inn Ct 🔢 TR18 ... 143 C1
Neal Cl PL7 .... 131 B4
Neath Rd PL4 .... 149 C4
Neeham Rd TR8 .... 56 B7
Nelson Ave PL1 .... 127 F3
Nelson Gdns 🔢 PL1 ... 127 F3
Nelson St PL4 .... 149 A4
Nelson Terr PL6 .... 125 E7
Nepean St 🔢 PL2 ..... 127 F3

Neptune Ave PL27 .... 31 F3
Neptune Pk PL9 .... 135 B8
Neswick St PL1 .... 148 B3
Neswick Street Ope PL1. 148 A3
NETHERCOTT 13 F7
Nethercott Cross EX21 . 13 F7
NETHERTON 38 D7
Netherton Est PL20 ..... 42 A3
Netherton Rd PL28 ..... 107 D4
Nettell's Hill TR15....... 140 B5
Nettlehayes PL9 .... 136 D7
Nevada Cl PL3 .... 129 D6
Nevada Pl 🔢 TR18 .... 143 C7
Nevada St PL3 .... 143 C7
Nevada Villas 🔢 PL24. . 60 C4
Newacott Cross EX22 ... 7 F5
New Barn Hill PL7 .... 130 F3
New Bglws PL30 .... 36 B3
NEWBRIDGE
  Callington.............. 39 D2
  Penzance............... 87 E6
  Truro................... 69 F3
Newbridge Hill PL18 ... 41 A6
Newbridge La TR1, TR3 . 69 F3
Newbridge St 🔢 TR1 ... 137 D4
Newbridge Way TR1 ... 69 F3
Newbury Ct PL1......... 124 B4
Newcastle Gdns PL5 ... 124 B5
New Connection St 🔢
  TR14................... 138 D3
New Cotts
  Gunnislake PL18 .... 41 A6
  Kilkhampton EX23....... 5 A6
New Cut TR11 .... 145 B4
New Cut TR15 .... 140 B5
New Dairy La TR17 ..... 89 B6
NEW DOWNS
  St Agnes.. .... 54 B2
  St Just................. 86 B6
New George St PL1 ..... 148 C3
Newham Est TR1........ 137 C3
New Ind Est TR1 .... 137 D2
Newham La
  Helston TR13 .... 146 A3
  Lostwithiel PL22 .... 49 A1
New Ind Est TR1 .... 137 C2
New Ind Est TR2 .... 72 A7
New Hos TR14 .... 139 B3
New Launceston Rd
  PL19................... 147 A5
NEWLYN 143 D4
Newlyn Art Gall★ TR18. 143 C3
Newlyn Halt Sta★ TR18. 56 C6
Newlyn Prim Sch TR18 . 143 C3
Newlyn Rd TR19 .... 97 B6
Newman Rd
  Plymouth PL5............ 123 E2
  Saltash PL12............ 122 F3
NEWMILL
  Penzance............... 76 B1
  Poundstock.............. 7 A1
Newmills Cl TR1 .... 137 B6
New Mills Farm Pk★
  PL15................... 18 D4
New Mills La TR1........ 137 A6
Newmills Sta★ PL15 .... 18 D4
New Molinnis PL26 ..... 47 C2
Newnham Ind Est PL7. . 130 F6
Newnham Rd PL7 .... 130 F6
New Northernmaye 🔢
  PL15................... 106 C6
New Park Rd
  Plymouth PL7............ 131 A4
  Wadebridge PL27 .... 108 C5
New Passage Hill PL1 . 127 E3
New Pk
  Horrabridge PL20 .... 42 C4
  Wadebridge PL27 .... 108 C4
NEW POLZEATH 21 E6
NEWPORT 106 B7
Newport
  Callington PL17 .... 39 E4
  St Germans PL12........ 65 A8
Newport Cl 🔢 PL12 ... 39 F4
Newport Ind Est PL15 . 106 C6
Newport Rd PL15 .... 106 B7
Newport Sq PL15 .... 106 B7
Newport St
  Millbrook PL10. .... 132 E5
  Plymouth PL1. .... 128 A1
Newport Terr 🔢 PL7 ... 39 F4
NEWQUAY 110 E7
Newquay Adult Ed Ctr
  TR7................... 110 F6
Newquay Airport TR8 ... 44 F8
Newquay Hospl TR7. ... 110 F5
Newquay Jun Sch TR7 . 110 F6
Newquay Sports & Com Ctr
  TR7................... 111 B6
Newquay Sta★ TR7 ..... 110 F6
Newquay Tretherras Sch
  TR7................... 111 B6
Newquay Zoo TR7. ..... 111 A5
New Rd
  Barripper TR14 .... 79 B5

New Rd continued
Bere Alston PL20 . . . . 41 B2
Boscastle PL35 . . . . 9 C2
Cadgwith TR12 . . . . 103 A4
Callington PL17 . . . . 39 E4
Camborne TR14 . . . . 139 B3
Cawsand PL10 . . . . 133 A1
Kingsand PL10 . . . . 133 B2
Lifton PL16 . . . . 19 F4
Liskeard PL14 . . . . 113 B5
Newlyn TR18 . . . . 143 C3
Perranporth TR6 . . . . 55 B4
Port Isaac PL29 . . . . 22 D7
Roborough PL6 . . . . 121 D2
Saltash PL12 . . . . 122 E3
St Columb Major TR9 . . . . 45 E6
St Hilary TR20 . . . . 89 F6
Stithians TR3 . . . . 80 F3
St Just TR19 . . . . 86 F6
Stratton EX23 . . . . 4 D1
Summercourt TR8 . . . . 57 D7
Tregony TR2 . . . . 71 F3
Troon TR14 . . . . 79 E4
New Road Cl PL10 . . . . . 133 A2
New Road Hall PL23 . . . . 116 C4
New Road Terr PL12 . . . . 53 C3
New Row
Gweek TR12 . . . . 92 C1
Mylor Bridge TR11 . . . . . . 82 A3
Nancledra TR 20 . . . . 76 F2
Redruth TR16 . . . . 139 D1
Summercourt TR8 . . . . 57 B6
New St
Bugle PL26 . . . . 47 C1
Falmouth TR11 . . . . 145 B4
Millbrook PL10 . . . . 132 E5
Padstow PL28 . . . . 107 D5
Penryn TR10 . . . . 144 D7
Penzance TR18 . . . . 143 E5
Plymouth PL1 . . . . 149 A2
Troon TR14 . . . . 79 E4
Newtake Rd PL19 . . . . . . 147 E2
Newton Ave PL5 . . . . . . 123 E2
Newton Ct
Dobwalls PL14 . . . . 50 E8
Redruth TR15 . . . . 140 A6
Newton Farm Cotts PL13 . . 62 E3
Newton Gdns PL5 . . . . . 123 F2
Newton Pk 19 TR2 . . . . . 95 A6
Newton Rd
St Mawes TR2 . . . . 95 A6
Troon TR14 . . . . 79 E5
Newton's Margate Ind Est
PL31 . . . . 35 B1
NEWTOWN
Coad's Green 27 D5
Praa Sands 90 B4
Newtown PL23 . . . . 60 F3
NEWTOWN-IN-ST
MARTIN 100 E6
Newtown La TR17, TR20 . . 89 A7
New Town La TR18 . . . . . 143 E5
New Windsor Terr 11
TR11 . . . . 145 A4
New Wood Cl PL6 . . . . . . 125 E8
New Zealand Ho PL3 . . . 128 B4
Nicholas Ave PL6 . . . . 80 A5
Nicholas Mdw PL17 . . . . . 40 A4
Nicholas Parc 3 TR18 . . 143 C7
Nicholson Rd PL6 . . . . . . 124 E2
Nicolls Flats PL15 . . . . . . 106 B5
Nightingale Cl PL9 . . . . . 136 C8
Nine Oaks PL20 . . . . 42 F3
NINNIS BRIDGE 77 B2
No Go By Hill TR19 . . . . . . 86 F7
NO MAN'S LAND 63 E7
No Mans' Land Rd TR11 . . 93 D5
Nook The PL19 . . . . 147 D6
NOONVARES 90 E7
Norfolk Cl PL3 . . . . 129 C5
Norfolk Rd
Falmouth TR11 . . . . 145 B4
Plymouth PL3 . . . . 129 C4
Norman Cotts PL15 . . . . . 106 C7
Normandy Hill PL15 . . . . 123 B2
Normandy Way
Bodmin PL31 . . . . 109 F2
Camborne TR14 . . . . 138 F3
Plymouth PL5 . . . . 123 C2
Norman's Way PL30 . . . . . 23 E3
NORRIS GREEN 40 E4
Northampton Cl PL5 . . . . 124 B5
NORTH BEER 12 F3
NORTH BRENTOR 30 E8
North Cl EX23 . . . . 5 A6
North Cliff 12 TR19 . . . . . 88 C1
North Cnr 1 TR18 . . . . . . 143 C2
NORTH CORNER 101 C2
North Cornwall Mus & Gall★
PL32 . . . . 105 C4
NORTHCOTT
Bude 4 C3
St Giles on the Heath 13 D3
Northcott Mouth Rd
EX23 . . . . 104 F8
NORTH COUNTRY 140 B8
NORTH DARLEY 38 D8
North Dimson PL18 . . . . . 40 F6
North Down Cres PL2 . . 127 F6
North Down Gdns PL2 . . 127 F6
North Down Rd PL2 . . . . 128 B6
Northesk St PL2 . . . . . . 128 A4
Northey Cl TR14 . . . . 69 F6
Northey Rd PL31 . . . . . . 109 D4
Northfield Cl TR16 . . . . . . 68 E1

Northfield Dr TR1 . . . . . . 137 D3
Northgate PI 1 PL15 . . . 106 C6
North Grange Ind Est TR3 . 81 F6
NORTH HILL 27 B3
North Hill
Blackwater TR4 . . . . 68 E5
Carharrack TR16 . . . . 80 F8
Chacewater TR4 . . . . 68 E5
4 Plymouth PL4 . . . . 149 A4
North Hill Pk PL25 . . . . . 114 D4
NORTHMOOR 3 F3
North Moor Cross EX22 . . . 3 F3
Northolt Ave PL5 . . . . . . 123 D4
North Orchard Ct 1 TR20 . 89 E5
North Par
Camborne TR14 . . . . 138 E3
Falmouth TR11 . . . . 145 A6
Penzance TR18 . . . . 143 E5
Portscatho TR2 . . . . 83 B2
North Parade Rear TR14 . 138 D3
North Park Villas PL12 . . 122 C4
NORTH PETHERWIN 18 A8
North Petherwin Ind Est
PL15 . . . . 18 A8
North Petherwin Prim Sch
PL15 . . . . 12 B1
North PI 15 TR26 . . . . . . 141 B6
North Pool Cl TR15 . . . . 139 C7
North Pool Rd TR15 . . . . 139 C7
NORTH PROSPECT 128 A6
North Prospect Rd PL2 . . 128 A6
North Quay
Hayle TR27 . . . . 142 B6
Padstow PL28 . . . . 107 D6
Plymouth PL4 . . . . 149 A2
North Quay Hill TR7 . . . . 110 D7
North Quay Par PL28 . . . 107 E6
North Rd
Camborne TR14 . . . . 138 D3
Goldsithney TR20 . . . . 89 E5
Landrake PL12 . . . . 53 C3
Lifton PL16 . . . . 19 F4
Looe PL13 . . . . 117 C3
Pentewan PL26 . . . . 73 C6
Redruth TR16 . . . . 140 E1
Saltash PL12 . . . . 122 F3
St Teath PL30 . . . . 23 E7
Torpoint PL11 . . . . 127 B3
Whitemoor PL26 . . . . 58 E8
Velverton PL20 . . . . 42 C3
North Road E PL4 . . . . . . 148 C4
North Road W PL1 . . . . . . 148 B4
North Roskear Mdw
TR14 . . . . 138 E5
North Roskear Rd TR14 . 138 F5
North Row TR19 . . . . 86 F6
North St
Fowey PL23 . . . . 116 D4
Launceston PL15 . . . . 106 A8
Lostwithiel PL22 . . . . 112 C2
Marazion TR17 . . . . 89 B5
14 Mousehole TR19 . . . . . 88 C1
Plymouth PL4 . . . . 149 A3
Redruth TR15 . . . . 140 B6
St Austell PL25 . . . . 114 C4
Tavistock PL19 . . . . 147 C5
Tywardreath PL24 . . . . 60 D5
NORTH TAMERTON 12 F8
North Terr
2 Penzance TR18 . . . . . . 143 E4
13 St Ives TR26 . . . . 141 B5
Whitemoor TR26 . . . . 58 E8
Northumberland St PL5 . 127 E8
Northumberland Terr
PL1 . . . . 148 B1
North View PL13 . . . . 117 D4
North Way TR8 . . . . 111 F4
North Weald Gdns PL5 . . 123 E5
Norton Ave PL4 . . . . 149 C4
Norton Ct 2 PL31 . . . . . 109 E5
Norwich Ave PL5 . . . . . . 124 B5
Notre Dame Cl PL6 . . . . . 124 F5
Notre Dame Ho PL1 . . . . 148 A3
Notre Dame RC Sch PL6 . 124 F5
Notte St PL1 . . . . 148 C2
Novorossisk Rd PL6 . . . . 125 E2
Noweth PI PL11 . . . . 144 E5
Nuffield Health Plymouth
Hospl PL6 . . . . 125 B4
NUMPHRA 87 A4
Nunnery Hill PL26 . . . . . . 72 F7
Nurseries The TR11 . . . . 144 D5
Nursery Cl
Plymouth PL5 . . . . 124 D7
Truro TR1 . . . . 137 D5
11 Tywardreath PL24 . . . . 60 D5
Nut La TR27 . . . . 77 E3
Nut Tree Hill PL12 . . . . . . 65 B8

O

Oakapple Cl PL7 . . . . 130 B7
Oak Apple Cl PL12 . . . . . 122 D4
Oak Ave PL12 . . . . 40 A1
Oakcroft Rd PL2 . . . . 128 B6
Oakdene Rise PL9 . . . . . 135 F6
Oakdene Villas 7 TR9 . . . 45 E1
Oak Dr
8 Liskeard PL14 . . . . 113 B5
Plymouth PL6 . . . . 124 F3
Oakey Orch PL7 . . . . 40 D4
Oakfield PL15 . . . . 27 D3
Oakfield Cl PL7 . . . . 131 C6
Oakfield PI PL4 . . . . 129 B1
Oakfield Rd
Falmouth TR11 . . . . 144 F5
Plymouth PL7 . . . . 130 C6

Oakfield Terrace Rd PL4 . 129 B1
Oak Ford PL30 . . . . 48 C7
Oakham Rd PL5 . . . . 124 B5
Oakhill PL30 . . . . 47 C6
Oak La
Truro TR1 . . . . 69 E4
Whitstone EX22 . . . . 7 F1
Oakland Pk TR11 . . . . . . 144 D5
Oaklands PL19 . . . . 147 D2
Oaklands Bsns Pk PL13 . . 63 D8
Oaklands Cl PL6 . . . . 125 C7
Oaklands Ct TR19 . . . . . . 45 E6
Oaklands Dr PL12 . . . . . . 122 C3
Oaklands Gn PL12 . . . . . . 122 C3
Oaklands Ind Est PL14 . . 113 E6
Oakleigh Terr TR7 . . . . . . 110 F6
Oak Park Terr TR14 . . . . 113 A6
Oak Pk PL30 . . . . 23 E3
Oak Rd PL19 . . . . 147 C2
Oakridge PL12 . . . . 53 C7
Oak Ridge PL16 . . . . 19 F4
Oaks The
17 Par PL24 . . . . 60 C4
Quintrell Downs TR8 . . . . 111 F3
St Austell PL25 . . . . 114 B3
Oak Tree Cl PL25 . . . . . . 115 B3
Oaktree Ct PL6 . . . . 124 F1
Oak Tree La PL19 . . . . . . 147 C3
Oak Tree Pk PL6 . . . . 125 D6
Oak Vale TR2 . . . . 72 A7
Oakwood Cl PL6 . . . . 125 D7
Oakwood Pk PL31 . . . . . . 109 F4
Oakwood Prim Sch PL6 . . 125 A6
Oakwood Rise PL32 . . . . 105 E5
Oates Rd
Helston TR13 . . . . 146 C6
Marazion TR17 . . . . 89 C5
Observer Cl TR1 . . . . 137 C3
Ocean Cres 22 TR13 . . . . 98 C8
Ocean Ct
Plymouth PL1 . . . . 133 F8
Porthtowan TR4 . . . . 68 A7
Ocean St PL2 . . . . 127 E6
Ocean View
Indian Queens TR9 . . . . . . 45 E1
Newquay TR7 . . . . 110 B5
Polruan PL23 . . . . 116 D2
Porthleven TR13 . . . . 98 B8
St Austell PL25 . . . . 114 E7
Ocean View Rd EX23 . . . 104 D7
Ocean View Terr TR26 . . 141 A6
Octagon St PL1 . . . . 148 B3
Octagon The PL1 . . . . . . 148 B2
Okehampton Cl PL7 . . . . 131 A4
Old Bakehouse Flats The
TR18 . . . . 143 F6
Old Barn Ct TR7 . . . . 110 D4
Old Barns The TR14 . . . . . 66 F2
Old Boat Yard The PL28 . 107 E4
Old Boys School TR16 . . . 67 E5
Old Brewery Yd 4 TR18 . 143 E5
Old Bridge St PL1 . . . . . 137 D4
Old Butchers Shop The
TR20 . . . . 89 B8
Old Cable La TR19 . . . . . . 96 E3
Old Callywith Rd PL31 . . . 35 B2
Old Canal Cl EX23 . . . . . . 7 F6
Old Carnon Hill TR3 . . . . . 81 F6
Old Chapel The TR4 . . . . . 68 F5
Old Chapel Way PL10 . . . 132 F6
Old Chough Flats TR7 . . . 111 B7
Old Church Rd PL15 . . . . . 13 A4
Old Church The TR18 . . . 143 D4
Old Coach Rd
Lanivet PL26, PL30 . . . . . . 47 D6
Playing Place TR3 . . . . 82 B8
Truro TR3 . . . . 70 F1
Old Coastguard Cotts
PL11 . . . . 65 A4
Old Coastguard Row
TR19 . . . . 96 B7
Old Corn Mill The TR12 . . 92 C1
Old Dairy The
Plymouth PL3 . . . . 129 B6
Sancreed TR20 . . . . 87 E4
Old Drovers Way EX23 . . . 4 E1
Old English Ind Est PL20 . 42 E3
Old Exeter Rd PL19 . . . . 147 D7
Old Falmouth Rd TR1 . . . 137 C1
Old Farm Rd PL25 . . . . . 127 C8
Old Ferry Rd PL12 . . . . . 123 A3
Old Foundry Ct TR19 . . . . 86 F6
Old Foundry The
Menheniot PL14 . . . . 51 E6
Tavistock PL19 . . . . 147 D6
Old George St PL1 . . . . . 148 C2
Old Grammar School Ct
PL22 . . . . 112 C2
Old Greystone Hill PL15,
PL19 . . . . 28 F6
Old Guildhall Mus★
PL13 . . . . 117 D3
Old Hill
Falmouth TR11 . . . . 144 F6
Grampound TR2 . . . . 72 A7
Helston TR13 . . . . 146 A6
Old Hill Cres TR11 . . . . . 144 F5
OLD KEA 82 E8
Old La PL26 . . . . 46 F3
Old Laira Rd PL3 . . . . 129 C4
Oldlands Cl PL6 . . . . 125 B6
Old Launceston Rd PL19 . 147 B6
Old Laundry The PL1 . . . 148 A3
Old Lawn School La
PL25 . . . . 114 B3

Old Market Rd PL31 . . . . 109 C4
Old Mill Cl PL15 . . . . 27 B3
Old Mill Ct PL7 . . . . 130 E5
Old Mill Herbary The★
PL30 . . . . 34 F6
Old Mill The
3 Boscastle PL35 . . . . 9 C2
Lerryn PL22 . . . . 61 D8
Old Mine La PL18 . . . . 40 E6
Old Nursery Cl TR13 . . . . 91 A1
Old Orchard Cl EX23 . . . . . 7 B6
Old Orchard The PL22 . . 112 C2
Old Park Rd PL3 . . . . 128 D6
Old Paul Hill TR18 . . . . . 143 C2
Old Plymouth Rd PL3 . . . 129 E5
Old Portreath Rd
Illogan TR16 . . . . 67 F5
Redruth TR15 . . . . 67 F4
Old Post Office Hill 8
EX23 . . . . 4 E1
Old Pound PL26 . . . . 58 E6
Old Priory PL7 . . . . 130 D5
Old Priory Jun Sch PL7 . 130 D5
Old Quarry Rd PL20 . . . . . 42 A3
Old Quay La PL12 . . . . 65 B8
Old Rd
Boscastle PL35 . . . . 9 C2
Liskeard PL14 . . . . 113 A6
Old Rectory Dr TR9 . . . . . 45 E6
Old Roselyon Cres PL24 . 60 B5
Old Roselyon Rd PL24 . . . 60 C4
Old Sandy La TR16 . . . . . 140 D3
Old School Cl PL27 . . . . . 21 F3
Old School Ct
Padstow PL28 . . . . 107 D5
Wadebridge PL27 . . . . . . 108 B5
Old School Ho The PL10 . 133 A1
Old Schoolhouse The
TR11 . . . . 145 B4
Old School Rd PL5 . . . . . 127 C8
Old School The 10 TR5 . . . 54 D1
Old Smithy Cl 4 TR17 . . . 89 C5
Old Smithy Cotts EX39 . . . 2 E4
Old Sta La TR17 . . . . 89 A6
Old Station Rd
Horrabridge PL20 . . . . 42 C4
1 Liskeard PL14 . . . . 51 A7
Old Station The PL20 . . . . 42 B4
Old Tannery Bsns Pk The 4
PL4 . . . . 149 A4
Old Town Hall The PL24 . . 60 B5
Old Town St PL1 . . . . 148 C3
Old Tram Rd PL12 . . . . . . 123 A3
Old Vicarage Cl TR3 . . . . . 80 F4
Old Vicarage Gate TR27 . 142 A1
Old Vicarage PI 11 PL25 . 114 C2
Old Vicarage The TR 26 . . . 76 E5
Old Warleigh La PL5 . . . . 124 B7
Old Well Gdns TR10 . . . . 144 C8
Old Wharf The PL9 . . . . . 135 C7
Old Woodlands Rd PL5 . . 124 D3
Old Workhouses The
TR13 . . . . 140 B8
Oliver Ct
Liskeard PL14 . . . . 50 E8
St Mellion PL12 . . . . 40 A1
Oliver's Terr TR13 . . . . . 146 C5
Olive Villas TR3 . . . . 81 F6
Olivia Pr PL11 . . . . 82 A3
Olivia Ct PL4 . . . . 149 B4
Omaha Rd PL31 . . . . 109 F3
Onslow Rd PL2 . . . . 128 C7
Ope's Ct 13 TR11 . . . . . . 145 B5
Opies La PL31 . . . . 109 C5
Opie's Terr TR16 . . . . 80 B5
Orange La TR26 . . . . 141 A6
Orchard Ave PL6 . . . . . . 129 B7
Orchard Cl
Helston TR13 . . . . 146 B7
3 Plymouth PL7 . . . . 131 C5
Poughill EX23 . . . . 4 D2
St Austell PL25 . . . . 114 E4
St Giles on the Heath PL15 . 13 F1
Tavistock PL19 . . . . 53 C8
Tideford PL12 . . . . 41 D8
Truro TR1 . . . . 69 F3
Orchard Cotts
Lamerton PL19 . . . . 30 B3
St Austell PL25 . . . . 114 F5
Orchard Cres PL9 . . . . . . 135 C7
Orchard Ct
Lamerton PL19 . . . . 30 A3
Penzance TR18 . . . . 143 C5
Orchard Gr PL25 . . . . 114 B4
Orchard Ho 11 TR18 . . . . 143 C2
Orchard La
Helford TR12 . . . . 93 B1
Plymouth PL7 . . . . 130 E6
Orchard PI 10 TR18 . . . . 143 C2
Orchard Rd PL2 . . . . 128 B7
Orchard Terr 20 TR18 . . 143 C2
Orchard The
Gunnislake PL18 . . . . 41 A6
Lerryn PL22 . . . . 61 D8
Newquay TR7 . . . . 111 B7
North Petherwin PL15 . . . . 18 B8
St Erth TR27 . . . . 77 E3
Orchardton Terr 2 PL9 . . 135 F5
Orchard Vale TR11 . . . . . 145 C7
Orchard Way
6 Goldsithney TR20 . . . . . 89 E5

Orchard Way continued
2 St Austell PL26 . . . . . . 115 A1
Orchard Wlk 13 PL27 . . . 108 B5
Orch The PL13 . . . . 117 D4
Ordnance St PL1 . . . . . . 127 E2
Ordulf Rd PL19 . . . . 147 A5
Oregon Way PL3 . . . . . . 129 D6
ORESTON 135 C7
Oreston Com Prim Sch
PL9 . . . . 135 C8
Oreston Rd PL9 . . . . 135 C8
Orion Dr PL27 . . . . 31 F3
Osborne Ct PL1 . . . . 148 C2
Osborne Parc TR13 . . . . 146 B7
Osborne PI PL1 . . . . 148 C2
Osborne Rd PL3 . . . . 128 A3
Osborne Villas
8 Falmouth TR11 . . . . . . 145 C3
2 Plymouth PL3 . . . . 128 A3
Osprey Gdns PL9 . . . . . . 136 C7
OTTERHAM 10 D1
Otterham Com Prim Sch
PL32 . . . . 16 C2
Otterham Pk PL32 . . . . . . 16 A8
OTTERHAM STATION 16 A8
OTTERY 30 A2
Ottery Cotts PL19 . . . . . . 30 A2
Ottery Park Ind Est PL19 . 30 A2
Outer Down PL19 . . . . . . 30 A3
Outland Rd PL2 . . . . 128 C7
Overcliff PL29 . . . . 22 D8
Overdale Rd PL2 . . . . 128 A7
Overton Gdns 3 PL3 . . . 128 F5
Overton Villas 6 PL15 . . 106 C5
Owen Dr PL7 . . . . 130 C7
Owen Sivell Cl PL14 . . . . 113 E6
Oxford Ave PL3 . . . . 128 E5
Oxford Gdns PL3 . . . . . . 128 E5
Oxford PI PL1 . . . . 148 A3
Oxford St PL1 . . . . 148 A3
Oxford Terr 4 TR1 . . . . . 148 B3
Oxland Rd TR16 . . . . 67 E5

P

Paardeburg Rd 1 PL31 . . . 48 D8
Packet La TR20 . . . . 89 F5
Packington St PL2 . . . . . 128 A4
Packsaddle TR10 . . . . 81 D2
Packsaddle Cl TR10 . . . . . 81 D2
Paddock Cl
Plymouth PL9 . . . . 135 E5
Saltash PL12 . . . . 122 D4
Paddock The
Helston TR13 . . . . 146 C7
Redruth TR15 . . . . 140 D2
Sticker PL26 . . . . 58 E1
Paddons Row PL19 . . . . . 147 C6
Padnover Terr 22 TR26 . . 141 B5
PADSTOW 107 C4
Padstow Harbour Ind Est
PL28 . . . . 107 D4
Padstow Mus★ PL28 . . . . 107 C5
Padstow School PL28 . . . 107 E4
Padstow Workshop Units
PL28 . . . . 107 D4
Page's Cross PL15 . . . . . 106 D6
Pagoda Dr PL26 . . . . 115 A1
Paiges Farm PL19 . . . . . . 135 C1
Painton Water EX39 . . . . . . 3 A8
Palace Rd PL25 . . . . 114 D4
Palace St PL1 . . . . 149 A2
Palm Ct TR1 . . . . 137 D3
PALMERSBRIDGE 25 F4
Palmers Terr PL34 . . . . . . 14 C6
Palmerston St PL1 . . . . . 148 A4
Palmers Way PL27 . . . . . 108 D6
PANCRASWEEK 8 C8
Pannier La TR26 . . . . 141 C2
Pannier Mkt PL19 . . . . . . 147 C5
Panson Cross PL15 . . . . . 13 E3
PANTERSBRIDGE 36 D3
PAR 60 C4
Parade PL1 . . . . 149 A2
Parade Bsns Pk 4 PL19 . 147 B4
Parade Hill TR19 . . . . 88 D1
Parade Ope PL1 . . . . 149 A2
Parade Pass 20 TR18 . . . 143 E5
Parade Rd PL5 . . . . 123 A3
Parade Sq PL22 . . . . 112 D2
Parade St TR18 . . . . 143 E5
Parade The
Helston TR13 . . . . 146 C5
Liskeard PL14 . . . . 113 C6
Lostwithiel PL22 . . . . 112 D2
Millbrook PL10 . . . . 132 E5
Milton Abbot PL19 . . . . . . 29 C6
Mousehole TR19 . . . . 88 D1
Truro TR1 . . . . 137 C4
**Paradise Park & The World
Parrot Trust**★ TR27 . . . . 142 A4
Paradise Pk EX22 . . . . 7 F1
Paradise PI PL1 . . . . 128 A2
Paradise Rd
Boscastle PL35 . . . . 9 C1
Plymouth PL1 . . . . 128 A2
PARAMOOR 72 E8
**Par Beach & St Andrews Rd
Nature Reserve**★ PL24 . . 60 D4
Parc-Abnac TR20 . . . . 88 B7
Parc-an-Bal TR14 . . . . . . 138 E4
Parc-an-Bre Dr PL26 . . . . 58 C8
Parc-an-Cady Est TR19 . . 97 A6
Parc-an-Chalow TR10 . . 144 B8
Parc-an-Creet TR26 . . . . . 77 A7
Parc-an-Dillon Rd TR2 . . . 83 B2
Parc-an-Dix La TR27 . . . 142 C7

Parc-an-Dower TR13 . . . 146 C6
Parcandover TR2 . . . . 57 E1
Parc-an-Forth 6 TR26. . . . 77 A6
Parc an Gate TR19 . . . . . . 88 C1
Parc-an-Gwarry 7 TR3 . . 81 F7
Parc-an-Ithan TR2 . . . . . . 102 F2
Parc-an-Maen 11 TR13. . . . 98 C8
Parc an Manns TR11 . . . . 93 D3
Parc-an-Peath TR19 . . . . . 97 A6
Parc-an-Stamps 4 TR26. . 77 A6
Parc an Yorth TR19 . . . . . 86 F8
Parc-Askell Cl TR12 . . . . . . 98 E5
Parc Bean Terr TR26 . . . 141 A6
Parc Behan Ct TR2 . . . . . 83 F6
Parc Bowen TR13 . . . . 92 A3
Parc-Bracket St TR14 . . 138 D3
Parc Brawse TR12 . . . . . . 102 F2
Parc Briwer TR10 . . . . . . 144 D7
Parc Eglos
  Helston TR13 . . . . 146 B6
  St Merryn TR8 . . . . 31 F8
Parc Eglos Sch TR13 . . . 146 C6
Parc Enys TR12 . . . . 99 B4
PARC ERISSEY 68 A3
Parc Erissey Ind Est TR16 68 A3
Parc Fer Cl TR23 . . . . 4 C5
Parc Godrevy TR7. . . . . . 110 C5
Parc Holland TR13 . . . . . 146 D8
Parc Ledden TR13 . . . . . . 146 C6
Parc Ledrak TR13 . . . . . . 146 B8
Parc Letta TR18. . . . . 143 C7
Parc Mellan TR18 . . . . . . 143 D7
Parc Mery TR2. . . . . 83 B2
Parc Monga Rd TR11 . . . 92 F3
Parc Morrep TR20 . . . . . . 90 B3
Parc Owles TR26. . . . . . . 141 D2
Parc Peneglos TR11. . . . . 82 A3
Parc Pennkarn PL33 . . . . 14 E3
Parc Rowan TR9 . . . . 57 E7
Parc Shady TR26. . . . . 77 C1
Parc Stepiney TR11. . . . 144 C2
Parc Terr 18 TR18. . . . . . 143 C1
Parc Trenance PL28. . . . . . 31 F7
Parc Trethias PL28. . . . . . 31 F7
Parc Vean PL30. . . . . 34 C1
Parc Venton Cl 2 TR14. . 138 F2
Parc Villas 17 TR18 . . . . 143 C1
Parc Wartha Ave TR18. . 143 D6
Parc Wartha Cres TR18. 143 D6
Par Gn PL24. . . . . 60 C4
Pargolla Rd TR7 . . . . 110 F6
Park 30 PL15 . . . . 106 A3
Parka Cl TR19 . . . . 45 E2
Park-an-Bans TR14. . . . . 138 E1
Parkancreeg 9 TR3. . . . . 81 F7
Park an Gonwyn TR26. . 141 E2
Park an Gorsaf TR14 . . . 138 D2
Park an Harvey TR13 . . 146 C6
Park-an-Mengleth TR15 140 D4
Park-an-Pyth TR19 . . . . . 75 A1
Park-an-Tansys TR14 . . 138 F2
Parka Rd
  Indian Queens TR9 . . . . 45 E1
  8 St Columb Road TR9. . 45 E2
Park Ave
  Plymouth, Devonport
    PL1. . . . . 127 E3
  Plymouth, Plymstock PL9 135 D7
  St Ives TR26 . . . . 141 B5
PARK BOTTOM 139 B8
Park Cl
  Illogan TR15. . . . . 139 B8
  Nancegollan TR13 . . . . . . 91 B7
  Plymouth PL7. . . . . 130 B7
Park Cnr TR18 . . . . 143 E5
Park Cres
  Falmouth TR11. . . . . 145 A4
  Helston TR13 . . . . 146 B5
  Plymouth PL9. . . . . 135 C7
  Ponsanooth TR3. . . . . . . 81 B4
Park Ct
  Chillaton PL16. . . . . 29 F8
  28 Penzance TR18. . . . . . 143 E5
Park Dr PL31 . . . . 109 B4
Parkenbutts TR2 . . . . 71 D7
Parkengear Vean TR2. . . 71 D6
Parkengue TR10. . . . . . . 144 A7
Parkenhead La PL28. . . . 20 F2
Park Ensklade 18 TR12. . 99 A2
Park en Venton TR12. . . 99 A2
Park-en-Vine PL27 . . . . . 32 C6
Parker Cl PL7. . . . . 130 B5
Parker Rd PL2. . . . . 128 B6
Parker's Gn PL18 . . . . . . 40 F6
Parkesway PL12 . . . . 122 D2
Park Fenton PL14 . . . . . 113 C5
PARKFIELD 39 A2
Parkfield Dr PL6. . . . . . . 125 F1
Park Gwyn PL26 . . . . 58 B4
Park Hill TR11 . . . . 145 A4
Park Ho PL25 . . . . 114 B3
Park Holly TR14. . . . . . . 138 B3
Parkins Terr 7 TR1 . . . . 137 D5
Park La
  8 Bere Alston PL20. . . . . 41 B1
  Bugle PL26. . . . . 47 C1
  Camborne TR14. . . . . . . 138 E2
  Plymouth PL3. . . . . 135 C7

Park Place La 12 PL3 . . . 128 A4
Park Rd
  Camborne TR14 . . . . . . 138 E4
  Fowey PL23 . . . . 116 C4
  Illogan TR15. . . . . 139 B7
  Lifton PL16. . . . . 19 F3
  Liskeard PL14 . . . . 113 C6
  11 Newlyn TR18. . . . . . 143 C1
  Plymouth PL3. . . . . 129 A6
  Ponsanooth TR3. . . . . . . 81 B4
  Redruth TR15. . . . . 140 C4
  St Austell PL25 . . . . 114 C3
  St Dominick PL12. . . . . . 40 D2
  Torpoint PL11. . . . . 127 B3
  Wadebridge PL27 . . . . . 108 B5
  Whitemoor PL26 . . . . . . 58 E8
Park Rd Hos PL22 . . . . . 112 C2
Park Rise TR11 . . . . 145 A4
Parkryn Rd 4 TR19 . . . . . 88 C1
Parkside PL2 . . . . 127 F5
Park St PL3. . . . . 128 A4
Park Stenak TR16 . . . . . . 80 F8
Parkstone La PL7 . . . . . . 130 F6
Park Street Ope 2 TR3. . 128 A4
Park Terr
  Falmouth TR11. . . . . 145 A4
  Truro TR1. . . . . 70 D1
Park The
  Penryn TR10. . . . . 144 B7
  Tregony TR2 . . . . 71 F4
Parkvedras Ho 6 TR1. . 137 B4
Parkvedras Terr 4 TR1 137 B4
Parkventon PL26. . . . . . . 47 C2
Park View
  Lifton PL16. . . . . 19 F4
  Liskeard PL14 . . . . 113 C6
  Perranarworthal TR3. . . 81 E6
  Plymouth PL4. . . . . 149 C3
  Summercourt TR8 . . . . . 57 B7
  Truro TR1. . . . . 137 C3
Parkview Apartments
  TR7 . . . . 110 F5
Park View Cl TR3 . . . . . . 82 A7
Park View Rd TR3 . . . . . 146 B5
Park View Terr PL27 . . . 108 B5
Park Villas TR3 . . . . 81 B4
Park Way PL25. . . . . 114 F5
Parkway Ind Est The
  PL6. . . . . 129 E7
Parkway The PL3, PL5,
  PL6. . . . . 124 B1
Park Wise TR10 . . . . 144 C8
Parkwood Cl PL6 . . . . . . 121 B2
Parkwood Ct PL19 . . . . . 147 D6
Parkwood Rd PL19 . . . . 147 D6
Park Wood Rise PL16 . . 19 F4
Parkwoon Cl PL6. . . . . . . 46 F3
Par La PL24. . . . . 60 B4
Par Moor Rd
  Par PL24, PL25 . . . . 60 B3
  St Austell PL24, PL25 . . 115 F4
PARNACOTT 8 E8
Parnell Cl PL6. . . . . 129 B2
Parr La PL4. . . . . 149 B2
Parr St PL4. . . . . 149 B2
Parsonage Ct PL16. . . . . 19 F4
Parsonage Way 4 PL14. 149 B2
Parsons Cl PL9 . . . . 136 A4
Parsons Ct PL10. . . . . . . 132 F6
Parsons Gn PL17. . . . . . . 39 E6
Par Sta PL24. . . . . 60 B3
Partwayes PL19. . . . . 30 A3
Pascoe Cl TR3 . . . . 69 D4
Pasley St E PL2 . . . . 127 F4
Pasley St PL2. . . . . 127 E4
Passage Hill TR11. . . . . . 82 A3
Passage La PL23 . . . . . . 116 B5
Passage St PL23 . . . . . . 116 D5
Passmore Cl
  Blackwater TR4 . . . . 68 E5
  Liskeard PL14 . . . . 113 D6
Pathfields EX23. . . . . . . 104 E5
Pathway Fields The
  TR27 . . . . 142 C5
Patna 9 PL1. . . . . 148 B4
Pato Point PL11. . . . . 127 A5
Patterdale Cl PL6 . . . . . 125 D3
Patterdale Wlk PL6 . . . 125 D3
Pattinson Cl PL6. . . . . . . 125 E2
Pattinson Ct PL6. . . . . . . 125 E2
Pattinson Dr PL6. . . . . . . 125 E2
PAUL 88 C2
Paull Rd PL31. . . . . 109 B4
Paulls Row 4 TR15. . . . . 140 C5
PAUL'S GREEN 90 E8
Paul's Row TR1 . . . . 137 D5
Paul's Terr TR1. . . . . 137 D5
Paviland Grange 6 PL1 128 A3
Pavilion Pk TR14. . . . . . 138 A4
Pavlova Cl PL14 . . . . 113 C5
Pavlova Ct 6 PL14. . . . . 113 C5
Paynter's Cross PL12. . . 53 E7
Paynter's Cross Cotts
  PL12. . . . . 53 E7
Paynters La TR16 . . . . . . 67 E4
PAYNTER'S LANE END . . 67 E4
Paynter's Lane End Est
  TR16 . . . . 67 D4
Paynter Wlk 5 PL7 . . . . 131 B5
Peacock Ave PL11 . . . . . 127 A3
Peacock Cl PL7. . . . . 130 F7
Peacock La PL4. . . . . 149 A2
Pearce's La PL24. . . . . . . 141 A5
Pearce's Row 3 PL24. . . 60 C4
Pearn Cotts 2 PL3. . . . . . 87 F3
Pearn Gdns PL3. . . . . . . 129 A7
Pearn Rd PL3. . . . . 129 A7

Pearn Ridge PL3. . . . . . . 129 A7
Pearson Ave 3 PL4. . . . . 128 F4
Pearson Rd PL4. . . . . 128 F4
Pebble Ct TR7 . . . . 111 C7
Pedlars Cl PL15. . . . . 18 B8
Pedna Carne Mobile Home
  Pk TR9. . . . . 57 E8
Pednandrea TR19 . . . . . . 86 E6
Pedn-m'n-du TR19 . . . . . 96 A7
Pedn-Moran TR2 . . . . 95 B6
Pedn-y-ke 1 TR12 . . . . . 99 A1
Peek Moor Cross EX22 . 13 E4
Peeks Ave PL9 . . . . 135 F7
Peel St PL1. . . . . 128 A1
Peguarra Cl PL28 . . . . . . 20 E1
Peguarra Ct PL28 . . . . . . 20 E1
Pelean Cross TR3 . . . . . . 81 B5
Pelham 11 TR11. . . . . . . 145 C3
Pellew Cl
  7 Falmouth TR11. . . . . . 145 A5
  Padstow PL28 . . . . 107 C5
Pellew Cres TR13 . . . . . 146 C4
Pellew Pl PL2. . . . . 127 F4
Pellew Rd TR11. . . . . 145 A5
Pellor Fields TR13 . . . . . 90 F3
PELYNT 62 D5
Pelynt Prim Sch PL13 . . 62 D6
Pembrey Wlk PL5. . . . . . 123 E4
Pembroke Cl 7 PL24. . . . 60 C4
Pembroke La PL1 . . . . . . 127 E1
Pembroke Rd TR7. . . . . . 111 C7
Pembroke St PL1 . . . . . . 127 E1
Pemros Rd PL5 . . . . 123 C1
Penair Cres TR1 . . . . 137 F6
Penair Sch TR1 . . . . 70 D4
Penair View TR1 . . . . . . 137 F4
Penally Ct PL5. . . . . 9 D2
Penally Hill PL35. . . . . . . 9 C9
Penally Terr PL35. . . . . . . 9 C2
Penalverne Ave TR18. . 143 D5
Penalverne Cres TR18. . 143 D5
Penalverne Dr TR18 . . . 143 D5
Penalverne Pl TR18 . . . 143 D5
Penamenye 15 TR26 . . 141 B6
Penare Gdns 2 TR18. . . 143 E6
Penare Rd 8 TR18. . . . . 143 E6
Penare Terr TR18 . . . . . 143 E6
Penarrow Cl TR11. . . . . 144 E2
Penarrow Rd TR11 . . . . 145 C8
Penarth PL13 . . . . 117 B3
Penarwyn Cres TR18 . . 143 B7
Penarwyn Rd PL24 . . . . 60 B4
Penarwyn Woods 6 PL24 60 B4
PENBEAGLE 141 A4
Penbeagle Cl 17 TR26. . 77 A6
Penbeagle Cres 8 TR26. 77 A6
Penbeagle Ind Est TR26 77 A6
Penbeagle La TR26. . . . . 77 A6
Penbeagle Terr 7 TR26. 77 A6
Penbeagle Way TR26. . 141 A4
PENBERTH 97 A3
Penberthy Cross TR27. . 89 F7
Penberthy Rd
  Helston TR13 . . . . 146 C5
  Portreath TR16 . . . . 67 D6
Penbothidno TR11 . . . . . 92 F3
Pen Brea Cl TR2 . . . . 95 B6
Penbrea Rd TR18 . . . . . 143 E7
Penbugle La PL31. . . . . 109 E7
Pencair Ave PL11. . . . . . 126 E2
Pencalenick Sped Sch
  TR1. . . . . 70 E4
Pencantol TR4. . . . . 81 C7
Pencarn Parc TR16. . . . . 80 A5
Pencarrick Cl TR1 . . . . . 137 B6
PENCARROW 105 D1
Pencarrow ★ PL30. . . . . 34 D6
Pencarrow Cl TR1 . . . . . 137 B6
Pencarrow Rd 8 TR16. . 67 E4
Pencavo Hill PL12. . . . . . 53 A3
Pencoys Prim Sch TR16 80 A5
Pencreber Rd 8 PL20. . 42 C4
PENCUKE 10 D5
Pendale Sq TR18 . . . . . 137 B4
Pendarves
  St Merryn TR8 . . . . 31 F7
  Tresillian TR2. . . . . 70 F5
Pendarves Flats TR18 . 143 D6
Pendarves Rd
  Camborne TR14 . . . . . . 138 C1
  Falmouth TR11. . . . . . . 144 F6
  Penzance TR18. . . . . . . 143 D6
  Truro TR1. . . . . 137 C6
Pendarves St
  Camborne, Beacon TR14 138 F1
  Troon TR14. . . . . 79 E4
Pendarves View TR14. . 138 C1
Pendean Ave PL14 . . . . 113 B6
Pendean Cl PL14. . . . . . 113 B6
Pendean Ct PL14. . . . . . 113 B6
Pendean Dr PL14 . . . . . 113 B6
PENDEEN 75 A1
Pendeen Cl
  Plymouth PL6. . . . . 124 F6
  Threemilestone TR3. . . . 69 D3
Pendeen Cres
  Plymouth PL6. . . . . 125 A6
  Threemilestone TR3. . . . 69 D3
Pendeen Ho TR13 . . . . . . 69 E4
Pendeen Pk TR13. . . . . . 146 B6
Pendeen Pl TR7. . . . . . . 110 F6
Pendeen Prim Sch TR19. 75 A1
Pendeen Rd
  Porthleven TR13 . . . . . . 91 B1
  Threemilestone TR3. . . . 69 D3
  Truro TR1. . . . . 137 E3

Pendennis Castle ★ TR11 145 E2
Pendennis Cl
  Penzance TR18. . . . . . . 143 E7
  Plymouth PL3. . . . . 128 F8
  Torpoint PL11. . . . . 126 F3
Pendennis Ct TR11. . . . 145 D3
Pendennis Pl TR18 . . . . 143 E7
Pendennis Rd
  Falmouth TR11. . . . . . . 145 D3
  Looe PL13 . . . . 117 D5
  Penzance TR18. . . . . . . 143 E7
Pendennis Rise TR11. . . 145 D3
Pender's La TR15 . . . . . . 140 B5
Pendilly Ave PL11 . . . . . 126 E2
Pendilly Dr PL25 . . . . . . 114 E7
Pendinnes Gdns PL15 . . 106 B8
PENDOGGETT. 23 A6
Pendola Wlk TR26 . . . . 141 B5
Pendour Pk PL22 . . . . . . 112 E2
Pendower Ct TR2 . . . . . . 83 D5
Pendower Rd
  Looe PL13 . . . . 117 E4
  Veryan TR2 . . . . 83 F6
Pendower Terr 4 TR18. . 138 E1
Pendragon Cres TR7 . . 111 A4
Pendragon Ho TR11. . . . 145 D3
Pendragon Rd PL14 . . . 113 D6
Pendra Loweth TR11 . . 144 D1
Pendray Gdns PL11. . . . . 50 E7
Pendrea Cl TR18. . . . . . . 138 F5
Pendrea Pk TR14 . . . . . . 138 F5
Pendrea Pl TR18 . . . . . . 143 F7
Pendrea Rd TR18 . . . . . 143 F7
Pendrea Wood TR1 . . . . 69 F3
PENDRIFT. 24 B1
Pendrim Rd PL13 . . . . . 117 D4
Pendruccombe Ct PL15. 106 D5
Pen-Eglos 8 TR2. . . . . . . 95 B6
PENELEWEY 82 C7
Penforth TR14 . . . . 138 E2
Penfound Gdns EX23 . . 104 F5
Pengannel Cl TR7 . . . . . 110 D3
Pengarrock Hill TR12 . . 101 D5
Pengarth 1 TR5 . . . . 54 D1
Pengarth Ct TR1 . . . . . . 137 C2
Pengarth Rd TR11. . . . . 145 A3
Pengarth Rise TR11 . . . 145 A3
PENGEGON. 138 F2
Pengegon Moor TR14 . . 138 F2
Pengegon Parc TR14. . . 138 F2
Pengegon Way TR14 . . 138 F2
PENGELLY 14 E2
Pengelly
  24 Callington PL17 . . . . 39 F4
  Delabole PL33 . . . . 14 E3
Pengelly Cl PL11. . . . . . . 126 F5
Pengelly Cross
  Godolphin Cross TR27 . . 90 F7
  Wadebridge PL27 . . . . . 108 C1
Pengelly Hill PL11 . . . . . 127 A5
Pengelly Pk PL11. . . . . . 126 F5
Pengelly Pl TR11. . . . . . 144 E5
Pengellys Row TR14 . . 139 A5
Pengelly Way TR3 . . . . . 69 D3
Pengeron Ave 1 TR14. . 138 F7
Pengersick Est TR20 . . . 90 C3
Pengersick La TR20. . . . 90 C3
Pengersick Parc TR20. . 90 C3
Pengliddon PL27. . . . . . . 33 B7
PENGOLD 10 A5
Pengover Cl PL14 . . . . . 113 D6
Pengover Gn PL14 . . . . . 51 E8
Pengover Hts PL14 . . . . 113 D6
Pengover Parc TR15 . . . 140 C6
Pengover Pk PL14 . . . . . 113 D6
Pengover Rd PL14 . . . . . 113 E6
Pengrowyn PL26 . . . . . . 59 D6
Pengwarras Rd TR14. . . 138 C3
Pengover 10 PL18. . . . . 143 C2
PENHALE
  Indian Queens 57 D8
  Millbrook 132 D7
  Mullion 99 D1
Penhale 1 TR6 . . . . 55 A5
Penhale Cl PL14 . . . . 37 F3
Penhale Cotts TR3 . . . . . 82 D6
Penhale Est TR15 . . . . . 140 B6
Penhale Gdns TR9 . . . . . 57 D8
Penhale Mdw TR3 . . . . . 37 F3
Penhale Rd
  Barripper TR14 . . . . 79 A4
  Carnhell Green TR14 . . . 78 F4
  Falmouth TR11. . . . . . . 144 F1
  Penwithick PL26 . . . . . . 59 D7
Penhaligon Cl TR15. . . . 140 D4
Penhaligon Ct TR1. . . . . 137 E5
Penhaligon Way PL25 . . 114 F4
PENHALLICK 139 C4
Penhall La TR4 . . . . 68 C6
PENHALLOW 55 B2
Penhallow TR15 . . . . . . 139 B8
Penhallow Cl
  Mount Hawke TR4 . . . . . 68 C6
  Veryan TR2 . . . . 83 C5
Penhallow Ct TR7. . . . . 111 C7
Penhallow Parc PL33. . . 14 D7
Penhallow Rd TR7 . . . . . 111 C7
Penhalls Way TR3 . . . . . 82 B8
PENHALVEAN 80 C4
Penharget Cl PL14 . . . . . 38 D5
Penhaven Ct TR18 . . . . . 56 B7
Penhaven Ct TR7 . . . . . 110 E6
Penhellaz Hill TR13 . . . 146 B6
Penhellaz Rd TR13 . . . . 146 B6
Penhole Cl PL15 . . . . 27 D3
Penina Ave PL14 . . . . . . 110 F4
Peninsula Medical Sch
  PL6. . . . . 125 C3

Peninsular Pk PL12 . . . . 122 C4
Penjerrick Gdns ★ TR11 . . 93 D5
Penjerrick Hill
  Budock Water TR11 . . . 144 C1
  Falmouth TR11. . . . . 93 E5
Penkenna Cl EX23 . . . . . 10 C5
Penkernick Cl TR18 . . . 143 B1
Penkernick Way TR9 . . . 45 E6
Penknight La PL22 . . . . 112 A2
Penlean Cl TR15 . . . . . . 140 D7
Penlea Rd TR10 . . . . 144 B8
Penlee Apartments PL23 116 C3
Penlee Cl
  13 Callington PL17 . . . . 39 F4
  Praa Sands TR20 . . . . . . 90 C3
  Tregony TR2 . . . . 71 F4
Penlee Cotts PL10 . . . . . 64 C2
Penlee Gdns PL3. . . . . . 128 A4
Penlee Ho TR1. . . . . 69 E4
Penlee House Gall & Mus ★
  TR18 . . . . 143 E5
Penlee Manor Dr TR18 . 143 E4
Penlee Pk PL11 . . . . 126 E4
Penlee Pl 4 TR18 . . . . . 128 F4
Penlee Rd PL3 . . . . 128 A4
Penlee St 10 TR18. . . . . 143 E6
Penlee View Terr 3
  TR18 . . . . 143 E4
Penlee Villas TR3 . . . . . . 82 B8
Penlee Way PL3 . . . . . . 128 B4
Penlu TR14. . . . . 138 F5
Penlu Ho TR14. . . . . 138 F5
Penluke Cl TR16 . . . . 80 A5
Penmare Cl TR27 . . . . . 142 E7
Penmare Ct TR27 . . . . . 142 E7
Penmare Terr 1 TR27 . . 142 E7
PENMARTH 80 C2
Penmayne Parc TR16. . 140 F1
Penmayne Villas TR7 . . 21 E3
Penmead Rd PL33. . . . . . 14 E2
Penmelen TR13 . . . . . . 105 C4
Penmenneth TR13 . . . . 146 F8
Penmenner Est 7 TR12 . 101 C4
Penmenner Rd TR12 . . 102 F2
Penmere Cl
  Helston TR13 . . . . 146 B8
  Penzance TR18. . . . . . . 143 E7
Penmere Cres TR11. . . . 144 F3
Penmere Ct TR11 . . . . . 145 A3
Penmere Dr TR7 . . . . . . 110 C5
Penmere Hill 7 TR11 . . 145 A3
Penmere Pl
  3 Falmouth TR11. . . . . . 145 A3
  Penzance TR18. . . . . . . 143 E7
Penmere Rd
  Penzance TR18. . . . . . . 143 E7
  St Austell PL25 . . . . 115 A4
Penmere Sta TR11 . . . . 144 F3
Penmerrin Ct TR7 . . . . . 110 E5
Penmeva View PL26. . . . 73 C3
Penmorvah TR11. . . . . . . 82 A2
Penmorvah Pl TR14 . . . 138 E2
Penmorvah Rd TR1 . . . 137 F6
PENNANCE 140 F1
Pennance Hill TR11. . . . 145 A2
Pennance Ho TR11. . . . 145 A2
Pennance La TR16 . . . . 140 F1
Pennance Parc TR16 . . 140 F1
Pennance Rd
  Falmouth TR11. . . . . . . 145 A2
  Lanner TR16. . . . . 80 E7
  Redruth TR16. . . . . 140 F1
Pennance Terr TR16 . . 140 F1
Penn an Drea TR13. . . . 146 D8
Pennant Farm PL29 . . . 22 E6
Pennard Villas PL27 . . . 33 B5
Penn Kernow PL15 . . . . 106 E4
Pennor Dr PL13 . . . . 114 C3
Pennoweth Prim Sch
  TR15. . . . . 140 C5
PENNYCOMEQUICK . . . 148 B4
Pennycomequick Hill
  PL4. . . . . 148 B4
PENNYCROSS 128 C8
Pennycross Cl PL2 . . . . 128 D8
Pennycross Park Rd PL2 128 C7
Pennycross Prim Sch
  PL2. . . . . 128 C8
Pennygillam Ind Est
  PL15. . . . . 106 A4
Pennygillam Way PL15 . 18 E2
Penny's La PL24 . . . . . . 115 F5
Penny's La PL9 . . . . 136 D6
PENNYTINNEY 23 A4
Penoweth TR11. . . . . 82 A2
PENPETHY 14 F5
PENPILLICK. 60 D7
PENPOL. 82 B6
Penpol Ave TR27 . . . . . 142 C5
Penpol Hill
  Crantock TR8. . . . . 110 B4
  Devoran TR3 . . . . 82 B6
PENPOLL. 61 D5
Penpol Prim Sch TR27 . 142 B5
Penpol Rd TR27 . . . . . . 142 B5
Penpol Terr TR27 . . . . . 142 C5
Penpol Vean TR27 . . . . 142 C5
PENPONDS 138 B1
Penponds Prim Sch TR14. 79 B5
Penponds Rd TR13. . . . . 91 A1
PENPONT 24 A1
Penpont Rd TR15 . . . . . 140 D6
Penpont View PL15 . . . . 26 C7

Pen Porth Ave TR26 . . . . . . 77 A7
Penquite Dr PL31 . . . . . . 109 F5
Penrice Com Coll PL25 . . 115 A3
Penrice Parc PL25 . . . . . . 115 A3
Penrith Cl PL6 . . . . 125 D3
Penrith Gdns PL6 . . . . . . 125 D3
Penrith Wlk PL6 . . . . 125 D3
PENROSE
St Breward 24 A3
St Eval 31 E5
Penrose Ct
Penzance TR18 . . . . 143 F6
2 South Tehidy TR14 . . 138 F7
Penrose Parc TR13 . . . . . 91 B1
Penrose Rd
Falmouth TR11 . . . . 145 A4
Helston TR13 . . . . 146 C6
Penrose St PL1 . . . . 148 B3
Penrose Terr TR18 . . . . . 143 F6
Penrose Villas 5 PL4 . . 128 F4
Penrose Walks★ TR12,
TR13 . . . . 98 D8
Penruan La TR2 . . . . 95 B6
PENRYN 144 B7
Penryn Coll TR10 . . . . . . 144 B7
Penryn Inf Sch TR10 . . . 144 B7
Penryn Jun Sch TR10 . . 144 B8
Penryn Mus★ TR10 . . . . 144 C7
Penryn St TR15 . . . . 140 B4
Penryn Sta TR10 . . . . . . 144 B8
Pensans Com Prim Sch
TR18 . . . . 143 D6
Penscombe Cross PL15 . 28 C6
Penscott La PL26 . . . . . . 114 C1
PENSILVA 38 E5
Pensilva Rd 38 E5
Pensilva Ind Est PL14 . . . 38 E4
Pensilva Prim Sch PL14 . . 38 E5
Pensilva Rd TR1 . . . . 137 E6
Penstowe Rd EX23 . . . . . . 5 A6
Penstrasse Pl 1 PL4 . . . 60 D5
PENSTRAZE 69 A4
Penstraze Bsns Ctr TR4 . . 69 A5
Penstraze La PL26 . . . . . . 47 A4
Pensylva PL25 . . . . 114 E3
Pentalek Rd TR14 . . . . . 138 D1
Pentamar St PL2 . . . . . . 127 E4
Pentargon Rd 1 PL35 . . . 9 C1
PENTEWAN 73 C6
Pentewan Hill PL26 . . . . . 73 D6
Pentewan Rd PL24, PL26 . 59 C1
Pentidna La TR27 . . . . . . 66 B2
Pentillie PL26 . . . . 73 C4
Pentillie Cl 6 PL20 . . . . . 41 B1
Pentillie Cres PL4 . . . . . 128 D4
Pentillie Gdns
14 Callington PL17 . . . . . 39 E4
St Austell PL25 . . . . . . 114 F6
Pentillie Rd
Bere Alston PL20 . . . . . . 41 B1
Plymouth PL4 . . . . 128 E4
Pentillie View 2 PL26 . . . 73 C4
Pentillie Way PL26 . . . . . 73 C4
PENTIRE 43 D4
Pentire Ave TR7 . . . . 110 A5
Pentire Cres TR7 . . . . . . 110 B5
Pentire Ct TR7 . . . . 110 B6
Pentire Gn TR8 . . . . 43 D3
Pentire Hts TR7 . . . . 110 A5
Pentire Rd
Newquay TR7 . . . . 110 C5
Penryn TR10 . . . . 144 B8
Torpoint PL11 . . . . 126 F3
Pentland Cl PL6 . . . . 124 F7
Pen Tor PL30 . . . . 35 C8
Pentor Ct PL30 . . . . 35 C8
Pentour 3 PL24 . . . . 60 B4
Pentowan Ctr TR26 . . . . 141 E2
Pentowan Gdns TR27 . . 142 E8
Pentowan Rd TR27 . . . . 142 E8
Pentreath Cl
Fowey PL23 . . . . 116 B5
Lanner TR16 . . . . 80 E7
Penzance TR18 . . . . 143 D7
Pentreath La
Lizard TR12 . . . . 102 F2
Praa Sands TR20 . . . . . . 90 B3
Pentreath Terr TR16 . . . . 80 E7
Pentre Ct EX23 . . . . 4 D4
Pentrevah Ct TR7 . . . . . 110 D6
Pentrevah Rd 8 PL26 . . . 58 E7
Pen-Tye TR27 . . . . 78 E3
Pentyre Ct PL4 . . . . 149 C4
Penvale 4 PL4 . . . . 38 E4
Penvale Cl TR14 . . . . 79 B5
Penvale Cres TR10 . . . . 144 B8
Penvale Ct 3 PL11 . . . . . 145 A4
Penvale Dr TR10 . . . . . . 144 B8
Penvean Cl TR10 . . . . 93 C8
Penvean La TR11 . . . . . . 144 C5
Penvenen 2 TR6 . . . . 55 A5
Penventinnie La TR1 . . . . 69 E4
Penventinue La PL23 . . . 116 B7
Penventon Terr
Four Lanes TR16 . . . . 80 B6
Redruth TR15 . . . . 140 A4
Penventon View TR13 . . 146 B5
Penview Cres TR13 . . . . 146 B5
Penvorder Cotts PL30 . . . 24 B2
Penvorder La PL30 . . . . . 24 B2
Penware Parc TR14 . . . . 138 C1
Penwarne Cl TR14 . . . . . 138 F7
Penwarne La PL26 . . . . . . 73 A5
Penwarne Rd TR11 . . . . . 93 D5

Penwartha TR12 . . . . . . 101 B2
Penwartha Cl
Constantine TR11 . . . . . . 92 F3
St Columb Minor TR7 . . 111 D7
PENWARTHA COOMBE . . 55 B3
Penwartha Ct TR11 . . . . . 92 F3
Penwartha Rd
18 Illogan TR14 . . . . . . 67 E4
Perranporth TR6 . . . . . . 55 B4
Penwartha Vean 14 TR16 67 E4
PENWEATHERS 69 F2
Penwerris Ct TR11 . . . . . 145 A6
Penwerris Farm TR11 . . 144 F5
Penwerris La TR11 . . . . . 145 A6
Penwerris Rd TR1 . . . . . . 69 F3
Penwerris Rise TR20 . . . . 90 B3
Penwerris Terr 10 TR11 . 145 A5
Penwethers La TR1 . . . . . 69 E2
Penwinnick Ct TR5 . . . . . 54 C1
Penwinnick Parc 4 TR5 . 54 D1
Penwinnick Rd
St Agnes TR5 . . . . 68 D8
St Austell PL25 . . . . . . 114 B3
Penwith Bsns Ctr TR20 . . 88 F6
Penwith Cl TR26 . . . . . . 141 A4
Penwith Coll TR18 . . . . . 143 D7
Penwithick Rd PL26 . . . . . 59 D7
Penwithian Cl TR27 . . . . 142 E6
PENWITHICK 59 E7
Penwithick Pk 6 PL26 . . 59 D7
Penwith Rd PL26 . . . . . . 141 A4
Penworth Cl PL15 . . . . . 106 C5
Penwyth TR12 . . . . 92 C1
Pen y Bryn PL27 . . . . . . 108 D6
PENZANCE 143 F5
Penzance L Ctr TR18 . . 143 D6
Penzance Rd
Helston TR13 . . . . 146 A6
St Buryan TR19 . . . . 97 C7
Penzance School of Art
TR18 . . . . 143 E5
Penzance Sta TR18 . . . . 143 F6
Pepo La TR2 . . . . 72 A7
Pepper Cl PL12 . . . . 40 C2
Pepper La PL9 . . . . 136 D7
Peppers Ct PL12 . . . . 40 C2
Peppers Hill Cl PL15 . . . . 18 F7
Peppers Park Rd PL14 . . 113 E6
Pepper St PL19 . . . . 147 C6
Pepys Pl PL5 . . . . 124 E1
PERCUIL 83 A1
Percuil View TR2 . . . . 95 B6
Percy Davy Cl TR6 . . . . . . 55 A5
Percy St PL5 . . . . 123 D1
Percy Terr PL4 . . . . 129 A4
Pergolla Ct 8 TR7 . . . . . 110 F6
Perhaver Pk PL26 . . . . . . 85 D5
Perhaver Way PL26 . . . . . 85 D5
Periwinkle Dr PL7 . . . . . 131 C5
PerkThen TR12 . . . . 102 F2
Permarin Rd PL10 . . . . . 144 C8
Perran-ar-worthal Prim Sch
TR3 . . . . 81 D6
Perran St PL3 . . . . 81 F6
Perrancombe Garden Ct
TR6 . . . . 55 A4
PERRANCOOMBE 55 A4
Perran Crossroads TR20 . 89 E5
PERRAN DOWNS 89 E5
PERRANPORTH 55 B5
Perranporth Cl PL5 . . . . 124 B2
Perranporth Prim Sch 15
TR6 . . . . 55 A4
PERRANUTHNOE 89 D4
PERRANWELL . . . .
Goonhavern 55 C3
Perranarworthal 81 C6
Perranwell Rd TR4 . . . . . . 55 D4
Perranwell Sta TR3 . . . . . 81 E6
PERRANZABULOE 55 B3
Perranzabuloe Mus★ TR6 55 A5
Perry Cl PL19 . . . . 147 B6
Perryman Cl PL12 . . . . . 130 E7
Perseverance Cotts 1
PL7 . . . . 130 E7
Peryn Rd PL19 . . . . 147 A5
Peter Hopper's Hill PL5 . 120 C2
Peter's Cl PL9 . . . . 136 C7
Petersfield Cl PL3 . . . . . 129 B6
PETER'S FINGER 19 C7
Peters Hill PL26 . . . . 58 E4
Peters Park Cl PL5 . . . . . 123 E1
Peter's Park La PL5 . . . . 123 E1
Peters Row TR19 . . . . 75 A1
PETERVILLE 54 D1
Petes Pl 21 TR26 . . . . . . 141 B5
Petherick Rd EX23 . . . . . 104 E7
Pethericks Mill EX23 . . . 104 E4
PETHERWIN GATE 18 B7
Pethick Cl PL6 . . . . 124 D6
Pethill Cl PL6 . . . . 125 F2
Pethybridge Dr PL31 . . . 109 B3
Petroc Ct PL18 . . . . 40 D6
PEVERELL 128 C6
Peverell Park Rd PL3 . . . 128 C5
Peverell Rd
Penzance TR18 . . . . 143 E7
7 Porthleven TR13 . . . . . 98 C8
Peverell Terr
Plymouth PL3 . . . . 128 D5
Porthleven TR13 . . . . 98 B8
Pew Tor Cl
Tavistock PL19 . . . . 147 E5
8 Yelverton PL20 . . . . . 42 C3
Phernyssick Rd PL25 . . . 114 F6
Philgray Cl TR27 . . . . . . 142 E7

Philip Cl PL9 . . . . 136 A5
Philip Gdns PL9 . . . . 135 F6
PHILLACK 142 D7
Phillack Hill TR27 . . . . . 142 D7
PHILLEIGH 83 B6
Phillimore St 3 PL2 . . . . 127 F4
Phoenix Bsns Pk PL6 . . 125 F4
Phoenix Cl 8 PL20 . . . . . 42 C4
Phoenix L Ctr PL15 . . . . 106 C4
Phoenix St PL1 . . . . 148 A2
Piala Pl TR27 . . . . 142 E7
Piazza 8 PL26 . . . . 141 B6
Piazza The 5 PL31 . . . . . 109 E5
Pickard Way EX23 . . . . . 104 D7
Pickering Villas TR4 . . . . 69 A3
Picketts Yd TR10 . . . . . . 144 D7
Pick Pie Dr PL25 . . . . . . 125 E8
PIECE 139 D2
Pier La PL10 . . . . 133 A1
Pier St PL1 . . . . 148 B1
Pigmeadow La PL14 . . . 113 C6
Pike Rd PL3 . . . . 129 D5
Pikes Hill PL23 . . . . 116 C4
Pike's Hill TR11 . . . . 145 B3
Pike St PL14 . . . . 113 C6
Pilchard Works The★
TR18 . . . . 143 C3
Pilgrim Cl PL2 . . . . 128 B6
Pilgrim Dr 11 PL20 . . . . . 41 B1
Pilgrim Dr PL20 . . . . 41 B1
Pilgrim Prim Sch PL1 . . 148 B3
Pilgrims Way TR27 . . . . . 78 C1
Pillars Cl TR8 . . . . 56 F5
Pillars Rd
Flushing TR11 . . . . 145 B8
Mylor Bridge TR11 . . . . . 82 A2
Pillar Wlk PL6 . . . . 124 D7
PILLATON 53 B6
PILLATONMILL 53 B6
Pill La PL12 . . . . 122 E4
Pillmere Dr PL12 . . . . . . 122 D4
Pillot Cotts PL28 . . . . 21 B4
Pinch Hill
Bude EX23 . . . . 104 F2
Marhamchurch EX23 . . . . 7 B7
Pinder Ct PL19 . . . . 147 B5
Pine Cl TR13 . . . . 146 D5
Pine Ct
Par PL24 . . . . 115 F6
Perranarworthal TR3 . . . . 81 C6
Pine Lodge Gdns★ PL25 115 D4
Pine Rd TR18 . . . . 143 B4
Pine Trees on the Lizard★
TR12 . . . . 99 F5
Pine View
Gunnislake PL18 . . . . . . 41 A6
St Dennis PL26 . . . . 46 D1
Pinewood Cl PL7 . . . . . 130 F6
Pinewood Dr PL6 . . . . . 125 E7
Pinewood Flats PL27 . . . 21 D5
Pinkhams Cotts PL12 . . 122 B6
Pink Moors TR16 . . . . 68 D1
Pin La PL1 . . . . 149 A2
Pinnacle Quay PL4 . . . . 149 B2
Pinsla Garden & Nursery★
PL30 . . . . 35 E1
Pinslow Cross PL15 . . . . 19 C8
Pintail Ave TR27 . . . . 77 E3
Pipers Cl PL15 . . . . 18 F3
PIPERS POOL 17 F3
Piran Cl PL18 . . . . 40 D6
Piran Hts EX23 . . . . 104 C3
Pitick Terr TR11 . . . . 145 B6
Pitland Cnr PL19 . . . . 30 D4
Pit Mdw TR11 . . . . 144 E3
Pits La PL10 . . . . 64 B2
Pitts Cleave Ind Est PL19 . 30 F3
PITYME 21 F3
Pityme PL27 . . . . 21 F3
Pityme Bsns Ctr PL27 . . . 21 F3
Pityme Farm Rd PL27 . . . 21 F3
Pityme Ind Est PL27 . . . . 21 F3
Pixie's Hall★ TR11 . . . . . 92 E4
Pixon La PL19 . . . . 147 B4
Pixon Trad Ctr 2 PL19 . 147 B4
Place de Brest PL1 . . . . 148 C3
Place Parc TR7 . . . . 111 D7
Place Rd PL23 . . . . 116 C4
Place Stables PL23 . . . . 116 C4
Place View PL23 . . . . . . 116 C4
Place View Rd 18 TR2 . . . 95 A6
PLAIDY 117 E4
Plaidy La PL13 . . . . 117 E4
Plaidy Park Rd PL13 . . . 117 E4
PLAIN-AN-GWARRY 140 B6
Plain-an-Gwarry TR15 . . 140 B5
Plaistow Cl PL5 . . . . . . 123 E2
Plaistow Cres PL5 . . . . . 123 E2
Plaistow Hill Inf Sch PL5 123 E2
Planet Pk PL3 . . . . 129 B8
Plantation La TR27 . . . . 142 B5
Plantings Sch The PL3 . . 128 E6
Plas Newydd Ave PL31 . 109 E3
Platt The PL27 . . . . 108 C5
Playingfield La TR7 . . . . 110 D5
PLAYING PLACE 82 B8
Pleasant Pl 8 TR18 . . . . 143 C7
Pleasure Hill Cl PL5 . . . 135 D8
Plestin Cl PL15 . . . . 106 C7
Pleyber Christ Way PL22 112 C2
Pleydon Cl PL13 . . . . 62 E2
Plintona View TR7 . . . . 130 E7
Plougastel Dr PL12 . . . . 122 E3
Plough Gn PL12 . . . . . . 122 E3
Plough Cn PL12 . . . . 81 C2
Plumer Rd PL6 . . . . 124 F2
PLUSHABRIDGE 38 F7
Plymbridge Gdns PL7 . . 130 C7

Plymbridge La PL6 . . . . 125 B4
Plymbridge Rd
Plymouth, Eggbuckland
PL6 . . . . 125 C1
Plymouth, Estover PL6 . . 125 E5
Plymouth, Mainstone PL6 125 F2
Plymouth, Plympton PL7 130 C7
Plym Cres PL19 . . . . . . 147 D5
PLYMOUTH 148 C3
Plymouth Arts Ctr★ PL4 149 A2
Plymouth Athenaeum &
Theatre★ PL1 . . . . 148 B2
Plymouth Business Sch
PL4 . . . . 149 A3
Plymouth City Airport
PL6 . . . . 125 C5
Plymouth City Mkt PL1 . 148 B3
Plymouth City Mus & Art
Gal★ PL4 . . . . 149 A3
Plymouth Coll PL4 . . . . 128 E4
Plymouth Coll Inf Sch 1
PL3 . . . . 128 F5
Plymouth Coll of Art &
Design PL4 . . . . 149 A3
Plymouth Coll of Art &
Design (Sutton Annexe)
PL4 . . . . 149 A3
Plymouth Coll of FE PL2 127 E5
Plymouth Coll Prep Sch
PL1 . . . . 148 A3
Plymouth Discovery Ctr★
PL3 . . . . 129 F6
Plymouth Drake Prim Sch
PL2 . . . . 127 F6
Plymouth Eggbuckland
Coll PL6 . . . . 129 A8
Plymouth Eggbuckland Vale
Prim Sch PL6 . . . . . . 125 B1
Plymouth Girls High Sch
PL4 . . . . 149 A4
Plymouth Keyham Barton RC
Prim Sch PL2 . . . . . . 127 E5
Plymouth Knowle Prim Sch
PL5 . . . . 124 A4
Plymouth Lipson Vale Prim
Sch PL4 . . . . 129 A4
Plymouth Medical & Tech Pk
PL6 . . . . 125 A3
Plymouth Pavilions PL1 148 B2
PlymouthRd
Liskeard PL14 . . . . 113 D5
Plymouth PL7 . . . . 130 B6
Tavistock PL19 . . . . . . 147 B4
Plymouth Road Ind Est
PL19 . . . . 147 C3
Plymouth St Andrew's CE
Prim Sch PL4 . . . . . . 149 A3
Plymouth St Joseph's RC
Prim Sch PL1 . . . . . . 127 E2
Plymouth St Paul's RC Prim
Sch PL5 . . . . 123 D1
Plymouth St Peters CE Prim
Sch PL1 . . . . 148 B3
Plymouth Ski & Snowboard
Ctr★ PL4 . . . . 129 E2
Plymouth Sta PL4 . . . . 148 C4
Plymouth Thornbury Prim
Sch PL6 . . . . 125 D4
Plymouth Trade Pk PL4 149 C1
Plymouth Whitleigh Prim
Sch PL5 . . . . 124 D4
PLYMPTON 130 E5
Plympton Hill PL7 . . . . . 130 F3
Plympton Hospl PL7 . . . 130 D5
Plympton St Mary CE Inf Sch
PL7 . . . . 130 D5
PLYMPTON ST
MAURICE 130 E4
Plympton St Maurice Prim
Sch PL7 . . . . 130 F3
Plym St PL4 . . . . 149 A3
PLYMSTOCK 135 E6
Plymstock Rd PL9 . . . . . 135 D7
Plymstock Sch PL9 . . . . 135 F8
Plymstock Sp Ctr PL9 . . 135 F8
Plymtree Dr PL7 . . . . . . 130 C7
Plym Valley Rly★ PL7 . . 130 A7
Poad's Trust PL14 . . . . . . 51 F5
Pochin Ho PL25 . . . . . . 114 F7
Pocklington Rise PL7 . . 130 E5
Pocohontas Cres 4 TR9 . 45 E1
Point 4 PL25 . . . . 82 B5
Point Neptune PL23 . . . 116 B3
Point Rd TR3 . . . . 82 A6
Polapit Tamar PL15 . . . . 19 A8
POLBATHIC 64 F8
Polbathic Rd TR15 . . . . 140 C6
POLBORDER 53 D7
Polbreen Ave TR5 . . . . . . 54 C1
Polbreen La TR5 . . . . 54 C1
POLBROCK 34 A4
Poldark Gdns 7 PL24 . . . 60 B4
Poldark Mine★ TR13 . . . 92 A6
Poldark Rd 12 TR16 . . . . 67 E4
Poldhu Cl TR26 . . . . 141 D1
Poldhu Rd
Liskeard PL14 . . . . 113 D6
Mullion TR12 . . . . 99 A2
Poldice La TR16 . . . . 68 E1
Poldice Terr TR16 . . . . . . 68 E1
Poldice Valley★ TR16 . . . 68 E1
Poldrissick Hill PL12 . . . 53 C2
Poldrissick La PL12 . . . . 53 C2
Poldue Cl TR15 . . . . 140 D6
Polean La PL13 . . . . 117 B4
Polean Trad Est PL13 . . 117 B4
Polecoverack La TR12 . . 101 C1

Polgarth
1 Camborne TR15 . . . . 139 C6
Newlyn TR18 . . . . 143 B3
Polgarth Cl TR26 . . . . . 141 D1
Polgaver Ho PL25 . . . . . 115 E3
POLGIGGA 96 D4
Polgine Cl TR14 . . . . 79 E5
Polgine La TR14 . . . . 79 E5
Polglase Wlk TR4 . . . . . . 70 D8
Polglaze Cl TR18 . . . . . 143 D7
Polgloth PL26 . . . . 58 D5
Polgoon Cl TR18 . . . . . . 143 C5
POLGOOTH 59 A1
Polgooth Cl TR15 . . . . . 140 D6
Polgover Way 5 PL24 . . . 60 B4
Polgrain Rd TR14 . . . . . 138 F6
Polgrean Pl PL24 . . . . . . 60 B5
Polhigey Terr TR16 . . . . . 80 C2
Polhorman La TR12 . . . . 99 A2
Police Ho TR11 . . . . 145 B4
Polisken Way TR4 . . . . . . 56 D1
POLKERRIS 60 E3
Polkerris Pk PL24 . . . . . . 60 C4
Polkerris Rd TR16 . . . . . . 80 F8
Polkirt Hill
Gorran Haven PL26 . . . . 73 B1
Mevagissey PL26 . . . . . . 73 C3
Polkirt Hts PL26 . . . . 73 C3
Polkyth L Ctr PL25 . . . . 114 E4
Polkyth Par PL25 . . . . . 114 E4
Polkyth Rd PL25 . . . . . . 114 F4
POLLADRAS 90 F5
Pollard Ct
Plymouth PL9 . . . . 135 B5
Saltash PL12 . . . . 122 B2
Pollard Rd 12 PL17 . . . . . 39 F4
Pollards Cl
Goonhavern TR4 . . . . . . 55 D4
Pensilva PL14 . . . . 38 E4
Pollards Way PL12 . . . . 122 E3
Polmark Dr PL28 . . . . . . 20 D2
Polmarth Cl PL25 . . . . . 114 F6
POLMASSICK 72 E4
Polmassick Vineyard★
PL26 . . . . 72 E4
POLMEAR 60 D4
Polmear Hill PL24 . . . . . . 60 D4
Polmear Parc PL24 . . . . . 60 D4
Polmear Rd
St Austell PL25 . . . . . . 114 F3
Tywardreath PL24 . . . . . 60 D4
Polmeere Ho TR18 . . . . 143 E7
Polmeere Rd TR18 . . . . 143 E7
Polmena La PL22 . . . . . 112 C2
Polmennor Dr TR26 . . . 141 D1
Polmennor Rd
Falmouth TR11 . . . . . . 144 F1
Heamoor TR18 . . . . . . 143 B5
Polmenor Downs N TR14,
TR27 . . . . 78 F5
Polmenor Downs S TR14 . 78 F4
Polmeor Cl TR26 . . . . . 141 D1
Polmewan Flats PL26 . . 59 A1
POLMORLA 108 A4
Polmorla Mews 10 PL27 108 B5
Polmorla Rd PL27 . . . . . 108 B5
Polmorla Wlk PL27 . . . . 108 C5
Polmor Rd TR20 . . . . 89 B8
POLPEOR 77 B3
Polpeor Row TR17 . . . . . 62 E1
POLPERRO 62 E1
Polperro Heritage Mus of
Smuggling & Fishing★
PL13 . . . . 62 E2
Polperro Model Village★
PL13 . . . . 62 D1
Polperro Prim Sch PL13 . 62 E2
Polperro Rd PL13 . . . . . 117 B4
Polpey La PL24 . . . . 60 D5
POLRUAN 116 C2
Polruan Cl TR26 . . . . 77 C4
Polruan Ctr TR1 . . . . . . 137 E2
Polruan Ho Prim Sch PL23 116 D2
Polruan Rd
Redruth TR15 . . . . 140 D6
Truro TR1 . . . . 137 E2
Polruan Terr PL1 . . . . . . 148 A3
POLSCOE 112 F3
Polscoe Rd PL22 . . . . . . 112 F3
Polsethow TR10 . . . . . . 144 B7
Polstain Cres TR3 . . . . . . 69 D3
Polstain Rd TR3 . . . . 69 D3
Polstain Villas TR3 . . . . . 69 D3
Polsue Way TR2 . . . . 70 F5
Poltair Ave PL25 . . . . . . 114 E4
Poltair Cl TR18 . . . . 143 C7
Poltair Cres PL25 . . . . . 114 D4
Poltair Ct PL25 . . . . 114 E4
Poltair Hospl PL20 . . . . 143 B8
Poltair Rd
Penryn TR10 . . . . 144 B7
St Austell PL25 . . . . . . 114 D4
Poltair Sports Coll PL25 114 D4
Poltair Terr 7 TR18 . . . . 143 C7
Poltarian Ct TR1 . . . . . . 106 D5
POLTESCO 103 B5
Poltesco La TR12 . . . . . 103 B5
Poltisco Cl TR1 . . . . 137 E3
Poltisco Wharf TR1 . . . . 137 E4
Poltisko Rd TR10 . . . . . 144 B7
Poltisko Terr TR10 . . . . 144 B7
Poltreen Cl TR26 . . . . . 141 D1
Polurrian Rd TR12 . . . . . 99 A1
Polvarth Est TR2 . . . . . . 95 B6
Polvarth Rd TR2 . . . . 95 A6
Polvean Cross PL15 . . . . 51 A4

Polvean Terr PL14 . . . . 51 A1
Polvella Cl TR7 . . . . 110 B5
Polvellan Manor PL13 . . 117 C4
Polvellan Terr PL13 . . . . 112 E7
Polvelyn Parc TR27 . . . . . 142 E7
Polventon Cl
 Falmouth TR11 . . . . 144 E4
 Heamoor TR18 . . . . 143 C7
Polventon Parc **6** TR12 . 101 C4
Polvillion Rd PL23 . . . . . . 116 B4
Polweath Cl TR18 . . . . 143 E7
Polwheal Rd TR18 . . . . 143 E7
Polwhaveral Terr **5**
 TR11 . . . . 145 A5
Polyne Cotts PL13 . . . . 62 F3
POLYPHANT 17 F1
POLZEATH 21 E5
Polzeath Ct PL27 . . . . 21 D6
Polzeath Gdns PL2 . . . . . 128 D8
POMPHLETT 135 E8
Pomphlett Cl PL9 . . . . . . 135 D8
Pomphlett Farm Ind Est
 PL9 . . . . 129 E1
Pomphlett Gdns PL9 . . . 135 D8
Pomphlett Rd PL9 . . . . . 135 E8
Ponchin Dr PL25 . . . . 114 E7
Pondbridge Hill **1** PL14 . 113 C5
Pondfield Rd PL12 . . . . . . 122 B3
Pondhu Cres PL25 . . . . . . 114 B3
Pondhu Prim Sch PL25 . . 114 B2
Pondhu Rd PL25 . . . . 114 C3
Pond La TR15 . . . . 140 A6
Pond Lanes End TR15 . . . 140 A6
Ponds Hill TR19 . . . . 75 B1
Pond View Terr PL26 . . . . 58 D5
Pond Wlk TR27 . . . . 142 D7
PONIOU 76 A5
Poniou La TR20 . . . . 88 F6
Poniou Rd TR20 . . . . 88 F6
Poniou Way TR20 . . . . 88 F6
Ponsandane Farm Mews
 TR18 . . . . 143 F7
PONSANOOTH 81 B5
PONSHARDEN 144 E7
Ponsharden Cotts TR11 . 144 F6
Ponsharden Ind Est
 TR11 . . . . 144 E6
Ponsmere Ct **9** TR6 . . . . 55 A5
Ponsmere Rd TR6 . . . . 55 A5
Ponsonby Rd PL3 . . . . . . 128 B4
PONSONGATH 103 E7
Ponstantual Hill TR12 . . . 99 D7
Ponsvale TR3 . . . . 81 B4
PONT 61 D3
Pontsmill Rd PL24 . . . . . . 60 C6
POOL 139 B5
Pool Bsns & Enterprise Coll
 TR15 . . . . 139 B4
Pool Bsns Pk TR15 . . . . . 139 B4
Poole Park Rd PL5 . . . . . . 127 C8
Pool Hall PL14 . . . . 51 F5
Pool Ind Est TR15 . . . . . . 139 C5
Pool's Ct TR27 . . . . 142 D6
Pool St PL31 . . . . 109 C4
Poplar Cl PL7 . . . . 131 B5
Poplar Terr TR11 . . . . 55 A5
Poplar Terr **1** TR11 . . . . 145 B7
Popplestone Pk PL8 . . . . 136 F5
Porcupine Rd PL4 . . . . 60 C6
Pordenack Cl TR26 . . . . . 141 E2
Porfell Wildlife Park &
 Sanctuary* PL14 . . . . . . 50 A2
Porhan Gn TR11 . . . . 144 E6
PORKELLIS 92 B8
Pork St PL12 . . . . 100 D6
Porsham Cl PL6 . . . . 121 B1
Porsham La PL5 . . . . 124 E8
Porspoder Pl PL10 . . . . . 133 A2
Portbigham PL13 . . . . 117 C3
Portbyhan Rd PL13 . . . . . 117 C3
PORTEATH 22 A6
Porteath Bee Ctr* PL27 . . 22 A6
Porteous Cl PL1 . . . . 127 F3
Porter Way PL12 . . . . 122 C3
PORT GAVERNE 22 A5
PORTH 111 C8
PORTHALLOW
 Looe 62 F2
 St Keverne 101 D6
Porth Beach Rd TR7 . . . . 111 B8
Porth Bean Cl TR7 . . . . . . 111 C7
Porth Bean Rd TR7 . . . . . 111 C7
Porthcollum La TR27 . . . . 78 A1
PORTHCOTHAN 31 C6
PORTHCURNO 96 E3
Porthcurno Telegraph Mus*
 TR19 . . . . 96 E3
Portheast Cl PL26 . . . . 85 C5
Portheast Way PL26 . . . . . 85 C5
Portherras Cross TR19 . . 75 A1

Portherras Terr TR19 . . . . 75 A1
Portherras Villas TR19 . . 75 A1
Porthgwidden TR3 . . . . . . 82 C4
Porthgwidden Studios
 TR26 . . . . 141 C6
Porthia Cl TR26 . . . . 141 A4
Porthia Cres TR26 . . . . . . 141 A4
Porthia Rd **12** TR26 . . . . 77 A6
PORTHILLY 21 F2
Porthilly Cvn Site PL27 . . 21 D2
Porthilly La PL27 . . . . 21 D2
Porthilly View PL28 . . . . 107 E4
PORTH KEA 70 B1
Porthkerris Divers*
 TR12 . . . . 101 E5
PORTHLEVEN 98 C5
Porthleven Cty Prim Sch
 TR13 . . . . 91 B1
Porthleven Rd TR13 . . . . 146 A5
Porthmellon Gdns PL17 . . 39 F4
PORTHMEOR 75 F4
Porthmeor Ct **51** PL26 . 141 B6
Porthmeor Hill TR26 . . . 141 A6
Porthmeor Rd
 St Austell PL25 . . . . 115 B3
 6 St Ives TR26 . . . . . . 141 B6
Porthmeor Sq **51** TR26 . 141 B6
Porthmeor Studios **50**
 TR26 . . . . 141 B6
Porthminster Terr **23**
 TR26 . . . . 141 B5
PORTH NAVAS 93 B2
PORTHOUSTOCK 101 E4
Porth Par TR7 . . . . 111 C8
Porthpean Beach Rd PL26 85 C8
Porthpean Rd PL24, PL26 114 F2
Porthrepta Rd TR26 . . . . 141 E1
Porth Sawle Flats TR2 . . 83 B2
PORTHTOWAN 68 A6
Porth View TR2 . . . . 95 B6
Porth Way TR7 . . . . 111 B7
PORTINGTON 29 E3
Port Isaac Prim Sch PL29 22 E7
Port La PL15 . . . . 27 B2
Portland Cl PL14 . . . . 113 D7
Portland Ct **9** PL1 . . . . . 127 F3
Portland Gdns TR11 . . . . 144 F4
Portland Pl **22** TR19 . . . . 88 C1
Portland Rd PL27 . . . . . . 108 C4
Portland Sq PL4 . . . . 148 C4
Portland Square Lane N
 PL4 . . . . 149 A4
Portland Terr PL14 . . . . . 113 C7
Portland Villas PL4 . . . . . 148 C4
PORTLOE 84 B3
PORTLOOE 117 A2
PORTMELLON 73 C3
Portmellon Pk PL26 . . . . . 73 C3
PORT QUIN 22 D8
PORTREATH 67 C6
Portreath Com Prim Sch
 TR16 . . . . 67 D6
PORTSCATHO 83 B2
Portuan Rd PL13 . . . . 117 D1
Portway Cl PL9 . . . . 136 D7
PORTWRINKLE 65 B4
Posses La PL18 . . . . 88 E6
Possession La PL12 . . . . . 53 C3
Post Box Row TR14 . . . . . 139 B3
Post Office Row PL26 . . . 58 D7
Potters La PL35 . . . . 9 C1
Potters Way PL7 . . . . 130 D5
Pottery Est PL10 . . . . 132 E6
Pottery Rd PL1 . . . . 127 D3
POUGHILL 4 D2
Poughill Rd EX23 . . . . . . 104 F7
Poultney Cl PL7 . . . . 131 A5
Pounda PL14 . . . . 51 B4
Pound Dean PL14 . . . . . . 113 A5
Poundfield Cl **2** EX23 . . . 4 D1
Poundfield Hill **1** EX23 . . 4 D1
Poundfield La EX23 . . . . . . 4 D1
Pound Hill PL12 . . . . 53 C3
Pound La
 Bodmin PL31 . . . . 109 E5
 Stoke Climsland PL17 . . 28 E1
 Threemilestone TR3 . . . . 69 E1
Pound Pk PL14 . . . . 51 F5
Pound Pk PL20 . . . . 42 B3
Pound's Cross PL6 . . . . . 120 E5
Pounds Park Rd
 1 Bere Alston PL20 . . . . 41 B1
 Plymouth PL3 . . . . 128 D7
Pounds Pk PL12 . . . . 122 F3
Pound St
 Liskeard PL14 . . . . 113 C6
 Plymouth PL1 . . . . 134 A8
POUNDSTOCK 6 E2
Poundstock Cl PL30 . . . . . 35 F3
Powderham Rd PL3 . . . . 128 F7
Powis Gdns PL5 . . . . 124 B2
Powisland Dr PL6 . . . . . . 125 A5
PRAA SANDS 90 C3
Praed Pl TR26 . . . . 77 E4
Praed's La TR17 . . . . 89 C5
Pras Coth TR16 . . . . 68 C3
PRAZE-AN-BEEBLE 79 C2
Praze-an-Creet TR26 . . . . 77 A7
Praze-an-Cronor TR9 . . . . 45 E5
Praze Bsns Centre TR15 . 79 B2
Prazegooth La PL12 . . . . 103 A4
Praze Mdw TR10 . . . . . . 144 C8
Praze Rd
 Leedstown TR27 . . . . 78 E1
 Newquay TR7 . . . . 111 B7
 Porthleven TR13 . . . . 91 B1
 Praze-an-Beeble TR14 . . 79 A2

Praze The TR10 . . . . 144 C8
Predannack Airfield*
 TR12 . . . . 102 D6
Predannack Rd **4** TR12 . . 99 A1
Preeze Cross PL30 . . . . . . 35 E6
Prestonbury Cl PL6 . . . . . 125 B7
Prevenna Rd **2** TR19 . . . 88 C1
Prideaux Cl PL12 . . . . 122 C5
Prideaux Place* PL28 . . . 107 C6
Prideaux Rd PL24 . . . . 60 B6
Pridham La PL21 . . . . 128 D7
Pridmouth Rd PL25 . . . . 114 E6
Priestacott Pk EX23 . . . . . 5 A6
Priesthood Terr PL10 . . . 132 E5
Priestley Ave PL5 . . . . . . 123 E2
Primitive Row TR14 . . . . 139 A5
Primrose Cl
 Camborne TR14 . . . . . . 138 B4
 3 Goldsithney TR20 . . . 89 E5
 Roche PL26 . . . . 47 A3
 Torpoint PL11 . . . . 126 E4
Primrose Cotts TR2 . . . . . 71 C6
Primrose Ct TR26 . . . . . . 141 B4
Primrose Dr PL28 . . . . 31 F7
Primrose Gdns
 Illogan TR16 . . . . 67 D4
 Truro TR19 . . . . 147 E4
Primrose Hill TR20 . . . . . . 89 E5
Primrose La **4** TR20 . . . . 89 E5
Primrose Rd EX23 . . . . . . 104 F5
Primrose Terr
 Newlyn TR18 . . . . 143 D1
 Portreath TR16 . . . . 67 D6
 Tresillian TR2 . . . . 70 F5
Primrose Valley TR26 . . 141 C4
Primrose Way PL15 . . . . . 27 A6
Primrose Wlk TR18 . . . . . 122 D4
Prince Charles Cl PL25 . 106 C7
Prince Charles Rd PL25 . 114 E5
Prince Charles Pk PL25 . 114 E5
Prince Maurice Ct PL4 . . 149 B3
Prince Maurice Rd PL4 . 128 F4
Prince of Wales Quarry
 Trail* PL34 . . . . 14 E5
Prince Philip Rd PL15 . . 106 C7
PRINCE ROCK 129 B1
Prince Rock Prim Sch
 PL4 . . . . 129 B2
Princes Rd PL6 . . . . 125 E6
Princes Row PL14 . . . . 38 B6
Princess Ave
 Plymouth, Plymstock PL9 135 C6
 Plymouth, West Park PL5 124 A3
Princess Cres PL9 . . . . . . 135 E6
Princess Sq PL13 . . . . . . 117 C3
Princess Rd PL14 . . . . 38 E4
Princess St PL1 . . . . 148 C2
Princess Street Ope PL4 148 C2
Princes St
 Bude EX23 . . . . 104 D6
 Looe PL13 . . . . 117 C3
 Penzance TR18 . . . . 143 E5
 Truro TR1 . . . . 137 C4
Prince's St TR1 . . . . 137 D4
Princes Terr **8** PL14 . . . . 38 E4
Princess Way PL1 . . . . . 148 C2
Prior's Barn PL31 . . . . . . 109 F4
Priors Cl **10** TR26 . . . . . . 77 A6
Priors Row TR13 . . . . 90 E3
Priory Cl
 Par PL24 . . . . 60 C5
 Tavistock PL19 . . . . 147 D3
Priory Cotts PL15 . . . . . . 106 B6
Priory Dr PL7 . . . . 130 D5
Priory Gdns PL19 . . . . . . 147 D3
Priory Lawn Terr PL3 . . . 129 A6
Priory Mews PL15 . . . . . . 106 B7
Priory Mill PL7 . . . . 130 D5
Priory Park Rd PL15 . . . . 106 B6
Priory Rd
 Bodmin PL31 . . . . 109 F4
 Plymouth PL3 . . . . 129 A6
 St Austell PL25 . . . . 114 C4
 St Columb Minor TR7, TR8 111 E7
Priory Ridge PL7 . . . . 130 D5
Prislow Cl TR11 . . . . 144 E2
Prislow Fields TR11 . . . . 144 E2
Prislow La TR11 . . . . 144 E2
PROBUS 71 C6
Probus Com Prim Sch
 TR2 . . . . 71 C6
Prospect Bldgs TR7 . . . . 110 E6
Prospect Cl TR27 . . . . . . 142 D6
Prospect Gdns TR11 . . . 137 E6
Prospect La PL12 . . . . . . 122 C3
Prospect Pl
 Ashton TR13 . . . . 90 E3
 3 Falmouth TR11 . . . . 145 B5
 Hayle TR27 . . . . 142 D6
 Helston TR13 . . . . 146 C5
 Mevagissey PL26 . . . . . . 73 C4
 26 Penzance TR18 . . . 143 E5
 5 Plymouth PL1 . . . . . 148 B2
 8 Porthleven TR13 . . . . 98 B8
 5 Truro TR1 . . . . 137 D5
Prospect Row
 Ashton TR13 . . . . 90 E3
 Plymouth PL1 . . . . 127 E1
Prospect St PL4 . . . . 149 A3
Prospect Terr
 Bodmin PL31 . . . . 109 E4
 Gunnislake PL18 . . . . . . 41 A6

Prospect Terr continued
 Gunnislake, St Ann's Chapel
 PL18 . . . . 40 E5
 Mevagissey PL26 . . . . . . 73 C4
Prospect Wlk PL12 . . . . . 122 C3
Prosper Cl PL26 . . . . 47 A2
Prosper Hill TR27 . . . . 66 B1
Prosper Rd PL26 . . . . 47 A2
Prouse Cres PL4 . . . . 106 C6
Prouse Rise PL12 . . . . . . 122 E2
Prouts Cl **4** PL15 . . . . . . 106 C6
Prout's La TR21 . . . . 78 D6
Prouts Mews **5** PL15 . . . 106 C6
Prouts Way PL15 . . . . 18 C2
Providence Pl
 Calstock PL18 . . . . 41 A3
 Plymouth PL1 . . . . 128 A3
Providence St PL4 . . . . . 149 A4
Provis Rd PL18 . . . . 143 C4
Prynne Cl PL1 . . . . 148 B3
Puckator La PL14 . . . . 38 A2
Puggis Hill PL14 . . . . 138 A5
Pulla Cross TR4 . . . . 81 B6
Putnam Cl PL14 . . . . 113 D5
Pydar Cl TR7 . . . . 111 B5
Pydar Mews **8** TR1 . . . . 137 C4
Pydar St TR1 . . . . 137 C5
Pym St
 Plymouth PL1 . . . . 127 F3
 Tavistock PL19 . . . . 147 C6
Pyramid Cl PL25 . . . . 58 F4
PYWORTHY 8 E5
Pyworthy CE Prim Sch
 EX22 . . . . 8 E4
PZ Gall* TR18 . . . . 143 F4

Q

Quakers Rd TR4, TR3 . . . . 81 B6
Quant Pk PL19 . . . . 147 C6
Quarry Cl EX23 . . . . 104 E7
Quarry Cnr PL20 . . . . 41 C2
Quarry Cotts
 Plymouth, Honicknowle
 PL5 . . . . 124 B2
 Plymouth PL1 . . . . 148 A3
Quarry Cres PL25 . . . . . . 106 A3
Quarry Ct TR11 . . . . 145 B4
Quarry Gdns TR18 . . . . . 143 D5
Quarry Hill
 Falmouth TR11 . . . . 145 B4
 Gulval TR18 . . . . 88 E7
Quarry House Flats TR1 . 137 E3
Quarry La
 Gunnislake PL18 . . . . . . 40 F6
 Landrake PL12 . . . . 53 D3
 Launceston PL15 . . . . . . 18 E3
 Sheffield TR19 . . . . 97 F7
 St Germans PL12 . . . . . . 65 A8
Quarrymans Cotts PL27 . 33 B7
Quarry Park Ave PL9 . . . 135 D7
Quarry Park Rd
 Newquay TR7 . . . . 110 F5
 Plymouth, Peverell PL3 . 128 D5
 Plymouth, Plymstock PL9 135 D7
Quarry Park Terr PL31 . . 109 C4
Quarry Rd
 Pensilva PL14 . . . . 38 E4
 Perranporth TR6 . . . . 55 B4
Quarry St
 St Germans PL12 . . . . . . 65 A8
 Torpoint PL11 . . . . 127 C3
Quarterdeck The PL1 . . . 134 A8
Quay Hill
 Falmouth TR11 . . . . 145 C4
 Penryn TR10 . . . . 144 D7
Quay La PL12 . . . . 53 D1
Quay Mews **8** TR1 . . . . 137 D4
Quay Rd
 Crumplehorn PL13 . . . . . 62 D1
 Devoran TR3 . . . . 81 F6
 Landrake PL12 . . . . 53 A2
 Looe PL13 . . . . 117 C3
 Mylor Bridge TR11 . . . . . 82 B4
 Plymouth PL1 . . . . 149 A2
 St Agnes TR5 . . . . 54 D2
 St Austell PL25 . . . . 115 B2
 St Germans PL12 . . . . . . 65 B8
 Tideford PL12 . . . . 52 F2
Quayside **6** PL19 . . . . . 147 B5
Quay St
 Falmouth TR11 . . . . 145 C4
 Looe PL13 . . . . 117 C3
 Lostwithiel PL22 . . . . . . 112 C2
 11 Mousehole TR19 . . . 88 C1
 Penzance TR18 . . . . 143 F4
 5 St Ives TR26 . . . . . . 141 C6
 20 Truro TR1 . . . . 137 D4
Quay The
 Pentewan PL26 . . . . 73 C6
 Penzance TR18 . . . . 143 F4
 Plymouth PL9 . . . . 135 C7
 Polruan PL23 . . . . 116 D3
 Portscatho TR2 . . . . 83 B2
 St Germans PL12 . . . . . . 65 B8
 St Mawes TR2 . . . . 95 A6
Queen Anne Gdns TR11 . 144 E3
Queen Anne's Quay PL4 . 149 B2
Queen Elizabeth Rd
 PL15 . . . . 106 C7
Queen Mary Rd PL11 . . . 145 B2
Queen Mary Rd TR11 . . . 145 B2
Queens Cl
 3 Indian Queens TR9 . . 45 E1
 Plymouth PL6 . . . . 125 E4
 St Austell PL26 . . . . 46 F3
Queen's Cres PL31 . . . . . 109 B3

Queen's Ct **6** TR18 . . . . 143 E4
Queen's Gate
 Plymouth, Lipson PL4 . . 149 B4
 Plymouth, Stoke PL3 . . . 148 A4
Queen's Gate Mews PL4 . 149 B4
Queen's Gate Villas PL4 . 149 B4
Queen's Gate Villas Rd
 PL4 . . . . 149 B4
Queens Pk PL27 . . . . 108 C4
Queens Rd
 Plymouth PL5 . . . . 123 F3
 St Austell PL25 . . . . 114 E3
 Queen's Rd PL4 . . . . 149 B4
 Queen's Sq **24** TR18 . . 143 E5
Queen St
 Bude EX23 . . . . 104 D6
 Goldsithney TR20 . . . . . 89 E5
 Lostwithiel PL22 . . . . . . 112 C2
 Penzance TR18 . . . . 143 E5
 Plymouth PL1 . . . . 127 D2
 St Just TR19 . . . . 86 E6
Queen's Way
 2 Goldsithney TR20 . . . 89 E5
 Hayle TR27 . . . . 142 C5
Queen Terr PL17 . . . . 40 C4
Quenchwell Rd TR3 . . . . . 81 F7
QUETHIOCK 52 C7
Quethiock Prim Sch PL14 52 C7
Quillet Rd TR18 . . . . 143 B3
Quilver Cl PL26 . . . . 85 D5
Quimperle Way PL14 . . . 113 E6
Quintrell Cl TR8 . . . . 44 E3
QUINTRELL DOWNS 44 E3
Quintrell Downs Sta TR8 111 F2
Quintrell Gdns TR8 . . . . . 44 E3
Quintrell Rd TR7, TR8 . . 111 E5
QUITHER 30 A8
QUOIT 45 F4

R

Rabys Row TR16 . . . . 140 F8
Race Hill
 Launceston PL15 . . . . . . 106 C5
 Truro TR4 . . . . 81 C8
Race Hill Terr PL15 . . . . . 106 C5
Rachel's Way **17** TR9 . . . 45 E6
Radcliffe Cl PL6 . . . . 124 E6
Radford Ave PL4 . . . . 129 B1
Radford La PL10 . . . . 132 D4
Radford Park Dr PL9 . . . 135 D6
Radford Park Rd PL9 . . . 135 D6
Radford Rd PL1 . . . . 148 B1
Radford View PL9 . . . . . . 135 D6
Radiant Ho PL1 . . . . 148 B2
Radland Cross PL12 . . . . 40 C3
Radnor Cl PL31 . . . . 109 F4
Radnor Hall PL4 . . . . 149 A3
Radnor Pl PL4 . . . . 149 A3
Redruth, North Country
 TR16 . . . . 140 C8
 Redruth, Scorrier TR16 . . 68 D3
Radnor St PL4 . . . . 149 A3
Raginnis Hill **25** TR19 . . 88 C1
Raglan Cl PL1 . . . . 127 F2
Raglan Gdns PL1 . . . . . . 127 F2
Raglan Rd PL1 . . . . 127 F2
Rail Way PL15 . . . . 17 F5
Railway Cotts
 Camborne TR14 . . . . . . 139 A3
 Falmouth TR11 . . . . 145 D3
 6 Plymouth, Ford PL2 . 127 F5
 Plymouth, Plymstock PL9 135 D7
 Tavistock PL19 . . . . 147 B6
Railway Cres PL14 . . . . . . 38 A4
Railway Terr
 Bodmin PL31 . . . . 109 D5
 Carharrack TR16 . . . . . . 80 F8
Railway Villas TR15 . . . . 139 B4
Rainham Cl TR15 . . . . . . 139 C8
Rainfields PL28 . . . . 107 D5
Rainy Fields Cl PL28 . . . 107 D5
Raleigh Cl PL28 . . . . 107 C4
Raleigh Ct PL12 . . . . 131 B6
Raleigh Pl **8** TR11 . . . . 145 A4
Raleigh Rd PL28 . . . . 107 C5
Raleigh St PL1 . . . . 148 B3
Ralph's Ct PL19 . . . . 147 B5
Ramage Cl PL6 . . . . 125 F3
RAME
 Cawsand 64 B2
 Stithians 92 E8
Rame Croft TR10 . . . . 80 E1
Ramehead Cotts PL10 . . . 64 B1
Ramehead La PL10 . . . . . 64 B1
Rame La
 Cawsand PL10 . . . . 132 F4
 Rame PL10 . . . . 64 B2
Rame Terr PL10 . . . . 80 E1
Rame View PL13 . . . . 117 E5
Ramillies Ave PL5 . . . . . . 124 A3
Ramoth Way TR6 . . . . 55 B5
Ramsey Gdns PL5 . . . . . 124 D1
Randwick Park Rd PL9 . 135 C6
Ranelagh Ct TR7 . . . . 111 C7
Ranelagh Mews PL31 . . 109 D5
Ranelagh Rd PL25 . . . . . 114 F4
Ransum Way PL19 . . . . . 147 B4
Raphael Cl PL9 . . . . 136 B5
Raphael Dr PL9 . . . . 136 A6
Raphael Rd PL13 . . . . 62 C1
Rapson Rd PL14 . . . . 113 D6

Rashleigh Ave
  Plymouth PL7 . . . . 130 F7
  Saltash PL12 . . . . 122 D1
Rashleigh Ct PL25 . . . . 115 C3
Rashleigh La PL23 . . . . 116 A4
Rashleigh Mews PL25 . . . . 115 A3
Rashleigh Pl PL25 . . . . 114 F4
Rashleigh Vale TR1 . . . . . . 137 E4
Ratcliffes La TR13 . . . . 146 A5
Rattle St PL26 . . . . 85 D5
Rawley Ct TR7 . . . . 110 E5
Rawley La TR7 . . . . 110 E5
Rawlin Cl PL6 . . . . 129 C8
Rawlings La PL23 . . . . 116 D5
Raymond Rd TR15 . . . . 140 C4
Raymond Way PL7 . . . . 130 D6
Raynham Rd PL3 . . . . 128 B4
Read Cl TR10 . . . . 144 B7
Reading Wlk PL5 . . . . 124 C4
READYMONEY 116 B3
Readymoney Rd PL23 . . . . 116 B3
REAWLA 78 E3
Reawla La TR27 . . . . 78 E3
Rebecca Cl PL24 . . . . 60 B6
Recreation Rd PL2 . . . . 128 C7
Recreation Road Ind Est
  PL2 . . . . 128 C7
Rectory Gdns
  Camborne TR14 . . . . 138 C2
  Lanreath PL13 . . . . 62 B8
  St Stephen PL26 . . . . 58 B4
Rectory La PL30 . . . . 34 D7
Rectory Rd
  Camborne TR14 . . . . 138 C2
  Lanivet PL30 . . . . 47 F6
  Plymouth PL1 . . . . 128 A2
  St Buryan TR19 . . . . 97 B6
  St Dennis PL26 . . . . 46 B1
  St Stephen PL26 . . . . 58 B4
Rectory The TR1 . . . . 137 C5
Redannack 2 TR12 . . . . 99 A2
Redannack N 1 TR12 . . . . . 99 A2
Redannack Cres TR1 . . . . . 137 B3
Redannack La TR1 . . . . 137 B4
Redbrooke Rd TR14 . . . . . . 138 E2
Redbrooke Terr TR14 . . . . . 138 E2
Redcliff Pl PL19 . . . . 135 E5
Reddicliff Rd PL9 . . . . 135 D5
Reddington Rd PL3 . . . . . . 129 B7
Redfern Ct 2 TR26 . . . . 141 B5
Redhill Cl PL5 . . . . 123 E4
Redinnick Gdns PL18 . . . . 143 E4
Redinnick Pl TR18 . . . . 143 D4
Redinnick Terr 1 TR18 . . . 143 E4
Red La
  Bugle PL26 . . . . 47 C2
  Rosudgeon TR20 . . . . 89 F5
REDMONSFORD 3 F2
Redmoor Cl PL19 . . . . 147 A7
Redmoor Rd PL17 . . . . 39 E6
Redmore Cl PL17 . . . . 39 E6
RED POST 7 F8
Red River Valley Nature
  Reserve ★ TR27 . . . . 66 D2
REDRUTH 140 D5
Redruth Cl PL5 . . . . 124 A5
Redruth Highway TR15 . . . 140 E7
Redruth Old Cornwall
  Society Mus ★ TR16 . . . . . 67 F5
Redruth Rd TR13 . . . . 146 D7
Redruth Sch TR15 . . . . 140 A5
Redruth Sta TR15 . . . . 140 C6
Redvale Rd PL30 . . . . 23 E3
Redvers Gr PL7 . . . . 130 E4
Redvers Hts TR15 . . . . 140 B3
Redwing Dr PL6 . . . . 125 D8
Redwood Cl EX23 . . . . 104 E5
Redwood Dr PL31 . . . . 131 B5
Redwood Gr EX23 . . . . 104 E5
Reeds Pk PL22 . . . . 112 C4
Reeds Way TR7 . . . . 110 D5
Reen Hill TR6 . . . . 55 B4
Reen La TR6 . . . . 55 B5
Reens Cres TR18 . . . . 143 D7
Reens Rd TR18 . . . . 143 C7
Reeves Cl TR13 . . . . 91 B1
Regal Ct PL12 . . . . 122 F2
Regal Theatre 1 TR18 . . . 143 E5
Regan Ct TR10 . . . . 144 A7
Regency Ho PL25 . . . . 115 E3
Regent Bldgs 10 TR18 . . . 143 E5
Regent Ct PL4 . . . . 149 A3
Regent Sq 21 TR18 . . . . . . 143 E5
Regent St PL4 . . . . 149 A3
Regent Terr
  Penzance TR18 . . . . 143 E4
  St Just TR19 . . . . 86 E6
Reigate Rd PL9 . . . . 135 E8
REJERRAH 55 F7
RELEATH 91 E8
Relistian La TR27 . . . . 78 E3
Relistian Pk TR27 . . . . 78 E3
RELUBBUS 90 A7
Relubbus Hill TR20 . . . . . . 90 A7
Relubbus La TR20 . . . . 90 A6
Renaissance Gdns PL2 . . . 128 C7
Rendlesham Gdns PL6 . . . 125 E3
Rendle St
  Delabole PL33 . . . . 14 E3
  Plymouth PL1 . . . . 148 B3
Renney Rd PL9 . . . . 135 C1
Rennie Ave PL5 . . . . 123 C1
Renoir Cl PL9 . . . . 136 A6
Renown St PL2 . . . . 127 E6
Reperry Cross PL30 . . . . . . 47 F6

Reppersfield Row TR13 . . . 90 F3
RESCASSA 72 F1
RESCORLA 59 D8
Rescorla Ct TR27 . . . . 142 C5
Research Way PL6 . . . . 125 C4
Reservoir Cres PL9 . . . . . . 136 B7
Reservoir La 1 PL3 . . . . . . 128 F6
Reservoir Rd
  Plymouth, Hartley PL3 . . . 128 F6
  Plymouth, Plymstock PL9 . 136 B7
Reservoir Way PL9 . . . . 136 B7
RESKADINNICK 138 B5
Reskadinnick Rd TR14 . . . 138 B4
RESKIVERS 71 F3
Resolution Ho PL4 . . . . . . 149 B3
Respryn Cl PL14 . . . . 113 D6
Respryn Rd PL31 . . . . 48 D8
RESTORMEL 112 C5
Restormel Castle ★ PL22 . 112 C5
Restormel Ind Est PL22 . . 112 D2
Restormel Rd
  Looe PL13 . . . . 117 D4
  Lostwithiel PL22 . . . . 112 C4
  Newlyn TR18 . . . . 143 C3
  Plymouth PL4 . . . . 148 C4
Restormel Terr
  Falmouth TR11 . . . . 145 B3
  Plymouth PL4 . . . . 148 C4
Restronguet Hill TR11 . . . . 82 B4
RESTRONGUET
  PASSAGE 82 A4
RESUGGA GREEN 59 D7
Resugga Green Residential
  Homes Pk PL26 . . . . 59 D7
Reswythen Wlk 1 TR14 . . 138 F7
Retallack Gdns 3 TR20 . . . 89 E5
Retallick Mdws PL25 . . . . 115 B5
Retanning La PL26 . . . . 58 E1
Retreat The
  8 Chacewater TR4 . . . . . . 69 A3
  Plymouth PL3 . . . . 129 B7
  St Columb Major TR9 . . . . 45 E6
Revell Park Rd PL7 . . . . 130 D6
Revel Rd PL3 . . . . 129 A6
Reynolds Gr PL5 . . . . 127 C8
Reynolds Rd PL7 . . . . 130 C6
REZARE 28 E4
Rheola Gdns PL6 . . . . 125 E5
Rhind St PL31 . . . . 109 E5
Rhodes Cl PL7 . . . . 130 E7
Rhubarb Hill TR8 . . . . 43 B1
Rhude Cross EX23 . . . . 3 B3
Rialton Hts TR7 . . . . 111 E7
Rialton Rd TR7, TR8 . . . . . 111 E6
Ribble Gdns PL3 . . . . 129 D7
Rice La PL3 . . . . 85 C5
Richard Lander Sch TR3 . . 69 D3
Richards Cres TR1 . . . . 69 E3
Richards La TR14 . . . . 67 E4
Richards Row PL3 . . . . 128 F7
Richards Terr PL10 . . . . . . 132 E5
Richmond Hill TR1 . . . . . . 137 B4
Richmond Pl
  40 St Ives TR26 . . . . 141 B6
  3 Truro TR1 . . . . 137 B4
Richmond Rd
  Pelynt PL13 . . . . 62 D6
  Plymouth PL6 . . . . 125 A2
Richmond St
  Heamoor TR18 . . . . 143 C7
  Penzance TR18 . . . . 143 E6
Richmond Terr
  Buckland Monachorum
  PL20 . . . . 41 F3
  Truro TR1 . . . . 137 B4
Richmond Way TR26 . . . . . 141 D1
Richmond Wlk PL1 . . . . . . 127 F1
Ricketts Rd PL26 . . . . 59 A1
Rick Mdw PL15 . . . . 18 E6
Ride The PL7, PL9 . . . . 129 D2
Ridge Cross PL9 . . . . 136 A3
Ridgegrove Hill PL15 . . . . 106 D6
Ridgegrove La PL15 . . . . . 106 C7
Ridge Ho PL4 . . . . 149 A3
Ridgeo Mill TR18 . . . . 143 F8
Ridge Park Ave PL4 . . . . . . 128 D4
Ridge Park Rd PL7 . . . . 130 E5
Ridge Pk PL7 . . . . 130 E5
Ridgevale Cl TR18 . . . . 143 F8
Ridgevale La TR18 . . . . 143 F8
Ridgeway
  22 Perranporth TR6 . . . . . 55 A5
  Plymouth, Plympton PL7 . 130 D5
  Plymouth, Plympton St Maurice
  PL7 . . . . 130 D5
  Probus TR2 . . . . 71 C6
  Saltash PL12 . . . . 122 D1
Ridgeway Sch PL7 . . . . 130 D5
Ridgeway Sp Ctr PL7 . . . . 130 E5
Ridgewell Terr TR9 . . . . 57 E8
Ridgewood Cl PL26 . . . . . . 114 F1
Riga Terr PL3 . . . . 129 C4
Rigdale Cl PL6 . . . . 129 A7
Rigmore Way PL5 . . . . 124 B3
Ringway Flats 8 PL31 . . . . 109 D5
RINSEY 90 D2
Rinsey La TR13 . . . . 90 D2
Risdon Ave PL4 . . . . 149 C3
Rivendell PL27 . . . . 108 C4
River Ct
  Saltash PL12 . . . . 122 D5
  Tavistock PL19 . . . . 147 D6
Riverford Cl PL6 . . . . 125 D7
River Pk 8 PL21 . . . . 42 C4
Riversdale Pl 8 PL27 . . . . 108 B5
RIVERSIDE 123 A1

Riverside
  Angarrack TR27 . . . . 78 C4
  8 Chacewater TR4 . . . . . . 69 A3
  Lanivet PL30 . . . . 47 F6
  Lelant TR26 . . . . 77 E4
  Padstow PL28 . . . . 107 E5
Riverside Ave TR7 . . . . 110 A5
Riverside Bsns Pk PL1 . . . 127 E3
Riverside Cl 1 PL20 . . . . . . 42 C4
Riverside Com Prim Sch
  PL25 . . . . 122 C1
Riverside Cott PL12 . . . . . 122 C1
Riverside Cres TR7 . . . . . . 110 A5
Riverside Ct PL22 . . . . 112 C2
Riverside Ho TR1 . . . . 137 D1
Riverside Mews
  Angarrack TR27 . . . . 78 C5
  Saltash PL12 . . . . 123 A3
Riverside Mills PL15 . . . . 106 B7
Riverside Pl PL1 . . . . 127 D2
Riverside View TR1 . . . . . . 137 E3
Riverside Wlk PL5 . . . . 124 B6
River St
  Mevagissey PL26 . . . . 73 C3
  Portscatho TR2 . . . . 83 B2
  Truro TR1 . . . . 137 C4
Rivers The PL12 . . . . 122 E1
Riverview TR11 . . . . 145 A6
River View
  Flushing TR11 . . . . 145 B7
  Gunnislake PL18 . . . . 40 E5
  Lerryn PL22 . . . . 61 C7
  Plymouth PL4 . . . . 129 B1
  Tresillian TR2 . . . . 70 E4
River View La PL4 . . . . 129 B1
River Wlk PL25 . . . . 114 B3
Riviera Apartments
  TR26 . . . . 141 D2
Riviera Cl 6 TR12 . . . . 99 A1
Riviera Est TR1 . . . . 70 D1
Riviera La TR2 . . . . 95 A6
Riviera Terr PL26 . . . . 73 C3
RIVIERE TOWANS 142 B7
Riviere Towans TR27 . . . . 142 B7
Roach's Ct TR26 . . . . 141 E1
Roach's Row TR15 . . . . . . 140 B5
Robartes St 13 TR1 . . . . . 137 C4
Robartes Gardens Flats
  PL25 . . . . 114 F4
Robartes Gdns PL25 . . . . 114 F4
Robartes Jun Sch PL31 . . 109 D4
Robartes Pl PL25 . . . . 114 E5
Robartes Rd
  Bodmin PL31 . . . . 109 D4
  Newquay TR7 . . . . 110 F5
  St Dennis PL26 . . . . 58 C8
Robartes Terr
  1 Illogan TR16 . . . . 67 E4
Lostwithiel PL22 . . . . 112 C3
Robert Adams Cl PL7 . . . 130 B5
Robert Eliot Ct PL25 . . . . 114 B3
Robert Hichens Rd TR11 . 145 A5
Roberts Ave PL11 . . . . 127 B3
Roberts Rd PL5 . . . . 127 D8
Robin Dr PL15 . . . . 106 E4
Robins Cl 1 PL24 . . . . 60 B4
Robins Way PL9 . . . . 135 E8
ROBOROUGH 121 D1
Roborough Ave PL6 . . . . . 125 B5
Roborough Cl PL6 . . . . . . 125 B5
Roborough Down La PL6 . 121 F5
Roborough La PL5 . . . . . . 124 D8
Robyns Cl PL7 . . . . 131 B5
ROCHE 46 F3
Roche Com Prim Sch
  PL26 . . . . 46 F2
Roche Rd
  Bugle PL26 . . . . 47 C2
  Stenalees PL26 . . . . 59 C7
Roche Rural Workshops
  PL26 . . . . 47 A4
Roche Sta PL26 . . . . 47 A4
Rochester Rd
  8 Plymouth PL4 . . . . 128 E4
  7 Plymouth PL4 . . . . 149 A4
Rochford Cres PL5 . . . . . . 123 F5
ROCK 21 D2
Rock Cl 1 TR14 . . . . 138 F2
Rock Close Ho TR27 . . . . 142 A1
Rockfield Ave PL6 . . . . 124 F6
Rock Gdns PL9 . . . . 135 E8
Rockhaven Gdns PL27 . . . 21 F3
ROCKHEAD 14 E3
Rockhead St PL33 . . . . 14 E3
Rock Hill PL5 . . . . 124 C7
Rockingham Rd PL3 . . . . . 129 A5
Rock La PL31 . . . . 109 C4
Rock Rd
  Newlyn TR18 . . . . 143 C3
  St Minver PL27 . . . . 21 E2
Rock Terr
  Heamoor TR18 . . . . 143 C7
  Plymouth PL7 . . . . 130 D4
Rock Twrs PL13 . . . . 117 D2
Rock View Parc PL26 . . . . . 47 A3
Rock Villas PL27 . . . . 21 D2
Rockville Pk PL9 . . . . 135 E8
Rockwood Rd PL6 . . . . . . 125 B8
Rocky Hill PL19 . . . . 147 B5
Rocky La
  Praa Sands TR20 . . . . 90 C6
  St Agnes TR5 . . . . 54 C2
  Veryan TR2 . . . . 83 D5
Rocky Park Ave PL9 . . . . . 135 E8
Rocky Park Rd PL9 . . . . . . 135 E8
Rodda's Rd TR14 . . . . 68 C6
Roddick Way 8 PL7 . . . . . 131 C5

Rodings The PL14 . . . . 51 F5
Rodney St PL5 . . . . 127 D8
Rodwell Cl TR15 . . . . 140 D5
Rodwell Ct TR27 . . . . 78 E1
Roebuck Villas PL11 . . . . . 145 D3
Roekindale Cl TR15 . . . . . 139 D6
Roeselare Ave PL11 . . . . . 127 A3
Roeselare Cl PL11 . . . . 127 A3
Rogate Dr PL6 . . . . 125 D4
Rogate Wlk PL6 . . . . 125 D4
Rogers Dr PL12 . . . . 122 D4
Roland Bailey Gdns
  PL19 . . . . 147 A6
Rollis Park Cl PL9 . . . . 135 C8
Rollis Park Rd PL9 . . . . 135 C8
Rolston Cl PL6 . . . . 124 D6
Roma Cl TR7 . . . . 111 C7
Roma Ct TR27 . . . . 142 B5
Roman Bridge PL13 . . . . . . 62 D1
Roman Dr PL31 . . . . 109 F2
Roman Rd PL5 . . . . 123 E2
Roman Way PL5 . . . . 123 E2
Romilly Gdns PL7 . . . . 130 B5
Romney Cl PL5 . . . . 124 B1
Ronald Terr PL2 . . . . 127 F5
Ronsdale Cl PL9 . . . . 135 D8
Roope Cl PL5 . . . . 127 C7
Ropehaven Cl PL25 . . . . . 114 E6
Ropehaven Rd PL25 . . . . . 114 E6
Roper Ave PL9 . . . . 135 D8
Ropewalk Ct 2 TR11 . . . . 145 C3
Ropewalk Rd TR3 . . . . 137 C1
Ropewalk The TR18 . . . . . 143 C4
Rope Wlk
  Mount Hawke TR4 . . . . 68 C6
  Padstow PL28 . . . . 107 D5
  8 St Austell PL26 . . . . . . 115 A1
Rope Wlk The
  3 St Ives TR26 . . . . 141 B6
  9 St Mawes TR2 . . . . 95 A6
Rorkes Cl PL5 . . . . 123 E2
Roscadghill Parc 1
  TR18 . . . . 143 C7
Roscadghill Rd TR18 . . . . 143 C6
Roscarrack Cl TR15 . . . . . 139 B8
Roscarrack Cl TR11 . . . . . 144 E2
Roscarrack Rd TR11 . . . . . 144 D1
Roscarrick Villas TR11 . . . 93 D3
Roscarrock Hill PL29 . . . . . 22 D7
ROSCROGGAN 138 D7
ROSE 55 C5
Rose Acre Dr 8 TR15 . . . . 140 C5
ROSE-AN-GROUSE 77 D8
Roseannon TR11 . . . . 93 D3
Rosebery Ave PL4 . . . . . . 149 C4
Rosebery La PL4 . . . . 149 C4
Rosebery Rd PL4 . . . . 149 C4
ROSECARE 10 C6
Roseclave Cl PL7 . . . . 131 C6
Rose Cottage PL27 . . . . . . 21 F5
Rosecott Pk EX23 . . . . 5 A6
Rose Cotts
  Camborne TR14 . . . . 138 E3
  Plymouth PL6 . . . . 129 B8
  Stithians TR3 . . . . 80 F3
Rosecraddoc View PL14 . . 38 A2
Rose Ct PL25 . . . . 115 A5
Rosedale Ave PL2 . . . . . . 128 D7
Rosedale Gdns PL31 . . . . . 35 B2
Rosedale Rd TR1 . . . . 137 C5
Rosedene Farm TR3 . . . . . 69 C4
ROSEDINNICK 45 E8
Rosedown Ave PL2 . . . . . 128 A7
Rose Eglos TR11 . . . . 144 C2
Rose Eglos Cl TR11 . . . . . 144 C2
Rose Gdns PL26 . . . . 125 E6
ROSEHILL 55 D5
  Goonhavern 55 D5
  Lostwithiel 112 C1
Rosehill
  Ladock TR2 . . . . 57 C1
  Lanivet PL30 . . . . 47 C6
  Marazion TR17 . . . . 89 B5
  Mylor Bridge TR11 . . . . . . 82 A2
Rose Hill
  Altarnun PL15 . . . . 26 C8
  Fowey PL23 . . . . 116 C4
  Par PL24 . . . . 60 B5
  Porthtowan TR4 . . . . 68 A6
  Port Isaac PL29 . . . . 22 D7
  Redruth TR15 . . . . 140 B5
  Sticker PL26 . . . . 58 F1
Rose Hill Cl PL22 . . . . 112 C2
Rosehill Gdns TR18 . . . . . 143 B6
Rosehill Mdw TR18 . . . . . 143 B6
Rose Hill Terr PL17 . . . . . . 41 A3
Rosehip Cl PL6 . . . . 125 E7
Rose In The Bush Pk
  TR12 . . . . 99 B8
Rose La 23 TR26 . . . . 141 B6
ROSELAND 51 E6
Roseland Com Sch The
  TR2 . . . . 72 A4
Roseland Cres
  6 Chacewater TR4 . . . . . . 69 A3
  Tregony TR2 . . . . 71 F3
Roseland Flats TR2 . . . . . . 82 E1
Roseland Gdns
  Bodmin PL31 . . . . 109 E6
  Redruth TR15 . . . . 140 D6
  Veryan TR2 . . . . 83 F6
Roseland Pk TR14 . . . . . . 138 D4
Roselands Rd PL31 . . . . . 109 F6
Roseland Terr TR14 . . . . . . 55 F2
Roselidden Parc TR13 . . . 146 B7
Roseline Est TR13 . . . . 80 D1
Roselyon Pl PL24 . . . . 60 C5
Roselyon Sch PL24 . . . . . . 60 C4

Rose Mdw TR3 . . . . 80 F3
Rose Mdws TR4 . . . . 55 C4
Rosemellen Terr PL14 . . . 113 B4
Rosemellin TR14 . . . . 138 E4
ROSEMELLING 59 F8
Rosemellin Prim Sch
  TR14 . . . . 138 E4
ROSEMERGY 75 D3
Rosemorran 28 TR26 . . . 141 B6
Rosemullion 4 TR6 . . . . . . 55 A5
Rosemullion Gdns 3
  TR14 . . . . 138 F7
Rose Mullion Gdns PL17 . 39 F5
Rosemullion Ho TR1 . . . . . 69 E4
Rosemundy TR5 . . . . 54 D1
ROSENANNON 33 A1
Rosenannon La TR15 . . . . 139 B8
Rosenannon Rd TR15 . . . 139 B8
Rose Row TR15 . . . . 140 B5
ROSERROW 21 E5
Rose Terr
  Gunnislake PL18 . . . . 40 E5
  Mitchell TR8 . . . . 56 F5
  22 Penzance TR18 . . . . . . 143 E6
Rosevale TR18 . . . . 143 D4
Rosevale Cres TR14 . . . . . 138 C4
Rosevale Gdns PL30 . . . . . 59 F8
Rosevalley TR3 . . . . 69 D3
Rose Valley TR19 . . . . 75 B2
Rosevallon La PL31 . . . . . 109 D5
ROSEVEAN 47 D1
Rosevean Ave TR14 . . . . . 138 E3
Rosevean Cl TR14 . . . . . . 138 E3
Rosevean Ct 8 PL25 . . . . 115 A3
Rosevean Gdns PL25 . . . 128 F6
Rosevean Ho 7 PL3 . . . . . 128 F6
Rosevean Rd TR18 . . . . . 143 E6
Rosevean Terr TR18 . . . . 143 E6
ROSEVEAR 99 C7
Roseveare Cl PL9 . . . . 136 A8
Roseveare Dr PL26 . . . . . . 46 D1
Roseveare Mobile Home Pk
  PL26 . . . . 46 D1
Roseveor Rd PL26 . . . . 47 C1
Rosevidney TR20 . . . . 89 B3
Rosewall Cotts 10 TR26 . 141 A5
Rosewall Terr 11 TR26 . . 141 A5
ROSEWARNE 78 F3
Rosewarne TR13 . . . . 91 A1
Rosewarne Cl TR14 . . . . . 138 D4
Rosewarne Gdns TR14 . . 138 D3
Rosewarne Mews TR14 . . 138 D4
Rosewarne Pk TR14 . . . . . 138 E4
Rosewarne Rd
  1 Camborne TR14 . . . . . 138 D3
  Carnhell Green TR27 . . . . . 78 F4
Rosewarne Terr TR14 . . . 138 D5
Rosewarne (Trng Ctr)
  TR14 . . . . 138 D5
Rosewin Mews 3 TR9 . . . . 45 E6
Rosewin Row
  2 St Columb Major TR9 . . 45 E6
  Truro TR1 . . . . 137 D5
Rosewithian Cl TR27 . . . . 78 B6
Rosewood Cl PL9 . . . . 135 F5
ROSEWORTHY
  Camborne 78 E6
  Shortlanesend 69 B3
ROSEWORTHY BARTON . . . 78 F6
Roseworthy Hill TR14 . . . . 78 F6
Rosina Way PL26 . . . . 59 D7
Roskear TR14 . . . . 138 E6
ROSKEAR CROFT 138 E6
Roskear Croft TR14 . . . . . 138 E6
Roskear Fields TR14 . . . . 138 E6
Roskear Parc TR14 . . . . . . 138 F5
Roskear Rd TR14 . . . . 138 E3
Roskear Sch TR14 . . . . . . 138 F3
Roskilling TR13 . . . . 146 D7
Roskilling Wartha TR13 . . 146 D7
Roskilly Cotts TR19 . . . . . . 88 C2
Roskilly's Ice Cream &
  Organic Farm ★ TR12 . . 101 D3
Roskrow Cl TR16 . . . . 80 A5
Roskruge Cl TR13 . . . . 146 D8
Ros Lyn TR26 . . . . 141 C1
Roslyn Cl
  St Austell PL25 . . . . 114 F5
  2 St Austell PL25 . . . . . . 115 A5
Rosparc TR2 . . . . 71 D6
Rosparvah Gdns TR18 . . . 143 C7
Rospeath Cres PL2 . . . . . 128 D8
Rospeath La TR20 . . . . 89 C7
Rossett Gdns PL31 . . . . . . 35 B1
Rossiter Ho TR19 . . . . 96 B6
Rosslyn Park Rd PL3 . . . . 128 F5
Ross St PL2 . . . . 127 E4
Rossventon TR14 . . . . 69 A1
Rostalek PL30 . . . . 24 B2
ROSUDGEON 89 F4
Rothbury Cl PL6 . . . . 125 D4
Rothbury Gdns PL6 . . . . . 125 D4
Rothesay Gdns PL5 . . . . . 124 D3
Rougemont Cl PL3 . . . . . . 129 B7
Rough La PL3 . . . . 81 B4
Rough St TR16 . . . . 80 D6
Roughtor Dr PL32 . . . . 105 C3
Roughtor Rd PL32 . . . . 15 D1
Roughtor View PL32 . . . . . 14 E2
Roundhayes Farm Cotts
  EX23 . . . . 10 C5
Round Ring TR10 . . . . 144 D8
Round's La PL34 . . . . 14 D7
Rous Rd PL12 . . . . 40 C2
ROW 24 B3
Rowan Cl
  Bodmin PL31 . . . . 109 B4
  Plymouth PL7 . . . . 131 B5

Rowan Cl continued
Tavistock PL19.............147 C3
Rowan Ct PL12.............122 C2
Rowans The
Bude EX23................104 E4
Lifton PL16.................19 F4
St Mellion PL12............53 C8
Rowan Way PL6............125 E7
Rowan Wood Rd PL19......30 F3
Rowden St PL3.............128 E5
Rowe Par PL1..............131 D4
Rowe's La TR13............146 E8
Rowe St PL11..............127 B3
Rowes Terr PL26............58 D5
Row La PL5................123 E2
Rowland Cl PL9............135 E5
Rowse Gdns PL18..........41 A3
Row The
Launceston PL15............17 F1
Pillaton PL12...............53 B7
Portloe TR2................84 A4
Royal Cornwall Hospl TR1 69 E4
Royal Cornwall Mus★
TR1.......................137 C4
Royal Cornwall
Showground★ PL27......33 C6
Royal Eye Infmy PL4.......128 E4
Royalist Ct **14** TR11.......145 C3
Royal Navy Ave PL2........127 F6
Royal Par PL1..............148 C2
Royal Talbot PL22..........112 C2
Royal William Rd PL1......134 A8
Roydon Cl PL15............106 B8
Roydon La PL15............106 B8
Roydon Rd PL15...........106 B8
Royffe Way PL31...........109 F3
RUAN HIGH LANES.........83 E6
RUAN LANIHORNE..........83 E8
RUAN MAJOR...............102 F6
RUAN MINOR...............103 B5
Ruby Terr TR13.............92 B8
RUDDLEMOOR..............59 B6
Rudyerd Wlk PL3..........129 D6
Rufford Cl PL2.............128 A7
Rule Cross EX23.............2 E2
RUMFORD..................32 A5
Ruminella View TR12......103 A4
Rumours Apartments
TR7.......................111 B7
Rundle Ct PL14............113 B4
Rundles Ct TR1............137 E3
Runnymede Ct PL6........125 E2
RUSHFORD.................30 A3
Rush Park Terr PL18........40 F7
Ruskin Cres PL5...........124 D2
Ruskin Ct TR9..............45 D5
Russell Ave PL3............128 F7
Russell Cl
Gunnislake PL18...........41 A7
Plymouth PL9..............136 B7
Saltash PL12...............122 C3
Russell Court Gdns PL19 147 B6
Russell Ct
Plymouth PL1..............148 C2
Saltash PL12...............122 C3
Tavistock PL19.............147 C5
Russell Mews PL31........109 C5
Russell Pl PL1.............148 B4
Russell St
7 Liskeard PL14.........113 C5
Tavistock PL19.............147 C5
Russell Way **4** TR10.....144 C7
Russet Wood PL5..........123 F4
Rutger Pl PL1...............87 A3
RUTHERNBRIDGE...........34 A1
Ruthern Valley PL30.........34 A1
Ruthven Cl PL6............128 F8
RUTHVOES.................45 F3
Ruthy's La PL28............107 D5
Rutland Rd PL4............128 F4
Rydal Cl PL6...............125 D2
Ryder Rd PL2..............127 F4
Rydon La EX22..............8 F7
Rye Hill
Ponsanooth TR3...........81 B4
Saltash PL12...............122 C2
Rylands Terr PL30..........24 B3

S

Saffron Cl PL23............116 C4
Sail Loft Flats **2** TR26...141 B6
ST AGNES..................54 D1
ST AGNES BEACON.........54 B1
St Agnes Mus★ TR5.......54 C1
St Agnes Prim Sch TR5....54 C1
St Albans Pk PL26..........42 D2
ST ALLEN...................56 B1
St Ambrusca Rd TR8.......110 A3
St Andrew's CE Prim Sch
PL20.......................41 B3
St Andrew's Cl
12 Bere Alston PL20......41 B1
Ponsanooth TR3...........81 B4
Saltash PL12...............122 C2
St Andrew's Cl PL18.......41 A3
St Andrew's Cross 1
PL1.......................149 A2
St Andrew's Pl PL11......133 A1
St Andrews Pl PL19........147 D2
St Andrew's Rd
Par PL24..................60 C5
2 Stratton EX23..........4 D1
St Andrew's St
Cawsand PL10.............133 A1
1 St Ives TR26...........141 B5
St Andrew St
Millbrook PL10............132 E5
Plymouth PL1..............148 C2
St Andrews Terr TR3........81 B4
St Andrew's Terr PL24.....60 C5
St Annes TR11..............93 D3
St Annes Cl
Lelant TR26................77 E4
Whitstone EX22.............7 B2
St Annes Rd **17** PL24.....60 B4
St Anne's Rd
Newquay TR7..............111 A7
Plymouth PL6..............125 D6
Saltash PL12...............122 E3
3 Trewoon PL25..........59 A3
ST ANN'S CHAPEL..........40 E6
St Ann's Hill EX23.........104 F3
St Anta Rd TR26...........141 E1
ST ANTHONY................95 B5
ST ANTHONY-IN-
MENEAGE................101 C8
St Anthony Way TR11......145 A2
St Aubyn Ave PL2..........127 F5
St Aubyn Cres TR7.........111 A6
St Aubyn Est TR14..........79 B2
St Aubyn Rd PL1...........127 E3
St Aubyns Rd TR7...........89 C5
St Aubyn's Rd PL1.........137 D3
St Aubyn's Rd TR1.........137 D3
St Aubyn's Vean TR1......137 D3
ST AUSTELL.................114 B5
St Austell Bay Bsns Pk
PL25.......................115 C4
St Austell Brewery Visitor
Ctr★ PL25................114 B4
St Austell Com Hospl
PL26.......................114 F1
St Austell Rd PL24.........115 F5
St Austell Row **2** TR2....95 A6
St Austell St
Summercourt TR8..........57 C6
Truro TR1..................137 D4
St Austell Sta PL25........114 D4
St Barnabas Ct PL1.........148 A4
St Barnabas Hospl PL12..122 F2
St Barnabas Terr PL1.......148 A4
St Benedicts Ct **13** PL24.60 D5
St Benets Cl PL30...........47 E6
St BLAZEY..................60 B5
ST BLAZEY GATE...........115 F6
St Blazey Rd PL24..........60 C4
St Boniface Cl PL2.........128 C7
St Boniface Dr PL2.........128 C7
St Boniface Rd RC Coll PL5 124 E1
St Breaca Cl TR13...........91 A3
ST BRECOCK................23 B3
St Brecok CP Sch PL27....108 B5
ST BREWARD...............24 B3
St Breward Prim Sch
PL30.......................24 B3
St Bridget Ave PL6.........124 F1
ST BUDEAUX................127 D1
St Budeaux Ferry Rd Sta
PL5.......................127 C2
St Budeaux Foundation Jun
Sch PL5...................123 F2
St Budeaux Victoria Rd Sta
PL5.......................123 D1
ST BURYAN...................97 B6
St Buryan Hill TR19........96 F4
St Buryan Prim Sch TR19..97 B6
St Cadocs PL28.............31 F7
St Carantoc Way TR8.......43 D3
St Catherine's Castle★
PL23.......................116 B2
St Catherine's CE Prim Sch
PL15.......................106 A4
St Catherines Ct PL23.....116 C3
St Clare Flats TR18.........143 D6
St Clare St TR18............143 D6
ST CLEER....................37 F2
St Cleer Dr PL27............108 D6
St Cleer Prim Sch PL14....38 A3
St Cleer Rd PL14...........113 C7
ST CLEMENT................70 D2
St Clement's Cl TR1........137 E4
St Clement's Hill TR1......137 E4
St Clements Parc TR1......137 E4
St Clement's Terr **3**
TR1.......................137 D5
St Clement Vean TR1......137 F6
ST CLETHER.................16 F4
St Columb Bsns Ctr TR9...45 E3
ST COLUMB MAJOR.........45 E5
St Columb Major Bsns Pk
TR9.......................45 D5
St Columb Major Ind Est
TR9.......................45 D5
St Columb Major Prim Sch
TR9.......................45 D5
ST COLUMB MINOR.........111 F7
St Columb Minor Sch
TR7.......................111 D7
ST COLUMB ROAD..........45 D2
St Columb Road Ind
Workshops TR9............45 D2
St Columb Road Sta TR9..45 D2
St Crewenna Terr TR27.....78 E1
St Cuthbert Cl PL15.......106 B7
St Cuthbert's Rd TR7.....110 D6
St Cyriac PL30...............47 F1
St Davids Cl PL24...........4 C8
St David's Rd PL19........147 E5
ST DAY......................68 E1
St Day & Carharrack Com
Sch TR16.................68 E1

St Day Rd TR15.............140 C5
ST DENNIS...................58 C8
St Dennis Com Prim Sch
PL26.......................58 C8
St Dennis Ind Est PL26....58 B8
St Dominic Cl PL31.........109 E5
ST DOMINICK...............40 D3
St Dominick CE Prim Sch
PL12.......................40 D2
St Dominic Pk PL17.........40 C4
St Dominic Sq **4** TR1.....137 C4
St Dominic St
8 Penzance TR18.........143 E6
5 Truro TR1..............137 C4
St Dunstan's Terr PL4......137 A3
St Edmunds La PL28.......107 D5
St Edward Gdns PL6.......125 B1
St Edward's CE Prim Sch
PL6.......................125 C1
St Eia St TR26..............141 C6
St Elizabeth Cl PL7.........130 F3
St Elvan Cres TR13.........91 A1
St Elwyns Rise TR27........142 B6
ST ENDELLION..............22 D5
ST ENODER..................57 B7
St Enodoc Cl PL27.........108 D6
ST ERME.....................70 E8
St Erme Terr St R4.........70 D8
ST ERNEY...................53 B2
ST ERTH.....................142 A1
St Erth Com Prim Sch
PL27.......................142 A1
St Erth Hill TR27...........77 F1
St Erth Ind Est TR27.......77 E2
ST ERTH PRAZE.............142 F1
St Erth Rd PL2.............128 D7
St Erth Sta TR27...........77 E2
ST EVAL.....................31 F3
St Eval Pl PL5..............123 E4
ST EWE......................72 B6
St Fimbarrus Rd PL23.....116 C3
St Francis CE Sch TR11....144 E3
St Francis Ct PL5...........124 B3
St Francis Mdw TR8.........56 F5
St Francis Rd TR9...........45 E2
St Francis St **5** TR18......143 E6
St Gabriel's Ave PL3.......128 D5
ST GENNYS..................10 C8
St George's Arc TR11......145 B4
St George's Ave PL2........128 C7
St George's CE Prim Sch
PL1.......................148 A1
St George's Cres PL31.....109 C4
St Georges Ct
Looe PL13..................117 D2
1 Plymouth PL2...........127 F4
St George's Hill TR6........55 A4
St Georges Hill **13** TR6..55 A4
St George's Pk PL12.......112 C3
St Georges Rd
Nanpean PL26...............58 D6
Saltash PL12...............122 D3
St George's Rd
Hayle TR27.................142 C5
Looe PL13..................117 D4
Newquay TR7..............110 D5
Saltash PL12...............122 E3
Truro TR1..................137 B5
St George's Terr
Perranporth TR6............54 F4
Plymouth PL2..............127 F4
ST GERMANS................65 A8
St Germans Prim Sch
PL12.......................65 A8
St Germans Rd PL17.......39 F3
St Germans Sta PL12.......65 B8
St Giles Dr PL27............108 C6
St Giles Mews PL27........108 C6
ST GILES ON THE HEATH...13 E1
St Giles on the Heath Prim
Sch PL15...................13 F1
ST GLUVIAS.................144 D3
St Gluvias Parc TR10......144 D8
St Gluvias St TR10.........144 D7
St Golder Rd TR18.........143 B3
St Gothian Sands Nature
Reserve★ TR27...........66 B2
St Grace's Ct TR2...........71 C6
St Helens Wlk PL5.........124 C5
St Henry St **4** TR18.......143 E6
ST HILARY...................89 E6
St Hilary Prim Sch TR20...89 F6
St Hilary Terr PL4..........149 C3
St Ia St TR26...............141 D1
St Issen CE Prim Sch
PL25.......................32 D6
ST ISSEY.....................32 E6
ST IVE........................38 F2
ST IVE CROSS...............39 A1
St Ive Rd PL14..............38 E4
ST IVES......................141 C6
St Ives Jun & Inf Schs
TR26.......................141 A5
St Ives La TR27.............66 B1
St Ives L Ctr TR26.........141 A5
St Ives Mus★ TR26........141 C6
St Ives Mushroom Farm
TR26.......................77 A5
St Ives Rd
Carbis Bay TR26...........141 D1
Pendeen TR19..............75 A1
St Ives Sch TR26...........141 B3
St Ives Sta TR26...........141 B5
St James Cl
Delabole PL33..............14 E2
Plymouth PL1..............148 B2
Torpoint PL11..............127 B3
St James Mews PL1........148 B2

St James' Place E PL1.....148 B2
St James' Place W PL1.....148 B2
St James Rd PL11..........127 B2
St James' St TR18..........143 E5
St James's Terr TR10.......144 E7
St James View TR9.........57 D8
ST JIDGEY...................32 C4
ST JOHN.....................132 C8
ST JOHNS...................146 A6
St Johns Ave PL19..........147 C5
St John's Bridge Rd PL4..108 B2
St Johns Bsns Pk TR13....146 B6
St Johns Cl PL6.............125 D4
St John's Ct
Helston TR13..............146 A6
Millbrook PL10............132 E5
St Johns Ct **7** TR18.......143 E5
St John's Ct
7 Falmouth TR11.........145 A4
Hayle TR27.................142 D6
St John's Dr PL9............135 B6
St Johns Gdns TR11.......145 B6
St Johns La PL11...........132 B8
St John's Rd PL15..........106 B4
St John's Rd
Helston TR13..............146 B6
Horrabridge PL20...........42 C4
Millbrook PL10............132 F5
Newquay TR7..............110 D5
Plymouth PL4..............149 B2
Plymouth, Turnchapel PL9 135 A6
St John's St
Hayle TR27.................142 D6
Plymouth PL4..............149 B2
St John's Terr
Devoran TR3................81 F6
Pendeen TR19..............75 A1
Plymouth, Milehouse PL4 128 F4
St John the Baptist RC Prim
Sch **4** TR14...............138 E2
St Joseph's Cl PL6.........124 F1
St Joseph's Rd PL15.......106 B8
St Joseph's Sch PL15.....106 B7
ST JUDE'S...................149 B3
St Jude's Rd PL4...........149 B2
St Julians Cres PL10.......133 E7
St Julitta PL30...............48 A1
ST JUST......................86 E6
ST JUST IN ROSELAND......82 F2
St Just Prim Sch TR19......86 E6
St Keri TR15.................18 A5
ST KEVERNE................101 C4
St Keverne Cty Prim Sch
TR12.......................101 D4
St Keverne Rd PL2..........128 D8
St Keverne Rural Workshops
TR12.......................101 C3
ST KEW......................23 A2
ST KEW HIGHWAY...........23 A2
St Kew Prim Sch PL30......22 F3
ST KEYNE....................51 A3
St Keyne Sta TR1...........137 A1
St Keyne Wishing Well Halt
PL14.......................51 C2
ST LAWRENCE..............34 D1
St Lawrence Rd
Bodmin PL30, PL31.......109 A4
Plymouth PL4..............149 A4
St Leonards PL31..........109 C5
St Leonard's Rd
Launceston PL15..........106 B8
Plymouth PL4..............149 C2
St Leonards Terr PL31.....109 C5
St Leo Pl PL2...............127 E4
ST LEVAN....................96 D3
St Levan Ct **3** TR17.......89 C5
St Levan Prim Sch TR19...96 E5
St Levan Rd
4 Marazion TR17..........89 C5
Plymouth PL2..............127 F5
ST MABYN...................34 C8
St Mabyn CE Prim Sch
PL30.......................34 D8
St Maddern's CE Sch
TR20.......................143 A8
St Margarets La PL26......59 A1
St Margarets Rd PL7.......130 B7
St Mark's CE Prim Sch
EX23.......................2 E2
St Marks Rd PL6...........125 D5
St Marnach's PL13.........62 B8
St Marnarch's Rd PL13....62 B8
ST MARTIN..................117 D7
St Martin Cl
Looe PL13..................117 D7
Mawgan TR12.............100 D6
St Martin-in-Meneage Prim
Sch TR12..................100 D6
St Martin's Ave PL7........128 D7
St Martin's CE Prim Sch
PL14.......................113 C5
St Martins Cl
Lewannick PL15............22 B7
Looe PL13..................117 D5
St Martin's Cl PL7.........130 F3
St Martin's Cres TR14.....138 C3
St Martins Ct PL14.........113 E5
St Martins Rd EX23.........7 B8
St Martin's Terr TR14.....138 C4
St Marwenne Cl EX23.......7 B6
St Maryhape PL19.........147 A5
St Mary's PL13.............117 D3
St Mary's CE Prim Sch
Penzance TR18.............143 E4
Truro TR1..................137 C6

St Mary's Cl PL31...........109 C4
St Mary's Cres PL31.......109 C4
St Mary's Ct PL7...........130 D5
St Mary's Gdns PL31......109 C4
St Mary's RC Prim Sch
Bodmin PL31..............109 C4
Falmouth TR11.............144 E3
St Mary's RC Sch TR18....143 E7
St Marys Rd PL24...........60 B4
St Mary's Rd
Bodmin PL31..............109 B3
Launceston PL15..........106 C8
Newquay TR7..............110 D5
Plymouth PL7..............130 C6
St Mary's St
Penzance TR18.............143 E6
12 Truro TR1..............137 D4
St Mary's Street Mews **10**
TR1.......................137 D4
St Mary St PL1..............148 A2
St Mary's Terr
Penzance TR18.............143 E5
4 Truro TR1..............137 C5
St Matthews Hill PL27.....108 D5
St Maurice Ct TR4.........130 F4
St Maurice Mews PL7......130 F4
St Maurice Rd PL7.........130 F3
St Maurice View PL7......131 B4
ST MAWES..................95 B6
St Mawes Castle★ TR2....95 A5
St Mawes Prim Sch TR2...95 A6
St Mawes Terr **8** PL2.....127 F5
ST MAWGAN.................45 A8
St Mawgan Cl PL31........109 F5
St Mellans Terr **5** TR12...99 A1
ST MELLION.................53 E8
St Mellion CE School
PL12.......................53 D8
ST MELLION PK.............53 C8
St Meriadoc CE Inf Sch
TR14.......................138 C2
St Meriadoc CE VA Jun Sch
TR14.......................138 B2
St Meriadoc Rd TR14......138 C3
ST MERRYN..................31 F8
St Merryn Airfield PL28....31 F6
St Merryn Prim Sch PL28..31 E8
ST MEWAN..................59 A2
St Mewan La PL24, PL26...59 A3
St Mewan Prim Sch PL26..59 A3
St Michael Ave PL2........127 F5
ST MICHAEL CAERHAYS....72 D1
ST MICHAEL PENKIVEL.....70 F1
St Michael's CE Prim Sch
TR13.......................146 C5
St Michaels Cl PL15........19 C1
St Michael's Cl
Hayle TR27.................142 B4
Plymouth PL4..............127 E1
St Michael's Cotts **11**
TR18.......................143 E5
St Michaels Ct
Mawnan Smith TR11.......93 D3
18 Penzance TR18........143 E5
St Michael's Ct **7** PL1...127 F2
St Michael's Hospl TR12..142 B4
St Michael's Mount★
TR17.......................89 B4
St Michael's RC Small Sch **17**
TR1.......................137 C4
St Michael's Rd
Newquay TR7..............110 D5
Perranporth TR6...........55 A4
Ponsanooth TR3...........81 C4
3 Stratton EX23..........4 D1
St Michael's St TR18.......143 E6
St Michael's Terr
Penzance TR18.............143 D6
6 Plymouth, Devonport
PL1.......................127 F3
Plymouth PL4..............148 C4
St Michaels Way PL26......47 A2
ST MINVER...................24 A2
St Minver Prim Sch PL27..21 F3
St Modwen Rd PL6........129 F7
St Moritz Ct PL27..........21 D5
St Moritz Villas PL27.......21 D5
St Nazaire App PL1........127 F2
St Nazaire Ct PL1..........127 E2
ST NEOT.....................36 F2
St Neot Com Prim Sch
PL14.......................36 F2
ST NEWLYN EAST...........56 C7
St Newlyn East Prim Sch
TR8.......................56 B7
St Nicholas' CE Prim Sch
PL11.......................64 C4
St Nicholas Cl TR7...........78 C6
St Nicholas Ct **1** TR26...141 B6
St Nicholas Pk PL22.......112 B3
St Nicholas St
Bodmin PL31..............109 C4
14 Truro TR1.............137 D4
St Nonna's Cl PL15..........26 C8
St Olaf's Rd **13** EX23......4 D1
St Paternus Ct PL15.......27 E8
St Pauls Cl PL3.............129 C5
St Paul St PL1..............134 A8
St Peter Cl PL7.............130 F4
St Peters Ct PL1............148 A3
St Peter's Hill TR18........143 C1
St Peter's RC Prim Sch
PL5.......................124 B5

St Peters Rd
  Plymouth PL5 . . . . 124 C2
  [11] Stratton EX23 . . . . 4 D1
St Peter's Rd TR11 . . . . . . 145 B7
St Peters St [18] TR26 . . . . 141 B6
St Peters Way TR13 . . . . . . 98 C8
St Petroc's CE Prim Sch
  PL31 . . . . 109 E4
St Petroc's Cl PL31 . . . . . . 109 E4
St Petrocs Mdw PL28 . . . . 107 C5
St Petroc's Sch EX23 . . . . 104 D7
St Petry TR20 . . . . 89 E5
St Philip St [7] TR18 . . . . . 143 E6
ST PINNOCK 50 D6
St Piran Cl PL3 . . . . 109 B4
St Pirans Cl [2] TR1 . . . . . 137 D4
St Piran's Cl PL25 . . . . . . 114 F6
St Pirans Ct
  Camborne TR14 . . . . 138 D3
  [1] Penzance TR18 . . . . . 143 E5
  Tintagel PL34 . . . . 14 E8
St Piran's Hill TR3 . . . . 81 D6
St Pirans Ho [15] TR5 . . . . . 55 A5
St Pirans Par [10] TR6 . . . . 55 A5
St Pirans Parc [14] TR13 . . . 98 C8
St Pirans Rd TR6 . . . . 55 A5
St Piran's Rd TR7 . . . . 110 D6
St Pirans Way TR20 . . . . . . 89 D4
St Pol de Leon View TR19 . . 88 C2
ST RUAN 103 A4
St Rumon's CE Inf Sch
  PL19 . . . . 147 C6
St Sampsons Cl [6] PL24 . . . 60 D5
St Sampson's Terr PL23 . . . 61 B5
St Saviour's Hill PL23 . . . . 116 D2
St Saviour's La PL28 . . . . . 107 D6
St Simon's La PL4 . . . . 149 C3
St Smithwick Way TR11 . . . 145 C3
ST STEPHEN 58 B4
St Stephen Churchtown Prim
  Sch PL26 . . . . 58 B4
St Stephen Rd PL7 . . . . . . 130 F3
ST STEPHENS
  Launceston 106 A8
  Saltash 122 D1
St Stephens Ct PL15 . . . . . 106 B7
St Stephen's Hill
  Launceston PL15 . . . . . . 106 B7
  Saltash PL12 . . . . 122 C1
St Stephen's Pl PL7 . . . . . 130 E5
St Stephens Prim Sch
  Launceston PL15 . . . . . . 106 B8
  Saltash PL12 . . . . 122 C2
St Stephens Rd PL26 . . . . . 58 E1
St Stephen's Rd PL12 . . . . 122 E2
St Stephen St PL1 . . . . . . 127 F1
St Sulien PL30 . . . . 48 A1
ST TEATH 23 E7
St Teresa Ho PL4 . . . . 149 A3
St Therese Cl [20] PL17 . . . . 39 F4
St Therese's Ct PL11 . . . . . 127 F2
ST THOMAS 106 B6
St Thomas Cl
  Plymouth PL7 . . . . 130 F3
  Truro TR1 . . . . 69 F3
St Thomas Hill PL15 . . . . . 106 B6
St Thomas Rd PL15 . . . . . 106 B6
St Thomas' Rd TR7 . . . . . . 110 F5
St Thomas St TR10 . . . . . . 144 C7
St Timney Farm PL32 . . . . . 10 D1
St Treath Prim Sch PL30 . . . 23 E7
ST TUDY 23 E3
St Tudy CE Prim Sch
  PL30 . . . . 23 E3
St Uny CE Sch TR26 . . . . . 141 D1
St Uny Cres TR15 . . . . 139 F5
ST VEEP 61 C6
St Vincent St PL2 . . . . 127 E4
St Warren St [6] TR18 . . . . 143 E6
ST WENN 46 D7
St Wenn Sch PL30 . . . . 46 D7
St Winnolls Pk PL13 . . . . . 117 D4
ST WINNOW 61 A8
St Winnow Barton Farm
  Mus* PL7 . . . . 61 A8
St Winnow CE Prim Sch
  PL22 . . . . 112 F2
Salamanca St PL11 . . . . . 127 B3
Salcombe Rd PL4 . . . . 149 C4
SALEM 68 F3
Salisbury Ope PL3 . . . . . . 128 B5
Salisbury Rd
  Plymouth PL4 . . . . 149 C4
  Truro TR1 . . . . 137 B4
Salisbury Road Jun Sch
  PL4 . . . . 149 C3
Salmon Row [3] TR1 . . . . . 137 D4
SALTASH 122 B1
Saltash Bsns Pk PL12 . . . . 122 C4
Saltash Com Sch PL12 . . . 122 C1
Saltash Her Mus* PL12 . . . 123 A2
Saltash Ind Est PL12 . . . . . 122 D4
Saltash L Ctr PL12 . . . . . . 122 E3
Saltash Parkway Ind Est
  PL12 . . . . 122 B4
Saltash Rd
  Callington PL17 . . . . 39 F4
  Plymouth, Keyham PL2 . . 127 E6
  Plymouth PL3 . . . . 148 C4
Saltash Sta PL12 . . . . 123 A2
Saltbox Cl TR11 . . . . 82 A2
Saltbox Rd TR11 . . . . 82 A2
Saltburn Rd PL5 . . . . 123 C1

Salt Cellar Hill [16] TR13 . . . 98 B8
Saltings Cl TR26 . . . . 77 E3
Saltings Reach TR26 . . . . . 77 E3
Saltings The TR26 . . . . 77 E4
Salt Mill PL12 . . . . 122 F4
Saltmill Cl PL12 . . . . 122 F3
Saltponds [27] TR19 . . . . . . 88 C1
Saltram House* PL7 . . . . . 130 A4
Saltram Terr PL7 . . . . 130 E5
Salts Mdw PL14 . . . . 50 B6
Sampford Gdns PL20 . . . . . 42 D5
SAMPFORD SPINEY 42 E7
Sampford Terr PL20 . . . . . . 42 C5
Sampson Cl PL18 . . . . 40 D6
Sampson Gdns TR3 . . . . . . 81 B4
Sampson's Ct TR27 . . . . . . 78 D6
Sampson Way TR3 . . . . 69 D3
Samprys Hill TR11 . . . . 93 D3
Samuel Bone Cl PL14 . . . . 113 D6
SANCREED 87 E4
Sanctuary Cl TR14 . . . . . . 138 C2
Sanctuary La
  Helston TR13 . . . . 146 C6
  [12] Stratton EX23 . . . . . . 4 E1
Sanctuary Lane Flats
  TR13 . . . . 146 C6
Sand Bay TR11 . . . . 145 C2
Sandercock Cl PL17 . . . . . . 39 F7
Sandfield Cres [3] TR14 . . . 138 C2
Sandford Rd PL9 . . . . 135 F8
Sand Hill PL18 . . . . 41 A6
Sand Hill PL5 . . . . 40 F5
Sandhole Cross EX39 . . . . . . 2 D8
Sandhurst Terr [1] TR1 . . . 137 C5
Sand La PL18 . . . . 41 A3
Sandon Wlk PL6 . . . . 125 A1
Sandows La [18] TR26 . . . . 141 A5
SANDPLACE 63 C7
Sandplace Rd
  Looe PL13 . . . . 117 C6
  Looe, Sandplace PL13 . . . 63 B7
  Sandplace Sta PL13 . . . . 63 B8
Sandra Way PL31 . . . . 109 C5
Sandyacres TR27 . . . . 78 B6
Sandy Acres TR27 . . . . . . 142 E8
SANDY BOTTOM 114 F4
Sandy Cl PL14 . . . . 51 B3
Sandy Cove TR4 . . . . 66 A7
Sandy Ct TR10 . . . . 31 B2
Sandy Hill PL25 . . . . 114 F4
Sandy Hill Prim Sch
  PL25 . . . . 114 F4
Sandyhills PL27 . . . . 21 E2
Sandy La
  Harlyn PL28 . . . . 20 D2
  Redruth PL15, TR16 . . . . 140 D5
  Trevone PL28 . . . . 20 F2
Sandylake La PL22 . . . . . . 112 F3
Sandymoor TR14 . . . . 139 B3
Sandy Rd
  Plymouth PL7 . . . . 131 C4
  Porthtowan TR4 . . . . 68 A7
Sango Cl PL10 . . . . 132 F6
Sango Rd PL11 . . . . 127 A2
San Sebastian Sq PL1 . . . . 148 C2
Saracen Cl PL14 . . . . 144 C7
Saracen Cres TR10 . . . . . . 144 C7
Saracen Ho [5] TR10 . . . . 144 C7
Saracen Pl TR10 . . . . 144 C7
Saracen Way TR10 . . . . . . 144 C7
Sarah Cl PL20 . . . . 41 B1
Sarahs Cl PL28 . . . . 107 D4
Sarah's Ct PL28 . . . . 107 D4
Sarah's Gate PL27 . . . . . . 32 C7
Sarah's La PL28 . . . . 107 D4
Sarah's Mdw PL28 . . . . . . 107 D4
Sarah's View PL28 . . . . . . 107 D4
Sargents Mdw EX23 . . . . . . 2 D1
Sarum Cl PL3 . . . . 128 F7
Saunders La PL11 . . . . 65 A5
Saunders Wlk PL6 . . . . . . 124 D6
Savage Rd PL5 . . . . 127 D7
SAVEOCK 69 B3
Savery Terr PL4 . . . . 129 A4
Savoy Bldg [3] PL25 . . . . . 114 C3
Sawles Rd PL25 . . . . 114 B2
Sawmills La TR16 . . . . 68 D3
Sawrey St PL1 . . . . 148 A2
Sawyers Ct TR13 . . . . 92 A6
Saxon Rd PL19 . . . . 147 A6
SCARWEATHER 57 E5
Scarletts Well Pk PL31 . . . 109 C6
Scarletts Well Rd PL31 . . . 109 C5
Scarlett's Well Rd PL31 . . 109 B5
Scarne Ind Est PL15 . . . . . 106 C3
Scholars Cl PL14 . . . . 38 F2
Scholar's La TR13 . . . . 91 C3
School Cl
  Par PL24 . . . . 60 B4
  Plymouth PL7 . . . . 130 D7
  St Columb Minor TR7 . . . 111 E6
  Tavistock PL19 . . . . 147 D5
School Dr PL6 . . . . 125 D7
School Hill
  Golant PL23 . . . . 61 B5
  Herodsfoot PL14 . . . . 50 E3
  Lanjeth PL26 . . . . 58 E4
  Mevagissey PL26 . . . . . . 73 C4
  Padstow PL28 . . . . 107 D5
  Perranarworthal TR3 . . . . 81 F6
  Shortlanesend TR4 . . . . . 69 F6
  South Petherwin PL15 . . . 27 E8
  St Buryan TR19 . . . . 96 E5
  St Keverne, Porthallow
    TR12 . . . . 101 D6
  St Keverne TR12 . . . . . . 101 D4
  St Neot PL14 . . . . 36 F2

School La
  Budock Water TR11 . . . . 144 C3
  Gulval TR18 . . . . 88 E6
  Jacobstow EX23 . . . . . . 11 A6
  Marazion TR17 . . . . 89 C5
  Plymouth PL7 . . . . 130 E4
  Polruan PL23 . . . . 116 D2
  Redruth TR15 . . . . 140 D5
  St Austell PL25 . . . . 115 C6
  St Erth TR27 . . . . 142 A1
  St Hilary TR20 . . . . 89 F6
  Troon TR14 . . . . 79 E4
  Truro TR1 . . . . 137 C3
School Rd
  Breage TR13 . . . . 90 F3
  Landrake PL12 . . . . 53 C3
  Pensilva PL14 . . . . 38 E5
  Summercourt TR8 . . . . . . 57 B7
  Tavistock PL19 . . . . 147 D2
School Wlk PL27 . . . . 108 D6
Sclerder La PL13 . . . . 62 E4
Scoble's Terr TR11 . . . . . . 70 D1
Sconner Rd PL11 . . . . 127 A3
Scoria Cl TR16 . . . . 68 D3
SCORRIER 68 D3
Scorrier House Workshops
  TR9 . . . . 46 A3
Scorrier St TR16 . . . . 68 E1
Scott Ave PL5 . . . . 127 C8
Scott Bsns Pk PL2 . . . . . . 128 A6
Scott Cl [2] PL14 . . . . 38 E4
Scott Hospl PL2 . . . . 128 A6
Scott Rd PL2 . . . . 128 A6
Scowbuds TR14 . . . . 138 F5
Scrations La PL22 . . . . 112 C2
SCREEDA 114 D8
Screech Owl Sanctuary*
  TR9 . . . . 46 A3
Seabank TR11 . . . . 145 B2
Seacroft Rd PL5 . . . . 123 C2
Sea Front Ct PL13 . . . . . . 117 D3
Seaholme Ct TR11 . . . . . . 145 A5
Sea La TR27 . . . . 142 D6
Seapoint Ho TR7 . . . . 110 E6
Sea Rd PL25 . . . . 115 D2
SEATON 64 B5
Seaton Ave PL4 . . . . 128 E4
Seaton Bsns Pk PL6 . . . . . 125 B3
Seaton La PL4 . . . . 128 E4
Seaton Pk PL11 . . . . 64 B5
Seaton Rd PL25 . . . . 127 F5
Seaton Valley North Nature
  Reserve* PL13, PL3 . . . . 64 B6
Seaton Way PL20 . . . . 42 A2
Sea Urchin TR26 . . . . 141 E2
Sea View
  Crackington Haven EX23 . . 10 C6
  Gunnislake PL18 . . . . . . 40 E5
Sea View Ave PL4 . . . . 149 C4
Seaview Cotts [10] TR11 . . 145 B5
Sea View Cotts PL6 . . . . . . 73 C3
Sea View Cres [11] TR2 . . . 95 A6
Sea View Ho [19] TR11 . . . 145 B3
Sea View Pl TR26 . . . . 141 C6
Sea View Rd
  Falmouth TR11 . . . . 145 B2
  [12] St Mawes TR2 . . . . . 95 A6
Seaview Terr TR8 . . . . 57 E6
Sea View Terr
  Camborne TR14 . . . . 138 E2
  Carn Towan TR19 . . . . . . 96 C7
  Helston TR13 . . . . 146 B6
  [6] Newlyn TR18 . . . . . . 143 C1
  Par PL24 . . . . 60 B6
  Penwithick PL26 . . . . . . 59 D7
  Plymouth PL4 . . . . 149 B4
  Redruth TR15 . . . . 140 C5
  [20] St Ives TR26 . . . . . . 141 B5
Seawell Rd EX23 . . . . 104 F7
Second Ave
  Plymouth, Billacombe
    PL9 . . . . 130 A1
  Plymouth, Devonport PL1 . 128 A2
  Plymouth, Weston Mill PL2 127 E7
Sedley Way PL5 . . . . 124 D3
Sefton Ave PL4 . . . . 129 B3
Sefton Cl PL4 . . . . 149 C4
Segrave Rd PL2 . . . . 128 B6
Selkirk Ho [5] PL9 . . . . 135 F7
Selkirk Pl PL5 . . . . 124 E2
SELLAN 87 E5
Selsden Cl PL9 . . . . 136 C6
Sendall's Way PL6 . . . . . . 124 F4
Seneschall Pk TR13 . . . . . 146 D8
SENNEN 96 B6
Sennen Cl PL11 . . . . 126 F4
Sennen Hts TR19 . . . . 96 B7
Sennen Pl PL2 . . . . 127 E5
Sennen Ret PL6 . . . . 125 A7
Sennen Sch TR19 . . . . 96 C7
Sentry Cl PL27 . . . . 32 D6
Sergeants Hill TR4 . . . . 68 F3
Serpell Cl PL6 . . . . 124 E6
Serpells Mdw PL15 . . . . . . 17 F1
Sethnoe Way TR13 . . . . . . 91 A3
Seton Gdns TR14 . . . . 138 B4
Setons The [3] TR14 . . . . . 138 B4
Seven Stars La PL5 . . . . . 124 C6
Seven Trees Ct PL4 . . . . . 149 B4
Severn Pl PL3 . . . . 129 C5
Sewell Ct PL3 . . . . 128 E5
SEWORGAN 92 C6
Seymour Ave
  Newquay TR7 . . . . 110 E6
  Plymouth PL4 . . . . 149 B4
Seymour Cl TR3 . . . . 69 C3
Seymour Dr PL3 . . . . 128 F5

Seymour Mews PL4 . . . . . 149 C4
Seymour Pk PL3 . . . . 129 A5
Seymour Pl PL1 . . . . 148 A4
Seymour Rd
  Plymouth, Mannamead
    PL3 . . . . 128 F5
  Plymouth, Plympton PL7 . 130 C6
Seymour St PL4 . . . . 149 A3
Shackleton Cres [9] PL27 . 31 F3
Shackleton Ct PL5 . . . . . . 124 E1
Shackleton Dr TR7 . . . . . . 111 B5
Shaft Downs La TR27 . . . . 78 F3
Shaftesbury Cotts PL4 . . . 149 A4
Shaftesbury St PL4 . . . . . 149 A4
Shakespeare Prim Sch
  PL5 . . . . 124 B2
Shakespeare Rd PL5 . . . . 124 C2
Shaldon Cres PL5 . . . . . . 124 B3
Shallowford Cl PL6 . . . . . 129 C8
Shallowford Rd PL6 . . . . . 129 C8
Shapleys Gdns PL9 . . . . . 136 A5
Shapters Rd PL4 . . . . 149 C2
Shapters Way PL4 . . . . . . 135 B8
Sharaman Cl PL25 . . . . . . 115 A5
Sharlands Rd EX23 . . . . . . 7 B6
Sharon Way PL6 . . . . 125 A5
Sharpitor Row PL20 . . . . . 42 E4
Sharrose Rd PL9 . . . . 135 B5
Shaw Way PL9 . . . . 135 A7
Shearwood Cl PL7 . . . . . . 131 B5
Sheep Fair Mdw [14] PL17 . 39 F4
Sheepstor Rd PL6 . . . . . . 125 D1
SHEFFIELD 97 F7
Sheila's Ct TR26 . . . . 141 D1
Shelburne Ct TR11 . . . . . . 144 F3
Shelburne Rd TR11 . . . . . 144 F3
Shell Cl PL6 . . . . 125 E1
Shelley Ave PL19 . . . . 147 D5
Shelley Rd PL25 . . . . 115 A4
Shelley Way PL5 . . . . 123 D1
Sherborne Cl PL9 . . . . . . 136 C6
Sherford Cres
  Plymouth, Elburton PL9 . 136 C7
  Plymouth, West Park PL5 . 124 A3
Sherford Rd PL9 . . . . 136 D6
Sherford Wlk PL9 . . . . . . 136 E7
Sheridan Rd PL5 . . . . 124 C1
Sherrell Pk PL20 . . . . 41 B1
Sherril Cl PL9 . . . . 135 F4
Sherwell La PL4 . . . . 149 A4
Sherwood Dr PL31 . . . . . . 109 C5
SHEVIOCK 65 B6
Sheviock La PL11 . . . . 65 B5
Shilla Pk PL32 . . . . 24 A8
Shilson Terr [7] PL15 . . . . . 106 C5
Shipley Wlk PL6 . . . . 125 A1
Ships & Castles L Ctr
  TR11 . . . . 145 E3
Shirburn Rd PL6 . . . . 125 A3
Shire Horse Farm & Carriage
  Mus The* TR16 . . . . 46 F3
Shires Way PL26 . . . . 46 F3
Shirley Gdns PL5 . . . . 124 C1
Shoemaker's La PL12 . . . . 122 E2
Shoemakers Row PL13 . . . 63 B7
Shoot Row TR15 . . . . 140 C5
SHOP
  Morwenstow 2 D1
  St Merryn 31 E8
Shop Hill [3] TR17 . . . . . . 89 C5
Shop Pk PL14 . . . . 38 A2
Shoreline TR7 . . . . 111 B8
Shores La PL27 . . . . 21 E3
Shortacross PL14 . . . . 38 A2
Short Cotts PL11 . . . . 127 A3
Short Cross Mews TR4 . . . 68 C6
Short Cross Rd TR4 . . . . . 68 C6
Shortlands SC22 . . . . 8 E5
SHORTLANESEND 69 F6
Shortlanesend Prim Sch
  TR4 . . . . 69 F6
Short Park Rd PL3 . . . . . . 128 D5
Shortwood Cres PL9 . . . . . 136 A7
Shrewsbury Rd PL5 . . . . . 124 C4
Shrubberies Hill TR13 . . . . 98 C8
Shute Hill
  Breage TR13 . . . . 90 F3
  Carharrack TR16 . . . . . . 80 E8
  Helston TR13 . . . . 146 C6
  Lostwithiel PL22 . . . . . . 112 C2
  Mawnan Smith TR11 . . . . 93 D3
  Pelynt PL13 . . . . 62 D5
Shute La
  Penryn TR10 . . . . 144 C8
  Pensilva PL14 . . . . 38 E4
  [6] Porthleven TR13 . . . . 98 B8
Shute Mdw TR10 . . . . 144 C7
Shute Park Rd PL9 . . . . . . 135 F6
SHUTTA 117 D4
Shutta Rd PL13 . . . . 117 C4
Sidings The
  Bugle PL26 . . . . 47 C2
  Delabole PL33 . . . . 14 E2
Sidmouth Cotts [9] PL4 . . . 128 F4
Sidney Terr [7] TR15 . . . . . 140 C5
Silvanus Jenkin Ave
  PL14 . . . . 113 E5
Silver Birch Cl PL6 . . . . . . 125 C7
Silver Ct [1] TR15 . . . . 140 B8
Silverdale Ct TR7 . . . . 110 E6
Silverdale Rd TR11 . . . . . . 145 A2
Silver Hill TR3 . . . . 81 D6
Silvershell Rd PL29 . . . . . 22 D7
Silvershell View PL29 . . . . 22 D7
Silver St
  Bere Ferrers PL20 . . . . . 120 A3
  Saltash PL12 . . . . 123 A2
Silver Terr PL10 . . . . 133 A6

Silverton Cl EX23 . . . . 104 E5
Silverton Rd EX23 . . . . . . 104 E5
Silver Way TR3 . . . . 69 C3
SILVERWELL 68 F7
Simms Terr PL18 . . . . 41 A6
Simon Cl PL9 . . . . 135 E6
Simpsons Ct [30] TR18 . . . 143 E5
Singlerose Rd PL26 . . . . . . 59 C7
Sir James Smith's Com Sch
  PL32 . . . . 105 C4
Sir John Hunt Com Sports
  Coll PL5 . . . . 124 D4
Sir Robert Geffery's CE Prim
  Sch PL12 . . . . 53 C3
Sir Williams Morles
  Almshouses PL12 . . . . . . 65 A8
SITHNEY 91 B3
SITHNEY COMMON 91 C3
Sithney Common Hill
  TR13 . . . . 91 C4
Sithney Old Hill TR13 . . . . 146 A6
Sithney Prim Sch TR13 . . . 91 B5
Sithney St PL5 . . . . 123 C1
Six Turnings TR11 . . . . 82 A2
Skardale Gdns PL6 . . . . . . 129 D8
Skardon Pl PL4 . . . . 149 A4
Skerries Rd PL6 . . . . 124 F7
Skidden Hill [18] TR26 . . . . 141 B5
Skinnard La PL18 . . . . 40 F5
SKINNERS BOTTOM 68 D5
Skitches Cnr EX23 . . . . 4 D1
Skyburriowe La TR12 . . . . . 99 C6
Skylark Rise
  Plymouth PL6 . . . . 125 E8
  Tavistock PL19 . . . . 147 D1
Slade Cl PL9 . . . . 136 A5
Slade Park Rd PL14 . . . . . . 38 E5
SLADESBRIDGE 34 A6
Slades La [2] TR10 . . . . . . 144 C7
Slades Rd PL25 . . . . 114 E5
Slate Cl PL33 . . . . 14 D2
Slate La PL1 . . . . 148 A2
Slatelands Cl PL7 . . . . 131 B3
SLAUGHTERBRIDGE 105 D7
Slipway PL27 . . . . 21 D2
Slipway Quay PL12 . . . . . . 119 B2
Smallack Cl PL6 . . . . 124 F2
Smallack Dr PL6 . . . . 124 F2
Smallridge Cl PL9 . . . . 135 F5
Smallridge La EX23 . . . . . . 4 F1
Smeaton Sq PL3 . . . . 129 D6
Smeaton's Twr* PL1 . . . . . 148 C1
Smithfield Ct TR18 . . . . . . 111 B3
Smithfield Dr PL12 . . . . . . 122 B3
Smithick Hill TR11 . . . . . . 145 B4
Smith's Cotts PL14 . . . . . . 113 C6
Smiths Way PL12 . . . . 122 B3
Smithy Cl PL12 . . . . 122 C4
Smithy Ct PL32 . . . . 105 D3
Smithy La TR3 . . . . 81 F7
Smugglers Row [8] PL15 . . 145 B5
Snell Dr PL12 . . . . 122 B3
Snowdrop Cres PL15 . . . . . 106 E4
Snow's Pas TR11 . . . . 145 B4
Socotra Dr [7] PL25 . . . . . . 59 A3
Solar Row [6] TR1 . . . . 137 D5
Somer Ct TR11 . . . . 145 A4
Somerset Cotts [10] PL3 . . 128 A4
Somerset Pl PL3 . . . . 128 A4
Somerset Place La [11]
  PL3 . . . . 128 A4
Somerville Rd TR16 . . . . . . 55 A4
Sona Merg Cl TR18 . . . . . . 143 C7
Soper's Hill PL5 . . . . 124 A1
South Albany Rd TR15 . . . 140 C3
Southbourne Bsns Pk TR15 140 C3
Southbourne Rd PL25 . . . . 114 E2
Southcliff TR11 . . . . 145 C2
South Cliff [18] TR19 . . . . . 88 C1
South Coombe La PL17 . . . 39 F8
SOUTHCOTT 11 A4
Southcott Mdws EX23 . . . . 11 A6
SOUTHDOWN 133 B6
Southdown Cl PL26 . . . . . . 58 E1
Southdown Cotts PL10 . . . 133 B6
Southdown Rd
  Millbrook PL10 . . . . 133 A6
  Sticker PL26 . . . . 58 E6
South Down Rd PL2 . . . . . 128 E6
South Downs TR15 . . . . . . 140 A2
Southdown Terr PL10 . . . . 133 A6
South Dr
  Redruth TR15 . . . . 140 D2
  South Tehidy TR14 . . . . . 138 E8
Southella Rd PL20 . . . . 42 D2
Southern Cl PL2 . . . . 127 F7
Southernhaye [8] PL15 . . . 106 C5
Southern Rd
  [8] Callington PL17 . . . . . 39 F4
  Southern Terr PL4 . . . . . 129 F4
Southernway PL9 . . . . 136 A8
Southern Way PL27 . . . . . 108 C5
Southfield PL12 . . . . 122 C3
Southfield Rd EX23 . . . . . . 104 E5
Southfields EX22 . . . . 8 A5
Southfields [3] TR26 . . . . . 141 A5
Southgate Ave PL9 . . . . . . 135 E4
Southgate Cl PL9 . . . . 135 E4
Southgate Pl [4] PL15 . . . . 106 C5
Southgate St
  Launceston PL15 . . . . . . 106 C5
  Redruth TR15 . . . . 140 C3
South Harbour TR10 . . . . . 144 D7
SOUTH HILL 39 C7
South Hill
  Plymouth, Hooe PL9 . . . . 135 C5

South Hill *continued*
Plymouth, Stoke PL1 . . . . . . 128 A3
South Hill Rd PL17 . . . . . . 39 E5
SOUTH HOLE 2 D7
Southlea Terr TR3 . . . . . . 80 F3
Southleigh Ho 18 TR1 . . . . 137 C4
Southleigh Mews 14
TR1 . . . . 137 C4
South Milton St PL4 . . . . . 149 C2
South Par 33 TR18 . . . . . . 143 E5
South Park Cl TR15 . . . . . 140 A4
Southpark Rd PL24 . . . . . . 60 C5
SOUTH PETHERWIN 27 E8
South Petherwin Prim Sch
PL15 . . . . 27 E8
SOUTH PILL 122 E3
South Pk
Jacobstow EX23 . . . . . . 11 A6
Redruth TR15 . . . . 139 F6
St Columb Major TR9 . . 45 E6
South Pl TR19 . . . . 86 E6
South Place Folly 5
TR18 . . . . 143 E4
South Place Gdns TR19 . . 86 E6
South Quay PL28 . . . . . . 107 D5
South Quay Hill TR7 . . . . 110 D6
South Rd
Goldsithney TR20 . . . . . . 89 E5
Stithians TR3 . . . . 80 F3
South Roskear Terr
TR14 . . . . 138 F4
Southside Ope 14 PL11 . . 149 A2
Southside St PL1 . . . . . . 149 A2
South St
Fowey PL23 . . . . 116 D4
Grampound Road TR2 . . 57 E1
Lostwithiel PL22 . . . . . . 112 C2
St Austell PL25 . . . . . . 114 C3
SOUTH TEHIDY 138 E7
South Terr
Camborne TR14 . . . . . . 138 D2
12 Penzance TR18 . . . . 143 E4
South Towan TR4 . . . . . . 68 A6
Southview PL10 . . . . . . 133 A6
South View
9 Horrabridge PL20 . . 42 C4
Liskeard PL14 . . . . 113 D7
Penryn TR10 . . . . 144 C8
Plymouth, Crownhill PL5 . . 124 E2
Plymouth, Elburton PL9 . . 136 B6
Porthleven TR13 . . . . . . 91 A1
South View Cl PL7 . . . . . . 130 D7
Southview Pl PL31 . . . . . . 109 E5
South View Parc TR4 . . . . 68 A6
South View Pk PL7 . . . . . . 130 D7
Southview Rd 15 PL24 . . 60 B4
Southview Terr 9 TR19 . . 88 C1
South View Terr
Blackwater TR4 . . . . 68 E5
Nancegollan TR13 . . . . . . 91 B7
Plymouth PL4 . . . . 149 C3
SOUTHWAY 124 F6
Southway PL28 . . . . 20 F2
South Way TR8 . . . . 111 F3
Southway Dr PL6 . . . . . . 124 E6
Southway La
Plymouth, Southway PL6 . . 125 B6
Plymouth, Tamerton Foliot
PL6 . . . . 124 C6
Southwell Rd PL6 . . . . . . 124 E1
SOUTH WHEATLEY 11 F3
Sovereign Ct PL7 . . . . . . 130 C5
Spargo Ct TR10 . . . . 93 C8
Spargo's La TR1 . . . . 137 E5
Sparkatown La PL20 . . . . 42 E7
Sparke Cl PL7 . . . . 131 B4
SPARKWELL 131 F8
Spar La TR15 . . . . 67 D4
SPARNON 96 F5
Sparnon Cl
Redruth TR15 . . . . 140 C4
St Austell PL25 . . . . . . 114 B4
Sparnon Cross TR13 . . . . 90 F5
Sparnon Ct TR15 . . . . . . 140 C4
SPARNON GATE 67 F4
Sparnon Hill 1 TR15 . . 140 C4
Sparnon Terr 2 TR15 . . 140 C4
Sparry La TR16 . . . . 80 F8
Spaven Mor TR14 . . . . . . 138 F5
Speares The PL12 . . . . . . 122 B2
Spear's Terr TR11 . . . . . . 144 F1
Speech La TR3 . . . . 81 C4
Speedwell Cl
Bude EX23 . . . . 104 F5
Millbrook PL10 . . . . . . 132 F5
Speedwell Cres PL6 . . . . 129 B7
Speedwell Wlk PL6 . . . . 129 B7
Spencer Gdns PL12 . . . . 122 F1
Spencer Rd PL9 . . . . . . 135 E8
Spernen Ct TR10 . . . . . . 141 C2
Spernen Wyn Rd TR11 . . 145 B2
Spicers La 8 EX23 . . . . . . 4 E1
Spindrift TR8 . . . . 44 C6
Spinnaker Quay PL9 . . . . 134 F7
Spinnakers TR7 . . . . . . 110 A5
Spinney The PL7 . . . . . . 131 A4
Spire Ct PL3 . . . . 129 C7
Spire Hill Pk PL12 . . . . 122 C2
Spire View PL13 . . . . . . 137 C6
Spitfire Row PL27 . . . . . . 31 F3
Splash Pool EX23 . . . . . . 104 F5
SPLATT
Rock 21 E3
Warbstow Cross 17 B7
Sportsmans PL32 . . . . . . 105 C3
Sportsmans Rd PL32 . . . . 105 C3
SPRIDDLESTONE 134 C4

Springfield
Horrabridge PL20 . . . . . . 42 C4
Portscatho TR2 . . . . . . 83 B2
12 Yelverton PL20 . . . . 42 C4
Springfield Ave PL15 . . 136 B6
Springfield Bsns Pk PL15 . . 18 E2
Springfield Cl
Dobwalls PL14 . . . . 50 E7
Lostwithiel PL22 . . . . . . 112 D2
Phillack TR27 . . . . 136 B7
Plymouth PL9 . . . . 136 B7
Polgooth PL26 . . . . 59 A1
St Austell PL25 . . . . . . 114 F5
Springfield Dr PL3 . . . . 128 A4
Springfield Gate PL13 . . 117 D5
Springfield La PL9 . . . . 136 B7
Springfield Pk
Barripper TR14 . . . . . . 79 B5
Mylor Bridge TR11 . . . . 82 A3
Widegates PL13 . . . . . . 63 E7
Springfield Pl 18 TR9 . . 45 E6
Springfield Rd
Falmouth TR11 . . . . . . 144 E5
Goldsithney TR20 . . . . . . 89 E5
Liskeard PL14 . . . . 113 E6
Looe PL13 . . . . 117 D6
Newquay TR7 . . . . 110 A5
Plymouth PL9 . . . . 136 B6
Springfield Rise PL9 . . 136 B7
Springfields PL26 . . . . . . 47 C2
Springfields Fun Pk & Pony
Ctr* TR9 . . . . 45 E4
Springfield Way
Roche PL26 . . . . 46 F3
St Day TR16 . . . . 68 D1
Threemilestone TR3 . . . . 69 C3
Springhill PL22 . . . . . . 128 C8
Springhill Gn PL22 . . . . 128 C8
Spring Pk PL6 . . . . 125 E7
Springwell View PL31 . . 109 F5
Springwood Cl PL7 . . . . 131 A3
Spruce Gdns PL7 . . . . . . 131 B5
Spurway Rd PL14 . . . . . . 113 D5
Square The
18 Bere Alston PL20 . . 41 B1
Cawsand PL10 . . . . 133 A1
2 Chacewater TR4 . . . . 69 A3
Grampound Road TR2 . . 57 E1
Gunnislake PL18 . . . . . . 41 A6
Gunnislake, St Ann's Chapel
PL18 . . . . 40 E5
Kilkhampton EX23 . . . . . . 5 A6
Landrake PL12 . . . . 53 C3
Leedstown TR27 . . . . . . 78 E1
Lizard TR12 . . . . 102 F2
Ludgvan TR20 . . . . 89 A8
Manaccan TR12 . . . . . . 101 A7
Marazion TR17 . . . . . . 89 B5
Pendeen TR19 . . . . 75 A1
Penryn TR10 . . . . 144 D7
Pentewan PL26 . . . . . . 73 B6
Plymouth, Stonehouse PL1 . . 128 A2
Portreath TR16 . . . . . . 67 C6
Portscatho TR2 . . . . . . 83 B2
Praze-an-Beeble TR14 . . 79 B2
Probus TR2 . . . . 57 D1
Roche PL26 . . . . 80 B5
Saltash PL12 . . . . 122 C3
St Keverne TR12 . . . . . . 101 D4
3 St Mawes TR2 . . . . . . 95 A6
St Stephen PL26 . . . . . . 58 B4
St Teath PL30 . . . . 23 E7
Tregony TR2 . . . . 82 F6
Veryan TR2 . . . . 83 C6
Week St Mary EX22 . . . . 11 E8
Squire La TR16 . . . . 80 F8
Squires La TR13 . . . . . . 91 C2
Stable Cotts PL7 . . . . . . 130 F5
Stable Ct PL27 . . . . . . 108 C6
Stables The TR14 . . . . . . 67 B4
STADDISCOMBE 135 F3
Staddiscombe Rd PL9 . . 135 F4
Staddon Cres PL9 . . . . . . 135 B6
Staddon Gn PL9 . . . . . . 135 D6
Staddon La PL9 . . . . . . 135 B4
Staddon Park Rd PL9 . . 135 D6
Staddon Terrace La PL1 . . 148 B4
Stafford Cl TR7 . . . . . . 111 D6
Staggy La PL31 . . . . . . 81 F7
Stag La
Plymouth, Elburton PL9 . . 136 B6
Plymouth, Plympton PL9 . . 130 B1
Stamford Cl PL9 . . . . . . 136 C6
Stamford Fort Cotts PL9 . . 135 A6
Stamford Hill EX23 . . . . 4 D1
Stamford La PL9 . . . . . . 135 A6
Stamps Hill
Fraddon PL26 . . . . 57 F8
Indian Queens TR9 . . . . 45 F1
Stamps La TR15 . . . . . . 139 D6
Stamps The PL17 . . . . . . 40 D5
Stanborough Cross PL9 . . 136 C7
Stanborough Rd PL9 . . . . 136 C7
Stanbury Ave PL6 . . . . . . 124 F1
Stanbury Cl PL15 . . . . . . 13 F1
Stanbury Cross EX23 . . 2 C1
Standarhay Cl PL9 . . . . 136 C7
Standarhay Villas PL9 . . 136 C7
Stanford Cl TR18 . . . . . . 143 D5
Stanford Mews TR9 . . . . 45 E6
Stanford Terr TR18 . . . . 143 D5
Stangray Ave PL4 . . . . . . 128 D4
Stanhope Cl TR7 . . . . . . 111 E6
Stanhope Rd PL5 . . . . . . 123 C1
Stanley Ct 4 PL31 . . . . 109 D5

Stanley Pl PL4 . . . . 129 B2
Stanley Terr 1 TR15 . . 140 B5
Stanley Way TR15 . . . . . . 140 C6
Stannary Bridge Rd
PL19 . . . . 147 D6
Stannary Rd PL26 . . . . . . 59 C8
Stantons Row PL14 . . . . 38 A3
Stanways Rd TR7 . . . . . . 111 D7
Staple Cl PL6 . . . . 121 C1
Stapleford Gdns PL5 . . 123 F5
Stapleton Rd EX23 . . . . 104 F4
Star Pk PL18 . . . . 41 A6
START 77 E3
Statham Rd PL31 . . . . . . 109 D4
Station App
9 Newquay TR7 . . . . . . 110 F6
3 St Columb Road TR9 . . 45 E2
St Erth TR27 . . . . 77 E2
Station Hill
Hayle TR27 . . . . 142 B5
Lelant TR26 . . . . 77 E4
Praze-an-Beeble TR14 . . 79 B2
Redruth TR15 . . . . 140 B4
Station La PL18 . . . . . . 41 A3
Station Par TR7 . . . . . . 110 F6
Station Rd
Bere Alston PL20 . . . . . . 41 B1
Bere Ferrers PL20 . . . . 119 E3
Bugle PL26 . . . . 47 C2
Camborne TR15 . . . . . . 139 C5
Carnhell Green TR14 . . 78 F4
Chacewater TR4 . . . . . . 68 F4
Fowey PL23 . . . . 116 D5
Grampound Road TR2 . . 57 E1
Gunnislake PL18 . . . . . . 40 F6
Helston TR13 . . . . 146 C7
Horrabridge PL20 . . . . . . 42 C4
Kelly Bray PL17 . . . . . . 39 F6
Launceston PL15 . . . . . . 106 C6
Liskeard PL14 . . . . 113 B4
Looe PL13 . . . . 117 C4
Mary Tavy PL19 . . . . . . 30 F5
North Brentor PL19 . . 30 E8
Padstow PL28 . . . . 107 D5
Par PL24 . . . . 60 C5
Penryn TR10 . . . . 144 B8
Penzance TR18 . . . . . . 143 F6
Perranarworthal TR3 . . 81 E6
Perranporth TR6 . . . . . . 55 B6
Plymouth, Elburton PL9 . . 136 C7
Plymouth, Keyham PL2 . . 127 E5
Plymouth, Plympton PL7 . . 130 E5
Plymouth, Tamerton Foliot
PL5 . . . . 124 A6
Redruth TR15 . . . . 140 C5
Saltash PL12 . . . . 123 A2
St Columb Major TR9 . . 45 E2
1 St Columb Road TR9 . . 45 E2
St Mabyn PL30 . . . . 34 C8
St Newlyn East TR8 . . 56 B7
Truro TR1 . . . . 137 B4
Yelverton PL20 . . . . . . 42 D2
Station View PL19 . . . . . . 30 E8
Station Yd 6 PL31 . . . . 109 D5
Steamers Mdw TR27 . . . . 78 C5
Steamers Mdw TR27 . . . . 78 C5
Steeple Cl
Plymouth PL9 . . . . 135 F4
St Ives TR26 . . . . 141 B3
Steeple La TR26 . . . . . . 141 B3
Steeple View Ct TR26 . . 141 C1
Steeple Woodland Nature
Reserve* TR26 . . . . . . 141 B3
Steer Park Rd PL7 . . . . 131 C5
Steer Point Cotts PL8 . . 136 F2
Stefan Cl PL9 . . . . 135 B5
STENALEES 59 B8
Stenalees Hill PL26 . . . . 59 C7
Stenlake Pl PL4 . . . . . . 129 B2
Stenlake Terr PL4 . . . . 129 B2
STENNACK 77 C7
Stennack Gdns 16 TR26 . . 141 A5
Stennack Parc TR19 . . . . 86 F8
Stennack Rd PL25 . . . . . . 115 B4
Stennack The TR26 . . . . 141 B5
Stentaway Cl PL9 . . . . . . 135 F8
Stentaway Dr PL9 . . . . . . 136 A8
Stentaway Rd PL9 . . . . 135 F8
STEPASIDE 58 B6
Stephens Rd PL14 . . . . . . 113 E7
Stephney Cl TR11 . . . . 144 C2
Steppy Downs Rd TR27 . . 78 A1
Sterts Theatre* PL14 . . 38 D7
Stewarts Rd EX22 . . . . . . 11 E8
STIBB 4 D5
STICKER 58 F1
Stiles The TR8 . . . . 54 D4
Stillman Cl 2 PL4 . . . . 149 A2
Stillman St PL4 . . . . . . 149 A2
Stippy Stappy 11 TR5 . . 54 D1
Stirling Ct PL5 . . . . . . 123 C1
Stirling Rd PL5 . . . . . . 123 C1
STITHIANS 80 F3
Stithians Com Prim Sch
TR3 . . . . 80 F4
Stithians Row TR16 . . . . 80 B5
Stockadon Farm Barns
PL3 . . . . 118 B4
Stoggy La PL7 . . . . . . 131 A6
STOKE 128 A3
Stoke Climsland Sch
PL17 . . . . 28 D1
Stoke Damerel Bsns Ctr 7
PL3 . . . . 128 A4
Stoke Damerel Com Coll
PL3 . . . . 128 B4

Stoke Damerel Prim Sch
PL1 . . . . 128 A3
Stoke Hill La PL20 . . . . . . 42 B2
Stoke Rd
Bray Shop PL17 . . . . . . 28 A1
Kelly Bray PL17 . . . . . . 39 E6
Linkinhorne PL17 . . . . . . 39 A8
Plymouth PL1 . . . . . . 125 A5
Stoke La PL6 . . . . 149 A6
Stokes La PL1 . . . . . . 149 A2
Stokes Rd TR1 . . . . . . 137 C5
Stoke Terr PL17 . . . . . . 39 E6
Stokingway Cl PL9 . . . . 135 E5
Stonebarton Cl PL7 . . . . 130 C6
Stonebarton Rd PL7 . . . . 130 C6
Stone Chair La TR19 . . 96 B7
Stone Cross PL16 . . . . . . 14 B3
Stonehall Flats PL1 . . . . 128 A1
Stone Hill EX23 . . . . . . 128 A1
STONEHOUSE 128 A1
Stonehouse Bridge PL1 . . 128 A1
Stonehouse St PL1 . . . . 148 A2
Stonerock Flats PL13 . . 117 C1
Stones Ct 10 TR26 . . . . 141 B5
Stonewood Ct 4 TR7 . . 45 E6
Stoney Hill PL25 . . . . . . 59 A4
Stoney La
Polgooth PL26 . . . . 59 A1
St Austell PL25 . . . . . . 114 C4
Stoney Lands PL12 . . . . 53 C3
Stony La
Bodmin PL31 . . . . 34 D1
Gunnislake PL18 . . . . . . 40 F5
Stopford Pl PL1 . . . . . . 127 F3
STOPTIDE 21 E2
Stott Cl PL3 . . . . 129 D5
Stour Cl PL3 . . . . 129 D6
STOURSCOMBE 106 F4
Stourscombe PL15 . . . . 106 F3
Stourscombe Wood
PL15 . . . . 106 F4
Stowe Gdns PL5 . . . . . . 124 B2
STOWFORD 5 E8
Stowford Cl PL20 . . . . . . 42 E3
Stowford Cross EX22 . . 5 F8
Stracey Rd TR11 . . . . . . 145 B2
Strafford Cl EX23 . . . . 104 C3
Strand TR18 . . . . 143 C2
Strand Sh Ctr The EX23 . . 104 D5
Strand St
Padstow PL28 . . . . 107 D5
Plymouth PL1 . . . . . . 134 A8
Strand The
Bude EX23 . . . . 104 D5
Falmouth TR11 . . . . . . 145 C2
Padstow PL28 . . . . 107 D5
Strangways Terr TR1 . . 137 D3
Strangways Villas TR1 . . 137 D3
STRATTON 4 E1
Stratton Hospl EX23 . . 4 D1
Stratton Pl TR11 . . . . . . 145 A6
Stratton Prim Sch EX23 . . 4 D1
Stratton Rd
Bude EX23 . . . . 104 F4
Stratton EX23 . . . . 4 D1
Stratton Terr
Falmouth TR11 . . . . . . 145 A6
Truro TR1 . . . . 137 B4
Stratton Wlk PL2 . . . . . . 128 D8
Strawberry Cl TR15 . . 140 B6
Strawberry Cres TR15 . . 140 B6
Strawberry Fields TR16 . . 140 E1
Strawberry Gdns TR16 . . 140 E1
Strawberry La
Hayle TR27 . . . . 142 D4
Lelant TR26 . . . . 77 E4
Redruth TR15 . . . . 140 B6
Stray Park Ct TR14 . . . . 138 F2
Stray Park La TR14 . . . . 138 E2
Stray Park Way TR14 . . 138 E2
Street-an-Garrow 17
TR26 . . . . 141 B5
Street-an-Pol 3 TR26 . . 141 B5
Stretyn 5 TR3 . . . . 81 F7
Strickland Cotts 6 TR18 . . 143 C2
Stringers Hill TR20 . . . . 88 A5
Strode Rd PL7 . . . . 130 F6
Stroma Cl PL6 . . . . 124 F7
Stroud Park Rd PL2 . . . . 128 C7
Stuart House Arts & Heritage
Ctr* PL14 . . . . 113 C5
Stuart Rd PL3 . . . . 148 A4
Stuart Road Prim Sch
PL1 . . . . 128 A4
Stuarts Way PL12 . . . . . . 53 E5
Stucley Rd PL21 . . . . . . 128 A1
Sturdee Rd PL2 . . . . . . 128 A5
Sturdon Cross EX23 . . 5 A8
Sugar Mill Bsns Pk PL9 . . 129 C1
SUMMERCOURT 57 C7
Summercourt Prim Sch
TR8 . . . . 57 C7
Summerfield Cl PL26 . . 73 B3
Summerfields 2 PL11 . . 122 D1
Summerheath TR10 . . . . 81 C1
Summerhill Rd PL15 . . 106 A5
Summer La PL3 . . . . . . 129 C8
Summerlands Cl PL7 . . 131 C5
Summerlands Gdns PL7 . . 131 C5
Summerlane Pk PL13 . . 62 D6
Summerleaze Ave EX23 . . 104 D6
Summerleaze Cres EX23 . . 104 D6
Summers Cl PL6 . . . . . . 129 F7
Summers St PL22 . . . . . . 112 C2
Summerville Cross EX39 . . 3 C6
Suncrest Cl PL14 . . . . . . 38 A4
Suncrest Est TR9 . . . . . . 45 E1

Sunderland Cl PL9 . . . . . . 135 A6
Sunderland Rd PL27 . . . . 31 F3
Sun Girt La PL14 . . . . . . 113 C5
Sunningdale TR1 . . . . . . 137 A4
Sunningdale Rd PL12 . . 122 C2
Sunnybank PL12 . . . . . . 98 C8
Sunny Bank
Bodmin PL30 . . . . 48 E8
Liskeard PL14 . . . . 113 A4
Sunnybanks PL12 . . . . . . 53 E4
Sunny Cnr
Goldsithney TR20 . . . . . . 89 F5
Truro TR4 . . . . 81 B7
Sunny Corner La TR19 . . 96 C7
Sunnycroft PL13 . . . . . . 117 C3
Sunny Dene PL5 . . . . . . 123 D1
Sunnyside
Carnkie TR13 . . . . 80 D1
Crantock TR8 . . . . 110 A3
Menheniot PL14 . . . . . . 51 F5
Menheniot PL14 . . . . . . 51 F5
2 Perranporth TR6 . . . . 55 A4
Portscatho TR2 . . . . . . 83 B2
7 Redruth TR15 . . . . . . 140 B4
Sunnyside Mdw PL32 . . 105 D4
Sunnyside Parc TR15 . . 139 C8
Sunnyside Rd PL4 . . . . . . 129 B2
Sunny Terr PL13 . . . . . . 143 B2
Sunnyvale Cl TR16 . . . . 67 C2
Sunnyvale Rd TR16 . . . . 67 D6
Sunrising Est PL13 . . . . 117 D5
Sunset Dr 8 TR13 . . . . 98 C8
Sunset Gdns 9 TR13 . . 98 C8
Sunshine Terr PL19 . . 147 D6
Sun Valley Pk TR9 . . . . 45 E6
Sunway Cl PL19 . . . . . . 147 A6
Sunwell La
Antony PL11 . . . . 65 E4
St John PL11 . . . . 132 A8
Surf View TR7 . . . . 110 A6
Sussex Pl PL1 . . . . . . 148 C2
Sussex Pl PL1 . . . . . . 148 C2
Sussex St PL1 . . . . . . 148 C2
Sussex Terr 8 PL2 . . . . 149 A4
Sutherland Rd PL4 . . . . 149 A4
Sutton Ct PL1 . . . . . . 127 F1
Sutton Mews 22 PL4 . . 149 B2
Sutton Pl PL4 . . . . . . 149 B2
Sutton Rd PL4 . . . . . . 149 B2
Sutton Wharf PL4 . . . . 149 A2
Swaindale Rd 8 PL3 . . 128 E6
Swale Cl PL4 . . . . 129 B6
Swallow Cl EX23 . . . . . . 104 D5
Swallowfield Cl PL24 . . 60 C5
Swallow Ho PL11 . . . . . . 145 C3
Swallows End PL9 . . . . 135 E6
Swan Cl PL10 . . . . 133 A6
Swan Gdns PL7 . . . . . . 130 F5
Swanpool Ct TR11 . . . . 145 A1
Swanpool Hill TR11 . . 145 A2
Swanpool Nature Reserve*
TR11 . . . . 144 F1
Swanpool Rd TR11 . . . . 144 F1
Swanpool St TR11 . . . . 145 C3
SWANVALE 144 F3
Swanvale Rd TR11 . . . . 144 F3
Sweet Briar Cres TR7 . . 111 A4
Swift Gdns PL5 . . . . . . 124 C2
Swinburne Gdns PL5 . . 124 C1
Swingate Cross EX22 . . 13 E8
Sycamore Ave
Plymouth PL4 . . . . . . 149 C2
St Austell PL25 . . . . . . 114 C5
Tavistock PL19 . . . . . . 147 C2
Sycamore Cl
Bodmin PL31 . . . . 109 B4
Polgooth PL26 . . . . 59 A1
Praze-an-Beeble TR14 . . 79 B2
Rock PL27 . . . . 21 E3
Sycamore Dr
Illogan TR15 . . . . 139 D7
Plymouth PL6 . . . . . . 125 C7
Redruth TR15 . . . . . . 140 D5
Torpoint PL11 . . . . . . 127 A3
Sycamore Gdns TR8 . . . . 57 B7
Sycamore Rd PL12 . . . . 122 B3
Sycamore The PL25 . . 114 C4
Sycamore Way PL6 . . . . 125 E6
Sydenham Cross PL19 . . 29 C2
SYDENHAM DAMEREL . . 29 D2
Sydney Cl
Plymouth PL7 . . . . . . 130 E4
St Austell PL25 . . . . . . 114 C3
Sydney Rd
Newquay TR7 . . . . 110 D6
Plymouth PL6 . . . . . . 127 B3
Sydney St PL1 . . . . . . 148 B4
Sylvan Cl PL25 . . . . . . 114 E6
Sylvan Ct PL1 . . . . . . 128 A3
Sylverton Pl 12 TR18 . . 143 C7
Symons Cl
Blackwater TR4 . . . . . . 68 E5
St Austell PL25 . . . . . . 115 A5
Symons Rd PL12 . . . . . . 122 F2
Symons Row PL14 . . . . 37 F3
Symons Terr TR15 . . . . 140 B5
Syra Cl PL30 . . . . 23 B2

T

Tabernacle St TR1 . . . . 137 D4
Tackbear Rd EX22, EX23 . . . 7 E4
Tailyour Rd PL6 . . . . 124 F2
Talbot Gdns PL5 . . . . 127 D7
Talexandra Terr PL15 . . . . 106 D5
Talgos Cl TR16 . . . . 140 E8
TALLAND 62 F2
Talland Ct 图 TR26 . . . . . 141 B5
Talland La PL13 . . . . 62 E2
Talland Rd TR26 . . . . 141 B5
Talland St PL13 . . . . 62 D1
Talmena Ave PL27 . . . . . . 108 A5
TALSKIDDY 45 E8
Talveneth
  Camborne TR14 . . . . 138 F3
  Pendeen TR19 . . . . 75 A1
  Redruth TR15 . . . . 140 C6
Talvenyth Cl TR31 . . . . . . 109 D5
Tamar Ave
  Plymouth PL2 . . . . 127 C5
  Tavistock PL19 . . . . 147 D5
Tamar Bridge PL5 . . . . . . 123 A2
Tamar Bsns Pk PL5 . . . . . . 18 E2
Tamar Cl
  圆 Bere Alston PL20 . . . . 41 B1
  图 Callington PL17 . . . . . 39 F4
Tamar Ho PL1 . . . . 127 E1
Tamarisk Ct PL28 . . . . 31 F7
Tamarisk La TR7 . . . . 111 A4
Tamar Otter & Wildlife Ctr★
  PL15 . . . . 18 B8
Tamar Science Pk PL6 . . . 125 C4
Tamarside Com Coll PL23 123 E1
Tamarside Sp Complex
  PL5 . . . . 123 F2
Tamar St
  Plymouth PL1 . . . . 127 E3
  Saltash PL12 . . . . 123 A2
  Torpoint PL11 . . . . 127 C3
Tamar Terr
  Calstock PL17 . . . . 41 A3
  Horsebridge PL19 . . . . . . 29 C1
  Launceston PL15 . . . . . . 106 D5
  Saltash PL12 . . . . 123 A2
Tamar Valley Ctr★ PL18 . 40 F5
Tamar Valley Discovery
  Trail★ PI20 . . . . 41 C1
Tamar Valley Donkey★
  PL18 . . . . 40 D5
Tamar Valley Sch PL5 . . . 123 B1
Tamar View
  Launceston PL15 . . . . . . 106 D5
  Milton Abbot PL19 . . . . . . 29 C6
  St Dominick PL12 . . . . . . 40 D2
Tamar View Ind Est
  PL12 . . . . 122 D5
Tamar Villas PL19 . . . . . . 135 D7
Tamar Way PL18 . . . . 41 A6
Tamar Wharf PL1 . . . . 127 D3
Tamblin Ave PL14 . . . . 50 E7
Tamerton Ave PL5 . . . . . . 123 D1
Tamerton Cl PL5 . . . . 124 A6
TAMERTON FOLIOT 124 B7
Tamerton Foliot Rd PL6 124 D5
Tamerton Rd PL6 . . . . 121 B2
Tangmere Ave PL5 . . . . . . 123 E5
Tangye Cl TR16 . . . . 67 E5
Tangye Rd TR15 . . . . 139 C6
Tanhouse Rd PL22 . . . . . . 112 C2
Tanwood View PL31 . . . . . 109 C5
Tanyard La 图 PL17 . . . . . 39 E4
Tapson Dr PL9 . . . . 135 A6
Taranto Rd TR15 . . . . 146 D4
Taroveor Rd TR18 . . . . . . 143 E6
Taroveor Terr 图 TR18 . . 143 E5
Tarr PL22 . . . . 112 C4
Tarrandean La PL15 . . . . . . 81 E6
Tarten Cross PL12 . . . . 53 B4
Tate St Ives (Gall)★
  TR26 . . . . 141 B6
Taunton Ave PL5 . . . . 124 B5
Taunton Pl PL5 . . . . 124 B5
Tavern Barn PL23 . . . . . . 116 C5
TAVISTOCK 147 E5
Tavistock Coll PL19 . . . . . 147 A3
Tavistock Com Prim Sch
  PL19 . . . . 147 B4
Tavistock Cross PL20 . . . . 41 C2
Tavistock Hospl PL19 . . . . 147 B5
Tavistock Mus★ PL19 . . . 147 C5
Tavistock Pl PL4 . . . . 149 A3
Tavistock Rd
  Callington PL17 . . . . 39 F4
  Launceston PL15 . . . . . . 106 D5
  Launceston, Stourscombe
    PL15 . . . . 106 E3
  Plymouth, Manadon PL5 . 124 E1
  Plymouth PL6 . . . . 125 B5
  Yelverton PL20 . . . . 42 C3
Tavistock St Peter's CE Jun
  Sch PL19 . . . . 147 D5
Tavy Pl PL4 . . . . 128 F4
Tavy Rd
  Saltash PL12 . . . . 123 A3
  Tavistock PL19 . . . . 147 D5
Tayberry Dr TR16 . . . . . . 140 F1
Tay Gdns PL3 . . . . 129 D7
Taylor Cl PL12 . . . . 122 C4
Taylor Rd PL12 . . . . 122 C4
Taylor's Cross EX23 . . . . . 5 B7

Taylor Sq PL19 . . . . 147 B6
Teachers Cl PL9 . . . . 135 F6
Teats Hill Flats PL4 . . . . . 149 B1
Teats Hill Rd PL4 . . . . 149 B1
Tedder Rd ⁴ PL26 . . . . . . 59 D7
Tees Cl PL3 . . . . 129 C7
Teetotal St TR26 . . . . 141 C6
Tehidy Cl TR14 . . . . 138 F7
Tehidy Copse TR14 . . . . . . 67 B4
Tehidy Country Park★
  TR14 . . . . 67 B4
Tehidy Gdns TR14 . . . . . . 138 F7
Tehidy Rd
  Camborne TR14 . . . . 138 D4
  Tywardreath PL24 . . . . . . 60 D5
Tehidy Terr TR11 . . . . 145 A6
Teign Rd PL3 . . . . 129 B6
Telcarne Cl TR27 . . . . 78 B6
Telegraph Hill TR16 . . . . . 68 E1
Telegraph Rd TR16 . . . . . . 68 D1
Telegraph Wharf PL1 . . . . 134 A8
Telephone La PL26 . . . . . . 59 C8
Telford Cres PL5 . . . . 123 F2
Temeraire Rd PL5 . . . . . . 124 D2
TEMPLE 36 B8
Tenacres La PL14 . . . . 38 E4
Tenby Rd PL5 . . . . 123 C1
TENCREEK 63 A3
Tencreek Ave TR18 . . . . . 143 E5
Tenderah Ct TR13 . . . . . . 146 C6
Tenderah Rd TR13 . . . . . . 146 C6
Tennyson Gdns PL5 . . . . . 124 B1
Tern Gdns PL7 . . . . 130 F5
Terrace The
  Chacewater TR4 . . . . 68 F3
  Crafthole PL11 . . . . 65 B5
  Dobwalls PL14 . . . . 50 D7
  Downderry PL11 . . . . 64 C5
  East Portholland PL26 . . . 84 E5
  Harrowbarrow PL17 . . . . . 40 D5
  Penryn TR10 . . . . 144 C7
  Pentewan PL26 . . . . 73 D6
  Port Isaac PL29 . . . . 22 E7
  Portwrinkle PL11 . . . . . . 65 A4
  Rock PL27 . . . . 21 D2
  St Ives TR26 . . . . 141 B5
  Yeolmbridge PL15 . . . . . . 18 E6
Terra Nova Gn PL2 . . . . . 128 B5
TERRAS 58 A4
Terras Hill PL22 . . . . 112 C3
Terras Rd PL26 . . . . 58 A4
TETCOTT 13 C7
Tethadene PL30 . . . . 23 E7
Tewington Pl PL25 . . . . . . 114 B4
Tewkesbury Cl PL2 . . . . . . 128 B4
Teyla Tor Rd TR26 . . . . . . 141 D1
Thackeray Gdns PL5 . . . . . 124 B1
Thames Gdns PL3 . . . . . . 129 D5
Thanckes Cl PL11 . . . . 127 A3
Thanckes Dr PL11 . . . . . . 127 A4
Theatre Ope PL1 . . . . 127 F1
Theatre Royal Plymouth
  PL1 . . . . 148 C2
THE BEACON 10 F6
Therlow Rd PL3 . . . . 129 B6
Thetford Gdns PL6 . . . . . 129 D8
Theydon Rd TR11 . . . . . . 144 F3
Third Ave
  Plymouth, Billacombe
    PL9 . . . . 130 A1
  Plymouth, Camels Head
    PL2 . . . . 127 E7
  Plymouth, Stoke PL1 . . . . 128 A2
Thirlmere Gdns PL6 . . . . . 124 F4
Thistle Cl PL5 . . . . 125 E7
Thomas Bullock Cl PL18 . . 48 C2
Thomas Johnson Ct ⁶
  TR1 . . . . 137 C8
Thomas St ⁴ TR13 . . . . . 98 C8
Thomas Terr ⁵ TR13 . . . . 98 C8
Thornberry Terr TR18 . . . 143 F6
Thornbury Park Ave PL3 128 D6
Thornbury Rd PL6 . . . . . . 125 E4
Thorn Cl PL15 . . . . 26 C7
Thorndon Cross EX22 . . . . . 8 F5
Thorne Cross EX23 . . . . . . 4 F2
THORNE MOOR 19 F8
Thornhill Rd PL3 . . . . 128 E6
Thornhill Way PL3 . . . . . . 128 E6
Thorn La PL12 . . . . 122 C3
Thorn Moor Cross PL15 . . 19 F7
Thornpark Rd PL15 . . . . . 114 E5
Thorn Pk PL3 . . . . 128 E5
Thorn Terr PL14 . . . . 113 B5
Thornton Ave PL4 . . . . . . 149 B4
Thornton Cl PL26 . . . . 46 F3
Thornville Terr PL9 . . . . . 135 C7
Thornwell La PL12 . . . . . . 53 E2
Thornyville Cl PL9 . . . . . . 135 C8
Thornyville Dr PL9 . . . . . . 135 D8
Thornyville Villas PL9 . . . 135 C8
Three Bridges Specl Sch ①
  TR10 . . . . 144 C8
THREE BURROWS 68 F5
Three Corners Cl PL32 . . . 105 B2
Three Cross TR13 . . . . 91 B3
THREE HAMMERS 17 C6
Three Holes Cross PL27 . . 34 A8
THREEMILESTONE 69 D4
Threemilestone Ind Est
  TR4 . . . . 69 C3
Threemilestone Prim Sch
  TR3 . . . . 69 D3
Threemilestone Ret Pk
  TR3 . . . . 69 C4
THREEWATERS 34 C1
THURDON 5 D5
Thurlestone Wlk PL6 . . . . 129 D8

Tiddy Brook Rd
  Plymouth PL19 . . . . 147 E2
  Whitchurch PL19 . . . . . . 147 E2
Tiddy Cl
  St Germans PL12 . . . . . . 65 B8
  Tavistock PL19 . . . . 147 B3
TIDEFORD 52 F2
Tideford Cross La PL12 . . . 52 F3
Tideford Dr
  Landrake PL12 . . . . 53 A2
  St Germans PL12 . . . . . . 65 B8
Tideford Rd PL12 . . . . 53 C3
Tidemill Ho TR11 . . . . . . 145 C3
Tides Reach TR7 . . . . 111 B7
Tillard Cl PL7 . . . . 131 C5
Tillie St ⁵ PL17 . . . . 39 E4
Tilly Cl PL9 . . . . 135 F4
Timber Cl PL25 . . . . 114 B4
Tincombe PL12 . . . . 122 C2
Tincroft Rd TR15 . . . . 139 B4
Tin La PL4 . . . . 149 A2
Tinners Dr PL27 . . . . 21 D6
Tinners Way
  Callington PL17 . . . . 39 F5
  New Polzeath PL27 . . . . . 21 D6
  ⑯ St Ives TR26 . . . . . . 77 A6
Tinners Wlk TR11 . . . . . . 145 D3
Tinney Dr TR1 . . . . 137 F5
Tinside Lido PL1 . . . . 148 C1
TINTAGEL 14 D6
Tintagel Castle★ PL34 . . . 14 B8
Tintagel Cres PL12 . . . . . 128 C8
Tintagel Hts PL34 . . . . . . 14 D6
Tintagel Old Post Office★
  PL34 . . . . 14 C7
Tintagel Prim Sch PL34 . . 14 C8
Tintagel Rd PL35 . . . . 9 F1
Tintagel Terr PL20 . . . . . . 22 C7
Tintagel Toy Mus★ PL34 . 14 C7
Tintagel Visitor Ctr★
  PL34 . . . . 14 C6
Tintern Ave PL4 . . . . 149 C2
Tiny Mdws
  Launceston PL15 . . . . . . 18 E1
  South Petherwin PL15 . . . 27 F8
Tipple Cross PL15 . . . . 19 C6
Tithe Rd PL7 . . . . 130 B7
TITSON 7 D4
Tiverton Cl PL6 . . . . 125 B8
Tobruk Rd PL12 . . . . 122 E3
Toby Way TR7 . . . . 110 D7
Toddington Lea PL35 . . . . . 9 E5
TODPOOL 68 E5
TOLBOROUGH 25 E4
TOLCARNE
  Camborne 79 D5
  Newlyn 143 C3
Tolcarne Cl PL25 . . . . 114 E3
Tolcarne Mews TR7 . . . . . 110 F6
Tolcarne Rd
  Camborne TR14 . . . . 79 D5
  Newquay TR7 . . . . 110 F6
  St Day TR16 . . . . 68 D1
Tolcarne St TR14 . . . . 138 D2
Tolcarne Terr TR18 . . . . . 143 C3
Tolcrows Ct TR7 . . . . 111 C7
TOLDISH 45 F2
Tolgarrick Rd TR14 . . . . . 138 E5
Tolgus Hill TR15 . . . . 140 A5
Tolgus Mount TR15 . . . . . 139 E8
Tolgus Pl TR15 . . . . 140 A6
Tolgus Tin★ TR16 . . . . 67 F5
Tolgus Vean TR15 . . . . . . 140 A5
Tolgus Wartha TR15 . . . . 140 A6
Tolgate Cl PL14 . . . . 113 B4
Tollox Pl PL3 . . . . 129 B4
Tollyfrank Hill TR2 . . . . . . 83 F6
Tolpedn Flats TR26 . . . . . 141 E2
Tolponds Rd PL13 . . . . 91 A1
Tolroy Rd PL27 . . . . 142 D1
TOLSKITHY 139 E7
Tolskithy La TR15 . . . . . . 139 E6
Tolticken Hill TR16 . . . . . . 67 E6
Toltuff Cres TR18 . . . . . . 143 C4
Toltuff Rd TR18 . . . . 143 C4
TOLVADDON 138 F6
TOLVADDON DOWNS 139 A7
Tolvaddon Energy Pk
  TR14 . . . . 138 F7
Tolvaddon Rd TR15 . . . . . 139 A5
Tolvan Cross TR12 . . . . . . 92 C2
Tolver Pl TR18 . . . . 143 E6
Tolver Rd TR18 . . . . 143 E6
Tolverth Terr PL30 . . . . . . 88 F6
Tolview Terr TR27 . . . . . . 142 B4
Tom Lyon Rd PL14 . . . . . . 113 E5
Tom Nicolls Cl ⁷ TR14 . . 38 A3
Top Hill TR2 . . . . 57 E1
Top of the Town Cytd
  PL12 . . . . 122 F2
Top Rd PL11 . . . . 64 C5
Torbridge Cl PL12 . . . . . . 122 D2
Torbridge Rd
  ⑥ Horrabridge PL20 . . . 42 C4
  Plymouth PL7 . . . . 130 E6
Torbryan Cl PL6 . . . . 129 E8
Tor Cl
  Plymouth, Hartley PL3 . . 128 E7
  Porthleven PL13 . . . . 91 B1
Tor Cres PL3 . . . . 128 E7
Tor La PL12 . . . . 122 B1
Torland Rd PL3 . . . . 128 E7
Torleven Rd TR13 . . . . 91 B2
TORPOINT 127 C3
Torpoint Com Sch PL11 . . 127 A4
Torpoint Inf Sch PL11 . . . 127 B3
Tor Rd
  Newquay TR7 . . . . 110 E6

Tor Rd continued
  Plymouth PL3 . . . . 128 E7
Torridge Cl PL7 . . . . 131 A6
Torridge Rd PL7 . . . . 130 F6
Torridge Way PL3 . . . . . . 129 C5
Torr La PL3 . . . . 128 E7
Torr Rd PL3 . . . . 128 E7
Torr View Ave PL3 . . . . . . 128 D7
Tors View Cl PL17 . . . . 39 F4
Torver Cl PL6 . . . . 125 D2
Tor View
  Bugle PL26 . . . . 47 C2
  Camelford PL32 . . . . 105 C2
  ⑦ Horrabridge PL20 . . . . 42 C4
  Tregadillett PL15 . . . . . . 18 C2
Torwood Cl PL31 . . . . 109 D4
Tory Brook Ave PL7 . . . . . 130 E6
Tory Brook Ct PL7 . . . . . . 130 E6
Tory Way PL7 . . . . 130 D6
TOSBERRY 3 B8
Tosberry Cross EX39 . . . . . 3 B8
Tothill Ave PL4 . . . . 149 B3
Tothill Rd PL4 . . . . 149 B3
Totnes Cl PL7 . . . . 131 B4
Tovey Cres PL5 . . . . 124 D2
Towan Blystra Rd TR7 . . . 111 A5
TOWAN CROSS 68 B7
Towan Cross TR8 . . . . 31 E8
Towan Rd
  Pentewan PL26 . . . . 73 D8
  Porthtowan TR4 . . . . 68 A7
Towans The PL28 . . . . 20 D1
TOWEDNACK 76 E5
Towednack Rd TR26 . . . . . 77 A6
Tower Cl
  Pelynt PL13 . . . . 62 D6
  Sennen TR19 . . . . 96 B6
Tower Ct PL12 . . . . 122 C2
Towerfield Dr PL6 . . . . . . 125 C8
Tower Hill
  Looe PL13 . . . . 117 D3
  Wadebridge PL27 . . . . . . 108 E5
Tower Hill Rd PL15 . . . . . . 13 F1
Tower Mdws TR19 . . . . . . 97 A6
Tower Park Est PL13 . . . . 62 D6
Tower Park Rd PL13 . . . . . 62 C6
Tower Pk
  Fowey PL23 . . . . 116 B3
  Lanivet PL30 . . . . 47 E7
  Pelynt PL13 . . . . 62 D6
Tower Rd
  Newquay TR7 . . . . 110 D6
  St Erme TR4 . . . . 70 D8
Towers Cl PL6 . . . . 125 F2
Tower St PL15 . . . . 106 C6
Tower View PL12 . . . . 122 D1
Town Arms Pas PL31 . . . . 109 E5
Town End PL31 . . . . 109 C5
Town Farm TR15 . . . . 140 C3
Town Farm Cl ⑧ PL20 . . . 42 C4
Townfield TR15 . . . . 139 C6
Town Hall TR5 . . . . 54 D1
TOWNLAKE 29 C1
Town Mill Gdns PL19 . . . . 147 C6
Town Mills Flats PL15 . . . 106 B7
Town Quay TR11 . . . . 145 D4
Townsend
  Polruan PL23 . . . . 116 D2
  ⑬ Stratton EX23 . . . . . . 4 E1
TOWNSHEND 90 D7
Townshend Ave PL2 . . . . . 127 E5
Townswell Cl PL12 . . . . . . 53 E2
Townswell La PL12 . . . . . . 53 E2
TRABOE 100 E4
Traboe Cross TR12 . . . . . 100 D3
Tracey Ct PL1 . . . . 148 B3
Trafalgar Fields TR20 . . . . 88 B7
Trafalgar Cl PL5 . . . . 127 D8
Trafalgar Pl ④ PL1 . . . . . 149 A4
Trafalgar Pl ③ PL1 . . . . . 127 F3
Trafalgar Place La PL1 . . . 127 F3
Trafalgar Sq TR1 . . . . 137 D4
Trafalgar St PL4 . . . . 149 A3
Traine Brake PL9 . . . . 136 C1
Traine Rd PL9 . . . . 136 B3
Traly Cl EX23 . . . . 104 F4
TRAMAGENNA 105 A1
Tram La TR16 . . . . 140 E1
Tramway Rd PL6 . . . . 125 E7
TRANNACK 91 D5
Trannack Mill Ind Est
  TR13 . . . . 91 E5
Trannack Prim Sch TR13 . 91 E5
Trannack Terr TR13 . . . . . 143 E7
Tranquil La PL31 . . . . 109 C5
Transit Way PL5 . . . . 124 C3
Trasdees Orch ⑩ PL17 . . 39 F4
Travers Cl PL14 . . . . 113 A6
Treago Gdns PL25 . . . . . . 125 C8
TREAL 103 A6
Trease TR19 . . . . 75 A1
Treassowe Rd TR18 . . . . . 143 E6
Treassowe Riding TR20 . . 88 F8
TREATH 93 C1
TREATOR 107 A5
Treator Cotts PL28 . . . . . 107 A5
Trebah Gdns★ TR11 . . . . . 93 C2
Treban Rd TR18 . . . . 143 C4
TREBARBER 44 F5
TREBARTHA 27 A4
Trebartha Cl PL17 . . . . 39 E3
Trebartha Rd TR1 . . . . . . 137 F5
Trebarthen Terr TR4 . . . . . 55 D5
Trebarva Cl TR15 . . . . . . 140 A6
Trebarvah Cl TR20 . . . . . . 89 E4
Trebarvah La TR20 . . . . . . 89 E4
Trebarvah Rd TR11 . . . . . . 92 E4
TREBARWITH 14 C5

Trebarwith Cres TR7 . . . . 110 E6
Trebarwith Rd PL33 . . . . . 14 E4
TREBEATH 17 F6
Treberran Gdns TR14 . . . . 138 F6
TREBETHERICK 21 D4
Treboul Cross PL12 . . . . . . 64 F8
Treboul Way PL12 . . . . 65 B8
TREBUDANNON 45 C4
TREBULLETT 28 A5
Treburdon Dr PL26 . . . . . . 46 F3
TREBURGETT 23 D6
Treburgie Water PL14 . . . . 50 D7
TREBURLEY 28 C4
Treburley Cl PL15 . . . . 28 C4
Treburley Ind Est PL15 . . . 28 C4
TREBURRICK 31 D5
TREBYAN 48 C6
Trebyan Bsns Pk PL30 . . . 48 C6
Trebyhan Parc TR3 . . . . . . 80 F3
Treby Rd PL7 . . . . 130 F4
Trecarn Cl PL15 . . . . 106 B5
Trecarne
  Falmouth TR11 . . . . 144 E5
  Tremar PL14 . . . . 38 A3
Trecarne Cl
  Polgooth PL26 . . . . 59 A1
  St Austell PL25 . . . . 115 B5
  Truro TR1 . . . . 137 E5
Trecarne Gdns PL33 . . . . . 14 E3
Trecarne View PL14 . . . . . 37 F3
Trecarrack Rd TR14 . . . . . 138 F3
Trecarrell PL15 . . . . 106 C4
Trecarrell Cl PL15 . . . . . . 106 C4
Trecerus Ind Est PL28 . . . 107 B4
Treclago View PL32 . . . . . 105 C2
TRECROGO 27 E7
Tredanek Cl PL31 . . . . . . 109 B5
Tredarrup Cross PL15 . . . . 11 A1
Tredarvah Dr TR18 . . . . . 143 C5
Tredarvah Rd TR18 . . . . . 143 C5
TREDAVOE 143 A2
Tredavoe La TR18 . . . . . . 143 B1
Tredenham Cl ④ PL24 . . . 60 C4
Tredenham Rd TR2 . . . . . . 95 B6
TREDETHY 34 F6
Tredethy Rd PL30 . . . . 34 F6
TREDINNICK
  Looe 63 A8
  Penzance 76 A1
  St Issey 32 D3
Tredinnick La PL12 . . . . . . 53 B2
Tredinnick Lane-End
  PL13 . . . . 64 A8
Tredinnick Way ⑧ TR6 . . . 55 A4
Tredinnick Wood Cl
  TR13 . . . . 146 D8
Tredour Rd TR7 . . . . 110 E4
Tredova Cres TR11 . . . . . 145 B2
TREDOWN 2 E5
Tredragon Cl TR8 . . . . 31 C2
Tredragon Rd TR8 . . . . . . 31 C2
Tredrea Gdns TR3 . . . . 81 D5
Tredrea La TR27 . . . . 77 E2
Tredrea Manor TR3 . . . . . . 81 D5
TREDRIZZICK 21 F3
Tredruston Rd PL27 . . . . . 33 B6
Tredydan Rd PL15 . . . . . . 106 B6
Tredynas Rd PL11 . . . . . . 145 D3
Tredyson Pl TR11 . . . . . . 145 A3
Tre-el-Verne Cl TR1 . . . . . 137 A4
TREEN
  Porthcurno 96 F3
  Zennor 75 F4
Treen Cotts TR26 . . . . 75 F4
Treen Flats TR14 . . . . 138 F3
Treen Hill TR19 . . . . 96 F4
TREESMILL 60 D6
Treetop Cl PL12 . . . . 122 D4
Treetops Hill PL13 . . . . . . 117 A3
Treeve La TR27 . . . . 78 C4
Treeve Lane Ind Est TR27 . 78 C6
TREFANNY HILL 62 D8
Treffry Ct TR7 . . . . 110 D6
Treffry Rd TR1 . . . . 137 D3
Treffry Rd TR1 . . . . 137 E2
Treffry Way ⑰ PL26 . . . . 60 B4
Trefinnick Rd PL17 . . . . . . 39 B8
Trefleur Cl ③ PL35 . . . . . . 9 C1
Trefloyd Cl PL17 . . . . 39 E6
TREFOFDA 24 A8
Treforda Rd TR7 . . . . 110 F4
Treforest Rd PL27 . . . . . . 108 A6
Treforthlan ⑦ TR16 . . . . . 67 E4
Treforthlan Cl ⑥ TR16 . . . 67 E4
TREFREW 105 D6
Trefrew Rd PL32 . . . . 105 D5
TREFRIZE 27 E3
Trefusis Cl TR11 . . . . 137 F5
Trefusis Ct TR11 . . . . 145 A6
Trefusis Gdns PL3 . . . . . . 129 A4
Trefusis Rd
  Falmouth TR11 . . . . 144 E2
  Flushing TR11 . . . . 145 C6
  Redruth TR15 . . . . 140 C4
Trefusis Terr
  Millbrook PL10 . . . . 132 C4
  Redruth TR15 . . . . 140 C5
TREGADILLETT 18 C2
Tregadillett Prim Sch
  PL15 . . . . 18 C2
Tregaer TR11 . . . . 145 C3
Tregainlands Pk PL30 . . . . 34 F3
TREGAJORRAN 139 D4
Tregalister Gdns PL12 . . . 65 B8
Tregaller La PL15 . . . . 18 E1
TREGAMERE 45 F7

Treganoon Rd TR15 140 D7
Tregargus View PL26 58 B4
TREGARLAND 63 C8
TREGARLANDBRIDGE 63 B8
Tregarland Cl
Camborne TR14 138 E2
Coad's Green PL15 27 D4
Tregarne Terr PL25 114 C4
Tregarrian Rd TR14 138 F7
Tregarrick PL13 117 B3
Tregarrick Cl TR13 146 B7
Tregarrick Ct PL13 117 B3
Tregarrick La PL13 62 D6
TREGARRICK MILL 62 D7
Tregarrick Rd PL26 46 F3
Tregarrick Way PL13 62 D6
Tregarth 12 PL26 59 D7
Tregartha Way PL14 113 D6
Tregarthen 2 TR26 141 A5
Tregarth Pl TR18 143 C4
Tregaskes Parc EX23 104 F5
Tregassack Rd TR20 88 F7
Tregassick Rd TR2 83 B1
TREGASWITH 45 C5
TREGATTA 14 C6
TREGAVARRAS 85 A5
Tregavarras Row PL26 85 A5
Tregavethan View TR3 69 C4
Tregay La PL14 113 C7
Tregeagle Rd PL26 47 A2
Tregea Hill TR16 67 C6
Tregear Cl TR12 99 D6
TREGEARE 17 D5
Tregear Gdns TR1 137 C4
Tregease Rd TR5 54 C1
Tregea Terr TR16 67 C6
Tregellas Rd TR12 99 B1
Tregellas Tapastry The★ 12
TR15 140 B4
Tregellast Cl TR12 101 D4
Tregellast Parc TR12 101 D4
Tregellast Rd TR12 101 D3
TREGELLIST 22 E4
Tregembo Hill TR20 90 A7
Tregender La TR20 89 B8
Tregender Rd TR20 89 B8
Tregenna Cl
Plymouth PL7 131 C4
Wainhouse Corner EX23 10 F6
Tregenna Ct
Camborne TR14 138 C2
Falmouth TR11 145 C3
Tregenna Fields TR14 138 C2
Tregenna Hill 16 TR26 141 B5
Tregenna La TR14 138 C2
Tregenna Parc TR26 141 C3
Tregenna Pl 4 TR26 141 B5
Tregenna Rd PL30 35 C8
Tregenna Terr TR26 141 B5
Tregenver Rd TR11 144 F4
Tregenver Terr TR11 144 F4
Tregenver Villas TR11 144 F4
TREGESEAL 86 F7
Tregeseal Hill TR19 86 F7
Tregeseal Row TR19 86 F6
Tregeseal Terr TR19 86 F6
TREGEW 145 B8
Tregew Cl TR11 145 B7
Tregew Rd
Flushing TR11 145 B8
Penryn TR10, TR11 81 F2
Treggodick Cotts TR20 143 A8
Tregian Cl TR1 137 F5
Tregidden Hill TR12 100 F5
Tregie TR18 143 B3
TREGISKEY 73 C5
Tregiskey Cotts PL26 73 C5
Tregisky La TR12 101 C1
Treglenwith Rd TR14 138 C4
Treglisson Rural Workshops
TR27 78 C3
Treglyn Cl TR18 143 B1
Treglyn Farm Cotts PL27 22 B3
Tregoddick Cl TR20 88 B7
Tregolds La PL28 31 F7
TREGOLE 6 E1
TREGOLLS 80 F3
Tregolls Cl TR1 137 E5
Tregolls Prim Sch TR1 137 F5
Tregolls Rd TR1 137 E5
TREGONCE 107 F2
TREGONETHA 46 C6
Tregoney Hill PL26 73 C3
Tregongeeves La PL26 59 A2
TREGONHAWKE 132 B4
Tregonhay PL14 38 C7
Tregonhayne Ct TR2 72 A4
Tregoniggie Ind Est
TR11 144 D4
Tregoning Rd PL11 126 F2
Tregonissey Cl PL25 114 D5
Tregonissey Rd PL25 114 E5
Tregonissy La End PL25 114 E6
TREGONNA 32 C7
Tregonning Cl TR13 90 E3
Tregonning Ct 8 TR6 55 A5
Tregonning Parc 9
TR12 101 C4
Tregonning Rd TR3 80 F3
Tregonning Terr TR13 90 F5
Tregonning View 17 TR13 98 C8
TREGONY 71 F4
Tregony Com Prim Sch
TR2 71 F4
Tregony Hill TR2 71 F3
Tregony Ind Est TR2 71 E3
Tregony Rd TR2 71 D6
TREGOODWELL 105 F4
TREGORRICK 114 D1
Tregorrick Pk (St Austell RFC) PL26 114 E1
Tregorrick Rd PL26 114 E1
Tregos Rd TR26 141 C2
TREGOSS 46 D3
Tregoss Rd TR7 110 F6
Tregothnan Rd
Falmouth TR11 145 A5
Truro TR1 137 E3
Tregowris Court Cotts
TR12 101 B5
Tregrea TR14 138 E1
TREGREENWELL 23 F7
Tregrehan Gdns★ PL24 115 E6
TREGREHAN MILLS 115 D6
Treguddock Dr PL27 108 D5
Tregullan TR15 139 C8
Tregullan View PL31 109 D3
Tregullow Rd TR11 144 F5
Tregundy Cl 21 TR6 55 A5
Tregundy Ct 20 TR6 55 A5
Tregundy La TR6 55 A5
Tregundy Rd TR6 55 A5
TREGUNE 10 F4
TREGUNNA 33 B8
Tregunna Cl TR13 91 B1
Tregunnel Hill TR7 110 D4
Tregunnick La PL11 64 B6
Tregunnus La PL11 64 D5
Tregunter Mews TR11 145 D3
Tregurra La TR1 137 E6
TREGURRIAN 44 E8
Tregurrian Hill TR8 44 D8
Tregurtha Farm Cotts
TR17 89 D6
Tregurtha View TR20 89 E5
Tregurthen Cl TR14 138 C2
Tregurthen Rd TR14 138 C2
TREGUSTICK 33 D1
Treguth Cl TR8 43 B1
Tregwary Rd TR26 141 A5
Tregye Rd TR3 82 A7
Trehaddle TR4 81 B7
TREHAN 122 A1
Trehane Rd TR14 138 B3
Trehannick Cl PL30 23 E7
Trehaverne Cl TR1 137 C5
Trehaverne La TR1 137 C5
Trehaverne Terr 3 TR1 137 C5
Trehaverne Vean TR1 137 C5
Trehawke La PL14 38 C1
Trehayes Mdw TR27 77 E2
Trehayes Parc TR27 142 E7
Trehaze-Na Cl PL32 10 C3
Treheath Rd PL14 50 E7
Trehill Cross PL12 40 C2
Trehill La PL10 64 B2
TREHUNIST 52 C6
Trehunsey Cl TR11 93 E2
Trehurst TR18 143 D4
Trekeen Rd TR10 144 B8
TREKEIVESTEPS 37 E4
TREKENNER 28 B5
Trekenner Prim Sch PL15 28 C5
TREKENNING 45 D5
Trekenning Rd TR9 45 D5
Trekestle Pk PL15 18 C2
TREKNOW 14 C5
Trekye Cl TR16 80 B5
Trelake La PL34 14 D5
Trelake Rd PL25 114 B4
TRELAN 100 E1
Trelan TR14 138 F3
Trelander Barton TR1 137 E5
Trelander E TR1 137 F4
Trelander Highway TR1 137 E4
Trelander N TR1 137 F4
Trelander S TR1 137 F4
Trelander Vean TR1 137 F4
Trelantis PL28 20 E1
Trelantis Est PL28 31 F8
TRELASH 10 F1
Trelaske La PL13 62 F4
Trelavour Prazey PL26 58 B8
Trelavour Rd PL26 58 C8
Trelavour Sq PL26 58 C8
Trelawne Cl 10 TR3 81 F7
Trelawne Cottage Gdns
PL13 62 E4
Trelawne Gdns PL13 62 E5
Trelawne Rd TR3 81 F7
Trelawney Apartments
TR7 110 F6
Trelawney Ave
Falmouth TR11 145 B3
Plymouth PL5 123 D1
Poughill EX23 4 C3
Redruth TR15 140 E7
St Ives TR26 141 A5
Trelawney Cl
Bodmin PL31 109 C4
Maenporth TR11 93 E3
Torpoint PL11 126 E3
Warbstow Cross PL15 11 B1
Trelawney Cotts PL15 106 D5
Trelawney Ct PL27 21 E3
Trelawney Est
Madron TR20 143 A8
Ponsanooth TR4 81 B7
Trelawney Gdns PL14 38 D4
Trelawney Hts 19 PL17 39 F4
Trelawney Parc
St Columb Major TR9 45 D5
Warbstow Cross PL15 11 B1
Trelawney Pl
Hayle TR27 142 C6
Penryn TR10 144 C8
Trelawney Pl *continued*
Plymouth PL5 123 D1
Trelawney Rd
Bodmin PL31 109 C3
Callington PL17 39 F4
Camborne TR14 138 D3
Chacewater TR4 69 A3
Helston TR13 146 C5
Newquay TR7 110 E5
Padstow PL28 107 D4
Plymouth PL3 128 D5
Ponsanooth TR3 81 B4
Saltash PL12 122 E2
St Austell PL25 114 E5
St Ives TR26 141 A5
St Mawes TR2 95 A6
Truro TR1 137 B5
Trelawney Rise
18 Callington PL17 39 F4
Torpoint PL11 126 E3
Trelawney Terr
Cury TR12 99 B4
Looe PL13 117 C4
Trelawney Way
Hayle TR27 142 C6
Torpoint PL11 126 E3
Trelawny Ct TR14 138 C3
Trelawny Rd
Falmouth TR11 145 B4
Menheniot PL14 52 A6
Plymouth PL7 130 C6
St Agnes TR5 54 C1
Tavistock PL19 147 C6
Treleaver Way TR1 69 F3
Trelee Cl TR27 142 E7
TRELEIGH 140 D8
Treleigh Ave TR15 140 B6
Treleigh Ind Est TR16 140 C7
Treleigh Prim Sch TR16 140 C8
Treleigh Terr TR15 140 A5
Trelevan Cl PL25 114 C3
Treleven Rd EX23 104 F4
TRELEW 82 B2
Treliddon La PL11 64 C5
Treliever Cross TR10 81 C1
Treliever Rd
Mabe Burnthouse TR10 81 C1
Penryn TR10 144 B8
TRELIGGA 14 C3
Treligga Downs Rd PL33 14 D2
TRELIGHTS 22 C6
Trelil Cvn Site TR13 146 E7
TRELILL 23 C5
Trelil La TR11 144 C2
Trelindon PL15 27 E8
Trelinnoe Cl PL15 27 E8
Trelinnoe Gdns PL15 27 E8
Treliske Ind Est TR1 69 E4
Treliske La TR1, TR4 69 F4
Treliske Rd TR15 140 D6
Trelispen Park Dr PL26 85 C5
Trelispen Pk PL26 85 C5
Trelissick Fields TR27 142 B3
Trelissick Gdns PL17 39 E3
Trelissick Gdns★ TR3 82 D6
Trelissick Rd
Falmouth TR11 144 F5
Hayle TR27 142 B3
Trelissick Woodland Wlk★
TR3 82 D6
TRELIVER 46 E8
Treloan La TR2 83 B1
Treloar Terr PL15 106 B6
Treloggan Ind Est TR7 111 B4
Treloggan La TR7 111 A5
Treloggan Rd TR7 111 A4
Trelorrin Gdns PL3 128 E5
Trelowarren★ TR12 99 F6
Trelowarren Ct 13 PL17 39 E4
Trelowarren St TR14 138 D3
Treloweck TR14 79 A4
Treloweth Cl
Plymouth PL2 128 D8
St Erth TR27 77 E2
Treloweth Com Prim Sch
TR15 139 D6
Treloweth Gdns TR15 139 C6
Treloweth La TR27 77 E2
Treloweth Rd TR15 139 C6
Treloweth Terr TR15 139 B7
Treloweth Way TR15 139 C7
Trelowth Rd PL26 59 A1
Treloyhan Cl TR26 141 C3
Treloyhan Park Rd TR26 141 C3
Trelyn PL27 21 E3
Trelyn Rd TR12 101 D4
TRELYON 141 B3
Trelyon Ave TR26 141 C4
Trelyon Cl TR19 97 B6
Tremabe La PL14 50 E7
Tremabe Pk PL14 50 E7
Tremadart Cl PL14 51 A1
Tremadart Farm Barns
PL14 51 A1
Tremaddock Cotts PL14 36 F3
Tremaddock Council Hos
PL14 36 F3
TREMAIL 16 B5
Tremaine Cl TR18 143 C7
Tremalic PL13 117 B3
Tremall Parc TR3 80 F3
Tremanor Way TR11 144 D5
TREMAR 38 A2
Tremar Cl PL14 38 A2
Tremar La
St Cleer PL14 37 F3
Tremar PL14 38 A3
Tremarle Home Pk TR14 138 F5
Tremarne Cl TR3 82 C5
Tremar Rd TR26 77 A7
Tremarren Rd PL27 108 B5
TREMATON 53 E2
Trematon Cl PL11 126 E4
Trematon Terr PL4 128 E4
TREMAYNE 79 C2
Tremayne Cl TR3 81 F6
Tremayne Ho PL31 109 B4
Tremayne Pk TR14 138 F2
Tremayne Rd
Carharrack TR16 80 F8
St Austell PL25 114 E4
Truro TR1 137 C5
Tremayne Rise PL19 147 B5
Tremayne Terr PL13 63 F8
Trembath Cres TR7 110 E5
Trembear Rd PL25 114 A4
Trembel Rd TR12 99 B2
Trembrase TR19 96 C7
TREMBRAZE 113 D8
Tremeadow Terr
Hayle TR27 142 B4
Liskeard PL14 113 D7
Tremear Gn 6 TR9 45 E2
Tremearne Rd 16 TR13 98 C8
Tremeddan Ct 2 PL14 113 C6
Tremeddan La PL14 113 C6
Tremeddan Terr PL14 113 B4
Tremeer La PL30 23 E3
Tremellin La TR27 77 F1
Tremena Gdns PL25 114 C4
Tremena Rd PL25 114 C4
Tremenheere Ave TR13 146 D8
Tremenheere Rd TR18 143 E6
Tremenva Ct 1 TR13 146 C5
TREMETHICK CROSS 88 A5
Tremewan 1 PL25 59 A3
Tremodrett Rd PL26 46 F3
Tremoh Ct TR2 71 C6
TREMOLLETT 27 D2
Tremollett Cotts PL17 28 B1
TREMORE 47 C7
Tremore Rd TR15 140 D6
Tremorva TR27 142 C6
Tremorvah Barton TR1 137 E5
Tremorvah Cres TR1 137 E5
Tremorvah Ct
Falmouth TR11 144 F1
Truro TR1 137 E5
Tremorvah Pk TR11 144 F1
Tremorvah Wood La
TR1 137 E5
Tremough Barton Cotts
TR10 81 C1
Tremoughdale TR10 144 B8
Trenale La PL34 14 D7
Trenalt Terr TR1 137 B5
TRENANCE
Newquay 110 E5
Roche 46 F7
St Issey 32 D5
Tregurrian 31 C2
Trenance Ave TR7 110 F5
Trenance Cl TR13 146 B7
Trenance Ct TR7 110 E4
Trenance Dr PL19 30 A3
Trenance Hill PL25 114 A5
Trenance Inf Sch TR7 110 E5
Trenance La
3 Mullion TR12 99 A1
Newquay TR7 110 E4
Trenance Leisure Park & Gdns★ TR7 111 A5
Trenance Pl PL25 114 B4
Trenance Rd
Camborne TR14 138 E4
Newquay TR7 110 E5
St Austell PL25 114 B4
TRENANT 37 C3
Trenant TR16 68 D1
Trenant Cl PL27 21 E5
Trenant Cross PL14 63 A6
TRENANT GIRT 108 C5
Trenant Ind Est PL27 108 D6
Trenant Rd
Looe PL13 117 D5
2 Tywardreath PL24 60 D5
Trenant Vale PL27 108 D6
TRENARREN 73 E7
Trenarren View PL25 115 A6
Trenarth TR10 144 C8
Trenarth Rd TR7 110 E5
Trenawin La TR27 78 E5
TRENCREEK 111 C4
Trencreek Cl TR4 56 D1
Trencreek La TR8 111 B4
Trencreek Rd TR7, TR8 111 B4
TRENCROM 77 B3
Trencrom La TR26 141 D1
Trencrom Row TR20 77 B3
TRENDEAL 57 C3
Trendeal Gdns 1 TR18 143 E5
Trendlewood Rd PL6 125 D7
Trendreath Cl TR26 77 E3
Treneague Pk PL27 108 B4
TRENEAR 92 A6
Trenear Cl TR15 140 D6
TRENEERE 143 E7
Treneere La TR18 143 D7
Treneere Rd TR18 143 D6
TRENEGLOS 16 F7
Treneglos TR4 81 C7
Treneglos Terr
Gulval TR18 88 E6
Newlyn TR18 143 C3
Trenerry Cl TR1 137 D6
TRENERTH 78 D2
Trenerth Rd TR27 78 E2
Trenethick Ave TR13 146 D8
Trenethick Bsns Pk
TR13 146 C8
Trenethick Cl TR13 146 D7
Trenethick Farm TR13 146 B8
Trenethick Parc TR13 146 D8
TRENEWAN 62 A4
TRENGALE 37 C2
Trengove PL26 47 C1
Trengove Cross TR11 92 D5
Trengrouse Ave PL11 126 F3
Trengrouse Way TR13 146 C5
TRENGUNE 11 A4
Trengwainton Gdns★
TR20 88 A6
Trenhaile Terr TR1 70 D1
Trenhayle La TR27 142 B2
Treningle View PL31 109 C3
TRENINNICK 111 A4
Treninnick Hill TR7 110 F5
Treninnow & Wiggle Chalets
PL10 132 C2
Trenithick Mdw TR4 68 C6
Trenithon La TR8 57 C6
Trennance Ct 6 TR12 99 A1
Trennick La TR1 137 E3
Trennick Row TR1 137 E3
Trennick Villas Ct TR1 137 E3
Trenode CE Prim Sch
PL13 51 F1
Trenouth Cl 5 PL14 38 A3
Trenovissick Rd PL24 60 B4
Trenowah Rd PL25 115 C5
TRENOWETH 93 B8
Trenoweth Ave TR14 138 B3
Trenoweth Cres TR18 143 B4
Trenoweth Ct TR12 102 F2
Trenoweth Est TR15 140 A8
Trenoweth La TR10 93 B8
Trenoweth Mdw TR12 102 F2
Trenoweth Rd
Falmouth TR11 144 F2
Penzance TR18 143 B5
Trenoweth Terr TR10 93 B8
Trenoweth Vean TR10 81 B1
Trenowth Terr TR2 57 E1
Trent Cl PL3 129 B6
Trentham Cl PL6 125 B6
Trentworthy Cross EX22 3 E2
TRENWHEAL 90 F7
Trenwith La TR26 141 A4
Trenwith Pl 14 TR26 141 B5
Trenwith Rd TR14 138 B3
Trenwith Sq TR26 141 A5
Trenwith Terr 11 TR26 141 B5
Trenython Rd 10 PL24 60 B4
Treore Cl PL30 23 A6
Treovis Cross PL14 38 C8
Tre-Pol PL26 58 F1
TREQUITE 23 B3
Treraven La PL27 108 C3
Trerew Rd TR18 143 C4
Trerice★ TR8 44 D1
Trerice Ct 15 PL17 39 E4
Trerice Dr TR7 111 B5
Trerice Fields TR14 79 B2
Trerice Holdings TR8 44 C1
Trerice Pl TR26 141 A5
Trerice Rd 6 TR26 141 A5
Trerice Terr PL26 58 A8
Trerieve PL11 64 C5
TRERISE 103 A7
Trerise Rd TR14 138 C3
Treroosel Rd PL30 23 D8
Trerose Coombe PL11 64 C5
Treruffe Hill TR15 140 B4
Treruffe Terr 9 TR15 140 B4
TRERULEFOOT 52 D2
Treryn Cl PL24 60 B5
Tresaderns Rd TR15 140 A6
Tresahar Rd TR11 145 A3
Tresamble Hill TR4, TR3 81 B6
TRESARRETT 35 B8
Tresavean Est TR16 80 E6
Tresavean Hill TR16 80 E6
Tresavean Terr TR16 80 E6
Tresawla Ct TR14 138 F6
TRESAWLE 71 C5
Tresawle Rd TR11 145 A6
Tresawls Ave TR1 69 F3
Tresawls Rd TR1, TR4 69 E4
Tresawna Terr TR11 145 B4
Tresawya Dr TR1 137 C4
Trescobeas Rd TR11 144 E5
Trescoe Rd TR20 88 F6
Tresco Pl TR11 144 F4
Trescore PL28 31 F7
TRESCOWE 90 B5
Trescowe Rd TR20 89 F5
Tresdale Parc TR27 78 D6
Treseder's Gdns TR1 137 D5
Tresevern Hill TR3 80 D4
Tresidder Cl TR11 144 E4
TRESILLIAN 70 F5
Tresillian Ho TR1 69 E4
Tresillian Rd TR11 144 F6
Tresillian St PL4 149 C2
TRESINNEY 24 C8
Tresithney Rd TR16 80 F8
Treskerby TR16 140 F7
Treskewes Est 1 TR12 101 C4
Treskewes Ind Est 10
TR12 101 C4
TRESKILLARD 139 C1

TRESKILLING PL30 .... 59 F8
TRESKINNICK CROSS 6 F1
TRESLOTHAN 79 D4
Treslothan Rd TR14 ..... 79 D4
Tresluggan Rd PL5 ..... 123 D1
Tresooth Ct TR10 .... 144 D7
Tresooth La TR10 .... 144 C8
Tresooth Ter TR10 ..... 144 D7
TRESOWES GREEN 90 D4
TRESOWES HILL 90 E4
Tresowgar La TR2 ...... 71 B6
TRESPARRETT 10 B2
TRESPARRETT POSTS 10 C4
Tresprison Ct TR13 .... 146 E5
Tressa Dowr La TR1 .... 137 F5
TRESWITHIAN 138 A3
Treswithian Barns TR14 . 138 A3
Treswithian Park Rd
 TR14 .... 138 B3
Treswithian Rd TR14 .... 138 B3
Tretawn Cl PL30 .... 23 B2
Trethannas Gdns TR14 .. 79 B2
TRETHELLAN 110 C6
Trethellan Hill TR7 ..... 110 C5
Trethern Ct TR14 .... 79 E4
Tretherras Cl TR7 ...... 111 A6
Tretherras Rd TR7 ..... 111 A6
TRETHEVEY 14 F8
Trethevy Cl PL14 .... 37 F3
Trethevy Quoit* PL14 ... 38 A3
TRETHEWEY 96 E4
Trethewey Ct TR9 ...... 45 E6
Trethewey Way TR7 .... 110 D5
Trethew Gdns TR14 .... 138 E4
Trethiggey Cres TR8 ... 111 D2
Trethill La PL11 .... 65 C5
Trethorne Leisure Farm*
 PL15 .... 18 B2
Trethorns Ct TR20 ...... 89 A8
TRETHOSA 58 A5
Trethosa Rd PL26 ...... 58 B4
Trethowan Hts TR1 ..... 69 F3
TRETHOWEL 114 C6
Trethurffe Terr TR9 .... 45 E5
Trethurffe Villas TR7 ... 57 C1
TRETHURGY 59 F6
Trethurgy Gdns [31] PL17 . 39 E4
Tretoil View PL31 ...... 109 E2
Tretorvic TR18 .... 143 C8
Tretower Cl PL6 .... 124 F5
TREVADLOCK 27 A6
Trevadlock Hall Pk PL15 . 27 A6
TREVAIL 43 D1
Trevail Cotts TR8 ...... 43 D1
Trevail Way PL25 ...... 114 E4
Trevale TR18 .... 143 C5
TREVALGA 9 B1
Trevalga Cl [3] TR8 .... 55 A4
Trevallack Parc [5] TR12 . 101 C4
Trevallack View [4] TR12 . 101 C4
Trevallion Pk TR3 ...... 82 B5
Trevallyn Rd PL15 ..... 106 B4
TREVANCE 32 E6
Trevance TR10 .... 144 A8
Trevance Pk PL24 ...... 60 D5
TREVANGER 21 F4
Trevanion Cl PL21 ..... 108 B4
Trevanion Ct
  Mawnan Smith TR11 ... 93 D3
 [1] Newquay TR7 ..... 110 F6
  Truro TR1 .... 69 F3
Trevanion La PL25 ...... 59 A3
Trevanion Pk PL27 ..... 108 C4
Trevanion Rd
  Liskeard PL14 .... 113 D5
  St Austell PL25 ...... 114 D2
 [2] Truro TR1 .... 59 A3
  Wadebridge PL27 ..... 108 B4
Trevanion Terr PL27 .... 108 C4
TREVANSON 33 C7
Trevanson Rd PL27 ..... 108 A6
Trevanson St PL27 ..... 108 B6
Trevarner Way PL27 .... 108 D6
Trevarno Cl PL25 ...... 59 A3
Trevarno Estate & Gdns*
  TR13 .... 91 C5
TREVARNON 78 D6
Trevarnon Cl TR27 ..... 78 D6
Trevarnon La TR27 ..... 78 D6
Trevarrack Ct TR18 .... 143 F8
Trevarrack La TR18 .... 143 F8
Trevarrack Pl TR18 .... 143 F8
Trevarrack Row TR18 ... 88 E6
TREVARREN 45 E3
Trevarren Ave TR16 .... 80 A5
TREVARRIAN 31 C1
Trevarrick Ct TR26 .... 141 C1
Trevarrick Dr PL25 .... 114 B4
Trevarrick Rd PL25 .... 114 B3
TREVARTH 80 E7
Trevarth Est PL26 ..... 73 C4
Trevarthian Ho TR17 ... 89 B5
Trevarthian Rd PL25 ... 114 C4
Trevarth Rd TR16 ...... 144 F5
Trevarth Terr TR16 .... 80 E7
Trevarweneth Rd [8] PL24 . 60 B4
Trevassack Ct TR27 .... 142 D6
Trevassack Hill PL26 .. 142 E6
Trevassack Parc TR27 .. 142 D6
Trevaunance Cl TR5 .... 54 C2
Trevaunance Cove* TR5 . 54 D2

Trevaunance Rd TR5 .... 54 C2
Trevaylor Ct TR11 ..... 137 E6
Trevaylor Rd TR11 ..... 144 F5
Trevean Cl TR14 .... 138 B3
Trevean Gdns [3] TR18 . 143 D5
Trevean La TR20 .... 89 F4
Trevean Rd
  Penzance TR18......... 143 D5
  Truro TR1 .... 69 F3
Trevean Way
  Newquay TR7 .... 110 C5
  Rosudgeon TR20 ...... 89 F4
Trevear Rd PL26 .... 58 B4
Trevecca Cotts PL14 ... 113 C8
Treveglos TR27 .... 142 B6
Treveglos Rd TR11 .... 144 E1
TREVEIGHAN 23 F6
Trevelga Ct TR7 .... 111 A7
Trevelgue Ct TR8 ...... 44 C6
Trevelgue Rd TR7, TR8 . 44 C6
Trevellan Rd TR11 ..... 82 A3
Trevella Rd EX23 ...... 104 E7
TREVELLAS 54 F2
Trevella Vean TR4 ..... 70 D8
TREVELMOND 50 D6
Trevelthan Rd [18] TR16 . 67 E4
Trevelva Rd TR1 .... 137 E2
Trevelveth Rd TR8 .... 110 B3
Trevelyan Cl [10] TR20 . 89 E5
Trevelyan Rd TR15, TR16 . 67 E4
Trevelyan Way [5] TR20 . 89 E5
TREVEMPER 110 E2
Trevemper Rd TR7, TR8 . 110 F2
TREVEN 14 C6
Trevena Cl TR18 .... 143 C4
Trevena Cross TR13 .... 90 F3
Trevena Dr [3] PL34 ... 14 C7
Trevena Gdns TR11 .... 93 D3
Trevena Lodge [6] PL34 . 14 C7
Trevena Terr TR7 ...... 110 D6
Trevendon PL27 .... 28 D1
Treveneague Gdns PL2 . 128 D8
Trevenen Rd TR13 ..... 146 C5
Treveneth Cres TR18 .. 143 C1
Treveneth Pl [9] TR18 . 143 C1
Treven La TR27 .... 78 B1
Trevenna Cross TR8 ... 45 A8
Trevenner Ho [8] TR15 . 143 C1
Trevenner La TR17 .... 89 C5
Trevenner Mews [6]
  TR15 .... 140 B5
Trevenner Sq TR17 .... 89 C5
TREVENNING 23 F5
Treven Noweth TR16 .. 68 C3
Trevenson Ct TR15 .... 139 B6
Trevenson La
  Camborne, Pool TR15 . 139 A6
  Camborne TR14 .... 138 D2
Trevenson Rd
  Camborne TR15 .... 139 B5
  Newquay TR7 .... 111 B6
  Camborne TR14 .... 138 D2
Treventon Cl
  Falmouth TR11 .... 144 E4
  Portscatho TR2 .... 83 B2
Treventon Rd TR2 ..... 83 B2
Treventon Rise [11] TR9 . 45 E6
TREVERBYN 59 C7
Treverbyn Cl
  Penwithick 59 C7
  St Cleer 37 B2
Treverbyn Ct
  Liskeard PL14 .... 113 E6
  Plymouth PL7 .... 130 E6
Treverbyn Com Prim Sch
  PL26 .... 59 C8
Treverbyn Gdns PL25 .. 114 E4
Treverbyn Rd
  Falmouth TR11 .... 144 E1
  Padstow PL28 .... 107 E4
  Plymouth PL7 .... 130 E6
  St Austell PL25 ...... 114 E7
  Stenalees PL26 ...... 59 C8
  St Ives TR26 .... 141 A5
Treverbyn Rise TR10 .. 144 A8
Trevere Cl TR27 .... 78 C6
Treverno Rd TR14 ..... 138 E6
TREVERVA 93 B6
Treveryn Parc TR11 ... 144 F7
TREVESCAN 96 B5
Trevessa Cl PL26 ..... 128 D8
Trevethan Cl TR11 .... 145 A4
Trevethan Ct [3] TR11 . 145 A5
Trevethan Gdns [7] TR11 . 145 A4
Trevethan Hill [1] TR11 . 145 B5
Trevethan Pk PL20 .... 119 F4
Trevethan Rise TR11 .. 145 A4
Trevethenick Rd TR11 . 137 E3
Treveth La TR13 ...... 146 B6
TREVETHOE 77 D3
Treveth Tean TR9 ..... 57 E8
Treveth Vlyn TR14 .... 138 E4
TREVIA 105 B4
TREVIADES 93 A3
Trevia La PL32 .... 105 B4
Trevian Cl [8] TR6 .... 55 A5
Trevia Pk Terr PL32 .. 105 C3
Treviglas Cl TR7 ...... 111 D7
Treviglas Com Coll TR7 . 111 D7
Treviglas La TR2 ..... 71 C6
Treviglas Rise TR7 ... 111 D7
TREVIGRO 39 C4
TREVILLA 82 C6
Trevilley La PL30, PL33 . 23 E8
Trevillick La PL14 .... 23 F6

Trevilling Rd PL27 .... 108 B6
Trevillis Pk PL14 ..... 113 B4
TREVILSON 56 D6
Trevilson Cl TR8 ...... 56 C7
Trevince Parc TR16 ... 80 F8
Trevingey Cl TR15 .... 140 A3
Trevingey Cres TR15 .. 140 A3
Trevingey Parc TR15 .. 140 A3
Trevingey Rd TR15 .... 140 A3
TREVISCOE 58 B7
Trevisker Prim Sch PL27 . 31 F3
Treviskey Hill TR2 .... 84 B3
Trevissome Ct TR11 ... 144 F6
Trevithick Ave PL11 .. 31 F8
Trevithick Ave PL11 .. 126 F4
Trevithick Cl
  Newquay TR7 .... 110 F4
  St Merryn PL28 .... 31 F8
  Truro TR1 .... 137 E6
Trevithick Cres TR27 .. 142 D5
Trevithick Ct
 [3] Camborne, Illogan Highway
  TR15 .... 139 C6
  Camborne TR14 .... 138 C3
  Truro TR1 .... 137 E6
TREWINT 10 F8
Trewint Cres PL13 .... 117 D4
Trevithick Jun & Inf Sch
  TR14 .... 138 D1
Trevithick Rd
  Camborne, Illogan Highway
  TR15 .... 139 C6
  Camborne TR14 .... 138 D3
  Chacewater TR4....... 69 A3
  Falmouth TR11........ 144 E5
  Plymouth PL5......... 123 E2
  St Austell PL25 ...... 114 E3
  Truro TR1 .... 137 E5
Trevollard La PL12 .... 61 F7
Trevollard PL12 ...... 53 D1
Trevol Pl PL11 .... 126 E3
Trevol Rd PL11 ...... 126 E3
TREVONE 20 E2
Trevone Cres PL25 ... 114 A4
Trevone Gdns PL2 ... 128 D8
Trevone Rd PL28 ..... 20 F2
Trevoney TR11 .... 144 C2
Trevor Cl PL28 .... 20 C1
Trevorder Cl TR11 ... 126 F2
Trevorder Dr PL25 ... 114 E7
Trevorder Rd PL11 ... 126 F2
Trevorgans Cross TR19 . 96 F8
TREVORRICK 107 E1
Trevose Ave TR7 ..... 110 C6
Trevose Cl TR5 ...... 54 C1
Trevose Ho TR1 ..... 69 E4
Trevose Rd TR1 ..... 69 F4
Trevose Way PL3 .... 129 C6
Trevowah Mdws TR5 . 110 A3
Trevowah Rd TR8 .... 43 D3
TREVOWHAN 75 D2
Trevozah Cross PL15 . 28 B8
Trevu Ho TR14 .... 138 E1
Trevu Rd TR14 .... 138 E2
Trevurvas La TR13 ... 90 C3
TREW 90 F4
TREWALDER 14 E1
Trewall Hill PL11 .... 64 D5
Trewans Terr TR11 ... 140 A6
Trewandrevra Cross TR11 . 92 F6
Trewarlett Cross PL15 . 28 A7
TREWARMETT 14 D5
Trewarne La TR11 .... 111 F3
Trewartha Cl TR26 ... 141 D1
Trewartha Ct [4] PL14 . 113 C6
Trewartha Flats TR26 . 141 D1
Trewartha Rd TR20 ... 90 C3
Trewartha Terr [12] TR18 . 143 E6
Trewarton Rd TR10 ... 81 D2
Trewarveneth Farm Cotts
  TR18 .... 88 C2
Trewarveneth St TR18 . 143 C2
TREWASSA 15 F5
Trewassa Flats PL32 . 15 F5
Trewavas Cres TR13 . 146 C5
Trewavas Rd TR18 ... 143 C1
Treweath Rd TR18 ... 143 D7
Treweege Row TR3 ... 80 E4
Treweeks Rd TR19 ... 75 A1
Treweese Cross PL14 . 52 A7
Treweese Rd
  Menheniot PL14 .... 52 B7
  Quethiock PL14 .... 52 B8
TREWELLARD 86 F8
Trewellard Hill PL11 . 77 A4
Trewellard Ind Est TR19 . 86 F8
Trewellard Rd TR19 .. 86 F8
Trewelloe Rd TR20 ... 90 C3
Trewen La TR16 ...... 68 E1
TREWEN 27 F2
TREWENNACK 146 F8
TREWENNAN 23 E8
Trewen Rd TR11 ..... 144 C2
Trewen Terr TR11 .... 144 C2
Trewern La TR20 .... 87 E6
TREWETHA 22 E7
Trewetha Farm Lodges
  PL26 .... 22 E7
Trewetha La PL29 .... 22 D7
TREWETHERN 22 E3
TREWEY 76 B5
Trewey Hill TR 26 .... 76 B4
Trewhela La TR20 .... 89 F7
Trewhella Terr TR20 . 90 A6
Trewhiddle Rd PL25 . 114 C2

Trewidden Cl TR1..... 137 E5
Trewidden Ct TR1 .... 137 E5
Trewidden Gdn* TR20 . 88 A4
Trewidden Rd TR26 ... 141 B5
TREWIDLAND 51 C2
Trewidland Prim Sch
  PL14 .... 51 C3
Trewince TR11 .... 93 B3
Trewince La
  Grampound Road TR2 . 57 E1
  Lostwithiel PL22 ..... 112 C3
  Porth Navas TR11 .... 93 B3
Trewince Manor TR2 .. 95 C6
Trewince Terr [8] TR18 . 143 C1
Trewince Villas PL27 .. 32 E6
Trewinnard Ct TR1 ... 137 B6
Trewinnard Gr TR1 ... 137 B6
Trewinnard La TR27 .. 77 E1
Trewinnard Rd TR3 ... 81 D5
Trewinnick Council Hos
  PL27 .... 32 A5
Trewinnick Rd PL27 .. 32 A5
Trewinnow Cross PL15 . 27 D6
TREWINT 10 F8
Trewint Cres PL13 .... 117 D4
Trewint Est PL14 .... 52 A5
Trewint La
  Landrake PL12........ 53 B2
  Rock PL27 .... 21 D3
Trewint Rd PL14 ..... 52 A6
Trewirgie Cty Jun Sch
  TR15 .... 140 B4
Trewirgie Gdns TR15 . 140 B4
Trewirgie Hill TR15 .. 140 B3
Trewirgie Rd TR15 ... 140 B3
Trewirgie Vean TR15 . 140 B4
Trewiston La PL27 ... 21 E3
Trewithen Parc PL22 . 112 D2
Trewithen Gdns* TR2 . 71 E6
Trewithen Parc TR8 .. 56 B7
Trewithen Rd TR18 ... 143 D5
Trewithen Terr TR13 . 90 D5
TREWITHIAN 83 B4
Trewithy Ct PL6 ..... 124 F1
Trewithy Dr PL6 ..... 124 F1
TREWOLD 9 F2
Trewollock Cl PL26 .. 85 C5
Trewollock La PL26 .. 85 C5
TREWOODLOE 39 B6
Trewoolsta Terr [6] PL14 . 38 E4
TREWOON
  Mullion 99 B2
  St Austell 59 A3
Trewoon Rd TR12 .... 99 B2
Treworden Cl EX23 ... 4 E1
Treworder La PL27 ... 108 F5
Treworder Rd TR1 ... 137 B3
TREWORGA 83 D7
Treworgan Ct TR1 ... 56 D1
Treworgan View TR4 . 56 D1
TREWORLAS 83 D5
Treworlis Cl TR13 ... 146 D8
Treworrick La PL14 . 38 E4
TREWORRICK 37 E3
TREWORTHAL 83 C5
Treworthal Rd TR3 ... 81 D5
Treworvenneth Dr [9]
  TR17 .... 89 C5
Trewrickle La PL11 .. 65 A5
Trewyn Flats [1] TR26 . 141 B6
Treyew Pl TR16 ...... 80 F8
Treyew Prim Sch TR1 . 137 A4
Treyew Rd TR1 ...... 137 B3
TREZAISE 47 A2
Trezaise Ave PL26 ... 47 A2
Trezaise Cl PL26 .... 47 A2
Trezaise Rd PL26 .... 46 F2
Trezaise Sq PL26 .... 47 A2
Treza Rd TR13 .... 91 A1
Trezela Rd TR18 .... 143 D6
Trinity Cl
  Bere Alston PL20..... 41 B1
  Carnkie TR16 .... 80 C2
Trinity Praze TR16 .. 80 C2
Trinity St PL25 ..... 114 C3
Trinity Way PL19 .... 147 A4
Tripp Hill PL14 ...... 36 F2
TRISPEN 56 D1
Trispen Hill TR4 .... 56 D1
Tristan Rd TR1 ...... 137 F5
Triumphal Cres PL7 . 130 A6
TROAN 57 C8
Trolver Hill TR3 .... 82 B6
Trolvis Vean TR10 ... 81 A1
TROON 79 E5
Troon Moor TR14 ... 79 E4
Troon Prim Sch TR14 . 79 E4
Troon Row TR13 .... 90 F3
Troubridge Rd TR13 . 146 C4
Trowbridge Cl PL5 .. 124 C4
Troy Ct PL23 .... 116 C4
Truck Hill TR2 ...... 71 B6
Trumglenoor Cotts TR9 . 68 A2
Trungle Parc TR19 .. 88 C2
Trungle Terr TR19 ... 88 C2
TRURO 137 E3
Truro Bsns Pk TR3 .. 69 C3
Truro Coll [23] TR1 . 137 D4
Truro Coll (Tregye Campus)
  TR3 .... 82 A7
Truro Dr PL5 .... 124 A5
Truro High Sch for Girls
  TR1 .... 137 C3
Truro Hill TR10 ..... 144 C8
Truro La TR10 ...... 144 C8
Truro L Ctr TR1 .... 69 E3
Truro Prep Sch TR1 . 69 F4

Truro Rd
  Lanivet PL30 .... 47 F7
  St Austell PL25 ...... 114 A2
Truro Sta TR1 .... 137 E3
Truro Sta TR1 .... 137 B4
Truro Vean Terr TR1 . 137 D5
TRUSCOTT 18 D4
TRUTHAN 56 C2
TRUTHWALL
  Marazion 89 D7
  St Just 86 E7
Truthwall La TR19 ... 86 F7
Tryelyn PL31 .... 109 F2
Tryhornek TR26 ..... 77 D4
Trythall Prim Sch TR20 . 76 B1
TRYTHOGGA 143 F8
Trythogga Hill TR18 . 143 F8
Trythogga Rd TR18 . 143 F8
Tubbon Hill TR3 .... 81 A4
TUBBS MILL 72 D2
Tucker Cl PL5 .... 127 F8
TUCKERMARSH 41 B2
Tuckers Ct TR18 .... 111 B4
TUCKINGMILL
  Camborne 139 A4
  St Breward 24 B4
Tuckingmill Terr TR13 . 91 E4
Tudor Cl PL9 .... 135 E5
Tudor Ct PL12 ...... 123 A2
Tudor Cl TR11 ...... 144 E5
Tunnels Through Time*
  TR7 .... 110 D5
Turbill Gdns [4] PL7 . 131 B5
TURFDOWN 48 E8
Turfdown Rd PL30 ... 48 E8
Turf St PL31 .... 109 C5
Turnavean Rd PL25 . 114 A5
Turnaware Rd TR11 . 144 E2
TURNCHAPEL 135 B7
Turnpike
  Gunnislake/Calstock PL18 . 40 E5
  Helston TR13 .... 146 C7
Turnpike Hill [2] TR17 . 89 C5
Turnpike Pl PL14 ... 113 B4
Turnpike Rd
  Connor Downs TR27 . 78 D6
  Marazion TR17....... 89 C5
Turnpike The TR19 .. 86 F6
Turnquay PL9 .... 135 C7
Turret Gr PL4 .... 128 F4
TUTWELL 29 A2
Tuxton Cl PL7 ...... 131 C3
TWELVEHEADS 69 B1
Twelvewoods Cl PL14 . 50 E8
Twelvewoods Pl PL14 . 50 E8
Twinbrook Pk TR11 . 93 B3
TWO BURROWS 68 E5
Two Hills Pk PL12 ... 122 C2
Two Trees PL27 .... 108 B4
Two Trees Rd PL22 . 112 F1
Tyacke Rd TR13 .... 146 B5
Tybesta TR2 .... 72 A7
Tye Hill Cl PL25 .... 59 A3
Tyland Rd PL12 .... 105 F4
Tylney Cl PL6 .... 125 B6
Tynance Ct PL26 ... 58 C8
Tyndale Cl PL5 ..... 124 B1
Tyringham Pl TR26 . 77 E4
Tyringham Rd TR26 . 77 E4
Tyringham Row TR26 . 77 F4
Tyshute La PL26 .... 59 A3
Tything Wlk [2] PL3 . 128 E6
TYWARDREATH 60 E5
Tywardreath Highway
  PL24 .... 60 D4
Tywardreath Hill PL24 . 60 D4
Tywardreath Prim Sch
  PL24 .... 60 D5
Tywarnhaile Way TR4 . 68 A6
Tywarnhayle Rd TR6 . 55 A5
Tywarnhayle Sq [23] TR6 . 55 A5

U

Uglow Cl TR14 ...... 138 C3
Ulalia Rd TR7 .... 110 F6
Ullswater Cres PL6 . 124 E4
Umfulla Pl [13] TR26 . 141 B5
Under Chapel Yd TR18 . 143 F4
Undercliff TR27 ..... 142 D7
Undercliff Rd PL9 .. 135 B7
Underhayes La PL15 . 106 A8
Underhill Rd PL3 ... 128 A4
Underhill Villas [3] PL3 . 128 A3
Under La PL15 ...... 18 C3
Underlane
  Boyton PL15......... 13 A3
  Marhamchurch EX23 . 7 B1
  Plymouth, Plympton PL7 . 130 C6
  Plymouth, Plymstock PL9 . 135 E6
Under Rd
  Boscastle PL35 .... 9 C1
  Bridgerule EX22....... 8 A5
  Gunnislake PL18 ...... 41 A6
Underways PL20 ..... 41 B1
UNDERWOOD 130 C3
Underwood Rd PL7 . 130 C4
Unicorn Cl PL7 ..... 130 B6
Union Cnr TR11 ..... 144 D5
Union Hill
  St Columb Major TR9 . 45 E6
 [6] Stratton EX23..... 7 A1
  Truro TR1 .... 70 D5
Union Pl
  Fowey PL23 .... 116 D4
  Plymouth PL1......... 148 A2
  Truro TR1 .... 137 D5

Union Rd TR11 . . . . . . 144 D6
Union Sq TR9 . . . . . . 45 E6
Union St
 Camborne TR14 . . . . . . 138 D2
 27 Penzance TR18 . . . . . . 143 E5
 Plymouth PL1 . . . . . . 148 A2
 Truro TR1 . . . . . . 137 C5
UNITED DOWNS 81 A8
United Downs Ind Pk
 TR16 . . . . . . 81 A8
United Rd TR16 . . . . . . 80 F8
Unit Hos PL7 . . . . . . 33 B5
Unity Cl PL6 . . . . . . 125 D5
Unity Rd TR13 . . . . . . 98 C8
University College Falmouth
 (Annexe) TR11 . . . . . . 145 B4
University College Falmouth
 (Tremough Campus)
 TR10 . . . . . . 144 A8
University College Falmouth
 (Woodlane Campus)
 TR11 . . . . . . 145 B3
University of Plymouth Prim
 Sch PL4 . . . . . . 148 C4
University of Plymouth
 (Cookworthy Bldg)
 PL4 . . . . . . 149 A3
UPCOTT 2 F4
Upcott Cross EX39 . . . . . . 2 F5
Upland Cl TR1 . . . . . . 137 F6
Upland Cres TR1 . . . . . . 137 E6
Upland Dr PL6 . . . . . . 125 A5
Uplands
 Lostwithiel PL22 . . . . . . 112 B2
 Saltash PL12 . . . . . . 122 E1
 Tavistock PL19 . . . . . . 147 A4
Uplands Vean TR1 . . . . . . 137 F5
Upper Castle Rd TR2 . . . . . . 95 A6
Upper Chapel PL15 . . . . . . 106 A4
Upper Dobbin Cl PL28 . . . . . . 20 F2
Upper Dobbin La PL28 . . . . . . 20 F2
Upper Eastcliffe Rd PL24 . . 60 D4
Upper Hillcrest 8 TR6 . . . . . . 55 A4
Upper Knollys Terrace La
 PL3 . . . . . . 128 C4
Upper Lemon Villas TR1 . 137 C3
Upper Ridings PL7 . . . . . . 131 B7
Upper School La TR1 . . . . . . 137 C3
Upperton La PL6 . . . . . . 121 F3
Upper Tredrea TR3 . . . . . . 81 D5
UPTON
 Bude 104 C2
 Upton Cross 38 C7
Upton Cl PL3 . . . . . . 129 B7
UPTON CROSS 38 D6
Upton Cross EX23 . . . . . . 104 C2
Upton Cross Prim Sch
 PL14 . . . . . . 38 C7
Upton Mdws EX23 . . . . . . 104 C3
Upton Terr EX23 . . . . . . 104 C2
UPTON TOWANS 78 B6
Upton Twrs Nature Reserve*
 TR27 . . . . . . 78 B6
Urban Terr PL17 . . . . . . 39 F5
Uxbridge Dr PL5 . . . . . . 123 E4
Uzella Pk PL22 . . . . . . 112 C2

V

Vaagso Cl PL1 . . . . . . 127 E2
Valency Row PL35 . . . . . . 9 C2
Valentine Row 4 PL17 . . . . . . 39 E4
Valiant Ave PL5 . . . . . . 124 A4
Vallard's La PL12 . . . . . . 53 E4
Valletort Flats PL1 . . . . . . 128 A2
Valletort Ho PL1 . . . . . . 148 A3
Valletort La PL1 . . . . . . 128 A3
Valletort La PL1 . . . . . . 128 A3
Valletort Pl PL1 . . . . . . 128 A3
Valletort Rd PL1, PL3 . . . . . . 128 A3
Valletort Terr PL1 . . . . . . 148 A4
Valley Bglws PL13 . . . . . . 117 F5
Valley Cl
 Goonhavern TR4 . . . . . . 55 C3
 Truro TR1 . . . . . . 69 F3
Valley La TR3 . . . . . . 81 F7
Valley Park La PL26 . . . . . . 73 C3
Valley Rd
 Bude EX23 . . . . . . 104 E5
 Carbis Bay TR26 . . . . . . 141 C2
 Mevagissey PL26 . . . . . . 73 C4
 Plymouth PL7 . . . . . . 130 B5
 Saltash PL12 . . . . . . 122 E2
Valley The TR19 . . . . . . 96 E3
VALLEY TRUCKLE 105 C2
Valley View
 Bodmin PL31 . . . . . . 109 E3
 10 Illogan TR16 . . . . . . 67 E4
 Plymouth PL6 . . . . . . 125 D7
 Redruth TR16 . . . . . . 140 E1
 St Keyne PL14 . . . . . . 51 A4
 St Teath PL30 . . . . . . 23 E1
 Wadebridge PL27 . . . . . . 108 C4
Valley View Cl PL3 . . . . . . 129 B6
Valley View Dr TR1 . . . . . . 69 F3
Valley View Pk
 Bodmin PL31 . . . . . . 34 D2
 St Austell PL26 . . . . . . 47 C2
Valley View Rd PL3 . . . . . . 129 B7
Valley View Terr TR3 . . . . . . 81 B5
Valley Wlk PL6 . . . . . . 125 E6
Vanguard Cl PL5 . . . . . . 124 D1
Vapron Rd PL3 . . . . . . 128 F6
Varfell La TR20 . . . . . . 89 A7
Varley La PL14 . . . . . . 113 B5
Varley Terr 1 PL14 . . . . . . 113 B5
Vauban Pl PL2 . . . . . . 127 F4

Vaughan Cl PL2 . . . . . . 128 C7
Vauxhall Ct 10 PL4 . . . . . . 149 A2
Vauxhall Quay PL4 . . . . . . 149 A2
Vauxhall St PL4 . . . . . . 149 A2
Vauxhall Street Flats 18
 PL4 . . . . . . 149 A2
Vear Rd TR14 . . . . . . 138 E2
Vean Terr TR14 . . . . . . 138 E2
Vear Ho TR14 . . . . . . 138 D2
Vellan Cl TR14 . . . . . . 79 B5
Vellandrucia TR3 . . . . . . 80 F3
Vellanhoggan Mews TR18 88 E4
VELLANOWETH 89 A8
Vellan Parc Ave TR27 . . . . . . 78 C5
Vellan Vrane TR27 . . . . . . 78 C5
Venn Cl 9 PL14 . . . . . . 38 A3
Venn Cl PL3 . . . . . . 128 E6
Venn Cres PL3 . . . . . . 128 E6
Venn Gdns PL3 . . . . . . 128 E7
Venn Gr PL3 . . . . . . 128 E6
Venn Hill PL19 . . . . . . 29 C6
Venn La PL2, PL3 . . . . . . 128 C6
Venn Way PL3 . . . . . . 128 E6
Venslooe Pl PL14 . . . . . . 113 B7
VENTERDON 28 D2
Ventnor Terr TR26 . . . . . . 141 A6
Venton Cl PL15 . . . . . . 18 B8
Venton East Sq TR19 . . . . . . 86 F6
VENTONGIMPS 55 C2
Venton Lace Rd TR2 . . . . . . 57 E1
VENTONLEAGUE 142 F7
Ventonleague Hill TR27 . 142 F7
Ventonleague Row TR27 142 E7
Ventonraze TR16 . . . . . . 67 E4
Ventonraze Terr 2 TR16 . . . . . . 67 E4
Venton Rd
 Falmouth TR11 . . . . . . 144 E4
 St Ives TR26 . . . . . . 141 C3
Ventonvase 6 TR16 . . . . . . 55 A5
Venton Vision Rise TR26 . . 77 A7
Veor Rd TR7 . . . . . . 111 C7
Verden Cl PL3 . . . . . . 128 E5
Verdun Terr PL14 . . . . . . 113 B5
Vernal Gdns PL2 . . . . . . 127 F7
Verna Pl PL5 . . . . . . 123 D2
Verna Rd PL5 . . . . . . 123 E2
Vernigo Cross PL12 . . . . . . 40 B1
Vernon Pl TR11 . . . . . . 145 B4
Vernon Villas PL24 . . . . . . 60 B4
Vernon Way TR10 . . . . . . 144 B7
VERYAN 83 F6
Veryan CE Prim Sch TR2 83 F6
VERYAN GREEN 83 F7
Viaduct Hill TR27 . . . . . . 142 E6
Viaduct La TR14 . . . . . . 138 A1
Vicarage Cl
 Budock Water TR11 . . . . . . 144 C3
 Menheniot PL14 . . . . . . 51 F5
Vicarage Gdns
 Milton Abbot PL19 . . . . . . 29 C6
 Plymouth PL5 . . . . . . 123 B1
Vicarage Hill
 Budock Water TR11 . . . . . . 144 C3
 Mevagissey PL26 . . . . . . 73 C4
 10 St Austell PL25 . . . . . . 114 C3
 St Day TR16 . . . . . . 68 E1
 9 Tintagel PL34 . . . . . . 14 C7
Vicarage La
 Lelant TR26 . . . . . . 77 E4
 Manaccan TR12 . . . . . . 101 A8
 Poundstock EX23 . . . . . . 6 F2
Vicarage Mdw PL23 . . . . . . 116 C4
Vicarage Rd
 Bude EX23 . . . . . . 104 D5
 Plymouth PL7 . . . . . . 130 C6
 Porthleven TR13 . . . . . . 91 A1
 St Agnes TR5 . . . . . . 54 D1
 Torpoint PL11 . . . . . . 127 B2
Vicarage Row TR13 . . . . . . 90 F3
Vicarage Terr TR11 . . . . . . 92 F4
VICTORIA
 Lostwithiel 112 B2
 Roche 46 F4
Victoria Ave PL1 . . . . . . 148 A4
Victoria Bsns Pk PL5 . . . . . . 47 A4
Victoria Ct PL14 . . . . . . 113 C6
Victoria Cotts
 Budock Water TR11 . . . . . . 144 C3
 Falmouth TR11 . . . . . . 145 B3
 Plymouth PL6 . . . . . . 129 B8
Victoria Ct 15 TR18 . . . . . . 143 E6
Victoria Gdns
 2 St Columb Road TR9 . . . . . . 45 E2
 Threemilestone TR3 . . . . . . 69 D3
Victoria La PL12 . . . . . . 122 F2
Victoria Mews 17 TR18 . 143 E6
Victoria Pk PL27 . . . . . . 108 D6
Victoria Pl
 31 Penzance TR18 . . . . . . 143 E5
 Plymouth, Devonport PL2 . 127 F7
 Plymouth PL1 . . . . . . 148 A2
 Ponsanooth TR3 . . . . . . 81 B4
 3 St Austell PL25 . . . . . . 114 C3
 32 St Ives TR26 . . . . . . 141 B6
Victoria Quay
 5 Falmouth TR11 . . . . . . 145 B5
 Truro TR1 . . . . . . 70 D1
Victoria Rd
 Bude EX23 . . . . . . 104 D7
 Camelford PL32 . . . . . . 105 E4
 Plymouth PL5 . . . . . . 123 D2
 Roche PL26 . . . . . . 46 F3
 Saltash PL12 . . . . . . 122 F2
 St Austell PL25 . . . . . . 114 F3
 11 St Ives TR26 . . . . . . 141 B6

Victoria Rd continued
 Threemilestone TR3 . . . . . . 69 D3
Victoria Road Prim Sch 1
 PL5 . . . . . . 123 D1
Victoria Row TR19 . . . . . . 86 E6
Victoria Sq
 Bodmin PL31 . . . . . . 109 F3
 16 Penzance TR18 . . . . . . 143 E6
 Truro TR1 . . . . . . 137 C4
Victoria St
 Camborne TR14 . . . . . . 138 D2
 St Columb Major TR9 . . . . . . 45 E6
 Torpoint PL11 . . . . . . 127 B3
Victoria Terr
 4 Liskeard PL14 . . . . . . 113 B5
 Nanpean PL26 . . . . . . 58 D6
 Plymouth PL4 . . . . . . 148 C4
 Portscatho TR2 . . . . . . 83 B2
 St Breward PL30 . . . . . . 24 B3
Victory Rd EX22 . . . . . . 13 A8
Victory St PL2 . . . . . . 127 E6
Vigo Bridge Rd PL19 . . . . . . 147 C6
Vigo Mews PL19 . . . . . . 147 C6
Village Dr PL6 . . . . . . 121 C1
Village Farm Cl EX23 . . . . . . 7 B6
Village The
 Buckland Monachorum
  PL20 . . . . . . 41 F3
 Duloe PL14 . . . . . . 51 A1
Villa Marina TR17 . . . . . . 89 B5
Villiers Cl PL9 . . . . . . 135 D7
Vincent Way PL12 . . . . . . 122 F2
Vine Cres PL2 . . . . . . 128 B6
Vinefield Ct TR11 . . . . . . 145 B7
Vine Gdns PL2 . . . . . . 128 B6
Vine Pl 10 PL24 . . . . . . 60 D5
Vinery La PL7, PL9 . . . . . . 130 E1
Vineyard The TR3 . . . . . . 80 F3
Vingoe's La TR20 . . . . . . 88 B7
Vinstone Way PL5 . . . . . . 123 D1
Violet Dr PL6 . . . . . . 125 E8
Violet La PL19 . . . . . . 147 E6
Virgin Hill TR17 . . . . . . 89 C6
Virginia Gdns PL2 . . . . . . 127 F7
Virgin Pl 16 TR19 . . . . . . 88 C1
Virgin St 20 TR26 . . . . . . 141 B6
Visicks Works TR3 . . . . . . 81 A4
Vivian Cl TR7 . . . . . . 110 E5
Vivian Ct TR1 . . . . . . 137 D3
Vivian Pk TR14 . . . . . . 138 F2
Vivian Rd PL31 . . . . . . 109 B4
Vixen Tor Cl PL20 . . . . . . 42 C3
VOGUE 68 D1
Vogue Cl TR16 . . . . . . 68 D1
Vogue Terr TR16 . . . . . . 68 D1
Vorfield Cl TR15 . . . . . . 140 B6
Vosporth Hill TR8 . . . . . . 110 A3
Voss Rd PL12 . . . . . . 53 E1
Vounder Glaze TR19 . . . . . . 86 E6
Voundervour La 20 TR18 . 143 E5
Vyvyan Dr TR8 . . . . . . 44 E3
Vyvyan Pl TR13 . . . . . . 146 C5
Vyvyan St TR14 . . . . . . 138 D3
Vyvyan's Terr TR14 . . . . . . 79 B2

W

Waddon Cl PL7 . . . . . . 130 E7
WADEBRIDGE 108 A6
Wadebridge Com Prim Sch
 PL27 . . . . . . 108 C6
Wadebridge L Ctr PL27 . 108 C7
Wadebridge Rd
 St Mabyn PL30 . . . . . . 34 C8
 St Tudy PL30 . . . . . . 23 E3
Wadebridge Sch PL27 . 108 D6
Wadeland Terr 8 PL14 . . . . . . 51 A7
Wadham Cl 4 PL14 . . . . . . 113 C5
Wadham Dr PL14 . . . . . . 113 C5
Wadham Ho 5 PL14 . . . . . . 113 C5
Wadham Rd PL14 . . . . . . 113 C5
Wadham Terr 6 PL2 . . . . . . 128 A5
Wagg La TR2 . . . . . . 71 C6
Waggon Hill PL7 . . . . . . 131 A4
WAINHOUSE CORNER 10 E6
Wain Pk PL7 . . . . . . 130 F4
Wainsway TR6 . . . . . . 55 A4
Wainways EX23 . . . . . . 10 F6
Wakefield Ave PL5 . . . . . . 123 E1
Wake St PL4 . . . . . . 148 B4
Walcot Cl PL5 . . . . . . 125 E3
Waldon Cl PL7 . . . . . . 131 B6
Walker Lines Ind Est 8
 PL31 . . . . . . 48 D8
Walker Terr 7 PL1 . . . . . . 148 B1
Walkham Bsns Pk PL5 . . . . . . 124 B1
Walkham Cl PL19 . . . . . . 147 D5
Walkham Mdws PL20 . . . . . . 42 C4
WALKHAMPTON 42 D4
Walkhampton Rd PL20 . . . . . . 42 C4
Walkhampton Wlk PL6 . . . . . . 125 E1
Walkham Terr 4 PL20 . . . . . . 42 C5
Walk Terr PL23 . . . . . . 116 C2
Walk The PL15 . . . . . . 106 C6
WALL 78 E3
Wallace Mews 1 PL3 . . . . . . 109 D5
Wallace Rd
 Bodmin PL31 . . . . . . 109 D5
 Plymouth PL7 . . . . . . 131 A4
Walled Gdn The TR10 . . . . . . 144 A8
Wall Gdn TR27 . . . . . . 78 E3
Wallpark Cl PL7 . . . . . . 130 F7
Wall Rd TR27 . . . . . . 78 E3
Wallsend Ind Est PL4 . . . . . . 149 C1
Wall Vean TR27 . . . . . . 78 E3
Walnut Cl PL7 . . . . . . 131 B5
Walnut Dr PL7 . . . . . . 131 C5

Walnut Gdns PL7 . . . . . . 131 C5
Walreddon Cl PL19 . . . . . . 147 B6
Walsingham Ct PL7 . . . . . . 131 B6
Walsingham Pl 15 TR1 . 137 C4
Walsingham Rd PL5 . . . . . . 18 D5
Walters La PL15 . . . . . . 18 B5
Walton Ct PL5 . . . . . . 123 C2
Walton Cres PL5 . . . . . . 124 C1
Wandle Pl PL3 . . . . . . 129 D5
Wansford Mdws PL26 . . . . . . 85 C5
WANSON 6 F3
Wanstead Gr PL5 . . . . . . 124 A2
Wantage Gdns PL1 . . . . . . 148 A3
WARBSTOW 11 B1
Warbstow Com Sch PL15 . . 11 B1
WARBSTOW CROSS 11 B2
Warburton Gdns PL5 . . . . . . 123 C1
Ward Cl 4 EX23 . . . . . . 4 D1
Wardlow Cl PL6 . . . . . . 128 F8
Wardlow Gdns PL6 . . . . . . 128 F8
Wardour Wlk PL6 . . . . . . 125 E7
Warfelton Cres PL12 . . . . . . 122 E2
Warfelton Gdns PL12 . . . . . . 122 E2
Warfelton Terr PL12 . . . . . . 122 E2
Waring Rd PL6 . . . . . . 124 D7
WARLEGGAN 36 C4
Warleigh Ave PL2 . . . . . . 127 E5
WARLEIGH BARTON 123 F8
Warleigh Cres PL5 . . . . . . 124 E5
Warleigh La PL2 . . . . . . 127 E5
Warleigh Rd 2 PL6 . . . . . . 128 E4
Warmwell Rd PL5 . . . . . . 123 E4
Warne Cl TR2 . . . . . . 71 F3
Warran La PL19 . . . . . . 147 C3
Warraton Cl PL12 . . . . . . 122 D3
Warraton Gn PL12 . . . . . . 122 D3
Warraton La PL12 . . . . . . 122 D3
Warraton Rd PL12 . . . . . . 122 D3
Warren 7 PL26 . . . . . . 141 B5
Warren Cl PL6 . . . . . . 124 D8
Warren La PL5 . . . . . . 124 A8
Warren Pk PL6 . . . . . . 125 D7
Warren Rd TR9 . . . . . . 45 F2
Warrens Field PL32 . . . . . . 105 D5
Warren St TR18 . . . . . . 98 C8
Warren The PL13 . . . . . . 62 E1
Warspite Gdns PL5 . . . . . . 124 D2
Warton Cl PL5 . . . . . . 124 D3
Warwick Ave
 Illogan TR16 . . . . . . 67 D4
 Plymouth PL5 . . . . . . 124 D3
Warwick Cl PL28 . . . . . . 31 F8
Warwick Cres 8 PL27 . . . . . . 31 F3
Warwick Dr PL25 . . . . . . 115 B5
Warwick Orchard Cl PL5 124 D3
Warwick Rd EX23 . . . . . . 104 E4
Wasdale Cl PL6 . . . . . . 125 D2
Wasdale Gdns PL6 . . . . . . 125 D2
WASHAWAY 34 C4
Washbourne Cl PL11 . . . . . . 127 B3
WATERGATE 24 E8
Watergate La PL30 . . . . . . 34 C8
Watergate Rd TR8 . . . . . . 44 C6
Watering Hill Cl PL25 . . . . . . 114 E3
Waterings Rd TR11 . . . . . . 82 A2
Water La
 Crantock TR8 . . . . . . 110 A3
 Delabole PL33 . . . . . . 14 E3
 Golant PL23 . . . . . . 61 B5
 Hayle TR27 . . . . . . 142 B3
 St Agnes TR5 . . . . . . 54 D1
WATERLOO 35 D7
Waterloo TR1 . . . . . . 137 E4
Waterloo Cl
 Plymouth PL1 . . . . . . 148 A3
 St Mawes TR2 . . . . . . 95 A6
Waterloo Ct PL1 . . . . . . 128 A2
Waterloo Pl TR11 . . . . . . 145 B4
Waterloo Rd PL5 . . . . . . 145 B5
Waterloo St
 Plymouth PL4 . . . . . . 149 A4
 Plymouth, Stoke PL1 . . . . . . 148 A3
Waterloo Yard Flats PL1 128 A2
Water-ma-Trout TR13 . . . . . . 146 C8
Water-ma-Trout Ind Est
 TR13 . . . . . . 146 C8
Waters Ct TR15 . . . . . . 140 E7
Waters Edge
 Newquay TR7 . . . . . . 110 A6
 Tavistock PL19 . . . . . . 147 D6
Water's Edge PL28 . . . . . . 107 E6
Watersedge PL25 . . . . . . 114 B4
Waterside Lane PL30 . . . . . . 47 E7
Waterside Mews PL11 . . . . . . 127 D3
Watersmead Parc TR11 144 C2
Watery La
 Bodmin PL31 . . . . . . 109 D5
 Milton Combe PL6 . . . . . . 120 D6
Watson Gdns PL4 . . . . . . 149 B3
Watson Pl PL4 . . . . . . 149 B2
Watts Park Rd PL12 . . . . . . 122 D3
Watts Rd PL4 . . . . . . 149 C3
Waveney Gdns PL5 . . . . . . 124 C3
Waverley Rd PL5 . . . . . . 124 B3
Wavish Pk PL11 . . . . . . 126 E3
Waycott Wlk PL6 . . . . . . 124 D6
Way Cross PL15 . . . . . . 27 B3
Wayfield Rd PL1 . . . . . . 148 B3
Wayside Cvn Pk TR7 . . . . . . 111 A4
Wayside Folk Mus* TR
 26 . . . . . . 76 B5
WEARDE 122 F2
Wearde Rd PL12 . . . . . . 122 E1
Webber Hill PL15 . . . . . . 145 B4
Webber St TR11 . . . . . . 145 B4
Webbs Ct 9 PL13 . . . . . . 113 C6

Webb St PL23 . . . . . . 116 D4
Wedgewood Rd PL25 . . . . . . 115 A4
WEEK GREEN 11 E8
Weeks Rise PL32 . . . . . . 105 B2
Weeks Row PL18 . . . . . . 41 A6
Weekstone Cross EX22 . . . . . . 8 C8
Weeth Cl TR14 . . . . . . 138 C3
Weethes Cotts 6 TR18 . . 143 D5
Weeth La TR14 . . . . . . 138 C3
Weeth Prim Sch TR14 . . 138 C4
Weeth Rd TR14 . . . . . . 138 C4
Weir Cl PL6 . . . . . . 125 F2
Weir Gdns PL6 . . . . . . 125 F2
Weir Rd PL6 . . . . . . 125 F2
Welbeck Ave PL4 . . . . . . 148 C4
WELCOMBE 2 D5
Welcombe Cross EX39 . . . . . . 3 B4
Welcome Ct TR4 . . . . . . 56 D1
Welland Gdns PL3 . . . . . . 129 C5
Weller Ct TR11 . . . . . . 145 B3
Wellfield Cl
 Coad's Green PL15 . . . . . . 27 D3
 Plymouth PL7 . . . . . . 131 C5
Well Gdns PL1 . . . . . . 148 B3
Wellhay Cl PL9 . . . . . . 136 C6
Wellhouse The 8 PL14 . . 113 C6
Wellington Cl TR14 . . . . . . 138 C3
Wellington Gdns PL11 . . 145 B4
Wellington Pl
 Falmouth TR11 . . . . . . 145 B4
 Penzance TR18 . . . . . . 143 D5
 Wadebridge PL27 . . . . . . 108 C4
Wellington Plantation
 TR11 . . . . . . 82 B7
Wellington Rd
 Camborne TR14 . . . . . . 138 D3
 Porthleven TR13 . . . . . . 91 B1
 St Dennis PL26 . . . . . . 58 C8
 2 St Eval PL27 . . . . . . 31 F3
Wellington St
 Plymouth PL4 . . . . . . 149 A4
 Plymouth, Stoke PL1 . . . . . . 128 A3
 Torpoint PL11 . . . . . . 127 B3
Wellington Terr
 Falmouth TR11 . . . . . . 145 B4
 Porthleven TR13 . . . . . . 91 B1
 Portscatho TR2 . . . . . . 83 B2
 2 Truro TR1 . . . . . . 137 C4
Well La
 Constantine TR11 . . . . . . 92 F4
 Falmouth TR11 . . . . . . 145 B4
 Goldsithney TR20 . . . . . . 89 F5
 Lamorna TR19 . . . . . . 97 E5
 Liskeard PL14 . . . . . . 113 C6
 St Cleer PL14 . . . . . . 37 F3
 St Keverne TR12 . . . . . . 101 D4
 Tregony TR2 . . . . . . 71 F3
 Tremar PL14 . . . . . . 38 A3
 Welcombe EX39 . . . . . . 2 E5
Well Mdw PL15 . . . . . . 18 A5
Wellpark Rd PL18 . . . . . . 40 F5
Well Park Rd PL11 . . . . . . 127 B3
Wellsbourne Pk PL3 . . . . . . 129 A6
Wells Ct PL10 . . . . . . 132 E4
Well St
 Callington PL17 . . . . . . 39 E4
 Delabole PL33 . . . . . . 14 E3
 Tregony TR2 . . . . . . 71 F3
 Tywardreath PL24 . . . . . . 60 D5
Well Way TR7 . . . . . . 111 C7
Welman Rd PL10 . . . . . . 132 F6
Welsby Terr PL14 . . . . . . 37 F3
WELSFORD 3 C8
Welsford Ave PL2 . . . . . . 127 F5
Welway TR6 . . . . . . 55 A4
WEMBURY 136 B1
Wembury Park Rd PL3 . . 128 D6
Wembury Rd PL9 . . . . . . 136 A4
WENDRON 81 A5
Wendron CE Prim Sch
 TR13 . . . . . . 91 F5
Wendron St TR13 . . . . . . 146 C6
WENFORDBRIDGE 24 A2
Wenlock Gdns PL2 . . . . . . 128 B8
WENMOUTH CROSS 37 A3
Wensum Cl PL7 . . . . . . 131 A4
Wentworth Gdns PL6 . . . . . . 125 E3
Wentwood Pl PL6 . . . . . . 125 E3
Wentworth Cl
 Lynstone EX23 . . . . . . 104 C3
 Polzeath PL27 . . . . . . 21 D5
 Redruth TR15 . . . . . . 140 C3
Wentworth Pl PL4 . . . . . . 129 B2
Wentworth Way PL12 . . . . . . 122 C2
WERRINGTON 18 F6
Werrington Dr PL17 . . . . . . 39 E4
Werrington Prim Sch
 PL15 . . . . . . 18 F7
Wesley Ave PL3 . . . . . . 128 E5
Wesley Cl
 Kelly Bray PL17 . . . . . . 39 F6
 Stenalees PL26 . . . . . . 59 C8
Wesley Cottage Mus*
 PL15 . . . . . . 26 B7
Wesley Ct
 Penryn TR10 . . . . . . 144 C8
 Pensilva PL14 . . . . . . 38 D4
 22 Porthleven TR13 . . . . . . 98 C8
 Torpoint PL11 . . . . . . 127 C3
Wesley La PL12 . . . . . . 122 F2
Wesley Pl
 5 Newlyn TR18 . . . . . . 143 C2
 Plymouth, Mutley PL4 . . 128 E5
 1 Plymouth, Stoke PL2 . . 128 A4

Wesley Pl continued
St Austell PL25 .... 114 F3
7 St Ives TR26 .... 141 B5
Wesley Rd
Cubert TR8 .... 55 D8
Pensilva PL14 .... 38 D4
Saltash PL12 .... 122 F2
Wesley St
Camborne TR14 .... 138 E3
11 Heamoor TR18 ..... 143 C7
Redruth TR15 .... 140 C5
Wesley Terr
Bugle PL26 .... 47 C2
Looe PL13 .... 117 D4
Wesley Way PL15 .... 26 B7
Wesley Yd TR7 .... 110 D6
West Ave 4 PL19 ... 147 B5
West Beach Rd TR4 ... 68 A6
West Beckon Cl EX23 .. 2 D1
West BLACKDOWN 30 F8
Westborne Hts TR15 .. 140 C5
Westborne Rd TR14 .. 138 B4
Westbourne Dr PL25 . 114 B3
Westbourne Rd PL3 ... 128 D5
Westbourne Terr
Fraddon TR9 .... 57 D8
Saltash PL12 .... 122 F3
Westbridge Cotts PL19 . 147 B4
Westbridge Ind Est 3
PL19 .... 147 B4
Westbridge Rd PL25 .. 59 A3
West Bridge Rd PL15 . 106 B7
Westbury Cl PL5 ...... 124 B4
Westby Rd EX23 ...... 104 E5
West Camps Bay PL11 . 64 C4
West Charles St TR14 . 138 D2
West Cl TR13 .... 146 D7
West Cliff TR4 .... 68 A6
Westcliff Flats EX23 .. 104 D6
West Cnr 1 TR3 .... 81 F7
Westcombe Cres PL9 . 135 D5
West Cornwall Hospl
TR18 .... 143 D6
Westcott PL27 .... 108 A6
Westcott Cl PL6 ...... 129 A8
Westcountry Cl PL2 .. 127 F7
Westcove Ho 2 TR7 .. 110 F6
Westcroft Rd PL5 .... 123 D1
West Ct TR7 .... 110 C6
WEST CURRY 12 D4
West Devon Bsns Pk
PL19 .... 147 B3
West Down Dr PL13 .. 117 C4
Westdown Rd PL33 ... 14 D2
West Down Rd PL26 .. 128 B6
WESTDOWNS 14 C1
Westella Rd PL20 .... 42 D2
West End
Goldsithney TR20 ...... 89 C5
Marazion TR17 .... 89 B5
Pentewan PL26 .... 73 C6
15 Porthleven TR13 ... 98 B8
Redruth TR15 .... 140 B4
St Day TR16 .... 68 D1
West End OfI TR10 .. 144 C8
West End Cotts PL11 . 64 B8
West End Rd PL5 ..... 124 B8
West End Ind Est TR10 144 B8
West End Sq 7 PL17 .. 39 E4
Westend Terr TR10 .. 144 C8
Westeria Terr PL2 .... 128 C7
Westerlands Rd PL27 . 108 B6
Western App PL1 ..... 148 B2
Western Ave 5 PL14 .. 51 A7
Western College Rd PL4 128 F5
Western Dr PL3 ...... 129 B4
Western Pl TR10 ..... 144 B8
Western Promenade Rd
TR18 .... 143 E4
Western Rd PL15 ..... 106 B5
Western Terr
Bodmin PL31 .... 109 C4
Falmouth TR11 .... 145 A4
Launceston PL15 ...... 106 B5
Western Wood Way PL7 131 D5
West Fairholme Rd EX23 104 E7
Westfield PL7 .... 131 A6
Westfield Ave PL9 ... 135 C6
Westgate Mews 2 PL5 . 106 C5
Westgate St PL5 ..... 106 C5
Westground Way PL34 . 14 D7
Westhampnett Pl PL5 . 123 F4
Westhaul Pk PL25 ... 115 E4
Westhays Cl PL9 ..... 135 F4
Westhead Rd PL10 ... 64 B2
Westheath Ave PL30,
PL31 .... 109 B3
Westheath Rd PL31 .. 109 B3
West Hill
St Austell PL25 .... 114 C3
Wadebridge PL27 ...... 108 A6
West Hill Ct 10 PL25 . 114 C3
West Hill Rd PL4 ..... 128 F4
WEST HOE 148 B1
West Hoe Rd PL1 ..... 148 B1
West Kitty TR5 .... 54 C1
West La
Crafthole PL11 .... 65 B5
Delabole PL33 .... 14 E2
Landrake PL12 .... 53 B3
Westlake Cl PL11 .... 126 F3
WEST LOOE 117 C3
West Looe Hill PL13 .. 117 B3
West Looe Sq PL13 ... 117 C3

West Malling Ave PL5 . 123 E5
Westmoor Cl PL7 ..... 131 C6
Westmoor Cres TR3 ... 81 D6
Westmoor Pk PL19 ... 147 C4
WESTON MILL 127 E8
Weston Mill Dr PL5 .. 127 F8
Weston Mill Hill PL5 . 123 A1
Weston Mill La PL5 .. 123 A1
Weston Mill Prim Sch
PL2 .... 127 E7
Weston Mill Rd PL5 .. 123 E1
Weston Park Rd PL3 . 128 D6
Westover Rd PL7 ..... 39 E4
WEST PANSON 13 D2
WEST PARK 124 A3
West Park Dr PL7 .... 131 C5
West Park Est PL27 .. 108 D5
West Park Hill PL7 ... 131 B7
Westpark Rd PL27 ... 108 A4
West Park Rd EX23 ... 104 D7
WEST PENTIRE 43 C3
West Pentire Rd TR8 . 43 D3
West Pk
Perranarworthal TR3 ... 81 D6
Redruth TR15 .... 139 F6
13 St Columb Major TR9 . 45 E6
Tideford PL12 .... 52 F2
Trewidland PL14 ...... 51 C3
West Pl
Falmouth TR11 .... 145 A4
48 St Ives TR26 ..... 141 B6
St Just TR19 .... 86 E6
West Point TR8 ...... 111 C4
West Porthmear Cotts
PL25 .... 115 B2
West Porthmear Ct PL25 115 B2
WEST PORTHOLLAND .. 84 D5
West Quay PL10 ..... 132 E5
West Rd
Looe PL13 .... 117 C4
Quintrell Downs TR8 .. 111 E3
West Rise TR11 ...... 144 F3
West St
Grimscott EX23 .... 5 B1
Liskeard PL14 .... 113 B6
Millbrook PL10 .... 132 E5
Penryn TR10 .... 144 C8
Polruan PL23 .... 116 C2
St Columb Major TR9 .. 45 E6
Tavistock PL19 .... 147 B5
Torpoint PL10 .... 132 E4
WEST TAPHOUSE 49 E6
West Tehidy TR14 ... 138 F7
West Terr
Hayle TR27 .... 142 B6
Newlyn TR18 .... 143 C3
WEST TOLGUS 139 D8
West Tolgus TR15 ... 139 D8
West Trevingey TR15 . 140 A3
West Trewrigle Rd TR15. 140 B4
Westview TR6 .... 55 B5
West View
Porthleven TR13 .... 91 A1
Tavistock PL19 .... 147 E2
Trevone PL28 .... 20 E2
West View Rd 5 PL20 . 41 B1
West Villas TR8 ...... 57 B7
West Way EX22 ..... 11 E8
West Wharf PL26 ... 73 C3
Westwinds PL32 ..... 16 A8
Westwood PL14 ...... 113 B6
Westwood Ave PL6 .. 125 C6
WEST YOULSTONE ... 3 B2
Wetherham La PL30 .. 23 E3
Whalesborough Parc
EX23 .... 104 F5
Wharf Rd
Penzance TR18 .... 143 F5
St Ives TR26 .... 141 B6
Wharfside 3 TR18 ... 143 E5
Wharfside Sh Ctr TR18 . 143 F5
Wharfside Village 9
TR18 .... 143 E5
Wharf The
22 Mousehole TR19 .... 88 C1
St Ives TR26 .... 141 B6
Wharf Theatre & Gall The ***
PL19 .... 147 B5
Wheal Agar TR15 .... 139 C6
Wheal Agar **5** TR14 . 138 F7
WHEAL ALFRED 142 F4
Wheal Alfred Rd TR27 . 142 F5
Wheal-an-Wens TR17 . 89 C5
Whealbrake Lodge PL26. 58 D6
Wheal Bull PL26 ..... 58 D5
Wheal Busy La TR4 ... 68 F3
Wheal Catherine Cl TR6. 55 B5
Wheal Damsel Rd TR16. 80 E8
Wheal Dance TR16 ... 140 D3
Wheal Dream TR26 .. 141 C6
Wheal Eliza Cl PL25 .. 115 B5
Wheal Fortune La TR15. 139 D6
WHEAL FRANCES 55 D3
Wheal Friendly La TR5 . 54 C2
Wheal Gerry TR14 ... 138 E4
Wheal Golden Dr TR8 . 43 C1
Wheal Gorland Rd TR16 . 80 E8
Wheal Harmony Terr
TR15 .... 140 B7
Wheal Jane Mdws TR3 . 69 C3
Wheal Jewel (Gipsy Site)
TR16 .... 68 E1
Wheal Kitty TR5 ...... 54 D1

Wheal Kitty La TR5 .... 54 D2
Wheal Kitty Workshops
TR5 .... 54 D2
Wheal Leisure TR6 .... 55 A5
Wheal Leisure Cl **25** TR6 . 55 A5
Wheal Margery TR26 . 141 C3
Wheal Maria Cotts PL19 . 29 D1
Wheal Martyn Mus * PL26 59 B6
Wheal Northey PL25 .. 115 B5
Wheal Oak TR13 ..... 146 B4
Wheal Quoit Ave TR5 . 54 C1
Wheal Ramoth 3 TR6 . 55 A5
Wheal Regent PL25 .. 115 D3
WHEAL ROSE 68 C3
Wheal Rose 16 TR13 . 98 C8
Wheal Silver TR15 ... 140 B5
Wheal Speed Rd TR26 . 141 C2
Wheal Tehidy La TR15 . 139 E6
Wheal Trefusis TR15 . 140 D2
Wheal Trelawney TR16. 140 D3
Wheal Venture Rd TR26 . 141 C3
Wheal View PL26 ..... 58 B4
Wheal Virgin Ho TR26 . 77 A6
WHEAL VOR 91 A5
Wheal Vor TR15 ..... 140 D3
Wheal Vyvyan TR11 .. 92 F4
Wheal Whidden TR26 . 141 C2
Wheatfield Cres TR7 . 111 A4
Wheatridge PL7 ...... 130 B7
Wheel Ayr TR26 ...... 141 C6
Wheeler Higman Cl PL26 . 59 C7
Wheelgate House Sch
TR8 .... 43 D2
Wheelwright Dr PL20 . 42 E4
Wherry Pl PL23 ...... 116 D2
WHERRY TOWN 143 D4
Wherry Way PL14 .... 50 E7
Whieldon Rd PL25 ... 115 A4
Whimple St PL1 ...... 148 C2
Whin Bank Rd PL5 ... 124 E2
WHIPSIDERRY 44 C6
Whipsiderry Cl TR7 .. 44 C6
Whistley Down PL20 . 42 B2
Whitby Cres PL11 .... 125 A1
Whitby Rd PL6 ...... 125 A1
WHITCHURCH 147 D3
Whitchurch Prim Sch
PL19 .... 147 D2
Whitchurch Rd
Horrabridge PL20 ..... 42 C5
Tavistock PL19 .... 147 C3
Whitcross Hill TR15 . 139 C3
Whitebarrow Cotts PL14. 37 A4
Whitecroft Way EX23 . 5 A6
WHITECROSS
Crowlas 77 C1
Wadebridge 33 B7
WHITE CROSS
Mullion 99 B4
St Columb Road 45 C2
Whitecross
Blisland PL30 .... 35 D7
Bodinnick PL23 .... 116 F6
White Cross
Cury TR12 .... 99 B4
Redruth TR16 .... 68 D3
White Cross Ct PL4 .. 149 A3
Whitecross Ind Est TR8 . 45 B2
Whitefield Terr PL4 .. 149 A4
Whiteford Cl 10 PL7 .. 39 E4
Whiteford Rd PL3 .... 128 E6
White Friars La PL4 .. 149 A3
Whitegate PL26 ...... 58 B8
Whitegate Mdws PL26. 58 B8
Whitegate Rd TR7 ... 111 A4
Whitegate Sh Complex
TR7 .... 111 A7
Whitehall Bglws PL30 . 23 B2
Whitehall Dr
8 Bere Alston PL20 .. 41 B1
Plymouth PL7 .... 136 B7
Whitehall Est PL30 ... 23 B2
White Hart Arc The 3
PL15 .... 106 C5
Whitehaven Way PL6 . 125 A7
WHITEHILL 146 C4
Whitehill Cross PL15 . 19 C6
Whitehill Terr TR13 . 146 C4
White Horse
Crowntown TR13 ...... 91 A6
Nancegollan TR13 .... 91 A6
White House Cl TR26 . 141 C2
White La PL1 .... 149 A2
White Lady Rd PL9 ... 135 D5
White Lodge EX23 .... 10 C7
WHITEMOOR 58 B8
Whitemoor Com Prim Sch
PL26 .... 58 B8
White River PL31 ..... 114 C3
White River PI Sh Ctr
PL25 .... 114 C3
WHITEROCK 108 A5
Whiterock Cl PL27 ... 108 B5
Whiterock Rd PL27 .. 108 B5
Whiterocks Pk PL18 .. 40 D6
Whiterock Terr PL27 . 108 B5
White's Cl 3 TR5 .... 54 C1
White Smock Mdw 7 PL9 . 9 C1
Whitestone Cres PL31. 109 C3
Whitestone Rd PL31 . 109 C3
White Walls Ct 16 TR6. 55 A4
Whitewater Ct PL7 ... 130 E6
WHITEWELL 22 C7
Whitham Pk PL19 ... 147 C4
WHITLEIGH 124 C5
Whitleigh Ave PL5 ... 124 E2
Whitleigh Cotts PL5 . 124 E2
Whitleigh Ct PL5 ..... 124 D4

Whitleigh Gn PL5 ..... 124 C4
Whitleigh Villas PL5 . 124 E2
Whitleigh Way PL5 ... 124 C4
Whitley Cl TR1 .... 137 D4
Whitley Grange PL14 . 113 A6
Whitlieburn Terr PL13. 117 C3
Whitpot Hill PL12 .... 64 F8
Whitsam Cross PL20 .. 41 A1
Whitsand Bay View PL11. 65 A4
Whitson Cross PL5 ... 124 C7
Whitsoncross La PL5 . 124 C7
WHITSTONE 7 F1
Whitstone Cty Prim Sch
EX22 .... 7 F1
Whitstone Head Sch EX22. 7 F1
Whittington St PL3 ... 148 B4
Whitworth Cl TR5 .... 54 C1
Whity Cross PL12 .... 122 A4
Widegate Nursery PL9 . 136 D8
WIDEGATES 63 F8
WIDEMOUTH BAY 6 F5
Widewell La PL6 ..... 125 C7
Widewell Prim Sch PL6. 125 B7
Widewell Rd PL6 ..... 125 C7
Widey Court Prim Sch
PL6 .... 124 F1
Widey Cross PL6 ..... 124 F1
Widey Ct PL6 .... 124 F1
Widey La PL6 .... 124 F2
Widey View PL3 ...... 128 F6
Widgeon Way TR27 .. 77 E3
Wiicove La PL11 ...... 126 E5
Widebeest Rd 6 PL27. 31 F3
Wilderness Rd PL3 ... 128 E5
Wilderness Trail * PL30. 48 C5
Wildflower La TR7 .... 111 A6
Wilkes Wlk TR1 ...... 137 D4
Wilkinson Cl PL17 .... 39 E6
Wilkinson Rd PL5 .... 127 D8
Willapark View PL35 .. 9 C1
Willas Rd PL16 .... 19 F4
William Edwards Cl
EX23 .... 104 E6
William Evans Cl PL6 . 124 D5
William Laundry Cl PL14. 52 A5
William Prance Rd PL6. 125 A3
Williams Ave PL4 ..... 129 B1
Williams Ho PL31 .... 109 B4
William St
Camborne TR14 .... 138 D2
Truro TR1 .... 137 D4
William Young Mews
PL14 .... 113 E5
Willis Vean TR12 ..... 99 A1
Willoughby Pl PL17 .. 39 E4
Willoughby Pk PL20 .. 42 D2
Willow Cl
22 Callington PL17 ... 39 F4
Mylor Bridge TR11 .... 82 A3
Plymouth PL3 .... 129 E5
Quintrell Downs TR8 .. 44 E3
Willow Cotts PL7 ..... 130 D4
Willow Ct PL6 .... 129 E7
Willow Dr TR14 ...... 138 B4
Willowfield TR18 ..... 143 C5
Willow Gn PL12 ...... 122 D2
Willow Rd PL19 ...... 147 C3
Willows The
Bugle PL26 .... 47 C1
Whipsiderry TR7 ...... 44 C6
Willow Way PL14 .... 113 B5
Willow Wlk PL6 ...... 125 D5
Wills Cl PL6 .... 124 D7
Wills La **18** TR26 ..... 141 B6
Wills Moor PL26 ..... 85 C5
Will's Row TR15 ..... 139 C8
WILMINSTONE 30 F3
Wilmstone Ind Est
PL19 .... 147 E7
Wilmot Gdns PL5 .... 124 D3
Wilsey View PL15 .... 17 B7
Wilson Cres PL2 ..... 128 B5
Wilson Way
Camborne TR15 .... 139 D5
14 Par PL24 .... 60 B4
Wilsworthy Cross EX22. 12 C7
Wilton Rd PL1 .... 128 A3
Wilton St PL1 .... 148 A4
Wilton Terr PL13 ..... 62 D6
Wiltshire Cl PL4 ..... 128 F4
Winchester Gdns PL5 . 124 A5
Windermere Cres PL6. 124 F4
Winding Terr PL10 ... 81 A1
WINDMILL 20 F1
Windmill PL23 .... 116 C4
Windmill Hill
Launceston PL15 ...... 106 C5
Saltash PL12 .... 122 E2
St Just in Roseland TR2. 82 F2
Windmill Hill Terr PL15. 106 C5
Windmill Ho PL23 ... 116 C4
Windmill Ind Est PL23. 116 C4
Windmill La PL15 .... 106 C5
Windsor Cl
Falmouth TR11 .... 145 B4
Newquay TR7 .... 110 D5
Plymouth PL25 .... 115 C3
Windsor Gr PL31 ..... 109 F5
Windsor Hill **8** PL26 . 141 B5
Windsor Ho PL31 .... 109 E5
Windsor La
Kelly Bray PL17 .... 39 F6
Plymouth PL12 .... 122 E2
Windsor Mews PL31 . 109 E5
Windsor Pl
Liskeard PL14 .... 113 C5
26 Penzance TR18 ... 143 E6

Windsor Pl continued
Plymouth PL1 .... 148 C2
Windsor Rd PL3 ...... 129 B7
Windsor Terr
Falmouth TR11 .... 145 B4
Penzance TR18 .... 143 D6
4 St Ives TR26 ...... 141 A5
Windsor Villas PL1 ... 148 C2
Windsworth PL24 .... 115 F7
Windy Ridge PL26 .... 46 D1
Wingfield PL31 .... 35 B2
Wingfield Mans PL3 . 128 A3
Wingfield Rd PL3 .... 148 A4
Wingfield Way PL3 ... 148 A4
Winifred Baker Ct 5
PL4 .... 149 A4
Winnard's Perch TR9 . 32 D1
Winnicott Cl PL6 ..... 124 E7
Winnow Cl PL9 .... 135 F4
Winns Row TR13 ..... 146 C6
Winsbury Ct PL6 ..... 125 A1
Winsor Cotts PL15 ... 106 B7
Winsor Est PL13 ..... 62 D5
Winstanley Wlk PL3 . 129 D6
Winston Ave PL4 ..... 148 C4
Winstone Terr TR8 ... 110 A3
Winwell Field PL27 .. 108 D6
Witham Gdns PL3 .... 129 C5
WITHEVEN 11 D3
WITHIEL 47 A8
WITHIELGOOSE MILLS . 47 C8
WITHNOE 132 A4
Withnoe La PL10 ..... 132 B6
Withnoe Terr PL10 ... 65 F3
Wixenford Ct PL9 .... 135 F8
Woburn Rd PL15 ..... 106 B4
Woburn Terr PL9 .... 135 C7
Wodehouse Terr TR11. 145 B4
Wolcocke Cl TR17 ... 89 D5
Wollaton Gr PL5 ..... 123 F3
Wolrige Ave PL7 ...... 131 B5
Wolrige Way PL7 ..... 131 A5
Wolsdon Pl PL1 ...... 148 A3
Wolsdon St PL1 ...... 148 A3
Wolsdon Street Sch PL1. 148 B3
Wolseley Bsns Pk 2
PL2 .... 128 A5
Wolseley Cl PL2 ..... 128 A5
Wolseley Rd
Plymouth, Camels Head
PL5 .... 127 F6
Plymouth, St Budeaux PL5 123 C1
Wolseley Road Flats PL2 127 F6
Wolverwood Cl PL7 .. 131 C3
Wolverwood La PL7 .. 131 B3
Wombwell Cres PL2 .. 127 E7
Wood Acre PL12 ..... 122 B4
Woodacre Ct PL12 ... 122 B4
Wooda La PL15 ...... 106 B6
Wooda Rd PL15 ...... 106 C6
Woodbine Cotts PL7 . 130 E4
Woodbine La PL7 .... 130 E4
Woodbury Gdns PL5 . 124 A3
Woodchurch PL20 ... 42 B3
Wood Cl PL12 .... 122 B3
Woodcock Cl PL10 ... 133 A6
Wood Dr
Saltash PL12 .... 53 C8
St Mellion PL12 .... 53 C8
Woodend Rd PL6 .... 125 D7
Woodfield Prim Sch PL5 124 C5
Woodfield Rd EX23 .. 104 E7
WOODFORD
Plymouth 130 C7
Shop 4 D8
Woodford Ave PL7 ... 130 A7
Woodford Cl PL7 .... 130 A7
Woodford Cres PL7 .. 130 A6
Woodford Cross EX23 . 2 C1
Woodford Gn PL7 .... 130 B6
Woodford Inf Sch PL7 . 130 B6
Woodford Jun Sch PL7. 130 B7
Woodford Rd PL6 .... 125 D6
Woodgate Rd PL14 .. 113 A5
Woodgrove Pk PL26 .. 59 A1
Woodhey Rd PL2 ..... 128 A7
Wood La
Landrake PL12 .... 53 D2
Truro TR1 .... 137 D3
Tywardreath PL24 .... 60 D5
Woodland Ave
Penryn TR10 .... 144 B6
Plymouth PL7 .... 136 A8
12 Tywardreath PL24 . 60 D5
Woodland Cl
Gunnislake PL18 ...... 40 F6
Lanivet PL30 .... 47 E7
St Austell PL25 .... 114 E3
Woodland Ct TR1 ..... 137 C7
Woodland Dr PL7 .... 130 B4
Woodland Glade PL30. 47 E7
Woodland Hts TR1 ... 137 C5
Woodland Rd
Plymouth PL7 .... 130 C6
St Austell PL25 .... 114 E3
Woodland Rise
Penryn TR10 .... 144 B7
Rilla Mill PL17 .... 38 E8
Woodlands
Dousland PL20 .... 42 E3
4 Mullion TR12 ..... 99 A2
10 Par PL24 .... 60 C4
Plymouth PL9 .... 135 F6
Woodlands Cl PL5 ... 124 A3
Woodlands End PL6 .. 125 D5
Woodlands La PL6 ... 125 D5
Woodlands Sch PL5 .. 124 B4
Woodlands Terr 3 TR16 140 F1

Woodlands The TR14..... 67 B4
Woodlands View PL13... 117 B4
Woodland Terr
　Plymouth PL4.......... 149 B4
　4 St Columb Road TR9.... 45 E2
Woodland Terr La PL4 . 149 B4
Woodland View
　Coombe PL26............ 58 C2
　Lanivet PL30............ 47 E6
Woodland Way
　Gunnislake PL18 .... 41 A7
　Torpoint PL11 .... 126 F3
Woodlane TR11.......... 145 B3
Woodlane CI TR11...... 145 B3
Woodlane Cres TR11.... 145 B3
Woodlane Dr TR11...... 145 B3
Woodley CI 8 EX23...... 4 D1
Woodman's Cnr PL20 .... 42 D3
Woodpecker Way PL19 . 147 D2
Woodridge CI TR27..... 78 E1
Woods-Browning Ind Est
　PL31................... 109 F2
Woodside
　Crapstone PL20......... 42 B2
　Penryn TR10............ 144 B7
　Plymouth PL4.......... 149 B4
Woodside Ave PL9...... 135 C6

Woodside Ct PL7 .... 130 E4
Woodside La PL4 ...... 149 B4
Woodstock Gdns PL5... 123 D1
Woodvale Terr PL15.... 106 C5
Wood View TR10........ 144 B7
Woodview Pk PL9....... 136 A6
Woodville CI PL2....... 127 F7
Woodville Rd
　Morwenstow EX23........ 2 C1
　Plymouth PL2........... 127 F6
　Woodford EX23 .... 4 D8
Woodway
　Penryn TR10........... 144 B7
　Plymouth PL9........... 136 A7
Woolacombe Cross PL20. 41 C1
Woolacombe Rd PL20... 41 C1
Woollcombe Ave PL7 .. 130 F4
WOOLLEY 3 A3
Woolster Ct 8 PL4.... 149 A2
WOOLSTON.............. 38 E3
WOOLWELL.............. 125 D7
Woolwell Cres PL6..... 125 C8
Woolwell Dr PL6....... 125 C7
Woolwell Rd PL6....... 125 D7
Woon La 3 TR3 .... 81 F7
Worcester Rd PL25..... 115 A4
Wordsworth Cres PL2... 127 F7

Wordsworth Rd PL2..... 127 F7
Wotton Cross PL12..... 53 B4
Wreford CI 11 TR9 ...... 45 D6
Wren Gdns PL7 .... 130 C6
Wren Ind Est TR1 ...... 69 E4
Wrens Gate PL9........ 135 E8
Wrey Ave PL14......... 113 C7
Wright CI PL1.......... 127 E3
WRINGSDOWN............ 18 E6
Wyatts La PL19 .... 147 B6
Wych Hazel Way TR7... 110 F4
Wycliffe Rd PL3........ 129 B4
Wye Gdns PL3 .... 129 D7
Wykeham Dr PL2 ...... 128 A7
Wyndham La PL1 ...... 148 A3
Wyndham Mews PL1.... 148 A3
Wyndham Pl PL1....... 148 A3
Wyndham Sq PL1 ...... 148 A3
Wyndham Street E PL1.. 148 B3
Wyndham Street W PL1. 148 B3
Wyndhurst Orch PL27 .. 108 B6
Wyoming CI PL3 .... 129 C6
Wythburn Gdns PL6.... 125 D3

Y

Yardley Gdns PL6....... 125 E3
Yarrow Mead PL9....... 136 D7
Yealmpstone CI PL7..... 131 B4
Yealmpstone Dr PL7... 131 B3
Yealmpstone Farm Prim Sch
　PL7................... 131 B3
Yeats CI PL5........... 124 C2
Yellow Tor Ct PL12..... 122 C2
Yellow Tor La PL12..... 122 C2
Yellow Tor Rd PL12 .... 122 B2
Yellow-Wort TR16 ...... 80 C3
YELVERTON 42 D3
Yelverton Bsns Pk PL20 . 42 B2
Yelverton CI PL5........ 123 E4
Yelverton Paperweight
　Mus* PL20............. 42 C2
Yelverton Terr
　Tavistock PL19......... 147 D6
　Yelverton PL20......... 42 D2
Yeo CI PL3 .... 129 B5
Yeoland Down PL20.... 121 E8
Yeoland La PL20 .... 42 C1
YEOLMBRIDGE 18 F6
Yeomdon Cross EX22 .....8 E4

Woo–Zod 181

Yeomans CI PL14 .... 113 D5
Yeomans Way PL7 ..... 131 A4
Yewdale Gdns PL6...... 125 D2
Yew Tree Ct TR1........ 137 F6
Yonder St PL9 .... 135 B6
York PI PL2............. 127 F4
York Rd
　Plymouth PL5.......... 127 E8
　Torpoint PL11 .... 127 B3
York St
　Penzance TR18......... 143 D6
　Plymouth PL1.......... 127 E2
York Terr 7 PL2........ 127 F5
Youldon Way PL20 ..... 42 C4

Z

Zaggy La PL17 .... 39 E4
ZELAH 56 A2
ZENNOR................ 76 B5
Zion St PL1............ 148 C2
Zodiac Ho TR19......... 96 E3